Content Area Reading Assessment

Content Area Reading Assessment

A FORMATIVE MEASURE OF THE COMMON CORE STATE STANDARDS

Lauren Leslie

Professor Emerita, Marquette University

JoAnne Schudt Caldwell

Professor Emerita, Cardinal Stritch University

PEARSON

Boston   Columbus   Indianapolis   New York   San Francisco   Upper Saddle River
Amsterdam   Cape Town   Dubai   London   Madrid   Milan   Munich   Paris   Montréal   Toronto
Delhi   Mexico City   São Paulo   Sydney   Hong Kong   Seoul   Singapore   Taipei   Tokyo

Vice President, Editor in Chief: Jeffery W. Johnston
Acquisitions Editor: Meredith D. Fossel
Editorial Assistant: Maria Feliberty
Director of Marketing: Margaret Waples
Marketing Manager: Christopher Barry
Project Manager: Karen Mason
Project Coordination: Electronic Publishing Services Inc., NYC
Operations Specialist: Deidra Skahill
Electronic Composition: Jouve
Interior Design: Electronic Publishing Services Inc., NYC
Cover Design: Nesbitt Graphics
Cover Image: Peter Frank / Corbis

Credits and acknowledgments borrowed from other sources and reproduced, with permission, in this textbook appear on page 452.

Library of Congress Cataloging-in-Publication Data

Leslie, Lauren.
   Content area reading assessment : a formative measure of the common core state standards / Lauren Leslie and JoAnne Schudt Caldwell.
      pages cm.
   Includes bibliographical references and index.
   ISBN 978-0-13-259646-6 — ISBN 0-13-259646-6
   1. Language arts—Correlation with content subjects.   2. Content area reading.   I. Title.
   LB1576.L486 2015
   372.6—dc23

                                                                                    2014014884

10 9 8 7 6 5 4 3 2 1

ISBN 10: 0-13-259646-6
ISBN 13: 978-0-13-259646-6

This book is dedicated to the following:

- the students and teachers who will be affected by the Common Core State Standards—may this book help in your transitions

- retired faculty who worry that they will have nothing to do in retirement

- Bill and Tim Caldwell, who love reading as much as their mother does

- Chris Leslie-Hynan, whose first novel was published in August 2014, for making parenting a wonderful experience

About the Authors

Lauren Leslie founded and directed the Hartman Literacy and Learning Center and its predecessor at Marquette University for over 25 years. She has published over 25 research articles and she is the co-author (with JoAnne Caldwell) of the *Qualitative Reading Inventory-5* and *Intervention Strategies to Follow Informal Reading Inventory Assessment: So What Do I Do Now?* She also co-authored (with JoAnne Caldwell) a chapter, Formal and Informal Measures of Reading Comprehension, in the *Handbook of Research on Reading Comprehension* (2009). She received the Albert J. Harris Award from the International Reading Association in 2001 for an article written with L. Allen, "Factors That Predict Success in an Early Literacy Intervention Program." In 2006, she received the Mary Neville Bielefeld Award for Career Achievement for her contributions to teaching, research, and service, particularly the mentoring of women faculty and students. She is professor emerita at Marquette University.

JoAnne Schudt Caldwell is the co-author (with Lauren Leslie) of the *Qualitative Reading Inventory-5* and *Intervention Strategies to Follow Informal Reading Inventory Assessment: So What Do I Do Now?* She is the author of *Reading Assessment: A Primer for Teachers and Coaches* and *Comprehension Assessment: A Classroom Guide*. She also co-authored *Reading Problems: Assessment and Teaching Strategies* with Joyce Jennings and Janet Lerner. She received her Ph.D. in Educational Psychology from Marquette University and is professor emerita at Cardinal Stritch University. She has published numerous articles as well as a chapter in *Quality Literacy Instruction for Students with Autism Spectrum Disorders* and a chapter in the *Handbook of Research on Reading Comprehension* (with Lauren Leslie). She received the Outstanding Service Award from the Wisconsin State Reading Association (1996), the Wisconsin Teacher Educator of the Year Award (1997) and the Achievement Award from Marquette University School of Education (2005).

Brief Contents

Contents

Chapter 8   Teacher Answer Keys   345

Foreword

But can they read the materials central to learning in my subject?

As a former high school literacy coach for over twenty years, I frequently fielded this question from my colleagues. Of course, as teachers we have long had access to reading achievement information for our students. Ostensibly, such student data can inform our instruction and help us meet the needs of a wide range of learners as we teach our discipline. But what exactly do reading achievement scores—whether from a state assessment or from instruments used within our district or school—tell us about students' likely ability to handle the reading demands inherent in the texts of specific subjects? We know that such assessments tend to offer "all-purpose" insights into a student's reading ability, based on a general mix of literary and informational samples. These assessments can perhaps be described as decontextualized glimpses at reading achievement that may, or often may not, provide teachers with the guidance they seek. A common concern from disciplinary teachers has been that these generalized assessments sometimes overestimated students' development as readers of the texts of their subject.

Lauren Leslie and JoAnne Caldwell, the authors of *CARA (Content Area Reading Assessment)* have created a formative assessment tool, carefully conceived and disciplinarily focused, that endeavors to address these needs of classroom teachers. An ambitious undertaking, *CARA* is a timely response to the remarkable convergence this decade of two significant cross currents impacting literacy instruction—Disciplinary Literacy and the Common Core. Disciplinary Literacy represents a re-examination of literacy practices that intersect with learning in content area subjects. The research base for Disciplinary Literacy has extended beyond a conceptualization of generalized reading behaviors to the literacy practices exemplified by readers engaged in disciplinary thinking. Such thinking might be typified as "reading through a disciplinary lens." In effect, readers approach the texts of a discipline in characteristic ways—drawing on certain pools of knowledge, interacting with specialized vocabulary, navigating text structures that are commonly employed to organize and communicate disciplinary knowledge, insights, and practices—to achieve comprehension of disciplinary texts. Instructional implications of Disciplinary Literacy emphasize mentoring students in customizing their thinking as readers: reading science texts through a scientific lens, history texts through a historian lens, and literature through a literary lens, for example.

The other major shift in the landscape of literacy instruction is the implementation of the rigorous expectations of the Common Core Literacy Standards (officially, *Common Core State Standards for English Language Arts and Literacy in History/Social Studies, Science, and Technical Subjects*). The standards' emphasis on the careful and critical reading of complex texts makes meaningful formative assessments even more valuable for teachers of different disciplines. The standards expect students to grow their capacity to read a variety of texts across the academic disciplines as well as express their comprehension of these texts as writers.

CARA is an exciting outgrowth of and response to these intertwining developments. The assessment is aligned with the ten Common Core reading standards and is designed to provide classroom teachers with disciplinary-specific indicators of their students' ability to read complex texts that are typical of the materials assigned for learning in science, social studies, and English language arts. *CARA* offers teachers a number of distinct advantages. Each subtest is designed to be group administered during a regular class period (although certainly this flexible instrument can be used in individual settings as well). Multiple passages for each discipline at each grade level permit teachers to use this formative tool to track progress during a school year. The specific standard being assessed in an item is clearly articulated, and all relevant standards are accounted for during the course of an assessment. The passages are segmented, with questions interspersed, to prompt careful reading and re-reading of an entire selection. Question stems directly relate to the comprehension processing mandated in the standards and standards' language is consistently applied across grade levels. The assessment relies on constructed responses, resulting in a more in-depth consideration of student thinking and performance. Thoroughly developed answer keys guide teachers in their analysis of individual results with strong fidelity to the demands of the standard. Finally, the assessments will generate individual student profiles regarding state of progress in meeting each standard, as well as assist teachers in deciding when more concerted instruction on specific standards will benefit an entire class. *CARA* aspires to fill a definite void in literacy assessment; no current measure accomplishes these worthy aims.

The pragmatic appeal of *CARA*—obtaining standards-based evaluations of reading achievement from disciplinary appropriate texts—will certainly be well-received by teachers. As busy folks, they are likely to eagerly turn to the assessment passages targeted for their grade level and subject, perhaps overlooking other features of this impressive resource. However, Leslie and Caldwell offer much in their preliminary chapters that teachers will find highly informative. First and foremost, the authors undertake to help teachers understand the intentions behind each of the reading standards, in effect building teacher confidence in and expertise with Common Core expectations. By doing so, the authors establish a groundwork for implementing the standards through developing classroom tasks and assessments that mirror the critical thinking expected by the standards. They thoughtfully examine the case for asking students to comprehend complex, grade level disciplinary texts. In particular, they examine the critical thinking—the closer consideration and analysis of an author's message—that is a hallmark of the standards. Especially useful are the instructional options detailed in Chapter 5 that can facilitate the development of each of the reading standards. In addition, the authors help teachers keep abreast of the burgeoning scholarship on reading comprehension and specific implications for disciplinary literacy.

Overall, *CARA* provides significant mentoring for classroom teachers through the carefully crafted assessment items developed for each disciplinary passage. The authors intend that these items will provide teachers with exemplars for writing their own classroom equivalents as part of course tasks and assessments. The extensive discussions for scoring each item are particularly valuable in helping teachers to truly appreciate the rigor and growth expected by each standard. Teachers may find this scoring process initially to be daunting, but working through this process will provide teachers with an outstanding professional development experience as well as important insights into their student's reading abilities. Teams of teachers collaborating to analyze results, share observations, and discuss instructional implications could be a natural outgrowth of administrations of *CARA* at specific grade levels or within a discipline.

Lauren Leslie and JoAnne Caldwell are well known and highly respected as the authors of the *Qualitative Reading Inventory (QRI)*, now in its fifth edition. With *CARA*, they have contributed a unique and much-needed addition to our library of professional assessment options. It was a special honor to be asked to review their work and share my enthusiastic observations.

Doug Buehl
Adolescent Literacy Consultant and Instructor
of Adolescent Literacy
Edgewood College, Madison, WI

Preface

The *Content Area Reading Assessment (CARA)* is a formative, group-administered assessment of reading comprehension that teachers can use to determine students' ability to answer questions based on the Common Core State Standards (CCSS) for English Language Arts and Literacy (ELA) in content areas. The content areas that are included in the ELA standards are literature, history/social studies, science, and technical Subjects. Thus, the *CARA* comprises literature, social studies, and science passages taken from representative textbooks at grades 4 through high school.

The *CARA* was developed to meet the needs of adolescent learners in the age of the Common Core State Standards. It was also designed in response to several critical issues facing education in the United States: the wide adoption of the CCSS; the latest reports of the National Assessment for Educational Progress (NAEP); reports of student performance on college entrance examinations; and as a response to two national reports that focused on adolescent literacy. The first report, *A Time to Act: An Agenda for Advancing Adolescent Literacy for College and Career Success* (2010) concluded, "Beyond grade 3, adolescent learners in our schools must decipher more complex passages, synthesize information at a higher level, and learn to form independent conclusions based on evidence. They must also develop special skills and strategies for reading text in each of the differing content areas (such as English, science, mathematics and history)—meaning that a student who 'naturally' does well in one area may struggle in another" (p. x). Another Carnegie report, *Measure for Measure: A Critical Consumers' Guide to Reading Comprehension Assessments for Adolescents* (2010), closely examined nine of the most commonly used literacy assessments and determined that none of them measured any degree of critical thinking, defined as "synthesizing knowledge across texts, critiquing an author's point of view, or composing an essay in response to literature" (p. 7). In addition, none of the tests estimated reading ability in specific content areas such as science and social studies.

These two national reports suggested several things. First, a group-administered test of reading comprehension was needed. Second, such an instrument should include specific attention to different content areas: literature, social studies, and science. It should also focus on critical thinking. The CCSS emerged concurrently with the publication of these reports (all were published in 2010) and we believed that the standards should be used to guide the development of a formative assessment. Accordingly, the *Content Area Reading Assessment (CARA)* was created in order to provide:

- A formative and group assessment of grade-appropriate and discipline-specific text comprehension based on the Common Core State Standards for grades 4 through high school
- A measure of comprehension in three distinct content areas: literature, social studies, and science that focuses on critical thinking
- A model that teachers can use for designing standards-based questions from their instructional materials
- Information from which teachers can plan standards-based instruction

The *CARA* was reviewed by teachers of fourth grade through high school and piloted with over 3900 students. Questions and answers were revised based on teacher feedback and student answers. In addition, we hired teachers to score students' answers to each of our text selections (18 each in literature, social studies, and science) to assess interrater reliability and to evaluate the clarity of answer keys.

Acknowledgments

Over 70 teachers were instrumental in the development of the *CARA*, but there were some whose contribution should be personally acknowledged. Teacher leaders participated by encouraging teachers in their schools to be involved in piloting. Classroom teachers piloted many sections of students from their schools and others served as scorers for our interrater reliability study. We are supremely grateful to these teachers, without whom the *CARA* would never have seen the light of day.

Jennifer Berthold, Burleigh Elementary School, Elm Grove, WI

Jeremy Buehl, Madison East High School, Madison, WI

Deborah Diven, Greenfield Middle School, Greenfield, WI

Megan Dixon, Greenfield School District, Greenfield, WI

Leslie Ferrell, Evansville Community School District, Evansville, WI

Pat Gilbert and the teachers at Wauwatosa West High School, Wauwatosa, WI

Tony and Danielle Gonzalez, Milwaukee College Prep, Milwaukee, WI

Laura Gutierrez, Assistant Principal, Bruce Guadeloupe Community School, Milwaukee, WI

Ralph Haas, Menomonie Middle School, Menonomie, WI

Wendy Hamilton, Cindy Wanie, and Erin Romenesko at Hawthorne STEM School, Waukesha, WI

Shandowlyon Hendricks-Williams, Urban Day School, Milwaukee, WI

Diane Hilbrink, Mahone Middle School, Kenosha, WI

Andy Hoey, Hingham High School, Hingham, MA

Scott Krueger, Greenfield High School, Greenfield, WI

Kristine Marver Lize, Menomonee Falls School District, Menomonee Falls, WI

Dan Manley, Greenfield High School, Greenfield, WI

Leann Neese and the teachers at Whitman Middle School, Wauwatosa, WI

Julie Norman, Port Washington High School, Port Washington, WI

Linda Simmons, Associate Professor, Retired, Cardinal Stritch University, who played an integral part in data analysis

And a special thank you to Doug Buehl for pushing us to address Standard 8.

We would also like to acknowledge and thank the reviewers who provided valuable feedback to this manuscript: David Hammond, East Jessamine Middle School, KY; Jodi Meyer-Mork, Luther College, IA; Lynette Miller, Licking Heights Central Middle School, OH; and Beth Pendergraft, Regents University, GA.

Content Area
Reading Assessment

Introduction to the Content Area Reading Assessment

What Is the *CARA*?

The Content Area Reading Assessment (CARA) is a formative, group-administered assessment that teachers and districts can use to determine students' ability to answer questions based on the Common Core State Standards (CCSS) for English Language Arts and Literacy (ELA) in content areas. The content areas included in the ELA standards are Literature, History/Social Studies, and Science and Technical Subjects. Thus, the *CARA* comprises literature, social studies, and science passages taken from representative textbooks at grades 4 through high school. The passages include questions based on the College and Career Readiness Anchor Standards for Reading (CCSSO & NGA, 2010, p. 10), which require constructed responses—that is, the students must write or type their answers to the questions. The *CARA* is not a high-stakes assessment; rather, it provides teachers a way to assess students' standards-based strengths as well as areas in which instruction is needed. In addition, the questions from each passage provide a model for composing standards-based questions. Therefore, teachers can use *CARA* passages and questions as examples from which to write their own questions, guide students' understanding of the demands of the standards, and provide standards-based instruction.

In summary, the *CARA* has several purposes. One purpose is to provide a formative assessment of reading comprehension in the content areas of literature, social studies, and science based on the CCSS in ELA. Second, it is designed to help teachers and students understand the CCSS in ELA. Third, it may serve as a model from which teachers can write standards-based questions from their instructional materials. Fourth, the information gained from classroom administration of the *CARA* can guide instruction toward standards where students appear to have the most difficulty.

Why Was the *CARA* Developed?

The *CARA* was developed because there was no assessment that met the needs of adolescent learners in the age of the Common Core State Standards. It was also designed in response to several critical issues facing education in the United States: the wide adoption of the Common Core Standards, the latest reports of the National Assessment for Educational Progress (NAEP), reports of student performance on college entrance examinations, and as a response to two national reports that focused on adolescent literacy.

As of this writing, 45 states have signed on to participate in the CCSS. This wide acceptance has occurred because student literacy performance has been of concern for some time. The National Assessment of Educational Progress (NAEP), often referred to as the Nation's Report Card, has monitored the academic progress of 9-, 13-, and 17-year-olds since the 1970s. Since the first assessment year, 9- and 13-year-olds have demonstrated progress in reading; 17-year-olds have not. A comparison of 2012 scores to 2008 scores indicates that only 13-year-olds demonstrated significant progress over the four-year span (NAEP, 2013).

Both the American College Test (ACT) and the Scholastic Aptitude Test (SAT) provide annual data on student readiness for college and career. Fifty-two percent of high school seniors met the ACT readiness benchmark for reading in 2012 (ACT, 2012) and forty-three percent met a similar SAT benchmark (SAT, 2012). "These results illustrate the need for common standards that will enable all students to develop the core competencies critical to college and career readiness" (SAT, 2012, p. 23).

The first national report, *A Time to Act: An Agenda for Advancing Adolescent Literacy for College and Career Success* (2010), examined the performance of adolescent readers on national tests and concluded,

> good early literacy instruction does not inoculate students against struggle or failure later on. Beyond grade 3, adolescent learners in our schools must decipher more complex passages, synthesize information at a higher level, and learn to form independent conclusions based on evidence. They must also develop special skills and strategies for reading text in each of the differing content areas (such as English, science, mathematics and history)—meaning that a student who "naturally" does well in one area may struggle in another. (Carnegie Council on Advancing Adolescent Literacy, 2010, p. x).

The authors of *A Time to Act* argued that, although we have a strong knowledge base of reading instruction for grades K–3, adolescent literacy presents greater instructional challenges.

> Middle and high school learners must learn from texts which, compared to those in the earlier grades:
>
> - are significantly longer and more complex at the word, sentence and structural levels;
> - present greater conceptual challenges and obstacles to reading fluency;
> - contain more detailed graphic representations (as well as tables, charts and equations linked to text); and
> - demand a much greater ability to synthesize information. (Carnegie Council on Advancing Adolescent Literacy, 2010, p. x).

The authors recommended that interim assessments be developed. Such assessments should be closely aligned to standards and provide data to guide instructional decision making. The *CARA* is such an assessment. It is aligned to the Common Core State Standards and its purpose is to identify the literacy instructional needs of adolescents.

Shortly following *A Time to Act,* another Carnegie-sponsored report emerged: *Measure for Measure: A Critical Consumer's Guide to Reading Comprehension Assessments for Adolescents* (Morsy, Kieffer, & Snow, 2010). This report closely examined nine of the most commonly used literacy assessments and determined that none of them measured any degree of critical thinking, which they defined as "synthesizing knowledge across texts, critiquing an author's point of view or composing an essay in response to literature" (p. 7). None of the tests measured reading ability in specific content areas such as science, social studies, and mathematics. If different content was included in the test, subject scores were summed so a user could not distinguish a student's ability in one content area as compared to another.

The two national reports suggested several things. First, a group-administered screening test of reading comprehension is needed. Second, this instrument should include specific attention to different content areas: literature, social studies, and science. Bransford, Brown, and Cocking (2000) state that "characterizing assessments in terms of . . . the content-process demands of the subject matter brings specificity to generic assessment objectives such as 'higher level thinking and deep understanding'" (p. 143). Third, the answering of test questions should require critical thinking.

Issues in Assessment of Adolescent Literacy

Concern about the nature of available assessments in the literacy field is not a recent occurrence. The influential Rand Report supported "an obligation to develop assessments that are embedded in and supportive of instruction" (Rand Reading Study Group, 2002, p. 55). Similarly, Sweet (2005) stressed the need for teachers to have assessment options that "inform instruction and . . . reflect the effect of instructional intervention" (p. 8). Afflerbach (2007) emphasized the importance of striking a balance between formative and summative reading assessments. Summative assessments help districts ascertain if students have met grade-level goals and state standards, but they do not inform instruction or focus on individual student needs, as formative assessments do. Formative assessments "can help teachers and schools demonstrate accountability on a daily basis" by providing a teacher with a "detailed sense of how well students are 'getting' the lesson" (p. 279).

The CCSS and Adolescent Literacy

The emergence of the Common Core State Standards for English Language Arts & Literacy in History/Social Studies, Science and Technical Subjects (2010) addressed two of the above needs identified by the national reports:

- A focus on literacy in the content areas of literature, social studies, science, and math
- A focus on higher-level thinking skills

The standards also addressed curriculum concerns voiced by ACT and SAT. The standards include reading standards for literature and for informational text (K–5 and 6–12). Standards are grouped into the following categories:

- Key Ideas and Details
- Craft and Structure
- Integration of Knowledge and Ideas
- Range of Reading and Level of Text Complexity

An examination of the standards illustrates that students are expected to engage in higher-level thinking in grade-level materials. The CCSS expect the students to:

- Read closely
- Make logical inferences
- Determine central ideas or themes
- Summarize
- Analyze how and why
- Interpret words and phrases
- Analyze text structure
- Assess point of view
- Integrate and evaluate content
- Delineate and evaluate arguments

Given the findings of the two foundation reports; concerns about student achievement raised by NAEP, ACT, and SAT; and the emergence of the Common Core State Standards, it is clear that new assessments are needed to address content area literacy, to assess critical thinking, and to provide formative measures for guiding instruction.

Accordingly, the *Content Area Reading Assessment (CARA)* was created in order to provide:

- A formative assessment of grade-appropriate and discipline-specific text comprehension based on the Common Core State Standards for Grades 4–9/10
- A measure of comprehension in three distinct content areas: literature, social studies, and science that focuses on critical thinking
- A tool that teachers can use to write standards-based questions from their instructional material
- Information from which teachers can plan standards-based instruction

Conley (2008) describes four characteristics of "fair" assessment for adolescents. Our intention was to construct such an assessment. Table 1.1 illustrates the relationship between each of Conley's four characteristics and how the *CARA* meets each of them.

Table 1.1   The Relationship Between Conley's (2008) Fair Assessment and the *CARA*

Characteristics of Fair Assessment	*Content Area Reading Assessment (CARA)*
1. Fair assessment is based on clear targets and goals.	*CARA* is grounded in the Common Core State Standards for English Language Arts and Literacy in History/Social Studies, and Science and Technical Subjects (2010), specifically the standards for Literature and Informational Text. The Common Core Standards provide the framework for the design of *CARA* questions.
2. Fair assessment should focus on what has been taught and learned by communicating information on performance and growth.	The purpose of the *CARA* is to identify those Common Core Standards that need to be taught. Because there are at least three passages at each level and in each discipline, a teacher can use the first passage as a measure of initial assessment. After identifying and teaching to areas of need, the second passage can be used as a specific assessment of improved performance in the standards. If more instruction is warranted, a third passage allows for additional assessment.
3. Fair assessment should provide students with useful and useable information.	Because each question on the *CARA* is tied to a specific standard, a student can identify his or her strengths and/or weaknesses with regard to each standard. In addition, because the *CARA* offers literature, social studies, and science passages, a student can determine which subject area may be more problematic and thus require more effort and attention on the student's part.
4. Fair assessment creates purposeful learning opportunities.	The *CARA* passages are drawn from typical textbooks at grades 4 through high school. The selections represent typical literature, social studies, and science passages. Even if a teacher does not administer a specific passage as a formative assessment measure, the teacher can use the passage as the focus of instruction in helping students understand the intent of the standards and in clarifying the cognitive activities that they must employ in order to meet them. The teacher can demonstrate, for example, what it means to analyze, the types of context needed to determine word meaning, and the different types of text structure.

Summary

In summary, the *CARA* was designed in direct response to:

- The lack of progress of 12th graders on national assessments (e.g., NAEP, SAT, ACT)
- The emergence of the Common Core State Standards
- The instructional and assessment concerns of two national reports on adolescent literacy

The *CARA* provides a formative, group-administered assessment that addresses content area literacy with a focus on critical thinking. It also represents fairness in adolescent assessment as described by Conley (2008). It is grounded in clear goals, offers useful information on performance and growth, and provides passages that can be used for both assessment and instruction. Finally, it provides teachers with a model for developing standards-based assessment and instruction.

Research Perspective for the *CARA*

Differences Between CCSS and Previous Standards

The purpose of the *CARA* is to assess comprehension of grade-level text using questions that are based on the Common Core State Standards for English Language Arts and Literacy in History, Social Studies, and Science and Technical Subjects (CCSSO & NGA, 2010), specifically the Reading Standards for Literature and Informational Text. There are four major differences between the Common Core Standards and previous standards.

1. The standards are text based; that is, they demand that readers comprehend explicit content and use this content to draw inferences. To put it another way, "the Common Core expects students to cite textual evidence as they explain what the text teaches" (Calkins, Ehrenworth, & Lehman, 2012, p. 41).
2. The standards focus on literacy in three distinct disciplines: language arts, social studies, and science. After first providing 10 general anchor standards that cross all three subject areas, the standards explain each anchor in more detail according to specific grade levels and subject areas.
3. The standards emphasize a higher level of comprehension—what has often been termed *critical thinking*.
4. The standards require that students attain proficiency in grade-appropriate text. For example, Standard 10 requires that grade 6 students "by the end of the year read and comprehend . . . in the grades 6–8 complexity band proficiently with scaffolding as needed at the high end of the range" (p. 37). Eighth graders are expected to do this "independently and proficiently."

Text Comprehension

What Does It Mean to Comprehend Text?

The *CARA* is primarily an assessment of student comprehension during and after reading literature, social studies, and science passages. Comprehension is a very general term and it is important that teachers and students understand specifically what it means to comprehend a text. Kintsch (2004) describes a text as composed of a series of ideas (the microstructure) that are organized as a narrative, an explanation, an argument, and so forth (the macrostructure). The ideas of the author and the author's choice of text organization together form what Kintsch refers to as the *text base*. "Forming a text base is the first step in the comprehension process. . . . A good text base is representative of the meaning of the text and its structure" (Kintsch, 2012, p. 22).

Readers must comprehend the text base; however, they also need to move beyond it and, depending on their purpose, interests, and world knowledge, construct a situation model, which is the reader's understanding of the text base integrated with the reader's knowledge. Two readers reading the same text can arrive at very different situation models. One reader interested in drama may read an account of ancient Greece and construct a situation model that focuses on Greek plays and their enactment. Another reader, involved in completing an assignment for a political science course, may concentrate on the organization of Greek government and build a situation model that compares the structure of the Athenian republic to present day democracy.

The standards require that readers use the text base, not their interests, opinions, or prior knowledge of the topic, as the foundation for constructing a situation model. Standard 1 states that students must "read closely to determine what the text says explicitly and to make logical inferences from it; cite specific textual evidence . . . to support conclusions (CCSSO & NGA, 2010, p. 10). This means that students must understand the text base, the author's ideas, and how they are organized. "Readers need to get their mental arms around the text, to be able to retell it, to cite it, to ground anything they have to say about the text with textual references" (Calkins, Ehrenworth, & Lehman, 2012, p. 39).

Perhaps an example will clarify how this process works. Consider the three *CARA* high school passages on Andrew Jackson; they form a text base. The author provides a summary of Jackson's beliefs and behavior prior to and during his two terms of office. The reader must comprehend this text base—what the author says were factors that led to Jackson's election in 1828 and his reaction to such issues as Native American rights, nullification, and the bank of the United States. Using comprehension of the text base as the foundation, the reader constructs a situation model. One possible situation model could be that the author's point of view of Jackson was less than favorable. This situation model might be influenced by the inclusion of Jackson's defiant remark regarding the Supreme Court (a remark one might identify as overly flippant), and by the absence of any quotation of Jackson's that would have presented him in a more favorable light. It could also be influenced by the author's use of the word *projected* in the passage: "He [Jackson] projected himself as a down-to-earth common man," rather than "He was a down-to-earth common man," which might indicate to a reader that the author felt Jackson's stance was somewhat suspect. Such a situation model would not be based on other accounts of Jackson's life or the reader's beliefs regarding political campaigns and the use or misuse of presidential power. The model is based on the text. Another reader may have constructed a different situation model, perhaps interpreting the author's text base as less biased and more objective. However, the critical element of the standards is that the text base was understood and the situation model was inferred from the text base.

The Comprehension Process (Kintsch, 2004)

Form a text base

    Understand the author's ideas (the microstructure)

    Understand the author's organization (the macrostructure)

Use the text base to build a situation model

    Analyze

    Apply

    Synthesize

    Evaluate

How Does Prior Knowledge Fit into Understanding the Text Base and Situation Model?

Does the requirement that a situation model be drawn from the text negate the extensive research base that indicates prior knowledge of the topic is a critical element in comprehension? In other words, do the standards expect students to rely on the text to the exclusion of what they already know? It is important, therefore, to clarify what is meant by *prior knowledge.*

Prior knowledge has often been interpreted in a narrow and somewhat limited fashion as knowledge of the specific topic or content of the passage. However, prior knowledge is much more than that. Alexander and Jetton (2000) describe prior knowledge as "a rich body of knowledge organized around pivotal concepts or principles" (p. 287). It involves linguistic knowledge of word meanings, sentence structure, and text structure. It involves schooled knowledge, which, as the name suggests, is knowledge gathered from school experiences. Perhaps the largest component is unschooled knowledge, the conceptual knowledge gleaned from everyday life experiences and from interactions with a variety of individuals. One can hypothesize that knowledge of specific comprehension strategies might be part of schooled knowledge, but such knowledge may actually be self-taught through wide reading and interaction with a variety of texts, thus falling into the category of unschooled knowledge. Readers construct a text base and a situation model using linguistic, schooled, and unschooled knowledge even if specific information on the topic of their reading is relatively unknown.

What Do Readers Do when They Build a Text Base and Situation Model?

Fisher, Frey, and Lapp (2012) describe comprehension as involving four reader roles: code breaker, meaning maker, text user, and text critic. Code breaker and meaning maker specifically refer to the reader's understanding of the text base. As code breaker, a reader draws a variety of linguistic inferences; "the reader recognizes words, retrieves their context-appropriate meanings, and builds phrases (parsing) from words" (Perfetti & Adlof, 2012, p. 6). As meaning maker, a reader constructs inferences that bridge text elements and "support the coherence necessary for comprehension" (p. 7). For example, consider the following excerpt from the second *CARA* passage on Andrew Jackson: "Jackson's political base lay in the South, where he captured 80 percent of the vote. Those voters expected Jackson to help them remove the 60,000 American Indians living in the region." Constructing an accurate text base requires inferring that "he" in the first sentence refers to Jackson, "those voters" refers to voters in the South, and "them" refers to "those voters." Readers frequently draw such bridging inferences without being overtly aware of the process. However, awareness often occurs when readers find themselves struggling to make sense of the text base.

As a text user and text critic, the reader constructs a situation model, which also involves drawing inferences. Many of these inferences are derived from prior knowledge. A reader of the Jackson passages possesses unschooled and schooled knowledge about many things, such as the purpose of authors, the motivations of individuals, the often contentious nature of political disagreements, and an understanding that text is rarely neutral. Using this world knowledge and assuming that an adequate and accurate text base has been constructed, a reader may infer a possible bias on the part of the author even if prior knowledge of Andrew Jackson is missing. But what about an individual who possesses prior knowledge about a specific topic such as Jackson's presidency? In that case, the reader infers whether the text agrees with, refutes, or adds to what the reader already knew.

What is involved in answering questions based on the standards? Teachers and students must realize that answering questions tied to the standards involves drawing text-based inferences. For example, if asked to analyze how two things are alike, the reader uses explicit statements in the text, not his or her prior knowledge of the topic. However, the ability to draw an inference is affected by understanding the demands of the task and the goals or purpose for reading (van den Broek, Lorch, Linderholm, & Gustafson, 2001). This suggests that students must be made aware of what is involved in answering questions based on the standards.

First, standards-based questions cannot be answered by simply matching the language of the question to similar language in the text. A student must identify text that is relevant to the question to compose an appropriate answer. This involves several components. First, students must understand the question stems. What is meant by *analyze, text evidence, text structure, point of view, central idea, context,* and so on? Next, the student must search the text and identify all content that may be relevant to the intent of the question. Finally, the student must select those text components that provide the best answer—that is, the text content that allows the student to clearly and effectively analyze, describe point of view, identify word meaning, and so on.

How do the standards address all the comprehension skills that are part of many curriculum standards and/or scope and sequence charts? The primary issue is whether all those skills are actually different and discrete entities, a question investigated in 1968 by Frederick Davis. Using what was then a new statistical tool, factor analysis, he identified eight separate sub-skills of the reading process. Table 2.1 indicates how Davis' eight factors closely align with the College and Career Readiness Anchor Standards for Reading.

Table 2.1   The Relationship Between Davis's (1968) Subskills of the Reading Process and the CCSS Anchor Standards

Davis's Subskills	Anchor Standards
Understanding content stated explicitly	**Standard 1:** Read closely to determine what the text says explicitly and to make logical inferences from it.
Weaving together ideas in the content	**Standard 2:** Determine central ideas or themes of a text and analyze their development. **Standard 7:** Integrate and evaluate content presented in diverse media.
Drawing inferences from the content	**Standard 1:** Read closely to determine what the text says explicitly and to make logical inferences from it. **Standard 3:** Analyze how and why individuals, events, and ideas develop and interact. **Standard 8:** Delineate and evaluate the argument and specific claims in a text including validity of reasoning as well as relevance and sufficiency of evidence.
Remembering word meanings in context	**Standard 4:** Interpret words and phrases as they are used in the text.
Following the structure of the content	**Standard 5:** Analyze the structure of texts.
Recognizing author's tone, mood, and purpose	**Standard 6:** Assess how point of view and purpose shape content and style. **Standard 9:** Analyze how two or more texts address similar themes or topics.
Recognizing literary techniques	**Standard 5:** Analyze the structure of texts. **Standard 6:** Assess how point of view and purpose shape content and style.

Comprehension of Discipline-Specific Text

How does reading differ in discipline-specific text? The standards focus on literacy in three distinct disciplines: English/language arts, history/social studies, and science. Similarly, the *CARA* is composed of text in three different disciplines: literature, social studies, and science. "Anchor standards for College and Career Readiness (CCR) define general, cross-disciplinary literacy expectations that must be met for students to be prepared to enter college and workforce training programs ready to succeed" (CCSSO & NGA, 2010, p. 4). The anchor standards are then explained in more specific terms for each grade level and each discipline. In the past, the ability to read and comprehend a single generic text was often considered to represent general reading ability. For example, a student's performance on a story-like passage from an informal reading inventory was used to determine overall reading level. Little attention was paid to the differences between text in different disciplines.

Understanding literature, social studies, and science passages is very different from the casual reading that many individuals engage in such as light fiction, newspaper accounts of football games, and magazine articles describing the tangled lives of Hollywood and reality television stars. "Disciplines of study such as social science, mathematics and science approach, represent and critique information in unique ways" (Shanahan, 2009, p. 240) and difficulty in comprehending them often occurs because students lack understanding of how information is created and shared in different disciplines.

Literature, social studies, and science are often and erroneously thought of as unitary disciplines; that is, they are each presumed to have a common structure and/or purpose. However, in reality, they represent a variety of sub-disciplines. For example, literature encompasses such disparate genres as short stories, plays, poetry, and novels. Social studies includes the disciplines of history and political science. Science comprises biology, chemistry, and physics, to name a few. Each of these sub-disciplines is characterized by a unique structure and content; a civics text is very different from a history text. For example, consider the difference between the chronological structure of an account of Andrew Jackson's term of office and explanations of how different political structures operate. A student who demonstrates skill in comprehending stories will not necessarily be as adept when asked to comprehend a play. A student who does well in a biology class may not do as well in physics.

Sub disciplines of broad areas of:

- Literature: short stories, plays, poetry, novels, memoirs, biography
- Social studies: history, political science, civics
- Science: biology, chemistry, physics, environmental science, technological studies.

It is true that reading involves some similar processes whether an individual is reading literature, social studies, or science. Readers identify words, attain a measure of automaticity in doing so, and comprehend connected text. However, additional and different skills are required in order to fully comprehend text in different disciplines. Reading comprehension is "context-dependent and influenced in part by the kind of text that one reads" (Shanahan, 2009, p. 257). History text, for example, often presents events and actions as chronological accounts and cause–effect relationships; science texts are structured with an emphasis on procedures and explanations.

Disciplinary experts read text differently. Dole, Nokes, and Drits (2009) described three strategies employed by historians: sourcing, corroboration, and contextualization. Historians identify and use the source of a text to draw inferences about its content. Corroboration involves noting similarities and differences between texts on the same topic. Contextualization entails comprehending an event through the lens of the specific historical and cultural context in which it occurred. In other words, historians "render judgments on the trustworthiness and reliability of the text and author" (Afflerbach & Cho, 2009, p. 78).

Other researchers asked teams of experts in the fields of history, chemistry, and mathematics to read disciplinary texts (Shanahan, Shanahan, & Misischia, 2011). Using think-alouds and focus group discussions, they identified important differences in how the experts read text in their specific discipline. The role of the author was important in each discipline, but how the expert used knowledge of the author was different. Historians paid attention to text authors' point of view and the possible source of their information. Chemists used the author as a possible predictor of quality. The date of the article also played a role in experts' evaluations of articles. Historians were concerned about when the text was written and how this might influence the content. Chemists were concerned with whether the content represented out-of-date material. Finally, the experts' knowledge base was used in interpreting the article. Historians focused on whether the text agreed or disagreed with their own opinions and whether the author represented a credible source. Chemists also were concerned with text credibility but they defined it as "plausibility or its congruence with scientific evidence" (p. 420).

What Is the Role of Academic Language in Discipline-Specific Text?

Different disciplines also employ different forms of academic language. Academic language is very different from social and/or spoken language. It is "the form of language expected in contexts such as the exposition of topics in the school curriculum, making arguments, defending propositions, and synthesizing information" (Snow, 2010, p. 450). Academic language is formal, complex, and impersonal. It is characterized by abstraction, conciseness, informational density, precision, and compression of ideas into as few words as possible. It contains morphologically complex words that are heavily dependent on Latin and Greek vocabulary. Nagy and Townsend (2012) argue that academic usage of the grammatical metaphor "is the largest diversion from social/conversational language and presents the most significant issue for students" (p. 94). Grammatical metaphor involves turning verbs and adjectives into nouns, generally by adding suffixes (*act/action*; *active/activity*): it allows a single word to express an entire sentence (Jackson *opposed* Adams, Jackson's *opposition*).

Reading in Different Disciplines

Literature	**Emphasis on**
	character motivation
	dialogue
	theme/message
	author's point of view
	figurative language
	connotative meaning
History	**Emphasis on**
	chronological events
	context of the event
	reliability of the source
	author perspective
	agreement/disagreement with author
Science	**Emphasis on**
	procedures and experiments
	accuracy of information
	author as a predictor of quality
	concern with out of date material
	value of information

What Does This Mean for Instruction?

Should instruction focus on generic strategies or discipline-specific strategies? Fang (2012) describes four approaches to content area literacy. The cognitive approach focuses on the use of generic strategies such as note taking, summarizing, and visual mapping. Based on the belief that such strategies are basically the same for all disciplines, "different comprehension activities are replicated from one content area to the next with little regard for the particular challenges to concepts, structure, genre or task within a content area or sub-discipline" (Conley, 2009, p. 538). The sociocultural approach promotes the use of students' unschooled knowledge and cultural practices "as both a bridge to and a resource for promoting the development of content area literacies (Fang, 2012, p. 104). The linguistic approach concentrates on the development of vocabulary and the analysis of grammatically complex sentences. The critical approach emphasizes that text must be understood in relation to the intention of the author and the context in which it is written.

A variety of studies showing improvement in overall comprehension as a result of teaching various comprehension strategies has been interpreted as evidence that teaching multiple strategies improves comprehension. However, this may occur not because of a specific strategy but because the emphasis on strategies promotes engagement with text and provides a vehicle for student dialogue (Wilkinson & Son, 2011). In fact, "the generic strategy approach can, indeed, be of infinite value to students when content area teachers and literacy specialists engage in thoughtful dialogue about how to contextualize these strategies" (Brozo, Moorman, Meyer, & Stewart, 2013, p. 355). However, a focus on generic strategies such as note taking, paraphrasing, and mapping developed from research on the comprehension process has been infused into different content areas "without considering what makes learning in content area contexts both diverse and often challenging" (Conley, 2009, p. 547). He suggests that the process needs to be reversed—that is, disciplinary practice should identify teaching and comprehension strategies germane to specific disciplines. Or putting it in another way, "strategies provide the tools to help students make sense of the content and the content gives meaning and purpose to the strategies" (Wilkinson & Son, 2011, p. 367).

Other authors have made similar arguments for discipline-focused reading instruction (Dole, Nokes, & Drits, 2009; Moje, 2008) suggesting that experts in a discipline should use knowledge of their field to guide student reading. "What that means instructionally is that secondary school teachers in the content areas need to work together with literacy specialists in joint efforts to improve reading comprehension" (Shanahan, 2009, p. 257; Snow, 2010). These comments parallel the conclusions of the authors of the national report *A Time to Act: An Agenda for Advancing Adolescent Literacy for College and Career Success* (Carnegie Council on Advancing Adolescent Literacy, 2010) discussed in Chapter 1.

What Does This Mean for Assessment?

The Carnegie-sponsored report, *Measure for Measure: A Critical Consumers' Guide to Reading Comprehension Assessments for Adolescents* (Morsy, Kieffer, & Snow, 2010) indicated that none of the most commonly used literacy assessments measure reading ability in different content areas. The assessments may have contained passages from different disciplines; however, the test scores were combined so there was no way to distinguish a student's ability in one discipline from another. This is unfortunate, because assessment of a student's ability to comprehend in one discipline may not generalize to a different one; that is, a student may demonstrate acceptable comprehension while reading a story but be less successful when reading a science text. Similarly, the ability to demonstrate mastery of the standards in one content area may not transfer to a different area.

If reading comprehension is context dependent—and it is—then reading comprehension assessment should be as well. The purpose of the *CARA* is to provide passages in literature, social studies, and science for the classroom teacher to use in determining the needs of his or her students. The teacher has the option to administer all or only a single passage. For example, a fifth-grade teacher may opt to administer only the science or social studies passage if he or she is concerned about student performance in that respective area. Another teacher may choose only to administer the literature passage. The *CARA* is not an informal reading inventory, as we will explain in the next chapter. It is a formative measure that teachers can use to suit their specific purpose: to examine which standards and which disciplines need instructional emphasis.

Factors Related to Critical Thinking

What Is Critical Thinking?

Besides stating that frequently used assessments did not address reading in the different disciplines, *Measure for Measure* (2010) concluded that none of the nine commonly used assessments evaluated critical thinking. An online search directed toward critical thinking identified numerous studies in disciplines other than education, as well as studies directed at college-level students. Few studies of critical thinking focusing on upper elementary, middle school, and high school levels were evident. One might hypothesize that the absence of interest or concern regarding critical thinking may reflect its absence in popular assessments. What is not regularly assessed may be viewed as having little relevance for classroom instruction.

The authors of *Measure for Measure* recommend that answering test questions requires a student to think critically and the standards have been described as focusing on critical thinking. What exactly does that mean? *Critical thinking* is generally recognized as an umbrella term that encompasses a variety of higher-level cognitive skills such as interpretation, analysis, and evaluation. It includes thinking about issues within specific disciplines as well as addressing the problems and challenges of our increasingly complex world. "Critical thinking or the ability to engage in powerful, self-regulatory judgment is widely recognized as an essential skill for the knowledge age" (Abrami, Bernard, Borokhovski, Wade, Surkes, Tamim, et al., 2008, p. 1102).

Critical thinking must be differentiated from critical literacy. Critical literacy involves preparing students to deal with the multiple uses of literacy in contemporary society. "This comprises knowledge of texts in a range of modalities, textual interpretation, construction and evaluation, and critical understandings about the reflexive relationship of interpretation to both textual and social practices and structures" (Freebody & Freiberg, 2011, p. 432). Critical literacy involves identification of multiple viewpoints, a focus on sociopolitical issues, and the promotion of social justice. Critical literacy has also been interpreted as identifying the viewpoints of textbook authors "that privilege some voices and silence others" (Sheridan-Thomas, 2008, p. 169). Obviously critical thinking is needed to foster critical literacy; however, the terms refer to different entities.

Critical thinking has been described as making use of many of the following cognitive processes that can be clearly linked to specific standards:

- Drawing inferences that bridge elements in the text or support the development of coherence (Perfetti & Adlof, 2012): Standards 1, 2, 3, 6, 7, 8, and 9
- Synthesizing information from various parts of the text and different texts (Pearson & Hamm, 2005): Standards 2, 3, 8, and 9
- Recognizing meaningful patterns of information (Bransford, Brown, & Cocking, 2000): Standards 5, 8, and 9

- Using higher-order, purposeful, and goal-directed operations requiring judgment, analysis, and synthesis (Gunn & Pomahac, 2008): Standards 3, 7, 8, and 9
- Employing metacognition, because critical thinking by definition involves reflecting on what is known and how that knowledge is justified (Kuhn, 1999): Standards 1, 6, 8, and 9
- Engaging in careful argumentation encompassing analysis, synthesis, inference, interpretation, evaluation, and reasoning; a skill that can be developed by teaching students "to think in terms of a series of mini-arguments as they collect evidence" (Yeh, 2001, p. 12): Standards 8 and 9

What Form Does Instruction in Critical Thinking Take?

Little consensus exists "about whether it is a set of generic skills that apply across subject domains . . . or whether it depends on the subject domain and context in which it is taught" (Abrami et al., 2008, p. 1105). Abrami and colleagues (2008) conducted a meta-analysis of four types of interventions involving critical thinking and concluded the following:

- General interventions focused on critical thinking as unrelated to a specific discipline.
- Immersion interventions included attention to disciplinary content but did not identify critical thinking as a specific learning objective. Instead, it was viewed as a byproduct of instruction.
- Infusion interventions included critical thinking as an explicit course objective presented with attention to content.
- A mixed approach taught critical thinking as an independent entity but within a specific content course.

Students who received mixed approaches that combined content and critical thinking instruction significantly outperformed all others. Immersion courses where critical thinking was not an explicit objective had the smallest effects: "Developing CT skills separately and then applying them to course content explicitly works best; immersing students in thought-provoking subject matter instruction without explicit use of CT principles was least effective" (p. 1210).

Supporting that conclusion, explicit instruction in critical thinking skills combined with science content was effective for middle school students (Gunn, Grigg, & Pomahac, 2006). Students examined case studies involving medical dilemmas and were guided to construct visual and text-based argument maps centered on the content. Analysis of the maps suggested improvement in critical thinking. In a follow-up study, seventh graders were taught to differentiate between memory questions and critical thinking questions. Then, using generic question stems, students created critical thinking questions based on science content. Analysis of the questions in relation to Bloom's taxonomy revealed that the experimental group produced more higher-level evaluation questions, whereas the control group generated more lower-level knowledge questions (Gunn & Pomahac, 2008).

These studies suggest that critical thinking skills as mandated by the standards can be taught if they are regarded as specific instructional components within the content of a discipline; they will not naturally develop as a result of instruction in disciplinary content. Kuhn (1999) states "it is essential that we know precisely what we mean when we refer to critical or thinking skills if the constructs are to be useful" (p. 17). The standards may act as a catalyst for formulating a more specific and agreed-on definition, as opposed to the vague and nebulous definitions that have proliferated. Using the Anchor Standards as a base, critical thinking may become associated with the following mental operations: supporting conclusions; analyzing the development of central ideas and themes; analyzing how word choice shapes meaning; analyzing how point of view shapes content; integrating and evaluating content; and evaluating arguments, claims, reasoning, relevancy, and sufficiency of evidence.

Grade-Appropriate Text

How Is the Difficulty of a Text Measured?

The standards require that, at the end of the year, students are able to read grade-appropriate text with support and/or independently and proficiently. Identification of grade-appropriate text has, for many years, rested on determination of text difficulty based on readability formulas. These include but are not limited to the following formulas: Dale-Chall (Chall & Dale, 1995); Fry (Fry, 2002); Flesch-Kincaid and Flesch Reading Ease (Farr, Jenkins, & Paterson, 1951; Flesch, 1948); Degrees of Reading Power (Questar Assessment, Inc., 2013) and Lexile levels (MetaMetrics, 2013). The authors of the Common Core Standards have adopted the Lexile readability formula as a measure of the text complexity band mentioned in Standard 10. Such formulas are based on word length, sentence length, and/or word frequency. They rest on the assumption that shorter sentences, words of few syllables, and words that are more frequent in speech and print translate into easier text. Readability formulas play an important part in determining which textbooks are considered appropriate for which grade level (Graesser, McNamara, & Louwerse, 2011).

What Are Other Factors That Contribute to the Difficulty of a Text?

Determining text difficulty, however, is considerably more complex than choosing a text that matches a grade-appropriate reading level as indicated by one or more readability formulas. Many other factors besides sentence length and word frequency play a part in making a text easy or difficult: "cohesive cues in text facilitate reading comprehension and help readers construct more coherent mental representations of text content" (McNamara, Graesser, & Louwerse, 2012, p. 90). These include but are not limited to syntax, coherence, the use of connectives, genre, and the complexity and familiarity of the concepts (Graesser, McNamara, & Louwerse, 2011). For example, given identical Lexile scores for two texts, one can certainly hypothesize that concepts included in an account of the Greek wars would be less difficult than those included in a description of the differences between prokaryotic and eukaryotic cells. Students are more knowledgeable about wars in general than about cell types. Also, the selection on cell types is more conceptually dense than the selection on the Greek wars. Similarly in literature, given comparable Lexile scores for two stories, one can estimate that the rather straightforward tale of a wounded animal would be less difficult to understand than a myth with an underlying message.

Narrative and expository texts differ in various components of complexity as suggested by text analysis using Coh-Metrix, a computer program that examines various indices of text difficulty. McNamara, Graesser, and Louwerse (2012) compared narrative, social studies, and science passages according to several indices: word frequency; sentence complexity; referential cohesion, or the overlap of words and concepts across the text; causal cohesion as indicated by use of connectives such as *because* and *therefore*; and verb cohesion, or the overlap between actions. Greater ease in comprehending literature may be due to word familiarity and the extensive use of connectives. Science texts, on the other hand, contain less frequent words and less supportive connectives. Although they are more cohesive, this does not necessarily compensate for their high level of difficulty. Social studies text, often as conceptually difficult as science, is less cohesive and offers only a moderate use of connectives. The authors concluded that "it is insufficient to define readability simply on the basis of word frequency, word length and sentence length. Text difficulty is also a result of cohesion" (p. 112). Research such as this suggests that future determination of text difficulty may become more finely tuned and better represent text difficulty.

The authors of the standards suggest that "reading texts have actually trended downward in difficulty in the last half century" (CCSSO & NGA, 2010, Appendix A, p. 3). The trend toward less difficult text may have resulted in an unintended consequence: lower reading levels on the part of students and adults. In an effort to make texts easier, publishing companies have engaged in such practices as making sentences shorter, providing definitions of vocabulary, and including directions or suggestions for comprehending the text. Coleman and Pimentel (2011) take issue with this: "the scaffolding should not preempt or replace the text by translating its contents for students or telling students what they are going to learn in advance of reading the text; that is, the scaffolding should not become an alternate, simpler source of information that diminishes the need for students to read the text itself carefully. Effective scaffolding aligned with the standards should result in the reader encountering the text on its own terms, with instructions providing helpful directions that focus students on the text" (pp. 7–8).

Fisher, Frey, and Lapp (2012) suggest that lowering the difficulty level of texts, probably a genuine attempt to produce more considerate and readable text, has actually removed "the struggle that is so important in developing habits" (p. 45). Similarly, Kintsch (2004) suggests that learning a new skill involves the "opportunity to face difficulties and learn to repair mistakes" (p. 1314). In other words, students can attain higher reading levels only by reading and grappling with difficult text under the guidance of a skilled and understanding teacher. The authors of the standards believe that "current standards, curriculum, and instructional practice have not done enough to foster the independent reading of complex texts so crucial for college and career readiness" (CCSSO & NGO, 2010, Appendix A, p. 3).

Reading Level

For many years, teachers and intervention specialists have attempted to match student instructional reading level with text written at the same level. The determination of a student's instructional level is based on criteria established and promulgated over 60 years ago by Emmet Betts (1946, 1957). The teacher asks a student to orally read a passage and answer questions about its contents. The teacher counts the number of oral reading mistakes (often called *miscues*) and errors in comprehension and translates them into percentages. An instructional level for word identification generally falls between 90 and 97 percent accuracy and at 70 percent or above for comprehension (Leslie & Caldwell, 2011). It has been long assumed that a student's instructional level and text level should match. That is, if a student has an instructional level of fifth grade, he or she should read fifth-grade text because that is the level at which, with teacher guidance, the student can experience success.

Text more difficult than an instructional level, often called *frustration text,* should be avoided. Fisher, Frey, and Lapp (2012) describe matching text to student instructional levels as "a commonly accepted practice" but state that "concerns about this reader-text match have proliferated . . . for decades" (p. 7). Similarly, Halladay (2012) questions assumptions underlying instructional-level text, including the idea that frustration text will lead to emotional upset on the part of the student. Is determination of instructional level an outworn concept? Should all students be expected to read the same text irrespective of their actual reading ability? It is important to put this in perspective.

First, determination of a student's instructional level serves more purposes than just matching reading level to text level. An instructional level below chronological grade level may indicate a need for instruction beyond what would be normally offered in the regular classroom. An instructional level below third grade, for example, suggests a need for instruction in decoding accuracy and fluency. An emphasis on such skills, a normal part of instruction in grades 1–3, would be inappropriate in higher-level classrooms.

Second, although the standards stress the need for reading at chronological grade level, they also include the caveat "with scaffolding as needed" (p. 14). An instructional level can suggest the degree of needed scaffolding. The extent of a gap between instructional level and chronological grade level indicates the seriousness of the problem. An eighth grader with an instructional level of fourth grade, for example, needs more intensive intervention/scaffolding than one reading at a sixth-grade level. A classroom teacher may be able to support students with instructional levels slightly below their chronological grade levels. Other students will probably need the more individualized and focused instruction offered by intervention specialists.

Third, determination of instructional level varies with the text used during the assessment process. Instructional level can vary depending on the student's familiarity with the text structure and the underlying concepts (Leslie & Caldwell, 2011). Students often have one instructional level for narrative text and a lower level for expository material. The complexity and cohesion of a text and the familiarity of the underlying concepts also play a significant role. For example, *CARA* science passages for fifth and sixth grades focus on relatively complex concepts: the structure and function of cells and Wegener's theory of continental drift. We suspect that even those reading comfortably at a fifth- or sixth-grade level will need support to comprehend these texts to the extent expected by the Common Core Standards.

Finally, using instructional level to match readers and texts has been interpreted as never asking a student to read a text beyond his or her instructional level. This seems to us to be an oversimplification of a basically good idea: providing the reader with a manageable text. However, frustration-level text can be manageable with the support and guidance of the teacher and/or intervention specialist. As schools transition into greater compliance with the standards, many readers presently viewed as capable, with instructional levels that match their chronological grade levels, may experience difficulties in meeting the demands of more complex text.

Engagement in Learning: What Will Motivate Students to Learn New Content?

Recently concerns have been raised about whether students will engage in close reading sufficiently to learn at the level demanded by the Standards. Most middle and high school teachers see the average student as not strongly motivated to learn difficult concepts. It is not that they are unable to learn such material, but they need to be motivated by interesting and important content with engaging questions that challenge them. "In my opinion, those are the hooks on which the new and challenging tasks can best be hung" (Snow, June 6, 2013, pg. 1). How can we reconcile the tenet of the Standards that requires students to read texts autonomously without the benefit of focusing questions or orienting information or an introductory activity designed to stimulate enthusiasm for the topic?

Similar concerns have been raised by a researcher who has spent his last decade studying factors that motivate students to engage in learning. In a report from the Literacy Panel, Guthrie argues that although students will have to learn new ways to read text closely, teachers cannot simply assign hard reading materials. Students will not learn by pouring concepts and new skills into them. "Teaching new skills is a must, but new skills must be balanced by inspiring students' passions and purposes for learning, (Guthrie, 2013, April 15, 2013, pg. 1).

One way that the *CARA* encourages students' attention to our materials is by providing one or more introductory sentences that direct them to read for a specific purpose.

The Development of Questions

The Common Core State Standards define what "students should understand and be able to do by the end of each grade" (CCSSO & NGA, 2010, p. 10). Assessing understanding involves asking questions; therefore, the clarity and quality of the questions are integral to the value of any assessment. An unclear question or a question that does not specifically relate to the purpose or content of the assessment is of little value. Although the ability to provide a correct answer to a question is regarded as a measure of comprehension, a student may offer an erroneous answer for several reasons. First, the student may not have comprehended the text on which the question is based. Second, the student may not have understood the question. Third, the student may have comprehended both text and question but did not possess specific skills demanded by the question, such as analyzing, summarizing, or defining a word through use of context.

Why can't students answer comprehension questions correctly?

1. The student may not have understood the text upon which the question is based.
2. The student may not have understood the question.
3. The student may have comprehended the text and the question but did not possess specific skills demanded by the question, such as analyzing, summarizing, or using context to define a word.
4. The student understood the elements of the answer, but was unable to put the pieces together to form a complete answer.

Educators have long realized that questions come in many forms. Answering different questions requires different skills on the part of the student and represents different levels of comprehension. The ability to answer a literal question by matching the question stem to what is explicitly stated in the text ("What are resources provided by the Northeast region of the United States?") is generally easier than answering a question where the evidence is not directly stated in the passage ("Explain how changes in climate were responsible for developing Niagara Falls").

What Are Different Kinds of Question Taxonomies?

A variety of question taxonomies have been developed with the purpose of clarifying different types of knowledge or comprehension activities required for answering a specific question. The foundation of these taxonomies comes from Davis (1968, 1972), who was one of the first to conceptualize comprehension as involving different processes. Although not specifically directed at question types, Davis identified eight relatively separate comprehension factors:

1. Remembering word meaning
2. Determining word meaning from context
3. Understanding explicitly stated content
4. Weaving together ideas in the text
5. Drawing inferences
6. Recognizing author's purpose, mood, and/or tone
7. Identifying literary techniques
8. Following the structure of the text

Presumably, different questions would be needed to assess each factor. As illustrated previously (see Table 2.1), the majority of Davis's processes match the Common Core Anchor Standards for Reading. For example, Standard 1 focuses on understanding explicitly stated content and drawing inferences; Standard 4 centers on determining word meaning from context; Standard 5 addresses text structure; and Standard 6 focuses on recognizing author purpose, mood, and tone.

One of the first and perhaps the most well-known taxonomy of question types is that of Bloom (Bloom & Krathwohl, 1956), who divided cognitive processing into six categories: knowledge, comprehension, application, analysis, synthesis, and evaluation. These categories were used by the authors of the Rand Report on Reading Comprehension (2002). A revision of Bloom's original work by Anderson and Krathwohl (2001) offered the following six levels: remembering, understanding, applying, analyzing, evaluating, and creating. A variety of question taxonomies followed Davis's and Bloom's work (Applegate, Quinn & Applegate, 2002; Ciardiello, 1998; Raphael, Highfield, & Au, 2006). Most frequently, question types were based on the cognitive processes needed to answer different kinds of questions, and were divided into two broad categories of literal and inferential.

A different question taxonomy (Graesser & Person, 1994) is based less on what the reader must do and where the answer may be found and more on "the nature of the information being sought in a good answer to the question" (Grasser, Ozuru, & Sullins, 2010). They offer 16 different question types differentiated as shallow, intermediate, and complex.

- Shallow questions employ such question stems as *who, what, where,* and *when.* The reader is expected to offer an example, state if something is true or false, or say if it occurred or existed.
- Intermediate questions focus on understanding of quantitative and qualitative properties; the value of variables; definitions; and comparisons.
- Complex questions concentrate on interpretation of data, causes, consequences, goals, instruments, and procedures; goals and resources; identification of why something did or did not occur; and placement of value on an idea.

Mosenthal (1996) also differentiated questions in terms of the type of information needed to provide an acceptable answer. He formed "a continuum of difficulty depending on how concrete or abstract different types of requested information are" (p. 323).

- Questions that asked an individual to identify persons, animals, or things were the easiest and most concrete in nature.
- The next level included questions that asked for the identification of amounts, attributes, times, actions, locations, and types.
- The third level included identification of manner, goal, purpose, alternatives, and conditions.
- The fourth level included questions that focused on identification of cause, effect, reason, result, explanation, and similarity.
- The highest level of difficulty included questions that asked individuals to identify equivalence, difference, and theme. An examination of the Graesser and colleagues (2010) and Mosenthal (1996) taxonomies suggests that higher levels of questions are clearly related to the standards.

This summary suggests that questions are primarily distinguished by what the student is asked to do in order to answer the question, the nature of the information demanded by the question, and/or where the answer may be found. How a question is phrased signals the type of answer that is required. The proper choice of a question stem and the student's understanding of that stem are critical components. For example, while *analyze* and *categorize* are possible question stems for Bloom and Krathwohl's higher levels of questions, the student must grasp exactly what they mean in order to answer a question correctly. Using uniform and structured question stems and teaching students the nature of answers required by a specific stem is recommended (Gunn & Pomahac, 2008).

Using Taxonomies to Write Question Stems

Question taxonomies can act as guides to educators for constructing question stems based on the standards. A question stem can use a question word, such as *who, what, when* or *where,* or it can include a direction such as *explain, describe,* or *analyze.* Using the taxonomies to write standards-based question stems involves two steps: matching a question type to a specific standard and selecting an appropriate question stem.

For example, Ciardiello's (1998) classification of questions representing convergent, divergent, and evaluative thinking are applicable to the higher level of thinking demanded by the standards. Convergent questions beginning with *why, how,* and *in what way* match with Standard 3. Evaluative questions beginning with *justify* and *defend* match with Standards 8 and 9. Similarly, questions that match the standards can be based on Bloom and Krathwohl's (1956) question categories using such stems as *compare, differentiate, analyze, explain, interpret,* and *summarize.*

Table 2.2   Classification of Question Taxonomies

Bloom & Krathwohl (1956)	Raphael (1982, 1986)	Ciardiello (1998)	Mosenthal (1991)	Graesser & Person (1994)	Anderson & Krathwohl (2001)	Applegate, Quinn, & Applegate (2002)
Knowledge	In the Book: Right There, Think and Search	Memory			Remembering	Literal
Comprehension	In My Head: Author and Me	Convergent	Identify persons, animals, things, time, attributes, actions, locations	Shallow: Who, what, when, where	Understanding	Low Level High Level
Application	In My Head: On My Own		Identify manner, goal, purpose, alternatives, condition		Applying	Response
Analysis		Divergent	Identify cause, effects, evidence, similarity, explanation	Intermediate: Quantitative, qualitative, properties, value, comparisons, definitions	Analyzing	
Synthesis			Identify equivalence, difference, theme	Complex: Causes, consequences, goals, instruments, reasons, value		
Evaluation		Evaluative			Evaluating Creating	

Question stems for the intermediate- and complex-level questions of Graesser and Person's (1994) taxonomy include: *What is the value of X? How is X similar to/different from Y? What can be inferred from X? Why did X occur? How did X occur? What are the consequences of X? What are the motives/goals of X?* In accord with the demands of the standards, answers to such questions must be text based—that is, they must ask the student to draw inferences based on text content. In addition, questions that match the standards must emphasize higher-level comprehension and focus on analysis and synthesis as opposed to identification of discrete pieces of information.

The challenge in writing question stems to match the standards is the appropriateness of a stem to the intent of the specific standard. It is often assumed that students understand the subtle differences between question stems. For example, how does *analyze* differ from *interpret*? Do *delineate* and *evaluate* carry the same or different meaning? A student's ability to answer a question obviously depends on ability to read the text, but it also depends on the student's understanding of the question stem.

The *CARA* uses uniform question stems across all passages and all levels, with one exception. For literature, *explain* or *describe* are the question stems used in grades 4–6, and *analyze* is the term used above grade 6. For informational text, *explain* is the question stem used for grades 4 and 5. It is replaced by *analyze* for the remaining grade levels. The *CARA* questions can be used as a model for teachers to construct their own standards-based questions.

Table 2.2 summarizes many question taxonomies and how each taxonomy presents similar concepts represented by different terms.

Summary

The research base for the *CARA* is broad. Because the CCSS require students to use the text to support their comprehension, we have reviewed studies showing that comprehension processes differ in discipline-specific texts. The review also included a discussion on critical thinking and the different ways researchers have defined and labeled it. The CCSS require that students be able to comprehend grade-level text, therefore we have described quantitative and qualitative measures of text difficulty and issues in using each. Finally, we describe the research on how to ask different levels of questions using different question taxonomies.

Chapter

3 Description of the *CARA*

A Formative Measure

The *Content Area Reading Assessment (CARA)* is a formative, group-administered assessment that teachers and/or districts can use to determine the extent to which their students can engage in critical thinking during and after reading representative textbooks currently in use in schools. Passages represent the content areas of literature, social studies, and science at grades 4 through early high school. The question format is constructed response, as opposed to selected response. Each passage is accompanied by 10 questions that address from five to six of the Common Core State Standards, a summary question, and, for middle school and high school history, an additional short passage that addresses Standard 8 for informational text. Some standards are assessed by more than one question. *CARA* questions are specifically aligned to the Common Core State Standards for English Language Arts and Literacy in History/Social Studies and Science and Technical Subjects (CCSSO & NGA, 2010). Specifically, questions for the literature passages are based on Reading Standards for Literature 4–12 (CCSSO & NGA, 2010, pp. 12, 36–38) and the social studies and science passages are based on Reading Standards for Informational Text 4–12 (pp. 39–40). The questions represent a strong focus on critical thinking.

Our primary purpose in designing the *CARA* was to craft an assessment of content area reading comprehension based on the Common Core Standards and composed of passages written for fourth grade through high school. We did not include kindergarten and grades 1–3 in our instrument. At these grade levels, primary attention is focused on the development of word recognition, accuracy, and fluency. In addition, *CARA* questions are constructed-response questions. Although younger children may be able to answer such items orally or as part of a class discussion, the *CARA* is a group-administered instrument and, as such, requires the students to individually write their answers to the questions. This may be beyond the abilities of younger children and the accuracy of the answer could be compromised by time constraints and difficulty in writing.

The *CARA* provides a model for integrating the Common Core Standards at a classroom level through the construction of questions that specifically address each standard. Present textbooks and many assessments primarily divide questions into the broad categories of literal and inferential, but the standards demand more specificity. They stipulate (and thus define) different forms of inferences that students should draw from the text. Examples of the format of Standard 3 questions in informational text are "Analyze why slavery was the unfinished business of the Constitution" or "Analyze why sediment is important in the formation of a fossil." An example of a Standard 2 question in informational text is "The topic of the above two paragraphs is the slave trade.

What is the central idea?" Teachers can use the format of *CARA* questions to design their own questions aligned to the standards; classroom questioning and discussion can focus on these.

The *CARA* is a formative measure. "Formative assessment involves instructional and evaluative practices that are used frequently and authentically by classroom teachers to gain information about the ever-evolving needs of individual students" (Wood, Taylor, Drye, & Brigman, 2007, p. 195). Formative assessments inform instruction; they provide insights about what students know and can do or what they do not know or cannot do. They emphasize diagnostic usefulness and are primarily used "to draw inferences about student performance and to inform instruction; that is, to make instructional modifications as suggested by student achievement" (Leslie & Caldwell, 2009, p. 410). The effective use of formative measures can have a positive effect on student achievement (Black & Wiliam, 1998).

Formative measures used in the classroom provide information about students that help the teacher design meaningful and useful instruction (Carpenter & Paris, 2005). They should demonstrate a "close relation to the domain they assess" (Afflerbach and Cho, 2011, p. 491). The focus of the *CARA* is to provide information to teachers and students about the extent to which their students meet the Common Core Standards. Specifically, the *CARA* focuses on the Reading Standards for Literature and for Informational Text. The 10 questions that follow each passage provide a specific match to the standards, incorporating the language of the standards as part of their question stems. The questions were examined, critiqued, and revised following examination by a variety of elementary and secondary classroom teachers, reading teachers, and content specialists. They were also revised following extensive piloting of students at all levels; a detailed description of such can be found in Chapter 6. The *CARA* provides a measure whereby teachers can ascertain which standards will need instructional emphasis with which students.

An Informal Measure

The *CARA* is an informal assessment, as opposed to a formal measure. Formal measures must be administered with strict adherence to directions in the test manual. Their validity and reliability is predicated on the fact that they are administered and scored in the same way to all students. Informal assessments allow for choice on the part of the test administrator/teacher with regard to selection of passage, format for administration, and selection of questions. For example, a teacher may choose to administer all questions for a *CARA* passage or only a subset. A teacher may choose to omit the summary question or the additional Standard 8 passage for middle school and high school social studies. A teacher may choose to administer two or more levels of *CARA* passages or only administer the level for a specific grade.

The *CARA* is a different instrument than the traditional informal reading inventory (IRI), as shown in Table 3.1. The purpose of an IRI is to determine a student's instructional and frustration reading levels. The purpose of the *CARA* is to determine a student's ability to read grade-appropriate text and answer text-based questions specifically aligned to the Common Core State Standards. An IRI is administered in an individual format. The *CARA* is a group-administered measure. The teacher orally asks questions when administering an IRI and the student answers in a similar manner. The *CARA* requires that the students read the questions on their own and write their own answers.

Table 3.1   A Comparison of *CARA* with Traditional Informal Reading Inventories

	CARA	**Informal Reading Inventory**
Purpose	To determine student ability to read and comprehend grade-level texts in three content areas	To identify the level of narrative and expository materials that students can read with at least 70 percent comprehension
Method of administration	Group	Individual
Response requirements	Written response to open-ended questions that provides text evidence for inferences; determines central idea or theme; summarizes; analyzes the text; determines meaning of vocabulary in context; identifies text structure; determines point of view or purpose; uses visual information to answer questions; and/or traces and evaluates arguments and specific claims in a text	Oral response to literal and inferential questions
Time requirements	45–50 minutes per passage for student administration; approximately 10 minutes per passage for teacher correction	Variable from 15 minutes to 2 hours

Validity and Reliability

Unfortunately, some individuals regard informal and/or formative assessments as less valid or reliable than standardized high-stakes assessments. This is a false assumption. Any assessment that is used to gather information about students must have a measure of validity and reliability (Afflerbach & Cho, 2011). Basically, *validity* means that an "individual's scores from an instrument make sense, are meaningful and enable you . . . to draw good conclusions" (Cresswell, 2008, p. 169). To put it another way, a valid assessment measures what it is supposed to measure (Salkind, 2011). *Reliability* refers to scoring that is stable, consistent, and relatively free of error.

CARA questions were designed to measure student performance on specific Common Core Standards. To establish content validity—that is, the match of each question to a specific Standard—we recruited teachers to evaluate questions and address two issues. First, did each question meet the intent of the specific standard? If not, then how could the question be rewritten to meet the standard? Suggestions of the reviewers were incorporated into the *CARA*.

One form of reliability important to the *CARA* is inter-rater reliability, or the extent to which teachers score the same student responses identically. Because constructed responses can vary in accuracy, completeness, and quality of expression, it was important to develop a clear yet concise answer key. We asked teachers to evaluate the answer key and they made a variety of suggestions for improvement. The most common suggestion was to include other options for correct answers. *CARA* answer keys were also refined through an examination of student answers across piloting sessions. When students provided answers that differed from the answer key but were substantially correct, they were added to the answer key. We compared different scorers on the same passage to determine the reliability of their scoring. When two scorers disagreed as to the accuracy of an answer, we carefully examined their responses and made adjustments to the question and/or the answer key. This is reported in more detail in Chapter 6.

Reliability is also focused "on how an assessment consistently informs teachers and students to foster student learning" (Afflerbach & Cho, 2011, p. 492). The overall purpose of the *CARA* is to inform students and teachers of the extent to which they meet specific standards in three different disciplines: literature, social studies, and science. The teacher can opt to focus assessment on one or more of these disciplines. Questions are directly related to specific standards. As described in Chapter 4, Parts 1 and 2, an analysis of student and class performance can identify those standards and disciplines that need instructional emphasis.

Choice of Texts

We chose *CARA* passages from existing textbooks. This decision was made because content validity of an assessment is increased when materials are drawn from typical textbooks that students read in their classroom. We chose literature, history (world and U.S.), and science (life and earth) textbooks published since 2005 by Pearson Education as representative of materials used in schools. We selected passages that were sufficiently long to enable 10 standards-based questions to be written. The length requirement was particularly challenging when choosing literature selections and, therefore, resulted in texts that varied in length from 590 words at grade 4 to 3173 words at high school. Depending on the grade level, informational passages ranged from 700 to 1200 words in length. Another requirement was that the assessment could be completed within a typical 45 to 50 minute class period. To stay within that time period, we chose a single text. This decision resulted in the exclusion of the assessment of Standard 9 that requires the examination of two or more texts.

Literature Passages

We chose three literature passages at each grade level (4 through 9/10). All passages were short stories with the exception of a fifth grade selection for which copyright permission was denied. The main character of this story was Leonardo daVinci and we replaced the selection with a biography of the artist, thus retaining much of the same content. We decided to include only short stories because there were more short stories than any other genre in the published materials. At fourth, fifth, and sixth grades, the term *short story* is used broadly to include historical fiction, realistic fiction, and trickster tales. From grade 7 on, the stories fit the short story genre. The decision to include only short stories resulted in Standard 5 not being addressed for literature at any grade level. At grade 4, Standard 5 states: "Explain major differences between poems, drama, and prose and refer to the structural elements of poems (e.g., verse, rhythm, meter) and drama (e.g., casts of characters, settings, descriptions, dialogue, stage directions) when writing or speaking about a text" (CCSSO & NGA, 2010, p. 12). Similarly, at grade 7, students were required to "analyze how a drama's or poem's form or structure contributes to its meaning" (p. 36). Also, at some grade levels students were asked to compare two or more texts. Because Standard 5 could not be addressed at all grade levels in literature, the decision was made to not include it at any grade level.

Informational Passages

We chose three passages at each level (4, 5, 6, middle school, and high school). The reason for labeling history texts as middle school, rather than grade 7 or grade 8, is that school districts vary in the grades at which they teach U.S. or world history. Similarly, science texts were labeled as middle school because school districts vary in when they teach earth or life science. In addition, the publishers of these texts also referred to them as *middle school texts*.

Passages within a specific subject were on the same topic. For example, the U.S. history passages for middle school were on the constitutional convention, the ratification debate, and the Bill of Rights. For life science at the middle school level, we chose the digestive system, the respiratory system, and the muscular system. We kept the same general topic so that if a teacher chose to administer all three passages over the school year as an assessment of progress, passages on the same topic would reduce the variability in comprehension.

Table 3.2 presents the titles of each literature, social studies, and science passage at each grade level and content area.

Table 3.2   *CARA* Passages According to Grade Level and Content Area

Grade Level	Literature	Social Studies	Science
Grade 4	Amelia and Eleanor Go for a Ride	The United States: Vast and Varied: The Northeast	Earth's Landforms: How Does Earth's Surface Change?
	Encyclopedia Brown and the Case of the Slippery Salamander	The United States: Vast and Varied: The Southeast	Earth's Landforms: How Does Water Affect Earth's Features?
	Grandfather's Journey	The United States: Vast and Varied: The Southwest	Earth's Landforms: How Do Waves Affect Coastal Landforms?
Grade 5	Leonardo daVinci Inventor and Artist	Inventions and Big Business	What Is Inside a Cell?
	Weslandia	Immigration	How Do Cells Work Together?
	Journey to the Center of the Earth	Workers and Unions	How Do Organs Work Together?
Grade 6	Arachne	An Expanding Nation: Rails Across the Nation	What Are Earth's Layers Made Of?
	The Wounded Wolf	An Expanding Nation: Conflict on the Plains	How Do Earth's Plates Help Create Landforms?
	Senor Coyote and the Tricked Trickster	An Expanding Nation: The Great Plains	How Do Scientists Explain Earth's Features?
Middle School Grade 7 Literature only	All Summer in a Day	The Constitutional Convention	The Digestive System
	The Californian's Tale	Debating the Constitution	The Muscular System
	The Third Wish	The Bill of Rights	The Respiratory System
Grade 8 Literature only	The Tell Tale Heart	The Roman Republic	Fossils
	The Drummer Boy of Shiloh	The Roman Empire	The Relative Age of Rocks
	The Story-Teller	The Fall of Rome	Radioactive Dating
High School	Sonata for Harp and Bicycle	Democracy and the Age of Jackson: The Election of 1824	Life Is Cellular
	Blues Ain't No Mockin Bird	Democracy and the Age of Jackson: Conflicts and Crises	Cell Structure

A Problem	Democracy and the Age of Jackson: More Conflicts and Crises	Organelles That Capture and Release Energy
	The Rise of the Greek City-States	The Vast World Ocean
	Conflict in the Greek World	Ocean Floor Features
	The Glory That Was Greece	Seafloor Sediments

Note: Middle school social studies and science passages are placed in the table representing middle school rather than levels seven and eight because textbook publishers designated them as such.

Question Placement

We decided to place questions throughout the body of the text instead of placing them all at the end. We made this decision for several reasons. First, high school English teachers reported to us that when they read a short story with their classes, they read a segment and then discuss it, read another segment and discuss it, and at the end ask questions about theme. Second, our texts are longer than typical assessment materials. Rereading or skimming to locate the answer to a question placed at the end of the passage would take much longer on the *CARA*. Third, because of text length, we did not want the time period of the assessment to be extended beyond a class period, as it might be if students reread or skimmed through the entire text to find answers. Finally, we did not want individual differences in skimming ability to interfere with students' ability to construct answers. At the end of each literature text there are questions on theme/lesson that require the student to understand the entire text. In addition, the final requirement is that students write a summary of the story. In informational text, the summary question indicates the specific information that should form the basis of the summary; that is, the student is asked to summarize a specific part of the text and not the entire text.

Example of a *CARA* Passage

The Roman Republic

The ancient city of Rome was at the center of the peninsula we now call Italy. After being ruled by kings, the Romans formed a republic. Read to find out what form this republic took.

Romans Form a Republic

Over several centuries Rome expanded its territory and found ways to govern that better represented the will of its citizens. The Romans wanted a government that did not rely on one ruler such as a king. They established a new form of government—a republic. In a republic, citizens who have the right to vote select their leaders. The leaders rule in the name of the people.

The Roman Senate.   In the Roman Republic, the most powerful part of the government was the senate. The Roman senate was the basis for our own legislative branch of government—the branch that proposes and votes on new laws. At first, the senate was made up only of 300 upper-class men called patricians. A patrician was a member of a wealthy family in the Roman republic. Ordinary citizens were known as plebeians. In the early republic, plebeians could not hold office or be senators.

The Roman Consuls.   Two chief officials called consuls led the government. The consuls were the chief executives of the government. They were responsible for enforcing the republic's laws and policies. The consuls were elected by the assembly of citizens. Before 367 B.C., plebeians could not be consuls. The senate advised the consuls on foreign affairs, laws, and finances, among other things.

1. **What point of view did the early Roman patricians have about plebeians holding office?**

Consuls ruled for one year only. They almost always did what the senate wanted them to do. Power was divided equally between the consuls. Both had to agree before the government could take any action. If only one consul said, "Veto" (I forbid), the matter was dropped. A veto is the rejection of any planned action by a person in power.

The Romans knew that their government might not work if the two consuls disagreed. For this reason, Roman law held that a dictator could be appointed to handle an emergency. In the Roman Republic, a dictator was a Roman official who had all the powers of a king but could hold office for only six months.

2. **What evidence in the text strongly supports that the senate primarily controlled the consuls?**

3. **What evidence in the text strongly supports that the Romans did not completely trust the office of consul?**

4. **The topic of the previous section is the "office of consul." What is the central idea?**

Praetors were other important officials. At first they functioned as junior consuls but later they served as judges in trials that settled disputes about money, business matters, contracts, and so on. Thus, the praetors helped to develop some of the first rules for Roman courts of law.

Patricians versus Plebeians.   The expansion of Rome's influence throughout Italy caused growing troubles between patricians and plebeians. Patricians and plebeians had different attitudes and interests. Patricians thought of themselves as leaders. They fought hard to keep control of the government. Plebeians believed they had a right to be respected and treated fairly. Plebeians did not trust the actions of the patrician senate. They believed the senate was often unfair to the plebeians. Therefore plebeians formed their own groups to protect their interests.

Many patricians grew wealthy because of Rome's conquests. They took riches from those they defeated in war. Then they bought land from small farmers and created huge farms for themselves. Plebeians did not work on these farms. Rather, the work was done by slaves brought back from conquests. Many plebeian farmers found themselves without work. The cities, especially Rome, were filled with jobless plebeians.

5. **The topic of the previous section is "patricians and plebeians." What is the central idea?**

6. **Analyze why patricians and plebeians were against each other. Give <u>two</u> reasons.**

Eventually jobless plebeians refused to fight in the Roman army. It was then that the patricians gave into one of the demands of the plebeians. This demand was for a written code of laws which was called the Laws of the Twelve Tables. The Twelve Tables applied equally to all citizens. They were hung in the marketplace so that everyone could know what the laws were. Despite this victory, the plebeians never managed to gain power equally to that of the patricians.

7. **Which text structure best explains how the author organized the previous passage?**

___**description of important features**

___**explanation of steps in a sequence**

___**account of cause and effect**

___**explanation of problem and solution**

___**comparison/contrast of two or more things**

Give a reason from the text for your answer. For example, if you choose description, tell what is being described. If you choose sequence, list one or two steps. For cause and effect, state a cause or effect mentioned in the text. For problem and solution, tell what the problem is or describe the solution. For comparison, tell what is being compared or contrasted.

8. **Analyze why the army was important to the patricians.**

The Decline of the Republic

By 120 B.C. Rome was in trouble. Roman generals gathered private armies and fought for power. Consuls no longer respected each other's veto power. Rome dissolved into **civil** war. As Rome seemed about to break up, Julius Caesar arose as a strong leader. Caesar became dictator of the Roman world in 48 B.C. Under Roman law, a dictator could rule for only six months but Caesar's rule lasted far longer than that. Although some **elements** of the republic remained, Caesar ruled with great power, taking much of the power that had once belonged to the senate. In 44 B.C., he became dictator for life. It seemed to many Roman senators that Rome once again had a king. They hated the idea. At a meeting of the senate, a group of senators stabbed Caesar to death. He had been a strong leader but many Romans felt that he had gone too far and too fast in gathering power.

9. What is the meaning of "civil" in the context of the previous passage?

10. What is the meaning of "elements" in the context of the previous passage?

Summarize what the text says about how the government of the Roman Republic was organized.

Reading Levels of *CARA* Selections

We chose *CARA* selections from representative textbooks clearly labeled for a specific grade by the publisher. Lexile levels for *CARA* passages are reported in Table 3.3 and are certified Lexile© levels by Metametrics. The original Lexile bands are in regular font and the "stretch" levels are in bold. "Stretch" levels represent the levels of text that students should be able to read in order to be college and career ready (MetaMetrics, 2013). *CARA* passage levels that are above Lexile grade levels and Lexile "stretch" levels are marked with a single asterisk; those that are below are marked with a double asterisk. The far right column displays the mean proportion correct on questions for each story. This allows a comparison between predicted difficulty (Lexile levels) and actual difficulty in students' ability to answer questions about the texts they read.

Table 3.3   Readability Levels for *CARA* Texts

| Passage Level and Title | Literature | | |
	Lexile Ranges: Regular and "Stretch"	Lexile Level	Mean Proportion Correct
Grade 4	640L–780L **740L – 940L**		
Amelia and Eleanor Go for a Ride		700L	.45
Encyclopedia Brown and the Case of the Slippery Salamander		700L	.44
Grandfather's Journey		660L	.52
Grade 5	730L–850L **830L – 1010L**		
Leonardo daVinci: Inventor and Artist		930L	.51
Weslandia		870L	.49
Journey to the Center of Earth		740L	.35

(Continued)

Table 3.3   (Continued)

Literature			
Passage Level and Title	Lexile Ranges: Regular and "Stretch"	Lexile Level	Mean Proportion Correct
Grade 6	860L–920L **925L – 1070L**		
Arachne		1060L	.51
The Wounded Wolf		710L**	.64
Senor Coyote and the Tricked Trickster		730L**	.47
Grade 7	880L–960L **970L – 1120L**		
All Summer in a Day		850L**	.56
The Californian's Tale		830L**	.62.
The Third Wish		1090L	.66
Grade 8	900L–1010L **1010L – 1185L**		
The Tell Tale Heart		830L**	.46
The Drummer Boy of Shiloh		1020L	.50
The Story-Teller		1050L	.47
Grade 9-10	960L–1120L **1050L – 1335**		
Sonata for Harp and Bicycle		920L**	.45
Blues Ain't No Mockin Bird		950L**	.42
A Problem		930L**	.35

Note: **Indicates that text is lower than the recommended Lexile level. www.lexile.com/about-lexile/grade-equivalent/grade-equivalent-chart. Note that all Lexile levels are certified by Metametrics.

Social Studies			
Passage Level and Title	Lexile Ranges: Regular and "Stretch"	Lexile Level	Mean Proportion Correct
Grade 4	640L–780L **740L – 940L**		
The United States: Vast and Varied: The Northeast		960L*	.37
The United States: Vast and Varied: The Southeast		980L*	.50
The United States: Vast and Varied: The Southwest		960L*	.44
Grade 5	730L–850L **830L – 1010L**		
Inventions and Big Business		860L	.40

Immigration		890L	.48
Workers and Unions		880L	.42
Grade 6	860L - 920L **925L – 1070L**		
An Expanding Nation: Rails Across the Nation		950L	.51
An Expanding Nation: Conflict on the Plain		880L	.45
An Expanding Nation: The Great Plains		920L	.43
Middle School	880L–1010L **970 – 1185**		
Constitutional Convention		840L	.46
Debating the Constitution		900L	.45
The Bill of Rights		1010L	.42
The Roman Republic		850L**	.43
The Roman Empire		880L	.36
The Fall of Rome		780L**	.37
High School	960L–1220L **1050L – 1385L**		
Democracy and the Age of Jackson: The Election of 1824		1030L	.45
Democracy and the Age of Jackson: Conflicts and Crises		1020L	.53
Democracy and the Age of Jackson: More Conflicts and Crises		1030L	NA
The Rise of the Greek City-States		990L	.60
Conflict in the Greek World		990L	.50
The Glory That Was Greece		1020L	.42

Note: *Indicates that text is higher than the recommended Lexile level.
Note: **Indicates that text is lower than the recommended Lexile level.
All Lexile levels are certified by Metametrics.
Note: NA: Pilot total less than 10

	Science		
Passage Level and Title	**Lexile Ranges: Regular and "Stretch"**	**Lexile Level**	**Mean Proportion Correct**
Grade 4	640L–780L **740L – 940L**		
Earth's Landforms: How Does Earth's Surface Change?		930L*	.50
Earth's Landforms: How Does Water Affect Earth's Features?		980L*	.35

(Continued)

Table 3.3   (Continued)

Passage Level and Title	Science Lexile Ranges: Regular and "Stretch"	Lexile Level	Mean Proportion Correct
Earth's Landforms: How Do Waves Affect Coastal Landforms?		950L*	.33
Grade 5	730L–850L **830L – 1010L**		
What Is Inside a Cell?		860L	.42
How Do Cells Work Together?		870L	.35
How Do Organs Work Together?		750L	.30
Grade 6	860L–920L **925L – 1070L**		
What Are Earth's Layers Made Of?		820L**	.51
How Do Earth's Plates Help Create Landforms?		920L	.41
How Do Scientists Explain Earth's Features?		950L	.41
Middle School	880L–1010L **970 – 1185**		
The Digestive System		930L	.53
The Muscular System		920L	.63
The Respiratory System		950L	.58
Fossils		930L	.41
The Relative Age of Rocks		970L	.46
Radioactive Dating		910L	.43
High School	960L–1220L **1050L – 1385L**		
Life Is Cellular		1010L**	.69
Cell Structure		1180L	NA
Organelles That Capture and Release Energy		1150L	NA
The Vast World Ocean		1170L	.70
Ocean Floor Features		1100L	.53
Seafloor Sediments		1150L	.51

Note: *Indicates that text is higher than the recommended Lexile level.
Note: **Indicates that text is lower than the recommended Lexile level.
All Lexile levels are certified by Metametrics.
Note: NA: Pilot total less than 10

What Lexile Levels Reveal About a Text

Lexile levels reflect word and sentence length, only two of several dimensions of text complexity. Total reliance on a readability score "overlooks the qualitative and reader-specific factors that should always be considered" (Fisher, Frey, & Lapp, 2012, p. 31). We must recognize these other components that influence a reader's comprehension, as obviously occurred with the fourth-grade selections.

The Common Core State Standards themselves do not regard text difficulty as totally defined by Lexile levels. They define text complexity as "the inherent difficulty of reading and comprehending a text combined with consideration of the reader and task variables" (CCSSO & NGA, 2010, p. 43) and offer a model that includes reader/task considerations, qualitative dimensions, and quantitative dimensions. Reader/task considerations include the motivation, knowledge, and experience of the reader. Task components include the purpose and complexity of the task and related questions. Qualitative variables include "levels of meaning or purpose; structure; language conventionality and clarity; and knowledge demands." Quantitative dimensions include "word length or frequency, sentence length, and text cohesion" (CCSSO & NGA, 2010, p. 4).

The authors of the Common Core Standards have adopted the Lexile readability formula as a quantitative measure of the text complexity band mentioned in Standard 10. Lexile measures range from 0L to 2000L. It is assumed that the lower the Lexile level of a book, the easier it is to comprehend. Thus, a text with a Lexile level of 750L would be easier than one written at a Lexile level of 950L. Lexile levels for specific grades are reported as ranges. Lexile bands, beginning at second grade through high school, were similarly stretched so that the highest 12th-grade Lexile level of 1360L meets the beginning level for college text (MetaMetrics, 2013). For example, the fifth-grade Lexile band of 730L to 850L was stretched to 830L to 1010L.

There are two Lexile levels, the text level and the reader level. Lexile levels for text are based on word familiarity and sentence length, two traditional predictors of text difficulty; we have reported these in Table 3.3. There are also Lexile levels for readers. A variety of standardized tests can be administered to determine a reader's score in Lexile units. If, for example, a reader attains a Lexile of 600L on a specific test, the reader will be expected to comprehend approximately 75 percent of a book with the same Lexile level (MetaMetrics, 2013).

Our analysis of Lexile levels for *CARA* passages is based on text levels, not reader levels. We did not have Lexile levels for our pilot students who read *CARA* passages; therefore, we could not assume that they would comprehend 75 percent of a text that fell within a Lexile level appropriate for their grade. We could not expect that sixth graders, for example, would be able to adequately comprehend all text within the sixth-grade Lexile band. Other factors affect comprehension: the topic and/or content of the book or passage, the interests and knowledge base of the reader, and how the book or passage is designed (MetaMetrics, 2013). A story may be easier to comprehend than a science passage. A social studies passage on a war may be easier than one on various ways of amending the Constitution.

There is a misconception that the readability of a text recommended for a specific grade level means that the entire text is written at that level. In other words, if a textbook is published as appropriate for fifth grade, are all selections in the text at a fifth-grade reading level? This is seldom so. The average readability level may be fifth grade, but individual passages in the text will vary. "This is an important point in considering quantitative text difficulty—the law of averages is at work. That does not mean that the entire text is readable just because the average suggests it is so" (Fisher, Frey, & Lapp, 2012).

Literature Passages

An examination of Table 3.3 reveals that the majority of *CARA* passages fit well within an appropriate Lexile range. At fourth and fifth grade, the literature passages were within the Lexile ranges for the respective grades. However, two of the sixth-grade stories had lower Lexiles than the Lexile range recommended for sixth grade. Recall that Lexile estimates are intended to predict the difficulty of text for the reader. However, the best measure of difficulty of a text for readers is their comprehension of the text.

The right-hand column of Table 3.3 presents the mean proportion correct from our pilot samples. We will refer to those results as we discuss the Lexile scores. For example, although the Lexile level for *Arachne* is much higher (1060L) than for *Senor Coyote* (730L), students' performance on the two passages was very similar, with mean proportions correct of .51 and .47, respectively. In contrast, the mean proportion correct on the fifth-grade stories was significantly different. The mean proportion correct on *Journey to the Center of the Earth* (740L) of .35

was lower than *Weslandia* (870L) at .49. If Lexiles were predictive of student scores on these passages, then *Weslandia,* which has a higher Lexile than *Journey to the Center of the Earth,* should have the lowest proportion correct. But that was not the case. Finally, notice in Table 3.3 that at the high school level, the Lexiles are very similar to each other, but students found *The Problem* to be more difficult with a mean proportion correct of .35. In conclusion, the difficulty of our literature passages is not directly associated with the Lexile levels, so other factors must be at work.

Science and Social Studies Passages

Similar to the results in literature, Table 3.3 reveals that the majority of *CARA* science and social studies passages fit well within appropriate Lexile ranges. The mean proportion correct for social studies and science passages showed a similar disconnect between Lexile levels and student performance as the literature selections. For example, Lexile levels for the three sixth-grade social studies passages differed by 70 points, but the proportions correct on the passages were not significantly different. Lexile levels for the six middle school social studies passages ranged from 840L to 1010L, but again the proportions correct were not significantly different. For the middle school science passages, higher Lexiles were connected to higher proportion correct, which is the opposite of what might be expected. The high school passages tended to follow the expected relationship of lower Lexiles receiving higher student scores, although the proportions correct were relatively similar.

Mismatch Between Grade Level and Lexile Level

In contrast to all of the literature and informational selections previously discussed, the fourth-grade passages for both social studies and science were well above recommended Lexile ranges. To determine if our passages were an anomaly, we examined other segments of text from the textbooks from which the passages were drawn. We also examined student proportion correct and compared this on passages of varying Lexile ranges.

Comparison of Passages in the Grade 4 Text.   We randomly selected passages of comparable length (approximately 700 words) from the same text and examined their Lexile levels. The social studies text was divided into six chapters corresponding to the five regions of the United States and an introductory chapter on the United States in general. Because the *CARA* passages were drawn from the Southwest, the Southeast, and the Northeast, we selected our random comparison passages from the Midwest, the West, and the introductory section. As indicated in Table 3.4, the comparison passages were also higher than Lexile levels recommended for grade 4.

Table 3.4   Readability Levels for Random Selection of Grade 4 Texts

Grade Four Lexile Ranges:
Regular: 640L–780L
Stretch: 740L–940L

Social Studies		Science	
Passage Title	Lexile Levels	Passage Title	Lexile Levels
Northeast	960L	Plate Tectonics	830L
Midwest	960L	Rocks and Minerals	870L
West	1000L	Earth's Resources	950L
		Climate and Weather	980L

In a similar fashion, we randomly selected passages from the same earth science text as our *CARA* passages. The earth science text is divided into five chapters. Our *CARA* passages were drawn from the chapter on the earth's surface. Additional passages were randomly drawn from the remaining four chapters on plate tectonics, rocks and minerals, earth's resources, and earth's climate. Table 3.4 shows that Lexile levels for these passages were all above Lexile levels recommended for fourth grade. Two science passages fell within the Lexile stretch range, one clearly at the high end of the range.

In summary, our comparison of *CARA* passages with other passages from the same content text indicates that, overall, fourth-grade social studies and science texts were rated as more difficult than recommended for fourth grade.

Students' Comprehension of Grade 4 Texts.   We examined our pilot data to see if fourth-grade students' proportions correct were lower on the fourth-grade texts compared to fifth-grade students who read the texts estimated to be within their recommended Lexile band. The proportions correct for fourth- and fifth-grade students were comparable, which suggests that, despite higher Lexile levels, the fourth- and fifth-grade passages represented similar levels of difficulty for students in the respective grades.

We were fortunate that our pilot contained scores from three fourth- and fifth-grade classrooms of students in the same school who each read a literature selection and a science selection. We compared their performance on the fourth-grade passages using a paired sample t-test statistic. Recall that the fourth grade literature selections were well within appropriate Lexile ranges, but the science selections were at higher-than-recommended Lexile levels. Comparison of student scores on *Amelia and Eleanor* (700L) and *How Does Earth's Surface Change?* (930L) and for *Encyclopedia Brown* (700L) and *How Does Water Affect Earth's Features?* (980L) showed no significant differences. This suggested that the texts did not differ in difficulty for the students despite differences in Lexiles. The comparison of *Grandfather's Journey* (660L) and *How Do Waves Affect Landforms?* (950L) found that *Grandfather's Journey* was the easier text. This may have occurred for two reasons. First, *Grandfather's Journey* had the lowest Lexile of the three literature passages; and second, the concepts in the science chapter, the cause and effect of wave action, were conceptually quite difficult.

We also examined whether the proportion correct scores of fourth graders in social studies and science were significantly different across the three passages within the content area. The resulting data are contrary to the expected relationship between text difficulty as measured by Lexiles and student performance. For the fourth-grade science passages, significant differences were found between the proportion correct on passage one and the other two passages, but no difference between passages two and three. Again, the Lexiles do not correlate with student performance and suggest that something other than Lexile levels may have played a part in students' comprehension. Although student's comprehension of passage one was greater than that of the other two passages, the Lexile difference between passage one and three was a minimal 10 points.

We also examined the proportion correct from fifth graders in the spring 2012 pilot. Recall that their passages were well within Lexile limits for fifth grade. For social studies, no significant differences in student proportion correct scores were evident for Lexiles that ranged from 860L to 890L. For science, student proportions correct on passage one were significantly less than on the other two passages despite having the lowest lexile. However, there were no significant differences in proportion correct between passage two (870L) and passage three (950L) despite a 120-point span in Lexile levels. This suggested to us that even within acceptable Lexile levels, something else besides word familiarity and sentence length is affecting student scores.

Beyond the Lexile: Other Measures of Text Difficulty

Hiebert's (2013) clarification of such factors offers a powerful argument why Lexile levels that are based on sentence length and vocabulary frequency offer only one measure of text difficulty. Another way to examine text difficulty is to compare a text to what Hiebert refers to as "benchmark texts"—that is, texts that are appropriate for a specific grade level. Similarity between the two may indicate that the text in question is suitable. While we were not able to make such a comparison for the fourth-grade texts, we did note the supportive nature of the teacher manuals and of text connected to student activities and content review. So, in addition to the traditional measures of text complexity, a third component of text complexity involves four components: levels of meaning, knowledge demands, language conventions, and clarity and structure. Table 3.5 provides descriptors of our fourth-grade texts within each of Hiebert's categories. Examination of each of the four categories summarized may provide indicators of why our students did not have significant problems understanding the fourth-grade social studies and science texts, despite their high Lexile levels. That is, because the texts included relatively familiar or concrete descriptions of concepts (levels of meaning), included familiar topics (knowledge demand), defined unknown words in the text (language conventions and clarity), and structured topics clearly with headings (structure), students were less affected by the higher Lexile level as they might be if these factors were not in play.

Decision.   Given the above findings and the limitations of readability formulas in general, we feel comfortable that the fourth-grade selections are appropriate choices for the *CARA*. First, if one examines the content of the fourth-grade social studies and science texts, it is easy to see why Lexile levels are high. All passages contained many unfamiliar and content-specific words such as *geyser, volcanoes, cascades,* and *plateau* (social studies) and *kilometers, magma, lithosphere, tectonic, precipitation, cumulonimbus,* and *humidity* (science). Many words referred to specific concepts that could not be substituted with easier or more familiar synonyms. This can lead to an inflated readability level because such key words not only are infrequent but "are often repeated which increases vocabulary load even though repetition of content words can support student learning" (Hiebert & Mesmer, 2013). Although passages

Table 3.5   **Descriptions of Fourth-Grade Social Studies and Science Texts Using Hiebert's (2013) Criteria of Text Complexity**

Levels of Meaning	
Social Studies: Relatively straightforward and concrete description: Landforms, resources, how Native Americans lived	Science: Relatively concrete topics: Effect of water on earth's surface; weathering, erosion and wave action
Knowledge Demands	
Social Studies: Relatively familiar concepts: Mountains, rivers, canyons, crops, oil, computers	Science: Relatively familiar concepts based on television weather channels: how land can be changed by wind and water
Language Conventions and Clarity	
Social Studies: Unfamiliar words and concepts clearly defined within the body of the text	Science: Unfamiliar words and concepts clearly defined within the body of the text
Structure	
Social Studies: Description and sequence; signaled by related topic headings	Science: Description and sequence; signaled by related topic headings

often provided a definition for an unfamiliar word by including it in a phrase immediately following the word, this tended to make sentences longer. Longer sentences raise readability levels; shorter sentences decrease levels. However, this does not always mean that text with shorter sentences is easier to comprehend (Hiebert & Mesmer, 2013); inclusion of definitions in the sentence may actually have helped student comprehension.

The argument could be made that we should have identified passages in the text that represented a suitable readability level. Given the conceptual content of the two series and the findings that other randomly selected text also had above-grade Lexile levels, this may not have been possible. Complex topics demand usage of unfamiliar words and such words increase readability levels. Specifically selecting only those portions of the text that represented an acceptable Lexile level would be contrary to the purpose of the *CARA*, which is to provide an assessment that mirrors textbook and classroom content.

Summary

In summary, the *CARA* is an informal and formative assessment of a student's ability to read grade level text, answer ten constructed response questions specifically based on the Common Core Standards for literature and informational text, and write a text based summary. It is composed of passages from grade 4 through high school. The validity of the questions as representative of the Common Core Standards and the reliability of scoring as based upon answer keys were evaluated by teachers and examined through careful analysis of student answers. The *CARA* can be used by teachers to evaluate which of the Common Core Standards needs specific instructional attention.

Administration and Scoring of the *CARA* Questions

Choice of Passage Level

The *CARA* offers passages at the following levels:

- Literature: Levels 4 through 9
- Social Studies: Levels 4 through 6, middle school, and high school
- Science: Levels 4 through 6, middle school, and high school

Standard 10 states that, by the end of the year, students should be reading grade-level text. For this reason, the first choice of passage level should be at your specific grade level. For example, sixth graders should read sixth-grade passages and high school students should read high school passages.

After the initial administration of the *CARA,* the teacher then has the following options:

- You can administer passages at lower levels to students who did not do well at their chronological grade level. It may be that inability to comprehend grade-level passages was responsible for their performance, not lack of cognitive skills required for answering standards-based questions. When given an easier passage, they may demonstrate ability to answer such questions.
- You can also administer higher-level passages to those students whose performance on the grade-level passage suggests a more advanced level of content area reading ability.

An intervention specialist has the option of initially selecting grade-level passages, reading-level passages, or both, depending on what is already known about a student. If a student's instructional level is based on reading narrative text, the specialist may choose to administer *CARA* science and/or social studies passages at an instructional level. Many students have different instructional levels for different content areas. The specialist may also administer *CARA* passages at the student's chronological grade level to determine the extent to which the student can handle grade-level material in different disciplines. You may find that the ability to handle reading-level and grade-level passages is heavily dependent on the content area. Students may be able to perform at a higher level in literature than in social studies or science.

Administration of additional passages is feasible because, as a group-administered as opposed to an individually-administered assessment, the *CARA* does not involve an extensive amount of administration time. In addition, if you choose to administer additional passages at different levels, you can distribute the passages to students without their being aware that some students are reading more difficult or less difficult selections.

Choice of Content Area

Your selection of which content area passage to administer depends on what you teach and what you need to know about your students. If you are a fourth-, fifth-, or sixth-grade teacher responsible for the instruction of literature, social studies, and science, you might decide to administer a passage from each content area. If you feel confident about your students' ability in literature, for example, you might choose to administer only the *CARA* social studies and science texts. If you are a content teacher at the middle school or high school level, your choice would obviously be passages in your specific discipline. If you are an intervention specialist, your choice of content area will depend on the nature of the instruction you are providing to your students and their specific needs. Students are often assessed for intervention instruction using relatively short narrative passages. You might find it helpful to move beyond this and evaluate their ability to read content area text as well as longer narratives.

At the middle school and high school levels, you have a choice of U.S. history or world history. In science, the *CARA* offers both life science and earth science passages. Your choice may depend on the curriculum of your school or district. For example, if the middle school curriculum focuses on U.S. history, you may select these passages for administration because they are specifically related to your curriculum. On the other hand, you may select world history in order to avoid the confounding of *CARA* results with prior instruction. If students have already been instructed in the topic of the *CARA* passages, familiarity could influence their performance. On the other hand, if the material is relatively unfamiliar, *CARA* results may provide a truer picture of student ability to understand and learn from unfamiliar text. Because the *CARA* is a formative assessment, the choice is yours.

Choice of Selection

Within each level of social studies and science, passages are sequential; that is, the content of the first passage conceptually precedes the other two selections. For example, the middle school passages on U.S. history are The Constitutional Convention, Debating the Constitution, and The Bill of Rights. Similarly, the high school life science passages are Life Is Cellular, Cell Structure, and Organelles That Capture and Release Energy. We suggest that you follow the *CARA* sequence and use the first passage for your initial administration and the two that follow as subsequent assessments for determining student progress after instruction. The literature selections are not sequential, so any of the three selections at a specific level would be appropriate.

Administrating the *CARA*

How should you introduce the selection? We do not suggest that you employ an extensive pre-reading activity such as asking students what they know and/or want to know about the topic. The purpose of the experience is for students to learn from the text—that is, use the text to answer the questions and compose a summary. If you engage in an extensive discussion of text content, you might not be able to distinguish what they learned from the text and what they learned from the preparatory discussion. Snow (2013), in a discussion of close reading, suggests that "we recognize the need to attend to student motivation and interest" by giving them an authentic purpose for the task at hand (p. 19). The basic purpose of the *CARA* is to determine students' ability to engage in close reading in order to provide answers to 10 questions based on the standards. It makes sense to share this with the students, as well as assure them that they are not going to be assigned a grade and their performance will not affect their report card. Their performance will provide information as to what they can do and what they need help with.

The *CARA* passages each begin with a short introduction telling students to read for a specific purpose that is connected to passage content. If you wish, you can read this to the students, but do not answer any questions that students might raise. For example, the introduction to a fifth-grade science passage is as follows: "Cells are the smallest living parts of any living thing. Cells have the same needs as any organism and carry out many of the same activities. Cells contain smaller parts, each with a specialized job. Read to find out more about how cells work." Following the reading, students may raise questions, such as "What does *specialized* mean?" "What is an organism?" "What needs do cells have?" Resist the temptation to engage in a lively prereading discussion. Simply tell the students that their job is to find out such answers on their own by reading the passage.

Administration, as indicated by *CARA* piloting, should take no longer than 45 to 50 minutes per passage, which is the relative length of many content classes. However, a teacher can choose to extend the time for a specific student. You may also choose to administer the questions on one day and ask the students to write the summary on another. Some pilot students did not write a summary; we don't know if they just decided not to do it or if they ran out of time. Of course, the students receive their papers/text again when they write their summary. Some students may change their answer to previous questions; however, the purpose of the *CARA* is to evaluate a student's best effort. If a student recognizes an error while rereading the text for the purpose of writing a summary, we have no difficulty with allowing the student to make a change. However, as a formative instrument, the teacher can decide what is an appropriate action.

For middle school and high school, we have provided an additional passage that assesses Standard 8, the ability to determine the validity of an argument. Our pilot data suggests that it is best to administer this separately. Though students were clearly able to read a passage, answer 10 questions, and complete the summary within a single period, many were not able to finish the Standard 8 task within that same period.

Scoring the *CARA*

The *CARA* is a constructed-response assessment; students write their answers instead of selecting one from several options. Selected-response questions are easy to correct; constructed-response questions often are not. In addition, correcting constructed-response questions takes more time; the average scoring time is 10 minutes per student. It should be noted that middle school and high school literature passages took longer than science or social studies texts. This is likely because of the differences in the lengths of the literature texts at the high school level and differences in the length of the summaries in literature versus nonfiction; a topic we will address in Chapter 4, Part 2. Correcting the first few papers will take longer as you familiarize yourself with the text; later ones will go faster. The acceptance and consistent use of the following scoring guidelines will increase the accuracy and consistency of scoring *CARA* questions.

Guidelines for Scoring of Constructed-Response *CARA* Questions

• **Clarify your understanding of each standard and what students should be able to do in order to meet it.** The majority of *CARA* questions related to a specific standard begin with the same question stem (e.g., *analyze, what evidence in the text indicates, what is the meaning of,* etc.) Be certain that you understand exactly what the question stem is asking students to do.

• **Engage in close reading of the text and the answer key prior to correcting student responses.** It was clear from our pilot data that, in some cases, scorers did not engage in close reading of the text and/or the answer key. They accepted answers that were contradicted by the text and/or did not recognize acceptable student paraphrases of text content. Prior to correcting *CARA* questions, carefully read each question, the relevant text, and the answer key to make certain that you understand question content. As you correct each student's responses, keep a copy of the passage close by for ready reference. Ambiguous answers can often be clarified as acceptable or not acceptable after rereading the passage.

- **Score all answers to question 1, then all answers to question 2, and so on.** This provides you with an understanding of how your students have interpreted the question and the variety of answers that are given. Often this will help you make a decision about ambiguous or confusing answers. It will also help to prevent scorer bias either in favor of or against a student.

- **Correct responses as if the student were a complete stranger to you.** Do not allow your knowledge of a student's classroom performance to influence your scoring decision. It is very easy to accept an ambiguous answer from students who perform well in class. Similarly, it is easy to reject the same answer from a struggling student. Teachers also want students to do well and when faced with a questionable answer, they may tend to accept it rather than mark it wrong. However, this can pose a problem for classroom instruction. Accepting erroneous answers as correct suggests that a classroom emphasis is not needed when it actually may be. It is better to mark a question wrong and make it the focus of instruction than to assume instruction is not needed when indeed it is.

- **Mark ambiguous and/or confusing answers as errors.** Answering constructed-response questions involves three things: understanding the question, knowing the correct answer, and adequately and clearly presenting the answer in writing. Unlike selected-response items, where the content of the answer is provided for the student to select, constructed-response questions require that the student compose his or her answer in a manner that can be understood by others. If the student knows the correct answer but is not able to frame a coherent response, the answer is wrong.

  Some pilot students talked "around the subject," or engaged in what has often been referred to as "bird walking." In other words, they hoped that if they wrote enough, they just might hit on an acceptable answer. Pilot scorers were not consistent with regard to ambiguous answers. In some cases the same scorer accepted an answer and then later rejected a similar one. Although we suspect that teachers tend to give students the benefit of the doubt, we need to promote strict adherence to the answer key. If the answer is not clear, it is wrong. Read ambiguous answers aloud; it is amazing how hearing their answer improves your scoring consistency. When uncertain about the acceptability of an answer, mark it wrong.

  If you are troubled by this recommendation, you can always discuss problematic answers with students to verify a decision. The *CARA* is a formative measure and, as such, you can modify the administration to suit your specific needs and concerns.

- **Do not allow extraneous information to obscure the accuracy of the answer.** Pilot students occasionally offered more information than was indicated by the question—that is, a correct answer was often followed or surrounded by extraneous information. Scorers reacted differently to this. Some marked the question wrong; others accepted it. If the extraneous information does not contradict the correct answer, give the student credit for the answer. If it does offer contradictory information, mark it wrong; the student is obviously unsure as to the most appropriate answer.

- **Only accept answers that are, as demanded by the standards, based on the text.** Answers that emanate from prior knowledge of the topic should be marked wrong. The answer may seem reasonable, but if there is no basis for it in the text, it should be marked as an error. Some scorers often accepted answers that made sense but were not present in the text. For example, a question asked for the points of view of the U.S. government with regard to gold discovered in the Black Hills. One student stated that the government was greedy and wanted gold for themselves. This answer was accepted as correct by a scorer. Although it may be true, it is not supported by the text, which ties the interests of the government to support of the miners and farmers.

Accepting answers to vocabulary items was another issue. The meaning of a specific word is based on its usage in the passage. *CARA* vocabulary items all carried multiple meanings, but the purpose of Standard 4 vocabulary items was to select the definition that matches word meaning as used in the text. For example, the word *respond* was used in a fifth-grade passage on cells. Although *respond* can mean "talk back," in the specific science passage this meaning is not appropriate; it referred to the way cells react, change, and adapt. Scorers often accepted a reasonable answer but not one that specifically addressed the use of the word in the context of the selection. Thus they were wrong.

• **Do not score on the basis of writing mechanics.** As constructed-response questions, there are issues of spelling, punctuation, sentence structure, and the like. Questions should be scored on the basis of accuracy and completeness, not on the mechanics of composition. You may wish to examine such issues and note areas where students seem to need instruction, but scoring on spelling and/or grammatical correctness is not germane to the *CARA*.

• **Score missing answers as errors.** Unintelligible answers are scored as wrong, as are missing answers. During the piloting process, we occasionally found students who elected to skip an answer and go on to one they felt they could answer. Missing answers are scored as wrong because it is not possible to determine why the answer was not completed—did they skip a question because they didn't know the answer, because they didn't want to attempt an answer, or because they ran out of time?

The following figure contains an abbreviated version of these guidelines. You may wish to make a copy to have on hand when you correct student papers.

Guidelines for Scoring *CARA* Questions

- Clarify your understanding of each standard and what students should be able to do in order to meet it.
- Engage in close reading of the text and the answer key prior to correcting student responses.
- Score all answers to question #1, then all answers to questions #2, etc.
- Correct responses as if the student was a complete stranger to you.
- Mark ambiguous and/or confusing answers as errors.
- Do not allow extraneous information to obscure the accuracy of the answer.
- Only accept answers that are, as demanded by the Standards, based on the text.
- Do not score on the basis of writing mechanics.
- Score missing answers as errors.

Two-Point Answers

CARA questions involve both one- and two-part answers. For example, questions measuring Standard 5 have two parts: identification of the text structure and explanation of the students' reason for their choice. Similarly, questions that measure Standard 3 often ask the students to provide two examples or reasons. A point table on the answer key of all passages

Table 4.1.1   Example of Point Table for a Sixth-Grade Science Text

Standard	Questions	Points per Question
1. Support an inference	2	1
	9	1
2. Determine main idea	1	1
	7	1
3. Explain why or how/ analyze	6	2
	8	1
	10	1
4. Determine word meaning	3	1
	4	1
5. Determine text structure	5	2
Total Questions	10	12
2. Summary		11
Total Summary		8 acceptable

indicates the number of points assigned to each question. In addition, there is a notation on the answer key when a question is a two-point question. The answers for each question indicate which question is related to which standard. Table 4.1.1 is the point table for the sixth-grade science passage on earth's features.

Scoring Issues for Specific Standards

Determining the acceptability of an answer is not always a clear-cut issue. There are some cases where the answer key, albeit quite specific, does not seem to provide sufficient guidance. We offer the following specific suggestions for deciding the acceptability of an answer based on our pilot data.

- **Standard 1: Cite textual evidence to support analysis of what the text says explicitly as well as inferences drawn from the text.** Students can rewrite or underline text evidence that indicates or supports the inference provided in the question stem. They can also paraphrase the text evidence, but the paraphrase must be accurate and clearly refer to the text components. If you are unsure about the validity of the paraphrase, mark it wrong. Sometimes students offer evidence from the same paragraph, but if it does not specifically refer to the evidence listed in the answer key, it should be regarded as an error. The student is clearly in the ballpark but unfortunately not on base.

- **Standard 2: Determine central idea/s or themes.** Many of our first pilot students who read nonfiction texts indicated confusion regarding the central or main idea. They either offered a one-word answer or listed a series of details from the paragraph as their version of the central idea. They did not seem to realize that topic and main idea are different things. The topic is one to three words long and is the subject of the paragraph/s; the central idea is a statement that summarizes what the author says about this subject. The topic is often contained in headings; the central idea, more often than not, has to be inferred from the details. In order to provide clarification, we changed the central idea question to include the topic. For example: "The topic of the previous paragraphs is Roman roads and aqueducts. What is the central idea?"

The central idea is not a running total of details contained in the paragraph. Rather a central idea is a single and unified statement that ties these details together, such as "Women had limited roles in Athenian society." To put it another way, the central idea reflects the author's purpose in selecting the details contained in the text. If a student provides a list of details, the answer is incorrect. In a similar fashion, if a student provides a single detail as the central idea, the answer is wrong. For example, the topic of two paragraphs in the middle school passage on the Constitutional Convention was the "slave trade." The fact that it would be barred in 1808 and that slave trade within the United States was unaffected are not central ideas; they are details supporting the central idea, which was that the North and South compromised about slavery. Also, because Standard 2 questions identify the topic of the paragraph, the central idea offered by the student should be clearly related to the topic. If it is not, the answer is wrong.

Becoming aware of a theme or what the author of a story wants the reader to think about after reading the story demands a level of abstraction. Younger students may not have heard the word *theme*; their teachers may have used the word *lesson* or *message* to describe the overarching theme in the story. At the higher-grade levels, students sometimes came up with themes that were different from those in the answer key, but were essentially correct. Therefore, be sure to consider the meaning of the answer, not simply the words used.

- **Standard 3: Analyze interactions/connections between individuals, events, and ideas.** In correcting questions based on this standard, you should remember that the standards are text-based. This means that the analysis must be primarily based on text content. Pilot students often included items that answered the question but were not present in the text. If the content of the student's response contains information that is obviously drawn from other sources, it is not correct and must be regarded as an error. In the high school passage on the rise of the Greek city-states, a question asked students to analyze how the military dominated Spartan society. One student answered that someone who did not want to become a soldier was probably killed or driven out from Sparta. Again, this is another probable answer but it is not stated in the text. Therefore, it is wrong and does not belong in the analysis. In some passages, Standard 3 questions take the form of two-point answers; students can receive one or two points depending on the completeness of their answer. The point table for each answer key indicates which questions require two points, as does the answer key for a specific passage.

- **Standard 4: Determine the meaning of words and phrases as they are used in the text.** The key to an acceptable answer is that it must refer to the word meaning as used in the text. Pilot students often offered a meaning that was correct but did not fit with the context of the passage. For example, *civil* in the high school selection on the Roman Republic means occurring within the state or political fighting between citizens. *Civil* also can mean courteous or social, but not in the context of this passage. Therefore a student who stated that *civil* means "being nice to someone" is in error and should be marked wrong. Students often offer answers that are not contained in the answer key. In determining whether such an answer is correct, remember that it must match the content of the selection. If it does not, it should be marked wrong.

Examples of students making similar kinds of mistakes were evident in a few questions from narrative text. Using *The Tell Tale Heart* as an example, the first questions asked what the following sentences meant in the paragraph in which they occurred: "Object there was none. Passion there was none." A couple of students wrote that there was no weapon around to kill the old man, interpreting the word *object* as a thing used to kill, rather than a purpose for the killing. Such answers should be marked wrong.

- **Standard 5: Analyze the structure of the text.** The first part of this question in informational text is selected response. The student chooses which of three or five text structures is best represented by a segment of the passage. Issues in correcting often involved the second part of the question, a constructed response in which the student offers a reason for choice of text structure. Pilot students often offered vague and general reasons for their choice.

For example, after selecting description, many students said "the author is describing something." A selection of cause/effect was explained as "because the author is saying what caused something." Vague and general answers such as these are wrong. A student's choice of structure should refer explicitly to the text as is indicated in the answer key.

- **Standard 6: Determine the author's point of view.** A point of view is an individual's opinion, attitude, purpose, or perspective. It is not an action; it is not what someone does. Point of view provides a reason or motivation for an individual's behavior. Many students described point of view in terms of what an individual did. For example, for the high school passage *The Rise of the Greek City-States,* they stated that Cleisthenes' point of view was broadening the role of ordinary citizens in government and making the assembly a genuine legislature. These are actions motivated by his particular point of view of government. One can infer from his actions that government should be open to ordinary citizens and/or government should actually do something. This may seem like a fine point, but it is an important one. Standard 6 focuses on the ability to infer motivation based on actions described in the text. Similarly, in the middle school passage on the Constitutional Convention, pilot students often described the Northern delegates' point of view of the Three-Fifths Compromise by describing their acceptance of the amendment itself, not the point of view that led them to their agreement, which was their belief in the importance of preserving the Union.

The author's point of view in literature requires students to be close readers of the author's language. For example, a question from the sixth-grade story *Arachne* is "What is the narrator's point of view of Arachne <u>and</u> what words from the text support your answer?" Students had to think about what language the author used to reflect his or her point of view. A correct answer was, "the author thinks she is self-centered and uses the words proud, she lived for praise, and she didn't believe that anyone could teach her anything." Students frequently interpreted the point of view but did not provide text evidence to support their interpretation. In such cases the students received one point out of the two possible points.

Determining Class Performance

All passages contain two separate indices of student performance: answers to 10 questions that are based on the standards and the contents of the summary.

Class Performance on the Standards

Because the primary focus of the *CARA* is to provide a formative assessment of the standards, your first need should be to determine how your class performed on each standard. This will allow you to focus your instruction on the specific needs of your class. Table 4.1.2 presents a class summary sheet that you can use to record and analyze the performance of your class. Table 4.1.3 presents a class summary sheet filled out with example data. Using the summary sheet has several advantages. First, it allows you to record and examine all *CARA* results on one page. Second, the uniform format allows you to easily compare *CARA* results on two passages (e.g., literature versus social studies) or passage 1 versus passage 2 administered at a later date. Third, if the *CARA* is administered across a grade level or even an entire school in order to address possible changes in instructional emphases, the uniform format fosters more efficient analysis of the results. The class summary sheet also contains space for recording Standard 8 information. We will address the class summary sheet again in Part 2 of this chapter.

Prepare the class summary sheet by entering the standard associated with each question and the number of points assigned to that question. You will find this information on the point table in the answer key for the passage that you are scoring (see Table 4.1.1 in this

Table 4.1.2 CARA Class Summary Sheet

Passage Title:

See end of specific passage answer key for standards, points, and total points.											Total Points Possible	
Points												
Standard												
Question	1	2	3	4	5	6	7	8	9	10		
Student Name	Enter number of points correct for each question.										Total Student Points Correct	% Correct (Points Correct Divided by Total Points Possible Multiplied by 100)
1												
2												
3												
4												
5												
6												
7												
8												
9												
10												
11												
12												
13												
14												
15												
16												
17												
18												
19												
20												
21												
22												
23												
24												
25												
etc.												
											Class Average %	
Total per question												
Class Percent: Total per question / (number of students* possible points) *100)												

Class Analysis by Standards: Each standard has one or more questions.
List standard; the questions tied to the standards with class % (the number of questions will vary); Average these %

Standard	Question # (class %)		Class Average		

Summary scoring is different between Literature and Social Studies/Science							
Points vary. See individual answer keys						Social Studies	Standard 8
Possible points			Possible points				
All summaries are Standard 2							
Literature Summary			Social Studies/Science Summary				
Number of Plot Elements	% of Plot Elements		Number of AK units	% Matches to Answer Key	Check, if at cut-off	Number of Arguments	Number of Valid Arguments
Total number of narrative elements varies with individual passages.			Assign a zero if summary is left blank, is not text related, or does not answer the question asked.				
Caution: Percent is the count divided by the total (varies) multipied by 100.							
Teacher Notes							

Table 4.1.3   Example of Completed *CARA* Class Summary Sheet

Passage Title:	Constitutional Convention											Total Points Possible
See end of specific passage answer key for standards, points, and total points.												12
Points		1	1	1	1	2	1	2	1	1	1	
Standard		4	4	1	2	3	1	5	6	2	3	
Question		1	2	3	4	5	6	7	8	9	10	

Student Name	Enter number of points correct for each question.											Total Student Points Correct	% Correct (Points Correct Divided by Total Points Possible Multiplied by 100)
1 J.J.	1	1	1	0	2	1	2	1	1	1		11	92%
2 P.L.	0	1	1	1	2	1	0	0	1	1		8	67%
3 A.D.	0	1	1	0	2	1	2	1	0	0		8	67%
4 E.D.	1	1	0	1	2	0	2	0	1	1		9	75%
5 R.T.	0	1	1	0	2	1	2	1	1	0		9	75%
6 B.B.	1	1	1	0	2	1	2	1	1	0		10	83%
7 T.C.	1	1	1	0	2	1	2	1	0	1		10	83%
8 K.L.	0	1	1	0	1	0	2	1	1	0		7	58%
9 J.R.	1	1	1	0	2	1	2	0	0	1		9	75%
10 W.J.	1	1	1	1	2	1	2	1	0	1		11	92%
11 C.C.	1	1	1	0	2	1	2	1	0	1		10	83%
12 C.L	0	1	1	0	2	0	2	0	0	1		7	58%
13 D.E	0	1	1	1	2	1	0	1	0	1		8	67%
14 A.H	1	1	1	0	2	1	0	1	0	1		8	67%
15 N.N	0	1	1	0	0	1	2	0	1	0		6	50%
16													
17													
18													
19													
20													
21													
22													
23													
24													
25													
etc.													
												Class Average %	73%

Total per question		8	15	14	4	27	12	24	10	7	10
Class Percent: Total per question / (number of students* possible points) *100)		53%	100%	93%	27%	90%	80%	80%	67%	47%	67%

Class Analysis by Standards: Each standard has one or more questions.
List standard; the questions tied to the standards with class % (the number of questions will vary); Average these %

Standard	Question # (class %)		Class Average
1	Q3 (93), Q4 (80)	(93 + 80)/2=	86.65
2	Q4 (27), Q9 (47)	(27 + 47)/2=	37
3	Q5 (80), Q10 (67)	(80 + 67)/2=	78.65
4	Q1 (53), Q2(100)	(53 + 100)/2=	76.5
5	Q7 (80)		80
6	Q8 (67)		67

Summary scoring is different between Literature and Social Studies/Science						Social Studies Standard 8	
Points vary. See individual answer keys							
Possible points		Possible points	9				
All summaries are Standard 2							
Literature Summary			Social Studies/Science Summary				
Number of Plot Elements	% of Plot Elements		Number of AK units	% Matches to Answer Key	Check, if at cut-off	Number of Arguments	Number of Valid Arguments
			8	89%		0	0
			1	11%		0	0
			5	56%		0	0
			6	67%		2	0
			0	0%		0	0
			2	22%		1	0
			7	78%		1	0
			5	56%		1	0
			0	0%		2	1
			0	0%		0	0
			3	33%		0	0
			2	22%		1	0
			6	67%		0	0
			7	78%		2	0
			4	44%		1	0
Total number of narrative elements varies with individual passages.			Assign a zero if summary is left blank, is not text related, or does not answer the question asked.				
Caution: Percent is the count divided by the total (varies) multipied by 100.							
Teacher Notes							

chapter for an example.) As we previously suggested, correct one question at a time and record each student's score. After correcting question 1, total the number of points, divide by the number of students, and multiply by 100 to arrive at a class percentage for that question. Then move on to the next question. Continue in this way until you have corrected and recorded all tests.

Some standards are assessed by multiple questions, notably Standards 1, 3, and 4 in informational text and Standards 1, 3, 4, and 6 in literature. You may want to determine your class average for a specific standard that is represented by more than one question. Simply add the class averages for each question and divide by the number of questions. For example, there are two questions that measure Standard 4 in informational text. If the class averages are 54 percent for one question and 18 percent for the other question, the overall average would be 36 percent (54 + 18 = 72, 72/2 = 36). Directions are on the lower left side of the class summary sheet.

How should we interpret these percentages? A majority of classroom and formative assessments are scored on a percentage basis—students' scores are totaled and translated into a percent. The percent is then used to assign a grade. Scores above 70 or 75 percent usually become grades of A, B, or C, with individual schools and districts establishing cut-offs and/or ranges for each grade. Informal reading inventories also translate summed scores into percentages that designate independent, instructional, and frustration levels for word identification and comprehension. Determining class performance on the *CARA* follows these practices. You may use the percentages in your school and district to determine student performance levels, or you may adopt the following percentage guidelines for advanced, proficient, or minimal level of performance. These are in accord with scoring practices for many informal instruments and classroom assessments (Leslie & Caldwell, 2011).

90% - 100%: Advanced and/or independent
70% - 89%: Proficient and/or instructional
Below 70%: Minimal and/or Frustration

Table 4.1.4 is the class summary section of Table 4.1.1 that summarizes data only on questions. It is placed here for your convenience as you read how to score and interpret class and individual percentages on the 10 questions.

Overall Class and Student Performance on the Passage

As illustrated by Table 4.1.4, the *CARA* can be used to determine an individual student's performance on a total passage. It can also be used to ascertain overall class performance. Thus, the *CARA* provides an answer to the following questions: What percentage correct did an individual student achieve on the passage? What percentage correct did the entire class achieve on the passage? Did the student/class do very well, perform adequately, or demonstrate below-level performance?

Determining an individual's performance level involves counting the number of points attained by the student (Total Student Points Correct) and dividing by the total number of points in the passage (Total Points Possible) and multiplying by 100. This gives you the percent correct (% Correct) for an individual student. For example, student 8 (K.L.) had seven correct answers for a percentage of 58 percent (7 divided by 12).

To determine the class average, add the percent correct for each individual student and divide by the number of students. This will give you the class average. Observe that in Table 4.1.4, the class percentage was 73 percent, but eight of 15 students scored above it and

Table 4.1.4   Example of Completed Class Summary Sheet for Each Question

Passage Title:	Constitutional Convention										Total Points Possible	
See end of specific passage answer key for standards, points, and total points.											12	
Points	1	1	1	1	2	1	2	1	1	1		
Standard	4	4	1	2	3	1	5	6	2	3		
Question	1	2	3	4	5	6	7	8	9	10		

Student Name	Enter number of points correct for each question.										Total Student Points Correct	% Correct (Points Correct Divided by Total Points Possible Multiplied by 100)
1 J.J.	1	1	1	0	2	1	2	1	1	1	11	92%
2 P.L.	0	1	1	1	2	1	0	0	1	1	8	67%
3 A.D.	0	1	1	0	2	1	2	1	0	0	8	67%
4 E.D.	1	1	0	1	2	0	2	0	1	1	9	75%
5 R.T.	0	1	1	0	2	1	2	1	1	0	9	75%
6 B.B.	1	1	1	0	2	1	2	1	1	0	10	83%
7 T.C.	1	1	1	0	2	1	2	1	0	1	10	83%
8 K.L.	0	1	1	0	1	0	2	1	1	0	7	58%
9 J.R.	1	1	1	0	2	1	2	0	0	1	9	75%
10 W.J.	1	1	1	1	2	1	2	1	0	1	11	92%
11 C.C.	1	1	1	0	2	1	2	1	0	1	10	83%
12 C.L	0	1	1	0	2	0	2	0	0	1	7	58%
13 D.E	0	1	1	1	2	1	0	1	0	1	8	67%
14 A.H	1	1	1	0	2	1	0	1	0	1	8	67%
15 N.N	0	1	1	0	0	1	2	0	1	0	6	50%
16												
17												
18												
19												
20												
21												
22												
23												
24												
25												
etc.												
											Class Average %	73%

Total per question	8	15	14	4	27	12	24	10	7	10		
Class Percent: Total per question / (number of students* possible points) *100	53%	100%	93%	27%	90%	80%	80%	67%	47%	67%		

Class Analysis by Standards: Each standard has one or more questions. List standard; the questions tied to the standards with class % (the number of questions will vary); Average these %						
Standard	Question # (class %)			Class Average		
1	Q3 (93), Q4 (80)	(93 + 80)/2=		86.65		
2	Q4 (27), Q9 (47)	(27 + 47)/2=		37		
3	Q5 (80), Q10 (67)	(80 + 67)/2=		78.65		
4	Q1 (53), Q2(100)	(53 + 100)/2=		76.5		
5	Q7 (80)			80		
6	Q8 (67)			67		

seven scored below. You can use the percent correct for individual students to form classroom groupings and/or to identify individuals for additional instruction.

It is important to understand that overall performance on the passage does not offer information on specific standards. It suggests a student's ability to read a grade-level selection in a specific discipline at an advanced, proficient, or minimal level. Overall passage performance for individual students identifies those who are experiencing difficulty with grade-level text in literature, social studies, and/or science. It may indicate the need for additional assessment by an intervention specialist. Thus the *CARA* offers a teacher the option to identify students who may need instruction beyond what is feasible for the classroom teacher. Similarly, overall class performance on a *CARA* passage suggests whether the average performance of the class is advanced, proficient, or minimal with regard to grade-level text in literature, social studies, or science. Minimal performance may be addressed through district-level adjustments to text, curriculum, allotted class time, teacher in-service, or other factors.

A teacher may choose to determine or ignore overall performance for individuals and/or the class. The more important analysis is class and individual performance on specific standards.

Analyzing Class and Student Performance on the Standards

If you review the completed example in Table 4.1.4, you will see the class showed weakness on two standards. The class score of 37 percent for Standard 2 (determine central idea/s) suggests the need for a strong instructional focus. The second score below 70 percent involved recognition of the delegates' point of view of the Three-Fifths Compromise. Some students interpreted point of view as an action, as opposed to the belief that motivated the action. Examining percentages on individual standards can help the teacher set a focus for instruction.

Examining individual student answers can also offer suggestions for instruction. This may be especially relevant to the intervention specialist. Three students (K.L., C.L., N.N.) scored below 60 percent; however, they demonstrated different profiles. Although all three indicated difficulty with regard to Standards 4 and 6, student C.L. had no issues with Standard 3; students K.L. and N.N. did. We recommend that you share individual performance privately with each student and let the entire group know the strengths and areas where they need instruction.

The following reports were written by a teacher about her class, which participated in the pilots. They indicate how *CARA* results can help the classroom teacher determine a focus for instruction.

SAMPLE REPORT ON SEVENTH GRADE SOCIAL STUDIES

Students experienced most difficulty in determining the central idea (11%) and determining point of view (31%). Relative strengths were evident with regard to determining text structure (64%) and determining word meaning from context (57%). Students often interpreted central idea as a summary of details contained in the paragraph, as opposed to one general statement that provided a purpose or rationale for inclusion of the details. They often confused point of view with a character's actions; that is, they did not seem to understand that a point of view is the reason or motivation for what a character does.

Students clearly experienced difficulty composing coherent answers to constructed-response questions. In some cases their responses were difficult to interpret; although an answer often seemed related to the question, it was not specific or detailed enough to provide an acceptable answer. Difficulties in paraphrasing the text were evident and it was

Example Report of Class Performance on the Standards: Middle School Social Studies

Class Performance on the Standards: Middle School Social Studies

Here is a summary of students' responses on the social studies passage. Below illustrates the average correct for each standard across the passage at a grade level.

The Constitutional Convention

Standard 1	Support an inference	53%
Standard 2	Determine central idea	11%
Standard 3	Explain why or how	50%
Standard 4	Determine word meaning	57%
Standard 5	Determine text structure	64%
Standard 6	Determine point of view	31%

Note: Some standards were measured by two questions: Standard 1, Standard 2, and Standard 3. The average correct for that standard was provided.

difficult to distinguish whether lack of comprehension or lack of writing skill was the issue. Answers also suggested that many students did not carefully read the question or perhaps did not understand the question stem. Answers also suggested that many did not engage in close reading and/or rereading of the text.

Students were asked to write a summary of a portion of the text. The majority of summaries were brief and relatively unfocused and many included personal comments and reactions. Inclusion of content that was unrelated to the topic of the summary was also common. This suggests that students do not understand the purpose and format of a summary.

SAMPLE REPORT FOR MIDDLE SCHOOL SCIENCE

Students experienced most difficulty in determining the central idea (25%) and analyzing why and how (39%). Relative strengths were evident with regard to determining text structure (53%) and determining word meaning from context (56%). For Standard 2 students tended to offer a topic, a single detail, or a list of details as opposed to a general statement or phrase that tied the details together and/or clarified the author's purpose. Standard 3 asks students to analyze the text by explaining how or why. In order to do this, the reader has to locate items from different sections of the text and draw them together to provide an answer. Students tended to offer one segment of the text as their answer, suggesting that they seemed to think that the answer can be found in one specific sentence. Standard 1 asks students to identify text support for an inference. This was also problematic for students. Locating text evidence requires close reading of the question as well as the text; many students simply offered their own opinions.

The standards demand a high level of comprehension involving close reading of the text to answer text-based questions. Similarities were evident across both social studies and science passages. Writing coherent answers to constructed-response questions were definite challenges for the students. Answers to questions were generally accurate if the answer could be found in text immediately preceding the question or in a single sentence. However, if the answer involved a larger segment of text, students experienced difficulty in pulling disparate sections together to form a coherent answer.

Students were asked to write a text-based summary. Summaries were evaluated on: whether they addressed the topic and/or answered the question, whether they were

Example Report of Class Performance on the Standards: Middle School Science

Class Performance on the Standards: Middle School Science

Here is a summary of students' responses on the science passage. Below illustrates the average correct for each standard across the passage at a grade level.

The Digestive System

Standard 1	Support an inference	45%
Standard 2	Determine central idea	25%
Standard 3	Explain why or how	39%
Standard 4	Determine word meaning	56%
Standard 5	Determine text structure	53%

Note: Some standards were measured by two questions: Standard 1, Standard 2, and Standard 3. The average correct for that standard was provided.

text-based, and whether they provided an adequate summary as measured by the number of Answer Key units contained in the summary versus the number of unrelated units. Seven students did not write a summary; perhaps they did not have enough time. Thirteen students did not address the topic or answer the question. Summaries of the remaining six students were inadequate in that they contained an equal number of or more unrelated pieces of information.

SAMPLE REPORT FOR SEVENTH GRADE LITERATURE

Students' relative strength was on using text information to support an inference. An example of a question used to measure Standard 1 was, "Cite two pieces of evidence from the paragraph above to explain why the man was so grateful to see the 45-year-old man and the cottage." Of the 27 students who answered this question, only five received no points for their answer. Nine students cited two pieces of text evidence; the other 50 percent provided one source. Students were similarly capable of determining a theme or message in

Example Report of Class Performance on the Standards: Grade 7 Literature

Class Performance on the Standards: Grade 7 Literature

Here is a summary of students' responses on the literature passages. Below illustrates the average correct for each standard across the three passages at a grade level.

All Summer in a Day
The Californian's Tale
The Third Wish

Standard 1	Support an inference	62%
Standard 2	Determine central idea	59%
Standard 3	Explain why or how	41%
Standard 4	Determine word meaning	55%
Standard 6	Determine point of view	59%

a story and determining point of view, with 59 percent getting these questions correct. The students who did not answer the theme question correctly on the fantasy story named the genre rather than the theme. This led scorers to suspect that they didn't understand the meaning of a theme.

The students' relative weakness was in explaining or analyzing why or how something happened. For example, a sample question was, "Analyze why the setting was important to a character in the story." Another question designed to measure this standard was, "Analyze how the location of the story relates to the narrator." In both of these questions, students must explain how two things related to each other. In several cases, students did not seem to understand the question.

The students were asked to write a text-based summary of the story. The summaries were scored by ascertaining whether a particular story element was contained in the summary. For example, in each story there was a main character, an event that began the plot of the story, other events that continued the action, and an ending. In the seventh-grade stories there was an initiating event and four other events, for a total of seven elements. The average number of elements contained in their summaries of the three stories were 3.8, 2.2, and 4.6, illustrating that one story was much harder to summarize than the other two. This difference occurred only on the summary, as each story was similar to the others on the percent correct answers to questions (average correct ranged from 60% to 66%).

Instruction should focus on analyzing or explaining how elements of the story relate to each other; for example, how a setting related either to a character or to an event in the story. Weaknesses in this area were also seen in social studies and science. Please be sure to read the standards to see how analysis questions may be written.

Summary

In this chapter we have described how to administer and score the *CARA*. We have explained how to choose a level of text or a content area depending on the purpose for administering the *CARA*. We have explained the process through which we developed the answer keys and the importance of adhering to them. We also provided detailed recommendations for scoring. Finally, we provided examples of reports that we have written to teachers about their classes' performance on some aspect of the *CARA*. We hope that these sample reports will help you understand how results of the *CARA* can be used to guide standards-based instruction. Chapter 4, Part 2, will explain the administration and scoring of the students' summaries.

Scoring of the *CARA* Options

Summaries

Standard 2 has two components. One is the assessment of central idea or theme of a selection. The second component is to summarize the text. According to Standard 2, a summary is text based; summary components are drawn from the text, not from other sources such as prior knowledge, student opinion, media, or other texts.

Evaluating the adequacy of any summary involves two components. One focuses on the mechanics of writing, such as spelling, punctuation, and sentence structure. The other focuses on the contents of the summary. Although admittedly important, the *CARA* does not deal with writing mechanics; a teacher can assess this component using his or her own method of doing so. The *CARA* focuses on evaluating the content of the summary: the extent to which the summary includes relevant and text-based components that adequately address the topic and/or intent of the summary question.

What are the components of a well-crafted summary? A summary includes only the most relevant or salient content about a specific topic (Ferretti & De La Paz, 2011). Another way of phrasing this is to describe a summary as including the main idea, usually in the form of an introductory statement, and the most significant or relevant details related to this idea (Helsel & Greenberg, 2007). For literature, a story summary focuses on the structure of a story: character, events, and resolution.

As a teacher, your purpose is to determine if a student understands how to write a text-based summary. This is seldom a simple decision. It is generally easy to recognize a good summary; we know one when we see one. However, from the point of view of a teacher who is expected to teach students how to write summaries, the issue is to identify what a student does not understand about the process. To put it another way, what is missing in the summary that you will have to teach to your students?

The student summary sheet provides space for recording student scores on the summary question. Because of structure differences between the two disciplines, summaries of informational text are evaluated and recorded differently than summaries of narratives.

Literature

In assessing students' ability to meet the standards for literature, the *CARA* focuses on short stories that include the typical narrative organization using settings (sometimes of importance and sometimes not), characters, goal and/or problem, a series of events where one or more characters try to reach a goal or solve the problem, and a resolution. After scoring numerous pilot summaries and using our judgments of their adequacy, we wrote a model summary for each answer key based on narrative structure, including at least one statement that represents each of the story elements. We made this decision rather than simply counting each statement that matched the answer key for two reasons. First, it would be possible for students to write several statements from one story element (e.g., characters) but not include a main event or an ending that was much more important to the story. Second, scoring by story elements provides the teacher with a clear path to instruction. For example, if your students frequently omit the initiating event in their story summaries, then you can address the importance of including this element.

For all of the literature selections, the narrative structure included settings (if they were important), character(s), an initiating event necessary for the story to unfold, one or more events where characters try to reach a goal or solve the problem, and an ending or resolution. In summary, each answer key was divided into the narrative elements (setting, character, initiating event, etc.) that were appropriate to the story. The number of events in an acceptable summary varied and increased as the passages became longer. Under each narrative element, the Answer Key provides appropriate summary units.

An acceptable summary should include at least 70 percent of the <u>narrative elements</u>. In addition, what the student says should be accurate. If a student makes an inaccurate statement about any narrative element, it does not count as an acceptable response. However, a student's comment should match narrative elements in meaning, not necessarily in exact wording. Valid inferences drawn from the text should also be counted as a valid element of the narrative structure. One scoring issue that may occur is a student who writes one or more accurate summary statements within an element, but also includes an error. In this situation, you should determine the importance of the accurate statements relative to the inaccurate one. If the inaccurate statement negates the accurate ones, then the answer is incorrect. However, if the inaccurate statement involves a minor detail, then the accurate statements take precedence and the story element is considered correctly included in the summary.

For example, at the fourth grade level the story, *Amelia and Eleanor go for a Ride,* one student described the characters stating, "Amelia was a pilot and Eleanor was the first lady and a pilot too." These are correct, but the student added that Eleanor was a pilot whereas in the story it says, "Mrs. Roosevelt just received her student pilot's license." Although a student license and a licensed pilot are not the same, a fourth grade student would be unlikely to understand the difference, so this addition does not negate the correct characterizations. At the sixth grade level, the story *Arachne* describes a contest between Arachne and the goddess Athena. One student described the behaviors of each character correctly, but at one point used the same name twice in a sentence. Although this could be considered an incorrect understanding of the actions of each character, the fact that other statements in this part of the summary were correct led us to consider this a minor detail and more likely a spelling error than an error in understanding. These scoring examples illustrate the complexity of scoring extended responses. Fortunately, these errors were very rare and occurred mostly on the names of characters. You must trust your instincts and score neither too stringently nor too leniently.

Using Story Structure

As you match a student's summary to the Answer Key, it is important to keep track of which student statements refer to which story element by marking abbreviations for each element. For example, if the student includes the characters, write CH beside that part of the summary. Similarly, if the student includes the initiating event, write IE beside it. Most stories have several event categories so mark a student's summary unit as EV1, EV2, and so on. When you have identified all acceptable student comments and matched these to an appropriate story element, count the number of narrative elements that were included in the student's summary and use this to determine a percent. The number of possible narrative elements varies across the grade levels, so refer to the point table in each answer key to find the number possible. As mentioned above, an acceptable summary should include 70% of the story elements. Divide the student's number of acceptable story units by the total number of units in the selection

Table 4.2.1   Guidelines for Scoring a Summary of Literature

Do	Don't
Count clause units	Count explanatory comments such as "I think"
Match clause units to answer key	Count connecting units such as "the next thing"
Accept paraphrases that match the answer key	Expect verbatim statements
Score on what student wrote	Score on what you think the student meant

to arrive at a percent. Do not confuse the number of student comments with narrative elements. For example, in *Amelia and Eleanor Go for a Ride,* there are five narrative elements: Characterization, Initiating Event, Event 1, Event 2, and Ending. If a student offers two accurate comments under Characterization, two under Event 1 and one under Ending, the score is three, not five, because two narrative elements were omitted (Initiating Event and Event 2).

After scoring each student's summary, the class summary sheet can be used to record student data on the summary (see Table 4.1.2 in Chapter 4, Part 1.). Write the number of correct story elements included in each student's summary followed by the percent of the elements included in the summary. The percent is calculated by the number of narrative elements included in the summary divided by the number of possible elements and multiplied by 100.

The sample summaries that follow provide examples of student work and how the summaries were scored. Guidelines for scoring a summary of literature are shown in Table 4.2.1.

Summary Examples from Literature

The following examples present students' summaries and their scoring. First, the student summary is organized into clauses and presented in italics. Next, the clauses from the summary are matched with the answers on the answer key. The answer key section is the same as that included for the story in the *CARA*. Finally, a checkmark is placed beside each story element included in the student's summary.

SUMMARY QUESTION FOR *AMELIA AND ELEANOR GO FOR A RIDE* (FOURTH GRADE): SUMMARIZE THE STORY

Student Summary 1:

Summary units are enclosed in parentheses. *(Eleanor and Amelia were best friends.) (Amelia was a pilot.) (Eleanor was the President's wife.) (Eleanor invites Amelia and her husband for dinner.) (Amelia took Eleanor on the plane for a ride.) (Then they came home) (and get in Eleanor's new car.) (And they come home for dessert.)*

Match to the Answer Key (Student units are in italics)

Characterization ___✓___

1. Amelia and Eleanor were alike
   Eleanor and Amelia were best friends (valid inference)

2. Because they were outspoken/determined/daring (any one of these)
3. Amelia was a pilot
   Amelia was a pilot.

4. Eleanor was the first lady of the United States
   Eleanor was the president's wife.

Initiating Event _✓_

5. Eleanor invited Amelia for dinner at the White House
   Eleanor invites Amelia and her husband for dinner.

6. Eleanor asked what it was like to fly over the Capitol at night

Event 1 _✓_

7. Amelia invited Eleanor to fly to Baltimore and back
8. The Secret Service men said it hadn't been approved
9. But Eleanor went anyway
   Amelia took Eleanor on the plane for a ride.

10. Eleanor enjoyed the beautiful flight

Event 2 _✓_

11. They returned home
    Then they came home

12. They went for a ride in Eleanor's new car
    and get in Eleanor's new car.

Ending _✓_

13. They returned to the White House for dessert
    And they come home for dessert.

Evaluation. This is an acceptable summary because it includes attention to all elements of story structure present in this passage for a score of 100 percent. Record this on the Class Summary Sheet.

Student Summary 2:

Summary units are enclosed in parentheses. *(This story is about two women and the adventures they take together.) (They are friends that do everything together) (for example, they flew a plane to Baltimore and back to Washington, D.C.) (They are very different) (one is the first lady) (and the other is a pilot.) (The first lady is named Eleanor Roosevelt,) (and the pilot was named Amelia Earhart.)*

Match to the Answer Key (Student units are in italics)

Characterization _✓_

1. Amelia and Eleanor were alike
   the women are friends (valid inference)
   they are very different (error; if this was the only statement made with regard to characters, it would not be acceptable)

2. Because they were outspoken/determined/daring (any one of these)
3. Amelia was a pilot
   the pilot was named Amelia Earhart

4. Eleanor was the first lady of the United States
   The first lady is named Eleanor Roosevelt

Initiating Event ____

5. Eleanor invited Amelia for dinner at the White House
6. Eleanor asked what it was like to fly over the Capitol at night

Event 1 ✓

7. Amelia invited Eleanor to fly to Baltimore and back
8. The Secret Service men said it hadn't been approved
9. But Eleanor went anyway
   They flew a plane to Baltimore and back to Washington D.C.
10. Eleanor enjoyed the beautiful flight

Event 2 ____

11. They returned home
12. They went for a ride in Eleanor's new car

Ending ____

13. They returned to the White House for dessert

Evaluation. The student begins his summary with a general statement. Although not on the answer key, it is considered an appropriate inferential summary statement of the story. The summary included seven statements that matched the answer key and one that did not. The student offers three accurate statements that describe the characters and one erroneous statement. One important event is addressed, but no other plot elements are mentioned. The summary is not acceptable because it does not include 70% of the narrative elements. An initiating event, an additional important event, and/or an ending are missing. The student addressed only two of the five plot elements, for a score of 40 percent.

SUMMARY QUESTION FOR *ALL SUMMER IN A DAY* (SEVENTH GRADE): SUMMARIZE THE STORY

Student Summary:

Summary units are enclosed in parentheses. *(It has been raining on Venus for 7 years.) (The children are sad because they want to see the sun.) (Margot told the children that the scientist predicted that the rain would stop and the sun would come out.) (The children didn't believe her,) (so they locked her up in a closet.) (All of a sudden the rain stopped and the sun came out.) (All the children were happy.) (They went out and played and let the sun be on them.) (Then they felt raindrops.) (They were all sad again.) (They remembered that Margot was in the closet.) (They went inside and let her out.)*

Match to the Answer Key (Student units are in italics)

Setting ✓

1. The story occurs on the planet Venus, where it rains all the time
2. Except for one hour every seven years when the sun comes out
   It has been raining on Venus for 7 years.
   The children were sad (valid inference)
3. The day is coming soon when the sun will come out
   Margot told the children that the scientist predicted that the rain would stop and the sun would come out.

Characterization ____

4. There is one child, Margot, who has been to Earth and seen the sun.
5. She is excluded by other children because she is different (she remembers the sun)
6. She is also very shy and withdrawn

Initiating Event _✓_

 7. There is a boy who is bullying her
 8. When she describes the sun no one believes her
 The children didn't believe her.

Event 1 _✓_

 9. The children gang up on Margot and put her in the closet so that she can't see the sun
 So they locked her up in a closet.

Event 2 _✓_

10. The sun comes out
 the sun came out

 All the children were happy (valid inference)

11. The children play (run among the trees, slip and fall, and play hide-and-seek, but mostly look at the sun)
 they went out and played and let the sun be on them.

12. After an hour they watch the sun fade and the rain comes again
 Then they felt raindrops. They were all sad again (valid inference)

Event 3 _✓_

13. They realize that Margo was right about the sun
14. They remember that they left Margot in the closet and they feel guilty
 they remembered that Margot was in the closet

Ending _✓_

15. They finally let her out of the closet
 They went inside and let her out.

Evaluation. This summary is an acceptable one because it includes six of the seven story elements described on the answer key, or 86 percent. The student did not describe Margo's character, but she was the main character in the summary.

Student Summary 2:

Summary units are enclosed in parentheses. *(The children didn't like Margot.) (One day when Margot said her poem the kids hated her even more.) (They told her that wasn't true.) (That the sun is like a flower blooming.) (They got angry and they locked her in a closet on her favorite day in which it didn't rain.) (After the kids played outside) (they felt guilty.)*

Match to the Answer Key (Student units are in italics)

Setting ____

 1. The story occurs on the planet Venus, where it rains all of the time
 2. Except for one hour every seven years when the sun comes out
 3. The day is coming soon when the sun will come out

Characterization _✓_

 4. There is one child, Margot, who has been to Earth and seen the sun
 5. She is excluded by other children because she is different (she remembers the sun)
 the children didn't like Margot (valid inference)

 6. She is also very shy and withdrawn

Initiating Event ____

7. There is a boy who is bullying her
8. When she describes the sun no one believes her

Event 1 ✓

9. The children gang up on Margot and put her in the closet so that she can't see the sun
   they got angry and locked her in a closet.

Event 2 ✓

10. The sun comes out
    on her favorite day in which it didn't rain.
11. The children play (run among the trees, slip and fall, and play hide-and-seek, but mostly look at the sun)
    the kids played outside
12. After an hour they watch the sun fade and the rain comes again

Event 3 ✓

13. They realize that Margo was right about the sun
14. They remember that they left Margot in the closet and they feel guilty
    they felt guilty

Ending ____

15. They finally let her out of the closet

Evaluation. This summary is not acceptable because it includes only characterization and events 1, 2, and 3, which is 4 out of 7, or 57 percent of the total plot components. The setting in this story is a central part, so it should be included in any summary. The ending is also important to the events of the story.

Student Summary 3:

Summary units are enclosed in parentheses. *(Margot and William and some other kids went to Venus.) (They were waiting for it to rain.) (Because the scientist predicted rain for the day we're going to be on a trip.) (So when they saw rain they were told that this was going to continue for all the days.) (They didn't come and start exploring.) (And until Margot was getting her attitude they decided to shut her up in the closet.) (They continued with the mission.) (They saw the water was pouring and it was getting worse each time.)*

Match to the Answer Key (Student units are in italics)

Setting ✓

1. The story occurs on the planet Venus, where it rains constantly
   kids went to Venus

2. Except for one hour every seven years when the sun comes out
3. The day is coming soon when the sun will come out

Characterization ____

4. There is one child, Margot, who has been to Earth and seen the sun
5. She is excluded by other children because she is different (she remembers the sun)
6. She is also very shy and withdrawn

Initiating Event ____

7. There is a boy who is bullying her
8. When she describes the sun no one believes her

Event 1 __✓__

9. The children gang up on Margot and put her in the closet so that she can't see the sun *they decided to shut her up in the closet.*

Event 2 ____

10. The sun comes out
11. The children play (run among the trees, slip and fall, and play hide-and-seek, but mostly look at the sun)
12. After an hour they watch the sun fade and the rain comes again

Event 3 ____

13. They realize that Margo was right about the sun
14. They remembered that they left Margot in the closet and they felt guilty

Ending ____

15. They finally let her out of the closet

Evaluation. This summary is clearly unacceptable because it has many errors of fact and includes only two elements (the setting and event 1), for a score of 13 percent. The summary names the two characters but says nothing about them, so it is not counted as characterization.

Informational Text

The summary question in literature asks the student to summarize the text. In contrast, the summary question in informational text requires that the student summarize only a portion of the text. Therefore, the teacher scoring summaries in informational text must ask two questions: Does the summary answer the *CARA* question? If the summary does answer the *CARA* question, what is the quality of the content?

Scoring Process

As you read the summary, underline, highlight, or identify in some way those components that match the summary units listed in the answer key. An easy method is to write the number of the answer key unit above or to the side of the relevant component. The answer key units are basically clausal units—that is, they take the form of a simple sentence: subject/ noun, verb, and/or object. After you have highlighted the summary you will ask yourself two questions, which are discussed next.

Scoring Informational Text: Challenges and Solutions

Does the Summary Address the CARA Question?   There are several reasons why a summary may not provide an acceptable answer to the *CARA* question and would result in a score of zero. First, the content of the summary may not focus on the topic as stated in the question stem. For example, the summary question for the middle school passage on the Roman Empire asks students to summarize the accomplishments of the Empire. A number of students in our pilot studies summarized the accomplishments of a specific emperor, Hadrian, which was not the intent of the question. When asked to summarize the issues that were debated during the process of ratifying the Constitution, several students summarized how ratification was celebrated and the subsequent choice of Washington as president. Similarly, when asked to summarize how skeletal muscle and smooth muscle are different, several students discussed the relationship of skeletal muscle and exercise and never mentioned smooth muscle. Clearly, these summaries did not address the specific topic of the question.

Second, a summary may focus on the topic of the question but be so general and/or vague in nature that it does not really address the question. For example, when asked to summarize what the text says about minerals in water, one student wrote, "Different minerals are allowed to carry different things. It can carry many different things like a rock or a boat. The reason we have salt is because things move to leave salt so it increases more and more." On the same question, another student wrote, "Minerals are in water and when they contract, they stay in water. Then they go somewhere else and change. The minerals help the water." It is difficult to even interpret such answers.

Often you will find a summary that contains one or two units that address the question, but because the summary also includes a large number of units that are unrelated to the question, the question basically remains unanswered. For example, a sixth-grade student summarizing the problems faced by the Union Pacific and Central Pacific began by stating one problem of the Union Pacific—conflict with the Native Americans—but then focused the entire summary on that issue without even mentioning the Central Pacific. In a similar fashion, when asked to summarize how fossils form, a middle school student began by stating that living things die and decay, but then went on to summarize what we can learn from fossils, which was irrelevant to the question. Another scoring issue you may face is an extremely brief summary, one that contains only one or two summary statements. Given the number of units in the *CARA* answer keys, such a summary would not be adequate to provide a satisfactory answer to the summary question.

Another situation you may encounter is a summary that is not text based. The *CARA* summary questions ask students to summarize "what the text says." Standard 2 is quite clear; students are expected to "summarize the key supporting details and ideas" (CCSSO & NGA, 2010, p. 13) and "provide an objective summary of the text . . . apart from personal opinions or judgments" (p. 39). Many students in our pilot studies summarized by offering personal opinions about the content of the text or what they saw as the importance of the information. Some included information in their summaries that was not drawn from the text. Such summaries do not answer the *CARA* question. The following examples are representative of summaries that are not text based.

Students were asked to summarize what the text says about the Great Compromise reached by delegates to the Constitutional Convention. The text clearly described the details of the compromise and the differences of opinion that led to it. The following summary is not text based and would be scored as incorrect. It is clearly based on the reader's general knowledge of the concept of compromise.

Compromise was always trying to solve problems. It helps settle things. Compromising did not always work. I think compromising is a great strategic role. Compromising was also not fair sometime. We should all compromise more. The delegates compromised and that was a good thing.

In a similar fashion, when asked to summarize the problems that led to the fall of Rome, one middle school student wrote the following personal commentary on the topic.

The fall of Rome started off with the emperors who declined. It was all their fault. The empire should have lasted longer. Most places need nurture. The emperors could have done that. Honestly I think that the empire would have done better if certain people weren't around and the emperors could have done a better job.

"The emperors who declined" could be interpreted as a loose paraphrase of the text that referred to emperors as corrupt, but the rest of the summary statements are clearly not text based. They reflect the writer's opinion of the Roman emperors.

When asked to summarize the role of tragic drama in the lives of ancient Greeks, one student wrote the following.

> *The three plays that they told about ended up not going well. Greeks started becoming afraid and fearful. They felt this way because of the stories the plays were telling, Audiences wanted gods to help them. But the plays were saying that the gods were mean. Many also conflicted with the laws of the state. Someone ends up dying. And that scared people.*

Although this summary is related to the summary question and actually answers it to some degree, none of the summary units are explicitly stated in the text and/or the answer key.

Therefore, if a summary does not address the summary question or is not text based, go no further with your evaluation. The summary should receive a score of 0. Such summaries strongly suggest a need for instruction in close reading of the summary question and/or in understanding of what is meant by text based.

What Is the Quality of the Summary?

The number of summary units that match the answer key units determines the quality of the summary. An acceptable summary contains at least 70 percent of the answer key units. Your role is to determine the number of text-based units that match the answer key. How should you proceed?

In some cases, it will be clearly evident that a summary addresses the *CARA* question and includes a majority of answer key units. In other cases, it will not be so apparent. The summaries written in response to the *CARA* question represent a first draft. They have not been fine-tuned or rewritten. They have not received input from a teacher or peer. As such, the summaries from our pilot studies tended to be somewhat disorganized and often displayed questionable sentence structure, ambiguous phrasing, and a certain amount of disorganization. For these reasons, a summary that contains a majority of units that match the answer key is not always apparent without some analysis.

Unacceptable information can take several forms:

- Statements that are related to the topic of the summary but are not present in the answer key because they lack specificity or importance
- Repetitions of previously stated information
- Information that is not germane to the intent of the summary
- Information that is inaccurate
- Information that is not text based

An acceptable summary contains at least 70 percent of acceptable units (i.e., units that match the *CARA* answer key). Divide the number of relevant summary units by the total number of units contained in the answer key summary and multiply by 100 to arrive at a percentage.

An important issue is how to determine what represents a summary unit. As mentioned previously, answer key units are basically clausal units consisting of a noun, verb, and object. We recommend using verbs to identify and separate clausal units. For example, consider the following: "The skeletal muscles are found by the bones because they help the body have a shape." This would include two clauses, one related to the verb *found* and one related to the verb *help*. Consider another example: "Skeletal muscles are attached to the skeleton to help in movement, whereas smooth muscles are found in organs and assist with bodily functions." This sentence includes four verbs and therefore four separate units: (1) skeletal muscles are attached to the skeleton (2) to help in movement (3) whereas smooth muscles are found in organs (4) and assist with bodily functions.

Identifying the verb as a signal for a unit occasionally poses difficulties. Students frequently prefaced a statement with "I think," "what happened was," "what I'm trying to say is," or similar statements. Do not count these as separate summary units. Similarly, students often connected a unit to a previous unit by saying "if that happened," "the next thing is," or "another problem was." Do not count such transition statements as separate units.

In some cases and depending on the specific passage, students included a list of nouns with no accompanying verb. If the nouns are listed separately in the answer key, count them as separate units. For example, the fourth-grade passage on the Southwest asks what the text says about how the Grand Canyon was formed; students often stated that "glaciers and river water caused erosion." Despite a common verb (*caused*), these are listed separately in the answer key, so count each of them. Similarly, students said that "water carries sand, gravel, and boulders." Because sand, gravel, and boulders are listed separately in the answer key despite a common verb (*carry*), count them as three separate units. Occasionally students omitted a verb and attached a noun or noun phrase to a verb that was clearly inappropriate. For example, in summarizing the fall of Rome, a student stated "money became worthless and even a bad army." Was the student saying that the bad army became worthless? In situations like this, use the answer key as your guide. If a "bad army" or an acceptable synonym is listed as a separate unit in the answer key, count the student's statement as a separate clausal unit.

One issue in evaluating summaries is the presence or absence of an introductory statement. Some students provided introductory statements that were often drawn from the question stem, such as *There were a lot of reasons why Rome fell*. Some placed a similar statement at the end to form a conclusion, such as *So Rome fell for a lot of reasons*. We suggest that an introductory or concluding statement clearly related to the question be counted as an acceptable unit. However, if a student places such a statement in the beginning and again at the end of the summary, do not count it twice. This can inflate the summary score.

Another issue is that of paraphrase. Do the students have to include the exact words of the text in their summary? Some of our pilot students carefully did this. Others did not but phrased the summary components in their own words. This is acceptable. In fact, it may demonstrate a clearer understanding of text meaning than copying directly from the text. However, the paraphrase should represent an accurate conceptual match to the answer key component.

Lack of clarity on the part of the student must also be considered. Our pilot process indicated that inability to clearly express themselves in writing often compromised the effectiveness and/or accuracy of student summaries. It is important that you judge a summary based on what the student actually wrote, not on what you think he or she really meant.

A final issue is the completeness of the summary. As we stated above, 70 percent of the summary units from informational text should match the answer key units. If they do not provide such a match, this suggests that students may need to engage in close reading of the text in order to identify as many components as possible that address the intent of the question. However, there may be times when slightly less than 70 percent of the summary units match the answer key. In cases where the score is close to the cut-off, we suggest you use your discretion. If you feel the summary is acceptable, mark it as such. Guidelines for scoring an informational text summary are shown in Table 4.2.2.

The following summarizes the scoring procedure for student summaries of informational text. Record these scores on the class summary sheet.

1. Does the summary address the summary question? Is it text based? If not, score it as 0, place a check in the appropriate column on the class summary sheet, and go to the next student. If so, move to the next step.
2. How many of the summary units match the answer key units? Divide the number of student summary units by the total number of Answer Key units possible and multiply by 100. A score of 70 percent or above indicates an acceptable summary.
3. Record the score on the summary portion of the *CARA* class summary sheet shown in Chapter 4, Part 1 (Table 4.1.2). A completed example is shown in Table 4.2.3. When all scores have been recorded, place a checkmark next to those that are acceptable. This allows you to see at a glance the number of students who seem to understand the components of a text-based summary of informational text.

Table 4.2.2   Guidelines for Scoring a Summary for Informational Text

Do	Don't
	Accept a summary that does not focus on the topic
	Accept a summary that does not address the question
	Accept a summary that is not text based
Count clausal units defined by the verb	Count explanatory comments such as "I think"
Count single nouns if listed as such in the answer key	Count connecting units such as "the next thing" or "another problem was"
Count introductions/conclusions (but not both)	Count introductions or conclusions as two separate units
	Count inaccurate repetitions or unclear information
Accept paraphrases that match the answer key	
Score on what student wrote	Score on what you think the student meant
Accept 70 percent of units that match the answer key as an acceptable summary	

Table 4.2.3   Completed Example: Summary Section of Class Summary Sheet for Literature and Social Studies

Summary scoring is different between literature and social studies/science

Points vary; see individual answer keys

Possible points   7   Possible points   9

All summaries are Standard 2

Literature Summary		Social Studies/Science Summary		
Number of plot elements	% of plot elements	Number of AK units	% matches to Answer Key	Check, if at cut-off
4	57%	8	89%	✓
6	86% ✓	1	11%	
7	100% ✓	5	56%	
5	71% ✓	6	67%	
3	43%	0	0%	
2	29%	2	22%	
4	57%	7	78%	✓
5	71% ✓	5	56%	
6	86% ✓	0	0%	
0	0%	0	0%	
7	100% ✓	3	33%	
5	71% ✓	2	22%	
3	43%	6	67%	
2	29%	7	78%	✓
6	86% ✓	4	44%	

Total number of narrative elements varies with individual passages.	Assign a zero If summary is left blank, is not text related, or does not answer the question asked.

Three students in Table 4.2.3 wrote acceptable summaries of informational text, as indicated by a score of 70 percent or above. The scores of two were borderline (67 percent) and warrant further examination. However, because this is a formative instrument, you may choose to accept 67 percent. Three students wrote summaries that did not address the question or were not text based. The remaining seven students wrote summaries that contained less than 70 percent of the answer key units. This strongly suggests the need for instruction in summary writing.

Summary Examples from Informational Text

The following text offers examples from our pilot of summaries that addressed the summary question and were text based.

SUMMARY QUESTION FOR *THE FALL OF ROME* (MIDDLE SCHOOL): SUMMARIZE WHAT THE TEXT SAYS WERE THE PROBLEMS THAT LED TO THE FALL OF ROME

Student Summary 1:

Summary units are enclosed in parentheses. *(These were the problems that led to the fall of Rome.) (A bad ruler.) (Senate wasn't too good.) (Economic problems.) (Not a lot of jobs.) (The size of the empire.) (A bad army.) (They were attacked a lot.) (They lost a lot of power during the years.)*

Match to the Answer Key (Student units are in italics)
1. An introductory statement of purpose
   These were the problems that led to the fall of Rome.

2. Roman emperors were corrupt
   A bad ruler

3. The senate lost power
   Senate wasn't too good.

4. The army was made up of mercenaries
5. Who had no loyalty to Rome
   A bad army

6. The Empire grew too big
   The size of the Empire

7. Enemies attacked Rome
   They were attacked a lot.

8. Conquered territories regained independence
9. There were serious economic problems
   Economic problems

10. Such as unemployment
    Not a lot of jobs

11. And inflation

No Match to the Answer Key
They lost a lot of power during the years.

Evaluation. The student did not write in sentence units. However, the summary phrases matched the answer key units. There were eight acceptable units, including the introductory sentence, and one unacceptable one for a percentage of 73 percent. Although the summary is not perhaps written in the best style, it is acceptable and indicates some student understanding of what a text-based summary entails.

Student Summary 2:

Summary units are enclosed in parentheses. *(There were many reasons for the Fall of Rome.) (Bad economy,) (bad emperors and many more.) (The Fall of Rome did have a few good impacts on us.) (Like we have magnificent arts and sculptures.) (Some bad things were that Rome was a great place.) (Money became worthless) (even a bad army.) (What I'm trying to say is Rome fell in many different ways.)*

Match to the Answer Key (Student units are in italics)

1. An introductory statement of purpose
   There were many reasons for the Fall of Rome.

2. Roman emperors were corrupt
   Bad emperors

3. The senate lost power
4. The army was made up of mercenaries
5. Who had no loyalty to Rome
   even had a bad army

6. The Empire grew too big
7. Enemies attacked Rome
8. Conquered territories regained independence
9. There were serious economic problems
   Bad economy

10. Such as unemployment
11. And inflation

No Match to the Answer Key.

The Fall of Rome did have a few good impacts on us.

Like we have magnificent arts and sculptures.

Some bad things were that Rome was a great place

Money became worthless

Rome fell in many different ways (repetition of introductory statement)

Evaluation. There were four acceptable units, including the introductory sentence for a score of 36 percent. Instead of including additional reasons for Rome's fall, the student repeated two items and added three other items that were not in the answer key, including a somewhat contradictory statement about bad things and Rome being a great place. It is not an acceptable summary.

SUMMARY QUESTION FOR *DEBATING THE CONSTITUTION* (MIDDLE SCHOOL): SUMMARIZE WHAT THE TEXT SAYS WERE THE MAIN ISSUES DEBATED DURING THE RATIFICATION PROCESS.

Student Summary 1:

Summary units are enclosed in parentheses. *(The first main issue was the weakening of states which was an anti-Federalist concern.) (Also there was no Bill of Rights to tell people their freedoms.) (Another was making sure that a president couldn't turn into a king.) (If that would have happened there would have been no reason to leave England.) (Federalists wanted a strong government.) (A government should make laws work.) (Lastly many were concerned about laws not having punishment.) (If they didn't, there wouldn't be a purpose for having laws.)*

Match to the Answer Key (Student units are in italics)

1. An introductory statement of purpose
2. The Federalists wanted a strong central government
   Federalists wanted a strong government.

3. A strong government could enforce laws.
   A government should make laws [*work.*]

4. Hamilton said laws must be attended with penalty
   Lastly many were concerned about laws not having punishment.

5. Antifederalists said strong government could weaken states' power
   The first main issue was the weakening of states which was an Anti-Federalist concern

6. A strong central government could also wipe out individual freedom
7. Mason said that government over an extensive territory could destroy people's liberty
8. There was no provision for a Bill of Rights
   Also there was no Bill of Rights to tell people their freedoms.

9. A president could be re-elected and become king.
   Another was making sure a president couldn't turn into a king

10. The government lacked checks and balances

No Match to the Answer Key

Because if that would have happened (connective) *there would have been no reason to leave England.*

If they didn't (connective) *there wouldn't be a purpose for having laws.*

Evaluation. There were six units that matched the answer key units for a score of 60 percent, which is close to the 70 percent cut-off. The units that did not match the answer key were conceptually related to the summary question. The scorer has the option of raising this score to 70 percent. Summary evaluation often involves a degree of ambiguity, as does the correction of many constructed-response questions in the *CARA*. As mentioned in Chapter 3, the *CARA* is a formative assessment designed for the purpose of determining student needs and for providing appropriate instruction; it is not a summative measure that assigns a final grade. You will often encounter uncertainty as you evaluate student answers; it is important to have a clearly stated reason for decision.

Student Summary 2:

Summary units are enclosed in parentheses. *(The main issues debated during the ratification process were the disagreements between the Federalists and Antifederalists.) (Federalists wanted a strong central government). (Antifederalists wanted a government where the people had more rights.) (When the Constitution was being ratified by nine states,) (the Antifederalists were trying to change the states' decision.) (But it didn't work.) (The Constitution was ratified.)*

Match to the Answer Key (Student units are in italics)

1. An introductory statement of purpose
   The main issues debated during the ratification process were the disagreements between the Federalists and Antifederalists

2. The Federalists wanted a strong central government
   Federalists wanted a strong central government.

3. A strong government could enforce laws

4. Hamilton said laws must be attended with penalty
5. Antifederalists said strong government could weaken states' power
6. A strong central government could also wipe out individual freedom
7. Mason said that government over an extensive territory could destroy people's liberties
8. There was no provision for a Bill of Rights
   Antifederalists wanted a government where people had more rights.
9. A president could be re-elected and become king
10. The government lacked checks and balances

No Match to the Answer Key

When the Constitution was being ratified by nine states,

the Antifederalists were trying to change the states' decision.

But it didn't work.

The Constitution was ratified.

Evaluation. There were three units that matched the answer key units, including an acceptable introductory statement, for a score of 30 percent. The units that did not match the answer key units did not address debated issues but rather explained events that occurred after the debates. The summary is not acceptable.

SUMMARY QUESTION FOR *THE GLORY THAT WAS GREECE* (HIGH SCHOOL): SUMMARIZE WHAT THE TEXT SAYS ABOUT THE ROLE OF TRAGIC DRAMA IN THE LIVES OF THE GREEKS

Student Summary 1:

Summary units are enclosed in parentheses. *(The rise of tragic drama in the lives of the Greeks was very important for different reasons.) (First it showed ideas on popular myths and legends) (which educated and entertained the audience with real life scenarios.) (Also playwrights discussed moral and social issues) (and the relationship between humans and the gods.) (The Greeks thought that the purpose of tragedy was to stir up and relieve the emotions of pity and fear.) (The audience saw how the powerful ones like warriors can be punished) (and be subject to horrifying misfortunes.) (Also how the wraths of the gods can bring down even the most powerful people.)*

Match to the Answer Key (Student units are in italics)

1. An introductory statement of purpose
   The rise of tragic drama in the lives of the Greeks was very important for different reasons

2. Greek dramas were often based on myths and legends
   First it showed ideas on popular myths and legends

3. Playwrights used these to discuss moral or social issues
   Also playwrights discussed moral and social issues

4. They also explored the relationship between people and the gods
   and the relationship between humans and the gods.

5. Aeschylus: The gods could bring down the greatest heroes
   The audience saw (transition) *how the powerful ones like warriors can be punished and subject to horrifying misfortunes* (paraphrase)

6. Sophocles: What could happen when individual moral duty conflicts with the law

7. Euripides: People were the cause of misfortune and suffering
8. The purpose of tragedy was to stir up and relieve emotions of pity and fear
   The Greeks thought (transition) *that the purpose of tragedy was to stir up and relieve the emotions of pity and fear.*

No Match to the Answer Key

which educated and entertained the audience with real life scenarios.

Also how the wraths of the gods can bring down even the most powerful people (repetition of previous statement)

Evaluation. Six units in the student's summary, including an introductory sentence, matched the summary units in the answer key; one was a paraphrase. The student's score was 75 percent. Two units did not match the answer key, but both were conceptually related to the topic and one was a repetition of what had previously been stated.

Student Summary 2:

Summary units are enclosed in parentheses. *(The text showed that tragic drama was very important to the Greeks.) (Tragedies were clearly important) (because many people attended.) (Also tragic drama showed opinions about important things.) (Also the play the Trojan Women showed that tragic drama showed an often untold side to a story.) (Tragedies showed how hard life could be for even important people.) (This showed people who were poor that they were not alone in their suffering.) (The tragedies made people afraid)*

Match to the Answer Key (Student units are in italics)

1. An introductory statement of purpose
   The text showed that tragic drama was very important to the Greeks

2. Greek dramas were often based on myths and legends
3. Playwrights used these to discuss moral or social issues
   Also tragic drama showed opinions about important things (loose paraphrase)

4. They also explored the relationship between people and the gods
5. Aeschylus: The gods could bring down the greatest heroes
   Tragedies showed (transition) *how hard life could be for even important people* (loose paraphrase)

6. Sophocles: What could happen when individual moral duty conflicts with the law
7. Euripides: People were the cause of misfortune and suffering
8. The purpose of tragedy was to stir up and relieve emotions of pity and fear

No Match to the Answer Key

Tragedies were important because many people attended.

Also the play the Trojan Women showed (transition) *that tragic drama showed an often untold side to a story.*

This showed (transition) *people who were poor that they were not alone in their suffering.*

The tragedies made people afraid.

Evaluation. Three units in the student's summary matched the summary units in the answer key. One was an introductory statement and two represented very general paraphrases, for a score of 38 percent. Four units did not match the answer key. There are more irrelevant than relevant units in the summary, although it addressed the question and was somewhat text based. However, it suggests that the student does not understand that a summary comprises the most significant or relevant information related to the topic of the summary.

SUMMARY QUESTION FOR *THE MUSCULAR SYSTEM* (MIDDLE SCHOOL): SUMMARIZE WHAT THE TEXT SAYS ABOUT HOW SKELETAL MUSCLE AND SMOOTH MUSCLE ARE DIFFERENT.

Student Summary 1:

Summary units are enclosed in parentheses. *(Skeletal muscle and smooth muscle are different in many ways.) (Our skeletal muscle is voluntary) (and smooth isn't.) (Smooth are found in the stomach and intestines in the body.) (Skeletal muscle is found on our bones.) (Skeletal muscles have tendons.) (Smooth muscle is also found in blood vessels.) (Smooth muscle is not striated) (unlike skeletal which is.) (Skeletal muscle gets tired fast.)*

Match to the Answer Key (Student units are in italics)

1. An introductory statement of purpose
   Skeletal muscle and smooth muscle are different in many ways.

2. Skeletal muscles are attached to bones
   Skeletal muscle is found on our bones.

3. Smooth muscles are inside internal organs
   Smooth are found in the stomach and intestines in the body.

4. Skeletal muscle is voluntary
   Our skeletal muscle is voluntary

5. Smooth muscle is involuntary
   And smooth isn't

6. Skeletal muscle is striated
   Unlike skeletal which is

7. Smooth muscle is not striated
   Smooth muscle is not striated

8. Skeletal muscle tires easily
   Skeletal muscle gets tired fast

9. Smooth muscle does not tire easily
10. Skeletal muscle reacts slowly
11. Smooth muscle reacts quickly

No Match to the Answer Key
   Skeletal muscles have tendons

   Smooth muscle is also found in blood vessels.

Evaluation. There were eight acceptable units, including an introductory statement, and two unacceptable ones, for a percentage of 72 percent.

Student Summary 2:

Summary units are enclosed in parentheses. *(One of the differences are smooth muscle are around the bones.) (Skeletal muscles are in organs.) (Smooth muscles are not striated) (but skeletal are.) (Skeletal muscles have tendons) (but smooth muscles don't.) (Smooth react fast.) (Skeletal get tired real soon.)*

Match to the Answer Key (Student units are in italics)

1. An introductory statement of purpose
2. Skeletal muscle are attached to bones
3. Smooth muscles are inside internal organs

4. Skeletal muscle is voluntary
5. Smooth muscle is involuntary
6. Skeletal muscle is striated
   but skeletal are.

7. Smooth muscle is not striated.
   Smooth muscles are not striated

8. Skeletal muscle tires easily
   Skeletal get tired real soon.

9. Smooth muscle does not tire easily
10. Skeletal muscle reacts slowly
    Smooth react fast
10. Smooth muscle reacts quickly

No Match to the Answer Key

One of the differences are smooth muscle are around the bones (erroneous statement)

Skeletal muscles are in organs (erroneous statement)

Skeletal muscles have tendons

but smooth muscles don't

Evaluation. There were four acceptable units and four unacceptable ones. It receives a score of 36 percent.

Evaluating Standard 8 for Middle School and High School Social Studies

You have the option to administer the Standard 8 passage as you see fit. Standard 8 focuses on identifying and evaluating arguments and claims in the text and assessing the validity of the reasoning. The first part of the Standard 8 question addresses identification of the text arguments. The student is asked to select two (middle school) or four (high school) arguments or reasons that indicate or support an author's point of view. The student's choice of arguments must match the arguments provided in the text and listed in the answer key. Some students answered the question by actually quoting the author's argument, underlining the argument in the text, and/or successfully paraphrasing the author's words. Paraphrasing was often an issue; students were not often successful in translating the words of the author into their own words. Our pilot data also indicated that students often did not draw their answers from the selection but simply invented an answer that had little connection to the passage. Some chose a passage segment that was inaccurate or inappropriate.

Standard 8 for informational text asks the reader to move beyond comprehending information to "evaluate the validity of the reasoning as the relevance and sufficiency of the evidence" (CCSSO & NGA, 2010, p. 10). Therefore, the second part of the Standard 8 question asks the students to select one (middle school) or two (high school) of the arguments they drew from the text and explain why the argument is or it is not valid. The issue is not whether students agree or disagree with the author's ideas; the issue is whether the author presents a valid argument. The answer key offers several examples of acceptable answers, but it would be impossible to cover all possibilities.

The first question that you should keep in mind when evaluating a student's reasoning is "Does it make sense?" Can you understand what the student is saying? Many pilot students wrote disorganized and rambling answers that seemed unconnected to the specific argument they were addressing.

The purpose of the standard is that, having identified an author's argument, the student can provide an acceptable reason for its validity or invalidity. Judging the validity of

Table 4.2.4   Completed Example: Summary Sheet for Social Studies Standard 8

Social Studies	Standard 8
Number of Arguments	Number of Valid Arguments
0	0
0	0
0	0
2	0
0	0
1	0
1	0
1	0
2	1
0	0
0	0
1	0
0	0
2	0
1	0

someone else's reasoning involves more than just stating an opinion. *Funk & Wagnalls New International Dictionary of the English Language* (1997) defines validity as "soundness in reasoning" (p. 138). Something that is valid is logical and can be supported. Conversely, something that is invalid lacks adequate verification. Many of our pilot students offered their opinion of why a specific argument was or was not valid without any explanation or evidence for their reasoning or any reference to a supportive source. We suggest that a judgment of validity requires an explanation and/or support from an external source.

You may not agree with the student's opinion; however, if it makes some sense from the student's point of view and contains an explanation, supporting evidence, or reference to an external source, accept it. We acknowledge that two teachers judging the same answer may have differences of opinion. As we mentioned earlier, correcting constructed response questions is somewhat of an inexact science. However, you will have an advantage that we did not have while correcting the answers of our pilot students: you can talk to a student and get additional clarification as to what he or she meant. We suspect that it will not take very long to ascertain if the student actually understood the argument and had any specific and relevant reason for describing it as valid or invalid.

Table 4.2.4 illustrates a filled out student summary sheet that has space for recording the number of arguments that were correctly identified and the number of those that were acceptable with regard to explanation of validity.

Three students correctly identified two arguments of Benjamin Franklin for signing the Constitution; five identified one argument. Only one student offered an acceptable reason for accepting the validity of Franklin's argument. This pattern was evident across middle school and high school pilot students and suggests that identifying and evaluating an argument is a somewhat foreign concept for students.

Summary Examples from Middle School World History

The *CARA* question for Standard 8 asked students to read the excerpt from Suetonius on the death of Julius Caesar, then explain two of Suetonius' reasons or arguments that indicate he thought Caesar was a great man and select one reason or argument and explain why it is valid or not valid. The following are examples of acceptable and unacceptable answers. Students' words are in italics.

Acceptable Answers

- "In fact the very night before his murder he dreamt now that he was flying above the clouds." *He dreamt he would die. It's not valid because people all have crazy dreams and they don't mean anything. They don't really come true.* (Acceptable because the student provided supporting evidence about dreams)
- When the funeral was announced . . . it was clear that the day would not be long enough for those who offered gifts." *I don't see what bringing gifts has to do with being great. People give gifts to people who are not great. I get gifts. I don't think you could call me great. It's not valid.* (Acceptable because the student provided supporting evidence about gift giving)

Unacceptable Answers

- "A little bird called the king-bird flew into the Curia [Senate chamber] . . . with a sprig of laurel, pursued by others of various kinds from the grove hard by, which tore it to pieces in the hall." *The birds meant he would die. I agree it's valid because some birds are very smart. Maybe it was a pet bird. A pet bird would know.* (Not acceptable because the reasoning about pet birds is inaccurate)
- "In fact the very night before his murder he dreamt now that he was flying above the clouds." *This is valid because it would be nice to fly like that.* (Not acceptable because the reason is not related to the argument; it is a personal opinion with no evidence to support flying as related to greatness)

Summary Examples from Middle School American History

The *CARA* question for Standard 8 asked students to read the excerpt from James Madison's letter to Thomas Jefferson, then explain two reasons or arguments that Madison presents for having or for not having a Bill of Rights and select one reason or argument and explain why it is valid or not valid. The following are examples of acceptable and unacceptable answers. Students' words are in italics.

Acceptable Answers

- "Perhaps too there may be a certain degree of danger, that a succession of artful and ambitious rulers may . . . finally erect an independent Government on the subversion of liberty. Should this danger exist at all, it is prudent to guard against . . ." *I agree it's valid because government isn't always right and bad people can get elected. So you should be very careful and cover all your bases.* (Acceptable because the student provided supporting evidence about governments)
- "Experience proves the inefficiency of a bill of rights on those occasions when its control is most needed." *I don't think it is valid. How does he know it was proved? I think it is almost impossible to prove anything. People always say "prove" but not how they are going to do that.* (Acceptable because the student provided an explanation about inappropriate usage of the word "prove")

Unacceptable Answer

- "Experience proves the inefficiency of a bill of rights on those occasions when its control is most needed." *It's valid because control is a good thing.* (Not acceptable; control as "a good thing" is a general statement and not specifically connected to the failure of the Bill of Rights)
- "Perhaps too there may be a certain degree of danger, that a succession of artful and ambitious rulers may . . . finally erect an independent Government on the subversion

of liberty. Should this danger exist at all, it is prudent to guard against . . ." *Well it's not valid because being an artist has nothing to do with running a government.* (Not acceptable; the reason is based on a misinterpretation of "artful")

Summary Examples from Middle and High School Social Studies

The *CARA* question for Standard 8 asked students to read the excerpt from Socrates' defense against the charges of corrupting the youth of Athens, explain four arguments that Socrates presents in support of his innocence, then select two arguments and, for each one, explain why it is erroneous or valid. The following are examples of acceptable and unacceptable answers. Students' words are in italics.

Acceptable Answer

- "And this is a duty which God has imposed upon me, as I am assured by oracles, visions, and in every sort of way in which the will of divine power was ever signified to anyone." *It's not valid to say an oracle told him what to do. Not all oracles are good; some could use their gifts for bad reasons. There is no proof they're right even though some people think so. And he could make up a story about visions.* (Acceptable; the student provided supportive evidence for not accepting oracles and visions)
- ". . . if anyone likes to come and hear me while I am pursuing my mission, whether he be young or old, he may freely come . . . anyone, whether he be rich or poor, may ask and answer me and listen to my word. . . . And if anyone says that he has ever learned or heard anything from me in private which all the world has not heard, I should like you to know that he is speaking an untruth." *This could be valid because philosophers like to share their opinions with others and love to spread knowledge. I don't think he would have kept things behind closed doors.* (Acceptable; the student provided supportive evidence regarding philosophers)

Unacceptable Answer

- "I would have you know that, if you kill such a one as I am, you will injure yourselves more than you will injure me." *This is valid because if you injure Socrates it's bad because you get a powerful person against you. Who would win? Socrates obviously.* (Not acceptable; evidence is unclear and suggests lack of understanding of what eventually happened to Socrates)
- "Someone will say: Yes, Socrates, but cannot you hold your tongue . . . . For if I tell you that this would be a disobedience to a divine command." *It's not valid because we should always obey God. He was wrong to disobey God.* (Not acceptable; the student misinterpreted the argument)

Summary

This chapter provides guidelines for scoring summaries of literature and informational text and for scoring students' responses to Standard 8. These elements of the *CARA* require close attention to how students express themselves in writing. The measurement of Standard 8 in informational text aligns with the College and Career Standards for Writing, under the first heading, *Text Type and Purposes: Write arguments to support a substantive claim with clear reasons and relevant and sufficient evidence* (CCSSO & NGA, 2010, p. 17).

General Suggestions for Classroom Instruction Focused on CCSS

We have divided this chapter into two parts. The first part provides general instructional recommendations on practices that focus on the CCSS and apply to all standards. The second part provides standards-specific strategies for helping students meet the requirements set forth in the CCSS.

A Focus on Comprehension

Comprehension Defined

The standards are fundamentally embedded in a reader's ability to comprehend the text. Although comprehension has been described as embodying a multitude of different mental operations, Paris and Hamilton (2009) state that the fundamental components of comprehension are drawing inferences and monitoring comprehension. After describing research that focused on identifying key aspects of the comprehension process, they concluded that "inference-making and comprehension monitoring were the only two independent variables to contribute unique variance to comprehension after removing the effects of decoding skill, verbal ability and working memory" (p. 39). The strong inferential nature of the standards aligns with this.

As we described in Chapter 2, Davis (1968, 1972) hypothesized that reading comprehension consisted of two major components: word knowledge and reasoning about reading. Factor analysis identified eight factors that comprised comprehension, seven of which can be specifically aligned to one of the nine standards.

What Must Teachers Know?

What must teachers understand about the standards in order to prepare their students to meet them? The standards are quite clear that they "define what all students are expected to know and be able to do, not how teachers should teach. . . . A great deal is left to the discretion of teachers" (CCSSO & NGA, 2010, p. 6). However, before teachers can begin to design instructional activities, they need to understand how the standards differ from previous curricular guidelines. These were explained in Chapter 2, but they bear repeating because the differences will have a serious impact on instruction. Teachers must know that:

1. The standards are text based
2. The standards focus on literacy in three distinct disciplines
3. The standards emphasize critical thinking
4. Students are expected to achieve grade-level proficiency.

Text Analysis, Not Text Response

A major difference from previous guidelines is that the Common Core Standards are text based; that is, they demand comprehension of what is explicitly stated in the text and what can be inferred based on information in the text. To put it another way, "the Common Core expects students to cite textual evidence as they explain what the text teaches" (Calkins, Ehrenworth, & Lehman, 2012, p. 41). This explicit comprehension forms the basis for meeting the standards; students draw inferences based on the content of the text, not on their previous knowledge of the topic or their personal opinions regarding it. To put it succinctly, they are expected to analyze the text, not personally respond to it (Calkins et al., 2012).

The standards demand that readers comprehend explicit content and use it to draw text-based inferences. As defined by the key verb in each standard, drawing inferences involves the following:

- Determine explicit text content (Standard 1)
- Explain central ideas and summarize (Standard 2)
- Analyze how and why (Standard 3)
- Interpret word meaning from context (Standard 4)
- Analyze text structure (Standard 5)
- Assess author point of view (Standard 6)
- Integrate material from diverse media (Standard 7)
- Evaluate arguments and claims in a text (Standard 8)
- Analyze two or more texts (Standard 9)

Curriculum materials "should include rigorous text-dependent questions that require students to demonstrate that they not only can follow the details of what is explicitly stated but also are able to make valid claims that square with all the evidence in the text" (Coleman & Pimental, 2011). Such questions can be answered only by close reading of the text and by supporting answers with evidence from the text.

This position stands in sharp opposition to the idea that specific prior content knowledge is necessary for text comprehension. Teachers often engage in extensive prereading activities to increase their students' knowledge of a topic before they begin reading. In fact, they often provide the text information verbally, which seems to negate the necessity for even reading the text. The standards are quite definite in this regard. "Teachers should never preempt or replace the text by translating its contents for students or telling students what they are going to learn in advance of the text" (Coleman & Pimentel, 2011, p. 8).

Are the standards asking too much? We think not. We believe that good readers have always engaged in the behaviors demanded by the standards. In a landmark book, Pressley and Afflerbach (1995) documented strategies used by proficient readers as they struggled to make sense of what they read. Using think-aloud and self-report data from a variety of studies, they organized reader comments into various categories. Reader behaviors listed under the categories of inference making, integrating, and interpreting are closely aligned to the standards.

Reader Behaviors Aligned to the Standards

Going beyond the information explicitly stated in the text (Standard #1)
Generating main ideas and summarizing the text (Standard #2)
Constructing explanations, examples and elaborations (Standard #3)
Inferring word meaning based on context (Standard #4)
Noting the macrostructure of the text (Standard #5)
Drawing inferences about author purpose and intention (Standards #6 and #8)
Looking for information elsewhere in the text (Standard #8).

(Pressley & Afflerbach, 1995)

Research described in Chapter 2 and in this chapter indicates that the behaviors of readers as they comprehend text are closely aligned to the standards (Davis, 1968, 1972; Kintsch, 2004; Paris & Hamilton, 2009; Pressley & Afflerbach, 1995). Instead of viewing the standards as something new and different, educators must realize that the behaviors employed by students in order to meet the demands of the Common Core Standards are the behaviors of all good readers who use the text base to draw inferences and comprehend what they read.

Instruction in Comprehension Strategies: What Kind?

Some readers develop these behaviors on their own, perhaps as a result of wide reading, trial and error, and high motivation to comprehend the text. Many readers do not. A variety of research studies have established that the strategies employed by proficient readers can be taught by explaining the nature and purpose of the strategy, modeling its use, and providing opportunities for guided practice (Wharton-McDonald & Swiger, 2009). Block and Pressley (2007) describe such strategies in terms of questions that readers should ask themselves about understanding words, interpreting sentences and paragraphs, comprehending the text, and using the knowledge gained through reading. Dole, Nokes, and Drits (2009) summarized studies of strategy instruction that have led to improved student performance. Many of the strategies are closely aligned to the standards, such as generating questions (all standards), summarizing the text (Standard 2), identifying and using text structure (Standard 5), and clarifying areas of confusion (all standards).

Despite evidence that teaching strategies can improve comprehension, some concerns have been raised. The deliberate and conscious attention to specific strategies that is part of such instruction is far different from the moment-by-moment activities of the readers studied by Pressley and Afflerbach (1995). Pressley and Afflerbach described the readers as "constructively responsive—that is, good readers are always changing their processing in response to the text they are reading; the result is complex processing" (p. 2). Though teaching strategies may promote active engagement and dialogue about text content, Sinatra, Brown, and Reynolds (2002) questioned whether allocating attention to specific strategies might actually weaken understanding of the text by diverting a student's cognitive resources away from text comprehension. There is also a danger that learning and applying specific strategies can become the primary focus of instruction, as opposed to learning content (Wilkinson & Son, 2011).

The standards suggest that the opposite should occur: "Rather than focusing on general strategies and questions disconnected from texts, strategies should be cultivated in the content of reading specific texts" (Coleman & Pimentel, 2011). Research evidence to support this position comes from McKeown, Beck, and Blake (2009), who compared strategies instruction to a focus on text content. Over a two-year period some students were exposed to content through open-ended and meaning-based questions; other students were taught specific comprehension strategies. The content students outperformed their peers in recall, quality of lesson discourse, comprehension monitoring, and strategy application. The authors concluded by saying that strategies should be taught, but they should not "lead the process of building understanding of a text" (p. 246). In other words, the focus should be on learning from text, with the strategies used as a means to the goal, not the goal itself.

If strategies instruction is to support students in meeting the standards, such instruction will have to be embedded into text content—that is, learning and practicing strategies will have to take a back seat to comprehending and learning what the text says. Strategies "provide the tools to help students make sense of the content and the content gives meaning and purpose to the strategies" (Wilkinson & Son, 2011, p. 397). This is not an either/or situation. Comprehension strategies can and should be taught in tandem, but with a focus on text content. At its most basic level, this involves using classroom texts as the basis for strategy instruction, as opposed to materials that are not specifically connected to curricular content. Teaching strategies can foster content knowledge by promoting active text engagement, fostering the construction of meaning, and providing a vehicle for engaging in dialogue (Wilkinson & Son, 2011).

There is an important distinction between reading comprehension strategies and instructional strategies (Jetton & Lee, 2012). Comprehension strategies "involve conscious, deliberate plans that readers use flexibly to understand text" (p. 4). These include summarization, generating questions, monitoring comprehension, and taking notes. On the other hand, instructional strategies are used by teachers to teach comprehension strategies. Instructional strategies include various forms of grouping, prereading activities, study guides, and teacher modeling. In the chapter that follows, we include both forms of strategies.

In summary, what conclusions can we draw regarding the role of strategy instruction? It is important, but only as a tool to comprehend text. This suggests that strategies should be taught using content textbooks, as opposed to selections on topics unrelated to the classroom curriculum. We cannot assume that a strategy taught using social studies content will transfer to literature or science material. We also cannot assume that instruction using material at a lower reading level will transfer to grade-level text. An intervention specialist may use such selections for initial instruction, but should then move into grade-appropriate classroom material (Caldwell & Leslie, 2013).

Grade-Appropriate Text

Instructional Level Versus Grade Level

We have identified a critical way in which the standards are different from former reading standards and curricular guidelines: They define comprehension as the ability to draw text-based inferences and they require that students analyze the text, not personally respond to it. However, the standards also require that readers do this in grade-appropriate text. For example, Standard 10 requires that grade 6 students "by the end of the year read and comprehend . . . in the grades 6–8 complexity band proficiently with scaffolding as needed at the high end of the range" (p. 37). Eighth graders are expected to do this "independently and proficiently." This is an important and troubling issue for teachers who match students to their instructional level whenever possible. It raises a valid question. How can students draw text-based inferences if they cannot read the text with some degree of comfort and skill?

Using instructional-level text to teach students how to perform the high-level inference skills required by the standards is not sufficient to enable students to do the same skills in grade-level text. Consider the concept of transfer, or "the ability to use what was learned in new situations" (Mayer & Wittrock, 2006, p. 289). Can readers transfer their knowledge of how to determine central ideas or themes (Standard 2), for example, from instructional-level to grade-level text? Probably not. A basic principle of transfer is that "transfer between tasks is a function of the degree to which the tasks share cognitive elements" (Bransford, Brown, & Cocking, 2000, p. 65). Familiarity with narratives, for example, will not transfer to comprehension of informational text because there is little similarity between their underlying structures. The ability to determine central ideas or summarize social studies text may not transfer to science material given the difference in text concepts, text structure, and author purpose. Similarly, a focus on the concepts and linguistic structure of instructional-level text may not provide sufficient knowledge to transfer to competence in higher-level text. It has been suggested that a total focus on instructional-level text "may bar access to concepts and ideas otherwise acquired by reading grade-level texts" and "lack of exposure to grade-level concepts, vocabulary and syntax may prevent children from acquiring information that contributes to their development of language, comprehension and writing" (McCormack, Paratore, & Dahlene, 2004, p. 119).

An examination of different grade-level texts on the same topic indicates that although identical topics may be presented at each level, the presentation quickly increases in complexity. For example, lower-level life science text describes the *jobs* performed by cells; higher-level text describes their *functions*. The number of *functions* also increases as text level rises. The number of new concepts introduced in a chapter or section increases as well. Vocabulary becomes more discipline specific and explanations become more detailed. Accompanying visuals move from colorful pictures with minimal text to complicated diagrams with detailed explanations.

An Instructional Shift

The International Reading Association Common Core State Standards Committee (2012) states that use of challenging text "represents a major shift in instructional approach" (p. 1). They caution that effective use of such text will require greater and more skillful scaffolding on the part of the teacher. Such scaffolding includes extensive use of rereading, explanation, encouragement, and other instructional supports. Shanahan (2011) agrees and emphasizes the need for teachers to identify what makes a book difficult and provide the motivation and scaffolding that students need to make sense of it. Robertson, Doughtery, Ford-Conners, & Paratore (2014) describe three key elements of effective scaffolded instruction: motivation and engagement, instructional intensity, and cognitive challenge.

Perhaps a solution would be a flexible approach to text levels (Glasswell & Ford, 2010). Instructional-level text may be best employed in initial instruction and certainly in intervention settings with struggling readers. However, instead of avoiding grade-level text and attempting to match text to student instructional levels, the teacher should offer instructional support for grade-level material through such practices as reading aloud, modeling strategies for analyzing text, and supporting students in their efforts to engage in text analysis as required by the standards. "Teaching with harder books is the way to go with the vast majority of kids," but only if "teachers know how to teach with such materials" and how to "provide the scaffolding and motivation that would sustain students' efforts" (Shanahan, 2011, p. 21).

Earlier we explained that transfer between tasks depends on the similarity between them (Bransford, Brown, & Cocking, 2000). Reading skills learned and practiced in literature passages will not effectively transfer to science material; the purpose, structure, and underlying concepts are too different. Instruction in interpreting the purpose and style of poetry will probably not improve comprehension of short stories or persuasive essays. Instruction in a science passage on the respiratory system will not effectively transfer to a social studies passage on the Bill of Rights. At an even more detailed level, a passage on life science may not effectively transfer to one on earth science, given the conceptual differences between the two fields of study. Similarly, using instructional-level text as a basis for instruction may not transfer to grade-level material unless there is some similarity between the structure and content of the text. Of course, the ideal situation would be to provide instruction at a student's instructional level and, using this as a basis, move to a grade-level selection on the same topic. For example, you might use a fifth-grade passage on the Constitutional Convention as a basis for reading a middle school passage on the same topic. However, this poses some difficult issues.

First, who would provide such instruction? Classroom teachers generally have one literature, social studies, or science text purchased by the district as a suitable fit for their specific grade levels. Students who find this text too difficult to read independently will probably represent different instructional levels. Assuming that the teacher or some other individual actually identifies these different instructional levels, the classroom teacher probably will not have appropriate texts to match the level of each student who struggles with grade-level text. Even if appropriate texts were available, providing initial instruction in instructional-level text before moving to an emphasis on grade-level material would involve serious issues regarding time and classroom organization.

This suggests that someone else—the intervention specialist, for example—should provide instruction in instructional-level text. There are two ways of doing this. After focusing on instructional-level text dealing with the same topic that will be covered in the classroom, the students then participate in their regular classroom activities using grade-level text. This would require extensive collaboration between the intervention specialist and the classroom teacher about the content that is taught and the chosen instructional emphasis. Ideally, the same standards and content emphases should take place in both formats if transfer is to occur to the highest extent possible.

Another possible paradigm would be for the intervention specialist to focus on both instructional-level and grade-level text. Initial instruction in determining central idea, for example, could occur in instructional-level text. Then, using read-alouds (described next), the intervention specialist could support students in finding the central idea in grade-level text on the same topic. This would not substitute for students' participation in grade-level activities; it would act as an additional support. Using instructional-level text as a bridge to grade-level text makes a lot of instructional sense, but it requires active collaboration between the classroom teacher and the intervention specialist.

Although the prevailing practice has been to provide text at an instructional level and to avoid text that seems to be difficult, some research suggests that grappling with difficult text can lead to more learning. Although research with young readers shows that coherent text is more easily understood than incoherent text (McKeown, Beck, Sinatra, & Loxterman, 1992), there are some conditions in which incoherent texts have been found to result in greater learning (McNamara, Kintsch, Songer, & Kintsch, 1996). Coherent text included definitions, explanations, elaborations, meaningful connectives between sentences, uniform references to key concepts, and the addition of titles and subtitles. High-knowledge readers performed better on the open-ended questions after reading the low-coherence text. These results were interpreted to mean that making things too easy could be an impediment to learning (McNamara, Kintsch, Songer, & Kintsch, 1996). Perhaps students who have a lot of relevant knowledge about a topic need to be challenged to engage in deep processing and difficult text can stimulate such processing if appropriately supported. "Learners learning a new skill must have the opportunity to face difficulties and learn to repair mistakes" (p. 1314). Of course, in order to avoid frustration, students need guidance and support as they grapple with difficult text.

The remainder of this chapter focuses on discussion and description of instructional activities for meeting the standards. It is organized in the following way. First, we provide a section on using grade-level text to foster student ability in meeting the standards. Then, we discuss general strategies that cross all standards and all text.

Scaffolding Grade-Level Text: Read-Alouds

The Joys of Reading Aloud

It is unfortunate that we read aloud to younger students in order to expose them to text that they cannot read on their own but neglect reading aloud to older students under the assumption that they are able to read the text independently and might be bored or even insulted by being read to. We should question these assumptions. First, many older students with instructional reading levels below their chronological grade levels cannot independently and successfully read their classroom texts. Second, many readers functioning at grade level would not be adverse to being read to, especially if it helped them better comprehend the text. Consider the popularity of audiobooks purchased primarily by adults for their own use and often downloaded to an iPod or similar device. The adults are obviously able to read the chosen selection on their own but choose to listen to books by favorite authors or about topics of interest as they drive, exercise, mow lawns, or relax comfortably. A quick perusal of audiobooks offered for sale reveals a wide range of topics and genres. They are not always fiction; often they are informational text on highly complex topics. Given that adults obviously value being read to, why should we hesitate to read aloud to older students? Why should we frown on reading aloud difficult sections of textbooks as a catalyst for discussion of content and for modeling strategies for understanding text?

One of the authors of this text often engaged in selected read-alouds with graduate students. These generally involved complex research reports on subjects relatively unfamiliar to the students. Students came to class having read the assigned articles or chapters but clearly dubious about their understanding of the content. She asked them to identify particularly problematic passages. She read these aloud and asked the students to read orally with her. This ensured that everyone was at the same place in the text when she stopped to ask questions, discuss concepts, and help them comprehend unfamiliar and difficult material. The students were not insulted, nor were they bored. In fact, as the semester progressed, they often came to class with certain sections and paragraphs marked for engaging in a read-aloud punctuated by an interactive discussion of the contents.

Some teachers may say that they do not have time for reading the text to students, given their need to teach specific content. However, the time spent reading aloud, modeling strategies, and discussing the text is probably no different than the time spent telling the students what is in the text and what they should have understood or the time spent preparing them to read the text by engaging in lengthy prereading explanations of text content.

Keys to Successful Read-Alouds

Several guidelines for effective read-alouds using informational text are offered by Stead (2014), and we will focus on two. The first is the selection of what you are going to read. The selection must contain some interesting information or the students will stop listening and the teacher must read with expression, showing his or her love of informational text. Because the purpose of this read-aloud is to address the CCSS, the second is the choice of standards that you will emphasize during the read-aloud. Let's examine each in turn.

Choice of the read-aloud selection seldom involves an entire chapter of information text. It may include what you feel are the most important parts of the chapter or it may be a chapter section that you know will pose difficulties for the students. It should be relatively short in order to hold students' attention. It is better to use two or three short selections than lose the students' attention during a longer read-aloud. Another way to maintain attention is to have the students read along with you. Consider the middle school *CARA* passage on fossils. You might choose to use the section on how a fossil forms, which represents three relatively short paragraphs. Discussion could focus on text structure (Standard 5) and word meaning (Standard 4). Or, you may ascertain that students understand what a fossil is and move directly to different types of fossils. This could involve four short read-aloud discussions based on text headings and a focus on Standards 1 and 3.

The key focus during the read-aloud is the standard or standards you are going to emphasize. In order to meet the standards, students must learn to analyze and draw high-level inferences from the body of the text. Your role is to maintain an emphasis on text analysis based on the standards. "Discussion of specific reading techniques should occur when and if they illuminate specific aspects of a text. They should be embedded in the activity of reading the text rather than being taught as a separate body of material" (Coleman & Pimentel, 2011, p. 8). As we discussed previously, if you intend to introduce and/or practice a specific strategy during the read-aloud session, your focus should be on what the students learn as a result of applying the strategy, not the strategy itself.

Classroom talk, including talk during read-alouds, should "turn students' attention to process" (Johnston, Ivey, & Faulker, 2011, p. 235). In other words, reading aloud should not involve the teacher asking literal questions and then providing the answers. Reading aloud is the venue for helping students recognize and utilize underlying processes for comprehending the text and using the text to draw inferences based on the CCSS.

The standards indicate what proficient readers should do. Based on the text, they should draw inferences, determine main ideas or themes, explain and analyze text, determine the meaning of unknown words through context, recognize text structure, and understand author point of view. These cognitive processes should guide the development of the read-aloud activities.

We suggest that you use the *CARA* question stems as your guide for the questions you ask and the strategies you model. Some strategies are quite standard specific. For example, using word and sentence context to determine word meaning refers only to Standard 4. Using *CARA* question stems actually makes planning a read-aloud more manageable. For example, if you focus on text structure (Standard 5), select two or more structures as described in the *CARA* stem. Point out signal words that are actually present in the text. Demonstrate how the author's purpose and/or central idea often indicate a specific structure. If you intend to use a graphic organizer or idea map to illustrate text structure visually, focus primarily on what the students learn through the process of constructing the organizer, not on the organizer itself. We suggest that you initially concentrate on one or two standards and then gradually address the entire range.

If the text is difficult to understand and if the topics are complex and unfamiliar, collaboration between readers can facilitate comprehension (Buehl, 2011). Collaboration is a give-and-take proposition. One individual does not provide all the input. A teacher who fosters collaboration during a read-aloud is a collaborator only when students are brought into the process. The collaborative teacher asks students to identify areas of confusion and helps them clarify the text by pointing out textual clues that guide them to figure out the answer, not by giving them the answer. Collaboration means that:

- Students ask as many or more questions than the teacher
- Students talk as much as the teacher
- Instead of giving the answer, the teacher helps students find the answer on their own and/or collaborate with each other in doing so

Teachers often ask for a read-aloud script to follow and we can understand why. Reading aloud and fostering interaction with students is not an easy task to plan or execute, although it does get easier with time. Unfortunately, there is no script that can be used with all text. A read-aloud varies depending on whether the text is narrative or informational. It varies according to the discipline, genre, and specific concepts involved. However, building a read-aloud around the standards and *CARA* question stems provides a measure of uniformity.

Expect to feel awkward at first. Awkwardness is always part of engaging in a new activity. It will pass. Don't look at a read-aloud as taking time way from instruction in the content of the text. You are helping students learn how to read text at a deeper level. You are showing them how to negotiate difficult parts. And as they do this, they will also learn the content.

Admit that you found certain parts difficult and explain how you attempted to resolve this. This lets students know that encountering problems during reading is a normal situation even for adults and "changes the power dynamic" by not placing yourself above the students (Johnston, Ivey, & Faulkner, 2011, p. 232).

What about those below-level struggling readers who cannot read grade-level text independently? Although the primary purpose of a collaborative read-aloud is to help students meet the standards, read-alouds serve a second extremely important function: they expose below-level readers to the vocabulary, language, structure, and concepts of grade-level material and provide direct and focused instruction in how to read such text. "By reading several challenging texts, students should build an infrastructure that enables them to approach new challenging texts with confidence and stamina" (Coleman & Pimentel, 2011, p. 8).

Guidelines for Successful Read-Alouds

Selection of passage
  Short
  Teacher and students read together
Selection of Standard focus
  Choice is dependent on text content
  Focus on process: what good readers do
  Use of *CARA* question stems
Focus on collaboration between students and teacher

General Strategies That Cross All Standards

Close Reading

A Definition of Close Reading.   "Among the highest priorities of the Common Core State Standards is that students be able to read closely and gain knowledge from texts" (Coleman & Pimental, 2011, p. 6). As we stated earlier, meeting the standards requires comprehension of what is explicitly stated in the text; students draw inferences based on text content, not on previous knowledge or opinions. Students must "understand what the author says and be able to defend their opinions and ideas with evidence from the text" (Fisher, Frey, & Lapp, 2012, p. 108).

"Close reading is an instructional routine in which students critically examine a text, especially through repeated readings" (Fisher & Frey, 2012, p. 179). Close reading is not fluent; it is a slow process of deliberate and analytic reading and rereading. Close reading is the type of reading you engage in when following instructions for filling out an income tax return. It is the type of reading you engaged in when taking the SAT, ACT, or GRE, knowing that your acceptance into a specific program or institution depended heavily on your score. Close reading is the type you do before using a chainsaw or some other form of dangerous equipment. You read closely the pharmacist's information on possible side effects and harmful reactions before taking a new type of medicine. You read closely when assembling a new and expensive piece of electronic equipment. You do not skim. You read slowly, often word for word. You reread, often perusing the same text multiple times. You stop and tell yourself what you understand and what you still find confusing. You move slowly and deliberately through the text and do not proceed until you have clearly understood what came before.

The primary purpose of close reading is to integrate new information with existing knowledge. However, a second purpose is "to build the necessary habits of readers when they engage with a complex piece of text" (Fisher & Frey, 2012, p. 179). Helping students move into close reading is not a quick fix. It involves engaging in rereading not once, but multiple times, as well as paying attention to detail, two elements that students often ignore.

Close Reading and Rereading

Read and reread to make sense of what the author is saying
Read and reread to make sense of details
Read and reread to cite textual evidence
Read and reread to engage in careful analysis and reanalysis
Read and reread to take notes
Read and reread to note and clarify confusing parts of the text
Read and reread many times for many purposes, i.e., structure, theme, motivation, etc.
Read and reread to defend opinions and ideas with text evidence
(Dobler, 2013; Fisher, Frey & Lapp, 2012)

Fostering Close Reading.   Close reading can be effective only if accompanied by supportive instructional practices. Two basic components are choice of passage and provision of "authentic and unique purposes for each of the rereadings" (Dobler, 2013, p. 14). It is important to start with "engaging questions, appealing topics and important ideas" (Snow, 2013, p. 19). Passages should be short and relatively complex, what Fisher, Frey, and Lapp (2012) describe as "worthy" (p. 108), so students can experience and learn how to address difficult text. The teacher should provide limited frontloading in the form of telling the students what the text says. The idea is for students to determine this on their own through close reading. Text-dependent questions based on the standards provide a context for close reading. Interactive read-alouds, shared reading, teacher modeling, think-alouds, and collaborative discussion can all play an integral part (Fisher & Frey, 2012). Taking notes in close reading is critical; the specific type of note taking is not. Many students do not know how to take notes as they read; teachers should offer different options such as text annotation and various forms of graphic organizers. Highlighting and underlining can be effective, but only if what is highlighted and underlined is important and understood.

A key component of close reading is recognition of what the reader does not understand. This can be an unknown word or a major idea. It can be the structure of a sentence, paragraph, or longer segment of text. Reader confusion can lead to teacher modeling of how to break apart a lengthy sentence or how to use context to suggest word meaning. It should not lead to the teacher rephrasing content in simpler language or explaining content the students are expected to grasp through their own close reading and careful thinking.

Helping students to approach reading with questions in mind can foster close reading. Such questions should focus on the standards. You can use the *CARA* question stems to formulate questions for close reading. Students should understand that these stems represent what readers should ask themselves about the text. Students are not used to asking questions; they see questions as emanating from the text or the teacher. Effective close reading begins with self-generated questions, such as the following:

- What is the author's central idea?
- How does the author structure the text?
- What process is the author analyzing?
- What is the author's point of view and what clues in the text suggest this?

Close reading can take many forms and there is no one way that is effective for everyone. Perhaps the only given is the acknowledgement that close reading is difficult, takes time, and is not always enjoyable. The enjoyment comes with the realization that a piece of text that once seemed impossible to understand now makes sense.

Guidelines for Close Reading

Definition
  Engaging in rereading multiple times
  Paying attention to detail
Supportive instructional processes
  Selection of an appropriate text
  Provision of authentic purpose
  Minimal frontloading
  Engaging questions
  Recognition of what the reader does not understand.

Classroom Discussion

Traditional Discussion.   Discussion in many classrooms does not promote the deeper level of comprehension that the standards demand. In too many classrooms, discussion consists of the teacher asking questions. If students offer an erroneous answer and no other students seem inclined to offer an alternative, the teacher provides the answer and moves on. This has often been described as an IRE pattern (initiation/response/ evaluation) and it is not as effective as might be suggested given its widespread use. In addition, discussion is generally focused on literal-level questions. This avoids ambiguity; the answer is either right or wrong. Unfortunately, though such questions abound in teacher manuals, the standards demand a higher level of comprehension. A review of research on the effects of classroom discussion indicated that "a student-centered, dialogic approach to discussion that moves beyond traditional I-R-E participant formats leads to a significant increase in comprehension. Accordingly, one might seriously question the value of the traditional teacher-led discussion format" (Almasi & Garas-York, 2009, p. 489).

Real Discussion.   What should "real" discussion consist of? Consider, for example, the discussion you might engage in during an adult reading group where members eagerly explain their understanding and evaluation of a chosen book. Group members generate the questions. They react to what their peers say, offer different interpretations, ask for clarification, and point out areas of confusion or misunderstanding. They evaluate the overall value of the text and often revise their initial impressions based on the comments of their peers. No one person does all the talking in an effective discussion group. Everyone's comments are valued, even if disagreed with, and all leave the session with a deeper understanding of the text: "it is from interaction and struggle among different, even competing voices that meaning and understanding emerge" (Wilkinson & Son, 2011, p. 367).

Differences in classroom discussion generally emanate from the degree of control exerted by the teacher or the students. As we have noted, most discussion is teacher controlled. We suspect that releasing control to students could be threatening to some teachers and they may not know how to proceed. Wilkinson and Son (2011) offer four components that can be gradually released to student control.

1. Who chooses the topic? Students can be allowed or encouraged to choose the discussion topic based on their interest and needs. Lack of understanding on the part of a student can be a powerful incentive to initiate a discussion.
2. Who is the interpretive authority? Who is the final arbiter of conflicting points of view? Is it the teacher, the text, the students, or a combination of all three? The standards would, of course, suggest that the text be the final authority.
3. Who controls turn taking? Is this dominated by the teacher or allowed to flow from the interactions of the students?
4. Who chooses the text? Obviously, in many cases, there is a single classroom text; however, who determines which specific section of the text should be the object of discussion? Is text choice determined by the teacher, who has specific curricular intentions, or the students, who need clarification of certain points, or both?

We are not suggesting that teachers relinquish discussion control in one fell swoop. We are, however, suggesting a gradual release of control dependent on the nature of the topic.

Discussion based on the standards uses the text to acquire information, identify arguments, and validate points of view. Teacher modeling supports the students, but only as necessary, and gradually releases responsibility to them for forming and answering questions. How does this play out in the classroom? Students take positions on word meaning, text structure, point of view, and arguments in the text; politely challenge those of other students; and offer evidence from the text to support their views. The topic of the discussion is the text and teachers and students "make visible their discipline-based comprehension strategies and processes in group discussions and other collaborative learning environments" (Wilkinson & Hye, 2011, p. 368).

Releasing Control of Discussion to the Students

Students choose topics.
The final arbiter is the text.
Control of turn-taking flows from student interactions
Choice of text is gradually released to students when appropriate.

Asking Questions

Question Quality.   Asking questions has traditionally been the teacher's role; students were expected to provide the answers. Our examination of a variety of textbooks presently in use in the schools suggests that the questions asked of students seldom meet the demands of the standards. The standards require "high-quality sequences of text-dependent questions . . . that move beyond what is directly stated to require students to make nontrivial inferences based on evidence in the text" (Coleman & Pimental, 2011, p. 6). Text-dependent questions are answered by text analysis; they are not answered by matching words in the question to words in the text and they are seldom answered with one or two words. The popular literal questions that begin with *who, what, when,* and *where*—described by Graesser, Ozuru, and Sullins (2010) as *shallow*—have given way to questions that ask students to *interpret, analyze, categorize, compare, describe, explain how,* and *explain why.* You may have to teach students what it means to categorize, to analyze, and to interpret. The meaning of specific question words can often be clarified by using everyday experiences. What does it mean to analyze the results of a football game? How could you interpret the actions or words of someone in the media? How could you categorize different types of music?

Question Before, During, or After Reading?   Teaching students to ask questions prior to reading has often been recommended as a way of fostering comprehension. The popular KWL strategy (Ogle, 1986) directs students to preface their reading by considering what they already know about a topic and what they want to learn about it. However, in using such a strategy, teachers must remember that what students already know or what they want to know is not a concern of the standards. The standards primarily focus on what students learn from the text and the higher-level inferences they draw. Rosenshine, Meister, and Chapman (1996) actually question the value of prereading questions "because generating such questions does not require inspecting text and monitoring one's comprehension" (p. 185).

As opposed to prereading questions, teaching students to ask questions during reading has been shown to be a valuable activity (Rosenshine, Meister, & Chapman, 1996). *Questioning the author* (Beck, McKeown, Hamilton, & Kucan, 1997) is perhaps the best example of a strategy to use while reading. Called *queries,* these questions take a variety of forms; however, they are all directed at the author of the text, such as *What is the author telling you and why?* Such questions "reinforce that reading is in many respects a dialogue between a reader and a writer" (Buehl, 2011, p. 175). We cannot deny the importance or effectiveness of such a practice; however, in order to more directly address the standards, you might consider formulating queries using the language of the standards.

- What is the author's central idea and how does the author indicate this?
- What processes or causes is the author analyzing?
- What text structure is the author using and how does the author indicate this?
- What clues to word meaning does the author include?
- What is the author's point of view? How do you know?
- What claims/arguments does the author present?

Teaching students to generate questions during reading significantly improves their comprehension (Rosenshine, Meister, & Chapman, 1996). The most effective practices included instruction in using signal words and generic question stems ("Another example of _____ was _____") to formulate questions (p. 198). Asking and answering questions may be the basis for all other strategies; "it is the process of asking and then answering questions of oneself and the text that brings the other strategies to life" (Neufeld, 2005, p. 304). A focus on the standards suggests that students should be taught to generate questions that are aligned with specific standards using appropriate signal words and question stems. Using the College and Career Anchor Standards for Reading as an example, (CCSSO & NGA, 2010, p. 10), teach students to formulate questions using the words and specific intent of each standard.

Questions Using the Words and Intent of the Standards

What does the text say explicitly?
What evidence in the text allows me to make inferences?
What is the central idea or theme of the text?
What process or causes does the author expect me to analyze?
What new words did I meet and what meaning clues are present in the text?
What is the structure of the text and how do I know this?
What is the point of view or purpose of the text and how is it developed in the text?
What information is presented in pictures, charts, graphs, etc?
What arguments or claims are presented in the text?
How is the text similar and different to others of the same theme but written in a
     different genre?

Similar questions can be constructed using the language and intent of each standard at a specific grade level for literature and informational text. These questions can be slightly modified for use as a basis for read-aloud activities and text discussion by simply substituting *you* for *I* or *me*.

There will be times when you will have to ask questions to ascertain if the students have learned text content. We are talking about tests that feed into grades. Many teacher manuals offer assessments that teachers can use for final summative measures. If these are not clearly related to the Standards (and they probably won't be at this point in time) we suggest you design your own test questions using question stems from specific Standards or drawn from the *CARA*.

Graphic Note Taking

From personal experience, all of us would agree that taking notes as we read helps both understanding and memory. Various formats for taking notes have been promoted and subsequently taught to students. Although we do not know of any research that supports this, we suspect that most students devise their own idiosyncratic strategies based on what works best for them. However, over the years, graphic forms of note taking in the form of visual diagrams and annotation formats have become more visible (Akhondi, Malayeri, & Samad, 2011; Caldwell & Leslie, 2013; Dymock & Nicholson, 2010).

Text Annotation.   Annotation involves marking the text in order to record one's comprehension, indicate points of confusion, and/or guide one's thinking. Although it can involve simple underlining or circling of text elements, systems of annotation usually move beyond this to include margin notes and symbols such as exclamation marks, question marks, and asterisks for indicating agreement, importance, or confusion. "Annotation is a structured way to mark up the text so it is more manageable" (Zywica & Gomez, 2008, p. 156). Annotation was a common practice until the advent of public libraries when "in the process of protecting the public books, we forgot about the gains to be had from writing in one that belongs to us alone" (Fisher, Frey, & Lapp, 2012, p. 112). Many teachers do not support annotation because of reluctance to mark a book that must be returned to the district at the end of the year. Similarly, students who purchase their own texts also feel hesitant to mark a book they hope to sell to another student at the end of the year. However, with the advent of ebooks and various forms of electronic note taking, annotation is now a viable note-taking option.

There are various types of annotation symbols. Underlining sentences and/or circling key words and phrases serve to highlight major points, as can symbols such as asterisks, stars, and exclamation marks. Writing in the margins can take the form of questions and statements of understanding. Zywica and Gomez (2008) list 12 different forms of annotation that can be used to increase comprehension of science text. Though some are specific to science material, others could be used with social studies text. They suggest that these be taught gradually. The forms are:

- Circling headings and subheadings
- Placing a square around key vocabulary
- Drawing a triangle around other difficult words
- Placing a double underline under main ideas and/or important facts
- Placing a single underline under supporting ideas
- Indicating procedural words with an arrow
- Marking definitions provided in the text with "def"
- Marking transition words with an asterisk
- Indicating conclusions with "concl"
- Marking inferences with "inf"

- Circling important formulas or equations
- Indicating confusing information with question marks

Mariage and Englert (2010) suggest six annotation symbols:

- BK for background knowledge (given the text-based nature of the standards, BK may not be a viable choice)
- CL for clarify
- I for inference
- MI for main idea
- P for prediction
- ? for questioning

Jennings, Caldwell, and Lerner (2014) recommend a very simple form of annotation that involves just three symbols:

- A plus sign (+) to mark what the reader already knew and/or understood
- An exclamation mark (!) to indicate something that was learned
- A question mark (?) to signal confusion

Annotation can be effectively combined with read-alouds and classroom discussions. You can indicate which annotation symbol you want the students to use. Start with one or two and gradually add symbols as students become more comfortable with the process. Model the process using a Smartboard, then read aloud another section and ask the students to reread it on their own and code it according to the chosen symbols. Students can compare annotations as part of postreading discussion. But what if your school still uses paper text? The value of annotation for helping students to interact with and learn from text is well worth the extra effort on your part to provide paper copies of the text. These copies, when annotated by the students, can provide effective study guides. Also, lengthy texts are not required; a one-page copy of a textbook segment can work very well.

How can you specifically tie annotation to the standards? Devise your own system of annotation prompts based on individual standards. While we suggest the ones shown here, we encourage you to devise a system with which you feel comfortable.

Tying Annotation to the Standards

Standard #1: Underline text evidence that leads to an inference and write I or the inference in the margin.

Standard #2: Indicate topic with a "T" and a main or central idea with "MI." If there is no explicit main idea, write one in the margin. For literature, underline text evidence of a theme and write "TH" in the margin.

Standard #3: Explanations or analyses can be annotated with "E" or "A" depending upon the term you choose to employ. You can provide more specific annotations by adding whether the analysis refers to a process (A-How), a cause (A-Why), a comparison (A-Comp), or a Purpose (A-Purp).

Standard #4: Circle new or difficult words and underline any context clues to their meaning.

Standard #5 (for informational text): In the margin, mark a paragraph or multiple paragraphs with a symbol that indicates the structure: Description (Desc); Cause-Effect (CE); Sequence (Seq or 1-2-3); Problem Solution (PSol); and Compare Contrast (CC).

Standard #6: Mark point of view as POV.

Standard #8: Mark ARG for Arguments and Ev for evaluation.

Standard #9: Mark CC where you can see a connection between how this author wrote about this event or theme and how another author expressed the same idea.

Of course, as we mentioned, gradually introduce such symbols and feel free to devise your own.

Visual Diagrams

There are many forms of diagrams that can be used as a graphic support for note taking (Caldwell & Leslie, 2013). However, at this point we need to offer a cautionary comment. Visual diagrams can be very helpful in guiding a student to organize his or her thoughts. In many cases, they offer a more focused form of note taking. However, the diagram is only a tool. The important component is the accuracy and relevance of the information that is inserted in the diagram. Like many things in life, some diagrams resonate with some students and others are less effective or motivating. We suggest that you offer a number of possible models and let the students select and/or devise their own. It is also important that the diagrams are helpful to the student in learning new content and in studying for a test, not viewed as something to complete in order to please the teacher. We realize that many teachers may totally disagree with the suggestion that visual note-taking efforts may be used during tests. Instead of an "open-book" test, the students take an "open-notes" test. However, such an option may well provide the motivation to design well-thought-out visual diagrams.

Summary

This chapter explains the type of reading required by the standards and differentiates it from other forms of reading.

- Standards-based comprehension is text based
- Students are expected to learn information from the text
- Strategy instruction should be based in the content areas
- Specific content-area strategies are more effective in improving comprehension than general strategies
- Standards require reading of grade-appropriate text
- Teachers need to scaffold texts for their students by modeling how they should engage in close reading
- Classroom discussion involves gradual release of control to the students
- Teachers should ask questions that use the words and intent of the standards
- Teachers should use text annotations and visual diagrams to support comprehension in grade-appropriate text

Strategies for Specific Standards

This chapter focuses on instructional strategies that apply to specific standards.

Strategies for Standard 1

"Read closely to determine what the text says explicitly and to make logical inferences from it; cite specific textual evidence when writing or speaking to support conclusions drawn from the text" (CCSSO & NGA, 2010, p. 10).

Drawing Text-Based Inferences

Standard 1 states that students should draw inferences based on the text, not on their knowledge about the topic or similar topics and not on their prior opinions or feelings. For example, consider the *CARA* middle school passage on debating the Constitution. The author did not explicitly state that Hamilton believed laws and advice were very different concepts. However, one can draw that inference from what Hamilton said about the powers of government. Similarly, in discussing how the process for ratifying the Constitution was carried out, the text does not explicitly say that state size and population were not factors. The reader can infer this based on the text statement that the Constitution went into effect as soon as the ninth state ratified it.

Helping students meet Standard 1 means teaching them how to draw text-based inferences. Few students find this an easy task. This may be because teachers and classroom texts often focus primarily on asking and answering literal questions that are assumed to be a proxy for students' understanding of the text. This may or may not be so. Students can become quite adept at matching question words to words in the text with only marginal understanding of the underlying concepts.

We suggest that you begin by providing the students with the definition of what an inference entails. The dictionary defines *infer* as "derive by reasoning; conclude or accept from evidence or premises; deduce" (*Funk & Wagnalls New International Dictionary of the English Language*, 1997, p. 647). Synonyms for inference include *conclusion, supposition, deduction, interpretation, implication,* and *assumption*. We draw inferences every day and offering some simple examples can help clarify the term. For example, if the day is cloudy, we infer from experience that it might rain. If a store advertises a clearance sale, we infer, again from experience, that a large number of people may attend the sale and make shopping somewhat difficult. Inferences derived from experience come naturally to us. However, inferences drawn from text often do not. In addition, inferences based on unfamiliar topics are even more problematic.

Questions designed to measure Standard 1 in *CARA's* texts present an inference and ask students to provide evidence from the text that supports it. We suggest that you follow this format. Begin with an inference that you generate and ask the students to find support for it in the text. Consider the following question from the sixth-grade passage *Señor Coyote and the Tricked Trickster*: "Using words from the text, how does the author tell us that Coyote thought he was better than the others were?" In this question we directly ask students to look for the words in the text that tell us about Coyote's view of himself. There are two sections where possible answers can be found. The best answer is, "But everyone would laugh at a big, brave, smart fellow like me working as a slave for a <u>mere</u> mouse!" The second possibility is where the coyote describes himself as "a big, brave, smart fellow like me." This question is helpful to students because it gives them something specific to look for in the text. In some cases, the answers must be found by putting together the ideas in several parts of the text. For example, the final section of *Señor Coyote* states,

> Then Coyote turned to Mouse. "So, my friend, I have now saved your life. We are now even and my debt to you is paid."
> "But mine is such a little life," Mouse protested. "And yours is so much *larger*. I don't think they balance. You should still pay me part."
> "This is ridiculous!" Coyote cried. "I—"
> "Wait!" Snake put in hopefully. "Let me settle the quarrel. Now you roll the rock away. I'll take Mouse in my coils just the way we were when Coyote came up. We'll be in a position to decide if—"
> "Thank you," said Mouse. "It isn't necessary to trouble everyone again. Señor Coyote, we are even."

The question asks students to use details from the story and explain why Mouse decided to accept that Coyote paid his debt at the end. To answer this question, students must infer the consequences of Mouse's unwillingness to take Coyote's saving his life as payment for Mouse saving Coyote's life. Mouse proclaims that his life is little compared to Coyote's, so Coyote should pay him. Coyote resists. Then Snake proposes that they arrange the situation as it was before Coyote came (Snake had Mouse in his grasp) and then decide again. At this point Mouse realizes that he could be back in the same predicament that he was in before, and decides to accept Coyote's payment. This answer is a much more complex process of working through an argument and understanding the consequences of each character's behavior.

Now, consider the *CARA* middle school passage *The Constitutional Convention*. The text states that "One part of the Virginia Plan nearly tore the convention apart. The plan called for representation based on population. The more people a state had, the more seats it would have in each house. Naturally this idea drew support from the big states." What inferences can be drawn from this? Delegates took such strong views that they were willing to walk away from the convention. The small states feared that the large states would dominate. The large states favored a position that would put them in control.

Modeling an inference that you drew and the text elements you used to do so will help students understand the process of forming text-based inferences. In a sense, you are moving backwards by providing the inference and then supporting it as opposed to identifying the support and using this to form an inference.

Once students are somewhat comfortable finding text support for inferences that you provide, move to the next step. Identify specific text elements and ask the students to use these as a basis for generating their inferences. For example, consider the *CARA* middle school passage *Debating the Constitution*. You could ask students to consider the following arguments against the Constitution: "a too-strong central government . . . would wipe out state power and individual freedom . . . destroying the liberties of the people . . . No Bill of Rights . . . offered no protections for basic freedoms." What could students infer about the concerns of the Antifederalists? The possibilities are that the Constitution was seriously flawed or the Antifederalists were afraid that individual rights would be ignored, or they did not trust government.

Finding text evidence to support and/or draw an inference can be an effective group activity. Different groups can examine the text in order to locate support for an inference or in order to draw an inference and justify the validity of their choice. You can provide them with an inference and have them locate text support for it, or you can identify sections of text for them to use to draw their own inference. Groups can then compare different responses and decide on the most acceptable text evidence or the inference from the text that has the most evidence. Of course, they will be learning the content as they go along.

In Chapter 5.1, we discussed transfer and how it works. Realize that generating an inference in a life science text may not transfer to an earth science passage. That is okay. What *will* transfer is the understanding that an inference must be based on explicit text content. Some content will lend itself to easier generation of inferences. This also may differ among students. A student interested in rocks, for example, may construct stronger text-based inferences in text about this subject than one of less interest or in a different discipline. Sometimes it is easier to draw text-based inferences from literature passages. Although the inference must be based on the text, it is often supported by life experiences similar to those portrayed in stories, novels, or plays. A teacher cannot assume that a student's ability in drawing inferences from literature indicates facility with the inference process as a whole. This argues that reading teachers and intervention specialists need to use a variety of texts to support the development of drawing inferences based on explicit text content.

Standard 1 Instruction in Drawing Text-Based Inferences

Provide a definition of *inference*
Offer examples of "everyday" inferences
Generate an inference; have students find text support for it
Identify specific parts of a text; ask students to use these to generate an inference
Use group activities to develop understanding of the inference process

Strategies for Standard 2

"Determine central ideas or themes of a text and analyze their development; summarize the key supporting details and ideas" (CCSSO & NGA, 2010, p. 10).

Differentiating Central Idea and Topic in Informational Text

Determination of central ideas in informational text is an activity that is often fraught with confusion, as various misconceptions exist regarding terminology. It is important to acknowledge that:

- Central idea and main idea are used synonymously. The standards have simply substituted *central idea* for the more commonly used *main idea*. We believe it is wise to use the term *central idea* given that standardized assessment based on the standards will, in all probability, use the same terminology as the standards.
- Topic and central idea are not the same things.
- Although each paragraph is believed to contain an explicitly stated central idea, usually as the initial sentence, many do not.

Topic and central idea are different entities. The topic is one or two words or a short phrase that indicates the content of the succeeding paragraphs. Textbook headings often signal topics. The central idea, however, is what the author says about the topic. It is tied to the author's purpose or point of view and the structure chosen by the author (Jitendra & Gajria, 2011). Finding the central idea "involves identifying the single most important idea in a section of text" (Klingner, Morrison, & Eppoloto, 2011, p. 234) and it is often inferred.

Identifying the central idea primarily involves generation, not recognition. Despite the prevailing belief that authors include central idea statements at the beginning of each paragraph, this seldom occurs. A single central idea can often cross several paragraphs of informational text or represent the content of a longer section of text. Central ideas are seldom recognized; they are inferred based on information in the text. Central ideas also differ in narrative and expository text. In narrative text, the reader identifies a theme based on the description and sequence of events. In expository material, the reader develops a generalization based on the "relationship of ideas about a topic" (Jitendra & Gajria, 2011, p. 199). Generating a central idea is often a difficult process. The reader cannot just select such a statement; they must construct it while ignoring the presence of extraneous textual information (Afflerbach, 1990).

Students in our pilot exhibited considerable difficulty in identifying the central idea across all grade levels and in both social studies and science. Despite being given the topic of the preceding paragraphs, they persisted in listing a series of details related to the topic instead of drawing them together in a single general statement tied to the author's purpose. Often they identified the first sentence of the paragraph as the central idea when it clearly was not an appropriate choice. They also chose the most salient or interesting detail and occasionally they virtually rewrote the paragraph instead of providing a single central idea statement.

We suggest a backward approach to determining the central idea, similar to what we recommended for teaching the inference process (Standard 1). Consider the "Soil Erosion" section from the fourth-grade science text *How Does Earth's Surface Change?* Tell the students the topic of the second paragraph is erosion and the central idea is that soil erosion causes destruction to land and people. Then ask the students to locate text details that support this. These could include the following: ". . . left many areas of soil bare . . . severe dust storms that blew for eight years . . . children wore dust masks to school . . . people couldn't see even during the day."

In the fifth-grade selection *What Is Inside a Cell?* the topic of paragraphs three and four under the heading "Some Parts of Animal Cells" is chromosomes and the central idea is that chromosomes control growth and change and play a part in heredity. The students should identify the following supporting details: "Chromosomes carry instructions for the cell . . . by telling every cell how to do its jobs, chromosomes control how the body grows and changes . . . has small sections of DNA called genes . . . heredity is the process of passing these genes. . . ."

After students become adept at identifying the details that support a given central idea, the next step is for them to identify the central idea based on the topic and text details. Because individuals often take notes in a format that lists details under the central idea (i.e., using the central idea as a heading for their notes), there is an assumption that this is the sequence for central idea identification. Actually, it is not. We cannot generate a central idea unless we have first read the details. We move from topic to details and then generate or recognize the central idea, even if we use a different placement for our note-taking efforts.

Standard 2 Process for Identifying or Generating a Central Idea

Check heading/s for topics

Read paragraphs

Identify details that are related to the topic

Identify/generate a central idea statement.

Determining the central idea demands rereading; such ideas do not leap out at you after you finish a paragraph. Like any difficult activity, breaking the process into separate steps helps. Identifying the topic is the first step. We have seldom encountered readers who could not identify the topic even in the absence of a heading; the topic is generally repeated numerous times throughout the paragraph. Because the topic is the support for all of the details provided by the author, once a student identifies the topic and connects it to relevant details, the central idea is often easily identified or generated.

Using a graphic organizer as a support for determining the central/main idea is extremely helpful as it provides the student with a visual representation of text structure (Caldwell & Leslie, 2013; Jennings, Caldwell, & Lerner, 2014).

Standard 2 Sequence for Filling Out a Central Idea Graphic Organizer

1. Identify the topic (one or two words) using the heading.
2. If there is no heading, the topic is generally the subject of the majority of sentences.
3. Write the topic on the top line of the organizer.
4. List relevant details under the topic.
5. Locate or generate a central idea statement.

In most cases, the central idea is not explicitly stated and it must be inferred or generated from the topic and details. It is important for students to realize there is no single way to express the main idea; different students will phrase their main idea statements in different ways. In the *CARA* we allowed for this. Correct answers to Standard 2 questions can be expressed as a sentence or as a phrase. What is critical is the association between the topic, the details that expand on the topic, and the central idea that expresses the author's overall purpose.

Determining a Theme in Literature Text

Determining a theme in literature is similar to inferring a central idea in informational text in that the reader must identify sentences or concepts that suggest the author's purpose in writing the story. One way of phrasing the question of a theme is, "What does the author want us to learn from reading this story?" or "What is the main point that the author is trying to convey to us?" Some themes are readily generated from reading a text; others require close reading, thinking, and reasoning. Consider two famous stories that are used in the *CARA*. First, *All Summer in a Day*, by Ray Bradbury, tells of life on Venus, where the weather is constant rain. Sunshine occurs for one hour every seven years. The students are waiting for that day, which is coming soon. The story revolves around a student who is different from the others and a boy who enjoys taunting her. On the day the sun comes out the boy, along with others from their class, lock her in a closet and forget about her until after the rain has started again. Bradbury includes several examples of how the children viewed the girl as different from her classmates, and two examples of how the boy taunted her. Most seventh-grade students in our initial pilot had no difficulty interpreting what Bradbury wants the reader to learn from his story, although they phrased it in different ways. For example, they said, "don't bully someone just because they are different from you," or "treat others the way you want to be treated."

Determining the theme in *The Tell Tale Heart*, by Edgar Allan Poe, is a bit more of a challenge. Literary fiction is more than simply telling a story. Poe wrote about events that scared people. What did he want his readers to come away with, other than fear? Why did he write the story of a man who argues he is not crazy and, in doing so, shows the reader that he *is* crazy? Poe is a master at creating tension as the reader knows what has happened, but the police don't, and it appears the man may get away with murder. The murderer begins very confident of his cleverness, yet as the police stay longer, he becomes more and more nervous, ultimately confessing even though the police never accuse him of the crime. One possible theme is that people who commit a crime often give their guilt away after a time, or as one student wrote, "what goes around, comes around." Is Poe trying to tell us that evil will be punished? Teachers must always propose to their students that stories have more than one possible theme. It is the students' job to find the evidence to support their theme.

Constructing Summaries of Informational Text

Standard 2 includes two separate components: recognizing the central idea and constructing a summary. A summary of informational text includes only the most relevant or salient content about a specific topic (Ferretti & De La Paz, 2011. Most individuals think of a summary as a written and shorter version of the text. However, summaries can be oral, visual, or written. Oral summaries are useful to the teacher for checking what students have understood or remembered; they can be similarly useful to the individual reader as a way of verbalizing what he or she has understood. Inability to construct an oral summary may indicate to the reader that rereading or a closer perusal of the text is necessary. Visual summaries such as diagrams and webs "capture both the important information from the text and the structure of the knowledge contained in the text" (Neufeld, 2005, p. 306)—that is, they include the main ideas and visually indicate the relationship between main ideas and explanatory details. The visual can be used later to write a summary.

How does one go about constructing a written summary of informational text? Perin (2007) describes several steps: Delete unnecessary and redundant material. Replace lists of items and/or verbs with general words. Select or write a topic sentence. These steps sound quite straightforward but, in reality, they do not always work for a specific passage. A passage may not contain a list of nouns or verbs that can be replaced with more generic terms. In addition, a key step is missing: that of determining the central idea or what the author has to say about the topic. Unless the reader is clear about the central idea, it is extremely difficult, if not impossible, to delete extraneous material. To put it another way, it is the relationship to the central idea that determines a text segment's necessity to the summary. Recognizing this, Helsel and Greenberg (2007) suggest building a summary on the central idea and details. Using the details as the basis for generating the central idea, construct a central idea statement. Then, review the details and only select those that pertain most specifically to the central idea. Once that is completed, you can replace lists of multiple items with single descriptors.

Steps in Constructing a Summary

- Identify the topic of a summary
- List all details that are related to the topic
- Generate or identify the central idea
- Review the details
- Select those that are most relevant to the central idea
- Replace lists with generic terms and/or combine details where appropriate

Visual summaries, often referred to as *idea maps,* can be an important first step in constructing a summary. Dymock and Nicholson (2010) describe several forms of visual summaries that act as the first step in writing a summary. The student reads the text, identifies its structure, and makes a diagram that summarizes both structure and content. Descriptive diagrams take the form of a list, a web, or a matrix. Sequential diagrams include squares connected by arrows. Cause and effect is represented by the cause written in a square with the effects placed in parallelograms joined by arrows. The same format is used to visualize the problem–solution pattern. Once a diagram is constructed, it is used as the guide for constructing a text summary. Caldwell and Leslie (2013) also offer some examples of idea maps that can form the basis for a summary.

Description Idea Map

Description

Sequence Idea Map

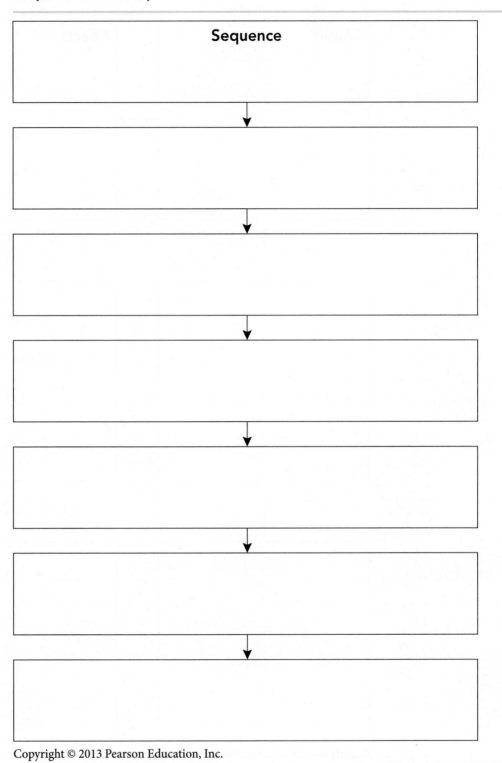

Sequence

Cause-and-Effect Idea Map

Problem–Solution Idea Map

Problem:

Solution:

Compare-and-Contrast Idea Map

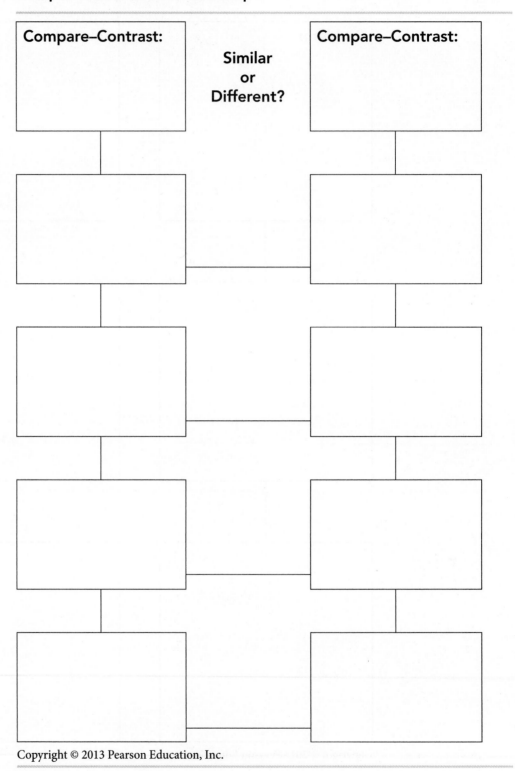

Main Idea Map

Topic:

Detail:

Detail:

Detail:

Main Idea Statement:

It is not easy to write a summary and we suspect that few teacher manuals offer examples of well-constructed summaries. We strongly suggest that you construct a summary before you ask students to do so and before you evaluate their work. In this way, you will be better able to understand the difficulties that students may have. In addition, you can describe your difficulties to the students and demonstrate how you solved them. Another suggestion is to construct the summary in front of the students using a Smartboard.

Chapter 4, Part 2, describes a process for evaluating the summaries written by pilot students as they answered the Standard 2 summary questions. You may want to use a similar process for classroom activities. Did the summary address and/or answer the question or the intent of the assignment? Was it text based? Were the majority of summary components related to the content of the summary? During *CARA* piloting, we often found that students misinterpreted summary writing as describing their particular response to the topic. For example, they commented about their interest in the topic or evaluated the actions of historical figures in terms of their own belief systems.

Constructing Summaries of Literature Text

Writing a summary of a literature text is more straightforward than writing a summary of informational text. Recall that our literature selections were all short stories, so they included the typical narrative organization: settings (sometimes of importance, sometimes not), characters, goal and/or problem, a series of events where one or more characters tried to reach a goal or solve the problem, and a resolution. There was a great amount of variability in the summaries of fourth and fifth graders. On average, they only included two elements in their summary: character and one event. Occasionally a group of students would appear to use some formula for writing a summary.

It appeared that summary writing at these grade levels is heavily dependent on good classroom instruction. The narrative structure can be used to teach students how to write summaries of the literature they read, and perhaps more importantly can be used as a guide for teaching them how to write stories. Teachers must provide explicit instruction on the elements of story and demonstrate, through modeling, how the elements are used to write stories (Caldwell & Leslie, 2013). It is vital that modeling and teacher-generated stories are included in instruction (Graham, 2006).

To teach students to summarize biographies, you should use a variant of the narrative structure that includes the most important elements of biographies. These elements vary from the information included in stories. For example, stories often include a setting, but biographies include where and when the main character was born. In addition to the main character, biographies often include people who were instrumental in helping the main character achieve his or her goal. Finally, implicit in all biographies is what the person is known or remembered for. In other words, why was the biography written about this person's life? Graphics are useful for helping students summarize stories and biographies: examples are presented here.

Character Perspective Chart

Three Billy Goats Gruff

Who are the main characters? The three billy goats.	**Who is the main character?** The troll.
Where does the story take place? By a bridge.	**Where does the story take place?** By a bridge.
What do the goats want? To get to the mountain to eat grass.	**What does the troll want?** To eat the goats.
What is the problem? The troll tries to stop them from crossing the bridge.	**What is the problem?** Each goat tells the troll to wait until his larger brother comes so that he will get a bigger meal. The goats trick the troll.
Events: Each time the goats try to cross the bridge, the troll stops them, but the goats trick him.	**Events:** Each time the goats try to cross the bridge the troll stops them and says he will eat them, but he doesn't.
Resolution: All of the goats get across the bridge safely because the largest goat kills the troll. The goats reach their goal as they go across the bridge and up the mountain to eat grass and get fat.	**Resolution:** The troll waits to eat the last goat, who is very large, and kills him. His goal is not met.

Map of Amelia Earhart Biography

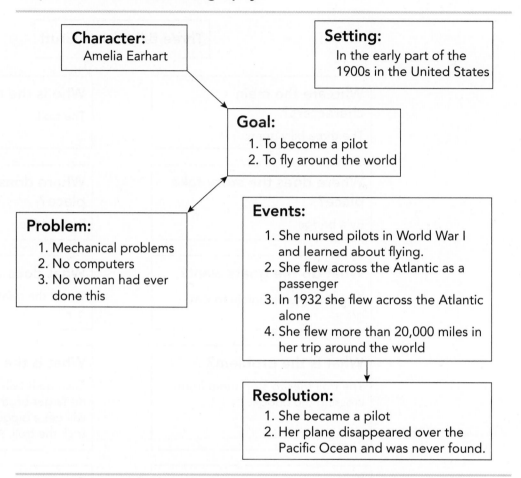

Character:
Amelia Earhart

Setting:
In the early part of the
1900s in the United States

Goal:
1. To become a pilot
2. To fly around the world

Problem:
1. Mechanical problems
2. No computers
3. No woman had ever
   done this

Events:
1. She nursed pilots in World War I
   and learned about flying.
2. She flew across the Atlantic as a
   passenger
3. In 1932 she flew across the Atlantic
   alone
4. She flew more than 20,000 miles in
   her trip around the world

Resolution:
1. She became a pilot
2. Her plane disappeared over the
   Pacific Ocean and was never found.

Strategies for Standard 3

"Analyze how and why individuals, events and ideas develop and interact over the course of a text" (CCSSO & NGA, 2010).

The Meaning of Analysis

What does it mean to analyze something? *The Funk & Wagnalls New International Dictionary of the English Language* (1997) defines *analyze* as "to resolve into constituent parts or elements" and "to examine minutely or critically, as a text" (p. 52). Common synonyms for *analyze* include *examine, study, evaluate, investigate, explore,* and *inspect.* However, one might suggest that all questions based on the standards involve analysis of some kind. How, then, is Standard 3 substantially different from the other eight standards?

Asking students to analyze promotes deeper learning only to the extent that students understand what they should be doing when they analyze. Chanock (2000) described confusion and ambiguity in definitions of *analyze* offered by both university teachers and their students. For example, "analysis for the purpose of essay writing means showing relationships and drawing conclusions" (Clancy & Ballard, 1981, p. 45), but analysis, for writing a summary or evaluating a process, involves other components. In addition, the word *analyze* is often considered analogous to other question stems such as *assess, compare, contrast, criticize, review, discuss, explain,* and *interpret.* This may be an inaccurate assumption; the words *review* and *discuss* could lead students to provide a description lacking in analysis.

As described in Chapter 2, the question taxonomy proposed by Graesser and Person (1994) differentiates 16 question types according to the nature of the information that is sought: shallow, intermediate, or complex. Similarly, Mosenthal (1996) classified questions as concrete or abstract, with abstract questions focused on identification of "purpose, pattern, difference, condition, reason or evidence" (p. 320). We believe that these two taxonomies clarify the concept of *analyze* by indicating that the results of an analysis should be complex and/or abstract and should focus on process, causality, purpose, and comparison of similarity and difference. Identification of how an event affected a story, the purpose for an event, why something occurred, how something occurred, and the comparison among concepts also differentiate Standard 3 from other standards that ask students to provide evidence for an inference, identify a central idea, determine word meaning, identify text structure, and clarify point of view.

Standard 3 The Analysis Process

Process:	How did something occur? Give examples.
Causality:	Why did something occur or not occur? Give reasons.
	What were the consequences of something? Give examples.
Purpose:	What were purposes behind an action? Give examples.
	What were motives and goals? Give reasons.
Comparison/Contrast:	How are things similar and different? Give examples.

How should teachers foster analysis? We believe that the first step is to clarify what is meant by analysis—that is, what a student should do when asked to analyze. We suspect that comparing, determining causality, and recognizing process or purpose are things they do quite naturally in their everyday life. Therefore, a teacher should use that knowledge to explain analysis. For example, if students were asked to analyze how a team's defense changed in the second half of a game, students would identify the strategies used in the first half and then draw a comparison to what was done in the second half. This is a compare–contrast analysis. If a character in a television series makes a surprising move, students can discuss purpose, motives, and goals based on prior words and actions of the character. Students can analyze the causes and consequences of events mentioned in the newspaper and familiar everyday processes such as learning to drive, running for class office, and practicing a sport. They need to carry over such activities to text-based comprehension. They also need to realize that such information will probably be found in different parts of the text and their role is to locate relevant information and consolidate it into a coherent whole.

Successful analysis presupposes that students understand the meaning of vocabulary used in questions, often referred to as question stems. What is meant by *why, how,* and *compare*? What is the difference between a purpose and a consequence? Before assuming that students clearly understand the specific differences between these concepts, it might be wise to ask some questions based on familiar concepts and activities. If students evince confusion, some interaction in the meaning of question stems is in order.

Analysis is not an easy task. Teachers should model the process, provide examples of acceptable analyses, and offer multiple opportunities for students to work together and individually to puzzle through the process.

Standard 3 Instruction in the Analysis Process

Clarify what it means to analyze.
Differentiate among process, causality, purpose and comparison/contrast.
Use examples from everyday life.
Move to examples from text.

Strategies for Standard 4

"Interpret words and phrases as they are used in the text including determining technical, connotative and figurative meanings and analyze how specific word choices shape meaning or tone" (CCSSO & NGA, 2010, p. 10).

Vocabulary in Informational Text

The text-based focus of the standards and the goal of preparing students for college and career literacy demands emphasize the importance of academic vocabulary. Academic vocabulary encompasses two broad concepts: content-specific academic vocabulary and general academic vocabulary (Baumann & Graves, 2010). Content-specific vocabulary refers to the words that are used in specific disciplines such as social studies, science, and literature and in subdisciplines such as biology, chemistry, and physics. General academic vocabulary includes words that appear across several disciplines, although the meaning may change slightly in different disciplines. For example, *features* in an earth science text takes on a different meaning than it does in a literature selection. Coxhead (2000) described academic vocabulary as "lexical items [that] occur frequently and uniformly across a wide range of academic material (p. 218). Vocabulary words for *CARA* Standard 4 questions in informational text were chosen from Coxhead's Academic Word List, a corpus of approximately 600 words most frequently found in academic text. Nagy and Townsend (2012) suggest that the list, composed of general academic words, "is best used as a list of one type of word that teachers should attend to as opposed to a list of the most important academic words" (p. 97). The Academic Word List does not include discipline-specific words that are exclusive to individual disciplines and important for text comprehension, such as *bathymetry, mitochondria, nullification,* and *oligarchy*.

Vocabulary in Literature Text

Vocabulary words chosen for Standard 4 questions in literature were based on the grade-level specification of the standard. For example, beginning at grade 5, the standard asks students to "determine the meaning of words and phrases as they are used in a text, including figurative language such as metaphors and similes." As the grade levels increase, students are often asked how specific words affect the meaning or tone of a story. Because of this emphasis on figurative language and word choice, we chose phrases that were to be understood figuratively, not literally, for the *CARA*. In some stories, figurative language only occurred once, and so the other word or phrase used to assess Standard 4 came from the Coxhead (2000) list or was a word determined to be critical to the meaning of the story.

Learning Word Meaning

Readers learn word meanings through reading; "word knowledge is acquired from context gradually, one small step at a time" (Nagy, 2010, p. 84). However, this poses a difficulty with regard to content-specific vocabulary; such words may be encountered less often in a single text or even across multiple texts in the same content area. For example, consider specific terminology related to the cell such as *prokaryotic, lysosomes,* and *mitochondria*. These may only occur in a single science unit. Similarly *patrician, plebeian,* and *consul* may only occur in a unit on ancient Rome. This suggests that such vocabulary may not be learned gradually over time but will need "high-quality instructional encounters involving repetition and review" (Nagy, 2010, p. 85).

Vocabulary instruction has been described as a stepping stone to disciplinary practices. Disciplinary learning often requires "in the moment" vocabulary support; that is, the teacher ascertains if students understand a word as they encounter it and clarifies meaning if needed. Research on teaching discipline-specific words indicates the importance of situating "academic vocabulary learning within the language of their respective content areas" (Nagy & Townsend, 2012, p. 101); that is, instruction supported student understanding of how the different disciplines use specific words differently.

Context Clues to Word Meaning

"Comprehension of text is a function of a reader's ability to efficiently locate and access word meaning when reading" (Baumann, 2009, p. 325). The words *locate* and *access* in the preceding quotation suggests that word meanings unknown prior to reading may be determined through the context of the text. However, students may not be aware of the power of context or understand how to use it.

Which words in a text should you select for emphasis and how should you present them? Typical instructional practice involves a teacher selecting a word, defining it, and providing a variety of activities for clarifying meaning and fostering student retention. One cannot argue about this; there are many instructional suggestions for developing understanding of and memory for specific words (Blachowicz & Fisher, 2007). However, the focus of Standard 4 is on the reader determining the meaning of words as they are used in the text, and the best way this can be done is through use of context. Of course, one can always use a dictionary, but dictionaries offer all possible meanings of a word and the reader still has to choose the definition that best fits a specific context. Besides, as we all know, stopping to peruse a dictionary can interrupt the flow of meaning.

In order to address Standard 4, teachers will have to offer explicit instruction in how to determine word meaning from context. This can involve words that cross all disciplines as well as technical words found in a single discipline. However, teachers should differentiate words that are accompanied by sufficient context from those that are not. Some words lack adequate context for determining their meaning. For example, in the *CARA* high school passage *The Vast World Ocean*, little context clarifies the meanings of *atmospheric, pulses,* and *hemisphere*. If students demonstrate confusion regarding these words, the teacher can explain the meaning and/or engage the students in dialogue that clarifies it. In contrast, the passage on ocean floor features contains the words *crust, shelf,* and *margin*. These carry meanings specific to oceanography, but the context of the passage is sufficient for students to infer their different meanings. The teacher should not define such words but demonstrate for students how context can unlock word meaning. It may not lead to a specific definition, but it often allows one to obtain a general sense of the word's meaning and thus continue reading with some measure of understanding. Inasmuch as rereading is a critical component of close reading, the word can be re-examined during subsequent readings of the text and through class discussion.

What type of context information may be present in a text? Baumann, Ware, and Edwards (2007) describe five types of context clues.

- The text author can provide a definition for a new and presumably important word; we noted that this often occurred in the informational text we examined as we constructed the *CARA*.
- The author can also provide a synonym; again, we noted this as a recurring pattern in science and social studies passages.
- The author can also include an antonym as contrast, provide an example of the word, or offer some general clues to meaning. All of these are examples of semantic context clues. However, there are other context clues as well.

- Morphological context includes meaning clues within the word itself, such as prefixes, suffixes, and roots.
- Syntactic context includes meaning clues derived from placement of the word in a sentence that signals a specific part of speech.

"There is considerable evidence that teaching students to develop their ability to use context clues holds promise for enhancing students' ability to acquire many word meanings through independent reading" (Baumann, 2009, p. 332).

As an example of the various forms of context, consider the word *features* in the following sentence from the *CARA* sixth-grade passage, *What Are Earth's Layers Made Of?*: "Victoria Falls is just one of Earth's many land features." Morphological context involves recognition of word parts such as *-ure* as in *future, pressure,* and *procedure.* It signals a possible noun. The ending *-s* also suggests a noun. The syntactic context or the position of the word in the sentence suggests a noun as well, in that *features* is preceded by the adjectives *many* and *land.* There is also strong semantic context in the passage. The text uses *landforms* as a synonym for *features* and offers a variety of feature examples such as *mountains, volcanoes, waterfalls,* and *canyons.*

As another illustration of the various forms of context, consider the word *elements* in the *CARA* middle school passage on the Roman Republic: "Although some elements of the republic remained, Caesar ruled with great power." The *-s* ending represents morphological context; it suggests that the word is plural. The placement of the word within the sentence indicates a noun; this represents syntactic context. Semantic context takes the form of an example of *elements.* By tying *elements* to the republic, the author provides an example of *elements* and limits its usage to government. Although *elements* can refer to weather and/or to chemical elements, in this context, those meanings do not fit. Similarly, consider the context surrounding the word *economic* in the *CARA* passage on the fall of Rome: "This change resulted in inflation, an **economic** situation in which more money circulates but the money has less value." The *-ic* suggests an adjective as in *realistic, basic,* or *heroic.* Sentence placement also suggests an adjective, as *economic* precedes a noun. The text offers a specific example of a characteristic of *inflation* and signals a meaning other than to inflate a balloon or exaggerate a claim.

The context clues in literature provide similar hints toward word meaning and in addition may extend over several sentences. In the fourth-grade selection *Encyclopedia Brown and the Case of the Slippery Salamander,* Encyclopedia says, "If he's a lizard expert, then I'm the queen of England!" The preceding sentences describe how Encyclopedia is trying to solve the case of the disappearance of the salamander. The three-sentence context preceding the quote provides meaningful context: "'Sam told me he's been taking care of salamanders and other lizards for more than 19 years.' That was all Encyclopedia needed to hear to conclude who was the thief. 'Oh, no he hasn't!' Encyclopedia declared with a satisfied smile. 'If he's a lizard expert, then I'm the queen of England!'" In the final sentence, Encyclopedia says, "Sam is lying and I can prove it!" The context indicates that Encyclopedia believed Sam lied and is using the expression to emphasize the point. As one student put it, "well Encyclopedia isn't the queen of England, so Sam must not be a lizard expert." Many students had great difficulty interpreting the meaning of the quote and tried to connect only the concepts in the quote.

Another example to illustrate how meaning clues can operate in literature comes from the high school text, *A Problem.* The context was, "He was sick of life and found it insufferably hard. He was inextricably involved in debt; he had not a farthing in his pocket; his family had become detestable to him; he would have to part from his friends and his women sooner or later, as they had begun to be too contemptuous of his sponging on them. The future looked black." The question asked: What does "they had begun to be too contemptuous of his sponging on them" mean? The words "insufferably hard . . . was inextricably involved in debt, he had not a farthing in his pocket . . . he would have to part with his friends" are all negative things that culminate in the final sentence, "The future looked black." This phrase has two stumbling blocks to comprehension, the meanings of the word *contemptuous* and *sponging*. The entire paragraph described how he had little money and he hated his life. In addition to these general meaning clues, the student would have to understand the use of the comma followed by the word *as* being used to provide a reason why he would have to leave his friends. In addition, if the student understood the word *contempt* he or she might realize its connection to *contemptuous* and identify it as describing his friends feeling negative toward him. Finally, the meaning of the word *sponging* could come from everyday experience, if they understood the figurative use of the word to describe how he was taking/absorbing from his friends.

Discussion of context clues present in a text as opposed to simply telling the students the meaning of a word will probably take more instructional time, but helping students understand the various forms of context may have a long-reaching effect and lead to some independence on their part. Selecting several words important to the text and having students work in pairs or groups to determine their meaning from context can be an effective activity.

Standard 4 Context Clues to Word meaning

Definition of a word
Synonym for a word
Antonym for a word
Examples of a word
General clues to meaning
Clues within a word: prefixes, suffixes, and roots
Placement in a sentence that suggests a noun, verb, adjective, etc.

Morphological Context

Morphological context demands special attention because of its importance and because it is often a neglected aspect of general literacy instruction as well as instruction that focuses on disciplinary literacy. Morphological awareness is "the ability to reflect on and manipulate meaningful parts of words, such as prefixes, roots and suffixes (Nagy, 2010, p. 87). Recognition of morpheme meaning is positively related to comprehension (Carlisle, 2010).

Many students, most likely the better readers, may have picked this up on their own. McCutchen and Logan (2011) found that fifth and eighth graders used morphological analysis to determine word meanings for real words and probable meanings for nonwords "even in the absence of instruction" (p. 343).

Teachers can help students learn how to use morphological context by instructing them in the components of morphology. Generative vocabulary instruction is based on Greek or Latin prefixes, suffixes, or roots. Using a single root, students, aided by the teacher, can generate a variety of words containing that root and carrying its basic meaning (Flanigan, Templeton, & Hayes, 2012). Rasinski, Padak, Newton, and Newton (2011) and Caldwell and Leslie (2013) provide lists of common prefixes, suffixes, and roots that they recommend teaching to students. Particularly in science, Latin and Greek roots such as *terr-* (earth), *-gress* (step), *-sect* (cut), and *-vert* (turn) carry strong meaning clues. Although content teachers may be somewhat adverse to taking time from content-focused lessons to teach morphemes, they can point out the morphemes in key vocabulary within a specific selection. However, intervention specialists should offer direct attention to morphology (Caldwell & Leslie, 2013) by providing examples of words containing the same morpheme

Table 5.2.1   Common Prefixes

Prefix	Meaning	Example
un-	not	unhappy
in-	not	incorrect
re-	again	reread
anti-	against	antibiotic
mis-	wrong	mistreat
pre-	before	predict
post-	after	postgame
dis-	opposite	disadvantage
circum-	around	circumference
inter-	between	interstate
intra-	within	intramural
sub-	under	submarine
super-	above	supernatural
uni-	one	uniform
bi-	two	bicycle
tri-	three	tripod

and helping students understand how knowledge of its meaning can act as a powerful context clue. For example, consider *circumference, circumnavigate, circumvent,* and *circumscribe.* Tables 5.2.1 through 5.2.3 provide examples of commonly used prefixes, suffixes, and roots.

Visuals can illustrate how word meaning is intimately connected to morphology. These do not have to be complex; in fact, simple visuals or diagrams work best. Place a word containing one or more morphemes at the top of a page. Underline the specific morphemes it contains and write the meanings underneath—or, better still, ask the students to provide a meaning based on their knowledge of other words. Then, brainstorm with the class other

Table 5.2.2   Common Suffixes

Suffix	Meaning	Example
-ed	past	jumped
-ing	present	jumping
-ful	full of, like	careful
-ly	like	sadly
-ness	condition	sadness
-less	without	hairless
-tion, -ion	state of	participation
-ism	belief	egotism
-logy	science	geology
-ician	specialist	pediatrician

Table 5.2.3   Common Roots

Root	Meaning	Example
aud-	hear	audition
chron-	time	chronicle
-cide	kill	homicide
dict-	tell, say	dictate
-duct	lead	conduct
flu-	flow	fluent
-gress	step	progress
-ject	throw	project
leg-	law	legal
man-	hand	manipulate
-mit	send	omit
mort-	death	mortician
ped-	foot	pedal
-pel	drive	expel
phil-	love	philosophy
-port	carry	transport
-rupt	break	erupt
-scrib	write	inscribe
-sect	cut	dissect
-spec	look	inspect
tele-	far	telescope
-tort	twist	distort
-trac	draw	distract
-vert	turn	convert
voc-	voice	vocal

words that contain the same morpheme and meaning. Offer suggestions if students cannot provide examples on their own. Place these under the respective morpheme and discuss how the morpheme indicates word meaning. This can be an effective group activity as different groups attempt to locate words that fit a specific morpheme meaning. Of course, they may locate words where the morpheme does not retain the same meaning, but that can also act as a learning experience and lead to another diagram.

Standard 4 Visual Illustrating Word Morphology

Comm**u**n**i**c**a**te	
together with	verb ending
commune	agitate
companion	duplicate
competition	dominate

(Continued)

Standard 4 Visual Illustrating Word Morphology (Continued)

	<u>Sub</u>mers<u>ible</u>
under	adjective ending
below	

submarine	corruptible
substitute	profitable
subordinate	terrible

Standard 4 Instruction in Determining Word Meaning from Context

Define words that lack adequate passage context.
Teach students how to use context to determine word meaning.
   Author provision of a definition
   Author provision of a synonym
   Author provision of an antonym
   Author provision of examples and/or general clues to meaning
   Use of morphological context
   Use of syntactic context

Strategies for Standard 5

"Analyze the structure of texts, including how specific sentences, paragraphs, and larger portions of the text (e.g., a section, chapter, scene, or stanza) relate to each other and the whole" (CCSSO & NGA, 2010, p. 10).

Sentence Structure

Usually when individuals consider text structure, they think of the overall structure of the text. Seldom do they consider sentence structure as a key variable in comprehension. However, understanding sentence structure and how various components such as modifiers, phrases, and conjunctions interact and affect meaning is a critical factor that crosses mastery of all of the standards. If a reader does not comprehend a sentence, it seems obvious that this will negatively affect text-level understanding. Research has demonstrated a strong association between oral language skills at the sentence level and reading comprehension (Scott, 2009).

What makes sentences difficult? Sentences can contain multiple and complex noun and verb phrases as well as numerous clauses joined by conjunctions. Nouns and verbs separated by words, phrases, and relative clauses can adversely affect comprehension. Verbs can take an active or passive voice. As the difficulty level of text increases, words in sentences become longer. Apart from the unfamiliarity of the concepts, consider the sheer length of the following words from *CARA* passages: *prokaryotes, cytoskeleton, microtubules, bathymetry, annihilation, unconstitutional,* and *nullification.* High school literature, especially that written by authors from long ago, can have very long sentences. Consider this sentence by Chekhov, from the second paragraph of the story *A Problem*: "Sasha Uskov, the young man of twenty-five who was the cause of all the commotion, had arrived some time before, and by the advice of kind-hearted Ivan Markovitch, his uncle, who was taking his part, he sat meekly in the hall by the door leading to the study, and prepared himself to make an open, candid explanation." Helping students parse this sentence into segments that describe Sasha and those that describe Ivan may help them understand it. For example, "Sasha: 25 years old; caused the commotion (as yet undefined); sat in the hall, preparing to explain himself. Ivan: Sasha's kind-hearted uncle." In addition, it is a wonderful example of the use of punctuation to aid the reader in understanding this 57-word sentence.

Realizing the possible negative effect of sentence length and complexity on comprehension, authors and publishers have attempted to shorten and simplify sentence structure in textbooks. However, the standards focus on students becoming college and career ready and the texts they will be expected to read and comprehend following high school will not always be user friendly with regard to sentence length.

What can a teacher do to address sentence complexity? Teachers can help students transform or paraphrase complex sentences into everyday language (Fang, 2008). They can also show how to parse a complex sentence into its constituent parts by identifying nouns and verbs and the words that describe or modify them. They can help students pay attention to conjunctions and how they can change or enhance meaning. They can demonstrate the importance of relating clauses to their specific referents. Such activities involve rereading, which is a key component of close reading.

An effective activity that has demonstrated a positive effect on writing is sentence combining. This activity helps students both produce and comprehend complex sentences (Nagy & Townsend, 2012; Saddler, 2007). For example, consider the following from a sixth-grade *CARA* passage:

> Wegener's **theory** stated that as Pangaea broke apart, its pieces moved to different parts of Earth to form today's continents. The shape of continents was **evidence** for Wegener's ideas, but it wasn't proof.

These two sentences could be combined as follows: The shape of the continents was evidence but not proof for Wegener's theory that the continents were formed when Pangaea broke apart. Sentence combining can also work in reverse. Consider the following sentence from a middle school *CARA* passage: "The expansion of Rome's influence throughout Italy caused growing troubles between patricians and plebeians." The teacher can guide the students to analyze or parse the sentence into two key ideas: "Rome expanded its influence" and "this (expansion) caused troubles." There are many examples of generic sentence-combining exercises on the web, but we are not suggesting that disciplinary specialists take time from content lessons to teach sentence combining. This is perhaps better suited to the intervention specialist as a way of easing struggling readers into comprehension of the longer and more involved sentences they will face in grade-level text. However, disciplinary specialists can take complex sentences in the text and help students understand how sentence units can be broken apart and/or combined.

Though textbook sentences are rarely of great length even in high school, the standards offer specific recommendations for the types of text that students should be able to read (CCSSO & NGA, Appendix B, 2010). The sentence and overall text structure of many of these recommended texts are complex and lend themselves to sentence combining/parsing. For example, consider the following single sentence from Benjamin Franklin's speech, the *CARA* text chosen for evaluating middle school students' ability to meet Standard 8: "For having lived long, I have experienced many instances of being obliged by better information, or fuller consideration, to change opinions even on important subjects, which I once thought right, but found to be otherwise." Consider the number of verbs contained therein: *lived, experienced, obliged, change, thought,* and *found.* What nouns or concepts do they refer to? Who else but the content specialist should help students to make sense of this and succeeding sentences in Franklin's speech? The teacher can project the text on a Smartboard, underline the verbs, and then help students determine the nouns or pronouns that match specific verbs. Attention to sentence structure that involves rereading, teacher demonstration, and discussion can also help students understand and remember text content.

Text Structure

Literature. Understanding the structure of a text involves moving beyond individual sentences to an understanding of overall text structure. There are a variety of subgenres in literature—for example, narratives, persuasive essays, poems, and plays—and therefore many different text structures. Just as students have been taught the structure of story (Stevens, Van Meter, & Warcholak, 2010) they need to be taught the elements of each subgenre. Evidence also exists that high school students who have been taught the structures of science fiction write stories that include more elements of that subgenre (Thomas, 1995). The facilitative effect of learning the structures of text is believed to be related to both the comprehension of and the memory of the text.

Constructing story maps is a recommended classroom practice in elementary schools (Dymock, 2007). Such maps include the basic components of story: character, setting, goal, problem, events, and resolution. A basic story map is illustrated here.

Generic Story Map

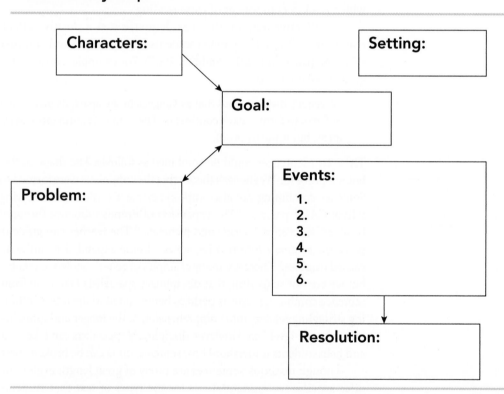

As the complexity of the stories that students read increases, so do the graphic aids that help them organize the story. Multiple-episode stories will be more complex and if the connection between the episodes is important, that relationship should be shown in the graphic.

Lesson Plan: Using a Multiple Episode Story to Teach Story Structure

Students: A group of five second graders who are having difficulty retelling a story.

Purpose: To teach students the episodic structure of folktales.

Overall Lesson Structure: This lesson represents the Reading for Meaning segment of the lesson.

Materials/Text: A well-known story, such as *The Three Little Pigs* or *Three Billy Goats Bluff; The Four Dragons,* a Chinese Folktale; and *Climbing the Mountain,* a Native American Folktale.

Explicit Review Instruction: Today we are going to examine how authors of folktales structure them. Folktales from the English language tend to have the same structure, and they are very similar to stories. Let's review what you already know about stories. What elements of story do you know? The elements listed below are the ones that should be reviewed. Use the definitions below found in Chapter 9 of *Intervention Strategies to Follow Informal Reading Inventory Assessment,* 3rd edition.

Teacher: "What is it that all stories have?"

Students: "A character"

Teacher: "Yes, and characters can be major or minor characters."

The teacher now reviews by asking what students remember and by restating the definitions of each of the story elements below.

- Character: A main character is the person or animal that the story is mostly about. This character appears more often in the story than any other. Minor characters are important to the story, but don't appear as often.
- Setting: The time and place in which a story takes place
- Goal/problem: Goal is what the main character wants. The problem is what stands in the way of the character achieving his or her goal.
- Events: What happens in the story that explains how the goal is met or the problem is solved.
- Resolution/Solution: Whether and how the goal is achieved; whether and how the problem is solved.

Explicit Instruction: What is an episode? An episode is a part of a story that relates a series of events. It usually begins with an event or action by the main character. An episode can look very different depending on the length of the story. Some stories have only two sentences in an episode and other stories have many more sentences in each episode. Let's look at a familiar story to find out what the episodes are. [Teacher should have a copy of a version of *The Three Little Pigs*.] "You all know *The Three Little Pigs*, right? How does it begin?" By showing the pictures, elicit the underlined answers below;

- Who are the main characters? <u>The Three Little Pigs</u>
- And what do they want? <u>To build houses and seek their fortunes</u>
- What happens first?
  - Episode #1: **Pig #1** <u>built house of straw. Wolf came and blew down Pig #1's house</u> because it was made of straw. Pig ran to second pig's house.
  - Episode #2: **Pig #2** <u>built house of sticks. The wolf came to the house made of sticks and blew it down too.</u> Both pigs ran to third pig's house.
  - Episode #3: And **Pig #3** <u>built his house of brick. The wolf came to Pig #3's house made of bricks and couldn't blow it down. So he went up on the roof and planned to come down the chimney.</u>
  - Episode #4: <u>The pigs built a fire in the fireplace and put a pot of water in it.</u>
- Resolution: <u>Wolf came down the chimney fell into the pot of boiling water</u> and was no more.

Guided Practice: "Now let's read longer stories and see if we can figure out where the episodes are. Remember at the end of an episode a story has been told. It may not include all of the elements of a story, but it will include main characters, setting, and an action or event."

Read *The Four Dragons* silently if the students are of similar abilities or an oral mode if necessary.

- Who are the characters? <u>Four Dragons: Long, Yellow, Black, Pearl</u>
- What is the setting? <u>Long ago on earth before lakes and rivers.</u>
- What is the problem? <u>The lack of rain on Earth so rice wouldn't grow. Goal: rain</u>
- So, what happens? <u>Dragons go to Jade Emperor to ask for rain.</u> **Beginning of E#1**

(Continued)

Lesson Plan: Using a Multiple Episode Story to Teach Story Structure (Continued)

Several events occur here

- And . . . .the dragons go back to the sea and wait for 10 days and no rain comes **End of E#1.**
- So what do the dragons do? They decide to scoop up water from the sea and send it into the sky. **(Beginning of E#2)**

Several events occur here

- And what happens? The dragons worked all day and made it rain. **End of Episode #2.**

Note that the story could end here because the goal was met. However, it doesn't.

- So, all's well, right? **Episode #3:** No, the Jade Emperor was mad that the dragons brought rain without his permission.

Several events occur here

- And what did he do? He had the dragons arrested and ordered the Mountain God to bring four mountains to lay on top of them so they couldn't escape. **End of Episode #3**
- Resolution: The dragons were imprisoned by the mountains, but they turned themselves into four rivers that flowed past high mountains. These rivers became China's four major rivers and are named after the dragons!

Note that each episode involves an action.

Day #2 (depending on class and length of time allotted)

Independent/Small group practice: To see if students can independently identify where episodes begin and end in a folktale.

Materials: *Climbing the Mountain*, a Native American folktale, and questions assessing elements of story and episodic structure (see below).

Introduction: Today I'm going to see if you can figure out where the episodes begin and end in a new folktale called *Climbing the Mountain*. Read the folktale and then we'll start the worksheet together.

- After reading: Get together with the 3–4 people around you, and you'll fill out the worksheet together.
- Using the worksheet, ask the first question. Lead discussion of the importance of the setting.

Procedures:

- Walk around the room to see what the groups are discussing. This may give you insight for what needs review.

Assessment: *Choose another folktale with several episodes, and develop questions or a story map that will guide them through the story.*

Names of group members: _____

Story Elements for *Climbing the Mountain*

What is the setting for this story and why is it important? _____
Who were the characters? _____
What was the goal? _____

How did the first episode begin? _____
How did the first episode end? _____
Describe each episode's beginning and end.
#2: _____   _____
#3: _____   _____
#4: _____   _____
#5: _____   _____
#6: _____   _____
#7: _____   _____
Resolution: _____
Moral: _____

Source: Caldwell & Leslie, *Intervention Strategies to Follow Informal Reading Inventory Assessment: So What Do I Do Now?,* Third Edition. Copyright © 2013 Pearson Education, Inc. All Rights Reserved.

Biographies also have structure and more specific information than that of a folktale or realistic fiction. A biography will have the following components in common with a generic story:

- Character (who is the biography about?)
- Setting (when and where was the person born; other important places that he/she lived before he/she became famous)
- Goals (what was the person's goal(s) and what happened that made the person choose a certain goal?)
- Problem (what problems prevented the person from reaching the goal(s) right away?)
- Events (what important events happened that led to the person becoming famous?)

In addition, a biography will include what the person is known for and what can be learned from the person's life. This final element demands an inference on the part of the reader: why did the author write about this person? A lesson plan written to develop an understanding of the structure of biographies is available in the Professional Development Toolkit that accompanies this book: *Intervention Strategies to Follow Informal Reading Inventory Assessment: So, What Do I Do Now?* (Caldwell & Leslie, 2013).

As stories become more complex, other structures come into play. Structure may no longer be canonical; stories may have flashbacks or foreshadowing. In addition, if students read literature from other cultures they will learn that not all stories are structured in familiar ways. In addition, students learn the terms *protagonist, antagonist, central conflict,* and *climax.* A graphic representing these elements can be found in the Professional Development Toolkit referred to previously. Because the *CARA* includes only narratives, we will not present teaching ideas for reading and writing persuasive essays and poetry. However, we can recommend one excellent reference on persuasive writing (Graham & Harris, 2007).

Informational Text.   Unfortunately, the overall structure of expository text is less clear cut because multiple structures exist. These include description, sequence, problem–solution, cause–effect, and comparison. Although the components of narrative structure often carry across the entire story, an expository selection can include different multiple structures. Text structure is often signaled by specific words (Caldwell & Leslie, 2013). For example, number words often suggest a sequence pattern, as do words such as *before, after, finally,* and *last.* Comparison is signaled by *alike, unlike, similar,* and *different. Because, as a result, therefore, since,* and *consequently* suggest a cause–effect pattern. Words such as *because, so that, as a result,* and *thereby* signal a problem–solution structure. In many cases, however, such explicit signal words are not present in the text and the reader has to consider the author's purpose in writing.

An author's choice of structure is often determined by his or her purpose: describing, comparing, listing steps, clarifying, or explaining causes and/or effects. Because author purpose often shapes a central idea, text structure and central idea recognition often go hand in hand. Recognition of structure can lead to a central idea statement; similarly, a central idea statement can suggest text structure.

Unfortunately, like so many things, determination of text structure is not an all-or-nothing proposition. Different readers can interpret a text as embodying different structures. For example, consider the *CARA* high school passage on Andrew Jackson's removal of Native Americans from their traditional lands. One reader may interpret the account of Cherokee removal as a sequential description of events. Another may interpret it as an issue of a problem encountered by Jackson and the solution he chose. However, this does not mean that all text segments have variable structures. In the third high school passage, the structure is clearly a comparison of Jackson's view of the bank versus his opponents' view. This suggests that when students choose a structure, they should be able to offer a valid reason for their choice based on signal words or the clear intention and purpose of the author.

There are many instructional suggestions for teaching text structure (Akhondi, Malayeri, & Samad, 2011; Moss, 2006; Neufeld, 2005; Williams and Pao, 2011). Some suggest teaching one structure at a time. But which one should it be? It should be the one in the text that you have chosen as the focus of your instruction. The formation of a graphic organizer for structure can also be an important first step in composing an effective summary. Caldwell and Leslie (2013) suggest some simple visual diagrams for fostering an understanding of structure. These are included in the discussion of summarization under Standard 2 on pages 100–108.

Standard 5 Instruction in Text Structure

Literature

    Teach the elements of story
    Teach the relationship of biography to story
    Model filling out story maps
    Have students fill out story maps
    Have students use maps to write their own stories
    Develop more graphics as the structures become more complex.

Informational text

    Teach words that signal different structures
    Use visual maps/diagrams to illustrate structure
    Ask students to offer reasons for their choice of structure, i.e., signal words
       or author's intent or purpose

Strategies for Standard 6

"Assess how point of view or purpose shapes the content and style of a text" (CCSSO & NGA, 2010, p. 10). It is important to recognize that Standard 6 is a broad interpretation of point of view. It is more than the perspective from which the story is told; rather, it is how the author uses language to convey his or her perspectives toward events and characters (historical or fictional) and how characters differ in points of view.

Teaching Point of View in Informational Text

This standard asks readers to assess how an author's point of view or purpose shaped the content and style of a text. This becomes a difficult issue when dealing with social studies and science textbooks. The purpose of such books is to teach a specific amount of content, usually interpreted as a series of facts such as the structure of a cell (science) or events connected to a specific historical period such as ancient Greece (social studies). If you ask students what is the purpose of the textbook author (and we have done this) they uniformly answer, "To teach." The author obviously chooses what to include and omit from any topic, but given the amount of space allotted to a specific topic, the most important or critical components are emphasized. The style of writing is relatively impartial. The author recounts that the Cherokee were forced to the Trail of Tears and that the U.S. government lied to the Native Americans, but words that signal approval or disapproval of such actions are missing from the text. Historians and scientists are concerned with point of view (Shanahan, 2009). However, this stance is missing in current textbooks. History texts focus on facts, what people did, and how they did it. Science is more authoritative and presents facts as not open to different interpretations.

This suggests that the teacher who intends to teach point of view in informational text needs to amass a variety of texts that present the point of view of different authors on the same topic—that is, "challenging, well crafted texts of varying views and perspectives" (Calkins et al., 2012, p. 97). Though this does not represent an impossible task, it can be a rather daunting one given the busy lives of teachers. A rich source of texts that represent different viewpoints can be found in the newspapers and magazines where sports and political columnists display very different opinions on the same general topics. Although these may be used effectively to teach point of view, they obviously are seldom connected to topics in the social studies or science curriculum. However, there are a variety of helpful websites for locating primary sources that represent different points of view and are connected to specific curricula:

- www.lib.berkeley.edu/instruct/guides/primarysources
- www.eduplace.com/ss/hmss/primary.html
- americanrhetoric.com
- www.yale.edu/collections_collaborative/primarysources/index.html

You can also find others or you can ask your students to search for them.

There is an alternative to locating texts that present different points of view of the same topic. The teacher who intends to focus on Standard 6 using his or her content textbook can recognize and discuss point of view as related to historical figures. Instead of evaluating the point of view of the author of the text, the reader identifies the point of view of the historical figures that were written about. This is a relatively straightforward process if an individual states his/her point of view as, for example, Benjamin Franklin did when offering reasons for signing the Constitution. But what if the text does not contain such an explicit statement? This requires a backward approach—that is, inferring point of view from the actions of historical figures. For example, we can infer from Andrew Jackson's decision to force the Cherokee from their tribal land that his point of view did not involve an understanding or appreciation of the Cherokee way of life. We can infer from the actions of the Northern delegates to the Constitutional Convention in agreeing to the Great Compromise that they understood the importance of maintaining the union of all 13 states. From the actions of Cleisthenes in changing the role of the Athenian assembly, we can infer his point of view regarding how a government should function. What this means for the teacher is that point of view can be taught to students by asking them to identify the actions of various individuals and working backwards to infer the point of view that motivated or drove the action. This approach is similar to determining the theme of a narrative passage in that both involve drawing an inference based on text content.

Our pilot indicated that point of view was an alien concept to many students. We suggest that defining what is meant by point of view is an important first step in instruction. Begin with what is familiar to students: sports figures, local politicians, movie and television stars, and the like. Identify and discuss specific things they said or did and model how to infer point of view from these.

Standard 6 Instruction in Point of View: Informational Text

Collect multiple texts that present the point of view of different individuals
   on the same topics; read and compare
Focus on the point of view of historical figures inferred from their action/words.
Work backwards from words and actions to point of view.

Teaching Point of View in Literature

An important judgment for a teacher to make is when to begin to teach point of view. Although the psychological literature demonstrates that preschool-age children can visually understand something from a point of view other than their own, there is no known transfer between that ability and children's understanding of point of view or perspective in literature. So, when can children read or listen to a story and be readily taught to recognize that the author had a particular point of view? The CCSS begin to assess point of view in third grade, so we will begin discussing ways to teach it at that point.

Intermediate Grades (3–5).   Helping a class create a common first-person narrative can occur when students have had some common experience. For example, students could write about a field trip, either in pairs or individually. After the stories are finished, groups of students could compare stories and discover that although they all experienced the same event, their telling of the story of the event was different. This occurs because children differ in what impressed them during the trip. This firsthand experience of discovering equally valid points of view of an event is a good segue into the concept that all writers have some point of view from which they tell a story. Because they are familiar with first-person writing (at least their own), perhaps we should use this knowledge to teach them how to identify stories written in the first person. The simple lesson tells the students to look for the word *I,* but hearing the voice of the author is more complex.

Moving from first-person writing to third-person writing could occur in a number of ways. Perhaps a beginning is helping children understand that someone tells the stories, and in contrast to the stories they wrote in the past, the author is not always the one telling the story. Authors *write* the story, yes, but they may or may not be the narrator, or the one telling the story. As in all instruction, the best way to teach a new skill is to use familiar content. The teacher could take a sample of the students' first-person stories describing the field trip and model combining them into a third-person narration of what happened. The teacher could draw the students' attention to the change in pronouns that signal the change from first person to third person.

A classic well-known fairy tale such as *The Three Little Pigs* would also be helpful to begin with because most everyone is familiar with it. Ask, who is telling the story? We should teach children that when the person telling the story is not named, the story is being told from the view of an outsider, called a *narrator*. Following the teacher's rewritten story, the students can be asked to do the same using the following guide from www.readwords.org

Kathy and Therese are very talented. Kathy has a beautiful singing voice and her teachers are always asking her to sing at assemblies or in school musicals. Therese doesn't have a good singing voice, but she is an amazing athlete. She is always the fastest runner in her class and she easily hits home runs when she plays baseball.

This paragraph is written in the _____ point of view. I will rewrite this paragraph in the _____ point of view.

_____

_____

_____

The CCSS Standard 6 description for third-grade students reads, "Distinguish their own point of view from that of the narrator or those of the characters." At fourth grade it becomes "Compare and contrast the point of view from which different stories are narrated, including the difference between first- and third-person narrations." The first line of the fourth-grade story *Grandfather's Journey* makes it clear that it is written in the first person by the grandson and the narrator is the author: "My grandfather was a young man when he left his home in Japan and went to see the world." Later in the story the author begins to talk directly about his life. "When I was a small boy, my favorite weekend was a visit to my grandfather's house." Most fourth-grade students in our pilot sample could not identify the point of view. Therefore, at the basic level students should be taught the signal words used by authors to distinguish first- from third-person point of view (see Table 5.2.4).

Middle School.   Standard 6 becomes more complex by sixth grade and requires close reading and attention to the author's language. It states, "explain how an author develops the point of view of the narrator or speaker in a text." A response to a question that taps this standard requires the student to examine how the author builds the narrator's point of view over the entire text. For example, in *The Wounded Wolf*, the narrator describes the wolf as weak because of lack of food during the late winter and shows his futile attempts to signal his pack that he is badly injured. Later in the story, she describes how other animals anticipate the wolf's death and surround him to pick at his wounds as he struggles to find

Table 5.2.4   Definitions and Examples of Points of View

Point of View	Pronouns Used	Example
First person: The narrator is a character in his/her own story.	I, me, my, mine, we, ours	I can still remember the taste of my grandma's chili.
Third person limited: The narrator is not a character in the story but observes what is happening.	he, his, him, she, hers, her, they, theirs	Jake can still remember the taste of his grandma's chili.
Third person omniscient: The narrator is not a character in the story but observes what is happening and knows the thoughts and feelings of the characters.	he, his, him, she, hers, her, they, theirs	Jake can still remember the taste of his grandma's chili and thought to himself he'd like to have a big bowl right now.

shelter. The author uses this vivid description of the events to signal to the reader her sympathy with the wolf. Therefore, teaching point of view at the sixth-grade level requires that the teacher first model how to find clues in the text that suggest the author's point of view and underline them. This involves looking at the words the author uses to describe a character, and using them to determine the author's point of view toward that character. An example of a teaching idea from www.readworks.org that uses *The House on Mango Street* is shown in Table 5.2.4.

Middle school teachers agree that one of the most important aspects of teaching point of view is finding short stories that excite the reader. A list of such stories can be found in Campbell (2007, p. 71). Other books recommended on the www.readworks.org website include: *The White Umbrella* (Gish, 1984), *Hamadi* (Shihab Nye, 1999), and *America Street: A Multicultural Anthology of Stories* (Mazer, 1993).

Even in middle school the use of children's picture books, especially *The True Story of the Three Little Pigs,* is recommended as a way to teach point of view (Campbell, 2007). Because the original story is so well-known to most students, *The True Story of the Three Little Pigs* can be used to show the point of view of the wolf. First, the teacher can read the title and the author. Right away the students recognize that the wolf is telling this story. One aspect of point of view at the upper level is to examine the reliability of the narrator. Reliability is considered important because "the moral and intellectual qualities of the narrator are more important to our judgment than whether the narrator is referred to as 'I' or 'she'" (Booth, 1983). If the narrator is discovered to be untrustworthy, then the total effect of the story is changed. In the case of *The True Story of the Three Little Pigs,* the question is, does the wolf have too much self-interest in the telling of the story to be a reliable narrator?

Point of view becomes even more complex in eighth grade, where students must "analyze how differences in the points of view of the characters and the audience or reader create effects such as suspense or humor." As described earlier, teachers should model looking for words in the text that indicate an author's point of view. An excellent example of how different points of view between the narrator and the reader create suspense comes from *The Tell Tale Heart.* Poe writes this story from the point of view of the main character/narrator, who is trying to convince the reader that he is not crazy. First, he tells us that he is dreadfully nervous, hears "all things in the heaven and in the earth. I heard many things in hell." Nevertheless, at the same time he tries to explain how carefully he planned a killing. "You should have seen how wisely I proceeded—with what caution—with such foresight . . ." In addition, his behavior each night leading up to the killing is extremely detailed. Poe describes the narrator's behavior to lead the reader to think that the man is mad—after all, he plans to kill someone he loves because the old man's eye looked strange. In addition, the narrator protests too much; he tries too hard to convince the reader that he isn't mad and in doing provides support for the opposite conclusion. Similarly, when the police are in the house after the killing, Poe describes the narrator as secure in his belief that he won't be caught: "for what had I to fear?" And later, "while I myself, in the wild audacity of my perfect triumph, placed my own seat upon the very spot beneath which reposed the corpse of the victim." These quotations signify the narrator's belief in himself, but suspense builds because the reader knows he's done the deed and wonders whether the police will figure it out. Teachers will need to model for students how to identify evidence that the man is crazy and also identify the opposing aspects of the personality that Poe presents.

High School.   Literary fiction is marked by its indirectness; that is, the author has an idea or belief about some facet of life that is indirectly told within the story. The author of literary fiction never comes out and says, for example, "I believe that the treatment of the Japanese in the United States during WWII was inhumane"; rather they will present a story of how the Japanese lived in internment camps in the United States during WWII, so as to lead the reader to the same conclusion. Literary fiction is in contrast to popular fiction, where the purpose is to tell a good story or to entertain the reader. Students are used to reading popular fiction and will need to be taught how to read literary fiction in such a way as to "get" the author's point of view. One component of analyzing point of view involves a determination of the reliability of the narrator. The reliability of the narrator is judged by considering the following questions (Smith & Wilhelm, 2010, p. 117):

1. Is the narrator too self-interested to be reliable?
2. Is the narrator sufficiently experienced to be reliable?
3. Is the narrator sufficiently knowledgeable to be reliable?
4. Is the narrator sufficiently moral to be reliable?
5. Is the narrator sufficiently emotionally balanced to be reliable?

Toni Cade Bambara provides an example of a narrator that meets many, but perhaps not all of the above criteria, in the *CARA* high school story, *Blues Ain't No Mockin Bird*. The story takes place in the Southern part of the United States in a time when black people were not considered equal to whites (at least by the whites). The narrator tells the story from the view of a black person. It illustrates that view through dialect, but more importantly by how one black family, especially the mother, was treated by white men employed by the county. For example, when the men tell Granny that they are filming for the county, they ask, "Mind if we shoot a bit around here?" But when Granny replies, "I do indeed," the man keeps taking pictures. And when Granny asks him to "shut that machine off," he points the camera at her and says, "Now, aunty." Granny retorts, "Your mamma and I are not related." There are many other examples of such treatment, but how should the narrator be evaluated?

When we ask, "Is the narrator experienced and knowledgeable about the likelihood of the events in the story?" we need to know the history of the time. It has been well documented that blacks were treated unequally to whites, so it is likely that the narrator qualifies as experienced and knowledgeable. We may assume the narrator to be the author, Toni Cade Bambara, who is African American and shows her identification with that culture by choosing the name Bambara, the African tribe known for its textiles. She takes the name after finding it in a sketchbook belonging to her great-grandmother. Bambara lived between 1939 and 1995, so she likely observed or experienced firsthand the type of events in the story. The only reliability question that might be of concern is the first one: is she too self-interested to be reliable? People with different views of African Americans might judge this differently, but we would say she is not too self-interested to be reliable.

As with middle school, students can read short stories to learn about how an author crafts point of view. The Bright Hub Education website (www.brighthubeducation.com/high-school-english-lessons/41476-short-stories-to-teach-point-of-view/#sthash.Hth9KwQI.dpuf) includes a list of short stories that are recommended for teaching point of view:

Contents of the Dead Man's Pocket by Jack Finney
The Secret Life of Walter Mitty by James Thurber
The Scarlet Ibis by James Hurst
The Cask of Amontillado by Edgar Allen Poe
The Celebrated Jumping Frog of Calaveras County by Mark Twain

An extension of the point of view standard is found at the high school level. At this level, the student must analyze a point of view reflected in a work of literature from outside the United States, drawing on a wide view of world literature. Literature anthologies of the future will include units that illustrate how to identify the point of view of cultures other than our own. Teaching point of view is very complex and has many dimensions. It is a perspective that readers will examine their entire literary lives.

Standard 6: Instruction in Point of View: Narrative

Begin with personal narratives
Extend to narratives of common experience
Model changing a third-person narrative into a first-person narrative
Teach signal words that indicate first person vs third person narratives
Model how to find clues in the text that suggest the author's point of view
Read stories from diverse view points

Strategies for Standard 8

"Delineate and evaluate the argument and specific claims in a text including the validity of the reasoning as well as the relevance and sufficiency of the evidence" (CCSSO & NGA, 2010, p. 10).

The informational passages that comprised the *CARA* did not contain arguments and claims that were open to evaluation with regard to their relevance and validity. As mentioned previously, informational text in social studies and science textbooks takes an authoritative stance, especially science. In social studies, text content primarily takes the form of event narration (e.g., the deliberations of the Constitutional Convention, the rise of labor unions, the fall of Rome, etc.). Seldom is the point of view or the stance of the textbook author evident. The student is expected to learn the content, not evaluate its validity. The *CARA* passages taken from typical middle and high school social studies and science textbooks clearly followed this pattern.

For this reason, we included additional social studies passages at the middle school and high school levels. These included original sources that presented an individual's arguments or reasons for taking a specific stance; all were conceptually associated with a specific *CARA* passage. These included Jackson's State of the Nation Address, which presented his reasons why the Electoral College should not elect a president in opposition to the popular vote (Election of 1824); arguments presented by the Corinthians for declaring war on Athens (Conflict in the Greek World) and Franklin's reasons for urging delegates to sign the Constitution (The Constitutional Convention). Students were asked to identify two (middle school) or four (high school) of the author's arguments and explain why they were or were not valid.

Piloting indicated that student ability to accurately identify an argument was heavily dependent on two things: the difficulty level of the passage and the student's writing ability. Students were less successful with passages that contained long and complex sentences, multiple examples of archaic language, and many unfamiliar words, such as James Madison's letter to Thomas Jefferson and Henry Clay's speech regarding Andrew Jackson's veto of the Bank of the United States. Writing ability played a significant part. Some students underlined the relevant arguments and/or wrote them verbatim on the test sheet; it was quite easy to judge the accuracy of such answers. However, many students chose to paraphrase an argument, usually in briefer terms, and it was not always possible to understand what they wrote or to match it with a relevant argument.

Standard 8 for informational text asks the reader to move beyond comprehending information to analyzing "the trustworthiness of the supports that the author provides for his or her claims and the soundness of the logic that links the supports to the claims" (Calkins et al., 2012, p. 87). The issue is not whether students agree or disagree with the author's ideas; the issue is "to trace the argument the author made and to assess its validity" (Calkins et al., 2012, p. 87). Our pilot students met with little success when asked to do this. It was impossible to determine if this was due to lack of comprehension of the text, poor understanding of what validity entails, or inability to clearly communicate one's ideas through writing. This suggests several avenues for instruction.

Understanding Complex Text

Consider what you do when faced with complex text. We refer to the type of text that, after reading, leaves you with the question, "now, what was that all about?" You probably break the text into smaller segments. Obviously you reread each segment multiple times. You may also highlight and/or annotate the text or take notes in a format that has worked for you in the past. You identify what you did not understand and probably write questions about what you need to know. Perhaps most importantly, you expect that arriving at an understanding of this text will require an extensive amount of time; in other words, it will not be a quick fix. In summary, you engage in close reading of the text.

The same strategies that you engaged in are those that you need to model and teach to your students. Rereading can take a variety of forms, as we described in an earlier segment on read-alouds. We also described other strategies that could be applied, such as close reading, graphic note taking, and use of context to determine the meanings of unfamiliar words. As previously mentioned, transforming or paraphrasing complex sentences into everyday language can make arcane texts more manageable. Parsing complex sentences into constituent parts by identifying nouns, verbs, and the words that describe or modify them can do the same (Fang, 2008). We particularly recommend the instructional use of sentence combining for dealing with the often long and complex sentences contained in primary source material. You can divide the sentence into its constituent parts and help the students combine them (Perin, 2007; Saddler, 2007) or you can guide the students to break apart a long sentence beginning with nouns and verbs and gradually identifying and adding words and phrases that modify them. You may also have to review punctuation. Commas and semicolons are often used to join multiple sentences. Consider Benjamin Franklin's speech to the Constitutional Convention. His first sentence contains nine commas and one semicolon!

Instructional Suggestions for Dealing with Complex Text

Engage in rereading
Engage in close reading
Use graphic note-taking
Break apart complex sentences; identify nouns and verbs
Use sentence combining; break apart complex sentences and have students
   combine them
Review punctuation

The Concept of Validity

Funk & Wagnalls New International Dictionary of the English Language (1997) defines validity as "soundness in reasoning" (p. 1386). Something that is valid is logical and can be supported. This suggests that instructing students on how to judge the validity of someone else's argument involves more than just stating one's personal opinion.

The standards require that "students understand what the author says and be able to defend their opinions and ideas with evidence from the text" (Fisher et al., 2012, p. 108). Standard 8 asks students to evaluate the validity, relevance, and sufficiency of text evidence, which often involves evidence external to the text, including the opinions and actions of others, historical events, and specific contexts that influence behavior. For example, historians evaluate a text based on the source of text information and when the text was written, whereas scientists focus on the match of text contents with present scientific evidence (Shanahan et al., 2011).

The performance of middle school students in our pilot strongly suggested that students have had little experience in dealing with a variety of arguments and in judging their validity. Many of our pilot students offered their opinion of why a specific argument was or was not valid without any explanation or evidence for their reasoning or any reference to a supportive source. We suggest that a judgment of validity requires an explanation for why one holds an opinion and/or support from an external source such as the ideas and/or actions of others.

Evaluating the arguments and claims in a text may require knowledge that is not actually present in the text, a position somewhat contradictory to the text-based emphasis of the standards. For example, understanding Xenophon's criticism of Athenian government depends on one's understanding of the relationship between aristocrats and commoners in ancient societies. Evaluating the validity of Tacitus's position on Tiberius Caesar involves some knowledge of the customs of ancient Rome. This suggests that brief but relevant frontloading on your part might be helpful. For example, you can preface the discussion of Xenophon's arguments by explaining that the ancient aristocrats actually believed themselves to be a higher form of being compared to commoners, much as many Southern slave owners felt about their slaves. You can explain that heads of ancient governments often gained power by force and other dubious methods as a preface to dialogue about the validity of Tiberius's actions.

In the absence of frontloading and without the presence of supportive information in the text, students can only judge the validity of claims and arguments based on what they do know. It is reasonable to expect that such judgments will be heavily based on the society in which they live. What is important with regard to Standard 8 is that students realize that they need to offer an explanation or reason for their opinion, unlike the majority of pilot students, who simply said what they thought with no accompanying explanation. At a somewhat more relaxed level, simply asking students to defend their opinions with the simple questions "Why do you think so" or "Why do you believe that" can foster understanding that opinions need to be supported.

Guiding students to understand that an opinion should be supported with some form of external evidence is not an easy task. Like all of us, students offer many opinions about many things with little explanation or rationale for what they say. You may wish to begin with everyday situations such as opinions about sports or entertainment figures, popular events like the Olympics, common but somewhat controversial activities like hunting, or current political issues such as immigration. Ask student to state their opinion and then have them locate support for that opinion. You may even divide the class into two groups and ask them to locate evidence for disparate opinions on the same topic. Given the vast wealth of information on the web, students can collect an amazing amount of information. Then they need to examine the value of that information. Using primary sources can also be an effective instructional tool. As mentioned previously, these are easily accessible from the web.

Four acts can help students assess the validity of primary source materials (or any materials, for that matter): identification, attribution, judging perspective, and assessing reliability (Morgan & Rasinski, 2012). These acts are not necessarily separate or sequential in nature. The teacher can use one or all to direct students' attention to identifying arguments and judging their validity. Identifying the type of source helps students understand what one can expect while reading it. Is the source a diary, a history, a public comment in a newspaper, an attempt to change an individuals' point of view? For example, the primary source associated with the *CARA* passage on the Constitutional Convention was Benjamin Franklin's speech urging delegates to sign the Constitution. The primary source associated with *Debating the Constitution* was an Antifederalist opinion piece written for a newspaper. The primary source for the passage on the Bill of Rights was a private letter written by James Madison to Thomas Jefferson. How might these differ with regard to purpose and style?

Attribution involves considering the context in which the text was written. The previous examples were written during the contentious process of debating and ratifying the Constitution. How is the language different in each one? What type of examples are offered? For example, Madison uses rather neutral language for liking and not liking a Bill of Rights. The author of the newspaper article, however, employs exaggeration and threat to convince readers of the evils of an elected president. Franklin prefaces his hope that the delegates would sign the Constitution by cleverly complimenting them on producing a "near perfect document." How does this affect your opinion of the validity of what each author said? Engaging in close reading of the three documents involves asking questions: What is the author trying to accomplish? Why did the author say what he did? Why did he choose particular words?

Judging perspective focuses on how the author's purpose shaped the way in which the document was written. The primary source attached to the *CARA* passage on the Roman Republic was Suetonius's account of Julius Caesar's death. One can infer from his description of omens that preceded Caesar's death, the behavior of the populace at his cremation, and the appearance of comets that he thought Caesar was a great man, if not a god. Contrast this with Tacitus's description of the reign of Tiberius and how he achieved power. Pay attention to the different words used to describe Julius Caesar and Tiberius Caesar. What were the authors attempting to accomplish?

The final act is that of reliability assessment. Is there corroborating evidence and/or information? Is the author's position a valid one? Why or why not? Where could one find more information? "Students must learn to seek out additional sources to support tentative conclusions about what they think they know" (Morgan & Rasinski, 2012, p. 589).

Evaluating the Validity of Primary Sources (Morgan & Rasinski, 2012)

Identification:	Identify the type of source
Attribution :	Consider the context
Perspective:	Identify the author's purpose
Reliability:	Consider corroborating evidence and information

Communication Through Writing

Writing to meet the demands of Standard 8 is purposeful. Throughout the piloting of the *CARA,* we were often concerned about students' ability to express themselves clearly and in writing. It was not because of spelling, punctuation, and other composition mechanics. Sentence structure was often disorganized. Incomplete and run-on sentences were common. Sentences were not logically connected by explanatory conjunctions and/or phrases. This was evident at all grade levels in answers to constructed-response questions, Standard 2 summaries, and opinions of validity on the Standard 8 passages.

The standards place "a tremendous emphasis on writing." They focus on opinion/argument writing, informational writing, and narrative writing and call for "extremely high levels of proficiency" (Calkins et al., 2012, pp. 102, 107). Simply put, students are expected to write often, across all disciplines, and for clearly defined purposes. Students must learn to clearly describe an argument, evaluate its validity, and coherently describe supporting evidence. Reasoning and writing go hand in hand. Monte-Sano and De La Paz (2012) found that writing facilitated students' overall historical reasoning and "that writing prompts focused on sourcing, corroborations of documents, and causation are more likely to elicit adolescents' attention to historical perspectives than prompts that ask students to imagine themselves as historical agents" (p. 290).

Summary

In this chapter, specific instructional recommendations for each of the standards measured by the *CARA* are provided. Teaching students to answer questions related to Standards 1, 2, 3, 4, and 6 are discussed for literature. In social studies, instructional recommendations are made related to Standards 1 through 6 and 8. Finally, recommendations for teaching science are provided for Standards 1, 2, 3, 4, and 5. Recall that Standard 9 was not addressed in any content area because it involves reading multiple texts, which is beyond the scope of the *CARA.*

Chapter 6

Challenges in the Development of the *CARA*

Development of Questions Allied to the Common Core State Standards

Which Standards?

We were faced with a choice when designing questions in science and social studies: should they be based on the Reading Standards for Informational Text (K–5, 6–12); or based on the Standards for Literacy in History/Social Studies, Science, and Technical Subjects? We chose the Reading Standards for Informational Text for two reasons. First, they provided a continuum of development for grades 4 through 12, which is the intent and the scope of our instrument. Second, the *CARA* is primarily a reading assessment, not an assessment of content knowledge specified by standards.

What Taxonomy Should Guide Question Development?

The cognitive demands of questions can be distinguished by what the student is asked to do in order to answer them, the nature of the information demanded by the question, and where the answer may be found (Graesser, Ozuru, & Sullins, 2010). A student may answer a question incorrectly because of three possible causes.

1. The text may be too difficult either because of a student's reading level or the conceptual difficulty of the text.
2. A student may not understand the question stem; they may not know what *analyze* entails or what a *theme* is. For example, our pilot data suggested that many students did not understand the meaning of *point of view* or *development of the plot*.
3. A student may lack the critical-thinking skills that the standards demand. For example, the student may not be able to determine a word's meaning by using word, sentence, and passage context.

Unfortunately, it is not possible to identify which of these might be responsible for an erroneous answer except discussion with individual students. This suggests that explanation of question stems and a focus on critical thinking should be an integral part of instruction based on the standards.

There is no dearth of suggestions and examples for composing questions at various levels of complexity and in different disciplines (Buehl, 2011; Fisher, Frey, & Lapp, 2012). However, the most important criterion for us was the relationship of each question to a particular Common Core State Standard. *CARA* questions were designed to address the specific cognitive activity demanded by each standard. If a teacher is to use the *CARA* to assess students' understanding of and ability to meet a particular standard, questions designed to assess one standard must be different from questions designed to measure other standards. To be specific, Standard 4 questions, designed to measure the ability to determine a word's meaning from context, must be clearly different from questions designed to assess Standard 5, understanding text structure. In addition, this differentiation must be consistent across levels of text. That is, Standard 4 questions for all levels must maintain a basic similarity. The *CARA* questions are relatively uniform across standards and texts, so a teacher will be able to compare a student's performance on one passage with later performance on a different passage at the same level.

Formulating questions that are closely aligned to the CCSS was not an easy task and we suspect that teachers and textbook authors will also find it difficult. Each standard begins with a main verb (e.g., *explain, determine, analyze*) and then describes in detail how that verb should be applied to the text. For example, in informational text, the primary question stem for Standard 2 is: *Determine a central idea of a text.* Though the primary question stem applies to almost any informational text, the additional information contained in a standard is different at each grade level. For example, the additional information added to the stem for grade 4 is "explain how it is supported by key details" (CCSSO & NGA, 2010, p. 14). At grades 9–10 the stem is further explained by the following: "analyze its development over the course of the text including how it emerges and is shaped or refined by specific details" (p. 40). The requirements for levels 11–12 are as follows: "determine two or more central ideas of a text and analyze their development over the course of the text including how they interact and build on one another to provide a complete analysis" (p. 40). However, middle and high school textbooks in science and social studies do not always provide texts supportive of standard demands. This suggests that teachers, who are often constrained to a specific district-imposed text, may have to adapt standards-based questions to textbook contents or select additional classroom material that provides a better match.

Not Any Text Will Do

The Common Core State Anchor Standards are general guidelines; however, they become specific when they are applied over the grade levels. Some passages provide an opportunity to assess a student's ability to meet a specific standard at the level of detail contained in the grade-level standard; other texts may not. For example, for fourth-grade literature, Standard 6 states: "compare and contrast the point of view from which different stories are narrated, including the difference between first- and third-person narrations" (CCSSO & NGA, 2010, p. 12). Because, in the interest of time and text length, we used a single text rather than multiple texts, ideally each text needed to include both first- and third-person narratives. Unfortunately we couldn't find a story like that so we used one story, *Grandfather's Journey*, that was written in first person, and the other fourth-grade stories were third-person narratives, like most stories in the fourth-grade basal text. We asked students to identify the point of view from which *Grandfather's Journey* was written and how students knew that. On the third person narratives, we designed questions to ask how the author illustrated a point of view in the story.

As this example illustrates, the author of the questions is limited by the contents of a text; therefore, it is not always possible to address the additional information included in each grade-level standard. In order to address some standards at some levels, multiple texts that offer different viewpoints are required. Although it is impossible to address all the specific and explanatory information addressed in each standard, it is possible to assess a student's ability to answer questions based on the anchor standard. One can assume that the basic ability required to meet each standard—for example, an ability to explain or analyze— are the first and requisite steps to determining standard mastery.

We chose to match the *CARA* question stems as closely as possible to the wording of the anchor standards for literature and informational text. The following delineates our rationale for the wording of each question, how it is specifically tied to a standard, and explanations of additional design issues. Although the standards for literature are similar to those for informational text, there are critical differences. For that reason, we have described the match of *CARA* questions to the standards separately for literature and informational text. Following the description of how we wrote questions to match each standard, we present the results of how our students in our pilot studies performed. It is important to remember that although we have data on how our questions performed, that does not imply that the *CARA* should be used like a standardized test. The *CARA* is formative; it gives the teacher an idea of how students perform on a sample of questions designed to meet the standards. Each standard is measured by three questions, at most. Therefore, the *CARA* cannot assess students' precise ability to write responses to standards-based questions. Rather, the results of the *CARA* can be used to suggest areas where teachers should develop similar kinds of questions from texts used in the classroom for further assessment of student performance.

Match of *CARA* Questions to Reading Standards for Literature Text

Table 6.1 presents the mean proportion correct on each story for each standard by grade level. Beneath the means we have indicated whether the difference among the means is significant or not.

The grand means at the bottom of Table 6.1 illustrate that students found point of view the most difficult of the standards. Standards 1 through 4 were similar in difficulty.

Standard 1

Standard 1 from the fourth-grade level through high school requires students to quote or cite evidence of what the text says explicitly, as well as when inferences are drawn. The *CARA* question stems are as follows:

- Using details from the story, provide evidence . . . (grades 4–6)
- Describe the evidence that . . . *or* What evidence in the text most strongly . . . (middle and high school)

We phrased questions designed to measure Standard 1 in the form of an inference. Instead of asking the student to draw a text-based inference, we provided an inference and asked the student to identify explicit textual support for it. There were several reasons for doing this. Formulating inferences is heavily dependent on the nature of the text (Vidal-Abarca, Martinez, & Gilabert, 2000). A coherent text allows the reader to draw inferences with greater ease than a less coherent passage. By providing an inference to the student and asking for identification of text support, we somewhat negate the influence of less coherent text on a student's answer. Second, finding textual support helps maintain reliability in correcting constructed-response questions. If students are asked to draw inferences on their own, a large variety of inferences may be offered. The individual who scores such items would first have to evaluate the validity of the inference (which may involve a fair amount of ambiguity) and then determine if it is suitably supported by the text. By providing an acceptable inference and asking for identification of textual support, we have provided teachers with a more reliable and somewhat easier scoring task. Third, we believe that the ability to find explicit textual support for an inference meets the intent of the standard. Our teacher reviewers at all levels unanimously agreed with us in this respect. We also suspect that finding explicit text to support an inference may be the first step to actually understanding the nature of an inference and may lend itself to instruction.

Table 6.1 Mean Proportion Correct on Each Literature Text and Each Standard by Grade

Grade Level	Standard 1	Standard 2	Standard 3	Standard 4	Standard 6	Standard 7
4	.43, .30, .53 No significant difference	.26, .39, .41 No significant difference	.55, .51, .71 No significant difference	.30, .56, .43 2 = 3 > 1	.48, .22, .39 1 > 2	.65, .49, .62 No significant difference
5	.49, .44, .31 1 = 2 > 3	.54, .63, .32 1 = 2 > 3	.59, .54, .22 1 = 2 > 3	.70, .64, .23 1 = 2 > 3	.36, .16, .20 1 = 2 > 3	.55, .62, .59 No significant difference
6	.39, .70, .33 2 > 1 = 3	.79, .50, .33 No significant difference	.44, .44, .25 No significant difference	.70, .64, .23 1 = 2 > 3	.36, .16, .20 1 > 2	NA
7	.66, .63, .64 No significant difference	.52, .51, .70 No significant difference	.98, .38, .61 1 > 3 > 2	.48, .51, .88 3 > 1	.61, .55, .50 No significant difference	NA
8	.39, .56, .80 3 > 2 > 1	.45, .53, .36 No significant difference	.60, .38, .29 1 > 2 = 3	.47, .49, .63 3 > 1 = 2	.40, .39, .40 No significant difference	NA
9	.56, .24, .31 1 > 2 = 3	.25, .34, .40 No significant difference	.20, .46, .28 2 > 1 = 3	.47, .46, .43 No significant difference	NA	NA
Grand mean	.51	.48	.50	.52	.38	NA

Note: The first mean proportion correct is from the first story in our listing at that grade level, the second mean is for the second story, etc. For example, at grade 4, under Standard 1, the mean of .08 refers to Story 1, *Amelia and Eleanor,* .30 refers to Story 2, *Encyclopedia Brown,* and .53 refers to Story 3, *Grandfather's Journey.* See Chapter 3 for a list of passages used at each grade level.

Pilot Study Results

Performance on Standard 1 on each text was based on two or three questions, depending on the text. As Table 6.1 illustrates, differences in difficulty in answering Standard 1 questions among stories at each grade level (except seventh grade) were common. Several features of the stories may explain why some questions were more difficult than others. First, to answer some questions, students needed to read very closely and/or reread sections to answer correctly. For example, in the fifth-grade story *Journey to the Center of the Earth,* the first question was, "Using details from the story, explain why the men thought that there were several animals in the water." To answer this question, students would need to go back to the preceding paragraph and examine the different clues that make the men believe there were many animals. This kind of close reading is likely unfamiliar to fifth graders.

At the upper-grade levels the differences in difficulty were likely because of how directly the text cued the answer. Students' ability to cite text evidence to support an inference was based on how directly the text provides the necessary cues and the complexity of interpretation that is required. At the eighth-grade level, questions designed to measure Standard 1 on *The Story-Teller* were directly cued by the text. In contrast, both Standard 1 questions on *The Tell Tale Heart* required that the students reread segments of the text and use general offhand cues in the text to answer the question correctly. For example, a directly cued Standard 1 question from *The Story-Teller* was, "Cite the evidence that most strongly suggests that the man is getting disturbed." In the paragraphs preceding this question the following cues were given: "The frown on the bachelor's face was deepening to a scowl" and "the bachelor had looked twice at her and once at the communication cord." In contrast, in *The Tell Tale Heart,* a question was, "Describe the evidence that most strongly suggests that the narrator is crazy." There were three paragraphs that provided information to answer the question. However, the question requires an interpretation of the narrator's description of himself, his attempt to convince the reader that he was not crazy, and his plan to kill the old man because of his strange eye.

Standard 2

Standard 2 across all levels requires students to determine a theme or central idea of the text and to write a text-based summary. The *CARA* question stems are as follows:

- What is the theme or message of the story? (grades 4–5)
- What is the theme or message of the story and provide details that show this (grade 6)
- What is the theme of the story and provide evidence of . . . (middle and high school)
- Summarize the story (grade 4 through high school)

At grades 4 through 6, the term *message* of the story was included so that students who had not specifically been taught the word *theme* would be able to understand the question. The terminology used in questions always presents a challenge to assessment designers. Teachers of younger students may use the term *message* or *lesson* to describe the concept of theme. Therefore, if only the term *theme* was used, a student who did not know this term might not answer a question correctly, but would have been able to answer the question if the term *message* was used. Students were also asked to summarize the stories.

Pilot Study Results

Performance on Standard 2 was usually based on one question (What is the theme or message in this story?); therefore, student performance on theme questions should be examined in other texts. However, as Table 6.1 indicates, the mean proportion correct on all stories at each grade level, except fifth, were not statistically different from each other. In the third text for fifth grade, *Journey to the Center of the Earth,* the theme was far more abstract. Students at this age have likely not read and analyzed stories where man is challenged by nature, a

Table 6.2   Mean Proportion of Story Elements Contained in Students' Summaries by Grade Level and Story

Grade Level	Story 1	Story 2	Story 3	Significant Differences	Grand Mean
4	.37	.45	.41	None	.41
5	.19	.37	.29	None	.28
6	.39	.48	.65	Story 3 greater than Story 1	.51
7	.55	.42	.65	Story 3 greater than Story 2	.54
8	.43	.38	.49	None	.43
9	.44	.35	.42	None	.40

theme that becomes common in higher-level texts. The difference among fifth-grade stories illustrates how stories within a basal reader or literature anthology differ in many ways and, therefore, making comparisons of students' ability across texts should be done with caution.

The performance on literature summaries was examined by averaging the proportion of elements of a story included in students' summaries. The data were converted to proportions to allow comparisons across grade levels because the numbers of elements varied in each story. Table 6.2 presents the mean proportion of story elements contained in students' written summaries of the three texts according to grade level.

An examination of the means in Table 6.2 suggest that students improved in their ability to write a summary of a story over the grades, but this ability fell when the length and complexity of the stories increased. Overall, it appears that students improve in their inclusion of story elements from grades 4 and 5 to grades 6 and 7, and drops again at grades 8 and 9. The lack of a developmental progression could be due to differences in the samples of students in these grades or represent an increase in the complexity of the stories in grades 8 and 9. To test the hypothesis of sample differences we examined only the data from one school that had students read all of the literature texts. The pattern of the data was the same as that presented in Table 6.2, suggesting a true developmental pattern.

Standard 3

Standard 3 at all levels requires students to describe, explain, or analyze some element of the story (e.g., character, setting, events, and/or plot). The *CARA* question stems are as follows:

- Describe or compare and contrast . . . (grades 4–6)
- Analyze how or why or how does . . . (middle and high school)

Describe, explain, and *analyze* are somewhat ambiguous terms. The use of *describe or compare/contrast* for grades 4 through 6 and *analyze* for middle and high school suggests that authors of the Common Core regard analysis as a more complex activity. Whether the cognitive processes used in analysis are tapped by the word *analyze* is highly debatable. Fortunately, additional information at each grade level offers specific directions for how explanation and analysis should occur. For example, at grade 6, Standard 3 asks the student to describe how a story's plot unfolds in a series of episodes, as well as how the character responds or changes as the plot moves toward a resolution. This requires the student not only to describe the plot, but also to identify how it developed and how the character responded or changed. A question designed to measure Standard 3 from a sixth-grade literature selection is, "Describe how Coyote's behavior has changed from the beginning of the story until now."

At Grade 8, the term *analyze* is used, but the task required of the student is quite similar. The Standard reads, "analyze how particular lines of dialog or incidents in the story propel the action, reveal aspects of a character, or provoke a decision" (CCSSO & NGA, 2010, p. 36). A question designed to measure Standard 3 from an eighth-grade literature selection focused on the use of dialogue. It was written as, "Analyze <u>what</u> the general believes about the war and <u>why</u> he feels that way, using words from the text." Another question designed to measure Standard 3 from an eighth-grade literature selection focused on an incident in the story: "How does the narrator's behavior, described in the two preceding paragraphs, reveal his beliefs about himself?"

Pilot Study Results

Standard 3 was measured by at least two questions. It appears that the common requirement is for the student to understand a writer's craft—specifically, how the author constructed elements of the plot and how characters changed because of certain events. It is clear that students have to do more than read the text; he or she must study and analyze it to recognize how the author constructed the story. The ability to do this varies with the content of the stories. Significant differences occurred among all stories at each grade level except at grades 4 and 6. Therefore, like Standard 1, teachers should be careful in ascribing differences in ability to explain or analyze how a story develops or how characters change during a story based on their reading of one story. Questions that included the word *describe* (a word used by the standards) were easier than those that asked the students to compare and/or contrast how one element of the story related to another. This finding suggests that teachers use the *CARA* to discuss the relationship of words in the question to the cognitive processes that they should use to answer the questions.

At eighth grade, most questions designed to measure Standard 3 were phrased the same way: "Analyze how _____ moves the plot along." Despite that similarity, student performance on the questions on *The Tell Tale Heart* was higher than on the other stories. Such differences can be explained by how directly the words in the story cue the reader to make the connection.

The term *plot* was introduced to the questions designed to assess Standard 3 at grade 6. Our pilot data suggest that performance at grade 6 was very similar to grade 5, where the term *plot* was not mentioned.

Standard 4

Standard 4 requires students to determine the meaning of words and phrases within the context of the text. The *CARA* question stems are as follows:

- What does _____ mean in the sentence . . .? (grade 4 through high school)
- What does the phrase _____ mean in the sentence . . .? (grade 4 through high school)

Beginning at grade 5, the student is asked to interpret figurative language such as metaphors and similes. At grade 6, the effect of word choice on meaning and tone is added to the basic question stem. Finally, at grades 9/10 the student is required to analyze the cumulative impact of a specific word choice on meaning and tone.

We chose several criteria to guide us in selecting the words or phrases to be included to measure this standard. First, beginning at grade 5, any word or phrase used figuratively was a primary candidate for selection. For example, in the sixth-grade text *The Wounded Wolf*, the author describes the setting: "He limps in blinding whiteness now. A ghostly presence flits around. 'Hahahahaha,' the white fox states—death is coming to the Ridge." The question written to assess Standard 4 is, "What does the phrase 'a ghostly presence flits around' mean?"

If no word or phrase was used figuratively, then we examined how important the word or phrase was in the text. When a word was related to the theme of the story and no other word was used figuratively, then the thematic word was chosen. For example, in the same sixth-grade story it says, "Gravely injured, Roko pulls himself toward the shelter rock. Weakness overcomes him and he stops." The question asks, "What does the word *gravely* mean in this sentence?" The word *gravely* was chosen because the severity of the wolf's injuries is central to the story.

At Grade 8, the effect of word choice on meaning and tone becomes part of the measurement of Standard 4. For example, in the eighth-grade selection *The Tell Tale Heart,* the following question was asked: "What does "Object there was none. Passion there was none" mean in the previous paragraph, and how does it set the tone of the story?" This two-part question required the student to determine the meaning of the sentences and then write how that meaning sets the tone of the story.

Pilot Study Results

Standard 4 was measured by at least two questions. As shown in Table 6.1, the grand mean proportion correct on questions of word or phrase meaning were similar to Standards 1 and 3, with an overall mean of .52. We must acknowledge that it is possible that the students knew some of the word meanings before they read the text and didn't need context to determine their meanings. Alternatively, context could have been stronger in some cases than others. Take the word *access,* used in the fourth-grade story, *Encyclopedia Brown and the Case of the Slippery Salamander.* One question that assessed Standard 4 asked, "What does the word *access* mean in the following sentence?" The sentence read, "Employees and volunteers are the only ones who have access to the back room in the Den of Darkness where Fred was being kept." The context here suggests that *access* has something to do with the back room in a place called the Den of Darkness and only certain people had something to do with the back room. This context may have provided sufficient clues to the meaning of *access.*

The variability in student performance on questions of word or phrase meaning was largely due to the use of figurative language and figures of speech. For example, in the fourth-grade text *Amelia and Eleanor Go for a Ride,* a question asked, "What does 'birds of a feather' mean in the sentence, 'Amelia and Eleanor were birds of a feather'?" The paragraph preceding the question explained in detail how similar Amelia and Eleanor were, but most students did not understand the figure of speech. The most common answer was it meant that they were best friends. Similarly, the phrase, "A bird in the hand is worth two in the bush" was not understood by most sixth graders. And finally, at the eighth-grade level students were asked how the use of certain words or phrases set the tone for the story. On *The Tell Tale Heart,* students were asked to determine the meaning of the following sentences and explain how they set the tone of the story: "Object there was none. Passion there was none." The word *object* has a more common meaning, referring to a physical object. The concept of *object* as a purpose was unfamiliar to many of our eighth graders.

Standard #5: was not assessed in literature.

Standard 6

The focus on Standard 6 is to determine point of view. The *CARA* question stems are as follows:

- Describe the author's point of view . . . (grades 4–6)
- Explain how a narrator's point of view . . . (grades 4–6)
- Explain how an author develops the point of view . . . (grades 4–6)
- Analyze how differences in the points of view of _____ create effects of suspense or humor (grades 7–8)
- Analyze a point of view reflected in work outside the U.S. (high school)

The CCSS concept of point of view is broad and encompasses not only the traditional perspective of from whose point of view a story is told, but is extended to include how the author develops and contrasts the points of view of different characters. For example, in a sixth-grade selection, the standard asks students to explain how an author develops the point of view of the narrator or speaker in a text. A question that was written for the myth *Arachne* is, "What is the narrator's point of view of Athene <u>and</u> how is it shown in the previous paragraph?" At the eighth-grade level, the standard asks students to analyze how differences in the points of view of the character and the reader create effects of humor or suspense. In the literature selection *The Tell Tale Heart,* a more complex use of point of view is illustrated when Poe presents the narrator as crazy and confident that he will get away with his crime compared to the reader's point of view that he is obviously guilty and will be found out. A question written to address this aspect of point of view is, "Analyze how your view of the narrator compares with his view of himself <u>and</u> explain how this increases the story's suspense."

Pilot Study Results

Standard 6 was measured by one or two questions. However, at grade 9, it was only measured on one of the three selections because the content of the other stories didn't allow the design of a point of view question. This standard was very difficult for students of all grades relative to the other standards, with a mean proportion correct across all grade levels of .38. At the fourth-grade level, the point of view questions were asked directly on one story, *Grandfather's Journey.* The questions were, "Describe the point of view from which the story is told <u>and</u> how you know it," and "What words does the author use in the last three paragraphs to signal that the author is talking about himself?" It was obvious that few students had learned the words that signal point of view, such as *I.* Because most of our stories were written in third person, most of our questions asked how the author implied his or her point of view of characters in the story. This required a close analysis of the author's language when writing about a character. It did not appear that students were used to considering how an author felt about a particular character and the words the author used to show that view. Our data suggest that the complexity of point of view will likely need explicit instruction throughout the grades (see Chapter 5, Part 2).

Standard 7

The focus of Standard 7 is analysis of how visuals and multimedia contribute to meaning, tone, and beauty of a text. We did not assess this standard and provide a more extensive explanation in the following section on informational text.

Standard 8

Standard 8 is not applicable to literature.

Standard 9

Standard 9 was not assessed because we chose to use a single text and the standard required a comparison of multiple authors or texts.

Standard 10

Standard 10 requiring the use of grade-level text was assessed by choosing materials for content texts designated for those grade levels. In addition, we assessed the readability of the materials using Lexiles. These estimates were described in Chapter 3.

Match of *CARA* Questions to Reading Standards for Informational Text

Standard 1

The common thread that crosses all iterations of Standard 1 from grades 4 through high school is citing, quoting, or referring to what the text says explicitly and when drawing inferences from the text. *CARA* question stems are as follows:

- What evidence in the text indicates that . . . followed by an inference (grades 4–6)
- What evidence in the text strongly supports that . . . followed by an inference (middle and high school)

As stated in the previous section discussing Standard 1 in literature, we phrased Standard 1 questions in social studies and science materials in the form of an inference. Instead of asking the student to draw a text-based inference, we provided an inference and asked the student to identify explicit textual support for it. Tables 6.3 and 6.4 present the mean proportion correct on each standard by grade level in social studies and science, respectively.

Pilot Study Results

Social Studies.   Performance on Standard 1 in each text was based on two questions. Significant differences between passages were evident for grade 6, middle school U.S. history, and high school world history. At all three levels, passage 1 was significantly easier than the remaining two passages, suggesting that the content of the initial passages may have been more familiar and/or less complex than the following passages. For example, at the middle school level, the first passage focused on the actions and attitudes of delegates to the Constitutional Convention, a somewhat easier concept than questions on the differences between law and advice and the most effective procedure for amending the Constitution. Similarly, a discussion of the differences between the societies of Athens and Sparta may have been conceptually easier than a focus on unsuccessful alliances and the philosophical and artistic accomplishments of Grecian society.

Science.   Significant differences were evident for all science passages except grade 5 and middle school life science. This suggests more conceptual variability across science passages with regard to Standard 1. For example, passage 2 for middle school earth science focused on the abstract and unfamiliar concept of determining the relative age of rocks.

Standard 2

The common thread in Standard 2 is determining the main or central ideas of a text and providing an objective summary. *CARA* question stems are as follows:

- The topic of (single paragraph) is . . . What is the main idea? (grade 4)
- The topic of (two paragraphs) is . . . What is the main idea? (grade 5)
- The topic of (two or more paragraphs) is . . . What is the central idea? (grades 6 through high school)
- Summarize what the text says about . . . (grades 4 through high school)

The standards vary by grade level in the number of central ideas that should be identified. Grades 5, 7, and 11/12 ask students to determine two or more central ideas. Grades 4, 6, 8, and 9/10 ask students to determine one central idea. Examination of texts indicated that the familiar paradigm of one central idea per paragraph is seldom the case.

Table 6.3 Mean Proportion Correct on Each Social Studies Text and Each Standard by Grade

Grade Level	Standard 1	Standard 2	Standard 3	Standard 4	Standard 5	Standard 6	Standard 7
4	.39, .54, .48 No significant difference	.32, .26, .35 No significant difference	.24, .47, .51 2 = 3 > 1	.52, .57, .56 No significant difference	.51, .50, .45 No significant difference	.15, .29, .22 No significant difference	.37, .77, .20 2 > 1 = 3
5	.41, .51, .65 No significant difference	.38, .36, .17 No significant difference	.34, .41, .35 No significant difference	.50, .59, .54 No significant difference	.27, .56, .38 2 > 1 = 3	.18, .21, .25 No significant difference	.91, .62, .50 2 = 3 > 1
6	.84, .64, .60 1 > 2 = 3	.41, .18, .31 1 > 2 = 3	.42, .41, .40 No significant difference	.66, .53, .72 3 > 1 = 2	.26, .28, .29 No significant difference	.73, .29, .13 1 > 2 = 3	.19, .86, .24 2 > 3 > 1
Middle school U.S. history	.49, .38, .40 1 > 2 = 3	.12, .46, .36 2 = 3 > 1	.47, .39, .34 1 > 2 = 3	.56, .57, .56 No significant difference	.61, .52, .57 No significant difference	.28, .51, .22 2 > 1 > 3	.45, .38, .35 No significant difference
Middle school world history	.43, .57, .50 No significant difference	.20, .27, .35 No significant difference	.48, .26, .44 1 = 3 > 2	.28, .27, .30 No significant difference	.62, .40, .36 1 > 2 = 3	.30, .38, .22 No significant difference	.60, .38, .20 1 > 2 > 3
High school U.S. history	.48, .58, NA No significant difference	.31, .60, NA 2 > 1	.55, .31, NA 1 > 2	.46, .50, NA No significant difference	.26, .66, NA 2 > 1	.17, .60, NA 2 > 1	.79, .97, NA 2 > 1
High school world history	.64, .41, .55 1 > 2 = 3	.44, .44, .21 1 = 2 > 3	.54, .72, .46 2 > 1 = 3	.75, .44, .37 1 > 2 = 3	.61, .40, .38 1 > 2 = 3	.34, .44, .73 3 > 1 = 2	.64, .29, .04 3 > 2 = 1
Grand mean	.50	.31	.40	.50	.43	.30	.47

Note: The first mean proportion correct is from the first passage in our listing at that grade level, the second mean is for the second passage, etc. For example, under Standard 1 the mean of .39 refers to passage 1, The Northeast, and .54 refers to The Southwest. See Chapter 3 for a list of passages used at each grade level.

Table 6.4 Mean Proportion Correct on Each Science Text and Each Standard by Grade

Grade Level	Standard 1	Standard 2	Standard 3	Standard 4	Standard 5	Standard 6	Standard 7
4	.42, .18, .43 1 = 3 > 2	.14, .27, .17 No significant difference	.52, .25, .30 1 > 2 = 3	.63, .50, .21 1 = 2 > 3	.73, .52, .65 1 = 3 > 2	.27, .19, .13 No significant difference	.45, .57, .13 1 = 2 > 3
5	.44, .42, .34 No significant difference	.22, .29, .48 3 > 1 = 2	.49, .31, .21 1 > 2 = 3	.40, .38, .23 1 = 2 > 3	.33, .28, .36 No significant difference	NA	.56, .57, .48 No significant difference
6	.63, .23, .30 1 > 2 = 3	.34, .49, .53 No significant difference	.45, .47, .48 No significant difference	.36, .54, .72 3 > 2 > 1	.60, .36, .16 1 > 2 > 3	NA	.81, .31, .16 1 > 2 = 3
Middle school life science	.68, .73, .79 No significant difference	.38, .40, .41 No significant difference	.37, .61, .65 2 = 3 > 1	.52, .38, .45 No significant difference	.68, .70, .56 No significant difference	NA	.80, .81, .37 1 = 2 > 3
Middle school earth science	.44, .60, .35 2 > 1 = 3	.31, .15, .26 No significant difference	.35, .41, .44 No significant difference	.34, .38, .66 3 > 1 = 2	.51, .63, .19 1 = 2 > 3	NA	.57, .58, .71 No significant difference
High school life science	.59, NA, NA	.28, NA, NA	.75, NA, NA	.75, NA, NA	.84, NA, NA	NA	.60, NA, NA
High school earth science	.74, .67, .46 1 = 2 > 3	.84, .50, .47 No significant difference	.57, .52, .52 No significant difference	.84, .38, .55 1 > 2 = 3	.76, .56, .55 No significant difference	NA	.79, .50, .42 No significant difference
Grand mean	.45	.29	.41	.45	.48	NA	.49

Note: The first mean proportion correct is from the first passage in our listing at that grade level, the second mean is for the second passage, etc. For example, under Standard 1, the mean of .42 refers to passage 1, How Does Earth's Surface Change? and .18 refers to passage 2, How Does Water Affect Earth's Features?. See Chapter 3 for a list of passages used at each grade level.

Central ideas were often drawn out across two or more paragraphs. Therefore, and in alignment with the rigor of the CCSS, we chose to ask students above grade 4 to identify the central idea of sections involving two or more paragraphs, as opposed to a single paragraph.

The standards state that students should not only identify central ideas but should also explain how the ideas are supported by details and how they are developed over the course of text. The purpose of the *CARA* is to provide teachers with a manageable formative assessment for determining which Common Core State Standards need classroom emphasis. Explanation of the support and/or development of a central idea requires longer text and more extensive answers than is feasible in a 50-minute formative assessment.

Another challenge is the phrasing of the central idea. Should it be expressed as a complete sentence, as an explanatory phrase, or as a topic? We believe that topic and central idea are two different entities. The topic indicates the subject of the paragraph/s, is usually expressed in one or two words, and is often included in a heading. The central idea explains or summarizes what the author says about the topic. Initial piloting indicated that students often confused topic with central idea. Because of this, we identified the topic of the paragraph/s for the students and asked them to identify the central idea.

We also believe that the central idea can be expressed either as a sentence or as an explanatory phrase as long as the topic and summary of content are clearly delineated. Thus, instead of saying "The U.S. government supported the settlers against the Native Americans," a student would be correct in stating the central idea as "government support (topic) of settlers against Native Americans (summary of content)."

Constructing a text-based summary of the entire text or of a portion of the text is offered as an additional assessment option. In contrast to literature text, where the student was asked to summarize the entire story, we chose to ask students to summarize a particular section of informational text. Piloting indicated that many students interpreted a summary as an individual and somewhat personal discussion of the text. We therefore included the term "what the text says" in the summary question to align with the text-based objectivity required by Standard 2.

As with the literature summaries, performance on informational summaries was examined by averaging the proportion of answer key elements that were included in students' summaries. The data were converted to proportions to allow comparisons across grade levels because the numbers of elements varied in each answer key.

Pilot Study Results

Social Studies.   Performance on Standard 2 was based on one question. Therefore, as with literature, students' ability to explain the central idea of a text should be examined in other texts. The mean proportion correct for students did not differ among passages in grades 4, 5, and middle school world history. For levels with significant differences, difficulty was often related to how clearly the central idea was signaled in the text. Some passages contained a distinctly phrased central idea as an introductory sentence. In others, central idea statements were either embedded in the passage or missing altogether, thus requiring a greater inference on the part of the reader. Topic familiarity and/or concept difficulty also may have played a part. Students found determining the central idea from an account of the philosophy and artistic accomplishments of ancient Greece more difficult than from descriptions of governments, wars, alliances, and broken treaties.

Science.   Significant differences in determining central idea were found only at grade 5, suggesting that science passages may consistently contain more explicitly signaled central ideas in the form of headings and introductory sentences.

Performance on Summaries.   The performance on informational summaries was examined by averaging the proportion of answer key elements that were included in students' summaries. The data were converted to proportions to allow comparisons across grade levels because the numbers of elements varied in each answer key. Table 6.5 presents the mean proportion of answer key elements contained in students' written summaries of the three social studies texts according to grade level; Table 6.6 presents the same results in science.

Examination of the data shows little improvement across the grades and suggests that the quality of a summary is somewhat dependent on the topic, with most comparisons showing one passage to result in a better summary than the other two. Lack of a developmental progression could be due to differences in the samples of students in these grades, represent an increase in the complexity of the passages, and/or reflect overall student inability to construct a coherent summary of informational text.

Table 6.5   Mean Proportion of Social Studies Answer Key Statements Contained in Students' Summaries by Grade Level and Texts

Grade Level	Text 1	Text 2	Text 3	Significant Differences	Grand Mean Weighted
4	.21	.12	.28	Text 3 greater than 2	.22
5	.09	.18	.12	Text 2 greater than 1	.14
6	.48	.49	.32	Text 2 greater than 1 and 3	.43
Middle school U.S. history	.09	.08	.20	Text 3 greater than 1 and 2	.13
Middle school world history	.15	.13	.12	None	.13
High school U.S. history	.13	.16	None	None	.14*
High school world history	.28	.11	.12	Text 1 greater than 2 and 3	.21

Note: * average of 2 passages.

Table 6.6   Mean Proportion of Science Answer Key Statements Contained in Students' Summaries by Grade Level and Texts

Grade Level	Text 1	Text 2	Text 3	Significant Differences Between	Grand Mean Weighted
4	.06	.04	.03	Text 1 and 2 greater than 3	.04
5	.04	.08	.12	Text 3 greater than 1	.07
6	.12	.33	.38	Text 2 and 3 greater than 1	.27
Middle school life science	.04	.06	.05	Text 2 and 3 greater than 1	.05
Middle school earth science	.13	.14	.08	None	.11
High school life science	.29	No data	No data	Only text 1 administered	
High school earth science	.23	.20	.10	ns	.18

Standard 3

The common thread in Standard 3 is explaining or analyzing individuals, events, ideas, and/or concepts. The main *CARA* stems are as follows:

- Explain what, why, or how . . . (grades 4–5)
- Analyze why or how . . . (grades 6 through high school)

Additional information for each level offers specific directions for how explanation and analysis should occur. This varies from level to level, such as including an anecdote (grade 6), explaining the influence of a specific idea or individual (grade 7), or using analogies or comparisons (grade 8). Although the text that a teacher is using may not lend itself to such specificity, a common variable is that all analyses are heavily dependent on the content of the text. Standard 3 requires higher-level thinking akin to Ciardiello's (1998) convergent question level, the analysis category of Bloom and Krathwohl (1956), and the intermediate and complex levels of Graesser, Ozuru, and Sullins (2010). Therefore, we interpreted Standard 3 as requiring an inference on the part of the student.

The nature of the inferences required by Standard 3 is determined by the content of the text, as opposed to prior knowledge. For many individuals, an inference involves taking information from the text and merging it with what they already know. This is clearly problematic for much informational text. In fact, one could argue that the purpose of informational text is to learn about something of which you know little. Readers seldom possess substantial prior knowledge of the topics of informational text, so their ability to infer based on prior knowledge is limited. The standards are text based and, as such, require that the primary source of an inference is the text. Thus, an analysis question that requires a reader to pull information from different parts of the text and/or make decisions about the relevance of pieces of text information demands inferential reasoning.

An additional issue is the depth and/or length of the answer. For some passages, an analysis could involve one explanation for an interaction, relationship, or connection. However, at higher levels, one could expect a more lengthy analysis. For middle school text, we made certain that at least one of the two analysis questions required an explanation that included a minimum of two examples or reasons. For high school, all Standard 3 questions required a minimum of two examples or reasons.

A final issue with this standard is the specificity of the primary question stem. At grade levels 5, 7, and 9 the focus is on interactions, relationships, and connections, but the question stem for grade 6 asks how an idea is introduced, illustrated, and elaborated. Like much information included in a specific standard, the text may or may not lend itself to this. So we chose to focus on interactions, relationships, and connections for grade 6 in order to produce continuity across questions at similar levels. This decision was made because two or more levels of the *CARA* may be administered to students in an attempt to find a level at which they can meet the standard. For this reason, the questions should be relatively similar across levels in order to ascertain that a wrong answer is primarily due to inability to engage in the underlying cognitive activity and not due to confusion regarding the format of the question.

Pilot Study Results

Social Studies.   Performance on Standard 3 was based on two questions. Significant differences among passages were found at all levels except 5 and 6. Answering Standard 3 questions requires close reading of the text as well as the question stem that asks students to analyze how or why. Standard 3 questions were also more variable with regard to where the answer was found. For example, the analysis questions in the first passage for middle school

U.S. history focused on differences between delegates and divergent opinions on slavery, items that were clearly signaled in the text. In passages 2 and 3, answers depended on inferences drawn from less obvious text components.

Science.   In science, Standard 3 was assessed by three questions with significant differences among passages evident at grades 4, 5, and middle school life science.

Standard 4

The common thread in Standard 4 is determining the meaning of words and phrases. The *CARA* question stem is as follows:

- What is the meaning of _____ in the context of the previous paragraph, section, or passage? (grades 4 through high school)

Current social studies and science texts are very factual and do not lend themselves to determining the impact of specific word choice, figurative language, analogies, and allusions as contained in the standards for grades 6 through high school. This may change as textbook authors adapt to the standards, but the purpose of *CARA* is to provide a valid formative measure for texts that are presently in use.

We chose vocabulary words from the Academic Word List (Coxhead, 2000) and asked students to provide a meaning specific to the context of the text. Our rationale for using these words was as follows. Due to their frequency, students will meet them in diverse texts so they are worthy of emphasis. Such words are tier 2 words (Beck, McKeown, & Kucan, 2002)—that is, "high-frequency useful words that appear in diverse and multiple contexts across a variety of content areas" (Caldwell & Leslie, 2013, p. 148). Second, although these words are not domain specific, their meanings can slightly change depending on the context of the passage. For example, the word *feature*, as found in a sixth-grade science passage, is a noun and carries the meaning of *structure*, *part*, or *landscape*. However, in a different context, the noun *feature* could mean a movie, part of a face, or a magazine article. *Feature* could also be a verb and take on the meaning of *give prominence to* or *highlight*. A student might know the word in one context but comprehension requires that the student is able to expand this knowledge to apply the word in a new context.

Unfortunately, we were not always able to select words that represented a clear change in meaning such as illustrated by *feature*. Some words on the Academic Word List, such as *individual* and *enforce*, maintained the same basic meaning irrespective of the context of the passage. This raises a question: How can we differentiate between the student who already knows the meaning of the word and the student who determines the meaning from the context of the passage? Unfortunately, we can't. Examination of our pilot data suggests that student answers tended to fall into three overlapping categories: exact definitions, definitions that were unclear or incomplete but hinted at some understanding of the word, and answers that were inaccurate. We might hypothesize that exact definitions represented words known prior to reading the selection and definitions that hinted at some understanding of the word represented initial learning through context. Although we have no definitive data to support our hypothesis, this may suggest a possible way to evaluate student performance on Standard 4.

But, what about students who were not able to provide an acceptable definition for a word? Given that at least two measures of context (morphological, syntactical, and/or semantic) were present in the text, we can assume that they did not use or were unable to use context as a guide for determining word meaning.

Most passages contained a variety of vocabulary from the Academic Word List. An issue was how to select specific words, thus we formulated the following guidelines for informational text. We did not repeat words chosen at other levels; that is, if a word had been selected in a previous level, we did not select it again. We also did not select words that were clearly defined in the text. Such definitions usually occurred in the same sentence as the target word or in the sentence that immediately followed. Obviously, a definition can be considered part of context, but it does not require the reader to use multiple context clues to determine word meaning. We believe the intent of Standard 4 is that readers determine meanings from the available context, not from a supplied definition.

If the word was repeated more than once in the passage, we selected it under the assumption that repetition signaled the importance of the word to passage content. An example is the choice of *layers* in a passage entitled *What Are Earth's Layers Made Of?* The word was repeated 10 times. However, in some cases, multiple repetitions of the word included a definition and, in such cases, we did not select it. If the occurrence of a word was widely spaced throughout the text, we used two guidelines for placement of the vocabulary question. Depending on the passage, we either placed the vocabulary question after the last incidence of the word, thus allowing the reader to make maximum use of context, or we placed the vocabulary question where the context was strongest.

In cases where a word was used only once, we attempted to select words that were surrounded by sufficient context clues to allow readers to arrive at a definition. We analyzed each word according to morphological context, syntactic context, and semantic context (Baumann, Edwards, Font, Tereshinski, Kame'enui, & Olejnik, 2002; Baumann, Ware, & Edwards, 2007). Morphological context included meaning clues within the word itself, such as prefixes, suffixes, and roots. Syntactic context included meaning clues derived from placement of the word in a sentence that signaled a specific part of speech. Semantic context included the following four components: synonyms, antonyms, examples, and general words or statements that offered clues to meaning. For a word to be selected, semantic context had to be present. However, the presence of synonyms, antonyms, and examples were rated higher than general clues. In addition to semantic context, either morphological or syntactic context had to be evident. In cases where several different words offered approximately the same level of context, we made a choice based on word frequency and word placement within a specific grade level (Zeno, Ivens, Millard, & Duvvuri, 1995).

Pilot Study Results

Social Studies.   Standard 4 performance was based on two questions with significant differences occurring only between passages at grade 6 and high school world history. This finding suggests that the words from social studies texts, chosen to be used to assess Standard 4, were similar in difficulty.

Science.   Significant differences were evident on all passages except Middle School life science. This may signal the greater unfamiliarity of the vocabulary in science and/or the difficulty in applying a new meaning to a previously familiar word. For example, for the middle school earth science passage, the words in passages 1 and 2 were relatively familiar words that took on very different meanings in the context of the passage. *Infer* in passage 1 means *reason, determine,* and/or *conclude,* not *guess* or *predict* as many pilot students stated. *Index* in passage 2 refers to a fossil used to organize or match rock layers.

Standard 5

The common thread in Standard 5 is describing and/or analyzing the structure of the text. The *CARA* question stem is as follows:

- *What text structure best explains how the author organized the previous passage?*

  - *Description of important features*
  - *Explanation of steps in a sequence*
  - *Account of cause and effect*
  - *Explanation of problem solution*
  - *Comparison of two or more things*

- *Give a reason from the text for your answer. For example, if you choose description, tell what is being described. If you choose sequence, list one or two steps. For cause and effect, state a cause or effect mentioned in the text. For problem and solution, tell what the problem is or describe the solution. For comparison, tell what is being compared or contrasted.* (grades 4 through high school)

At each level we asked students to identify the structure of specific paragraph/s. We realize that paragraph structure may be a relatively unfamiliar concept for students, so we included options as part of the question. For grade 4, students were given three structure options; for grades 5 through high school, they were asked to choose from five structure options. We also asked students to give a reason for their answer. Unfortunately, initial piloting suggested that students seldom were able to offer a coherent reason for their choice of structure. Therefore, we also inserted general directions for doing so.

The question stems for Standard 5 at grades 9/10 and 11/12 pose a problem. The factual nature of much social studies and science classroom text does not allow for specific attention to how an author's ideas are developed or refined as well as any evaluation of their effectiveness. We believe that identification of the structure with an accompanying rationale for choice is a necessary first step to analysis and evaluation and thus addresses the intent of the standard.

Pilot Study Results

Social Studies.   Significant differences in mean proportions correct were found for all passages except for grades 4, 6, and middle school U.S. history. Standard 5 was assessed by one question that had two parts: choice of a text structure and explanation for the choice. Offering an acceptable explanation for the choice requires identification of the author's underlying purpose in crafting a specific text segment. It also requires understanding of different expository structures and the words and paragraph organization that signal a specific structure.

Science.   No significant differences in mean proportion correct were found among passages in grade 5 and middle school life science. Significant differences for both social studies and science suggest that some texts do not clearly signal structure.

Standard 6

The common thread in Standard 6 is determining an author's point of view or purpose. The *CARA* question stems for social studies are as follows:

- How are _____ and _____ alike or different? (grades 4–5)
- What was the point of view/purpose of . . . (grades 6 through high school)

Given the factual nature of informational text in present textbooks, the point of view of the text author is not always evident. The standards for high school levels include analysis of effective rhetoric, style, and content with regard to point of view. However, this, like the author's point of view, is not always possible with the factual nature of typical social studies and science textbooks.

Social studies texts, for example, do not present two authors' versions of the same issue. That is, they do not present a text about Andrew Jackson written by someone who is pro-Jackson and one written by someone who takes a more negative view. However, they do contain the points of view of individual historical figures, political parties, government policies, and the like. We believe asking students to determine such differences is in accord with Standard 6 of the CCSS and may provide an initial step to recognizing author point of view.

Science texts, however, are primarily factual and do not allow for contrasting points of view or purposes. Their purpose is to provide the most recent factual and/or explanatory information about a topic in as clear and unambiguous a manner as possible. In fact, scientists report that "school science time should not be devoted to critical analysis of science texts—texts that they note should be 'clearly authoritative'" (Shanahan, Shanahan, & Misischia, 2011, p. 422). Given this and the fact that science texts clearly do not allow for interpretation of author purpose or viewpoint, we did not include a Standard 6 question for science text. Instead, we added an additional Standard 3 question for science passages, reasoning that analysis is a key component of understanding science information. One small segment of fourth-grade students piloted a point of view question in science early in the piloting process, but this question was withdrawn. The majority of grade 4 science passages did not include a Standard 6 question.

Pilot Study Results

Social Studies.   Standard 6 was assessed by one question, therefore students' abilities to interpret point of view should be examined in other social studies materials. This standard was only assessed in social studies. No significant differences in mean proportion correct were found among texts in grades 4, 5, and middle school world history. Students may have found point of view easier to determine when it was signaled by what someone said as differentiated from what someone did. For example, the point of view of Jackson was clearly signaled by his words in passage 2 regarding the Supreme Court and the removal of the Native Americans. His point of view in passage 1 was less obvious and required a deeper inference based on his actions and those of his supporters.

Standard 7

The common thread in Standard 7 is interpreting or analyzing information presented visually or quantitatively. We originally included a single question based upon Standard 7. Visuals were taken from the same textbook and chapter as the written text. They included photographs, pictures, drawings, diagrams, maps, charts, graphs, and political cartoons. Visuals of the same type, such as photographs, graphs, maps, and diagrams, differed in both clarity and style. Because of the diversity in format across all visuals, a student's response could only be interpreted with regard to the specific nature of the visual attached to the text. Student ability to interpret a map, for example, could not be extended to other visual formats or even, in some cases, to other maps.

Pilot data indicated that significant differences between passages occurred for most levels in both social studies and science text. It is impossible to determine if differences were due to the type of visual, the style of the visual, the nature of the question, or a combination of all three. However, student performance on a single visual that may or may not be representative of other visuals of the same general nature clearly offers rather limited information to the teacher. Given the wide diversity across visuals in current textbooks, one cannot assume instruction in a specific visual format will transfer to other visuals even of the same general nature.

We reasoned that deleting the Standard 7 question and substituting a second Standard 2 question would offer more instructional input. Determining the central idea was clearly a weakness for our pilot students. Was this a function of the text, of student knowledge, or a combination of both? By offering two questions on central idea, a teacher could compare individual or class performance on two questions as opposed to one and perhaps gain greater understanding of the extent to which central idea across single or multiple paragraphs is understood.

Pilot Study Results

Social Studies.   Differences were significant at all levels except middle school world history.

Science.   Significant differences were noted for all levels except grade 5, middle school earth science, and high school earth science. Significant differences across all passages were probably due to the fact that visuals differed in format and content.

Conclusions

What conclusions can be drawn from the pilot data on informational text? Significant differences among passages were apparent across all levels in both social studies and science. This may reflect the difficulty and unfamiliarity of the topics as well as the unfamiliar nature of the questions themselves. Our pilot students may not have had experience with explaining the basis of an inference, analyzing how and why, and/or differentiating text structure as Standards 1, 3 and 5 asked them to do. Third, pilot results for informational text may reflect student lack of experience in reading such texts as opposed to stories.

Many factors interact to render a question easy or difficult and one cannot assume that the nature of the question is the primary source of difficulty. One cannot expect that Standard 3 analysis questions, for example, will always be more difficult than Standard 2 questions. The questions may ask students to do things such as analyze how and why and determine central idea; however, the difficulty of any question is clearly related to the student's understanding of the question, the way the answer is signaled in the text, and the ability of the students to engage in close reading to identify relevant text components.

As suggested by this analysis, a variety of text elements may play a significant role in student ability to answer a question; such elements cross all questions. Obviously, the complexity and/or familiarity of the topic play a key role. Another critical component is the degree to which the answer is clued in the text by the presence of headings, inclusion of preliminary questions, and statements of intention. Text organization, if clearly signaled, can provide additional support. Placement of relevant information is another factor. Is the answer found in a single paragraph or does it cross several paragraphs? Is it stated once or repeated several times, perhaps in different terms? The nature and extent of contextual support for unfamiliar word meanings is also an issue. Some forms of context may be more helpful than others. Is the purpose of the author clearly signaled or does it have to be inferred by the reader? Do connectives such as *because* and *therefore* enhance comprehension? And, of course, even if the reader understands what it means to analyze or what point of view entails, reader interest, motivation, and previous knowledge will always affect the ability of students to answer any of the standards-based questions in the *CARA*.

This suggests two issues. First, teachers will need to show students how to read text in order to answer standards-based questions. They will need to model the close reading process and show students what to look for. Second, helping students understand text from the point of view of the Common Core Standards is not a one-time issue. One cannot assume that success in answering Standard 3 questions in one text or in one discipline will transfer to other selections. Questions answered in one text may pose difficulty in text on another topic or in a different discipline. What may transfer, however, is reader understanding of question stems and the process of searching for text components that are relevant to specific questions.

Standard 8

The common thread in Standard 8 is explaining and evaluating arguments or claims in a text. We assessed this standard in social studies text only at the middle school and high school levels. The *CARA* question stems are as follows:

- Read the excerpt from _____. Explain two reasons or arguments that _____ presents. Select one reason or argument and explain why it is valid or not valid. (<u>middle school</u>)
- Read the excerpt from _____. Explain four reasons or arguments that _____ presents. Select two reasons or arguments and explain why they are valid or not valid. (<u>high school</u>)

We limited our assessment of Standard 8 to middle school and high school because of difficulty in finding lower-level passages that presented a specific position supported by arguments. Few textbooks at any level provided passages appropriate for assessing Standard 8. Science passages, as mentioned previously with Standard 6, are factual and do not present material as contrasting arguments to be evaluated, accepted, and/or rejected. They are authoritative and do not lend themselves to critical analysis (Shanahan, Shanahan, & Misischia, 2011). As with Standard 6, we chose not to assess Standard 8 in science text.

We found that an authoritative stance was also present in many social studies texts; the primary concern of authors seems to be transmittal of information about events and individuals with an emphasis on understanding and retaining information, not critically examining it. However, we addressed Standard 8 for middle school and high school social studies by adding a separate, relatively short second passage to each of the U.S. and world history passages. We chose primary sources for this addition, such as Jackson's State of the Union speech and Suetonius' description of the death of Julius Caesar, and asked students to identify reasons or arguments put forward by the author to justify his position. We then asked the students to choose one or more arguments and explain why they considered them to be valid or not valid. Primary sources were clearly inappropriate for grades 4 through 6. They were too difficult, with long, complicated, and somewhat archaic sentence structure.

Pilot Study Results

Pilot student performance at the middle school level suggested that students found the archaic language and concept density of primary sources to be difficult. Students performed better when identifying arguments in the text, with mean proportion correct ranging from .17 to .40 for world history and .19 to .33 for U.S. history. Judging the validity of an argument was even a greater challenge, with means ranging from .02 to .21 for world history and .13 to .16 for U.S. history.

Performance of high school students was somewhat better. Mean proportion of identification of arguments in the texts ranged from .44 to .58 for world history and .28 to .76 for U.S. history. Similar to the pattern at the middle school level, performance on evaluating the validity of arguments was lower: .11 to .28 for world history and .24 to .69 for U.S. history. One of the U.S. history selections, *Memorial of the Cherokee Nation,* was obviously much easier than Jackson's State of the Union address and the address of Clay criticizing Jackson's veto of the Bank of America. Overall pilot results suggest that identification and evaluation of text arguments based on the somewhat archaic language and relatively unfamiliar concepts in primary sources will need strong classroom emphasis.

Standard 9

Standard 9 was not assessed because we chose to use a single text and this standard required a comparison of multiple authors or texts.

Standard 10

Standard 10 requiring the use of grade-level text was assessed by choosing materials for content texts designated for those grade levels. In addition, we assessed the readability of the materials using Lexiles. These were described previously in Chapter 3.

Development of Answer Keys and Explanation of Pilot Studies

Pilot Study 1

The development of answer keys to accompany *CARA* questions occurred throughout our piloting process. We composed initial versions of the *CARA* answer keys during 2011 and the winter of 2012. In March of 2012, we recruited teachers to review the questions to determine if they matched the standards and to review the accuracy and sufficiency of the answer keys. Each teacher was given an explanation of our project and its goals and timelines.

We recruited teachers in a number of ways. There were teachers in the states of Massachusetts and Washington with whom we had previous contact and who expressed interest in our continued research. In addition, we sent a message to upper elementary, middle school, and high school teachers who were members of the Wisconsin State Reading Association (WSRA) and on the WSRA listserv. A notice was also put on the website of the Wisconsin Society of Science Teachers. We also contained the principals of four Catholic high schools in the Milwaukee area, and finally, we contacted past graduate students of ours who were in leadership positions in their school districts.

The initial invitation to WSRA members led to 56 responses, of which 40 teachers reviewed materials at their grade level, for a response rate of 71 percent—an excellent response. Personal contacts led to the addition of five additional school districts in Wisconsin, Massachusetts, and Washington. Their district personnel gave us names of 17 teachers who indicated preliminary interest and we contacted them via email. Eighty-two percent of those teachers reviewed the materials.

The feedback provided by the teachers was invaluable. Suggestions for rephrasing of questions and additional answers were the most common type of feedback. We had placed the comprehension questions throughout the text as opposed to at the end of the passage; teachers often suggested a different placement to provide more context for answering the question. After examining science and social studies text, teachers recommended a different format for the text structure question. Occasionally literature teachers identified that a question contained part of a standard, but not all of it. Seldom did social studies or science teachers question the relationship of the question to the specific standard. It was very gratifying that teachers were very interested in participating.

Student Pilot Methodology

After revising our materials based on teacher feedback, we solicited the same teachers to test the materials with their students. Of the 54 teachers who reviewed the materials, 66 percent indicated an interest in piloting them with their students and 77 percent of that group returned data to us by the end of the 2012 academic year. Table 6.7 presents the number of classrooms that participated in the spring 2012 pilot study.

Student responses to questions guided our modification of answer keys. As we were scoring the answers to questions we found answers different from the ones we had originally written that were also correct. This occurred in part because students' manner of

Table 6.7   Number of Classrooms in Spring 2012 Pilot

Grade Level	Literature	Social Studies	Science
4	9	8	6
5	5	4	4
6	2	0	0
7	8	2	2
8	3	2	1

Note: Total number of students = 936.

expression was quite different from ours. For example, on a question that asked students to identify the theme of *The Tell Tale Heart,* the answer that we'd written was, "The theme that emerges is that despite careful planning a murderer often either gives him/herself away by his/her own behavior OR his/her guilt may eventually consume him/her." An answer provided by several students was "What goes around comes around." Although this response is not as detailed as the ones we had written, it sums up the theme rather nicely.

Students' responses to Standard 5 in informational text also led to changes in the answer key. Quite often students offered acceptable answers that we had not even thought of. Standard 5 asked students to select the structure of a passage and provide a reason for their choice. In several cases, students chose structures that were not included in the original answer key, but they provided valid reasons for doing so. If this occurred for a reasonable number of students and if we saw sufficient evidence in the text to support their view, we adjusted the answer key. For example, sequence was not an original option for the high school world history passage on the rise of the Greek city-states, but numerous students chose it and offered a viable reason for their choice. We examined the text and agreed with them. Although the passage compared different forms of government in the city-states and described causes that led to their evolution, it did so in a sequential account from monarchy to aristocracy to oligarchy. Therefore, we changed the answer key to include sequence.

Similarly, we added description to the answer key for the middle school passage on debating the Constitution. A number of students chose this option and provided a well-thought-out reason for doing so. When we examined the passage, we concurred with their choice. However, we did not always agree with students' responses. In the middle school passage on fossils, many students stated that the text structure was sequence. Although two sentences in the passage referred to the sequence of dying and decaying and burial by sediments, most of the passage dealt with description and/or cause–effect. We could not agree with our pilot students in this respect.

We also added to the answer key responses to Standard 4 questions that asked for a definition. Students often provided definitions and/or synonyms we had not thought of. Accordingly, we adjusted the answer key. In many respects, the answer key was the joint effort of two *CARA* authors, teacher reviewers, and students.

Finally, we conducted item analyses to determine the alpha reliability of our assessments. The scale analysis examines the correlations between each item and the total score. If there are high positive correlations between how students performed on each item and the total score, then the overall reliability will be high. The degree of variability among the students is a factor in the analysis, so if all students answered a question correctly, or if all students were incorrect on their answers to a question, the alpha reliability estimate is reduced by one question. If our analyses found that the reliability estimates were low, we analyzed whether certain items were too hard or too easy, or whether the entire scale did not seem to be measuring one construct. Therefore, many of the questions were different for the second pilot.

Pilot Study 2

We solicited teachers to administer the *CARA* in grades 4 through 9/10. As Table 6.7 illustrates, we had a minimal amount of students in grades 6 and no high school students participate in the first pilot study, so we sought many classrooms on which to pilot passages from these grades. Classrooms were administered grade-appropriate materials in the fall of 2012, winter of 2013, and spring of 2013. The total number of students who participated in the second pilot study was 3,012.

Interrater Reliability: Scoring of Answers to Questions.   After we corrected student responses we sent a random sample of 15 student protocols from each story and nonfiction text to a classroom teacher or literacy specialist for rescoring; they were paid $25 per hour for their work. Each teacher scored every question in the manner described in Chapter 4, Parts 1 and 2—that is, they scored all answers to question 1, then all answers to question 2, and so on. This format allowed the teachers to observe the quality of answers to each question across all students and prevented either halo effects or devil effects, which in this case means to be positively or negatively influenced by students' performance on other questions. It is important that teachers follow the same procedures in scoring their students' papers.

Literature Text.   Scorings were compared on each question on each text at each grade level and the percent agreements were averaged over the number of questions measuring each standard. So, for example, on the fifth-grade literature passages, there were two questions that measured Standard 1. The percent agreement was calculated for each question within a story and then the percents were averaged to obtain a percent agreement for Standard 1 on the story. Finally, an overall agreement was determined by averaging the percents across the three literature texts. An identical procedure was used for the informational texts. Table 6.8 presents the interrater reliability on the literature texts by grade level and standard.

Whenever the interrater reliability of a single question dropped below 70 percent, we examined our answer key to determine what information needed to be added to make scoring more clear. Most frequently we added a clarifying statement to the answer key. In some cases, notes were added to the answer key to signal an area where scorer confusion occurred. For example, question 8 from the eighth-grade short story *The Story-Teller* was, "Analyze how the man's description of the park keeps the children interested in his story."

Table 6.8   Interrater Reliability by Standard and Grade Level of Literature Text

Grade Level	Standard 1	Standard 2	Standard 3	Standard 4	Standard 6	Standard 7
4	86%	99%	91%	95%	80%	87%
5	95%	91%	95%	92%	91%	100%
6	97%	84%	91%	89%	80%	NA
7	89%	90%	87%	86%	89%	NA
8	93%	84%	78%	82%	86%	NA
9	92%	87%	89%	91%	87%	NA

The answer in the key is, "His description is detailed and he has an unusual explanation for why there were no sheep in the park and this keeps the children paying attention to the story OR The detailed descriptions make a picture in the children's mind and that keeps them attending to the story. *Note:* The student's response needs to be more general than simply listing characteristics of the pigs; it must refer to the descriptive quality of the man's story."

Similarly, on Poe's *The Tell Tale Heart,* question 6 asked, "How does the narrator's behavior, described in the two preceding paragraphs, reveal his beliefs about himself?" The answer in the key is, "When he describes how he hides the body he tells us how clever he was OR His behavior shows that he is very confident that what he'd done won't be discovered." Some students wrote that his behavior shows he isn't crazy. Such an answer does not describe a behavior of the narrator and therefore isn't correct. The note on this answer key is, "The answer must describe the man's behavior and what it says about his beliefs about himself." Notes such as these were added to answer keys whenever scorers overlooked a generalization expected for a correct answer.

There were several general challenges that scorers faced in scoring literature text. First, vague answers were more difficult to score. For example, on the seventh-grade text, *The Third Wish,* question 2 asks the student to "Analyze how the king's gift will affect the story's plot." One answer that scorers differed on was, "The King's gift will affect Mr. Peters in some way that he uses them." Although generally correct, this answer is vague and doesn't reveal understanding of how wishes are used in other stories. This same student answered "Analyze how the setting is important to a character in the story" by writing, "it explains why these animals are here." For this answer to be correct the student would need to tie the setting (by a river) to the character of a swan (needs water to live in). This student is on the right track, but in order for his answer to be correct the scorer needs to infer what this answer means. Such is always a challenge when scoring constructed responses. A final example from this student is his response to the question, "How did the author develop the characters of Leita and Mr. Peters to illustrate their different points of view toward being human?" He wrote: "he showed us that Mr. Peters was giving her things but Leita just wanted to be a swan." The answer does not directly address the personal characteristics of Mr. Peters and Leita. As a reader, we can infer that if Mr. Peters was giving her things, he was generous. However, there is nothing about who Leita is other than she wanted to be a swan.

Another problem area is when students include correct information and also an error in their answer to a two-part question. On *The Californian's Tale,* question 9 asks the students to "Cite two sources of evidence that the people of the town cared about Henry." The answer on the key is, "They've been coming to his house for 19 years to help him over the anniversary of her not returning from the trip OR They plan a party/dance for her homecoming OR They fix up the house with flowers for the party OR Men come by his house and ask him to read her letter to them OR They drug him so he will sleep so he won't go wild OR They encourage him that she will come." One student wrote, "they come every (error) Saturday and fix up the house with flowers (correct) and they encourage him that she will come (correct)." So, does she receive the full credit of two points, despite her error?

Informational Text.   Scorings for informational text were compared on each question on each text at each grade level and the percent agreements were averaged over the number of questions measuring each standard. Tables 6.9 and 6.10 present the percent agreements in social studies and science, respectively.

Analysis of interrater reliability of social studies and science passages revealed some distinct patterns. Average agreement between scorers across three passages in a single discipline and at a single grade level was above 70 percent, ranging from 71 to 88 percent.

Table 6.9   Interrater Reliability by Standard and Grade Level on Social Studies Text

Grade Level	Standard 1	Standard 2	Standard 3	Standard 4	Standard 5	Standard 6	Standard 7
4	83%	90%	72%	95%	73%	92%	92%
5	82%	79%	84%	78%	79%	81%	90%
6	84%	79%	57%	63%	78%	69%	87%
Middle school U.S. history	86%	77%	66%	81%	80%	83%	75%
Middle school world history	91%	84%	85%	91%	88%	83%	100%
High school U.S. history	90%	64%	70%	83%	79%	79%	86%
High school world history	81%	75%	64%	82%	80%	87%	82%

However, as indicated in Tables 6.9 and 6.10, average agreement between scorers for specific standards occasionally fell below 70 percent. This primarily occurred for questions measuring Standard 3, which asks the reader to analyze how or why something occurred by drawing information from different parts of the text. It can be argued that student answers tended to be more ambiguous to the scorer because the students found them more difficult. Standard 3 questions also required both students and scorers to differentiate between *how* and *why*. Students clearly found this difficult, often explaining how something occurred rather than why it occurred or vice versa. Scorers also seemed to experience the same difficulty accepting a why answer for a how answer or vice versa.

Two-point answers also represented an issue for scorers, who often accepted a single answer as adequate. Lack of scorer agreement on two-point passages clearly lowered interrater scores for Standards 3 and 5. Our interrater percentages reflect the total agreement between scorers with regard to both answers. However, there was high agreement between scorers on a single answer (that is, the majority of scorers agreed on at least one answer).

Table 6.10   Interrater Reliability by Standard and Grade Level on Science Text

Grade Level	Standard 1	Standard 2	Standard 3	Standard 4	Standard 5	Standard 6	Standard 7
4	81%	73%	62%	88%	71%	NA	75%
5	74%	80%	54%	86%	84%	NA	98%
6	81%	76%	75%	69%	73%	NA	78%
Middle school U.S. history	81%	94%	79%	82%	93%	NA	98%
Middle school world history	93%	87%	83%	87%	87%	NA	89%
High school U.S. history	77%	74%	64%	94%	91%	NA	100%
High school world history	79%	71%	62%	85%	75%	NA	82%

We carefully examined scorer answers to ascertain, if possible, why they differed. This led to general guidelines for correcting student answers, which we have included in Chapter 4, Part 1. These guidelines include:

- Close reading of the question and text content prior to reading students' responses
- Dealing with ambiguous and/or confusing answers
- Maintaining a focus on text-based answers
- Adhering to the answer key

Examination of student answers in informational text and how scorers reacted to them was used to clarify the *CARA* answer keys. We added additional instructions regarding what constitutes acceptable answers for specific questions. For example, a majority of students offered "proof" as an acceptable definition of *evidence* even though this is contradicted several times in the sixth-grade passage, *How Do Earth's Plates Help Create Landforms?* As a result, we included specific directions in the answer key stating that "proof" was not an acceptable answer. Scorers often accepted answers that clearly emanated from prior knowledge. When asked for evidence why trees were a valuable resource on the Great Plains, students cited shade, fruit, and firewood. The text only mentioned houses and fences. As a result, for all Standard 1 questions, we inserted: "Answer should include information from the text." Some questions required two-point answers and scorers often gave full credit for a single answer. To address this, we included the following in the answer key for all two point items: "As a two-point question, there should be two clearly defined answers." For Standard 5, students often gave extremely vague and nonspecific answers for their choice of structure ("because it said so in the text") and scorers occasionally accepted it. We clarified Standard 5 questions to include the following: "Reasons that are not present in the text are inaccurate." We also added additional examples of acceptable answers based on student response. Students often contributed answers that did not match the answer key but made sense in the context of the passage. This was most evident with regard to Standards 4 and 5.

Although adjustments to answer keys represented the majority of changes resulting from our interrater analysis, we also clarified some questions by rewording them in more specific terms. There were occasions when scorers and students misread the question. For example, a question in a middle school earth science text asked; "Analyze how fossils formed by tar and resin are alike." A majority of students explained how tar and resin, not fossils, were alike and the scorer accepted this answer. The question was modified. Similarly, low scorer agreement and/or low student scores or ambiguous student answers led to revisions of questions. For example, we altered "Explain why the oceans will always be salty" to "Explain how the oceans become salty." "What evidence in the text indicates that working conditions were not good?" was changed to "What evidence in the text indicates that workers had little time for recreation?" Similarly, we simplified and/or clarified vocabulary in some questions. "Explain the effect of wind on waves" was changed to "Explain how wind changes waves." "Explain the role of chromosomes in the cell" was rewritten as "Explain how chromosomes work in the cell."

Alpha Reliability of Tests

The reliability of a test can be measured in several ways, but within-test reliability typically uses the alpha estimate. The estimate examines the correlation between student performance on each item with the total score. Another way of thinking about it is: do all of the items measure the same construct? If so, then the alpha will be high, approaching .90. The alpha estimates are based on the number of items on a test and the variability among student data. A question that every student answers correctly or incorrectly results in no variance among students and is dropped from the analysis, reducing the number of items. This is one reason for conducting the analysis, so that items that fail to discriminate can be rewritten or removed. The *CARA* is a 10-question assessment; therefore, the alpha estimates were not expected to be high (above .80). However, we wanted to see the extent to which questions measuring different standards would be related to a total score.

Alpha reliability of each text was determined on pilot data from the spring of 2012, and also on data from the 2012–2013 school year. When there were no changes to questions or answer keys the data from the two years were collapsed. This did not happen very often, as many changes were made to the questions and answer keys as a result of the first pilot. Table 6.11 presents the mean proportion correct, number of students, and alpha reliability of each text by grade level and content area.

Table 6.11 Mean Proportion Correct, Number of Students, and Alpha Reliability for Each Modified Text by Grade Level and Content Area: Fall 2012 and Spring 2013 Testing

Grade Level	Name of Text	Content Area	Mean Proportion Correct	No. of Students	Alpha
4	Amelia and Eleanor Go for a Ride	Literature	.45	43	.76
	Encyclopedia Brown and the Case of the Slippery Salamander	Literature	.44	44	.63
	Grandfather's Journey	Literature	.52	34	.67
	The Northeast*	Social Studies	.37	41	.77
	The Southeast*	Social Studies	.50	35	.78
	The Southwest*	Social Studies	.44	54	.55
	How Earth's Surface Change?	Science	.50	49	.73
	How Does Water Affect Earth's Features?	Science	.35	49	.68
	How Do Waves Affect Coastal Landforms?	Science	.33	53	.45
5	Leonardo da Vinci: Inventor and Artist	Literature	.51	56	.59
	Weslandia	Literature	.49	35	.75
	Journey to the Center of the Earth	Literature	.35	54	.69
	Inventions and Big Business*	Social Studies	.40	34	.63
	Immigration*	Social Studies	.48	47	.66
	Workers and Unions**	Social Studies	.42	24	.43
	What Is Inside a Cell?*	Science	.42	116	.63
	How Do Cells Work Together? (Q10 missing)	Science	.35	79	.54 n(67)
	How Do Organs Work Together?* (Q1 missing)	Science	.30	60	.32 n(48)
6	Arachne	Literature	.51	91	.50
	The Wounded Wolf	Literature	.64	.88	.37
	Señor Coyote and the Tricked Trickster	Literature	.42	64	.42
	Rails Across the Nation*	Social Studies	.51	74	.57
	Conflict on the Great Plains*	Social Studies	.46	73	.51
	The Great Plains* (Q10 missing)	Social Studies	.43	72	.33 (n=45)
	What Are Earth's Layers Made Of?*	Science	.51	83	.67
	How Do Earth's Plates Help Create Landforms?*	Science	.41	88	.70
	How Do Scientists Explain Earth's Features?*	Science	.41	58	.33

(Continued)

Table 6.11   (Continued)

Grade Level	Name of Text	Content Area	Mean Proportion Correct	No. of Students	Alpha
7	All Summer in a Day	Literature	.56	73	.64
	The Californian's Tale	Literature	.53	54	.67
	The Third Wish	Literature	.66	50	.72
	The Constitional Convention	History	.46	155	.56
	Debating the Constitution	History	.45	118	.66
	The Bill of Rights	History	.42	153	.70
	The Digestive System	Life Science	.53	64	.49
	The Muscular System (Q10 missing)	Life Science	.63	57	.35 (n=13)
	The Respiratory System	Life Science	.58	41	.37
8	The Tell Tale Heart	Literature	.46	86	.79
	The Drummer Boy of Shiloh	Literature	.47	113	.81
	The Story-Teller	Literature	.50	47	.73
	The Roman Republic	History	.43	30	.73
	The Roman Empire	History	.36	53	.66
	The Fall of Rome	History	.37	51	.57
	Fossils	Earth Science	.41	54	.56
	The Relative Age of Rocks	Earth Science	.46	40	.49
	Radioactive Dating	Earth Science	.43	62	.65
9	Sonata for Harp and Bicycle	Literature	.45	52	.67
	Blues Ain't No Mockin Bird	Literature	.42	56	.68
	A Problem	Literature	.35	60	.69
	The Rise of the Greek City-States	World History	.60	105	.69
	Conflict in the Greek World	World History	.50	41	.60
	The Glory That Was Greece	World History	.42	48	.72
	The Vast World Ocean	Earth Science	.70	19	.32
	Ocean Floor Features	Earth Science	.53	16	.67
	Seafloor Sediments	Earth Science	.51	19	.82
10	The Election of 1834	American History	.45	42	.66
	Conflicts and Crises	American History	.53	37	.59
	More Conflicts and Crises	American History	None	None	None
	Life Is Cellular	Life Science	.69	64	.68
	Cell Structure	Life Science	None	None	None
	Organelles That Capture and Release Energy	Life Science	None	None	None

Note: * indicates data from pilots 1 and 2 were combined; ** indicates pilot 2 only. When a question is missing, it means that the student copy did not include the question (copying error).

What Do These Data Mean?

There were several passages where the alpha reliability estimate did not reach .60 or above. An analysis of these scales did not find specific questions that were negatively related to the total score. This means that all of the items were related to the total score, but which items varied from text to text, and we did not find a pattern. That is, we didn't find that questions designed to measure any particular standard to be more or less related to the total score. The low reliability estimates (those below .50) suggest that the ability to answer some questions was not related to the ability to answer others. A review of Tables 6.2, 6.3, and 6.4 illustrates that some standards were more difficult than others, especially in informational text.

Challenges in Scoring Summaries

After looking at student responses, scoring changes were deemed necessary for both literature and informational text. Although students were similarly able to answer questions across the content areas, their abilities to summarize what they read were greater for literature texts (mean = .27) than for informational texts (mean = .12). We changed the scoring system so that students would be given points for each statement that was included in the exemplar summaries, but some scoring differences between fiction and nonfiction were warranted. In the literature texts, students were given one point for each clause they wrote that matched the meaning of the exemplar summary and one point was subtracted for each error statement written. Most students summarized literature by citing the most important events, but occasionally students would respond with their reaction or opinion of the story rather than summarize it.

Literature Text.   Scoring systems for extended texts range from broad global evaluations (i.e., holistic scoring) to refined measures such as propositional analysis (Kintsch & van Dijk, 1978). We tried three different scoring systems to see which best measured a student's ability to summarize literature. We began with a scoring system based on clauses (Trabasso & Magliano, 1996), which parsed a story into clauses based on verbs. Each story was parsed using the clause system and summaries were compared to the parsed text. Using this system, each clause in a student's summary that matched (in meaning, not in exact words) a clause in the text was given one point. The total score was a simple summation of points. This system seemed to work, but what did it mean for instruction? What sense could a teacher make based on a number of points?

Next, we kept the clause system, but wrote exemplar summaries that included only those clauses that captured the important elements of the story. An example is shown below for the fourth-grade story *Amelia and Eleanor Go for a Ride.*

1. Amelia and Eleanor were alike   _____
2. Because they were outspoken/determined/daring (any one of these)   _____
3. Amelia was a pilot   _____
4. Eleanor was the first lady of the United States   _____
5. Eleanor invited Amelia for dinner at the White House   _____
6. Eleanor asked what it was like to fly over the Capitol at night   _____
7. Amelia invited Eleanor to fly to Baltimore and back   _____
8. The Secret Service men said it hadn't been approved   _____
9. But Eleanor went anyway   _____
10. Eleanor enjoyed the beautiful flight   _____
11. When they returned Amelia and Eleanor   _____
12. Went for a ride in Eleanor's new car   _____
13. They returned to the White House for dessert   _____

Again, we scored students' summaries by matching each statement to our exemplar summaries, giving one point for each match. This worked out better, but still left a teacher without clear implications for instruction. Finally, we took these exemplar summaries and organized them according to the elements of story. The basic story includes setting, character, initiating event (that event which must occur for the story plot to develop), events in which the main character attempts to reach a goal or solve a problem, and an ending or resolution. We used this system to rescore 20 percent of the data and found that it resulted in reliable scoring among scorers: different scorers came within one point of each other over 90 percent of the time. The final form of an exemplar summary looks like this.

Characters

1. Amelia and Eleanor were alike   _____
2. Because they were outspoken/determined/daring (any one of these)   _____
3. Amelia was a pilot   _____
4. Eleanor was the first lady of the United States   _____

Initiating Event

5. Eleanor invited Amelia for dinner at the White House   _____
6. Eleanor asked what it was like to fly over the Capitol at night   _____

Event 1

7. Amelia invited Eleanor to fly to Baltimore and back   _____
8. The Secret Service men said it hadn't been approved   _____
9. But Eleanor went anyway   _____
10. Eleanor enjoyed the beautiful flight   _____

Event 2

11. When they returned Amelia and Eleanor   _____
12. Went for a ride in Eleanor's new car   _____

Ending

13. They returned to the White House for dessert   _____

Informational Text.   Because of the structures of informational text, propositional analysis (Kintsch, 1998, 2004; Kintsch & van Dijk, 1978) was used to score the first round of data from informational text. However, the paucity of summaries of informational text led to a change in scoring. We awarded one point for an introductory statement and one point for each relevant clause. The words used in the summary did not need to be identical to the text, but the same underlying semantic content was required. Many summaries of informational texts contained material that was in the text but not specifically related to the summary question. In addition, students often included information that was not present in the text; one can only hypothesize that such information was drawn from prior knowledge. Erroneous information was also included and suggested poor understanding of text content. These results indicated lack of experience with writing text-based summaries.

Summary

This chapter describes the challenges that we faced in designing the *CARA* and how we addressed those challenges. Explanations of how we piloted the *CARA* with teachers and several samples of students were described and the results of the pilot studies were presented for each standard in literature and informational text. In literature, the most difficult standard was Standard 6, point of view. In informational text, the most difficult standard was Standard 2, identifying the central idea in sections of text and writing a text-based summary. In addition, determining the point of view in social studies was also very difficult for students. We also recruited teachers to score our data and we present the percent agreement of their scoring with ours on all standards for literature, social studies, and science passages. Our final table presents alpha reliability of all texts and explains why some of the estimates are low. We end with a discussion of the challenges in scoring summaries.

Chapter

7 Student Materials

ANSWER SHEET

Name _____ Class _____ Date _____

Name of Text _____

Write your answer to each question in the following spaces.

1. _____
   _____
   _____
   _____
   _____

2. _____
   _____
   _____
   _____
   _____

3. _____
   _____
   _____
   _____
   _____

4. _____
   _____
   _____
   _____
   _____

5. _____
   _____
   _____
   _____
   _____

6. _____
   _____
   _____
   _____

7. _____

8. _____

9. _____

10. _____

Summarize. _____

Literature, Part I

Amelia and Eleanor Go for a Ride (Adapted)
by Pam Muñoz Ryan

This story is about two remarkable women and their friendship. Read to discover the adventures they share.

Amelia and Eleanor were birds of a feather. Eleanor was outspoken and determined. So was Amelia. Amelia was daring and liked to try things other women wouldn't even consider. Eleanor was the very same. So when Eleanor discovered that her friend Amelia was coming to town to give a speech, she naturally said, "Bring your husband and come to dinner at my house!" It wasn't unusual for two friends to get together. But Eleanor was Eleanor Roosevelt, the First Lady of the United States, who lived in the White House with her husband President Franklin Roosevelt.

Amelia was Amelia Earhart, the celebrated aviator who had been the first female pilot to fly solo across the Atlantic Ocean. Many people didn't understand why a woman would want to risk her life in a plane. But Amelia had said it more than once: "It's for the fun of it." Besides, she loved the feeling of independence she had when she was in the cockpit.

In a guest room at the White House, Amelia and her husband, G.P., dressed for dinner.

1. What does "birds of a feather" mean in the sentence, "Amelia and Eleanor were birds of a feather"?

Eleanor dressed for dinner. Her brother, Hall, would be escorting her this evening because the President had a meeting to attend. Then she peeked out the window at the brand-new car that had just been delivered that afternoon. She couldn't wait to drive it.

Many people thought it was not appropriate and too dangerous for a woman to drive a car, especially the First Lady of the United States. But Eleanor always gave the same answer. "It's practical, that's all." Besides she loved the feeling of independence she had when she was behind the wheel.

2. Describe two ways that the author shows the similarities between Amelia and Eleanor.

3. What is the central idea of the story so far?

It was a brisk and cloudless April evening. The guests had gathered in the Red Room. Eleanor and Hall greeted Amelia Earhart and G.P., as well as several reporters and a photographer.

Dinner started with George Washington's crab chowder.

"This is delicious," said Amelia. "But if soup at the White House has such a fancy name, what will dessert be called?" Perhaps Abraham Lincoln's peach cobbler? Or maybe Thomas Jefferson's custard? They laughed as everyone took turns guessing.

4. Describe the setting of the story so far.

5. Using details from the story, provide one reason why there were reporters and photographers at the dinner.

"Mrs. Roosevelt just received her student pilot's license," said one of the reporters.

Amelia wasn't surprised. She had been the one to encourage Eleanor. She knew her friend could do anything she set her mind to.

"I'll teach you myself," offered Amelia.

"I accept! Tell us, Amelia, what's it like to fly at night in the dark?"

Everyone at the table leaned closer to hear. Very few people in the whole world had ever flown at night, and Amelia was one of them. Amelia's eyes sparkled. "The stars glitter all about and seem close enough to touch. At higher elevations, the clouds blow shiny white with dark islands where the night sea shows through. I've seen the planet Venus setting on the horizon, and I've circled cities of twinkling lights."

"And the capital city at night?" asked Eleanor.

"There's no describing it," said Amelia. "You just have to experience it on a clear night, when you can see forever. Why we should go tonight! We could fly the loop to Baltimore and back in no time!"

The Secret Service men protested. "This hasn't been approved!"

"Nonsense!" said Eleanor. "If Amelia Earhart can fly solo across the Atlantic Ocean, I can certainly take a short flight to Baltimore and back!"

Before dessert could be served, Amelia had called and arranged a flight. Within the hour, Amelia and Eleanor boarded the Curtis Condor twin-motor airplane. For a moment, both women looked up at the mysterious night sky.

> 6. Using details from the story, provide evidence that Eleanor Roosevelt did not allow others to control her behavior.

The plane rolled down the runway, faster and faster. And they lifted into the dark.

Amelia made a wide sweep over Washington, D.C., and turned off all the lights in the plane. Out the window, the Potomac River glistened with moonshine. The capitol dome reflected a soft golden halo. And the enormous, light-drenched monuments looked like tiny miniatures.

And even though they knew it wasn't so, it seemed as if the plane crawled slowly through star-struck space.

Eleanor marveled, "It's like sitting on top of the world!" When it was time to land, Amelia carefully took the plane down. A group of reporters had gathered, anxious to ask questions.

> 7. What does the phrase, "It's like sitting on top of the world!" mean in the previous paragraph?

"Mrs. Roosevelt, did you feel safe knowing a girl was flying that ship?"

"Just as safe!" said Eleanor.

"Did you fly the plane, Mrs. Roosevelt?" asked one reporter.

"What part of it did you like best?" said another.

"I enjoyed it so much, and no, I didn't fly the plane. But someday I intend to. I was thrilled by the city lights, the brilliance of the blinking pinpoints below."

Amelia smiled. She knew just how Eleanor felt.

As the Secret Service agents drove them slowly back to the White House, Amelia and Eleanor agreed that there was nothing quite as exciting as flying. What could compare? Well, they admitted, maybe the closest thing would be driving in a fast car on a straight-away road with a stiff breeze blowing against your face.

Arms linked, they walked up the steps to the White House. Eleanor whispered something to Amelia, and then they hesitated, letting the rest of the group walk ahead of them.

"Are you coming inside, Mrs. Roosevelt?" someone asked.

But by then they were hurrying toward Eleanor's new car. Eleanor quickly slipped into the driver's seat and took her turn at the wheel. With the wind in their hair and the brisk air stinging their cheeks, they flew down the road.

And after they had taken a ride about the city streets of Washington, D.C., they finally headed back to the White House for dessert! Eleanor Roosevelt's pink clouds on angel food cake.

8. Describe the personality of Eleanor Roosevelt using two details from the text.

9. Describe how the author shows the similarity between the two women toward the end of the story.

10. What is the message or theme of this story?

Summarize the story.

Literature, Part II

Encyclopedia Brown and the Case of the Slippery Salamander
by Donald Sobol

Read to find out what clues led to solving the case of the Slippery Salamander.

To a visitor, Idaville looked like an ordinary seaside town. It had churches, two car washes, and a movie theater. It had bike paths, beaches, and good fishing spots. But there was something out of the ordinary about Idaville. For more than a year no one had gotten away with breaking a law.

How did Idaville do it? The secret resided in a red brick house at 13 Rover Avenue. That's where Idaville's police chief lived with his wife and son. Chief Brown was a smart, kind, and brave man. But he wasn't the one solving the crimes. No, the brains behind it all was his ten-year-old son, Encyclopedia.

Encyclopedia's real name was Leroy. But only his parents and teachers called him that. Everyone else called him "Encyclopedia" because his brain was filled with more facts than a reference book. Sometimes the Brown family was tempted to tell the world about Encyclopedia's amazing talent as a crime-solver. But so far they hadn't leaked a word. Who would believe that Idaville's top detective was a fifth-grader?

1. Whose point of view is the story told from and how do you know?

2. Describe the type of man Chief Brown was and use at least two details from the story.

One Monday night Chief Brown sat at the dinner table, staring at his plate. So far he hadn't eaten anything. Encyclopedia and his mother knew the reason. The chief wasn't eating because he had come up against a crime that he couldn't solve.

At last Chief Brown looked up. "There was a theft at the aquarium today," he said, rubbing his forehead. Last summer an aquarium had opened near the beach. The most popular attractions were the giant shark tanks, the dolphin shows, and the Den of Darkness. The Den of Darkness was a huge indoor exhibit of reptiles and amphibians. Encyclopedia liked visiting the frogs and salamanders in the amphibian section.

"I hope the great white sharks weren't stolen," Mrs. Brown said with a smile. "That would certainly take a bite out of business!"

Chief Brown shook his head. "It wasn't the sharks."

Encyclopedia listened carefully as his father explained that Fred, a tiger salamander, had been stolen.

"Fred was shipped to the aquarium only two days ago," Chief Brown said. "He was being kept apart from the other animals until we were sure he was healthy. If he got a clean bill of health, he was to go on display next month."

"Do you have any clues, dear?" Mrs. Brown asked.

The chief frowned. "Not many. All we know is that the salamander disappeared this morning between ten-thirty and eleven forty-five."

3. Using details from the story, explain why the salamander was not on display in the aquarium like the others.

"Why would someone steal a salamander?" Mrs. Brown wondered.

"Fred is the aquarium's only tiger salamander," her husband explained. "From what the director of the aquarium told me, someone could steal him for a lot of money."

"Really?" Mrs. Brown's eyes widened. "Do you think a visitor might have stolen him?"

"It's very unlikely," Chief Brown replied. "Employees and volunteers are the only ones who have access to the back room in the Den of Darkness where Fred was being kept."

4. What does the word *access* mean in the following sentence? "Employees and volunteers are the only ones who have access to the back room . . . "

Chief Brown explained that three people had been working at the exhibit that morning: Mrs. King, who volunteered at the aquarium every Monday; Sam Maine, the man in charge of cleaning and maintaining the exhibits; and Dr. O'Donnell, an expert on reptiles and amphibians.

"Did you question the three of them?" Mrs. Brown asked.

The chief nodded. "Dr. O'Donnell spent the morning examining a new crocodile from Australia. Sam Maine told me he was busy cleaning out exhibits and feeding some of the lizards. Several people saw him working," Chief Brown added, "so it looks like he's telling the truth."

5. What is the central idea of the story so far?

"What about Mrs. King?" his wife prodded.

Chief Brown frowned. "Actually, Sam Maine seems very suspicious of Mrs. King," he confided. "After talking with her I can see why. Mrs. King is fascinated with salamanders. She told me that she has dozens of them at home as pets, and Fred is the first tiger salamander she's ever seen." He shook his head. "Mrs. King does seem kind of odd—she thinks salamanders are sacred creatures with magical powers."

Encyclopedia spoke up. "In ancient times, people used salamanders for medicine."

6. Describe how Encyclopedia's comment about "ancient times" shows support for Mrs. King's belief that salamanders are sacred creatures.

"Maybe Fred wasn't stolen for money," Mrs. Brown said. "Maybe Mrs. King took Fred just because she thinks he's a special specimen!"

"That's exactly what I've been thinking," Chief Brown admitted. "But there's no proof that Mrs. King had the opportunity to steal Fred. She was with a group of children from ten-thirty to eleven-fifteen. Then one of the cashiers saw her in the cafeteria."

7. Describe two reasons why people thought Mrs. King stole the salamander.

Chief Brown sighed with frustration. "I hate to admit it, but this case has me baffled!"

Encyclopedia closed his eyes. His parents watched him hopefully. They knew that when Encyclopedia closed his eyes, it meant he was doing his deepest thinking. A moment later Encyclopedia was ready. He opened his eyes and asked one question.

"Has Sam Maine been working at the aquarium long, Dad?"

"Actually, he was hired only two weeks ago," Chief Brown answered. "But he has a lot of experience. Sam told me he's been taking care of salamanders and other lizards for more than 19 years."

That was all Encyclopedia needed to hear to conclude who was the thief. "Oh, no he hasn't!" Encyclopedia declared with a satisfied smile. "If he's a lizard expert, then I'm the queen of England! Sam is lying and I can prove it!"

8. What does the phrase "if he's a lizard expert, then I'm the queen of England!" mean?

9. What did Encyclopedia hope to learn when he asked how long Sam Maine had been working at the aquarium? Provide text details to support your answer.

Encyclopedia knew that Sam was lying because he told Chief Brown he'd been taking care of "salamanders and other lizards for 19 years." Anyone who had been caring for salamanders that long would know that salamanders are not lizards, they are amphibians, and lizards are classified as reptiles.

Sam admitted stealing the new tiger salamander that morning. After he returned Fred to the aquarium, he was fired!

10. What is the message or theme of this story?

Summarize the story.

Grandfather's Journey (Adapted)

by Alan Say

Where does a grandfather's journey take him and what does he learn along the way? Read this story to find out.

My grandfather was a young man when he left his home in Japan and went to see the world. He wore European clothes for the first time and began his journey on a steamship. The Pacific Ocean amazed him. For three weeks he did not see land. When land finally appeared it was the New World.

He explored North America by train and riverboat, and often walked for days on end. Deserts with rocks like huge sculptures amazed him. The endless farm fields reminded him of the ocean he had crossed. Huge cities of factories and tall buildings confused and yet excited him.

He marveled at the high mountains and rivers as clear as the sky. He met people along the way. He shook hands with black men and white men, with yellow men and red men. The more he traveled, the more he wanted to see new places, and never thought of returning home.

1. Using details from the story, explain how we know that the trip from Japan to the New World was a long one.

2. Describe what kind of person the narrator's grandfather is and how he reacts to new things.

Of all the places he visited, he liked California best. He loved the strong sunlight there, the Sierra Mountains, the lonely seacoast. After a time, he returned to his village in Japan to marry his childhood sweetheart. Then he brought his bride to the new country. They made their home by the San Francisco Bay and had a baby girl.

As his daughter grew, my grandfather began to think about his own childhood. He thought about his old friends. He remembered the mountains and rivers of his home. He surrounded himself with songbirds, but he could not forget. Finally, when his daughter was nearly grown, he could wait no more. He took his family and returned to his homeland.

Once again he saw the mountains and rivers of his childhood. They were just as he had remembered them. Once again he exchanged stories and laughed with his old friends. But the village was not a place for a daughter from San Francisco. So my grandfather bought a house in a large city nearby. There, the young woman fell in love, married and sometime later I was born.

3. Describe the point of view from which the story is told and how you know it.

4. What is the central idea of the story so far?

When I was a small boy, my favorite weekend was a visit to my grandfather's house. He told me many stories about California. He raised warblers and silvereyes, but he could not forget the mountains and rivers of California. So he planned a trip.

But a war began. Bombs fell from the sky and scattered our lives like leaves in a storm. When the war ended, there was nothing left of the city and of the house where my grandparents had lived. So, they returned to the village where they had been children. But my grandfather never kept another songbird.

5. What do the words "scattered our lives like leaves in a storm" mean?

The last time I saw him, my grandfather said that he longed to see California one more time. He never did. And when I was nearly grown, I left home and went to see California for myself. After a time, I came to love the land my grandfather had loved, and I stayed on until I had a daughter of my own.

But I also miss the mountains and rivers of my childhood. I miss my old friends. So I return now and then, when I cannot quiet the longing in my heart.

The funny thing is, the moment I am in one country, I am homesick for the other. I think I know my grandfather now. I miss him very much.

6. What does "when I cannot quiet the longing in my heart" mean?

7. Using details from the story, explain why the author feels that he knows his grandfather now.

8. What words does the author use in the last three paragraphs to signal that he is talking about himself?

9. Describe two ways that the narrator of the story (the author) and his grandfather were alike.

10. What is the theme or message of this story?

Summarize the story.

Literature, Part I

Leonardo da Vinci: Inventor and Artist

This is a biography of Leonardo da Vinci, a famous painter who lived in the 1400s.
Read to find out about his life and what he is most known for.

Leonard da Vinci was born in 1452 close to the town of Vinci, Italy. Little is known about Leonardo's early life. He wrote down only two childhood memories. One occurred while exploring in the mountains. He discovered a cave and was terrified that some great monster might live there. However, he was also curious to find out what was inside. He showed that kind of curiosity throughout his life. He looked at things closely and was interested in how things worked. His father was busy working, so he spent his days with his uncle Francesco who taught him to observe nature. Later he would sketch these memories. His father recognized Leonardo's talents and sent him to study with a painter and sculptor.

1. Using details from the story, why do you think Leonardo's last name was da Vinci?

2. Compare and contrast how his uncle, Francesco, and his father influenced da Vinci's life.

Da Vinci's interests ranged far beyond fine art. He studied all forms of science, architecture, weaponry and more. All his life Leonardo tried to discover the secret of flying so he could create a flying machine for himself. He was successful at creating workable designs for machines like the bicycle and submarine that would not come into being for centuries. He also had beliefs that challenged current thinking. He saw science and art as complementary rather than distinct disciplines. His varied interests and talents led to a quote by Sigmund Freud. He described daVinci as a man who awoke too early in the darkness, while the others were all still asleep.

3. What does the phrase "a man who awoke too early in the darkness, while the others were all still asleep" mean?

Around 1482, he was hired to paint his first painting, the Adoration of the Magi. However, shortly after he began the work, he moved to Milan so he never completed the painting. He developed a habit of starting a project but not finishing it. He loved the planning of the project better than painting it. The Duke of Milan asked da Vinci to create a magnificent statue of a horse, in bronze, to honor his father. Da Vinci did not consider himself a sculptor, but he loved the challenge. He wanted to know all about his subjects so he visited stables, to study horses' bodies. He measured and drew pictures until he knew where all the bones and muscles of a horse were. He also visited statues of horses to see how other artists had designed them.

4. Describe how the author's point of view of da Vinci's abilities is described in the story so far.

5. What do the details in the paragraph above tell you about how Leonardo researched the object he was going to make?

When daVinci was ready to begin the Duke decided that he wanted a horse three times bigger than life. No one had attempted such a monumental project before. He worked on the project on and off for 12 years, and in 1493 a clay model was ready to display. However, by then a war with France was coming. His bronze for the sculpture went into cannons. Da

Vinci and the duke fled Milan, but the horse couldn't move. So, when the French entered Milan they used the clay model as target practice. Between their arrows and rain, the horse was destroyed.

Probably because of his many interests, da Vinci didn't complete many paintings. His most widely known painting is of the Mona Lisa, the woman with the mysterious smile. Despite its power over the ages the painting is only 2.5 feet by 1.75 feet, small for the paintings of the day. His second famous painting is The Last Supper, which he created in three years for a hall in Milan. The painting measuring 15 feet by 29 feet shows the Passover dinner during which Jesus Christ addressed the Apostles. The scene illustrates when Christ delivered the shocking message that one disciple would betray him. The Apostles reacted to the news with different degrees of horror and shock. Da Vinci created each Apostle's distinct facial expression and body language. However, Leonardo, always the inventor, tried using new materials. Instead of using wet plaster, the preferred method of fresco painting, he thought he'd use *dry* plaster. His experiment resulted in more varied colors, which was his intent. What he didn't know was that this method wouldn't last. The painted plaster began to flake off the wall almost immediately, and people have been attempting to restore it ever since.

6. Describe the theme of the story so far using text evidence to support your statement.

7. Compare and contrast daVinci's work on the horse with his painting of *The Last Supper.*

Michelangelo was another famous artist who lived at the same time. Although da Vinci was a lot older than Michelangelo, the two men were in competition. Michelangelo grew up hearing of da Vinci as the greatest artist in Europe, so he strove to better him. Michelangelo was very critical of da Vinci's tendency to start a project and not finish it. He told da Vinci he should be ashamed of not finishing the bronze horse. Da Vinci was probably jealous of all of the attention that the young Michelangelo was getting for his sculptures, especially for his divine sculptor of *David*. As if to rub salt into a wound, da Vinci was asked to help decide where to place the statue. It all was too much for him and Leonardo left Florence. He died grieving that he never finished the horse.

8. What does "rub salt into a wound" mean in the paragraph above?

9. What is a theme of this story and how does da Vinci's life show it?

10. How would this story be different if Michelangelo had written it?

Summarize the story.

Weslandia

by Paul Fleischman

This story is about a boy who is very unusual and makes a world all his own.
Read to find out what he does and how others react to it.

"Of course he's miserable," moaned Wesley's mother. "He sticks out."

"Like a nose," snapped his father.

Listening through the heating vent, Wesley knew they were right. He was an outcast from the civilization around him.

1. **What does the phrase "like a nose" mean?**

He alone in his town disliked pizza and soda, alarming his mother and the school nurse. He found professional football stupid. He'd refused to shave half his head, the hairstyle worn by all the other boys, despite his father's bribe of five dollars.

Passing his neighborhood's two styles of housing—garage on the left and garage on the right—Wesley alone dreamed of more exciting forms of shelter. He had no friends, but plenty of tormentors.

Fleeing them was the only sport he was good at.

2. **Describe two ways that Wesley was different from other boys his age.**

Each afternoon his mother asked him what he'd learned in school that day.

"That seeds are carried great distances by the wind," he answered on Wednesday.

"That each civilization has its staple food crop," he answered on Thursday.

"That school's over and I should find a good summer project," he answered on Friday.

As always, his father mumbled, "I'm sure you'll use that knowledge often."

Suddenly, Wesley's thoughts shot sparks. His eyes blazed. His father was right! He could actually use what he'd learned that week for a summer project that would top all others. He would grow his own staple food crop—and found his own civilization!

3. **Describe how Wesley's attitude toward learning was different from his father's attitude.**

The next morning he turned over a plot of ground in his yard. That night a wind blew in from the west. It raced through the trees and set his curtains snapping. Wesley lay awake, listening. His land was being planted.

Five days later the first seedlings appeared.

"You'll have almighty bedlam on your hands if you don't get those weeds out," warned his neighbor.

"Actually, that's my crop," replied Wesley. "In this type of garden there are no weeds."

4. **What is the central idea of the story so far?**

Following ancient tradition, Wesley's fellow gardeners grew tomatoes, beans, Brussels sprouts, and nothing else. Wesley found it thrilling to open his land to chance, to invite the new and unknown.

The plants shot up past his knees, then his waist. They seemed to be all of the same sort. Wesley couldn't find them in any plant book.

"Are those tomatoes, beans, or Brussels sprouts?" asked Wesley's neighbor.

"None of the above," replied Wesley.

Fruit appeared, yellow at first, then blushing magenta. Wesley picked one and sliced through the rind to the juicy purple center. He took a bite and found the taste an entrancing blend of peach, strawberry, pumpkin pie, and flavors he had no name for.

Ignoring the shelf of cereals in the kitchen, Wesley took to breakfasting on the fruit. He dried half a rind to serve as a cup, built his own squeezing device, and drank the fruit's juice throughout the day.

Pulling up a plant, he found large tubers on the roots. These he boiled, fried, or roasted on the family barbecue, seasoning them with a pinch of the plant's highly aromatic leaves.

It was hot work tending to his crop. To keep off the sun, Wesley wove himself a hat from strips of the plant's woody bark. His success with the hat inspired him to devise a spinning wheel and loom on which he wove a loose-fitting robe from the stock's soft inner fibers.

Unlike jeans, which he found scratchy and heavy, the robe was comfortable, reflected the sun, and offered myriad opportunities for pockets.

5. Describe how the author feels about Wesley, how you know that, and how the author's feelings influence how the story is told so far.

His schoolmates were scornful, then curious. Grudgingly, Wesley allowed them ten minutes apiece at his mortar, crushing the plant's seeds to collect the oil.

This oil had a tangy scent and served him both as a suntan lotion and mosquito repellant. He rubbed it on his face each morning and sold small amounts to his former tormentors at the price of ten dollars per bottle.

"What's happened to your watch?" asked his mother one day.

Wesley admitted that he no longer wore it. He told time by the stalk that he used as a sundial and had divided the day into eight segments—the number of petals on the plant's flowers.

He'd adopted a new counting system as well, based likewise upon the number eight. His domain, home to many such innovations, he named "Weslandia."

6. What does the word *segments* mean in the sentence, ". . . divided the day into eight segments—the number of petals on the plant's flowers"?

7. Using details from the story, explain why "Weslandia" was a good choice as a name for Wesley's domain.

Uninterested in traditional sports, Wesley made up his own. These were designed for a single player and used many different parts of the plant. His spectators looked on with envy.

Realizing that more players would offer him more scope, Wesley invented other games that would include his schoolmates, games rich with strategy and complex scoring systems. He tried to be patient with the other players' blunders.

August was unusually hot. Wesley built himself a platform and took to sleeping in the middle of Weslandia. He passed the evenings playing a flute he'd fashioned from a stalk or gazing up at the sky, renaming the constellations.

His parents noted Wesley's improved morale. "It's the first time in years he's looked happy," said his mother.

Wesley gave them a tour of Weslandia.

"What do you call this plant?" asked his father. Not knowing its name, Wesley had begun calling it "swist," from the sound of its leaves rustling in the breeze. In like manner, he named his new fabrics, games, and foods until he'd created an entire language. Mixing the plant's oil with soot, Wesley made a passable ink. As the finale to his summer project, he used the ink and his own eighty-letter alphabet to record the history of his civilization's founding.

In September, Wesley returned to school.

He had no shortage of friends.

8. Describe how the author feels about Wesley at this point in the story providing evidence from the last few paragraphs.

9. Using details from the story, explain why Wesley had no shortage of friends when he returned to school.

10. What is the theme or message of this story?

Summarize the story.

Literature, Part III

Journey to the Center of the Earth

by Jules Verne

This is a science fiction story written in 1864, before people knew what the center of the earth was made of. The author was very interested in science and based it on scientific knowledge at the time. The story is about characters going to explore the center of the earth to see what's there. Read to find out what they find in this excerpt from the book.

Tuesday, August 20.

At last it is evening—the time of day when we feel a great need to sleep. Of course, in this continuing light, there is no night, but we are very tired. Hans remains at the rudder, his eyes never closed. I don't know when he sleeps: but I find I am dozing myself.

And then . . . an awful shock! The raft seems to have struck some hidden rock. It is lifted right out of the water and even seems to be thrown some distance. "Eh!" cries my uncle. "What's happening?" And Hans raises his hand and points to where, about two hundred yards away, a great black mass is heaving. Then I know my worst fears have been realized.

"It's some . . . monster!" I cry.

"Yes," cries my uncle, "and over there is a huge sea lizard!"

"And beyond it . . . a crocodile! But who ever saw such a crocodile! Such hideous jaws! Such terrible teeth!"

"And a whale!" my uncle shouts. "See those enormous fins! And see how it blows air and water!"

And indeed two columns of water rise from the surface of the sea as he speaks, reaching an immense height before they fall back into the sea with an enormous crash. The whole cave in which this great sea is set, its walls and roof invisible to us, echoes with the sound of it. We are at the center of the most tremendous uproar! And then we see—and how tiny we feel!—that we are in the middle of a great circle of these creatures. Here, a turtle, forty feet wide: here, a serpent even longer, its ghastly head peering out of the water. Wherever we look, there are more of them: great teeth, frightful eyes, great coiling bodies! They are everywhere! I snatch up my rifle and think at once how useless it is. What effect would a bullet have on the armor that encases the bodies of these monsters?

1. **Using details from the story, explain why the men thought that there were several animals in the water.**

There seems no hope for us. Though, suddenly, most of the creatures have plunged under the surface and are no longer to be seen, they leave behind a mighty crocodile and a prodigious sea serpent; and they are making their way toward us, and the end seems near. I think that, useless though it is, I will fire a shot. But Hans makes a sign for me to wait. For these monsters, having come so close to the raft, suddenly turn and make a rush at each other. In their fury they appear not to have seen us. And at that moment we realize how very small we are. To their great eyes, we must seem nothing bigger than an inch or so of floating scrap.

2. **Using details from the story, explain how we know that the narrator respects Hans.**

And so, in a thunder of broken water, the battle begins. At first I think all the creatures have come to the surface and are taking part. *There* is a whale!—*there* is a lizard!—a turtle!—and other monsters for which I can find no name. I point them out to Hans. But he shakes his head.

"*Tva!*" he cries.

"*Tva?* Two? Why does he say two? There are more than two!" I cry.

"No, Hans is right," says my uncle. "One of those monsters has the snout of a porpoise, the head of a lizard, the teeth of a crocodile. . . . It is the ichthyosaurus, or great sea lizard."

"And the other?"

"The other is a serpent, but it has a turtle's shell. It is the plesiosaurus, or sea crocodile."

He is right! There seems to be half a dozen monsters, or more, but the truth is there are only two!

And ours are the first human eyes ever to look at these great primitive reptiles! I am amazed by the flaming red eyes of the ichthyosaurus, each bigger than a man's head. Those eyes, I know are of enormous strength, since they have to resist the pressure of water at the very bottom of the ocean. The creature is a hundred feet long, at least, and when I see his tail rise out of the water, angrily flicked like the hugest whip you could imagine, I can guess at his width. His jaw is larger than I'd ever dreamed a jaw could be, and I remembered that naturalists have said the jaw of the ichthyosaurus must have contained at least one hundred and eighty-two teeth. They were making their calculations, of course, from the fossilized bones of creatures they imagined had been extinct for millions of years. Now I, Hans, and my uncle are gazing, from out our tiny raft, at a living ichthyosaurus rising from an ocean deep inside the Earth!

3. **What is the central idea of the story so far?**

4. **What does the phrase ". . . when I see his tail rise out of the water, angrily flicked like the hugest whip you could imagine" mean?**

5. **Describe how the interaction between the narrator and his uncle show which of them knows more about the creatures.**

6. **Describe how the narrator's point of view toward the events in *Journey* is shown.**

The other creature is the mighty plesiosaurus, a serpent with a trunk like an immensely long cylinder, and a short thick tail and fins like the banks of oars in a Roman galley. Its body is enclosed in a shell, and its neck, flexible as a swan's, rises thirty feet above the surface of the sea.

7. **What does the phrase, "and its neck, flexible as a swan's" mean?**

No other human being has ever seen such a combat! They raise mountains of water, and time and again the raft seems about to be upset. Time and again we imagine we are drowned. The creatures hiss at each other—and the hissing is worse than the sound of the wildest wind you can imagine, all blowing together. Then they seize each other in a terrible grip, giant wrestlers: and then, break away again. And again comes the great hissing, the furious disturbance of the water!

8. Contrast how the appearance of the sea creatures at the beginning of the story was different from the second appearance described above.

And in the middle of it all, how tiny we are! We crouch on the raft, expecting that any moment it will be overturned and we shall drown in that wildly disturbed sea, hundreds of miles below the surface of the Earth: far, far from the sky, trees, the blessed fresh air!

And then, suddenly, ichthyosaurus and plesiosaurus disappear together under the waves. Their going down, in one enormous plunge, draws the sea down with them, as if a great hole had been made in the water, and we are nearly dragged down with them. For a while there is silence. The water grows calmer. And then, not far from the raft, an enormous shape appears. It is the head of the plesiosaurus.

The monster is mortally wounded. All we can make out is its neck, a serpent's. It is twisted and coiled in the agonies of death. With it the creature strikes the water as if with some great whip. Then it wriggles, as some vast worm might do, cut in two. Every dreadful movement stirs the sea violently, and we are nearly blinded as the tormented water sweeps over the raft. But bit by bit the great writhings die down, and at last the plesiosaurus lies dead on the surface.

As for the ichthyosaurus, he was surely recovering from the struggle in some deep cave. He could not have been unhurt. He must need to lick his wounds.

Or was he on his way to the surface again, to destroy us?

9. Compare and contrast how the events in the last three paragraphs suggest different endings to the rest of this story.

10. What is the theme or message of the story?

Summarize the story.

LITERATURE

Arachne (Adapted)

by Olivia E. Coolidge

This story is a myth about a talented young woman who believes that her weaving is better than anyone else's, including the goddess Athene. Read to find out what happens when a human challenges a goddess.

Arachne was a maiden who became famous throughout Greece, though she was neither wellborn nor beautiful. She lived in an obscure little village, and her father was a humble dyer of wool. In this he was very skilled, producing many varied shades. Above all he was famous for the clear, bright, scarlet which is made from shellfish. It was the most glorious of all the colors used in ancient Greece. Even more skillful than her father was Arachne. It was her task to spin the fleecy wool into a fine, soft thread and to weave it into cloth on the loom within the cottage. Arachne was small and pale from much working. Her eyes were light and her hair was a dusty brown, yet she was quick and graceful. Her fingers, roughened as they were, went so fast that it was hard to follow their flickering movements. So soft was her thread, so fine her cloth, that soon her products were known all over Greece. No one had even seen the like of them before.

1. Using words from the text, explain how Arachne's success depended on her father.

At last Arachne's fame became so great that people used to come from far and wide to watch her working. Even the graceful nymphs would steal in from stream or forest and peep shyly through the dark doorway. They watched in wonder the white arms of Arachne as she stood at the loom and threw the shuttle from hand to hand. "Surely, Athene herself must have taught her," people would murmur to one another. "Who else could know the secret of such marvelous skill?"

Arachne was immensely proud of her skill that had brought so many to look on her. Praise was all she lived for, and it displeased her greatly that people should think anyone, even a goddess, could teach her anything. Therefore, when she heard them murmur, she would stop her work and turn round indignantly to say, "With my own ten fingers I gained this skill, and by hard practice from early morning till night. I never had time to stand looking as you people do while another maiden worked. Nor if I had, would I give Athene credit because the girl was more skillful than I. As for Athene's weaving, how could there be finer cloth or more beautiful embroidery than mine? If Athene herself were to come down and compete with me, she could do no better than I."

2. Describe how what Arachne said about Athene in the last sentence sets up the plot of the story.

3. What does the word *credit* mean in this sentence? "Nor if I had, would I give Athene credit because the girl was more skillful than I."

4. What is the narrator's point of view of Arachne and what words in the text support your answer?

One day when Arachne turned round with such words, an old woman answered her. The gray old woman, bent and poor, stood leaning on a staff and peering at Arachne amid the crowd of onlookers. "Reckless girl," she said, "how dare you claim to be equal to the immortal gods themselves? I am an old woman and have seen much. Take my advice and ask pardon of Athene for your words. Rest content with your fame of being the best spinner and weaver that mortal eyes have ever beheld."

"Stupid old woman," said Arachne indignantly, "who gave you a right to speak in this way to me? It is easy to see that you were never good for anything in your day, or you would not come here in poverty and rags to gaze at my skill. If Athene resents my words, let her answer them herself. I have challenged her to a contest, but she, of course, will not come. It is easy for gods to avoid matching their skill with that of men."

5. What does the word *challenged* mean in this sentence? "I have challenged her to a contest, but she, of course, will not come."

At these words the old woman threw down her staff and stood erect. The wondering onlookers saw her grow tall and fair and stand clad in long robes of dazzling white. They were terribly afraid as they realized that they stood in the presence of Athene.

Arachne herself flushed red for the moment, for she had never really believed that the goddess would hear her. Before the group that was gathered there she would not give in; so pressing her pale lips together in obstinacy and pride, she led the goddess to one of the great looms and set herself before the other.

6. Describe how Arachne's reaction to Athene in the last paragraph moves the plot along.

Without a word both began to thread the long woolen strands that hung from the rollers, and between which the shuttle moved back and forth. Many skeins lay heaped beside them to use, bleached white, and gold, and scarlet and other shades, varied as the rainbow. Arachne had never thought of giving credit for her success to her father's skill in dyeing, though in actual truth the colors were as remarkable as the cloth itself.

Soon there was no sound in the room but the breath of the onlookers, the whirring of the shuttles, and the creaking of the wooden frames. The excited crowd in the doorway began to see that the skill of both in truth was very nearly equal. But however the cloth might turn out the goddess was the quicker of the two. A pattern of many pictures was growing on her loom. There was a border of twined branches of the olive, Athene's favorite tree, while in the middle figures began to appear. As they looked at the glowing colors, the spectators realized that Athene was weaving into her pattern a last warning to Arachne. The central figure was the goddess herself competing with Poseidon, the Greek god of the seas and horses, for possession of the city of Athens. But in the four corners were mortals who had tried to strive with gods and pictures of the awful fate that had overtaken them. The goddess ended a little before Arachne and stood back from her marvelous work to see what the maiden was doing.

7. What is the narrator's point of view of Athene and how is it shown in the previous paragraph?

Never before had Arachne been matched against anyone whose skill was equal, or even nearly equal to her own. As she stole glances from time to time at Athene and saw the goddess working calmly, but always a little faster than herself. Arachne became angry instead of frightened, and an evil thought came into her head. Athene stepped back a pace to watch Arachne finishing her work. She saw that the maiden had taken for her design a pattern of scenes which showed evil or unworthy actions of the gods. The patterns showed how the gods had deceived fair maidens, and resorted to trickery. The patterns showed that gods appeared on earth from time to time in the form of poor and humble people. When the goddess saw this insult glowing in bright colors on Arachne's loom, she did not wait while the cloth was judged. She stepped forward, her gray eyes blazing with anger, and tore Arachne's work across. Then she struck Arachne across the face. Arachne stood there for a moment, struggling with anger, fear, and pride. "I will not live under this insult," she cried, and seizing a rope from the wall, she made a noose and would have hanged herself.

8. Describe how Arachne's choice of a design for her weaving added to the development of the plot.

The goddess touched the rope and touched the maiden. "Live on, wicked girl," she said. "Live on and spin, both you and your descendents. When men look at you they may remember it is not wise to strive with Athene." At that the body of Arachne shriveled up, and her legs grew tiny, spindly, and distorted. There before the eyes of the spectators hung a dusty brown spider on a slender thread.

All spiders descend from Arachne. As the Greeks watched them spinning their thread wonderfully fine, they remembered the contest with Athene. They thought that it was not right for even the best of men to claim equality with the gods.

9. Why was Arachne the cause of her own downfall? Provide supporting evidence from the text.

10. What is the theme or central idea of the story? Provide two details from the text that support the theme.

Summarize the story.

The Wounded Wolf

by Jean Craighead George

This story is about a wolf that gets injured and his fight for survival. Read to find out the benefits of wolves living in a pack.

A wounded wolf climbs Toklat Ridge, a massive span of rock and ice. As he limps, dawn strikes the ridge and lights it up with sparks and stars. Roko, the wounded wolf, blinks in the ice fire, then stops to rest and watch his pack run the thawing Arctic valley. They plunge and turn and fight the mighty caribou that struck young Roko with his hoof and wounded him. He jumped between the beast and Kiglo, leader of the Toklat pack. Young Roko spun and fell with hooves, paws, and teeth roaring over him. And then his pack and the beast were gone.

Gravely injured, Roko pulls himself toward the shelter rock. Weakness overcomes him and he stops. He and his pack are thin and hungry. The winter's harvest has been taken so this is the season of starvation. The produce of spring has not begun.

1. What does the word *gravely* mean in this sentence? "Gravely injured, Roko pulls himself toward the shelter rock."

Young Roko glances down the valley, droops his head, and stiffens his tail to signal to his pack that he is badly hurt. A frigid blast of wind picks up long shawls of snow and drapes them between young Roko and his pack. Winds wail and so his message is not read.

2. Using words from the story, explain how the weather interfered with Roko's signal.

A raven scouting Toklat Ridge sees Roko's signal. "Kong, kong, kong," he bells—death is coming to the ridge; there will be flesh and bone for all. His voice rolls out across the country and penetrates the rocky cracks where the Toklat ravens rest. One by one they hear, spread their wings, and beat their way to Toklat Ridge. They alight upon the snow and walk behind the wounded wolf.

"Kong," they toll with keen excitement, for the raven clan is hungry, too. "Kong, kong"— there will be flesh and bone for all.

Roko snarls and hurries toward the shelter rock. A cloud of snow envelopes him. He limps in blinding whiteness now.

A ghostly presence flits around. "Hahahahahaha," the white fox states—death is coming to the Ridge. Roko smells the fox tagging at his heels.

The cloud whirls off and two golden eyes look up at Roko. The snowy owl has heard the ravens and joined the deathwatch.

3. What does the phrase "a ghostly presence flits around" mean?

Roko limps along. The ravens walk and the white fox leaps. The snowy owl flies and hops along the rim of Toklat Ridge. Roko stops. Below the ledge out on the flats the musk-ox herd is circling. They form a ring and all face out, a fort of heads and horns and fur that sweeps down to their hooves. Their circle means to Roko that an enemy is present. He squints and smells the wind. It carries scents of thawing ice, broken glass—and earth. The grizzly bear is up! He has awakened from his winter's sleep and craving need for flesh will drive him.

Roko sees the shelter rock. He strains to reach it, and stumbles. The ravens move in closer and the white fox boldly walks beside him. "Hahaha," he yaps. The snowy owl flies ahead, alights, and waits.

The grizzly bear hears the eager fox and rises on his flat hind feet. He twists his powerful neck and head and his great paws dangle at his chest. He sees the animal procession and hears the ravens knell of death. Dropping to all fours, he joins the march up Toklat Ridge.

Roko stops; his breath comes hard. A raven alights upon his back and picks the open wound. Roko snaps and the raven flies and circles back. The white fox rips at Roko's toes and the snowy owl inches closer. The grizzly bear, still dulled by sleep, stumbles onto Toklat Ridge.

Only yards from the shelter rock, Roko falls.

Instantly the ravens mob him. They scream and peck and stab at his eyes. The white fox leaps upon his wound. The snowy owl sits and waits.

4. What is the narrator's point of view towards the ravens, fox, and owl, and which words in the text show it?

Young Roko struggles to his feet. He bites the ravens, snaps at the fox, and lunges at the stoic owl. He turns and warns the grizzly bear. Then he bursts into a run and falls against the shelter rock. The wounded wolf wedges down between the rock and barren ground. Now protected on three sides, he turns and faces all his foes.

The ravens step a few feet closer. The fox slides toward him on his belly. The snowy owl blinks and waits, and on the ridge rim roars the hungry grizzly bear.

Roko growls.

5. What is the narrator's point of view towards Roko and which words in the text show it?

6. Using words from the story, explain why Roko has the courage to face his foes.

The sun comes up. Far across the Toklat Valley, Roko hears his pack's "hunts ended" song. The music wails and sobs, wilder than the bleating wind. The hunt song ends and next comes the roll call. Each member of Toklat's pack barks to say that he is home and well.

"Kiglo here," Roko hears his leader bark. There is a pause. It is young Roko's turn but he cannot lift his head to answer. The pack is silent and the leader starts the count once more. "Kiglo here." A pause. Roko cannot answer.

The wounded wolf whimpers softly. A mindful raven hears. "Kong, kong, kong," he tolls—this is the end. His booming sounds across the valley. The wolf pack hears the raven's message that something is dying. They know it is Roko, who has not answered roll call.

7. Describe how the "roll call" moves the plot along.

The hours pass. The wind slams snow on Toklat Ridge and massive clouds blot out the sun. In their gloom Roko sees the deathwatch move in closer. Suddenly he hears the musk-oxen thundering into their circle. The ice cracks as the grizzly leaves. The ravens bust into the air, the white fox runs, and the snowy owl flaps to the top of the shelter rock. And Kiglo rounds the knoll.

In his mouth he carries meat. He drops it close to Roko's head and wags his tail excitedly. Roko licks Kiglo's chin to honor him. Then Kiglo puts his mouth around Roko's nose. This gesture says, "I am your leader." And by mouthing Roko, he binds him and all the wolves together.

The wounded wolf wags his tail. Kiglo trots away.

Already Roko's wound feels better. He gulps the food and feels his strength return. He shatters bone, flesh, and gristle and shakes the scraps out on the snow. The hungry ravens swoop upon them. The white fox snatches up a bone and the snowy owl consumes flesh and fur. And Roko wags his tail and watches.

8. Describe how AND why Roko's behavior toward the animals changed from earlier in the plot to now.

For days Kiglo brings young Roko food. He gnashes, gorges, and scatters bits upon the snow. A purple sandpiper winging north see ravens, owl, and fox and he drops in upon the feast. The long-tailed jaeger gull flies down and joins the crowd on Toklat Ridge. Roko wags his tail.

One dawn he moves his wounded leg. He stretches it and pulls himself into the sunlight. He walks—he romps. He runs in circles. He leaps and plays with chunks of ice. Suddenly he stops. The "hunt's end" song rings out. Next comes the roll call.

"Kiglo here."

"Roko here," he barks out strongly.

The pack is silent.

"Kiglo here," the leader repeats.

"Roko here."

Across the distance comes the sound of whoops and yips and barks and howls. They fill the dawn with celebration and Roko prances down the Ridge.

9. Describe four events that are necessary to the plot of the story.

10. What is the message or theme of this story? Include evidence from the story to support your answer.

Summarize the story.

Señor Coyote and the Tricked Trickster: A Mexican Folktale

by I.G. Edmonds

One day long ago in Mexico's land of sand and giant cactus, Señor Coyote and Señor Mouse had a quarrel. None now alive can remember why, but recalling what spirited caballeros (gentlemen) these two were, I suspect that it was some small thing that meant little. Be that as it may, these two took their quarrels seriously and for a long time would not speak to each other. Read to find out what caused them to speak to each other again.

Then one day Mouse found Señor Coyote caught in a trap. He howled and twisted and fought, but he could not get out. He had just about given up when he saw Señor Mouse grinning at him.

"Mouse! *Mi Viejo amigo*—my old friend!" he cried. "Please gnaw this leather strap in two and get me out of this trap."

"But we are no longer friends," Mouse said. "We have quarreled, remember?"

"Nonsense!" Señor Coyote cried. "Why, I love you better than I do Rattlesnake, Owl, or anybody in the desert. You must gnaw me loose. And please hurry, for if the *peon* (worker) catches me I will wind up a fur rug on his wife's kitchen floor."

Mouse remembered how mean Señor Coyote had been to him. He was always playing tricks on Mouse and his friends. They were very funny to Señor Coyote for he was a great trickster, but often they hurt little Mouse.

"I'd like to gnaw you free," he said, "but I am old and my teeth tire easily."

"Really, Señor Mouse, you are ungrateful," said Señor Coyote reproachfully. "Remember all the nice things I have done for you."

"What were they?"

"Why—" Coyote began and stopped. He was unable to think of a single thing. There was a good reason for this. He had done nothing for Mouse but trick him. But Señor Coyote was a sly fellow. He said quickly, "Oh, why remind you of them? You remember them all."

"I fear my memory of yesterday is too dim," Mouse said, "but I could remember very well what you could do for me tomorrow."

"Tomorrow?" Coyote asked.

"Yes, tomorrow. If I gnaw the leather rope holding you in the trap, what will you do for me tomorrow, and the day after tomorrow and the day after the day after tomorrow and the day. . ."

"Stop!" Señor Coyote cried. "How long is this going to go on?"

"A life is worth a life. If I save your life, you should work for me for a lifetime. That is the only fair thing to do."

"But everyone would laugh at a big, brave, smart fellow like me working as a slave for a mere mouse!" Señor Coyote cried.

"Is that worse than feeling sad for you because your hide is a rug in the peon's kitchen?"

Señor Coyote groaned and cried and argued, but finally agreed when he saw that Mouse would not help him otherwise.

"Very well," he said tearfully, "I agree to work for you until either of us dies or until I have a chance to get even by saving your life."

Mouse said with a sly grin, "That is very fine, but remember what a great trickster you are. So you must also promise that as soon as I free you that you will not jump on me, threaten to kill me, and then save my life by letting me go!"

"Why, how can you suggest such a thing?" Coyote cried indignantly. And then to himself he added, "This mouse is getting too smart!"

"Very well, promise," said Mouse.

1. **Describe how the interaction between Coyote and Mouse sets up the plot.**

2. **Using words from the text, how does the author tell us that Coyote thought he was better than Mouse?**

3. **What is the narrator's point of view of Coyote, and which words in the story tell you about his point of view?**

"But I am not made for work," Señor Coyote said tearfully. "I live by being sly."

"Then be sly and get out of that trap yourself," Mouse retorted.

"Very well," Señor Coyote said sadly. "I will work for you until I can pay back the debt of my life."

And so Mouse gnawed the leather strap in two and Coyote was saved. Then for many days thereafter Señor Coyote worked for Mouse. Mouse was very proud to have the famous Señor Coyote for a servant. Señor Coyote was greatly embarrassed since he did not like being a servant and disliked working even more.

There was nothing he could do since he had given his promise. He worked all day and dreamed all night of how he could trick his way out of his troubles. He could think of nothing.

4. **Describe how Coyote's behavior has changed from the beginning of the story until now.**

Then one day Baby Mouse came running to him. "My father has been caught by Señor Snake!" he cried. "Please come and save him."

"Hooray!" cried Coyote. "If I save him, I will be released from my promise to work for him."

He went out to the desert rocks and found Señor Rattlesnake with his coils around Señor Mouse.

"Please let him go and I will catch you two more mice," Coyote said.

"My wise old mother used to tell me that a bird in the hand is worth two in the bush," Snake replied. "By that same reasoning, one mouse in Snake's stomach is worth two in Coyote's mind."

5. **What does the phrase "a bird in the hand is worth two in the bush" mean?**

"Well, I tried, Mouse," Coyote said. "I'm sorry you must be eaten."

"But you must save me, then you will be free from your promise to me," Mouse said.

"If you're eaten, I'll be free anyway," Coyote said.

"Then everyone will say that Coyote was not smart enough to trick Snake," Mouse said quickly. "And I think they will be right. It makes me very sad, for I always thought Señor Coyote the greatest trickster in the world."

This made Coyote's face turn red. He was very proud that everyone thought him so clever. Now he just *had* to save Mouse.

6. **Describe how Mouse changes to become more like the sly Coyote.**

So he said to Snake, "How did you catch Mouse anyway?"

"A rock rolled on top of him and he was trapped," Mouse said. "He asked me to help him roll it off. When I did he jumped on me before I could roll away."

"That is not true," Snake said. "How could a little mouse have the strength to roll away a big rock? There is the rock. Now you tell me if you think Mouse could roll it."

It was a very big rock and Coyote acknowledged that Mouse could not possibly have budged it.

"But it is like the story *Mamacita* tells her children at bedtime," Mouse said quickly. "Once there was a poor burro who had a load of hay just as large as he could carry. His master added just one more straw and the poor burro fell in the dirt. Snake did not have quite enough strength to push the rock off himself. I came along and was like that last straw on the burro's back and together we rolled the rock away."

"Maybe that is true," Snake said, "but by Mouse's own words, he did only a very little of the work. So I owe him only a very little thanks. That is not enough to keep me from eating him."

7. **What is the narrator's point of view of Mouse, and which words in the text show you his point of view?**

"Hmmm," said Coyote. "Now you understand, Snake, that I do not care what happens, myself. If Mouse is eaten, I will be free of my bargain anyway. I am only thinking of your own welfare, Snake."

"Thank you," said Señor Rattlesnake, "but I do enough thinking about my welfare for both of us. I don't need your thoughts."

"Nevertheless," Coyote insisted. "Everyone is going to say that you ate Mouse after he was kind enough to help you."

"I don't care," Snake said. "Nobody says anything good of me anyway."

8. **What does the word *welfare* mean in these sentences? "I am only thinking of your own welfare, Snake." . . . "but I do enough thinking about my welfare for both of us."**

"Well," said Coyote. "I'll tell you what we should do. We should put everything back as it was. Then I will see for myself if Mouse was as much help as he said he was or as little as you claim. Then I can tell everyone that you were right, Snake."

"Very well," said Señor Snake. "I was lying like this and the rock was on me—"

"Like this?" Coyote said, quickly rolling the rock across Snake's body.

"Ouch!" said Snake. "That is right."

"Can you get out?" Coyote asked.

"No," said Snake.

"Then turn Mouse loose and let him push," said Coyote.

This Snake did, but before Mouse could push, Coyote said, "But on second thought, if Mouse pushes you, you would then grab him again and we'd be back arguing. Since you are both as you were before the argument started, let us leave it at that and all be friends again!"

Then Coyote turned to Mouse. "So, my friend, I have now saved your life. We are now even and my debt to you is paid."

"But mine is such a little life," Mouse protested. "And yours is so much *larger*. I don't think they balance. You should still pay me part."

"This is ridiculous!" Coyote cried. "I—"

"Wait!" Snake put in hopefully. "Let me settle the quarrel. Now you roll the rock away. I'll take Mouse in my coils just the way we were when Coyote came up. We'll be in a position to decide if—"

"Thank you," said Mouse. "It isn't necessary to trouble everyone again. Señor Coyote, we are even."

9. Using details from the story, explain why Mouse decided to accept that Coyote paid his debt at the end.

10. What is the theme or message of this story?

Summarize the story.

Literature, Part I

All Summer in a Day

by Ray Bradbury

This is a story about children who live on the planet Venus, where it rains constantly except for a few hours on one day every seven years. Read how the children respond to such weather.

"Ready?"

"Ready."

"Now?"

"Soon."

"Do the scientists really know? Will it happen today, will it?"

"Look, look: see for yourself!"

The children pressed to each other like so many roses, so many weeds, intermixed, peering out for a look at the hidden sun.

It rained.

It had been raining for seven years; thousands upon thousands of days compounded and filled from one end to the other with rain, with the drum and gush of water, with the sweet crystal fall of showers and the concussion of storms so heavy there were tidal waves come over the islands. A thousand forests had been crushed under the rain and grown up a thousand times to be crushed again. And this was the way life was on the planet Venus and this was the schoolroom of the children of the rocket men and women who had come to a raining world to set up civilization and live out their lives.

1. Using details from the story, provide two reasons why the setting of the story is unusual.

"It's stopping. It's stopping!"

"Yes, yes!"

Margot stood apart from them, from these children who could not remember a time when there wasn't rain and rain and rain. They were all nine years old, and if there had been a day, seven years ago, when the sun came out for an hour and showed its face to the stunned world, they could not recall. Sometimes, at night, she heard them stir, in remembrance, and she knew they were dreaming and remembering gold or a yellow crayon or a coin large enough to buy the world with. She knew they thought they remembered warmness, like a blushing in the face, in the body, in the arms and legs and trembling hands. But then they always awoke to the tatting drum, the endless shaking down of clear bead necklaces upon the roof, the walk, the gardens, the forests, and their dreams were gone.

2. What does, "endless shaking down of clear bead necklaces upon the roof, the walk, the garden" describe in the previous sentence above?

All day yesterday they had read in the class about the sun. About how like a lemon it was, and how hot. And they had written small stories or essays or poems about it:

I think the sun is a flower.

That blooms for just one hour.

That was Margot's poem, read in a quiet voice in the still classroom while the rain was falling outside.

"Aw, you didn't write that!" protested one of the boys.

"I did," said Margot. "I did."

"William!" said the teacher.

But that was yesterday. Now the rain was slackening, and the children were crushed in the great thick windows.

"Where's teacher?"

"She'll be back."

"She'd better hurry, we'll miss it!"

They turned on themselves, like a feverish wheel, all fumbling spokes.

3. **Analyze how the setting has shaped the children's lives.**

Margot stood alone. She was a frail girl who looked as if she had been lost in the rain for years and the rain had washed out the blue from her eyes and the red from her mouth and the yellow from her hair. She was an old photograph dusted from an album, whitened away, and if she spoke at all her voice would be a ghost. Now she stood, separate, staring at the rain and the loud wet world beyond the huge glass.

"What're you looking at?" said William.

Margot said nothing.

"Speak when you're spoken to." He gave her a shove. But she did not move; rather she let herself be moved only by him and nothing else.

They edged away from her; they would not look at her. She felt them go away. And this was because she would play no games with them in the echoing tunnels of the underground city. If they tagged her and ran, she stood blinking after them and did not follow. When the class sang songs about happiness and life and games her lips barely moved. Only when they sang about the sun and the summer would her lips move as she watched the drenched windows.

4. **Describe how the author shows Margo and William are different.**

And then, of course, the biggest crime of all was that she had come here only five years ago from Earth, and she remembered the sun and the way the sun was and the sky when she was four in Ohio. And they, they had been on Venus all their lives, and they had been only two years old when last the sun came out and had long since forgotten the color and heat of it and the way it really was. But Margot remembered.

"It's like a penny," she said once, eyes closed.

"No, it's not!" the children cried.

"It's like a fire," she said, "in the stove."

"You're lying, you don't remember!" cried the children.

But she remembered and stood quietly apart from all of them and watched the patterning windows. And once, a month ago, she had refused to shower in the school shower rooms, had clutched her hands to her ears and over her head, screaming the water mustn't touch her head. So after that, dimly, dimly, she sensed it, she was different and they knew her difference and kept away.

There was talk that her father and mother were taking her back to Earth next year; it seemed vital to her that they do so, though it would mean the loss of thousands of dollars to her family. And so the children hated her for all of these reasons of big and little consequence. They hated her pale snow face, her waiting silence, her thinness, and her possible future.

"Get away!" the boy gave her another push. "What're you waiting for?"

Then for the first time, she turned and looked at him. And what she was waiting for was in her eyes.

"Well, don't wait around here!" cried the boy savagely. "You won't see nothing!"

Her lips moved.

"Nothing!" he cried. "It was all a joke, wasn't it?" He turned to the other children. "Nothing's happening today. Is it?"

They all blinked at him and then, understanding, laughed and shook their heads. "Nothing, nothing!"

"Oh, but," Margot whispered, her eyes helpless. "But this is the day, the scientists predict, they say, they know, the sun . . ."

"All a joke!" said the boy, and seized her roughly.

"Hey everyone, let's put her in a closet before the teacher comes!"

"No," said Margot, falling back.

5. Explain the relationships among the children and how their relationships have begun to develop the plot.

They surged about her, caught her up and bore her, protesting and then pleading, and then crying, back into a tunnel, a room, a closet, where they slammed and locked the door. They stood looking at the door and saw it tremble from her beating and throwing herself against it. They heard her muffled cries. Then smiling, they turned and went out and back down the tunnel, just as the teacher arrived.

"Ready, children?" She glanced at her watch.

"Yes," said everyone.

"Are we all here?"

"Yes!"

The rain slackened still more.

They crowded to the huge door.

The rain stopped.

It was as if, in the midst of a film concerning an avalanche, a tornado, a hurricane, a volcanic eruption, something had, first, gone wrong with the sound apparatus, thus muffling and finally cutting off all the noise, all of the blasts and repercussions and thunders, and then, second, ripped the film from the projector and inserted in its place a peaceful tropical slide which did not move or tremor. The world ground to a standstill. The silence was so immense and unbelievable that you felt your ears had been stuffed or you had lost your hearing altogether. The children put their hands to their ears. They stood apart. The door slid back and the smell of the silent, waiting world came in to them. The sun came out.

It was the color of flaming bronze and it was very large. And the sky around it was a blazing blue tile color. And the jungle burned with sunlight as the children, released from their spell, rushed out, yelling, into the springtime.

"Now, don't go too far," called the teacher after them. "You wouldn't want to get caught out!"

But, they were running and turning their faces up to the sky and feeling the sun on their cheeks like a warm iron; they were taking off their jackets and letting the sun burn their arms.

"Oh, it's better than the sun lamps, isn't it?"

"Much, much better!"

They stopped running and stood in the jungle that covered Venus that grew and never stopped growing, tumultuously, even as you watched it. It was a nest of octopi, clustering up great arms of fleshlike weed, wavering, flowering in this brief spring. It was the color of rubber and ash, this jungle, from the many years without sun. It was the color of stones and white cheeses and ink, and it was the color of the moon.

6. What does the phrase "a nest of octopi" mean in the following sentences? "They stopped running and stood in the jungle that covered Venus that grew and never stopped growing, tumultuously, even as you watched it. It was a nest of octopi, clustering up great arms of fleshlike weed, wavering, flowering in this brief spring."

The children lay out, laughing, on the jungle mattress, and heard it sigh and squeak under them, resilient and alive. They ran among the trees, they slipped and fell, they pushed each other, they played hide-and-seek and tag, but most of all they squinted at the sun until tears ran down their faces, they put their hands up to that yellowness and that amazing blueness and they breathed of the fresh, fresh air and listened and listened to the silence which suspended them in a blessed sea of no sound and no motion. They looked at everything and savored everything. Then, wildly, like animals escaped from their caves, they ran and ran in shouting circles. They ran for an hour and did not stop running.

And then—

In the midst of their running one of the girls wailed. Everyone stopped. The girl, standing in the open, held out her hand.

"Oh, look, look," she said, trembling.

They came slowly to look at her opened palm.

In the center of it, cupped and huge, was a single raindrop.

She began to cry, looking at it.

They glanced quietly at the sky.

"Oh. Oh."

A few cold drops fell on their noses and their cheeks and their mouths. The sun faded behind a stir of mist. A wind blew cool around them. They turned and started to walk back toward the underground house, their hands at their sides, their smiles vanishing away.

A boom of thunder startled them and like leaves before a new hurricane, they tumbled upon each other and ran. Lightning struck ten miles away, five miles away, a mile away, a half mile. The sky darkened into midnight in a flash.

They stood in the doorway of the underground for a moment until it was raining hard. Then they closed the door and heard the gigantic sound of the rain falling in tons and avalanches.

"Will it be seven more years?"

"Yes. Seven."

Then one of them gave a little cry.

"Margot!"

"What?"

"She's still in the closet where we locked her."

"Margot."

They stood as if someone had driven them, like so many stakes, into the floor. They looked at each other and then looked away. They glanced out at the world that was raining now and raining and raining steadily. They could not meet each other's glances. Their faces were solemn and pale. They looked at their hands and feet, their faces down.

7. What does the phrase "they stood as if someone had driven them, like so many stakes, into the floor" describe?

8. Contrast how the children were feeling when they first put Margo in the closet to how they are feeling now.

"Margot."

One of the girls said, "Well . . . ?"

No one moved.

"Go on," whispered the girl.

They walked slowly down the hall in the sound of cold rain. They turned through the doorway to the room in the sound of the storm and thunder, lightning in their faces, blue and terrible. They walked over to the closet door slowly and stood by it.

Behind the closet door was only silence.

They unlocked the door, even more slowly, and let Margot out.

9. Using two details from the story, explain why locking Margot in the closet on this day was an especially cruel thing to do.

10. What is the theme or message of the story?

Summarize the story.

LITERATURE

The Californian's Tale (Adapted)

by Mark Twain

This story takes place during the gold rush in California. A man who has been there for many years is walking and finds a well-cared-for house and a welcoming owner. Read to find out what happens during his visit.

Thirty-five years ago I was out prospecting in California, tramping all day long with pick and pan and horn, and washing a hatful of dirt here and there, always expecting to make a rich strike, and never doing it. It was a lovely region, woodsy, balmy, delicious, and had once been populous, long years before, but now the people had vanished. In the country neighborhood one found at intervals the prettiest little cottage homes, snug and cozy, and cobwebbed with rose vines—sign that these were deserted homes, forsaken years ago by defeated and disappointed families who could neither sell them nor give them away. Now and then, half hour apart, one came across solitary log cabins of the earliest mining days, built by the first gold-miners. In some few cases these cabins were still occupied; and when this was so, you could depend upon it that the occupant was the very pioneer who had built the cabin.

1. Analyze how the story's location relates to the narrator.

It was a lonesome land! Not a sound in all those peaceful expanses of grass and woods but the drowsy hum of insects; no glimpse of man or beast; nothing to keep up your spirits and make you glad to be alive. And so at last, when I caught sight of a human creature, I felt a most grateful uplift. This person was a man about forty-five years old, and he was standing at the gate of one of those cozy little rose-clad cottages of the sort already referred to. However, this one hadn't a deserted look; it had the look of being lived in and petted and cared for and looked after; and so had its front yard, which was a garden of flowers, abundant, gay and flourishing. I was invited in, of course, and required to make myself at home—it was the custom of the country.

2. Cite two pieces of evidence from the previous paragraph to explain why the man was so grateful to see the 45-year-old man and the cottage.

It was delightful to be in such a place, after long weeks of daily and nightly familiarity with miners' cabins—with all which this implies of dirt floor, tin plates and cups, bacon and beans and black coffee, and nothing of ornament but war pictures tacked to the log walls. That was all hard, cheerless, materialistic desolation, but here was a nest which had aspects to rest the tired eye and refresh that something in one's nature which, after long fasting, recognizes, when confronted by the belongings of art, howsoever cheap and modest they might be, that it has unconsciously been famishing and now has found nourishment.

3. What does the following sentence mean? ". . . but here was a nest which had aspects to rest the tired eye and refresh that something in one's nature which, after long fasting, recognizes, when confronted by the belongings of art, howsoever cheap and modest they might be, that it has unconsciously been famishing and now has found nourishment."

The delight that was in my heart showed in my face, and the man saw it and was pleased; saw it so plainly that he answered it as if it had been spoken.

"All her work," he said caressingly; "she did it all herself—every bit," and he took the room in with a glance which was full of affectionate worship. One of those soft Japanese fabrics with which women drape with careful negligence the upper part of a picture frame was out of adjustment. He noticed it, and rearranged it with cautious pains, stepping back several times to gauge the effect before he got it to suit him. Then he gave it a light finishing pat or two with his hand, and said: "She always does that. You can't tell just what it lacks, but it does lack something until you've done that—you can see for yourself after it's done."

He took me into a bedroom so that I might wash my hands; such a bedroom as I had not seen for years: white counterpane, white pillows, carpeted floor, papered walls, pictures, dressing-table, with mirror and pin-cushion and dainty toilet things; and in the corner a wash-stand, with real china-ware bowl and pitcher, and with soap in a china dish, and on a rack more than a dozen towels—towels too clean and white for one out of practice to use without some vague sense of profanation. So my face spoke again, and he answered with gratified words:

"All her work; she did it all herself—every bit. Nothing here that hasn't felt the touch of her hand. But I mustn't talk so much."

By this time I was wiping my hands and glancing from detail to detail of the room's belongings, as one is apt to do when he is in a new place, where everything he sees is a comfort to his eye and his spirit; and I became conscious that there was something there somewhere that the man wanted me to discover for myself. I knew he was trying to help me by furtive indications with his eye, so I tried hard to get on the right track, being eager to gratify him. I failed several times, as I could see out of the corner of my eye without being told; but at last I knew I must be looking straight at the thing—knew it from the pleasure issuing in invisible waves from him. He broke into a happy laugh, and rubbed his hands together, and cried out:

"That's it! You've found it. I knew you would. It's her picture."

I went to the little black-walnut bracket on the farther wall, and did find there what I had not yet noticed—a daguerreotype-case. It contained the sweetest girlish face, and the most beautiful, as it seemed to me, that I had ever seen. The man drank the admiration from my face, and was fully satisfied.

4. **Explain the phrase "drank the admiration from my face."**

"Nineteen her last birthday," he said, as he put the picture back; "and that was the day we were married. When you see her—ah, just wait till you see her!"

"Where is she? When will she be in?"

"Oh, she's away now. She's gone to see her people. They live forty or fifty miles from here. She's been gone two weeks today."

"When do you expect her back?"

"This is Wednesday. She'll be back Saturday, in the evening—about nine o'clock, likely."

I felt a sharp sense of disappointment.

"I'm sorry, because I'll be gone then," I said, regretfully.

"Gone? No—why should you go? Don't go. She'll be disappointed."

She would be disappointed—that beautiful creature! If she had said the words herself they could hardly have blessed me more. I was feeling a deep, strong longing to see her—a longing so supplicating, so insistent, that it made me afraid. I said to myself: "I will go straight away from this place, for my peace of mind's sake."

"You see, she likes to have people come and stop with us—people who know things, and can talk—people like you. She delights in it; don't go; it's only a little while, you know, and she'll be so disappointed."

I heard the words, but hardly noticed them, I was so deep in my thinkings and strugglings. He left me, but I didn't know. Presently he was back, with the picture case in his hand, and he held it open before me and said:

"There, now, tell her to her face you could have stayed to see her, and you wouldn't."

That second glimpse broke down my good resolution. I would stay and take the risk.

5. **Cite one piece of information that suggests why the narrator is afraid to stay until the wife comes home.**

That night we smoked the tranquil pipe, and talked till late about various things, but mainly about her; and certainly I had had no such pleasant and restful time for many a day. The Thursday followed and slipped comfortably away. Toward twilight a big miner from three miles away came and gave us warm salutation, clothed in grave and sober speech. Then he said:

"I only just dropped over to ask about the little madam, and when is she coming home. Any news from her?"

"Oh, yes, a letter. Would you like to hear it, Tom?"

"Well, I should think I would, if you don't mind, Henry!"

Henry got the letter out of his wallet, and said he would skip some of the private phrases, if we were willing; then he went on and read the bulk of it—a loving, sedate, and altogether charming and gracious piece of handiwork, with a postscript full of affectionate regards and messages to Tom, and Joe, and Charley, and other close friends and neighbors.

6.   How does the letter show the woman's point of view toward her neighbors?

As the reader finished, he glanced at Tom, and cried out:

"Oho, you're at it again! Take your hands away, and let me see your eyes. You always do that when I read a letter from her. I will write and tell her."

"Oh no, you mustn't, Henry. I'm getting old, you know, and any little disappointment makes me want to cry. I thought she'd be here herself, and now you've got only a letter."

"Well, now, what put that in your head? I thought everybody knew she wasn't coming till Saturday."

"Saturday! Why, come to think, I did know it. I wonder what's the matter with me lately? Certainly I knew it. Ain't we all getting ready for her? Well, I must be going now. But I'll be on hand when she comes, old man!"

Late Friday afternoon another gray veteran tramped over from his cabin a mile or so away, and said the boys wanted to have a little gaiety and a good time Saturday night, if Henry thought she wouldn't be too tired after her journey to be kept up.

"Tired? She tired! Oh, hear the man! Joe, you know she'd sit up six weeks to please any one of you!"

When Joe heard that there was a letter, he asked to have it read, and the loving messages in it for him broke the old fellow all up; but he said he was such an old wreck that that would happen to him if she only just mentioned his name. "Lord, we miss her so!" he said.

Saturday afternoon I found I was taking out my watch pretty often. Henry noticed it, and said, with a startled look:

"You don't think she ought to be here soon, do you?"

I felt caught, and a little embarrassed; but I laughed, and said it was a habit of mine when I was in a state of expectancy. But he didn't seem quite satisfied; and from that time on he began to show uneasiness. Four times he walked me up the road to a point whence we could see a long distance; and there he would stand, shading his eyes with his hand, and looking. Several times he said:

"I'm getting worried, I'm getting right down worried. I know she's not due till about nine o'clock, and yet something seems to be trying to warn me that something's happened. You don't think anything has happened, do you?"

I began to get pretty thoroughly ashamed of him for his childishness; and at last, when he repeated that imploring question still another time, I lost my patience for the moment, and spoke pretty brutally to him. It seemed to shrivel him up and cow him; and he looked so wounded and so humble after that, that I detested myself for having done the cruel and unnecessary thing. And so I was glad when Charley, another veteran, arrived toward the edge of the evening, and nestled up to Henry to hear the letter read, and talked over the preparations for the welcome. Charley did his best to drive away his friend's bodings and apprehensions.

"Anything happened to her? Henry, that's pure nonsense. There isn't anything going to happen to her; just make your mind easy as to that. What did the letter say? Said she was well, didn't it? And said she'd be here by nine o'clock, didn't it? Did you ever know her to fail of her word? Why, you know you never did. Well, then, don't you fret; she'll be here, and that's absolutely certain, and as sure as you are born. Come, now, let's get to decorating—not much time left."

7.   Analyze how the narrator and Charley differ in their reaction to Henry's asking, "You don't think anything has happened, do you?"

Pretty soon Tom and Joe arrived, and then all hands set about adoring the house with flowers. Toward nine the three miners said that as they had brought their instruments they might as well tune up, for the boys and girls would soon be arriving now, and hungry for a good, old-fashioned break-down. A fiddle, a banjo, and a clarinet—these were the instruments. The trio took their places side by side, and began to play some rattling dance-music, and beat time with their big boots.

It was getting very close to nine. Henry was standing in the door with his eyes directed up the road, his body swaying to the torture of his mental distress. He had been made to drink to his wife's health and safety several times, and now Tom shouted:

"All hands stand by! One more drink, and she's here!"

Joe brought the glasses on a waiter, and served the party. I reached for one of the two remaining glasses, but Joe growled under his breath:

"Drop that! Take the other."

Which I did. Henry was served last. He had hardly swallowed his drink when the clock began to strike. He listened till it finished, his face growing pale and paler; then he said:

"Boys, I'm sick with fear. Help me—I want to lie down!"

They helped him to the sofa. He began to nestle and drowse, but presently spoke like one talking in his sleep, and said: "Did I hear horses' feet? Have they come?"

8. **Analyze how the Saturday night party advances the plot.**

One of the veterans answered, close to his ear: "It was Jimmy Parish come to say the party got delayed, but they're right up the road a piece, and coming along. Her horse is lame, but she'll be here in half an hour."

"Oh, I'm so thankful nothing has happened!"

He was asleep almost before the words were out of his mouth. In a moment those handy men had his clothes off, and had tucked him into his bed in the chamber where I had washed my hands. They closed the door and came back. Then they seemed preparing to leave; but I said: "Please don't go, gentlemen. She won't know me; I am a stranger."

They glanced at each other. Then Joe said:

"She? Poor thing, she's been dead nineteen years!"

"Dead?"

"That or worse. She went to see her folks half a year after she was married, and on her way back, on a Saturday evening, the Indians captured her within five miles of this place, and she's never been heard of since."

"And he lost his mind in consequence?"

"Never has been sane an hour since. But he only gets bad when that time of year comes round. Then we begin to drop in here, three days before she's due, to encourage him up, and ask if he's heard from her, and Saturday we all come and fix up the house with flowers, and get everything ready for a dance. We've done it every year for nineteen years. The first Saturday there was twenty-seven of us, without counting the girls; there's only three of us now, and the girls are gone. We drug him to sleep, or he would go wild; then he's all right for another year—thinks she's with him till the last three or four days come round; then he begins to look for her, and gets out his poor old letter, and we come and ask him to read it to us. Lord, she was a darling!"

9. **Cite two sources of evidence that the people of the town cared about Henry.**

10. **What is the theme or message of the story? Provide an example of how the theme developed over the story.**

Summarize the story.

The Third Wish

by Joan Aiken

This is a fantasy story about a man who receives three wishes and has to decide how to use them. Read to find out how he uses them, the conflicts that result, and how his life changes.

Once there was a man who was driving in his car at dusk on a spring evening through part of the forest of Savernake. His name was Mr. Peters. The primroses were just beginning but the trees were still bare, and it was cold; the birds had stopped singing an hour ago.

As Mr. Peters entered a straight, empty stretch of road he seemed to hear a faint crying, and a struggling and thrashing, as if somebody was in trouble far away in the trees. He left his car and climbed the mossy bank beside the road. Beyond the bank was an open slope of beech trees leading down to thorn bushes through which he saw the gleam of water. He stood a moment waiting to try and discover where the noise was coming from, and presently heard a rustling and some strange cries in a voice which was almost human—and yet there was something too hoarse about it at one time and too clear and sweet at another. Mr. Peters ran down the hill and as he neared the bushes he saw something white among them which was trying to extricate itself; coming closer he found that it was a swan that had become entangled in the thorns growing on the bank of the canal.

The bird struggled all the more frantically as he approached, looking at him with hate in its yellow eyes, and when he took hold of it to free it, it hissed at him, pecked him, and thrashed dangerously with its wings which were powerful enough to break his arm. Nevertheless he managed to release it from the thorns, and carrying it tightly with one arm, holding the shaky head well away with the other hand (for he did not wish his eyes pecked out), he took it to the verge of the canal and dropped it in.

> 1. What does the word *release* mean in this sentence? "Nevertheless he managed to release it from the thorns . . . "

The swan instantly assumed great dignity and sailed out to the middle of the water, where it put itself to rights with much dabbling and preening, smoothing its feathers with little showers of drops. Mr. Peters waited, to make sure that it was all right and had suffered no damage in its struggles. Presently the swan, when it was satisfied with its appearance, floated in to the bank once more, and in a moment, instead of the great white bird, there was a little man all in green with a gold crown and long beard, standing in the water. He had fierce glittering eyes and looked by no means friendly.

"Well, sir," he said threateningly, "I see that you are presumptuous enough to know some of the laws of magic. You think that because you have rescued—by pure good fortune—the King of the Forest from a difficulty, you should have some fabulous reward."

"I expect three wishes, no more and no less," answered Mr. Peters, looking at him steadily and with composure.

"Three wishes he wants, the clever man! Well, I have yet to hear of the human being who made any good use of his three wishes—they mostly end up worse off than they started. Take your three wishes then"—he flung three dead leaves in the air—"don't blame me if you spend the last wish in undoing the work of the other two."

> 2. Analyze how the king's gift will affect the story's plot.

Mr. Peters caught the leaves and put two of them carefully in his briefcase. When he looked up, the swan was sailing about in the middle of the water again, flicking the drops angrily down its long neck.

Mr. Peters stood for some minutes reflecting on how he should use his reward. He knew very well that the gift of three magic wishes was one which brought trouble more often than not, and he had no intention of being like the forester who first wished by mistake for a sausage, and then in a rage wished it on the end of his wife's nose, and then had to use his last wish in getting it off again. Mr. Peters had most of the things he wanted and was very content with his life. The only thing that troubled him was that he was a little lonely, and had no companion for his old age. He decided to use his first wish and to keep the other two in case of emergency. Taking a thorn he pricked his tongue with it, to remind himself not to utter rash wishes aloud. Then holding the third leaf and gazing round him at the dusky undergrowth, the primroses, great beeches and the blue-green water of the canal, he said: "I wish I had a wife as beautiful as the forest."

A tremendous quacking and splashing broke out on the surface of the water. He thought that it was the swan laughing at him. Taking no notice he made his way through the darkening woods to his car, wrapped himself up in the rug and went to sleep.

When he awoke it was morning and the birds were beginning to call. Coming along the track towards him was the most beautiful creature he had ever seen, with eyes as blue-green as the canal, hair as dusky as the bushes, and skin as white as the feathers of the swans.

"Are you the wife that I wished for?" asked Mr. Peters.

"Yes, I am," she replied. "My name is Leita."

She stepped into the car beside him and they drove off to the church at the outskirts of the forest, where they were married. Then he took her to his house in a remote and lovely valley and showed her all his treasures—the bees in the white hives, the Jersey cows, the hyacinths, the silver candlesticks, the blue cups and the luster bowl for putting primroses in. She admired everything, but what pleased her most was the river which ran by the foot of his garden.

"Do swans come up there?" she asked.

"Yes, I have often seen swans there on the river," he told her, and she smiled.

3. **Using two details from the story, explain who Leita was before she was Mr. Peters's wife.**

Leita made him a good wife. But as time went by Mr. Peters began to feel that she was not happy. She seemed restless, wandered much in the garden, and sometimes when he came back from the fields he would find the house empty and she would return after half an hour or so with no explanations of where she had been. On these occasions she was always especially tender and would put out his slippers to warm and cook his favorite dish—Welsh rarebit with wild strawberries—for supper.

One evening he was returning home along the river path when he saw Leita in front of him, down by the water. A swan had sailed up to the verge and she had her arms around its neck and the swan's head rested against her cheek. She was weeping, and as he came nearer he saw that tears were rolling, too, from the swan's eyes.

"Leita," he asked, very troubled.

"This is my sister," she answered. "I can't bear being separated from her."

4. **Analyze how the setting is important to a character in this story.**

Now he understood that Leita was really a swan from the forest, and this made him very sad because when a human being marries a bird it always leads to sorrow.

"I could use my second wish to give your sister human shape, so that she could be a companion to you," he suggested.

"No, no," she cried. "I couldn't ask that of her."

"Is it so hard to be a human being?" asked Mr. Peters sadly.

"Very, very hard," she answered.

"Don't you love me at all, Leita?"

"Yes, I do, I love you," she said, and there were tears in her eyes again. "But I miss the old life in the forest, the cool grass and the mist rising off the river at sunrise and the feel of the water sliding over my feathers as my sister and I drifted along."

"Then shall I use my second wish to turn you back into a swan again?" he asked, and his tongue pricked him to remind him of the old King's words, and his heart swelled with grief inside him.

"Who will take care of you?"

"I'd do it myself as I did before I married you," he said, trying to sound cheerful.

She shook her head. "No, I could not be as unkind to you as that. I am partly swan, but I am also partly a human being now. I will stay with you."

5.   What is the central conflict within one of the main characters in this story?

Poor Mr. Peters was very distressed on his wife's account and did his best to make her life happier, taking her for drives in the car, finding beautiful music for her to listen to on the radio, buying clothes for her and even suggesting a trip around the world. But she said no to that; she would prefer to stay in their own house near the river.

He noticed that she spent more and more time baking wonderful cakes—jam puffs, petits fours, éclairs, and meringues. One day he saw her take a basketful down to the river and he guessed that she was giving them to her sister.

He built a seat for her by the river, and the two sisters spent hours together there, communicating in some wordless manner. For a time he thought that all would be well, but then he saw how thin and pale she was growing.

6.   How did the author develop the characters of Leita and Mr. Peters to illustrate their different points of view toward being human?

One night when he had been late doing the accounts he came up to bed and found her weeping in her sleep and calling: "Rhea! Rhea! I can't understand what you say! Oh, wait for me, take me with you!"

Then he knew that it was hopeless and she would never be happy as a human. He stooped down and kissed her goodbye, then took another leaf from his notecase, blew it out of the window, and used up his second wish.

Next moment instead of Leita there was a sleeping swan lying across the bed with its head under its wing. He carried it out of the house and down to the brink of the river, and then he said, "Leita! Leita!" to waken her and gently put her in the water. She gazed round her in astonishment for a moment, and then came up to him and rested her head lightly against his hand; next instant she was flying away over the trees towards the heart of the forest.

7.   Using two pieces of evidence, explain why Mr. Peters used his second wish to set Leita free.

He heard a harsh laugh behind him, and turning round saw the old King, looking at him with a malicious expression.

"Well, my friend! You don't seem to have managed so wonderfully with your first two wishes, do you? What will you do with the last? Turn yourself into a swan? Or turn Leita back into a girl?"

"I shall do neither," said Mr. Peters calmly. "Human beings and swans are better in their own shapes."

But for all that he looked sadly over towards the forest where Leita had flown, and walked slowly back to his house.

8.   Explain the phrase, "human beings and swans are better in their own shapes."

9.   Analyze the contrast between the King's and Mr. Peters's points of view of turning Leita back into a swan.

Next day he saw two swans swimming at the bottom of the garden, and one of them wore the gold chain he had given Leita after their marriage; she came up and rubbed her head against his hand.

Mr. Peters and his two swans came to be well known in that part of the country; people used to say that he talked to swans and they understood him as well as his neighbors. Many people were a little frightened of him. There was a story that once when thieves tried to break into his house they were set upon by two huge white birds which carried them off bodily and dropped them into the river.

As Mr. Peters grew old everyone wondered at his contentment. Even when he was bent with rheumatism he would not think of moving to a drier spot, but went slowly about his work, with the two swans always somewhere close at hand.

Sometimes people who knew his story would say to him:

"Mr. Peters, why don't you wish for another wife?"

"Not likely," he would answer serenely. "Two wishes were enough for me, I reckon. I've learned that even if your wishes are granted they don't always better you. I'll stay faithful to Leita."

One autumn night, passers-by along the road heard the mournful sound of two swans singing. All night the song went on, sweet and harsh, sharp and clear. In the morning Mr. Peters was found peacefully dead in his bed with a smile of great happiness on his face. In his hands, which lay clasped on his breast, were a weathered leaf and a white feather.

10. What is the theme of this story?

Summarize the story.

The Tell-Tale Heart

by Edgar Allan Poe

This story is one of the most famous of Edgar Allan Poe, who wrote short stories and poems. Read to observe how Poe uses words to bring tension into the story.

True!—nervous—very nervous, very dreadfully nervous I had been and am; but why *will* you say that I am mad? The disease had sharpened my senses—not destroyed—not dulled them. Above all was the sense of hearing acute. I heard all things in the heaven and in the earth. I heard many things in hell. How, then, am I mad? Hearken! and observe how healthily—how calmly I can tell you the whole story.

It is impossible to say how first the idea entered my brain; but once conceived it haunted me day and night. Object there was none. Passion there was none. I loved the old man. He had never wronged me. He had never given me insult. For his gold I had no desire. I think it was his eye! Yes, it was this. One of his eyes resembled that of a vulture—a pale blue eye, with a film over it. Whenever it fell upon me, my blood ran cold; and so by degrees—very gradually—I made up my mind to take the life of the old man and thus rid myself of the eye forever.

1. What does "Object there was none. Passion there was none" mean in the previous paragraph, and how does it set the tone of the story?

Now this is the point. You fancy me mad. Madmen know nothing. But you should have seen *me.* You should have seen how wisely I proceeded—with what caution—with such foresight—with what dissimulation I went to work! I was never kinder to the old man than during the whole week before I killed him. And every night, around midnight, I turned the latch of his door and opened it—oh, so gently! And then, when I had made an opening sufficient for my head, I put in a dark lantern, all closed, so that no light shone out, and then I thrust in my head. Oh, you would have laughed to see how cunning I thrust it in! I moved it slowly—very, very slowly, so that I might not disturb the man's sleep. It took me an hour to place my whole head within the opening so far that I could see him as he lay upon his bed. Ha!—would a madman been so wise as this? And then, when my head was well in the room, I undid the lantern cautiously—oh, so cautiously—cautiously (for the hinges creaked)—I undid it just so much that a single thin ray fell upon the vulture eye.

2. Describe the evidence that most strongly suggests that the narrator is crazy.

3. Analyze how the author creates a feeling of suspense through how carefully the narrator planned the murder compared to how nervous and "mad" the narrator seems in other parts of the story.

And I did this for seven long nights—every night just at midnight—but I found the eye always closed; and so it was impossible to do the work; for it was not the old man who vexed me, but his evil eye. And every morning, when the day broke, I went boldly into the chamber, and spoke courageously to him, calling him by name in a hearty tone, and inquiring how he had passed the night. So you see he would have been a very profound old man, indeed, to suspect that every night, just at twelve, I looked in upon him while he slept.

Upon the eighth night I was more than usually cautious in opening the door. A watch's minute hand moves more quickly than did mine. Never, before that night, had I *felt* the extent of my own powers—of my sagacity. I could scarcely contain my feelings of triumph. To think that there I was opening the door, little by little, and he not even to dream of my secret deeds or thoughts. I fairly chuckled at the idea; and perhaps he heard me; for he moved on the bed suddenly, as if startled. Now you may think that I drew back—but no. His room was as black as pitch with the thick darkness (for the shutters were close fastened, through fear of robbers), and so I knew that he could not see the opening of the door and I kept pushing on steadily, steadily.

I had my head in, and was about to open the lantern, when my thumb slipped upon the tin fastening, and the old man sprang up in the bed, crying out—"Who's there?"

4. **Analyze how the events of the eighth night move the plot along.**

I kept quite still and said nothing. For a whole hour I did not move a muscle, and in the meantime I did not hear him lie down. He was still sitting up in the bed, listening—just as I have done, night after night, hearkening in the deathwatches beetles in the wall.

Presently I heard a slight groan of pain or of grief—oh, no!—it was the low stifled sound that arises from the bottom of the soul when overcharged with awe. I knew the sound very well. Many a night, just at midnight when all the world slept, it has welled up from my own bosom, deepening, with its dreadful echo, the terrors that distracted me. I say I knew it well. I knew what the old man felt, and pitied him, although I chuckled at heart.

I knew that he had been lying awake ever since the first slight noise, when he had turned in the bed. His fears had been ever since growing upon him. He had been trying to fancy them causeless, but could not. He had been saying to himself—"It is nothing but the wind in the chimney—it is only a mouse crossing the floor," or "it is merely a cricket which has made a single chirp." Yes, he has been trying to comfort himself with these suppositions: but he had found all in vain. *All in vain;* because Death, in approaching him, had stalked with his black shadow before him, and enveloped the victim. And it was the mournful influence of the unperceived shadow that caused him to feel—although he neither saw or heard—to *feel* the presence of my head within the room.

When I had waited a long time, very patiently, without hearing him lie down, I resolved to open a little—a very, very little crevice in the lantern. So I opened it—you can't imagine how stealthily, stealthily—until at length, a single dim ray, like the thread of the spider, shot out from the crevice and fell upon the vulture eye.

It was open—wide, wide open—and I grew furious as I gazed upon it. I saw it with perfect distinctness—all a dull blue, with a hideous veil over it that chilled the very marrow in my bones; but I could see nothing else of the old man's face or person for I had directed the ray as if by instinct, precisely upon the . . . spot.

And now—have I not told you that what you mistake for madness is but overacuteness of the senses?—now, I say, there came to my ears a low, dull, quick sound, such as a watch makes when enveloped in cotton. I knew *that* sound well, too. It was the beating of the old man's heart. It increased my fury, as the beating of a drum stimulates the soldier into courage.

But even yet I refrained and kept still. I scarcely breathed. I held the lantern motionless. I tried how steadily I could maintain the ray upon the eye. Meantime the hellish tattoo of the heart increased. It grew quicker and quicker, and louder and louder every instant. The old man's terror *must* have been extreme! It grew louder, I say, louder every moment—do you mark me well?

5. **What does the phrase "do you mark me well" mean in the previous sentence?**

I have told you that I am nervous: so I am. And now at the dead hour of the night, amid the dreadful silence of that old house, so strange a noise as this excited me to uncontrollable terror. Yet for some minutes longer I refrained and stood still. But the beating grew louder, louder! I thought the heart must burst. And now a new anxiety seized me—the sound would be heard by a neighbor! The old man's hour had come! With a loud yell, I threw open the lantern and leaped into the room. He shrieked once—once only. In an instant I dragged him to the floor, and pulled the heavy bed over him. I smiled gaily, to find the deed so far done. But, for many minutes, the heart beat on with a muffled sound. This however, did not vex me; it would not be heard through the wall. At length it ceased. The old man was dead. I removed the bed and examined the corpse. Yes, he was stone, stone dead. I placed my hand upon the heart and held it there many minutes. There was no pulsation. He was stone dead. His eye would trouble me no more.

If still you think me mad, you will think so no longer when I describe the wise precautions I took for the concealment of the body. The night waned, and I worked hastily, but in silence. First of all I dismembered the corpse. I cut off the head and the arms and the legs.

I then took up three planks from the flooring of the chamber, and deposited all between the scantlings, small beams. I then replaced the boards so cleverly, so cunningly, that no human eye—not even his—could have detected anything wrong. There was nothing to wash out—no stain of any kind—no blood spot whatever. I had been too wary for that. A tub had caught all—ha! ha!

6. How does the narrator's behavior, described in the two preceding paragraphs, reveal his beliefs about himself?

When I had made an end of these labors, it was four o'clock—still as dark as midnight. As the bell sounded the hour, there came a knocking at the street door. I went down to open it with a light heart—for what had I *now* to fear? There entered three men, who introduced themselves, with perfect suavity, as officers of the police. A shriek had been heard by a neighbor during the night; suspicion of foul play had been aroused; information had been lodged at the police office, and they (the officers) had been deputed to search the premises.

I smiled—for *what* had I to fear? I bade the gentlemen welcome. The shriek, I said, was my own in a dream. The old man, I mentioned, was absent in the country. I took my visitors all over the house. I bade them search—search *well*. I led them, at length, to *his* chamber. I showed them his treasures, secure, undisturbed. In the enthusiasm of my confidence, I brought chairs into the room, and desired them *here* to rest from their fatigues, while I myself, in the wild audacity of my perfect triumph, placed my own seat upon the very spot beneath which reposed the corpse of the victim.

7. Analyze how your view of the narrator compares with his view of himself and explain how this increases the story's suspense.

The officers were satisfied. My *manner* had convinced them. I was singularly at ease. They sat, and while I answered cheerily, they chatted of familiar things. But, ere long, I felt myself getting pale and wished them gone. My head ached, and I fancied a ringing in my ears: but still they sat and still they chatted. The ringing became more distinct:—it continued and became more distinct: I talked more freely to get rid of the feeling: but it continued and gained definitiveness—until, at length, I found that the noise was *not* within my ears.

No doubt I now grew *very* pale;—but I talked more fluently, and with a heightened voice. Yet the sound increased—and what could I do? It was a *low, dull, quick sound—much such a sound as a watch makes when enveloped in cotton.* I gasped for breath—and yet the officers heard it not. I talked more quickly—more vehemently; but the noise steadily increased. I arose and argued about trifles, in a high key and with violent gesticulations; but the noise steadily increased. Why *would* they not be gone? I paced the floor to and fro with heavy strides, as if excited to fury by the observations of the men—but the noise steadily increased. Oh! what could I do? I foamed—I raved—I swore! I swung the chair upon which I had been sitting and grated it upon the boards, but the noise arose over all, and continuously increased. It grew louder—louder—*louder!* And still the men chatted pleasantly, and smiled. Was it possible they hear not? no, no! They heard!—they suspected!—they *knew!*—they were making a mockery of my horror! This I thought, and this I think. But anything was better than this agony! Any thing was more tolerable than this derision! I could bear those hypocritical smiles no longer! I felt that I must scream or die!—and now—again!—hark! louder! louder! louder! *louder!*—

"Villains!" I shrieked, "dissemble no more! I admit the deed!—tear up the planks—here, here!—it is the beating of his hideous heart!"

8. Cite the evidence that most strongly supports the inference that the source of the sound getting louder and louder was the narrator's own heart.

9. Analyze how the differences between the police's behavior and the narrator's behavior develop suspense in the story.

10. What is a theme of this story and how does it relate to the plot of the story?

Summarize this story.

Literature, Part II

The Drummer Boy of Shiloh

by Ray Bradbury

This story is about a young boy who is a soldier in the Civil War. He is thinking about the battle that will be fought the next day when the General approaches and begins to talk with him. Read what the boy learns from the General about his role in the war.

In the April night, more than once, blossoms fell from the orchard trees and lit with rustling taps on the drumskin. At midnight a peach stone left miraculously on a branch through winter, flicked by a bird, fell swift and unseen, struck once, like panic, which jerked the boy upright. In silence he listened to his own heart ruffle away, away—at last gone from his ears and back in his chest again. After that, he turned the drum on its side, where its great lunar face peered at him whenever he opened his eyes. His face, alert or at rest, was solemn. It was indeed a solemn time and a solemn night for a boy just turned fourteen in the peach field near the Owl Creek not far from the church at Shiloh.

1. Cite evidence that strongly supports that the boy was afraid.

". . . thirty-one, thirty-two, thirty-three . . ."
Unable to see, he stopped counting.
Beyond the thirty-three familiar shadows, forty thousand men, exhausted by nervous expectations, unable to sleep for romantic dreams of battles yet unfought, lay crazily askew in their uniforms. A mile yet farther on, another army was strewn helter-skelter, turning slow, basting themselves with the thought of what they would do when the time came: a leap, a yell, a blind plunge their strategy, raw youth their protection and benediction.

Now and again the boy heard a vast wind come up, that gently stirred the air. But he knew what it was—the army here, the army there, whispering to itself in the dark. Some men talking to others, others murmuring to themselves and all so quiet it was like a natural element arisen from south or north with the motion of the earth toward dawn.

What the men whispered the boy could only guess, and he guessed that it was: Me, I'm the one. I'm the one of all the rest who won't die. I'll live through it. I'll go home. The band will play. And I'll be there to hear it.

Yes, thought the boy, that's all very well for them, they can give as well as they get!

For with the careless bones of the young men harvested by night and bindled around campfires were the similarly strewn steel bones of their rifles, with bayonets fixed like eternal lightning lost in the orchard grass. Me, thought the boy. I got only a drum, two sticks to beat it, and no shield.

There wasn't a man-boy on this ground tonight who did not have a shield he cast, riveted or carved himself on his way to his first attack, compounded of remote but nonetheless firm and fiery family devotion, flag-blown patriotism and cocksure immortality strengthened by the touchstone of very real gunpowder, ramrod, minnieball and flint. But without these last, the boy felt his family move yet farther off away in the dark, as if one of those great prairie-burning trains had charged them away never to return—leaving him with this drum which was worse than a toy in the game to be played tomorrow or someday much too soon.

2. What does the phrases "compounded of remote but nonetheless firm and fiery family devotion, flag-blown patriotism and cocksure immortality," mean in the previous paragraph?

3. Analyze how the boy's point of view of the other soldiers' protection differs from his view of his own protection and how these views create suspense in the story.

The boy turned on his side. A moth brushed his face, but it was a peach blossom. A peach blossom flicked him, but it was a moth. Nothing stayed put. Nothing had a name. Nothing was as it once was.

If he lay very still, when the dawn came up and the soldiers put on their bravery with their caps, perhaps they might go away, the war with them, and not notice him lying small here, no more than a toy himself.

"Well now," said a voice.

The boy shut up his eyes, to hide inside himself, but it was too late. Someone, walking by in the night, stood over him.

"Well," said the voice quietly, "here's a soldier crying *before* the fight. Good. Get it over. Won't be time once it all starts."

And the voice was about to move on when the boy, startled, touched the drum at his elbow. The man above, hearing this, stopped. The boy could feel his eyes, sense him slowly bending near. A hand must have come down out of the night, for there was a little *rat-tat* as the fingernails brushed and the man's breath fanned his face.

"Why, it's the drummer boy, isn't it?"

The boy nodded, not knowing if his nod was seen. "Sir, is that *you*?" he said.

"I assume it is." The man's knees cracked as he bent still closer. He smelled as all fathers should smell, of salt sweat, ginger tobacco, horse and boot leather, and the earth he walked upon. He had many eyes. No, not eyes—brass buttons that watched the boy. He could only be, and was, the General.

"What's your name, boy?" he asked.

"Joby," whispered the boy, starting to sit up.

"All right, Joby, don't stir." A hand pressed his chest gently, and the boy relaxed. "How long you been with us, Joby?"

"Three weeks, sir."

"Run off from home or joined legitimately, boy?"

Silence.

" . . . Fool question," said the General. "Do you shave yet, boy? Even more of a . . . fool. There's your cheek, fell right off the tree overhead. And others here not much older. Raw, raw . . . the lot of you. You ready for tomorrow or the next day, Joby?"

"I think so, sir."

4. Cite strong evidence that shows that the General is aware of the youth of his soldiers.

"You want to cry some more, go on ahead. I did the same last night."

"*You*, sir?"

"It's the truth. Thinking of everything ahead. Both sides figuring the other side will just give up, and soon the war done in weeks, and us all home. Well, that's not how it's going to be. And maybe that's why I cried."

"Yes, sir," said Joby.

The General must have taken out a cigar now, for the dark was suddenly filled with the smell of tobacco unlit as yet, but chewed as the man thought what next to say.

"It's going to be a crazy time," said the General. "Counting both sides, there's a hundred thousand men, give or take a few thousand out there tonight, not one as can spit a sparrow off a tree, or knows a horse clod from a minnieball. Stand up, bare the breast, ask to be a target, thank them and sit down, that's us, that's them. We should turn tail and train four months, they should do the same. But here we are, taken with spring fever and thinking it blood lust, taking our sulfur with cannons instead of with molasses, as it should be, going to be a hero, going to live forever. And I can see all of them over there nodding agreement, save the other way around. It's wrong, boy, it's wrong as a head put on a hindside front and a man marching backward through life. More innocents will get shot out of pure enthusiasm than ever got shot before. Owl Creek was full of boys splashing around in the noonday sun just a few hours ago. I fear it will be full of boys, again, just floating, at sundown tomorrow, not caring where the tide takes them."

5. Analyze what the General believes about the war and why he feels that way, using words from the text.

The General stopped and made a little pile of winter leaves and twigs in the darkness, as if he might at any moment strike fire to them to see his way through the coming days when the sun might now show its face because of what was happening here and just beyond.

The boy watched the hand stirring the leaves and opened his lips to say something, but did not say it. The General heard the boy's breath and spoke himself.

"Why am I telling you all this? That's what you wanted to ask, eh? Well, when you got a bunch of wild horses on a loose rein somewhere, somehow you got to bring order, rein them in. These lads, fresh out of the milkshed, don't know what I know, and I can't tell them: men actually die in war. So each is his own army. I got to make *one* army of them. And for that, boy, I need you.

"Me!" The boy's lips barely twitched.

"Now, boy," said the General quietly, "you are the heart of the army. Think of that. You're the heart of the army. Listen, now."

6. Analyze how Joby's and the General's different points of view of Joby's role in the war creates suspense.

And, lying there, Joby listened.

And the General spoke on.

If he, Joby, beat slow tomorrow, the heart would beat slow in the men. They would lag by the wayside. They would drowse in the fields on their muskets. They would sleep forever, after that, in those same fields—their hearts slowed by a drummer boy and stopped by enemy lead.

But if he beat a sure, steady, ever faster rhythm, then, then their knees would come up in a long line down over that hill, one knee after the other, like a wave on the ocean shore! Had he seen the ocean ever? Seen the waves rolling in like a well-ordered cavalry charge to the sand? Well, that was it, that's what he wanted, that's what was needed! Joby was his right hand and his left. He gave the orders, but Joby set the pace!

7. Cite evidence from the text of how Joby's drumming could result in the loss of soldiers' lives.

So bring the right knee up and the right foot out and the left knee up and the left foot out. One following the other in good time, in brisk time. Move the blood up the body and make the head proud and the spine stiff and the jaw resolute. Focus the eye and set the teeth, flare the nostrils and tighten the hands, put steel armor all over the men, for blood moving fast in them does indeed make men feel as if they'd put on steel. He must keep at it, at it! Long and steady, steady and long! Then, even though shot or torn, those wounds got in hot blood—in blood he'd helped stir—would feel less pain. If their blood was cold, it would be more than slaughter, it would be murderous nightmare and pain best not told and no one to guess.

8. What do the phrases, "Move the blood up the body and make the head proud and the spine stiff and the jaw resolute. Focus the eye and set the teeth, flare the nostrils and tighten the hands," mean in the previous paragraph?

The General spoke and stopped, letting his breath slack off. Then, after a moment, he said, "So, there you are, that's it. Will you do that, boy? Do you know now you're the general of the army when the General's left behind?"

The boy nodded mutely.

"You'll run them through for me then, boy?"

"Yes, sir."

9. Analyze how the General shows his leadership when he explains Joby's role.

"Good. And maybe, many nights from tonight, many years from now, when you're as old or far much older than me, when they ask you what you did in this awful time, you will tell them—one part humble and one part proud—'I was the drummer boy at the battle of Owl Creek,' or the Tennessee River, or maybe they'll just name it after the church there, 'I was the drummer boy at Shiloh.' Good grief, that has a beat and sound to it fitting Mr. Longfellow. 'I was the drummer boy at Shiloh.' Who will ever hear those words and not know you, boy or what you thought this night, or what you'll think tomorrow or the next day when we must get up on our legs and *move*!"

The General stood up. "Well, then. Bless you, boy. Good night."

"Good night, sir."

And, tobacco, brass, boot polish, salt sweat and leather, the man moved away through the grass.

Joby lay for a moment, staring but unable to see where the man had gone. He swallowed. He wiped his eyes. He cleared his throat. He settled himself. Then at last, very slowly and firmly, he turned the drum so that it faced up toward the sky.

He lay next to it, his arm around it, feeling the tremor, the touch, the muted thunder as, all of the rest of the April night in the year 1862, near the Tennessee River, not far from Owl Creek, very close to the church named Shiloh, the peach blossoms fell on the drum.

10. **What is a theme of this story and how do the characters reveal it?**

Summarize the story.

Literature, Part III

The Story-Teller

by Saki (H.H. Monroe)

This story is about three children who are traveling with their aunt on a train. She tries to keep them busy by telling them stories but is a poor story-teller. Read to find out who is able to entertain them and how.

It was a hot afternoon and the railway carriage was correspondingly sultry, and the next stop was at Templecombe, nearly an hour ahead. The occupants of the carriage were a small girl, and a smaller girl, and a small boy. An aunt belonging to the children occupied one corner seat, and the further corner seat on the opposite side was occupied by a bachelor who was a stranger to their party, but the small girls and the small boy emphatically occupied the compartment. Both the aunt and the children were conversational in a limited, persistent way, reminding one of the attentions of a housefly that refused to be discouraged. Most of the aunt's remarks seemed to begin with "Don't," and nearly all of the children's remarks began with "Why?" The bachelor said nothing out loud.

1. **What does "but the small girls and the small boy emphatically occupied the compartment" mean in the previous paragraph?**

"Don't, Cyril, don't," exclaimed the aunt, as the small boy began smacking the cushions of the seat, producing a cloud of dust at each blow.

"Come and look out of the window," she added.

The child moved reluctantly to the window. "Why are those sheep being driven out of that field?" he asked.

"I expect they are being driven to another field where there is more grass," said the aunt weakly.

"But there's lots of grass in that field," protested the boy; "there's nothing else but grass there. Aunt, there's lots of grass in that field."

"Perhaps the grass in the other field is better," suggested the aunt fatuously.

"Why is it better?" came the swift, inevitable question.

"Oh, look at those cows!" exclaimed the aunt. Nearly every field along the line had contained cows or bullocks, but she spoke as thought she were drawing attention to a rarity.

"Why is the grass in the other field better?" persisted Cyril.

2. **Analyze how the dialogue between the aunt and Cyril reveals their personalities.**

The frown on the bachelor's face was deepening to a scowl. He was a hard, unsympathetic man, the aunt decided in her mind. She was utterly unable to come to any satisfactory decision about the grass in the other field.

The smaller girl created a diversion by beginning to recite "On the Road to Mandalay." She only knew the first line, but she put her limited knowledge to the fullest possible use. She repeated the line over and over in a dreamy but resolute and very audible voice; it seemed to the bachelor as though someone had a bet with her that she could not repeat the line aloud two thousand times without stopping. Whoever it was who had made the wager was likely to lose his bet.

"Come over here and listen to a story," the aunt said, when the bachelor had looked twice at her and once at the communication cord.

3. **Cite the evidence that most strongly suggests that the man is getting disturbed.**

The children moved listlessly toward the aunt's end of the carriage. Evidently her reputation as a story-teller did not rank high in their estimation.

In a low confidential voice, interrupted at frequent intervals by loud, petulant questions from her listeners, she began an unenterprising and deplorably uninteresting story about a little girl who was good, and made friends with everyone on account of her goodness, and was finally saved from a mad bull by a number of rescuers who admired her moral character.

4. **What does the story reveal about how the children and the narrator feel about the aunt's storytelling ability?**

"Wouldn't they have saved her if she hadn't been good?" demanded the bigger of the small girls. It was exactly the question that the bachelor had wanted to ask.

"Well, yes," admitted the aunt lamely, "but I don't think they would have run quite so fast to help if they had not liked her so much."

"It's the stupidest story I've ever heard," said the bigger of the small girls with immense conviction.

"I didn't listen after the first bit, it was so stupid," said Cyril.

The smaller girl made no actual comment on the story, but she had long ago recommended a murmured repetition of her favorite line.

"You don't seem to be much of a success as a story-teller," said the bachelor suddenly from his corner.

The aunt bristled in instant defense at this unexpected attack.

"It's a very difficult thing to tell stories that children can both understand and appreciate," she said stiffly.

"I don't agree with you," said the bachelor.

"Perhaps *you* would like to tell them a story," was the aunt's retort.

"Tell us a story," demanded the bigger of the small girls.

5. **How does the man's comment about the aunt's ability to tell stories move the plot forward?**

"Once upon a time," began the bachelor, "there was a little girl named Bertha, who was extraordinarily good."

The children's momentarily aroused interest began at once to flicker; all stories seemed dreadfully alike, no matter who told them.

"She did all that she was told, she was always truthful, she kept her clothes clean, ate milk puddings as though they were jam tarts, learned her lessons perfectly, and was polite in her manners."

"Was she pretty?" asked the bigger of the two small girls.

"Not as pretty as any of you," said the bachelor, "but she was horribly good."

There was a wave of reaction in favor of the story; the word *horrible* in connection with goodness was a novelty that commended itself. It seemed to introduce a ring of truth that was absent from the aunt's tales of infant life.

6. **What does the phrase "wave of reaction" mean in the previous paragraph and how does it affect the tone of the story?**

"She was so good," continued the bachelor, "that she won several medals for goodness, which she always wore, pinned on to her dress. There was a medal for obedience, another medal for punctuality, and a third for good behavior. They were large metal medals and they clinked against one another as she walked. No other child in town where she lived had as many as three medals, so everybody knew that she must be an extra good child."

"Horribly good," quoted Cyril.

"Everybody talked about her goodness, and the Prince of the country got to hear all about it, and he said that as she was so very good she might be allowed once a week to walk in his park, which was just outside the town. It was a beautiful park, and no children were ever allowed to go there."

"Were there any sheep in the park?" demanded Cyril.

"No," said the bachelor. "There were no sheep."

"Why weren't there any sheep?" came the inevitable question arising out of that answer.

The aunt permitted herself a smile, which might almost have been described as a grin.

7. **Cite the two pieces of evidence that most strongly explain why the aunt is smiling.**

"There were no sheep in the park," said the bachelor, "because the Prince's mother had once had a dream that her son would either be killed by a sheep or else by a clock falling on him. For that reason the Prince never kept a sheep in his park or a clock in his palace."

The aunt suppressed a gasp of admiration.

"Was the Prince ever killed by a sheep or by a clock?" asked Cyril.

"He is still alive, so we can't tell whether the dream will come true," said the bachelor unconcernedly; "anyway, there were no sheep in the park, but there were lots of little pigs running all over the place."

"What color were they?"

"Black with white faces, white with black spots, black all over, gray with white patches, and some were white all over."

8. Analyze how the man's description of the park keeps the children interested in his story.

The story-teller paused to let a full idea of the park's treasures sink into the children's imaginations; then he resumed:

"Bertha was rather sorry to find that there were no flowers in the park. She had promised her aunts, with tears in her eyes, that she would not pick any of the kind Prince's flowers, and she had meant to keep her promise, so of course it made her feel silly to find that there were no flowers to pick."

"Why weren't there any flowers?"

"Because the pigs had eaten them all," said the bachelor promptly. "The gardeners had told the Prince that you couldn't have pigs and flowers, so he decided to have pigs and no flowers."

There was a murmur of approval at the excellence of the Prince's decision; so many people would have decided the other way.

"There were lots of other delightful things in the park. There were ponds with gold and blue and green fish in them, and trees with beautiful parrots that said clever things at a moment's notice, and hummingbirds that hummed all the popular tunes of the day. Bertha walked up and down and enjoyed herself immensely, and thought to herself: 'If I were not so extraordinarily good, I should not have been allowed to come into this beautiful park and enjoy all that there is to be seen in it,' and her three medals clinked against one another as she walked and helped to remind her how very good she really was. Just then an enormous wolf came prowling into the park to see if it could catch a fat little pig for its supper."

"What color was it?" asked the children, amid an immediate quickening of interest.

"Mud color all over, with a black tongue and pale gray eyes that gleamed with unspeakable ferocity. The first thing that it saw in the park was Bertha; her pinafore was so spotlessly white and clean that it could be seen from a great distance. Bertha saw the wolf and saw that it was stealing toward her, and she began to wish that she had never been allowed to come into the park. She ran as hard as she could, and the wolf came after her with huge leaps and bounds. She managed to reach a shrubbery of myrtle bushes, and she hid herself in one of the thickest of the bushes. The wolf came sniffling among the branches, its black tongue lolling out of its mouth and its pale gray eyes glaring with rage. Bertha was terribly frightened and thought to herself: 'If I had not been so extraordinarily good, I should have been safe in the town at this moment.' However, the scent of the myrtle was so strong that the wolf could not sniff out where Bertha was hiding, and the bushes were so thick that he might have hunted about in them for a long time without catching sight of her, so he thought he might as well go off and catch a little pig instead. Bertha was trembling very much at having the wolf prowling and sniffing so near her, and as she trembled the medal for obedience clinked against the medals for good conduct and punctuality. The wolf was just moving away when he heard the sound of the medals clinking and stopped to listen; they clinked again in a bush quite near him. He dashed into the bush, his pale gray eyes gleaming with ferocity and triumph, and dragged Bertha out and devoured her to the last morsel. All that was left of her were shoes, bits of clothing, and the three medals for goodness."

"Were any of the pigs killed?"

"No, they all escaped."

"The story began badly," said the smaller of the small girls, "but it had a beautiful ending."

"It is the most beautiful story that I ever heard," said the bigger of the small girls, with immense decision.

"It is the *only* beautiful story that I have ever heard," said Cyril.

A dissentient opinion came from the aunt.

"A most improper story to tell to young children! You have undermined the effects of years of careful teaching."

"At any rate," said the bachelor, collecting his belongings preparatory to leaving the carriage, "I kept them quiet for ten minutes, which was more than you were able to do."

"Unhappy woman!" he observed to himself as he walked down the platform of Templecombe station; "for the next six months or so those children will assail her in public with demands for an improper story!"

9. How do the differences between the children's and the aunt's points of view toward the man's story create humor at the end?

10. What is the central theme of *The Story-Teller*? Support your answer with evidence from the text.

Summarize the story.

Literature, Part I

Sonata for Harp and Bicycle

by Joan Aiken

This story is about an advertising copywriter who goes to work at a company that has strict rules about when its employees are to leave the building. The secret to this policy is not told to employees until they've been with the company for a long time. The copywriter is so curious that he takes it upon himself to find out what the secret is. Read to find out what happens because of his curiosity.

"No one is allowed to remain in the building after five o'clock," Mr. Manaby told his new assistant, showing him into the little room that was like the inside of a parcel.

"Why not?"

"Directorial policy," said Mr. Manaby. But that was not the real reason.

Gaunt and sooty, Grimes Buildings lurched up the side of a hill toward Clerkenwell, a district of London. *Every little office within its dim and crumbling exterior owned one tiny crumb of light—* such was the proud boast of the architect—but toward evening the crumbs were collected as by an immense vacuum cleaner, absorbed and demolished, yielding to an uncontrollable mass of dark that came tumbling in through window and doors to take their place. *Darkness infested the building like a flight of bats returning willingly to roost.*

1. Analyze how the segments in italics affect the mood of the story's setting.

"Wash hands, please. Wash hands, please," the intercom began to bawl in the passages at a quarter to five. Without much need of prompting, the staff hustled like lemmings along the corridors to green- and blue-tiled washrooms that mocked with an illusion of cheerfulness the encroaching dusk.

"All papers into cases, please," the voice warned, five minutes later. "Look at your desks, ladies and gentlemen. Any documents left lying about? Kindly put them away. Desks must be left clear and tidy. Drawers must be shut."

A multitudinous shuffling, a rustling as of innumerable bluebottle flies might have been heard by the attentive ear after this injunction, as the employees of Moreton Wold and Company thrust their papers into cases, hurried letters and invoices into drawers, clipped statistical abstracts together and slammed them into filing cabinets, dropped discarded copy into waste baskets. Two minutes later, and not a desk throughout Grimes Buildings bore more than its customary coating of dust.

"Hats and coats on, please. Hats and coats on, please. Did you bring an umbrella? Have you left any shopping on the floor?" At three minutes to five the homegoing throng was in the lifts and on the stairs; a clattering, a staccato-voiced flood darkened momentarily the great double doors of the building, and then as the first faint notes of St. Paul's came echoing faintly on the frosty air, to be picked up near at hand by the louder chimes of St. Biddulph's-on-the-Wall, the entire premises of Moreton Wold stood empty.

2. What does the word *rustling* mean in the following sentence? "A multitudinous shuffling, a rustling as of innumerable bluebottle flies might have been heard by the attentive ear after this injunction as the employees of Moreton Wold and Company thrust their papers into cases, hurried letters and invoices into drawers . . . "

"But why is it?" Jason Ashgrove, the new copywriter, asked his secretary one day. "Why are the staff herded out so fast? Not that I'm against it, mind you; I think it's an admirable idea in many ways, but there is the liberty of the individual to be considered, don't you think?"

"Hush!'" Miss Golden, the secretary, gazed at him with large terrified eyes. "You mustn't ask that sort of question. When you are taken onto the Established Staff you'll be told. Not before."

"But I want to know now," Jason said in discontent. "Do you know?"

"Yes, I do," Miss Golden answered tantalizingly. "Come on, or we shan't have finished the Oat Crisp layout by a quarter to." And she stared firmly down at the copy in front of her, lips folded, candyfloss hair falling over her face, lashes hiding eyes like peridots, a girl with a secret.

Jason was annoyed. He rapped out a couple of rude and witty rhymes which Miss Golden let pass in a withering silence.

"What do you want for your birthday, Miss Golden? Sherry? Fudge? Bubble bath?"

"I want to go away with a clear conscience about Oat Crisps," Miss Golden retorted. It was not true; what she chiefly wanted was Mr. Jason Ashgrove, but he had not realized this yet.

"Come on, don't tease! I'm sure you haven't been on the Established Staff all that long," he coaxed her. "What happens when one is taken on, anyway? Does the Managing Director have us up for a confidential chat? Or are we given a little book called *The Awful Secret of Grimes Buildings*?"

Miss Golden wasn't telling. She opened her drawer and took out a white towel and a case of rosy soap.

"Wash hands, please! Wash hands, please!"

Jason was frustrated. "You'll be sorry," he said. "I shall do something desperate."

"Oh no, you mustn't!" Her eyes were large with fright. She ran from the room and was back within a couple of moments, still drying her hands.

"If I took you out for a coffee, couldn't you give me just a tiny hint?"

Side by side Miss Golden and Mr. Ashgrove ran along the green-floored passages, battled down the white marble stairs among the hundred other employees from the tenth floor, the nine hundred from the floors below.

3. **Analyze how the interaction between Miss Golden and Mr. Ashgrove advances the plot.**

He saw her lips move as she said something, but in the clatter of a thousand feet the words were lost.

"—fire escape," he heard, as they came into the momentary hush of the carpeted entrance hall. And "—it's to do with a bicycle. A bicycle and a harp."

"I don't understand."

Now they were in the street, chilly with the winter dusk smells of celery on carts, of swept-up leaves heaped in faraway parks, and cold layers of dew sinking among the withered evening primroses in the bombed areas. London lay about them wreathed in twilit mystery and fading against the barred and smoky sky. Like a ninth wave the sound of traffic overtook and swallowed them.

"Please tell me!"

But, shaking her head, she stepped onto a scarlet homebound bus and was borne away from him.

Jason stood undecided on the pavement, with the crowds dividing around him as around a pier of a bridge. He scratched his head, looked around him for guidance.

An ambulance clanged, a taxi hooted, a drill stuttered, a siren wailed on the river, a door slammed, a brake squealed, and close beside his ear a bicycle bell twinkled its tiny warning.

A bicycle, she said. A bicycle and a harp.

Jason turned and stared at Grimes Buildings.

Somewhere, he knew, there was a back way in, a service entrance. He walked slowly past the main doors, with their tubs of snowy chrysanthemums, and up Glass Street. A tiny furtive wedge of darkness beckoned him, a snicket, a hacket, an alley carved into the thickness of the building. It was so narrow that at any moment, it seemed, the overtopping walls would come together and squeeze it out of existence.

Walking as softly as an Indian, Jason passed through it, slid by a file of dustbins, and found the foot of the fire escape. Iron treads rose into the mist, like an illustration to a Gothic fairy tale.

He began to climb.

When he had mounted to the ninth story he paused for breath. It was a lonely place. The lighting consisted of a dim bulb at the foot of every flight. A well of gloom sank beneath him. The cold fingers of the wind nagged and fluttered at the tails of his jacket, and he pulled the string of the fire door and edged inside.

4. **What does the phrase "a well of gloom sank beneath him" mean in the previous paragraph and how does it affect the tone of the story?**

Grimes Buildings were triangular, with the street forming the base of the triangle, and the fire escape the point. Jason could see two long passages coming toward him, meeting at an acute angle where he stood. He started down the left-hand one, tiptoeing in the cave-like silence. Nowhere was there any sound, except for the faraway drip of a tap.

No night watchman would stay in the building; none was needed. Burglars gave the place a wide berth.

Jason opened a door at random; then another. Offices lay everywhere about him, empty and forbidding. Some held lipstick-stained tissues, spilled powder, and orange peels; others were still foggy with cigarette smoke. Here was a Director's suite of rooms—a desk like half an acre of frozen lake, inch-thick carpet, roses, and the smell of cigars. Here was a conference room with scattered squares of doodled blotting paper. All equally empty.

He was not sure when he first began to notice the bell. Telephone, he thought at first, and then he remembered that all the outside lines were disconnected at five. And this bell, anyway had not the regularity of a telephone's double ring; there was a tinkle, and then silence; a long ring, and then silence; a whole volley of rings together, and then silence.

Jason stood listening and fear knocked against his ribs and shortened his breath. He knew that he must move or be paralyzed by it. He ran up a flight of stairs and found himself with two more endless green corridors beckoning him like a pair of dividers.

5.   Cite evidence to show why Jason becomes afraid when he hears the bell.

Another sound now: a waft of ice-thin notes, riffling up an arpeggio like a flurry of snowflakes. Far away down the passage it echoed. Jason ran in pursuit, but as he ran the music receded. He circled the building, but it always outdistanced him, and when he came back to the stairs he heard it fading away to the story below.

He hesitated, and as he did so heard again the bell; the bicycle bell. It was approaching him fast, bearing down on him, urgent, menacing. He could hear the pedals, almost see the shimmer of an invisible wheel. Absurdly, he was reminded of the insistent clamor of an ice-cream vendor, summoning children on a sultry Sunday afternoon.

There was a little fireman's alcove beside him, with buckets and pumps. He hurled himself into it. The bell stopped beside him, and then there was a moment while his heart tried to shake itself loose in his chest. *He was looking into two eyes carved out of expressionless air; he was held by two hands, knotted together out of the width of the dark.*

6.   **What do the sentences in italics suggest Jason was looking at?**

"Daisy, Daisy?" came the whisper. "Is that you Daisy? Have you come to give me your answer?" Jason tried to speak, but no words came.

"It's not Daisy! Who are you?" The sibilants were full of threat. "You can't stay here. This is private property."

He was thrust along the corridor. It was like being pushed by a whirlwind—the fire door opened ahead of him without a touch, and he was on the openwork platform, clutching the slender railing. Still the hands would not let him go.

"How about it?" the whisper mocked him. "How about jumping? It's an easy death compared to some."

Jason looked down into the smoky void. The darkness nodded to him like a familiar [spirit].

"You wouldn't be much loss, would you? What have you got to live for?"

Miss Golden, Jason thought. She would miss me. And the syllables Ber-en-ice Gold-en lingered in the air like a chime. Drawing on some unknown deposit of courage he shook himself loose from the holding hands and ran down the fire escape without looking back.

7.   **Analyze how Jason's interactions with the bicyclist advance the plot of the story.**

Next morning when Miss Golden, crisp, fragrant, and punctual, shut the door of Room 492 behind her, she stopped short of the hat-pegs with a horrified gasp, "Mr. Ashgrove, your hair!"

"It makes me look more distinguished, don't you think?" he said.

It had indeed this effect, for his impeccable dark cut had turned to stippled silver which might have been envied by many a diplomat.

"How did it happen? You've not—" her voice sank to a whisper— "you've not been in Grimes Building after dark?"

"Miss Golden—Berenice," he said earnestly. "Who was Daisy? Plainly you know. Tell me the story."

"Did you see him?" she asked faintly.

"Him?"

"William Heron—The Wailing Watchman. Oh," she exclaimed in terror. "I can see that you did. Then you are doomed—doomed."

"If I'm doomed," said Jason, "let's have coffee, and you tell me the story quickly."

"It all happened over fifty years ago," said Berenice, as she spooned out coffee powder with distracted extravagance. "Heron was the night watchman in this building, patrolling the corridors from dusk to dawn every night on his bicycle. He fell in love with a Miss Bell who taught the harp. She rented a room—this room and gave lessons in it. She began to reciprocate his love, and they used to share a picnic supper every night at eleven, and she'd stay on a while to keep him company. It was an idyll, among the fire buckets and the furnace pipes.

"On Halloween he had summoned up the courage to propose to her. The day before he had told her he was going to ask her a very important question, and he came to the Buildings with a huge bunch of roses and a bottle of wine. But Miss Bell never turned up.

"The explanation was simple. Miss Bell, of course, had been losing a lot of sleep through her nocturnal romance, so she used to take a nap in her music room between seven and ten, to save going home. In order to make sure that she would wake up, she persuaded her father, a distant relative of Alexander Graham Bell, to attach an alarm-waking fixture to her telephone which called her every night at ten. She was too modest and shy to let Heron know that she spent those hours in the building, and to give him the pleasure of waking her himself.

"Alas! In this important evening the line failed, and she never woke up. The telephone was in its infancy at that time, you must remember.

"Heron waited and waited. At last, mad with grief and jealousy, having called her home and discovered that she was not there, he concluded that she had betrayed him; he ran to the fire escape, and cast himself off it, holding the roses and the bottle of wine.

"Daisy did not long survive him but pined away soon after. Since that day their ghosts have haunted Grimes Buildings, he vainly patrolling the corridors on his bicycle, she playing her harp in the room she rented. *But they never meet.* And anyone who meets the ghost of William Heron will himself, within five days, leap down from the same fatal fire escape."

She gazed at him with tragic eyes.

"In that case we must lose no time," said Jason, and he enveloped her in an embrace as prompt as it was ardent. Looking down at the gossamer hair sprayed across his pin-stripe, he added, "Just the same it is a preposterous situation. Firstly, I have no intention of jumping off the fire escape—" here, however, he repressed a shudder as he remembered the cold, clutching hands of the evening before— "and secondly, I find it quite nonsensical that those two inefficient ghosts have spent fifty years in this building without coming across each other. We must remedy the matter, Berenice. We must not begrudge our new-found happiness to others."

He gave her another kiss so impassioned that the electric typewriter against which they were leaning began chattering to itself in a frenzy of enthusiasm.

"This very evening," he went on, looking at his watch, "we will put matters right for that unhappy couple and then, if I really have only five days to live, which I don't for one moment believe, we will proceed to spend them together, my bewitching Berenice, in the most advantageous manner possible."

She nodded, spellbound.

"Can you work a switchboard?" he added. She nodded again. "My love, you are perfection itself. Meet me in the switchboard room then, at ten this evening. I would say, have dinner with me, but I shall need to make one or two purchases and see an old R.A.F. friend. You will be safe from Heron's curse in the switchboard room if he always keeps to the corridors."

"I would rather meet him and die with you," she murmured.

"My angel, I hope that won't be necessary. Now," he said, sighing, "I suppose we should get down to our day's work."

Strangely enough the copy they wrote that day, although engendered from such agitated minds, sold more packets of Oat Crisps than any other advertising matter before or since.

That evening when Jason entered Grimes Building he was carrying two bottles of wine, two bunches of red roses, and a large canvas-covered bundle. Miss Golden, who had concealed herself in the switchboard room before the offices closed for the night, eyed these things with surprise.

8. Cite evidence in the text that suggests that Jason plans a celebration for two couples.

"Now," said Jason, after he had greeted her, "I want you first to ring our own extension."

"No one will reply, surely."

"I think she will reply."

Sure enough, when Berenice rang Extension 170 a faint, sleepy voice, distant and yet clear, whispered, "Hullo?"

"Yes."

Berenice went a little pale. Her eyes sought Jason's and, prompted by him, she said formally, "Switchboard here, Miss Bell. Your ten o'clock call."

"Thank you," the faint voice said. There was a click and the line went blank.

"Excellent," Jason remarked. He unfastened his package and slipped its straps over his shoulders. "Now plug in the intercom."

Berenice did so, and then said, loudly and clearly, "Attention. Night watchman on duty, please. Night watchman on duty. You have an urgent summons to Room 492. You have an urgent summons to Room 492." The intercom echoed and reverberated through the empty corridors, then coughed itself to silence.

"Now we must run. You take the roses, sweetheart, and I'll carry the bottles."

Together they raced up eight flights of stairs and along the passages to Room 492. As they neared the door a burst of music met them—harp music swelling out, sweet and triumphant. Jason took a bunch of roses from Berenice, opened the door a little way, and gently deposited them, with a bottle, inside the door. As he closed it again Berenice said breathlessly, "Did you see anyone?"

"No, "he said. "The room was too full of music." She saw that his eyes were shining.

They stood hand in hand, reluctant to move away, waiting for they hardly knew what. Suddenly the door opened again. Neither Berenice nor Jason, afterward, would speak of what they saw but each was left with a memory, bright as the picture on a Salvador Dali calendar, of a bicycle bearing on its saddle a harp, a bottle of wine, and a bouquet of red roses, sweeping improbably down the corridor and far, far away.

"We can go now," Jason said.

9. Provide strong evidence that Mr. Heron and Miss Bell were actually in Room 492.

He led Berenice to the fire door, tucking the bottle of Medoc in his jacket pocket. A black wind from the north whistled beneath them as they stood on the openwork platform, looking down.

"We don't want our evening to be spoiled by the thought of a curse hanging over us," he said, "so this is the practical thing to do. Hang onto the roses." And holding his love firmly, Jason pulled the ripcord of his R.A.F. friend's parachute and leaped off the fire escape.

A bridal shower of rose petals adorned the descent of Miss Golden, who was possibly the only girl to be kissed in midair in the district of Clerkenwell at ten minutes to midnight on Halloween.

Summarize the story then return to answer question 10.

10. What is the theme of this story and how does the author communicate it to the reader?

Blues Ain't No Mockin Bird

by Toni Cade Bambara

This story takes place in the South many decades ago. It illustrates how black people were treated by white authorities. Read to find out how one black family reacts to such treatment.

The puddle had frozen over, and me and Cathy went stompin in it. The twins from next door, Tyrone and Terry, were swingin so high out of sight we forgot we were waitin our turn on the tire. Cathy jumped up and came down hard on her heels and started tap-dancin. And the frozen patch splinterin every which way underneath was kinda spooky. "Looks like a plastic spider web," she said. "A sort of weird spider, I guess, with many mental problems." But it really looked like the crystal paperweight Granny kept in the parlor. She was on the back porch, Granny was, making the cakes drunk. The old ladle dripping rum into the Christmas tins, like it used to drip maple syrup into the pails when we lived in the Judson's woods, like it poured cider into the vats when we were on the Cooper place, like it used to scoop buttermilk and soft cheese when we lived at the dairy.

"Go tell that man we ain't a bunch of trees."

"Ma'am?"

"I said to tell that man to get away from here with that camera." Me and Cathy look over toward the meadow where the men with the station wagon'd been roamin around all mornin. The tall man with a huge camera lassoed to his shoulder was buzzin our way.

"They're makin movie pictures," yelled Tyrone, stiffen his legs and twistin so the tire'd come down slow so they could see.

"They're makin movie pictures," sang out Terry.

"That boy don't never have anything original to say," say Cathy grown-up.

1. **What does Granny mean by "we ain't a bunch of trees?"**

By the time the man with the camera had cut across our neighbor's yard, the twins were out of the trees swingin low and Granny was onto the steps, the screen door bammin soft and scratchy against her palms. "We thought we'd get a shot of the house and everything and then . . . "

"Good mornin," *Granny cut him off. And smiled that smile.*

"Good mornin," he said, head down all the way Bingo does when you yell at him about the bones on the kitchen floor. *"Nice place you got here, auntie. We thought we'd take a—"*

"Did you?" said Granny with her eyebrows. Cathy pushed up her socks and giggled.

2. **How do the three segments in italics affect the meaning and tone of the story?**

"Nice things here," said the man, buzzin his camera over the yard. The pecan barrels, the sled, me and Cathy, the flowers, the printed stones along the driveway, the trees, the twins, the toolshed.

"I don't know about the *thing*, the *it*, and the *stuff*," said Granny still talking with her eyebrows. "Just people here is what I tend to consider."

Camera man stopped buzzin. Cathy giggled into her collar.

"Mornin', ladies," a new man said. He had come up behind us when we weren't lookin. "And gents," discoverin the twins givin him a nasty look. "We're filmin for the county," he said with a smile. "Mind if we shoot a bit around here?"

"I do indeed," said Granny with no smile. Smilin man was smiling up a storm. So was Cathy. But he didn't seem to have another word to say, so he and the camera man back on out the yard, but you could hear the camera buzzin still. "Suppose you just shut that machine off," said Granny real low through her teeth, and took a step down off the porch and then another. "Now, aunty," Camera said, pointin the thing straight at her.

"Your mamma and I are not related."

3. Analyze how the author has portrayed Granny's personality by how she interacts with the photographer and provide one example of her behavior.

4. Analyze how the author develops the character of the camera man by how he interacts with Granny.

Smilin man got his notebook out and a chewed-up pencil. "Listen," he said movin back into our yard, "we'd like to have a statement from you . . . for the film. We're filmin for the county, see. Part of the food stamp campaign. You know about the food stamps?"

Granny said nothing.

"Maybe there's something you want to say for the film. I see you grow your own vegetables," he smiled real nice. "If more folks did that, see, there'd be no need—"

Granny wasn't sayin nuthin. So they backed on out, buzzin at our clothesline and the twins' bicycles, then back on down to the meadow. The twins were dangling in the tire, lookin at Granny. Me and Cathy were waitin too, cause Granny always got somethin to say. She teaches steady with no let-up.

5. Analyze how the interaction between Granny and the men in the previous scene advances the plot of the story.

"I was on this bridge one time," she started off. "Was a crowd cause this man was goin to jump, you understand. And a minister was there and the police and some other folks. His woman was there, too."

"What was they doin?" asked Tyrone.

"Tryin to talk him out of it was what they was doin. The minister talkin about how it was a mortal sin, suicide. His woman takin bites out of her own hand and not even knowin it, so nervous and cryin and talkin fast."

"What happened?" asked Tyrone.

"So here comes . . . this person . . . with a camera, takin pictures of the man and the minister and the woman. Takin pictures of the man in his misery about to jump, cause his life so bad and people been messin with him so bad. This person takin up the whole role of film practically. But savin a few, of course."

"Of course," said Cathy, hatin the person. Me standin there wonderin how Cathy knew it was "of course" when I didn't and it was my grandmother.

After a while Tyrone say, "Did he jump?"

"Yeh, did he jump?" say Terry all eager. And Granny just stared at the twins till their faces swallow up the eager and they don't even care anymore about the man jumpin.

6. Cite evidence to explain the connection between the story Granny is telling above and the incident between Granny and the men doing the filming.

Then she goes back onto the porch and lets the screen door go for itself. I'm lookin to Cathy to finish the story cause she knows Granny's whole story before me even. Like she knew how come we move so much and Cathy ain't but a third cousin we picked up on the way last Thanksgivin visitin. But she knew it was on account of people drivin Granny crazy till she'd get up in the night and start packin. Mumblin and packin and wakin everybody up sayin, "Let's get on away from here before I kill me somebody." Like people wouldn't pay her for things like they said they would. Or Mr. Judson bringin us boxes of old clothes and raggedy magazines. Or Mrs. Cooper comin in our kitchen and touchin everything and sayin how clean it all was.

Granny goin crazy, and Grandaddy Cain pullin her off the people sayin, "Now, now, Cora." But the next day loadin up the truck with rocks all in his jaw, madder than Granny in the first place.

7. Cite evidence that explains Granny's anger in the past.

"I read a story once," said Cathy soudin like the Granny teacher. "About this lady Goldilocks who barged into a house that wasn't even hers. And not invited, you understand. Messed over the people's groceries and broke up the people's furniture. Had the nerve to sleep in the folks' bed."

"Then what happened?" asked Tyrone. "What they do, the folks, when they come in to all this mess?"

"Did they make her pay for it?" asked Terry, makin a fist. "Id've made her pay me."

I didn't even ask. I could see Cathy actress was very likely to just walk away and leave us in mystery about this story which I heard was about some bears.

"Did they throw her out?" asked Tyrone, like his father sounds when he's bein extra nasty-plus to the washin machine man.

"Woulda," said Terry. "I woulda gone upside her head with my fist and—"

"You woulda done whatch always do—go cry to Mamma, you big baby," said Tyrone. So naturally Terry starts hittin on Tyrone, and next thing you know they tumbling out the tire and rollin on the ground. But Granny didn't say a thing or send the twins home or step out on the steps to tell us about how we can't afford to be fightin amongst ourselves. She didn't say nuthin. So I get into the tire to take my turn. And I could see her leanin up against the pantry table, starin at the cakes she was puttin up for the Christmas sale, mumbin real low and grumpy and holdin her forehead like it wanted to fall off and mess up the rum cakes.

Behind me I hear before I can see Granddaddy comin through the woods in his field boots. Then I twist around to see the shiny black oilskin cuttin through what little left there was of yellows, reds, and oranges. His great white head not quite round cause of this bloody thing high on his shoulder, like he was wearin a cap on sideways. He takes the shortcut through the pecan grove, and the sound of twigs snapping overhead and underfoot travels clear and cold all the way up to us. And here comes Smilin and Camera up behind him like they was goin to do somethin. Folks like to go for him sometimes. Cathy say it's because he's so tall and quiet and like a king. And people just can't stand it. But Smilin and Camera don't hit him in the head or nuthin. They just buzz on him as he stalks by with the chicken hawk slung over his shoulder, squawkin, drippin red down the back of the oilskin. He passes the porch and stops for a second for Granny to see he's caught the hawk at last, but she's just starin and mumblin, and not at the hawk. So he nails the bird to the tool shed door, the hammerin crackin through the eardrums. And the bird flappin himself to death and droolin down the door to paint the gravel in the driveway red, then, brown, then black. And the two men movin up on tiptoe like they was invisible or we were blind, one.

"Get them persons out of my flower bed, Mister Cain," say Granny moanin real low like at a funeral.

"How come your grandmother calls her husband 'Mr. Cain' all the time?" Tyrone whispers all loud and noisy and from the city and don't know no better. Like his mother, Miss Myrtle, tell us never mind the formality as if we had no better breeding than to call her Myrtle, plain.

And then this awful thing—a giant hawk—come wailin up over the meadow, flyin low and tilted and screamin, zigzaggin through the pecan grove, breakin branches and hollerin, snappin past the clothesline, flyin every which way, flyin into things reckless with crazy.

"He's come to claim his mate," says Cathy fast, and ducks down. We all fall quick and flat into the gravel driveway, stones scrapin my face. I squinch my eyes open again at the hawk on the door, tryin to fly up out of her death like it was just a sack flown into by mistake. Her body holdin her there on that nail, though. The mate beatin the air overhead and clutchin for hair, for heads, for landin space.

The camera man duckin and bendin and runnin and fallin, jiggling the camera and scared. And Smilin jumpin up and down swipin at the huge bird tryin to bring the hawk down with just his raggedy cap. Grandaddy Cain straight up and silent, watchin the circles of the hawk, then aimin the hammer off his wrist. The giant bird fallin, silent and slow.

Then here comes Camera and Smilin all big and bad now that the awful screechin thing is on its back and broken, here they come. And Granddaddy Cain looks up at them like it was the first time noticing, but not payin them too much mind cause he's listenin, we all listenin, to that low groanin music comin from the porch. And we figure any minute, somethin in my back tells me any minute now, Granny gonna bust through that screen with something in her hand and murder on her mind. So Granddaddy say above the buzzin, but quiet, "Good day, gentlemen." Just like that.

Like he'd invited them in to play cards and they'd stayed too long and all the sandwiches were gone and Reverend Webb was droppin by and it was time to go.

8. What does the sentence, "Like he'd invited them in to play cards and they'd stayed too long and all the sandwiches were gone and Reverend Webb was droppin by and it was time to go" mean?

They didn't know what to do. But like Cathy say, folks can't stand Granddaddy tall and silent and like a king. They can't neither. The smile the men is smiling is pullin the mouth back and showin the teeth. Lookin like the wolf man, both of them. The Granddaddy holds his hand out—this huge hand I used to sit in when I was a baby and he'd carry me through the house to my mother like I was a gift on a tray. Like he used to on the trains. They called the other men waiters. But they spoke of Granddaddy separate and said, The Waiter. And said he had engines in his feet and motors in his hands and couldn't no train throw him off and couldn't nobody turn him round. They were big enough for motors, his hands were. He held that one hand out all still and its getting to be not at all a hand but a person in itself.

"He wants you to hand him the camera," Smilin whispered to Camera, tiltin his head to talk secret like they were in the jungle or somethin and come upon a native that don't speak the language. The men started untyin the straps, and they put the camera into that great hand speckled with the hawk's blood all black and crackly now. And the hand don't even drop with the weight, just the fingers move, curl up around the machine. But Granddaddy lookin straight at the men. They lookin at each other and everywhere but at Granddaddy's face.

"We filmin for the county, see," says Smilin. "We putting together a movie for the food stamp program . . . filmin all around these parts. Uhh, filmin for the county."

"Can I have my camera back?" say the tall man with no machine on his shoulder, but still keepin it high like the camera was still there or needed to be. "Please, sir."

Then Grandaddy's other hand flies up like a sudden and gentle bird, slaps down fast on top of the camera and lifts off half like it was a calabash cut for sharing.

"Hey," Camera jumps forward. He gathers up the parts into his chest and everything unrollin and fallin all over. "Whatcha tryin to do? You'll ruin the film." He looks down into his chest of metal reels and things like he's protectin a kitten from the cold.

"You standin in the misses' flower bed," says Granddaddy. "This is our own place."

9. Cite strong evidence that the author's initial portrayal of Granddaddy makes it surprising that he opened the man's camera.

The two men look at him, then at each other, then back at the mess in the camera man's chest, and they just back off. One sayin over and over all the way down to the meadow. "Watch it, Bruno. Keep ya fingers off the film." Then Granddaddy picks up the hammer and jams it into the oilskin pocket, scrapes his boots, and goes into the house. And you can hear the squish of his boots headin through the house. And you can see the funny shadow he throws from the parlor window onto the ground by the string-bean patch. The hammer draggin the pocket of the oilskin out so Granddaddy looked even wider. Granny was hummin now—high not low and grumbly. And she was doin the cakes again, you could smell the molasses from the rum.

"There's this story I'm goin to write some day," says Cathy dreamer. "About the proper use of the hammer."

"Can I be in it?" Tyrone say with his hand up like it was a matter of first come, first serve.

"Perhaps," says Cathy, climbin onto the tire to pump us up. "If you there and ready."

Summarize this story then return to answer question 10.

10. What is the theme of the story and how does Granddaddy's behavior support it?

Literature, Part III

A Problem

by Anton Chekhov

Translated from Russian by Constance Garnett

This story is about a family who struggles with what to do with their irresponsible nephew. Read to find out what the nephew has done and what the family members believe should be done about it.

The strictest measures were taken that the Uskov's family secret might not leak out and become generally known. Half of the servants were sent off to the theater or the circus; the other half were sitting in the kitchen and not allowed to leave it. Orders were given that no one was to be admitted. The wife of the Colonel, her sister, and the governess, though they had been initiated into the secret, kept up a pretense of knowing nothing; they sat in the dining room and did not show themselves in the drawing room or the hall.

Sasha Uskov, the young man of twenty-five who was the cause of all the commotion, had arrived some time before, and by the advice of kind-hearted Ivan Markovitch, his uncle, who was taking his part, he sat meekly in the hall by the door leading to the study, and prepared himself to make an open, candid explanation.

The other side of the door, in the study, a family council was being held. The subject under discussion was an exceedingly disagreeable and delicate one. Sasha Uskov had cashed at one of the banks a false promissory note, and it had become due for payment three days before, and now his two paternal uncles and Ivan Markovitch, the brother of his dead mother, were deciding the question whether they should pay the money and save the family honor, or wash their hands of it and leave the case to go to trial.

To outsiders who have no personal interest in the matter such questions seem simple; for those who are so unfortunate as to have to decide them in earnest they are extremely difficult. The uncles had been talking for a long time, but the problem seemed no nearer to decision.

"My friends!" exclaimed the uncle who was a colonel, and there was a note of exhaustion and bitterness in his voice. "Who says that family honor is a mere convention? I don't say that at all. I am only warning you against a false view; I am pointing out the possibility of an unpardonable mistake. How can you fail to see it? I am not speaking Chinese; I am speaking Russian!"

"My dear fellow, we do understand," Ivan Markovitch protested mildly.

"How can you understand if you say that I don't believe in family honor? I repeat once more: fa-mil-y ho-nor false-ly un-der-stood is a prejudice! Falsely understood! That's what I say: whatever may be the motives for screening a scoundrel, whoever he may be, and helping him to escape punishment, it is contrary to law and unworthy of a gentleman. It's not saving family honor; it's civic cowardice! Take the army for instance . . . the honor of the army is more precious to us than any other honor, yet we don't screen our guilty members, but condemn them. And does the honor of the army suffer in consequence? Quite the opposite!"

The other paternal uncle, an official in the Treasury, a taciturn, dull-witted, and rheumatic man, sat silent, or spoke only of the fact that the Uskovs' name would get into the newspapers if the case went for trial. His opinion was that the case ought to be hushed up from the first and not become public property; but apart from publicity in the newspapers, he advanced no other argument in support of his opinion.

The maternal uncle, kind-hearted Ivan Markovitch, spoke smoothly, softly and with a tremor in his voice. He began by saying that youth has its rights and its peculiar temptations. Which of us has not been young, and who has not been led astray? To say nothing of ordinary mortals, even great men have not escaped errors and mistakes in their youth. Take, for instance, the biography of great writers. Did not every one of them gamble, drink, and draw down upon himself the anger of right-thinking people in his young days? If Sasha's error bordered upon crime, they must remember that

Sasha had received practically no education; he had been expelled from the high school in the fifth class; he had lost his parents in early childhood, and so had been left at the tenderest age without guidance and good, benevolent influences. He was nervous, excitable, had no firm ground under his feet, and above all, he had been unlucky. Even if he were guilty, anyway he deserved indulgence and sympathy of all compassionate souls. He ought, of course, to be punished, but he was punished as it was by his conscience and the agonies he was enduring now while waiting the sentence of his relations. The comparison with the army made by the Colonel was delightful, and did credit to his lofty intelligence; his appeal to their feeling of public duty spoke for the chivalry of his soul, but they must not forget that in each individual the citizen is closely linked with the Christian. . . .

"Shall we be false to civic duty," Ivan Markovitch exclaimed passionately, "if instead of punishing an erring boy we hold out to him a helping hand?"

1. Explain, using textual evidence, how the Colonel's views of Sasha's behavior differ from the views held by Ivan Markovitch.

2. What did Ivan Markovitch assume Sasha was feeling during the family meeting? Cite evidence from the text.

Ivan Markovitch talked further of family honor. He had not the honor to belong to the Uskov family himself, but he knew their distinguished family went back to the thirteenth century; he did not forget for a minute, either, that his precious, beloved sister had been the wife of one of the representatives of that name. In short, the family was dear to him for many reasons, and he refused to admit the idea that, for the sake of a paltry fifteen hundred rubles, a blot should be cast on the escutcheon, family shield with coat of arms, that was beyond all price. If all the motives he had brought forward were not sufficiently convincing, he, Ivan Markovitch, in conclusion, begged his listeners to ask themselves what was meant by crime? Crime is an immoral act founded upon ill-will. But is the will of man free? Philosophy has not yet given a positive answer to that question. Different views were held by the learned. The latest school of Lombroso [an Italian physician and criminologist], for instance, denies the freedom of the will, and considers every crime as the product of the pure anatomical peculiarities of the individual.

3. What does the word *blot* mean in the phrase, "a blot should be cast on the escutcheon, family shield with coat of arms"?

4. Analyze how the Russian philosophy that criminals are not responsible for their actions because they have no free will and every crime is considered as "the product of the pure anatomical peculiarities of the individual" is similar to and different from a crime you have heard about locally or nationally

"Ivan Markovitch," said the Colonel, in a voice of entreaty, "we are talking seriously about an important matter, and you bring in Lombroso, you clever fellow. Think a little; what are you saying all this for? Can you imagine that all your thundering and rhetoric will furnish an answer to the question?"

5. Analyze how the arguments between the uncles advance the plot.

Sasha Uskov sat at the door and listened. He felt neither terror, shame, nor depression, but only weariness. It seemed to him that it made absolutely no difference to him whether they forgave him or not; he had come here to hear his sentence and to explain himself simply because kind-hearted Ivan Markovitch had begged him to do so. He was not afraid of the future. It made no difference to him where he was: here in the hall, in prison, or in Siberia.

"If Siberia, then let it be Siberia, damn it all!"

He was sick of life and found it insufferably hard. He was inextricably involved in debt; he had not a farthing in his pocket; his family had become detestable to him; he would have to part from his friends and his women sooner or later, as they had begun to be too contemptuous of his sponging on them. The future looked black.

6. What does "they had begun to be too contemptuous of his sponging on them" mean?

Sasha was indifferent, and was only disturbed by one circumstance; the other side of the door they were calling him a scoundrel and a criminal. Every minute he was on the point of jumping up, bursting into the study and shouting in answer to the detestable metallic voice of the Colonel:

"You are lying!"

Criminal is a dreadful word—that is what murderers, thieves, robbers, are; in fact, wicked and morally hopeless people. And Sasha was very far from being all that. . . . It was true he owed a great deal and did not pay his debts. But debt is not a crime, and it is unusual for a man not to be in debt. The Colonel and Ivan Markovitch were both in debt. . . .

"What have I done wrong besides?" Sasha wondered.

He had discounted a forged note. But all the young men he knew did the same. Handrikov and Von Burst always forged IOU's from their parents or friends when their allowances were not paid at the regular time, and then when they got their money from home they redeemed them before they became due. Sasha had done the same, but had not redeemed the IOU because he had not got the money which Handrikov had promised to lend him. He was not to blame; it was the fault of circumstances. It was true that the use of another person's signature was considered reprehensible; but still, it was not a crime but a generally accepted dodge, an ugly formality which injured no one and was quite harmless, for in forging the Colonel's signature Sasha had had no intention of causing anybody damage or loss.

"No, it doesn't mean that I am a criminal . . ." thought Sasha. "And it is not in my character to bring myself to commit a crime. I am soft, emotional. . . . When I have the money I help the poor. . . . "

> 7. **Analyze how Sasha's thinking, as explained in the previous paragraph, will advance the plot of the story.**

"But, my friends, this is endless," the Colonel declared, getting excited. "Suppose we were to forgive him and pay the money. You know he would not give up leading a dissipated life, squandering money, making debts, going to our tailors and ordering suits in our names! Can you guarantee that this will be the last prank? As far as I am concerned, I have no faith whatever in his reforming!"

The official of the Treasury muttered something in reply; after him Ivan Markovitch began talking blandly and suavely again. The Colonel moved his chair impatiently and drowned the other's words with his detestable metallic voice. At last the door opened and Ivan Markovitch came out of the study; there were patches of red on his cleanshaven face.

"Come along," he said, taking Sasha by the hand. "Come and speak frankly from your heart. Without pride, my dear boy, humbly and from your heart."

Sasha went into the study. The official of the Treasury was sitting down; the Colonel was standing before the table with one hand in his pocket and one knee on a chair. It was smoky and stifling in the study. Sasha did not look at the official or the Colonel; he felt suddenly ashamed and uncomfortable. He looked uneasily at Ivan Markovitch and muttered:

"I'll pay it . . . I'll give it back . . . "

"What did you expect when you discounted the IOU?" he heard a metallic voice.

"I . . . Handrikov promised to lend me the money before now."

Sasha could say no more. He went out of the study and sat down again on the chair near the door. He would have been glad to go away altogether at once, but he was choking with hatred and he awfully wanted to remain, to tear the Colonel to pieces, to say something rude to him. He sat trying to think of something violent and effective to say to his hated uncle, and at that moment a woman's figure, shrouded in the twilight, appeared at the drawing room door. It was the Colonel's wife. She beckoned Sasha to her, and, wringing her hands, said, weeping:

"*Alexandre,* I know you don't like me, but . . . listen to me; listen, I beg you. . . . But my dear, how can this have happened? Why it's awful, awful! For goodness' sake, beg them, defend yourself, entreat them."

Sasha looked at her quivering shoulders, at the big tears that were rolling down her cheeks, heard behind his back the hollow, nervous voices of worried and exhausted people, and shrugged his shoulders. He had not in the least expected that his aristocratic relations would raise such a tempest over a paltry fifteen hundred rubles! He could not understand her tears nor the quiver of their voices.

An hour later he heard that the Colonel was getting the best of it; the uncles were finally inclining to let the case go for trial.

"The matter's settled," said the Colonel, sighing. "Enough."

After this decision all the uncles, even the emphatic Colonel, became noticeably depressed. A silence followed.

"Merciful Heavens!" sighed Ivan Markovitch. "My poor sister."

And he began saying in a subdued voice that most likely his sister, Sasha's mother, was present unseen in the study at that moment. He felt in his soul how the unhappy, saintly woman was weeping, grieving, and begging for her boy. For the sake of her peace beyond the grave, they ought to spare Sasha.

The sound of a muffled sob was heard. Ivan Markovitch was weeping and muttering something which it was impossible to catch through the door. The Colonel got up and paced from corner to corner. The long conversation began over again.

But then the clock in the drawing room struck two. The family council was over. To avoid seeing the person who had moved him to such wrath, the Colonel went from the study, not into the hall, but into the vestibule. . . . Ivan Markovitch came out into the hall. . . . He was agitated and rubbing his hands joyfully. His tear-stained eyes looked good-humored and his mouth was twisted into a smile.

"Capital," he said to Sasha. "Thank God!" You can go home, my dear, and sleep tranquilly. We have decided to pay the sum, but on condition that you repent and come with me tomorrow into the country and set to work."

A minute later Ivan Markovitch and Sasha in the greatcoats and caps were going down the stairs. The uncle was muttering something edifying. Sasha did not listen, but felt as though some uneasy weight were gradually slipping off his shoulders. They had forgiven him: he was free! A gust of joy sprang up within him and sent a sweet chill to his heart. He longed to breathe, to move swiftly, to live! Glancing at the street lamps and the black sky, he remembered that Von Burst was celebrating his name day that evening at the "Bear," and again a rush of joy flooded his soul. . . .

8. What does the phrase "some uneasy weight were gradually slipping off his shoulders" mean?

"I am going!" he decided.

But then he remembered he had not a farthing, that the companions he was going to would despise him at once for his empty pockets. He must get hold of some money, come what may!

"Uncle, lend me a hundred rubles," he said to Ivan Markovitch.

His uncle, surprised, looked into his face and backed against a lamppost.

"Give it to me," said Sasha, shifting impatiently from one foot to the other and beginning to pant. "Uncle, I entreat you, give me a hundred rubles."

"Won't you?" he kept asking, seeing that his uncle was still amazed and did not understand. "Listen if you don't, I'll give myself up tomorrow! I won't let you pay the IOU! I'll present another false note tomorrow!"

Petrified, muttering something incoherent in his horror, Ivan Markovitch took a hundred-ruble note out of his pocket and gave it to Sasha. The young man took it and walked rapidly away from him. . . .

Taking a sledge [a heavy sled], Sasha grew calmer, and felt a rush of joy within him again. The "rights of youth" of which the kind-hearted Ivan Markovitch had spoken at the family council woke up and asserted themselves. Sasha pictured the drinking party before him, and among the bottles, the women, his friends, the thought flashed through his mind:

"Now I see that I am a criminal; yes, I am a criminal. "

Summarize the story then return to answer questions 9 and 10.

9. Determine the central ideas of the story and analyze how they are developed over the course of the entire story. Cite textual evidence to support your answer.

10. Cite strong and thorough text evidence to explain whether Sasha was a criminal.

Social Studies, Part I

The United States, Vast and Varied: The Northeast

The United States is divided into five regions. Today you will read about the landforms, crops, and early settlers in the Northeast.

The Northeast

The United States is divided into five regions. A region is an area that shares certain characteristics such as landforms and climate. Landforms are natural features on the Earth's surface such as a mountain or a river. Most regions have several landforms. Climates are the weather patterns that the region has over a long period of time. The regions are the Northeast, Southeast, Midwest, Southwest, and West. These regions have many different landforms and climates that result in different crops being grown.

1. Which text structure best explains how the author organized the above passage?

    ____   description of important points
    ____   account of cause and effect
    ____   comparison/contrast of two or more things

    Give a reason from the text for your answer. For example, if you choose description, tell what is being described. For cause and effect, state a cause or an effect mentioned in the text. For comparison, tell what is being compared or contrasted.

The Northeast has mountains, lakes and ocean beaches. The northern part of the Appalachian Mountains begins in Canada and extends through the Northeast into the Southeast region of our country. The highest mountain in the northern section of the Appalachian Mountains is Mt. Washington in New Hampshire.

2. What evidence in the text indicates that landforms can cross from one region to another?

Each region of the country has certain landforms for which it is known. In the Northeast one of the most well known landforms is Niagara Falls. It is **located** between two of the Great Lakes, Lake Erie and Lake Ontario, on the border between the United States and Canada. Many thousands of years ago glaciers, huge sheets of ice, covered the Northeast. As the Earth warmed, ice melted and carved out the Great Lakes and the Niagara Gorge. A gorge is a deep narrow valley that usually includes a stream or river. The Niagara River plunges 188 feet down from Horseshoe Falls on the Canadian side into the Niagara Gorge. On the American side the river plunges between 70 feet and 100 feet down into the Gorge. More than 6 million cubic feet of water goes over the falls each minute. The depth of the gorge and the amount of water moving over the falls makes them an amazing sight. After visiting Niagara Falls, the poet Carl Sandburg wrote, "the tumblers of the rapids go white, go green, go changing over the gray, the brown, the rocks."

3. What is the meaning of *located* in the context of the above paragraph?

4. Explain how two changes in temperature formed Niagara Falls.

5. How is Carl Sandburg's description of Niagara Falls ("go white, go green, go changing over the gray, the brown, the rocks") different from the description in most of the paragraph? Your answer should include both Sandberg and the author of the text.

The Narragansett People

For hundreds of years the Narragansett Indians lived in the Northeast in the area which is now Rhode Island. They hunted, fished, and grew corn and vegetables for food. The Narragansett lived in a cooperative society that worked together to get things done. Whenever a family needed something done all of their neighbors as well as family members helped. The first Europeans to set foot on Narragansett lands were Dutch, French, and English fishermen and fur traders. The traders brought goods such as iron axes and hoes. They traded these goods with the Narragansett in exchange for their animal furs. In 1636, an English settler named Roger Williams came to buy land from the Narragansett to form a colony that would become Rhode Island. Williams learned their language and earned their trust. He helped keep peace between the Native Americans and the colonists. For a while they got along; however, some Europeans took part of the Narragansett's land. The Narragansett tried to keep their land and independence. Eventually fights broke out and many Narragansett were killed in battles that followed. The Narragansett scattered. Many moved to Canada or joined other Native American groups. Some remained on their lands and live there today.

6. The topic of the above paragraph is "The Narragansett People." What is the central idea of the paragraph?

7. What evidence in the text indicates that the Narragansett would not allow a member of their community to go without food?

8. Explain why early Europeans and the Narragansett lived in peace.

Resources of the Northeast

The Northeast provides many **resources** for the rest of the country. The hilly land near Lake Erie has just the right climate for growing grapes, which need up to 205 days to mature. The lake keeps the temperature from not getting too cold in winter so the grapes have the necessary time to grow and ripen. Another berry that grows in the Northeast is the cranberry. The berries grow in bogs, which are areas of soft, wet, spongy ground. To prepare a bog, swampy land must be leveled of trees and cleared of remaining plants. Then it is covered with sand to allow for good drainage. Small cranberry plants are pressed into the sand and as they grow they produce a covering over the bottom of the bog. In addition to grapes and cranberries, lobster and clams are bountiful resources from the Northeast.

9. What in the meaning of *resources* in the context of the above paragraph?

10. The topic of the above paragraph is "Resources of the Northeast." What is the central idea of the paragraph?

Summarize what the text says about how the relationship between Europeans and Narragansett changed over time.

Student Materials

Social Studies, Part II

SOCIAL STUDIES

The United States, Vast and Varied: The Southeast

Today you will read about the landforms, crops, and early settlers in the Southeast region of the United States.

The Southeast

The Southeast has mountains, rivers, and two large bodies of salt water, the Atlantic Ocean and the Gulf of Mexico. Four Southeastern states border the Gulf of Mexico. The Southeast has several important landforms, but perhaps the greatest is the Mississippi River.

The Big River

The Mississippi River affects the land and people of the Southeast. It is the largest river in the United States. It is wide, a mile and a half in some places. The Mississippi River starts at Lake Itasca in Minnesota and goes south to the Gulf of Mexico, a distance of 2,350 miles. When the Mississippi approaches the Gulf of Mexico, its waters fan out into smaller marshy rivers called bayous. As the Mississippi flows south, it carries dirt, sand and mud rich with nutrients. These materials are deposited at the mouth of the river, the place where the river flows into the Gulf of Mexico. Over thousands of years, the land has benefited from the build-up of these deposits. This rich, flat land is called a delta and it covers thousands of square miles. Because of the length of the Mississippi, it acts as a water highway. Native Americans used it as a main trade route. Today the river is still a **major** route for ships and barges loaded with goods. One of the nation's busiest ports is located on the Mississippi.

1. The topic of the above paragraph is "The Mississippi River." What is the central idea of the paragraph?

2. What is the meaning of *major* in the context of the above paragraph?

3. Explain why the Mississippi River is still important today. Give two reasons.

4. What evidence in the text indicates that the delta of the Mississippi River is a good place to grow crops?

The Cherokee People

The Cherokee made their homes in the mountains of southern Appalachia. They hunted deer and other animals and made clothing from the skins and fur. Cherokee hunters travelled for hundreds of miles through shared territory that no single group claimed but many used. Like in other regions of the United States, their lives began to change when European settlers came to the region. Spanish explorers traveled through the Southeast and traded their knives, hoes, guns, and cloth for the Cherokee's deerskin to make outerwear. The Spanish also brought new diseases to the Native Americans and the Cherokee became ill from them. Like in the Northeast, conflicts occurred between the settlers and the Native Americans because the settlers wanted Cherokee land. The Cherokees were forced to move westward.

In the late 1700s, George Washington tried to help end the conflicts. He encouraged the Cherokee to give up hunting and to focus more on farming instead. The government gave the Cherokee horses, plows, and other tools to farm. Some built large farms, learned English and were successful in **adapting** to the surrounding culture. Although many Cherokee took up new ideas and changed their way of life, conflicts remained between them, the settlers and government. After gold was discovered on Cherokee land, settlers were even more determined to force the Cherokee off their land. In the 1830s, the United States government ordered them to give up their land. American soldiers forced the Cherokee to move west to what is now Oklahoma. Forced to walk thousands of miles without enough food or warm clothing, thousands of Cherokee died. Their journey came to be called the Trail of Tears.

5. The topic of the above paragraph is "The Cherokee People." What is the central idea of the paragraph?

6. What is the meaning of *adapting* in the context of the above passage?

7. Explain how the Cherokee and the European settlers felt differently about using land.

8. What evidence in the text indicates that the U.S. government treated the Cherokee unfairly?

Resources of the Southeast

In his poem *Evangeline,* Henry Wadsworth Longfellow described the Southeast as "beautiful is the land, with its prairies and forests of fruit-trees; Under the feet a garden of flowers. . . " The Southeast contains wide stretches of good farmland. The coastal plains have warm temperatures and plenty of rain, which makes the area excellent for farming. Most parts of the coastal plains have a long growing season which makes it possible to grow crops like cotton, peanuts and sugar cane which cannot grow well in colder regions. Farming has been an important industry ever since the first settlers came to the Southeast. Today the major crops of the region include cotton, corn, peanuts, rice, soybeans and citrus fruits such as oranges, lemons, limes and grapefruits. Directly north of Florida, Georgia produces more peanuts than any other state. Rice is especially grown along the Mississippi River in Arkansas and Louisiana.

9. How is Henry Wadsworth Longfellow's description of the Southeast different from the description in most of the paragraph?

10. Which text structure best explains how the author organized the above previous passage?

_____ description of important points

_____ account of cause and effect

_____ explanation of a problem and solution

Give a reason from the text for your answer. For example, if you choose description, tell what is being described. For cause and effect, state a cause or an effect mentioned in the text. For problem and solution, tell what the problem is or describe the solution.

Summarize what the text says about how the Mississippi River has influenced or changed the Southeast.

SOCIAL STUDIES

Social Studies, Part III

The United States, Vast and Varied: The Southwest

Today you will read about the landforms, crops, and early settlers in the Southwest region of the United States.

The Southwest

Some parts of the Southwest are desert and other parts have an arid, or dry, climate. Its most well known landforms are mountains and canyons. One of the seven natural wonders of the world, the Grand Canyon, is in the Southwest.

The Grand Canyon

The Grand Canyon is about 277 miles long and 18 miles across at its widest point. It is 6,000 feet deep at its deepest point. Scientists don't exactly know how the Grand Canyon was formed, but they do know that erosion was **involved.** This gradual process of wearing away soil and rock can be caused by gravel and sand, by water from rushing rivers, by rainwater, by melting and moving glaciers, and even by wind. Many scientists believe that the rushing water of the Colorado River helped dissolve and wear away the rock of the Grand Canyon. The sand, gravel and boulders carried by the river most likely helped cut the canyon as well. Rainwater also causes erosion by dissolving certain kinds of rock. Wind may also play a part. Blowing sand can wear away the surface of the rock. Because erosion takes place all the time, the Grand Canyon may never stop changing. However, these changes happen very slowly over thousands of years.

1. What is the meaning of *involved* in the context of the above paragraph?

2. Explain how sand and rainwater eroded the Grand Canyon in different ways.

3. What evidence in the text indicates that someone who visited the Grand Canyon several times might not notice any changes from erosion?

There was not much interest in the Grand Canyon until 1869 when John Wesley Powell explored it. He made a dangerous trip by boat down the Colorado River and through the canyon. He said, "The Grand Canyon is a land of song. . . . This is the music of waters." His report led others to want to see this natural wonder. In 1903, President Theodore Roosevelt visited the Grand Canyon. Impressed with its beauty, he stated, "Keep it for your children, your children's children, and for all who come after you as one of the great sights which every American should see." In 1919, the Grand Canyon became a national park.

4. The topic of the above paragraph is "The Grand Canyon." What is the central idea of the paragraph?

5. How were Roosevelt's comments on the Grand Canyon different from the author's description of the Grand Canyon?

The Navajo People

When European explorers came to North America, the Navajo lived in the hot, dry land of the Southwest. The Navajo were mainly hunters and gatherers but they learned farming, pottery making, and basket weaving from their neighbors, the Pueblo who lived nearby. The Navajo got sheep and horses from the Spanish colonists who settled in the area and raising sheep became very important to them. They used the sheep for food and wool. The Navajo were organized into clans or family groups. Each clan had a leader but there was no primary Navajo leader. When white settlers came, the United States government made a treaty with the Navajo but only a few clans knew about it. This led to **conflict.**

6. What evidence in the text indicates that the U.S. government did not understand how the Navajo lived?

In 1863, a soldier named Kit Carson was ordered by the United States government to stop the conflicts between the Navajo and the white settlers. Carson and his men forced the Navajo to walk 300 miles to a new site in eastern New Mexico. It was a difficult journey and many Navajo died. When they arrived, they found that the soil was poor for growing crops, and the water was not safe to drink. Many more Navajo died. Finally the United States government allowed the Navajo to return home. The Navajo signed a treaty with the government. They would live on their own land and in return they promised to end any **conflict** with white settlers.

7. The topic of the above paragraph is "The Navajo People." What is the central idea of the paragraph?

8. Which text structure best explains how the author organized the above paragraph?

   ____ explanation of problem and solution

   ____ account of cause and effect

   ____ comparison/contrast of two or more things

   Give a reason from the text for your answer. For example, if you choose problem and solution, tell what the problem is or describe the solution. If you choose cause/effect, state a cause or an effect mentioned in the text. For comparison/contrast, tell what is being compared or contrasted.

9. What is the meaning of *conflict* in the context of the passage entitled "The Navajo People?"

Resources of the Southwest

A gusher is an oil well that produces a large amount of oil. The first gusher in the Southwest was drilled near Beaumont, Texas in 1901. By 1902, over 500 Texas companies were involved in the business of drilling for and refining oil. Oil comes out of the ground in the form of a thick black liquid called crude oil. This liquid must be separated, or refined, into different groups of chemicals. The factory that does this is called a refinery. From the refinery the chemicals go to other factories to be made into many different products. The oil industry is important to the economy of the Southwest. Technology is another important part of the economy. Texas industries make computers, computer chips, radios, calculators, electronic equipment, aircraft, space vehicles and missiles.

10. Explain why the Southwest did not develop farming as a major resource.

Summarize what the text says about how the Grand Canyon was formed.

SOCIAL STUDIES

Social Studies, Part I

Inventions and Big Business

Read to find out how new inventions and big business changed our country in the late 1800s.

Alexander Graham Bell was always interested in sound and speech. He built a talking-machine when he was 16. By the time he was in his twenties, he had a new idea. He believed it was possible to make a machine that would allow people to talk to each other across wires. He called this idea the "talking telegraph."

He continued to work on his invention and he hired Thomas Watson to help him. On March 10, 1876, Bell tested his invention. Bell and Watson stood in separate rooms, with the doors closed. Into one end of the telephone, Bell shouted, "Mr. Watson, come here, I want to see you." Watson raced into Bell's room and announced that he had heard the sentence clearly.

The telephone quickly changed the way people communicated with each other. By the time Bell died in 1922, there were over 13 million telephones in use in the United States and Canada.

1. The topic of the above section is "Bell's invention of the telephone." What is the central idea?

Another inventor who helped change the country was Thomas Edison. In his workshop in Menlo Park, New Jersey, Edison developed hundreds of inventions, including the phonograph and the movie camera. Of all his inventions, however, the most difficult was the electric light bulb. All the bulbs he built burned out quickly or exploded. "I've tried everything," Edison wrote. "I have not failed. I've just found 10,000 ways that won't work."

In 1879 Edison solved the problem. He built a bulb that glowed for two days. In 1882 Lewis Latimer, whose father had escaped slavery, invented a bulb that lasted much longer. The work of both Edison and Latimer helped make electric lights practical for everyday use.

2. Explain why Edison is a good model or example for any inventor. Give two reasons.

3. Which text structure best explains how the author organized the above section?

   ____ description of important features

   ____ explanation of steps in a sequence

   ____ account of cause and effect

   ____ explanation of problem and solution

   ____ comparison/contrast of two or more things

Give a reason from the text for your answer. For example, if you choose description, tell what is being described. For sequence, list one or two steps explained in the text. For cause and effect, state a cause or an effect mentioned in the text. For problem/solution, tell what the problem is or describe the solution. For comparison, tell what is being compared or contrasted.

The Rise of Steel

People knew that steel was stronger than iron. For example, steel railroad tracks lasted 20 times longer than tracks made from iron. But steel was very expensive to produce, so it could not be used for huge projects like railroad building. That changed in 1856, when an

English inventor named Henry Bessemer discovered a new way of making strong steel at affordable prices. It was now possible to produce steel in massive quantities.

Andrew Carnegie saw that there could be a huge market for steel in the rapidly growing United States. In the 1870s, Carnegie began using the Bessemer process. His goal was to produce steel at the lowest possible price. He bought mines to provide his steel mills with necessary resources, such as iron and coal. He bought ships and railroads to bring the resources to his mills, and to deliver the finished steel all over the country.

Carnegie helped steel-making become a **major** industry in the United States. By 1900, the United States was producing more steel than any other country in the world. Carnegie became one of the world's richest men. He believed he should use his wealth to help others. He often said, "The man who dies rich dies disgraced."

4. The topic of the above three paragraphs is "the rise of the steel industry." What is the central idea?

5. Explain why Carnegie chose Bessemer's way of making steel.

6. What evidence in the text indicates that producing steel involves other industries?

7. What is the meaning of *major* in the context of the passage entitled "The Rise of Steel"?

Rockefeller and the Oil Industry

In 1859, oil was discovered in western Pennsylvania and a new industry was born. Oil pumped from the ground is called crude oil. Crude oil was shipped to oil **refineries,** where it was turned into useful products such as kerosene. Kerosene lamps were the main source of lighting in the United States. This was before Edison had invented the light bulb.

John D. Rockefeller saw an opportunity to make a fortune. He built his first oil refinery in 1863. Using the profits from this business, he bought other refineries. By the early 1880s, Standard Oil controlled about 90 percent of the oil business in the United States. Standard Oil had become a monopoly. A monopoly is a company that has control of an entire industry and stops competition.

By the early 1900s, a new invention, the automobile, was creating a growing demand for products made from oil. Automobiles needed gasoline and motor oil. **Refineries** began turning crude oil into these valuable products. The oil industry continued to grow, and it remains one of the biggest and most important industries in the country today.

8. What is the meaning of *refineries* in the context of the above passage?

Big businesses were important in other industries as well, such as railroad building and coal mining. Many of these businesses were corporations. A corporation is a business that is owned by investors. People can invest in a corporation by buying shares of the company, called stocks. People buy stock in a corporation, hoping the price of the stock will go up. Today, many of the nation's biggest businesses are corporations.

9. What evidence in the text indicates that the invention of the automobile helped the oil industry?

10. How were Andrew Carnegie and John D. Rockefeller's points of view alike?

Summarize what the text says about how the inventions of Bell and Edison affected people.

Social Studies, Part II

Immigration

Read about how the population of the United States changed in the late 1800s.

The late 1800s was a time of rapid change in the United States. Before the Civil War, most Americans had lived and worked on farms. By 1900, more Americans worked in industries than on farms. And as growing industries continued creating new jobs in cities, people moved to cities by the thousands. Chicago, for example, had been a town of 30,000 people in 1850. By 1900, Chicago was home to nearly 2 million people.

New Americans

Over 23 million immigrants arrived in the United States between 1880 and 1920. During the late 1800s, the largest numbers of immigrants came from the countries of northern and western Europe, including Ireland, Great Britain, Germany, and Sweden. In the early 1900s, the greatest numbers came from southern and eastern European countries, such as Italy, Austria-Hungary, and Russia.

Why did so many people leave their homelands? Many were escaping hardships at home, such as poverty, hunger, lack of jobs, or lack of freedom. Many Jewish immigrants left Europe to escape religious persecution.

1. The topic of the above two paragraphs is "immigration." What is the central idea?

For millions of immigrants from Europe, the first stop in the United States was Ellis Island, a small island in New York Harbor. At Ellis Island, immigrants were checked for diseases and asked questions about where they planned to live and work.

For immigrants from Asia in the early 1900s, the first stop was Angel Island in San Francisco Bay. Many Asian immigrants spent weeks or months on Angel Island, waiting for permission to enter the United States. Some expressed their frustration by writing poems. One person wrote: "Counting on my fingers, several months have elapsed. Still I am at the beginning of the road."

2. What evidence in the text indicates that immigrants thought life in the United States would be better than life in their homeland?

3. Explain why Ellis and Angel Islands were important steps in the immigration process.

Arriving and Settling

What was it like for immigrants to arrive in a big American city in the late 1800s or early 1900s? For many, it was like stepping into a different world. This was a time when American cities were growing and changing. Cities like New York and Chicago were beginning to build skyscrapers. Boston built the nation's first underground train, or subway, in 1897. In many cities, passengers rode electric streetcars to and from work. And in the early 1900s, automobiles began competing for space on the crowded city streets.

An immigrant from Poland named Walter Mrozowski never forgot how he felt during his first few minutes in New York. "I was in a new world," he remembered. "I kept my courage up. I had to. There was no one to help me."

4. What was Walter Mrozowski's point of view regarding his new world?

Recent arrivals needed to do two things right away, find a place to stay and find a job. Some immigrants had friends or relatives whom they could go to for help. Those who did not know anyone usually headed to a neighborhood where there were other people from their homeland. Living in a community where the language and traditions were familiar made it a little easier for immigrants to **adjust** to life in a new country.

5. Which text structure best explains how the author organized the above previous paragraph?

   ____   description of important points

   ____   explanation of steps in a sequence

   ____   account of cause and effect

   ____   explanation of problem and solution

   ____   comparison/contrast of two or more things

   Give a reason from the text for your answer. For example, if you choose description, tell what is being described. For sequence, list one or two steps explained in the text. For cause and effect, state a cause or an effect mentioned in the text. For problem/solution, tell what the problem is or describe the solution. For comparison, tell what is being compared or contrasted.

6. What is the meaning of *adjust* in the context of the above paragraph?

Life in the Cities

Most immigrants settled in the cities, where there were busy factories and many jobs. People were also moving to the cities from small towns and farms all over the United States. With so many people moving to cities, there was soon a shortage of housing. New arrivals crowded into tenements, or buildings that are divided into small apartments. In tenements, families of eight or more often lived together in one tiny apartment. Some apartments lacked heat. Others had no windows, making it hard to get enough fresh air. Diseases spread quickly in such unhealthy living conditions.

When looking for work, immigrants sometimes faced the added hardship of prejudice. Prejudice is an unfair **negative** opinion about a group of people. For example, job advertisements sometimes included phrases like "No Irish need apply." Immigrants from many different countries faced similar kinds of prejudice.

7. The topic of the above two paragraphs is "immigrant life." What is the central idea?

8. What is the meaning of *negative* in the context of the above passage?

9. What evidence in the text indicates that immigrants faced many hardships even if they found a job?

At the same time, many Americans across the country worked to help immigrants improve their lives. Christian and Jewish organizations started schools, gave aid, and worked for change, and groups of successful immigrants aided struggling newcomers. Settlement houses were centers that provided help for those who have little money. Immigrants could take free English classes and get help finding work. A daycare center was available for the children of families where both parents worked.

10. Explain how some immigrants met the same hardships in the United States that they had faced in their homeland. Give two examples.

Summarize what the text says about the difficulties faced by immigrants.

SOCIAL STUDIES

Workers and Unions

Read how life was very difficult for US workers in the late 1800s and how people tried to improve it.

Industry created millions of new jobs. Both immigrants and people born in the United States found work in factories and mines. But it was a difficult time for workers.

Andrew Carnegie's steel mills were very successful. Many workers at Carnegie's mills, however, barely earned enough money to survive. At Carnegie's Homestead Steel Works in Homestead, Pennsylvania, steelworkers put in 12-hour days, seven days a week. They got two vacation days a year—Independence Day and Christmas. The average salary was $10 a week.

Many women worked in clothing factories, where they earned even less. Women operated sewing machines in hot, cramped workshops known as sweatshops. A teenager named Sadie Frowne talked about what it was like to work in a sweatshop in New York City. "The machines go like mad all day because the faster you work the more money you get. Sometimes in my haste I get my finger caught and the needle goes right through it. . . . I bind the finger up with a piece of cotton and go on working."

Sweatshops could be very dangerous places to work. At a sweatshop run by the Triangle Shirtwaist Company in New York, workers worried about fires. They asked the owners to construct fire escapes and keep the workshop doors unlocked. The owners refused. On a Saturday afternoon in March, 1911, a fire started. Workers were trapped inside. The fire killed 146 people, mostly young women.

1. The topic of the above two paragraphs is "sweatshops." What is the central idea?

2. What evidence in the text indicates how the owners of the Triangle Shirtwaist Company caused the death of 146 people?

Low wages, long workdays, and disasters like the Triangle Shirtwaist Company fire encouraged many workers to join labor unions. In labor unions, workers join together to fight for improved working conditions and better wages.

Unions along with others also worked to end child labor. In 1910, nearly 2 million children were working in the United States. Children performed dangerous jobs in places like cotton mills and coal mines, earning just 10 to 20 cents a day.

3. What evidence in the text indicates that workers had little time for recreation activities?

Going on Strike

One of the first union leaders in the United States was Samuel Gompers. As a teenager, Gompers worked in a cigar factory in New York City. He helped form a union of cigar factory workers. When owners cut cigar makers' wages in 1877, Gompers helped lead his union on a strike. In a strike, workers refuse to work until business owners meet their demands.

This strike did not work. Factory owners ignored the union's demand for better wages. Gompers realized that unions would have more power if they joined together. In 1886, Gompers brought many workers' unions together to form the American Federation of Labor, or AFL. The AFL fought for better wages, an 8-hour work day, safer working conditions, and an end to child labor.

4. The topic of the above two paragraphs is "unions." What is the central idea?

5. Which text structure best explains how the author organized the above two paragraphs?

____ description of important features

____ explanation of steps in a sequence

____ account of cause and effect

____ explanation of problem and solution

____ comparison/contrast of two or more things

Give a reason from the text for your answer. For example, if you choose description, tell what is being described. For sequence, list one or two steps explained in the text. For cause and effect, state a cause or an effect mentioned in the text. For problem/solution, tell what the problem is or describe the solution. For comparison, tell what is being compared or contrasted.

At times, **tensions** between striking union workers and business owners erupted into violence. This happened at Carnegie's Homestead Steel Works in 1892. Workers went on strike for higher wages, but the factory manager refused to bargain with the striking workers. Instead, he hired armed guards to break up the strike. The guards clashed with workers, and people on both sides were killed. The Homestead Strike lasted several months, but the workers were not able to win higher wages.

6. What is the meaning of *tensions* in the context of the above paragraph?

7. Explain why many business owners were unwilling to raise wages.

Coal miners were also struggling to improve their working conditions. A woman named Mary Harris Jones helped lead this effort. When she was in her 50s, Jones began traveling to mining towns in the Appalachian Mountains. "Join the union, boys," she urged the miners. Miners began calling her "Mother Jones." Mine owners threatened Jones, but she refused to stop her work. Well into her 90s, she continued organizing unions and speaking out in support of better treatment for workers.

8. How were the points of view of Samuel Gompers and Mary Harris Jones alike?

Improving Conditions

Along with labor unions, some business owners, religious organizations, and political leaders also helped to improve life for workers. Slowly, conditions began to improve. New laws shortened hours and improved safety in the workplace.

People from all over the world continued coming to the United States in search of work. Even if the pay was not high, it was more than most immigrants could have hoped to earn in their native country.

A new holiday was created to honor the **contribution** of workers in the United States. The first Labor Day celebration was held in New York City in September 1882. Within a few years, workers were holding Labor Day celebrations in many cities. In 1894, Congress declared Labor Day a national holiday.

9. What is the meaning of *contribution* in the context of the above passage?

10. Explain why working conditions gradually improved. Give two examples.

Summarize what the text says about the difficult conditions that workers faced.

Social Studies, Part I

An Expanding Nation: Rails Across the Nation

In the early days of our country, traveling across the United States was a long, difficult, and often dangerous process. Read to find out how the building of the transcontinental railroad changed this.

Rails Across the Nation

There was no easy way to get across the United States in the 1850s. To travel from the East Coast to the West Coast, you had two choices. You could take the train west to Missouri where the railroad tracks ended. From there you could continue traveling west by stagecoach, horse-drawn wagons that traveled in regular stages or sections of a route.

Your second choice was to sail south to Central America, travel west across Panama by train, and then get on another boat and sail north to California. You might also sail all the way around South America. Just like traveling by stagecoach, the ocean voyage was long, expensive and often dangerous. People began looking for faster ways to move people, mail, and goods across the United States.

1. The topic of the previous section is "traveling across the United States." What is the central idea?

2. Which text structure best explains how the author organized the above passage?

     ____   description of important features

     ____   explanation of steps in a sequence

     ____   account of cause and effect

     ____   explanation of problem and solution

     ____   comparison/contrast of two or more things

   Give a reason from the text for your answer. For example, if you choose description, tell what is being described. For sequence, list one or two steps explained in the text. For cause and effect, state a cause or an effect mentioned in the text. For problem/solution, tell what the problem is or describe the solution. For comparison, tell what is being compared or contrasted.

The Transcontinental Railroad

It took people or goods weeks and even months to cross the country. Many people believed that the best way to link East and West would be to build a transcontinental railroad, a railroad across the continent.

In 1862 the United States government gave two companies the job of building the transcontinental railroad. The Union Pacific began building track west from Omaha, Nebraska. The Central Pacific began building east from Sacramento, California.

Across the Plains

The United States government paid the Central Pacific and the Union Pacific for every mile of track completed. The companies were paid in land and money. As a result, the two companies raced against each other. Each company tried to build track more quickly than the other.

Geography gave the Union Pacific an advantage in this race. The Union Pacific began building on the broad, flat plains of Nebraska. The Central Pacific had the difficult job of building in the rugged Sierra Nevada mountain range in California.

3. **What evidence in the text indicates that paying for each mile of track completed may have been unfair?**

The Union Pacific did face **challenges,** however. One problem was finding enough workers in a region that was far from big towns and cities. This problem was solved when the Civil War ended in 1865. Thousands of Irish immigrants who had served in the Union Army moved west to work on the railroad. The Union Pacific workers also included former Confederate Army soldiers and formerly enslaved African-Americans.

A more serious challenge was conflict with Native Americans. As the railroad moved west, tracks began cutting across traditional hunting grounds of such groups as the Lakota and Cheyenne. A Lakota chief named Red Cloud told Union Pacific workers, "We do not want you here, you are scaring away the buffalo."

The Union Pacific was determined to continue building and the United States government fully supported the railroad. General William Tecumseh Sherman warned Native American leaders: "We will build iron roads, and you cannot stop the locomotive." Soldiers began guarding Union Pacific workers and the tracks continued moving west.

4. **The topic of the previous section is "the Union Pacific." What is the central idea?**

5. **What is the meaning of *challenge* in the context of the previous passage?**

6. **What was the point of view of the U.S. government regarding land that the railroad crossed?**

Over the Mountains

While the Union Pacific built track across the Great Plains, the Central Pacific was stuck in the steep slopes of the Sierra Nevada. Like the Union Pacific, the Central Pacific had a hard time finding enough workers. Many of the people in California had come there to search for gold. They were not interested in railroad jobs that paid $35 a month. But thousands of young Chinese **immigrants** were interested in these jobs. Like many other people they had come to California with dreams of finding gold. Most, however, were treated unfairly at gold mining camps so they began looking for other opportunities.

Chinese immigrants made up about 80% of the Central Pacific workforce. Most of them were teenagers. These young men did the difficult work of blasting tunnels through the solid rock of the mountains. Many workers were killed in accidents but the work never stopped.

7. **Analyze how the workers of the Union Pacific and Central Pacific were alike and different.**

8. **What is the meaning of *immigrants* in the context of the previous passage?**

9. **What evidence in the text suggests why Chinese immigrants were willing to work on the railroad?**

The Central Pacific finally finished building track through the mountains in 1867. Work then sped up, as tracks were built east across the Nevada desert. Almost every day, the newspapers around the country printed stories about the transcontinental railroad. The project was a source of pride for many Americans.

The Golden Spike

On May 10, 1869, the tracks of the Union Pacific and Central Pacific met at Promontory Point, Utah territory. A special golden railroad spike was made to symbolize the success of the project. Leland Stanford, president of the Central Pacific, was given the honor of hammering the golden spike into the tracks. Stanford lifted a hammer, swung at the spike and missed. People began celebrating anyway—the railroad was finished. The message "Done" was telegraphed from Utah to cities around the country.

10. Analyze why newspapers knew that describing daily progress on the railroad would sell papers.

Summarize what the text says about the problems faced by the Union Pacific and the Central Pacific.

Social Studies, Part II

An Expanding Nation: Conflict on the Plains

Farmers, ranchers, and miners moved in great numbers to the Great Plains. Railroads and telegraph lines crossed the land and the great herds of buffalo began to disappear. Read to find out what happened to the Native Americans who lived on the Plains.

Thousands of settlers began moving to the Great Plains in the 1860s. This led to conflict between new settlers and Native Americans who could see that their traditional way of life was threatened. Battles between Native Americans and settlers became more and more common on the Great Plains.

The United States government was determined to support the settlers. The government wanted the region to be open for expanding railroad lines, growing farms and ranches, and new towns. At first, the government offered money and goods to Native Americans. However, Native Americans did not value the white man's goods. So government leaders decided that Native Americans should move onto reservations. The government was ready to use military force to do this.

    1. The topic of the previous two paragraphs is "conflict between Native Americans and the U.S. government." What is the central idea?

Realizing that they could not defeat the United States army, many Native Americans agreed to move to reservations. In 1868 Lakota leaders signed a treaty with the United States creating the Great Lakota Reservation. This large reservation included the Black Hills in what is now South Dakota and Wyoming. According to the treaty, this land was to belong to the Lakota people forever.

Then gold was found in the Black Hills in 1874. About 15,000 gold miners illegally rushed onto the Lakota reservation.

The United States government now hoped that the Lakota would be willing to sell the Black Hills. A government representative told Lakota leaders, "Gold is useless to you and there will be fighting unless you give it up." But Lakota leaders refused to move again.

    2. What was the point of view of the U.S. government regarding gold found on the Lakota reservation?

    3. What evidence in the text indicates that money meant little to the Native Americans?

The Battle of Little Bighorn

Led by Colonel George Custer, the Seventh Cavalry's mission was to defeat the Lakota and force them onto a new reservation.

The Lakota were camped on the banks of the Little Bighorn River in Montana. The American soldiers were badly outnumbered, but Custer decided to attack anyway. He was killed along with his entire force of more than 200 soldiers.

Little Bighorn was an important battle for two reasons. First, it was the biggest victory Native Americans ever won over United States forces. Second, it soon led to the end of freedom for Native Americans of the Great Plains. Custer's defeat convinced the United States government to take stronger action against the Lakota and other Native American groups.

More soldiers were sent to the Great Plains. By the end of 1877, most Lakota had been forced onto reservations. The Black Hills were now open to gold miners and settlers from the United States.

4. **Which text structure best explains how the author organized the previous passage?**

____   description of important features

____   explanation of steps in a sequence

____   account of cause and effect

____   explanation of problem and solution

____   comparison/contrast of two or more things

Give a reason from the text for your answer. For example, if you choose description, tell what is being described. For sequence, list one or two steps explained in the text. For cause and effect, state a cause or an effect mentioned in the text. For problem/solution, tell what the problem is or describe the solution. For comparison, tell what is being compared or contrasted.

Chief Joseph

West of the Great Plains, other Native American groups were also struggling to hold on to their land. The Nez Perce lived in the Wattowa Valley of Oregon. In 1877 the United States government decided to move the Nez Perce to a reservation in Idaho Territory. The government wanted the Wallowa Valley to be open to settlers. Many Nez Perce, however, did not want to leave their **traditional** land.

5. **What is the meaning of** *traditional* **in the context of the previous paragraph?**

In June 1877 United States soldiers were sent to capture the Nez Perce and take them to a reservation. The Nez Perce refused to be taken. For the next three months, the army chased Chief Joseph and about 700 Nez Perce. Several fierce battles were fought. Finally they were surrounded by American soldiers.

General Nelson Miles promised Chief Joseph that if the Nez Perce surrendered, they would be allowed to return to Oregon. This **convinced** Chief Joseph to stop fighting. He told the American soldiers, "I am tired; my heart is sick and sad. From where the sun now stands I will fight no more forever." General Miles's promise was not kept, however. The Nez Perce were taken to a reservation in Oklahoma where many became sick and died. Chief Joseph spent the rest of his life working and speaking for a fair and equal treatment of Native Americans. During a visit to the president in 1879, he said. "Treat all men alike. Give them the same laws. Give them all an even chance to live and grow. . . . You might as well expect all rivers to run backward as that any man who was born a free man should be contented penned up and denied liberty to go where he pleases. . . . Let me be a free man . . . free to talk, think and act for myself and I will obey every law."

6. **The topic of the previous two paragraphs is "Chief Joseph." What is the central idea?**

7. **What is the meaning of** *convinced* **in the context of the previous paragraph?**

8. **Analyze what results when a person is denied liberty, according to Chief Joseph.**

9. **What evidence in the text indicates that the U.S. government lied to the Native Americans?**

After the Wars

In 1890, a group of Lakota families decided to leave their reservation. They were soon surrounded by soldiers at Wounded Knee, South Dakota. While the Lakota were giving up their weapons, someone fired a shot. United States soldiers began firing their guns, and about 300 Lakota were killed.

The fighting at Wounded Knee marked the end of the wars between United States forces and Native Americans. Native Americans all over the western half of the United States had been moved onto reservations.

10. Analyze why the Native Americans probably distrusted the U.S. government. Give two examples from the text.

Summarize what the text says about how the U.S. government treated the Lakota.

Social Studies, Part III

An Expanding Nation: The Great Plains

In the 1800s, few people lived in the central part of the United States. Read to find out how this area was developed by pioneers and immigrants.

In the mid-1800s, many Americans called the Great Plains the "Great American Desert." They looked at the plains and saw a vast region of dry grassland in the middle of the country. They saw few trees, harsh weather and low rainfall. People could not conceive that the Great Plains would ever make good farmland.

The United States government wanted to encourage pioneers, or new settlers, to move to the Great Plains. Leaders hoped that with hard work, pioneers could transform the plains into productive farmlands. New railroad lines could then carry farm goods to growing cities in the east.

But what would **motivate** people to move to the "Great American Desert"? The government's solution was to give the land away. In 1862, President Abraham Lincoln signed the Homestead Act. This law offered free land to American citizens and immigrants who were willing to start new farms on the Great Plains.

If you were a man over the age of twenty-one or a woman who was the head of a family, you could claim 160 acres of land. You had to pay a small fee—usually $10. You had to farm your land and live on it for five years. Then the land was yours.

Settlers who claimed land through the Homestead Act were called Homesteaders.

1. The topic of the previous three paragraphs is "The Homestead Act." What is the central idea?

2. What is the meaning of *motivate* in the context of the previous passage?

3. Analyze how development of the Great Plains would benefit the United States.

4. Which text structure best explains how the author organized the previous passage?

    ____   description of important features

    ____   explanation of steps in a sequence

    ____   account of cause and effect

    ____   explanation of problem and solution

    ____   comparison/contrast of two or more things

Give a reason from the text for your answer. For example, if you choose description, tell what is being described. For sequence, list one or two steps explained in the text. For cause and effect, state a cause or an effect mentioned in the text. For problem/solution, tell what the problem is or describe the solution. For comparison, tell what is being compared or contrasted.

Settling on the Plains

Before they could plant crops on their properties, homesteaders had to rip up the grass on their land. The grasses on the Great Plains had thick tangled roots that reached several inches down into the soil. Because they had to burst through this sod before planting crops, Great Plains farmers were called sodbusters.

Most sodbusters used the ripped up sod to construct houses. In regions with few trees, sod was a very useful building material. Sod houses stayed cool in the summer and warm in winter and they were fireproof. Unfortunately for homesteaders, the sod walls were often home to bugs, mice and snakes.

Once homesteaders were able to plant crops, they found that the soil was very fertile. This was not the "Great American Desert" after all.

Life on the Plains

The Great Plains may have had fertile soil but homesteaders had to work hard to **survive.** A pioneer from England put it simply: "You must make up your mind to rough it."

Roughing it included facing the harsh weather and natural disasters of the Great Plains. Bitter cold and deadly blizzards swept across the plains in winter. Spring often brought tornadoes, hailstorms and flooding. Summer could mean blazing heat and little rain. In fall grasses dried and settlers had to watch out for fires.

If the weather was not enough to worry about, farmers also faced the dreaded grasshopper. In the mid-1870s, millions of grasshoppers swarmed across the Great Plains and consumed everything in their path—crops, grass and even fences and axe handles.

5. What is the meaning of *survive* in the context of the previous passage?

6. What was the point of view of pioneers about staying on the Great Plains?

7. What evidence in the text indicates that many sodbusters may have given up and left the Great Plains?

Technology on the Great Plains

Farming the Great Plains presented many new challenges. Iron plows used in the East did not work well in the tough sod and thick soil. An inventor named John Deere built stronger steel plows. Most of the water in the Great Plains is deep underground. New types of windmills were designed to pump this water up to the surface. Steady winds made windmills a useful power source. Farmers always need fences to keep animals away from their crops. In a region with little wood, however, farmers had a hard time finding material to build fences. John Glidden invented barbed wire in 1874. Barbed wire fences were cheap and easy to build.

8. What evidence in the text indicates why trees are a valuable resource for farmers?

American Fever

Stories about the fertile soil of the Great Plains spread quickly to Europe. The desire to move to this region was so intense that it became known as "American Fever." Thousands of families from European countries crossed the Atlantic Ocean to begin new lives on the Great Plains.

Many of these immigrants brought valuable farming skills to the United States. Farmers from Russia, for example, brought seeds for a hardy type of wheat they had grown at home. American farmers were having a hard time finding a type of wheat that could survive the weather on the Great Plains. The wheat brought from Russia grew well on the plains. The Great Plains soon became one of the world's most productive wheat growing regions.

9. The topic of the previous two paragraphs is "Immigrants on the Great Plains." What is the central idea?

The Homestead Act also provided opportunities for African American homesteaders who continued to face unfair treatment after the end of slavery. Thousands of African American pioneers started new lives in communities on the Great Plains.

10. Analyze how the success of the Great Plains was due to the efforts of different people. Give two examples from the text.

Summarize how the Great Plains was settled. Include difficulties as well as factors that led to success.

American History, Part I

The Constitutional Convention

After the Declaration of Independence from Britain, the states created a plan for governing their new nation. This plan, called the Articles of Confederation, was adopted in 1777. When the Revolutionary War ended in 1783, the states called a meeting to revise the Articles. Read how the delegates created a new Constitution.

Aims of the Convention   Congress called the meeting "for the sole and express purpose of revising the Articles of Confederation." However, many delegates argued that revising the Articles would not be enough.

Delegates   In all, 55 delegates from 12 states took part in the convention. Only Rhode Island did not send any representatives.

The Virginia Plan

On the third day of the convention, Edmund Randolph of Virginia proposed a plan for a new, strong central government called the Virginia Plan. James Madison was the principal author of this plan.

Three Branches of Government   The Virginia Plan called for the central government to have three separate branches. Congress would continue to be the **legislative** branch. But two additional branches would be created. The executive branch would carry out the laws. The judicial branch would consist of a system of courts to interpret the law.

    1. **What is the meaning of *legislative* in the context of the previous paragraph?**

Randolph proposed that Congress appoint three people to serve jointly as chief executive. One person alone, he said, would never able to win the people's confidence. Others objected. A single executive, they said, could act more quickly when urgent action was required. Eventually, the delegates voted to have one person, called the President, serve as executive.

A Two-House Legislature   The Virginia Plan called for change in the composition of Congress. Rather than a single legislative body, it would consist of two parts—a lower house and an upper house.

Delegates argued long and hard about methods of choosing members of the two houses. Some wanted state legislatures to elect both houses. Roger Sherman of Connecticut said the people "should have as little to do" with the selection process as possible because they can be misled.

On the other hand, James Wilson of Pennsylvania warned against shutting the people out of the process. According to Wilson, election of the legislature by the people was "not only the cornerstone but the **foundation** of the fabric."

    2. **What is the meaning of *foundation* in the context of the previous passage?**

    3. **What evidence in the text strongly supports that some delegates did not trust future voters?**

The Great Compromise

One part of the Virginia Plan nearly tore the convention apart. The plan called for representation based on population. The more people a state had, the more seats it would have in each house. Naturally this idea drew support from big states.

New Jersey Plan   The smaller states strongly opposed this idea. They wanted each state to have the same number of votes in Congress. William Paterson of New Jersey introduced a modified plan on behalf of the small states. It called for a single house of Congress, with equal representation for each state.

Terms of the Compromise   Finally, the delegates agreed to a compromise, which came to be known as the Great Compromise. A compromise is an agreement in which each side gives up part of what it wants. The solution was a two-house Congress. To please large states, the lower house, called the House of Representatives, was to be based on population. Representatives would serve two year terms and bigger states would thus have more votes. To please the small states, each state would have two seats in the upper house, or Senate. Senators would serve six-year terms. The Great Compromise was a vital step in creating a new Constitution. Now, small-state delegates were willing to support a strong central government.

    4. The topic of the previous section is "The Great Compromise." What is the central idea?

    5. Analyze how the delegates differed with regard to forming a government. Offer two examples.

    6. What evidence in the text strongly supports that small states feared the larger states would have more power?

    7. Which text structure best explains how the author organized the previous passage?

        ____ description of important features

        ____ explanation of steps in a sequence

        ____ account of cause and effect

        ____ explanation of problem and solution

        ____ comparison/contrast of two or more things

    Give a reason from the text for your answer. For example, if you choose description, tell what is being described. For sequence, list one or two steps explained in the text. For cause and effect, state a cause or an effect mentioned in the text. For problem/solution, tell what the problem is or describe the solution. For comparison, tell what is being compared or contrasted.

Debates Over Slavery

Other issues divided the delegates; none more so than the question of slavery. The issue of slavery touched off bitter debates between northerners and southerners.

Three-Fifths Compromise   Southern delegates said that enslaved people should be counted in calculating how many representatives a state should have in Congress. Northern delegates said that because enslaved people could not vote, they should not be counted toward a state's representation.

    Finally, delegates agreed to a plan called the Three-Fifths Compromise. Each enslaved person would be counted as three-fifths of a free person. Thus, 500 enslaved people would count as 300 free people. The Three-Fifths Compromise was a gain for the South, which got more seats in the House. Northern delegates reluctantly agreed in order to keep the South in the Union.

    The Three-Fifths Compromise was a blow to African Americans. It helped preserve slavery in the new Constitution by making a distinction between free persons and "all other persons." The compromise was finally overturned when slavery was banned in 1865.

    8. What was the Northern delegates' point of view regarding the Three-Fifths Compromise?

Slave Trade   Some northern delegates wanted to ban the buying and selling of people anywhere in the country. Southern delegates protested that the ban would ruin the South's economy.

Once again a compromise was reached. Ships would be allowed to bring enslaved people into the country for a period of 20 years. After 1808, Congress would bar the importation of enslaved people. But the slave trade *within* the United States was not affected. After many more weeks of debate, the delegates agreed on all terms.

9. The topic of the previous section is "Three-Fifths Compromise." What is the central idea?

10. Analyze why slavery was the unfinished business of the Constitutional Convention.

Summarize what the text says about the Great Compromise.

Optional Standard 8 Assessment

Benjamin Franklin's Speech to the Constitutional Convention on September 17, 1787

When the Constitutional Convention finished its deliberations and all that remained was for the delegates to sign the Constitution, Benjamin Franklin asked for permission to address the delegates.

I confess that there are several parts of this constitution which I do not at present approve, but I am not sure I shall never approve them. For having lived long, I have experienced many instances of being obliged by better information, or fuller consideration, to change opinions even on important subjects, which I once thought right, but found to be otherwise. It is therefore that the older I grow, the more I am apt to doubt my own judgment, and to pay more respect to the judgment of others. . . .

In these sentiments, Sir, I agree to this Constitution with all its faults, if they are such; because I think a general Government necessary for us, and there is no form of Government but what may be a blessing to the people if well administered, and believe farther that this is likely to be well administered for a course of years, and can only end in Despotism, as other forms have done before it, when the people shall become so corrupted as to need despotic Government, being incapable of any other. I doubt too whether any other Convention we can obtain may be able to make a better Constitution. For when you assemble a number of men to have the advantage of their joint wisdom, you inevitably assemble with those men, all their prejudices, their passions, their errors of opinion, their local interests, and their selfish views. From such an assembly can a perfect production be expected? It therefore astounds me, Sir, to find this system approaching so near perfection as it does. . . . Thus I consent, Sir, to this Constitution because I expect no better and because I am not sure that it is not the best. . . . I hope, therefore that for our own sakes as a part of people, and for the sake of posterity, we shall act heartedly and unanimously in recommending this Constitution . . . wherever our influence may extend and turn our future thoughts and endeavors to the means of having it well administered.

On the whole, Sir, I can not help expressing the wish that every member of the Convention who may still have objections to it, would with me, on this occasion, doubt a little of his own infallibility and to make manifest our unanimity, put his name to this instrument.

Read the excerpt from Benjamin Franklin's speech to the delegates of the Constitutional Convention. Explain two reasons or arguments that Franklin presents for signing the Constitution.

Select one of the reasons or arguments you chose and explain why it is valid or not valid.

American History, Part II

Debating the Constitution

After the Revolutionary War ended, the Constitution of the United States was written and approved by delegates to the Constitutional Convention. Read what happened when Americans were asked to approve the Constitution.

Once the Constitution had been signed, Americans debated whether or not to ratify, or approve, the Constitution. Many of the delegates who signed the Constitution had doubts about parts of the document. For example, Benjamin Franklin agreed "to this Constitution with all its faults." As the Constitution's supporters soon learned, the battle for approval would be hard-fought and bitter. In the end, however, the Constitution was ratified.

Federalists Versus Antifederalists

The convention had set a process for states to ratify, or approve, the Constitution. Each state was to hold a convention. The Constitution would go into effect once it was ratified by nine states.

The Federalist Position   Supporters of the new Constitution called themselves Federalists because they favored a strong federal, or national, government. James Madison, Alexander Hamilton, and John Jay published the *Federalist Papers,* a series of 85 newspaper essays in support of the Constitution.

At the heart of the Federalist position was the need for a stronger central government. For the Union to last, they argued, the national government had to have powers denied to it under the Articles of Confederation, including the power to **enforce** laws. Hamilton wrote: "Government implies the power of making laws. It is essential to the idea of a law, that it be attended with . . . a penalty or punishment for disobedience. If there be no penalty . . . the resolutions or commands which pretend to be laws will, in fact, amount to nothing more than advice."

1. The topic of the previous section is "the Federalist position." What is the central idea?

2. What is the meaning of *enforce* in the context of the previous passage?

3. What evidence in the text strongly supports that law and advice are different?

The Antifederalist Position   Opponents of ratification were called Antifederalists. Leading Antifederalists, such as George Mason and Patrick Henry of Virginia, agreed that the Articles of Confederation were not strong enough. However, they felt the Constitutional Convention had gone too far.

Antifederalists were not all united in their reasons for opposing the Constitution. Some of their most frequent arguments included:

- Weakening the States. Antifederalists argued that the Constitution dangerously weakened the state governments. They feared that a too-strong central government, like that of England, would wipe out state power and **individual** freedom. "There never was a government over a very extensive country without destroying the liberties of the people," warned Mason.
- No Bill of Rights. Some Antifederalists pointed out that the proposed Constitution offered no protections for basic freedoms. Unlike the constitutions of many states, it had no bill of rights.
- President or King? Another objection was that the Constitution provided for a President who could be reelected again and again. Said Henry, "Your President *may* easily become a king."

4. The topic of the previous section is "the antifederalist position." What is the central idea?

5. What is the meaning of *individual* in the context of the previous passage?

6. Which text structure best explains how the author organized the previous passage?

    ___   description of important features

    ___   explanation of steps in a sequence

    ___   account of cause and effect

    ___   explanation of problem and solution

    ___   comparison/contrast of two or more things

    Give a reason from the text for your answer. For example, if you choose description, tell what is being described. For sequence, list one or two steps explained in the text. For cause and effect, state a cause or an effect mentioned in the text. For problem/solution, tell what the problem is or describe the solution. For comparison, tell what is being compared or contrasted.

7. What was Mason's point of view regarding a strong central government?

8. Analyze why the Antifederalists did not support ratification of the Constitution. Give two reasons.

The Ratification Debate

The debate between Federalists and Antifederalists heated up as states held their ratification conventions. Without the approval of nine states, the Constitution would not go into effect.

Delaware acted first. Its convention unanimously approved the Constitution on December 7, 1787. Pennsylvania, New Jersey, Georgia, and Connecticut quickly followed.

Antifederalists hoped to win in Massachusetts. Opposition to the Constitution was strong in the rural areas. Only a major campaign by Constitution supporters won ratification by the state.

All eyes moved to Virginia. By then, Maryland and South Carolina had ratified, which made a total of eight state ratifications. Only one more was needed. But if large and powerful Virginia rejected the pact, New York and other remaining states might do so, too.

Patrick Henry led the attack on the Constitution in Virginia. "There will be no checks, no real balances, in this government," he said. James Madison supported the Constitution and warned of the possible breakup of the Union. In the end, the Federalist view narrowly won out. Virginia's convention approved the Constitution by a vote of 89 to 79.

Meanwhile, in June 1788—while Virginia was still debating—New Hampshire became the ninth state to ratify. The Constitution could now go into effect. In time, New York and North Carolina followed. Finally, in May 1790, Rhode Island became the last of the original 13 states to ratify the Constitution.

On July 4, 1788, Philadelphia celebrated the ratification of the Constitution. A huge parade snaked along Market Street, led by soldiers who had served in the Revolution. Benjamin Rush, a Philadelphia doctor and strong supporter of the Constitution, wrote to a friend, "Tis done. We have become a nation."

Once the Constitution was ratified, Congress took steps to prepare for a new government. George Washington was elected the first president, with John Adams as vice president.

9. What evidence in the text strongly supports that state population did not matter in the ratification process?

10. Analyze why it was important that all 13 states ratified the Constitution.

Summarize what the text says were the main issues debated during the ratification process.

Optional Standard 8 Assessment

SOCIAL STUDIES

Essay in The New York Journal, December 11, 1787

As states began to decide whether or not to ratify the Constitution, the opinions of many individuals were published in a variety of newspapers.

In the first place the office of president of the United States appears to me to be clothed with such powers as are dangerous. To be the fountain of all honors in the United States—commander in chief of the army, navy, and militia; with the power of making treaties and of granting pardons; and to be vested with an authority to put a negative upon all laws, unless two thirds of both houses shall persist in enacting it, and put their names down upon calling the yeas and nays for that purpose—is in reality to be a king and a king too of the worst kind: an elective king. If such powers as these are to be trusted in the hands of any man, they ought, for the sake of preserving the peace of the community, at once to be made hereditary. . . . The election of a king whether it be in America or Poland, will be a scene of horror and confusion. . . . I say that our future president will be as much a king as the king of Great Britain. . . . All the difference is, that we shall be embroiled in contention about the choice of the man, while they are at peace under the security of an hereditary succession. To be tumbled headlong from the pinnacle of greatness and be reduced to a shadow of departed royalty is a shock almost too great for human nature to endure. It will cost a man many struggles to resign such eminent powers, and ere long, we shall find some one who will be very unwilling to part with them. Let us suppose this man to be a favorite with his army, and that they are unwilling to part with their beloved commander in chief . . . and this country will be involved at once in war and tyranny. . . . We may also suppose . . . that this man may not have the means of supporting, in private life, the dignity of his former station. . . . Such a man would die a thousand deaths rather than sink from the heights of splendor and power, into obscurity and wretchedness. . . . in the course of less than twenty years we shall find that we have given him enough to enable him to take all. I would therefore advise my countrymen seriously to ask themselves this question: Whether they are prepared to receive a king?

Read the excerpt from the newspaper. Explain two reasons or arguments that the author presents for not ratifying the Constitution.

Select one of the reasons or arguments you chose and explain why it is or is not valid.

SOCIAL STUDIES

The Bill of Rights

During the debate that surrounded the ratification of the Constitution, many states had insisted that a bill of rights be added. After the states ratified the Constitution, the new Congress met. Read to find out how they added a Bill of Rights and what this Bill guarantees.

The delegates to the Constitutional Convention are often called the Framers because they framed or shaped our form of government. Although the Framers were pleased with the government they had established through the Constitution, some were dissatisfied with the final document. For one thing, while establishing the powers of the state and federal governments, the document said nothing about the rights of the American people. In 1791, the new nation would do something about the omission when it added the Bill of Rights, the first ten amendments to the Constitution.

This addition was possible because the founders had written a Constitution that allowed for change. The Constitution was flexible enough to be changed but not so flexible that it could be *easily* changed. Article 5 of the Constitution laid out the method for amending the Constitution.

1. The topic of the previous section is "the Constitution." What is the central idea?

The Amendment Process

The Constitution can be changed in one of four ways. There are two different **procedures** for proposing amendments to the Constitution. There are also two different **procedures** for ratifying, or approving, amendments to the Constitution, the second step in the process.

Proposing an Amendment   Congress can propose an amendment if both the House and Senate vote for a change to the Constitution. Each of the Constitution's 27 amendments has been proposed in this way.

The second way to propose an amendment begins at the state level. Currently, the legislatures of 34 states must call for a national convention. It is then up to the national convention to formally propose an amendment.

Ratifying an Amendment   An amendment can be ratified through the action of state legislatures. Currently, the *yes* vote of 38 states is needed. Twenty-six of the 27 amendments to the Constitution have been ratified in this way.

An amendment can also be ratified through the action of state conventions rather than through state legislatures. Conventions are special meetings that are called to address a specific issue. Only the Twenty-first Amendment was added through the process of state conventions.

2. The topic of the previous section is "The Amendment Process." What is the central idea?

3. What is the meaning of *procedures* in the context of the previous passage?

4. What evidence in the text strongly supports that ratification of amendments by state legislatures was the most effective procedure?

5. Analyze why it is not easy to amend the Constitution. Offer two reasons.

The Bill of Rights

The Preamble of the Constitution begins with the words, "We the people of the United States." However, the seven articles of the original document deal mostly with issues involving the structure and powers of the branches of government, not with the rights of individuals. The Bill of Rights, the name given to the first 10 amendments to the Constitution, addresses the freedoms guaranteed to citizens.

First Amendment: freedom of religion, speech, and the press; right of petition and assembly

Second Amendment: right to bear arms

Third Amendment: government cannot force people to quarter troops in their homes

Fourth Amendment: protects against unreasonable search and seizure

Fifth Amendment: rights of people accused of crimes

Sixth Amendment: right to trial by jury in criminal cases

Seventh Amendment: right to trial by jury in civil cases

Eighth Amendment: forbids excessive bail and cruel or unusual punishment

Ninth Amendment: people's rights are not limited to those listed in the Constitution

Tenth Amendment: states or people have all powers not denied or given to federal government by the Constitution

6. **What point of view of the Framers of the Constitution is reflected in the Ninth and Tenth Amendments?**

The First Amendment

The colonial past was very much on the minds of American leaders when they set out to write the Bill of Rights. It is not surprising, therefore, that the colonial experience inspired the very first amendment to the Constitution. The first amendment states: Congress shall make no law respecting an establishment of religion, or prohibiting the free exercise thereof; or abridging the freedom of speech, or of the press; or the right of the people peaceably to **assemble**, and to petition the government for a redress of grievances.

7. **What is the meaning of *assemble* in the context of the previous paragraph?**

Freedom of Religion

Many individuals had come to North America because they wanted to practice their religion freely. Yet, colonial religious leaders were later driven from Massachusetts after clashing with community leaders over religious questions. The Founders wanted to avoid such church-versus-state disputes. Thus, the First Amendment affirms freedom of religion as a basic right. Americans are free to follow religion or no religion, as they choose.

8. **Which text structure best explains how the author organized the previous passage?**

____ **description of important features**

____ **explanation of steps in a sequence**

____ **account of cause and effect**

____ **explanation of problem and solution**

____ **comparison/contrast of two or more things**

Give a reason from the text for your answer. For example, if you choose description, tell what is being described. For sequence, list one or two steps explained in the text. For cause and effect, state a cause or an effect mentioned in the text. For problem/solution, tell what the problem is or describe the solution. For comparison, tell what is being compared or contrasted.

Freedom of Speech and Freedom of the Press

Dictators will often shut down newspapers and jail people who criticize the government. By contrast, the First Amendment protects the right of Americans to speak without fear of punishment.

The First Amendment also protects the press from government censorship. Freedom of the press also means that journalists cannot be arrested for criticizing the government or public officials. However, the press has a responsibility to present the news fairly and accurately. Individuals may sue journalists for libel, or the publication of false and malicious information that damages a person's reputation.

9. What evidence in the text strongly supports that freedom of the press is limited?

Peaceful Assembly and Petition

King George III and Parliament ignored the colonists' petition protesting the Stamp Act. Such experiences had a powerful effect on the leaders who wrote the Bill of Rights. The First Amendment thus guarantees the right of Americans to assemble in peaceful protest. It also protects their right to petition the government for a change in policy.

10. Analyze how the colonial past influenced what was included in the Bill of Rights.

Summarize what the text says about how the Constitution can be changed.

Optional Standard 8 Assessment

James Madison's Letter to Thomas Jefferson, October 17, 1788

The absence of a Bill of Rights in the Constitution was thought by many to be a strong reason for not ratifying it. During the ratification debates, James Madison set forth his position on a Bill of Rights.

My own opinion has always been in favor of a bill of rights; provided that it be so framed as not to imply powers not meant to be included in the enumeration. At the same time I have never thought the omission a material defect, nor been anxious to supply it even by *subsequent* amendment, for any other reason than that it is anxiously desired by others. I have favored it because I suppose it might be of use, and if properly executed could not be of disservice.

I have not viewed it in an important light because . . . I conceive that in a certain degree . . . the rights in question are reserved by the manner in which the federal powers are granted. . . . the limited powers of the federal Government and the jealousy of the subordinate [state] Governments afford a security. . . . experience proves the inefficiency of a bill of rights on those occasions when its control is most needed. Repeated violations of these parchment barriers have been committed by overbearing majorities in every State. In Virginia I have seen the bill of rights violated in every instance where it has been opposed to a popular current. . . .

What use then it may be asked can a bill of rights serve in popular Governments? I answer the two following . . . .

1. The political truths declared in that solemn manner acquire by degrees the character of fundamental maxims of free Government, and as they become incorporated with the national sentiment, counteract the impulses of interest and passion.

2. Although it be generally true as above stated that the danger of oppression lies in the interested majorities of the people rather than in usurped acts of the Government, yet there may be occasions on which the evil may spring from the latter source; and on such, a bill of rights will be good ground for an appeal to the sense of the community. Perhaps too there may be a certain degree of danger, that a succession of artful and ambitious rulers may by gradual and well timed advances, finally erect an independent Government on the subversion of liberty. Should this danger exist at all, it is prudent to guard against it especially when the precaution can do no injury. At the same time I must own that I see no tendency in our Governments to danger on that side.

Read the excerpt from James Madison's letter to Thomas Jefferson. Explain two reasons or arguments that Madison presents for having or for not having a Bill of Rights.

Select one of the reasons or arguments you chose and explain why it is or is not valid.

SOCIAL STUDIES

The Roman Republic

The ancient city of Rome was at the center of the peninsula we now call Italy. After being ruled by kings, the Romans formed a republic. Read to find out what form this republic took.

Romans Form a Republic

Over several centuries Rome expanded its territory and found ways to govern that better represented the will of its citizens. The Romans wanted a government that did not rely on one ruler such as a king. They established a new form of government—a republic. In a republic, citizens who have the right to vote select their leaders. The leaders rule in the name of the people.

The Roman Senate   In the Roman Republic, the most powerful part of the government was the senate. The Roman senate was the basis for our own legislative branch of government—the branch that proposes and votes on new laws. At first, the senate was made up only of 300 upper-class men called patricians. A patrician was a member of a wealthy family in the Roman Republic. Ordinary citizens were known as plebeians. In the early republic, plebeians could not hold office or be senators.

The Roman Consuls   Two chief officials called consuls led the government. The consuls were the chief executives of the government. They were responsible for enforcing the republic's laws and policies. The consuls were elected by the assembly of citizens. Before 367 B.C., plebeians could not be consuls. The senate advised the consuls on foreign affairs, laws, and finances, among other things.

  1. **What point of view did the early Roman patricians have about plebeians holding office?**

Consuls ruled for one year only. They almost always did what the senate wanted them to do. Power was divided equally between the consuls. Both had to agree before the government could take any action. If only one consul said, "Veto" (I forbid), the matter was dropped. A veto is the rejection of any planned action by a person in power.

The Romans knew that their government might not work if the two consuls disagreed. For this reason, Roman law held that a dictator could be appointed to handle an emergency. In the Roman Republic, a dictator was a Roman official who had all the powers of a king but could hold office for only six months.

  2. **What evidence in the text strongly supports that the senate primarily controlled the consuls?**

  3. **What evidence in the text strongly supports that the Romans did not completely trust the office of consul?**

  4. **The topic of the previous section is "the office of consul." What is the central idea?**

Praetors were other important officials. At first they functioned as junior consuls but later they served as judges in trials that settled disputes about money, business matters, contracts and so on. Thus, the praetors helped to develop some of the first rules for Roman courts of law.

Patricians versus Plebeians   The expansion of Rome's influence throughout Italy caused growing troubles between patricians and plebeians. Patricians and plebeians had different attitudes and interests. Patricians thought of themselves as leaders. They fought hard to keep control of the government. Plebeians believed they had a right to be respected and treated fairly. Plebeians did not trust the actions of the patrician senate. They believed the senate was often unfair to the plebeians. Therefore plebeians formed their own groups to protect their interests.

Many patricians grew wealthy because of Rome's conquests. They took riches from those they defeated in war. Then they bought land from small farmers and created huge farms for themselves. Plebeians did not work on these farms. Rather, the work was done by slaves brought back from conquests. Many plebeian farmers found themselves without work. The cities, especially Rome, were filled with jobless plebeians.

5. The topic of the previous section is the "Patricians versus Plebeians." What is the central idea?

6. Analyze why patricians and plebeians were against each other. Give two reasons.

Eventually jobless plebeians refused to fight in the Roman army. It was then that the patricians gave into one of the demands of the plebeians. This demand was for a written code of laws which was called the Laws of the Twelve Tables. The Twelve Tables applied equally to all citizens. They were hung in the marketplace so that everyone could know what the laws were. Despite this victory, the plebeians never managed to gain power equally to that of the patricians.

7. Which text structure best explains how the author organized the previous passage?

____ description of important features

____ explanation of steps in a sequence

____ account of cause and effect

____ explanation of problem and solution

____ comparison/contrast of two or more things

Give a reason from the text for your answer. For example, if you choose description, tell what is being described. For sequence, list one or two steps explained in the text. For cause and effect, state a cause or an effect mentioned in the text. For problem/solution, tell what the problem is or describe the solution. For comparison, tell what is being compared or contrasted.

8. Analyze why the army was important to the patricians.

The Decline of the Republic

By 120 B.C. Rome was in trouble. Roman generals gathered private armies and fought for power. Consuls no longer respected each other's veto power. Rome dissolved into **civil** war. As Rome seemed about to break up, Julius Caesar arose as a strong leader. Caesar became dictator of the Roman world in 48 B.C. Under Roman law, a dictator could rule for only six months but Caesar's rule lasted far longer than that. Although some **elements** of the republic remained, Caesar ruled with great power, taking much of the power that had once belonged to the senate. In 44 B.C., he became dictator for life. It seemed to many Roman senators that Rome once again had a king. They hated the idea. At a meeting of the senate, a group of senators stabbed Caesar to death. He had been a strong leader but many Romans felt that he had gone too far and too fast in gathering power.

9. What is the meaning of *civil* in the context of the previous passage?

10. What is the meaning of *elements* in the context of the previous passage?

Summarize what the text says about how the government of the Roman Republic was organized.

Optional Standard 8 Assessment

Suetonius: The Lives of the Caesars

Julius Caesar became very powerful and some Romans believed his power destroyed their republican form of government. A group of Roman senators stabbed him to death at a meeting of the Senate. Read the excerpt from Suetonius on the death of Julius Caesar.

Now Caesar's approaching murder was foretold to him by unmistakable signs. . . . Shortly before his death, . . . the herds of horses which he . . . had let loose without a keeper, stubbornly refused to graze and wept copiously. Again, . . . a soothsayer . . . warned him to beware of danger, which would come not later than the Ides of March; and on the day before the Ides of that month a little bird called the king-bird flew into the Curia [Senate chamber] . . . with a sprig of laurel, pursued by others of various kinds from the grove hard by, which tore it to pieces in the hall. In fact the very night before his murder he dreamt now that he was flying above the clouds, and now that he was clasping the hand of Jupiter; and his wife Calpurnia thought that the pediment of their house fell, and that her husband was stabbed in her arms; and on a sudden the door of the room flew open of its own accord. . . .

When the funeral was announced . . . it was clear that the day would not be long enough for those who offered gifts. . . . The bier [body] was carried down into the Forum . . . on a sudden two beings with swords by their sides and brandishing a pair of darts set fire to it with blazing torches, and at once the throng of bystanders heaped upon it dry branches. . . . Then the musicians and actors tore off their robes . . . rent them to bits and threw them into the flames, and the veterans of the legions; many of the women too, offered up the jewels which they wore and the amulets and robes of their children. . . .

He died in the fifty-sixth year of his age, and was numbered among the gods, not only by a formal decree, but also in the conviction of the common people. For at the first of the games which his heir Augustus gave in honor of his apotheosis [change into a god], a comet shone for seven successive days. . . .

Hardly any of his assassins survived him for more than three years, or died a natural death. They were all condemned, and they perished in various ways—some by shipwreck, some in battle; some took their own lives with the self-same dagger with which they had impiously slain Caesar.

Explain two of Suetonius's reasons or arguments that indicate he thought Caesar was a great man.

Select one reason or argument and explain why it is or is not valid.

The Roman Empire

Thirteen years of civil war followed the death of Julius Caesar. When the war ended, Caesar's adopted son, Augustus, became the first emperor of Rome. His rule marked the beginning of the Roman Empire and the end of the Roman Republic. Read to find out how the Roman emperors ruled their vast empire.

When Augustus came to power, Roman control had already spread far beyond Italy. Under Augustus and the emperors who followed him, Rome gained even more territory. With pride, the Romans called the Mediterranean Sea "our sea."

The Power of Augustus   Augustus was an intelligent ruler. When he was struggling for power, he often ignored the senate and its laws. But after he won control, he changed his manner. He showed great respect for the senate and was careful to avoid acting like a king. Augustus often said that he wanted to share power with the senate. He even said that he wanted to restore the republic.

What really happened was quite different. Romans were so grateful for Rome's peace and prosperity that they gave Augustus as much power as he wanted.

Governing Conquered Peoples   The Romans took some slaves after a conquest but most of the conquered people remained free. To govern, the Romans divided their empire into provinces. Each province, or area of the empire, had a Roman governor supported by an army. Often the Romans built a city in a new province to serve as its capital.

Wisely, the Romans did not usually force their way of life on conquered peoples. They allowed these people to follow their own religions. Local rulers ran the daily affairs of government. As long as there was peace, Roman governors did not interfere in the conquered peoples' lives. Rather they kept watch over them. Rome wanted peaceful provinces that would supply the empire with the raw materials it needed. Rome also wanted the conquered people to buy Roman goods and to pay taxes. Many of the conquered people adopted Roman ways.

1. The topic of the previous two paragraphs is "governing conquered peoples." What is the central idea?

2. Analyze why conquered peoples did not rise up against Rome and attempt to gain their freedom. Give two reasons.

3. Which text structure best explains how the author organized the previous passage?

     _____ description of important features

     _____ explanation of steps in a sequence

     _____ account of cause and effect

     _____ explanation of problem and solution

     _____ comparison/contrast of two or more things

   Give a reason from the text for your answer. For example, if you choose description, tell what is being described. For sequence, list one or two steps explained in the text. For cause and effect, state a cause or an effect mentioned in the text. For problem/solution, tell what the problem is or describe the solution. For comparison, tell what is being compared or contrasted.

4. What was Rome's point of view regarding the treatment of conquered people?

Roman Architecture and Technology   Under the Romans, architecture and engineering blossomed. With these skills, the Romans built their empire. The Romans made advances in the use of the arch—a curved **structure** used as a support over an open space. Romans used arches to build larger structures. They developed an important new building material—concrete. Concrete was a mix of stone, sand, cement and water that dried hard as a rock. Concrete helped the Romans construct buildings that were taller than any previously built.

Possibly the greatest Roman building was the Colosseum, the site of contests and combats between people and between people and animals. The giant arena held 50,000 spectators. Its walls were so well built that the floor of the arena could be flooded for mock naval battles in real boats. Stairways and ramps ran through the building and there were even elevators.

5. What evidence in the text strongly supports that the ancient Romans enjoyed watching fights?

Roads and Aqueducts Roman engineers build roads from Rome to every part of the empire. These roads allowed the Roman military to maintain firm control by travelling quickly to all parts of the empire. These roads also helped trade to spread throughout the empire and made the empire more prosperous.

Romans were famous for their aqueducts, **structures** that carried water over long distances. The aqueducts were huge lines of arches, often many miles long. A channel along the top carried water from the countryside to the cities. Roman aqueducts tunneled through mountains and spanned valleys.

6. The topic of the previous section is "roads and aqueducts." What is the central idea?

7. What is the meaning of *structure* in the context of the previous passage?

8. What evidence in the text strongly supports that Romans were skilled in matters of science?

9. Analyze why Roman technology helped the empire last for a long time.

Roman Law Roman law spread throughout the empire. The great Roman senator Cicero expressed Roman feeling about law when he said, "What sort of thing is the law? It is the kind that cannot be bent by influence, or broken by power, or spoiled by money." Under Roman law, persons accused of crimes had the right to face their accusers. If reasonable doubt existed about a person's guilt, that person would be considered innocent. Roman law was passed on to other cultures, including our own.

The Five "Good Emperors." Augustus died in A.D. 14. For eighty-two years after his death, Roman history was a story of good, bad, and terrible emperors.

In A.D. 96, Rome entered what is called the age of the five "good emperors." Perhaps the greatest of these was Hadrian. He worked hard to build a good government. His laws protected women, children, and slaves. He issued a **code** of laws so that all laws were the same throughout the empire. Hadrian reorganized the army so that soldiers were allowed to defend their home provinces. This gave them a greater sense of responsibility. Hadrian traveled throughout his empire, commissioning many buildings and other structures. He even traveled to the British Isles, where he commissioned a great wall to be built, parts of which still stand today. Hadrian also encouraged learning. The last of the "good emperors" was Marcus Aurelius who chose his son Commodus to follow him. During the reign of Commodus, things started going badly for the Roman Empire.

10. What is the meaning of *code* in the context of the previous paragraph?

Summarize what the text says were the accomplishments of the Roman Empire.

SOCIAL STUDIES

Optional Standard 8 Assessment

Tacitus: The Reign of Augustus

After the death of Julius Caesar, the Roman Republic fell into civil war. Caesar's adopted son, Augustus, became the first Roman emperor. Read the excerpt from the historian Tacitus on how Augustus rose to power.

Augustus . . . when the world was wearied by civil strife, subjected it [the Republic] to empire under the title of "Prince." . . . Hence my purpose is to relate a few facts about Augustus . . . without either bitterness or partiality . . .

Giving out that he was a Consul, and was satisfied with a tribune's authority for the protection of the people, Augustus won over the soldiers with gifts, the populace with cheap corn, and all men with the sweets of repose, and so grew greater by degrees, while he concentrated in himself the functions of the Senate, the magistrates, and the laws. He was wholly unopposed, for the boldest spirits had fallen in battle, or in the proscription [were condemned], while the remaining nobles . . . were raised the higher by wealth and promotion, so that . . . they preferred the safety of the present to the dangerous past. Nor did the provinces dislike that condition of affairs. . . .

Augustus meanwhile, as supports to his despotism, raised to the pontificate [government office] . . . his sister's son, while a mere stripling [boy]. . . . his stepsons, he honored with imperial titles. . . . In his stepson Tiberius everything tended to center. He was adopted as a son, as a colleague in empire and a partner in . . . power. How few were left who had seen the republic!

Thus the State had been revolutionized, and there was not a vestige left of the old sound morality. Stripped of equality, all looked up to the commands of a sovereign without the least apprehension for the present. . . . Augustus in the vigor of life, could maintain his own position, that of his house, and the general tranquility. When in advanced old age, he was worn out by a sickly frame, and the end was near. . . . the popular gossip of the large majority fastened itself variously on their future masters. Agrippa was savage . . . and neither from age nor experience in affairs was equal to so great a burden. Tiberius Nero was of mature years . . . and had established his fame in war, but he had . . . many symptoms of a cruel temper. . . . They must, it seemed, be subject to two striplings . . . who for a while would burden, and some day rend asunder the State.

Explain two of Tacitus's reasons or arguments that indicate he did not admire Augustus.

Select one reason or argument and explain why you think it is or is not valid.

World History, Part III

The Fall of Rome

The Roman Republic and Empire existed for over 1,000 years. Read to learn what caused the fall of the Empire.

When Marcus Aurelius died he left his son in power in A.D. 180. Commodus allowed others to help him rule the empire, but he made poor choices. He stood by as others worked to destroy the power and prestige of the senate. Commodus himself showed little use for the senate by not seeking its approval before he acted. He kept a grip on power by bribing the army to support him. His bold, extravagant and savage ways were his downfall. Commodus was assassinated in A.D. 192.

The Empire Crumbles

The decline of the Roman Empire began under Commodus. Historians do not agree on any one cause for this decline. They believe that several problems led to the fall of Rome.

Weak, Corrupt Rulers   After Commodus, emperors were almost always successful generals, not politicians. They often stole money from the treasury. They used the money to enrich themselves and pay for the loyalty of their soldiers. The government and the economy became weak and the senate lost power. Between A.D. 180 and AD. 284, Rome had 29 emperors. Most were assassinated.

1. Analyze why so many of the Roman emperors after Commodus were assassinated.

A Mercenary Army   In earlier times the Roman army had been made up of citizen soldiers ready to defend their land. Now the army was filled with mercenaries, foreign soldiers who serve for pay. Mercenaries were motivated by money, not by loyalty to any cause. They often switched sides if so doing could work for their personal advantage. Rome's strength had depended on a strong army that was loyal to the empire. This was now a memory.

2. What evidence in the text strongly supports why a mercenary army was less effective than one loyal to the empire?

The Size of the Empire   The Roman Empire had grown too large. Enemies launched attacks all over the empire. Many conquered territories regained their independence. The Roman army spent its time defending the empire instead of extending its authority. Consequently, the empire shrank.

Serious Economic Problems   When Rome stopped conquering new lands, new sources of wealth were no longer available. The empire struggled to pay its army. To raise money, the government raised taxes. Meanwhile, the people of the empire suffered severe unemployment.

Food was scarce, so its price went up. To pay for food, the government produced more coins. The value of these coins was dependent upon the amount of silver in them. But because the government did not have much silver, less of the metal was put in each coin. This change resulted in inflation, an **economic** situation in which more money circulates, but the money has less value. When inflation is not controlled, money buys less and less. Roman coins soon became worthless.

3. What is the meaning of *economic* in the context of the previous passage?

4. The topic of the previous section is "economic problems." What is the central idea?

5. Analyze why Rome experienced economic problems. Give two reasons.

6. Which text structure best explains how the author organized the previous passage?

   ____ description of important features

   ____ explanation of steps in a sequence

   ____ account of cause and effect

   ____ explanation of problem and solution

   ____ comparison/contrast of two or more things

Give a reason from the text for your answer. For example, if you choose description, tell what is being described. For sequence, list one or two steps explained in the text. For cause and effect, state a cause or an effect mentioned in the text. For problem/solution, tell what the problem is or describe the solution. For comparison, tell what is being compared or contrasted.

Efforts to Stop the Decline   Some emperors tried to stop the empire's **decline.** Diocletian worked to strengthen Rome. He enlarged the army, built new forts at the borders, and improved the tax system. Diocletian also divided the empire into two parts to make it easier to rule. He ruled the wealthier eastern part of the empire, and appointed a co-emperor to rule the western part.

Diocletian and his co-emperor stepped down in A.D. 305. A struggle for power followed for seven years. Generals fought one another for power until one, Constantine, became the winner. Constantine reigned for 25 years. He moved the capital of the Roman Empire east to the city of Byzantium in what is now Turkey. He called the city New Rome but it soon became known as Constantinople, "the city of Constantine." With the emperor and the empire's capital in Constantinople, the power of the Roman Empire was now firmly in the East.

7. The topic of the previous two paragraphs is "efforts to stop the decline." What is the central idea?

8. What is the meaning of *decline* in the context of the previous passage?

9. What evidence in the text strongly supports that Constantine was a strong and powerful ruler?

10. What was Constantine's point of view with regard to saving the empire?

Invasion and Collapse   Constantine struggled to keep the empire together but the forces pulling it apart were too great. After his death, invaders swept across Rome's borders and overwhelmed the empire. The invaders belonged to northern tribes. Today we call them Germanic tribes. The Romans called them barbarians. In the past, the Roman army had been able to defeat these tribes. Now, however, they could not stop the intruders. In the 400s, the Germanic tribes overran the empire. One tribe, the Visigoths, captured and looted Rome in 410. The Vandals, another Germanic tribe, took Rome in 455. The Roman emperor was almost powerless.

The last Roman emperor was 14-year-old Romulus Augustus. In 476, a German general took power and sent the emperor to work on a farm. After Romulus Augustus, no emperor ruled over Rome and the western part of the empire. However, even after Rome fell, the eastern part of the empire remained strong. Its capital, Constantinople, remained the center of another empire for a thousand years, the Byzantine Empire.

Summarize what the text says were the problems that led to the fall of Rome.

SOCIAL STUDIES

Optional Standard 8 Assessment

Ammianus Marcellinus: The Luxury of the Rich in Rome

Many reasons were offered for the fall of Rome, such as weak rulers, a mercenary army, and economic problems. Marcellinus offers another reason. Read the excerpt from Marcellinus on how Roman citizens lived.

The whirlpool of banquets, and divers other allurements of luxury I omit, lest I grow too wordy. Many people drive on their horses recklessly, as if they were post horses, with a legal right of way, straight down the boulevards of the city, and over the flint-paved streets, dragging behind them huge bodies of slaves, like bands of robbers. And many matrons, imitating these men, gallop over every quarter of the city, . . .

Those few mansions which were once celebrated for the serious cultivation of liberal studies, now are filled with ridiculous amusements of torpid indolence [laziness] reechoing with the sound of singing, and the tinkle of flutes and lyres. You find a singer instead of a philosopher; a teacher of silly arts is summoned in place of an orator, the libraries are shut up like tombs, organs played by waterpower are built, and lyres so big that they look like wagons! and flutes, and huge machines suitable for the theater. The Romans have even sunk so far, that not long ago, when a dearth [famine, starvation] was apprehended, and the foreigners were driven from the city, those who practiced liberal accomplishments were expelled instantly, yet the followers of actresses and all their ilk were suffered to stay; and three thousand dancing girls were not even questioned . . . along with the members of their choruses, and a corresponding number of dancing masters. . . .

So much for the nobles. As for the lower and poorer classes some spend the whole night in the wine shops, some lie concealed in the shady arcades of the theaters. They play at dice so eagerly as to quarrel over them, snuffing up their nostrils, and making unseemly noises by drawing back their breath into their noses . . . or (and this is their favorite amusement by far) from sunrise till evening, through sunshine or rain, they stay gaping and examining the charioteers and their horses; and their good and bad qualities. Wonderful indeed it is to see an innumerable multitude of people, with prodigious eagerness, intent upon the events of the chariot race!

Explain two of Marcellinus's reasons or arguments why this contributed to the fall of Rome.

Select one reason or argument and explain why you think it is or is not valid.

American History, Part I

Democracy and the Age of Jackson: The Election of 1824

Read about the election of Andrew Jackson, the first president of our country who was not an aristocrat from Virginia or Massachusetts but rather a common man from the Tennessee frontier.

As the presidential election of 1824 approached, two-term President James Monroe announced that he would not seek a third term. His presidency was marked by what appeared to be general political harmony. There was only one major political party, and the nation seemed to be united in its purpose and direction. Beneath this surface, however, there were differences. These would become obvious in the election of 1824.

A Four-Way Race   Four leading Democratic Republicans hoped to replace Monroe in the White House. John Quincy Adams, Monroe's Secretary of State, offered great skill and experience. A caucus of Democratic Republicans in Congress preferred William Crawford of Georgia. A caucus is a closed meeting of party members for the purpose of choosing a candidate. War hero Andrew Jackson of Tennessee and Henry Clay of Kentucky provided greater competition for Adams.

A Troubled Outcome   The crowded race produced no clear winner. Jackson won more popular votes than did Adams, his next nearest competitor. Jackson did well in many southern states and in the western part of the country. Adams was strongest in the Northeast. But neither won a majority of the electoral votes needed for election. As a result, for the second time in the nation's history, the House of Representatives had to determine the outcome of a presidential election. There, Clay threw his support to Adams, who became President. When Adams appointed Clay as Secretary of State, Jackson accused them of a "corrupt bargain," in which he thought Clay supported Adams in exchange for an appointment as Secretary of State.

Jackson's opposition weakened Adams's presidency. Taking a broad, nationalist view of the Constitution, Adams pushed for an aggressive program of federal spending for internal improvements and scientific exploration. Jackson and other critics denounced this program as "aristocratic" for allegedly favoring the wealthy over the common people. This would become a growing theme in national politics.

1. What evidence in the text strongly supports that Jackson had little respect for John Quincy Adams or Henry Clay?

Jackson Begins His Next Campaign   Much of the criticism of Adams's presidency came from Andrew Jackson. Indeed, Jackson and his supporters spent much of Adams's term preparing for the next election. Jackson especially relied upon New York's Martin Van Buren, who worked behind the scenes to build support for Jackson. Meanwhile, Jackson traveled the country drumming up support among the voters—a new practice.

Jackson hoped to exploit the increasingly democratic character of national politics. In the 1824 presidential election, a growing number of states had chosen their presidential electors based on popular vote. This was a shift from the method used in the first presidential elections, in which state legislatures chose electors. By 1836, every state but South Carolina was choosing electors based on the popular vote. Voters also had an increased role in choosing other state and local officials across the country. For example, the use of caucuses was replaced in many cases by more public conventions in which voters had a greater say in who became a candidate for office.

During the 1810s and 1820s, many states rewrote their constitutions. Those documents had originally restricted the right to vote and hold office to men who owned property. In 1776, about three fourths of all free men could meet the property ownership requirement because they owned a farm or a shop. But that qualified proportion slipped as more men worked for wages in the expanding industries. Without their farm or shop, they could not vote. The economic losses caused by the Panic of 1819 had also removed many voters from the rolls.

The new state constitutions expanded the electorate by abolishing the property requirement. In many states, any white man who paid a tax could vote and hold office. These changes increased participation in elections. Male voter turnout that had been less than 30 percent in the elections of the early 1800s reached almost 80 percent in 1840.

Unfortunately, the expansion of democracy did not benefit all Americans. Most of the new constitutions also took the vote away from free blacks—even those with property. Nor did the new constitutions allow women to vote. In addition, American Indians, who were not citizens of the United States, were denied the vote. Democracy was limited to white men.

2. The topic of the previous three paragraphs is "new state constitutions." What is the central idea?

3. Analyze how the new state constitutions both expanded and limited the democratic process.

Jackson Emerges

During the mid-1820s, Andrew Jackson became the symbol of American democracy. Historians refer to the movement as Jacksonian Democracy. In his speeches and writings, Jackson celebrated majority rule and the dignity of the common people. He **projected** himself as a down-to-earth common man with humble roots, which contrasted with the image of the aristocratic leaders of the past. Jackson believed in a strong presidency and used his power to veto 12 congressional acts—more than all the previous six presidents combined.

Jackson's life reflected the nation's own story of expanding opportunity. He was born in a log cabin, orphaned as a boy, and wounded during the American Revolution. Moving west to the then-frontier, he had become a wealthy lawyer and planter in Tennessee. Jackson won military fame in the War of 1812 and in the wars against the Creeks and Seminoles.

4. What is the meaning of *projected* in the context of the previous passage?

5. The topic of the previous section is "Jackson Emerges." What is the central idea?

6. Analyze why Jackson was an appealing candidate. Give two reasons.

The Election of 1828   By the election of 1828, Jackson's supporters called themselves Democrats, not Democratic Republicans. Jacksonian Democracy triumphed in the presidential election of 1828. With 56 percent of the popular vote and two thirds of the electoral votes, Jackson defeated Adams. A rowdy crowd attended Jackson's inauguration in Washington, D.C. Their raucous conduct symbolized the triumph of the democratic style over the alleged aristocracy represented by John Quincy Adams.

Jackson owed his victory to his campaign manager Martin Van Buren, who revived the Jeffersonian partnership of southern planters and northern common people. The party promised a return to Jeffersonian principles: strong states and a weak federal government that would not interfere in slavery. Only those principles, Van Buren argued, could keep sectional tensions from destroying the Union.

A New Party Structure   While returning to old principles, the Democrats **innovated** in party structure. They developed a disciplined system of local and state committees and conventions. The party cast out anyone who broke with party discipline. While becoming more democratic in style, with carefully planned appeals to voters and great public rallies, elections also became the business of professional politicians and managers.

The new party rewarded the faithful with government jobs. Where Adams had displaced only a dozen government officials when he became President, Jackson replaced hundreds. He used the government jobs to reward Democratic activists. Van Buren's "reward" was appointment as Secretary of State, the coveted steppingstone to the presidency. The Democrats defended the use of jobs as rewards for political loyalty. Senator William Learned Marcy of New York addressed the issue in a speech before Congress in 1832: "They boldly preach what they practice. When they are contending for victory, they avow the intention of enjoying the fruits of it. If they are defeated, they expect to retire from office. If they are successful, they claim, as a matter of right, the advantages of success. They see nothing wrong in the rule, that to the victor belongs the spoils of the enemy." Critics, however, denounced the use of political jobs as a reward for party loyalty, a practice they called the spoils system.

7. Which text structure best explains how the author organized the previous passage?

   ____ description of important features

   ____ explanation of steps in a sequence

   ____ account of cause and effect

   ____ explanation of problem and solution

   ____ comparison/contrast of two or more things

   Give a reason from the text for your answer. For example, if you choose description, tell what is being described. For sequence, list one or two steps explained in the text. For cause and effect, state a cause or an effect mentioned in the text. For problem/solution, tell what the problem is or describe the solution. For comparison, tell what is being compared or contrasted.

8. What is the meaning of *innovated* in the context of the previous passage?

9. What was the point of view of William Marcy regarding the Democrats' use of jobs as rewards for political loyalty?

10. What evidence in the text strongly supports that Jackson and his party initiated new practices for political campaigning? Include at least two kinds of evidence.

Summarize what the text says about how Andrew Jackson won the presidency in 1828.

Optional Standard 8 Assessment

Andrew Jackson's State of the Nation Address, 1829

In the election of 1824, Jackson won more popular votes than John Quincy Adams, but there was no clear winner in the electoral college. The election was decided by the House of Representatives and Adams was named president. Jackson became president in 1828.

I consider it one of the most urgent of my duties to bring to your attention the propriety of amending that part of the Constitution which relates to the election of President and Vice-President. Our system of government was by its framers deemed an experiment, and they therefore consistently provided a mode of remedying its defects.

To the people belongs the right of electing their Chief Magistrate; it was never designed that their choice should in any case be defeated, either by the intervention of electoral colleges or by the agency confided, under certain contingencies, to the House of Representatives. Experience proves that in proportion as agents to execute the will of the people are multiplied there is danger of their wishes being frustrated. Some may be unfaithful; all are liable to err. So far, therefore, as the people can with convenience speak, it is safer for them to express their own will.

The number of aspirants to the Presidency and the diversity of the interests which may influence their claims leave little reason to expect a choice in the first instance, and in that event the election must devolve on the House of Representatives, where it is obvious the will of the people may not be always ascertained, or, if ascertained, may not be regarded. From the mode of voting by States the choice is to be made by 24 votes, and it may often occur that one of these will be controlled by an individual Representative. Honors and offices are at the disposal of the successful candidate. Repeated ballotings may make it apparent that a single individual holds the cast in his hand. May he not be tempted to name his reward?

But even without corruption, supposing the probity of the Representative to be proof against the powerful motives by which it may be assailed, the will of the people is still constantly liable to be misrepresented. One may err from ignorance of the wishes of his constituents; another from a conviction that it is his duty to be governed by his own judgment of the fitness of the candidates; finally, although all were inflexibly honest, all accurately informed of the wishes of their constituents, yet under the present mode of election a minority may often elect a President, and when this happens it may reasonably be expected that efforts will be made on the part of the majority to rectify this injurious operation of their institutions. But although no evil of this character should result from such a perversion of the first principle of our system—that the majority is to govern—it must be very certain that a President elected by a minority can not enjoy the confidence necessary to the successful discharge of his duties.

In this as in all other matters of public concern policy requires that as few impediments as possible should exist to the free operation of the public will. Let us, then, endeavor so to amend our system that the office of Chief Magistrate may not be conferred upon any citizen but in pursuance of a fair expression of the will of the majority.

Read the excerpt from Andrew Jackson's State of the Nation Address. Explain four reasons or arguments that Jackson presents for amending the Constitution.

Select two arguments and, for each one, explain why you think it is or is not valid.

American History, Part II

Democracy and the Age of Jackson: Conflicts and Crises

Andrew Jackson's presidency featured a number of conflicts and crises. Read to learn about two of these.

Native American Removal

Jackson's political base lay in the South, where he captured 80 percent of the vote. Those voters expected Jackson to help them remove the 60,000 American Indians living in the region. These Indians belonged to five nations: the Cherokee, Chickasaw, Creek, Choctaw, and Seminole.

Southern voters had good reason to expect Jackson's help with Indian removal. Jackson's victory in the Creek War of 1814 had led to the acquisition of millions of Creek acres in Georgia and Alabama. His war with the Seminoles in 1818 paved the way for American control of Florida.

Still, many Native Americans had remained in the South. In many cases, they had even adopted white American culture. For example, many practiced Christianity, established schools, owned private property, and formed constitutional, republican governments. A Cherokee named Sequoyah invented a writing system for the Cherokee language so they could print their own newspaper and books. These Native Americans in the five southeastern tribes became known as the "five civilized tribes."

Many southern whites, however, denounced the Indian civilizations as a sham. Indians could never be civilized, southerners insisted. President Jackson agreed that the Indians should make way for white people. "What good man would prefer a country covered with forests and ranged by a few thousand savages to our extensive Republic?" he asked. Indeed, southern whites wanted the valuable lands held by the Indians. In 1829, white settlers discovered gold on Cherokee lands in Georgia.

1. The topic of the previous four paragraphs is "Native Americans in the South." What is the central idea?

2. What evidence in the text strongly supports that Jackson's view of Native Americans as "savages" was not true? Include at least two reasons.

Between 1827 and 1830, the states of Georgia, Mississippi, and Alabama dissolved the Indian governments and seized these lands. In 1832, after the Indians appealed their case to the federal courts, John Marshall's Supreme Court tried to help the Indians. In Worcester vs. Georgia, the Court ruled that Georgia's land seizure was unconstitutional. The federal government had treaty obligations to protect the Indians, the Court held, and federal law was superior to state law. President Jackson, however, ignored the Court's decision. "John Marshall has made his decision, now let him enforce it," Jackson boldly declared. Although often a nationalist, Jackson favored states' rights in this case.

Even before this ruling, Jackson had urged Congress to pass the Indian Removal Act of 1830. This act sought to peacefully negotiate the exchange of American Indian lands in the South for new lands in the Indian Territory (modern-day Oklahoma).

In a message to Congress in 1830, Jackson stated: "Rightly considered, the policy of the General Government toward the red man is not only **liberal**, but generous. He is unwilling to submit to the laws of the States and mingle with their population. To save him from this alternative, or perhaps utter annihilation, the General Government kindly offers him a new home." The Choctaws and Chickasaws reluctantly agreed to leave their southeastern homelands for new lands in the West. A few stayed behind, but they suffered violent mistreatment by whites.

3. The topic of the previous three paragraphs is "Indian land." What is the central idea?

4. Analyze why many white men, including Jackson, wanted Native Americans removed from the southeast. Include at least two reasons.

5. **What is the meaning of *liberal* in the context of the previous paragraph?**

The Jackson administration continued pressuring remaining Indian groups to sell their lands and move west. In 1835, a small group of Cherokees who did not represent their nation made an agreement with the government under which all Cherokees would leave the South for Oklahoma. Though the rest of the Cherokees protested, the federal government sought to enforce the treaty. In 1838, U.S. soldiers forced 16,000 Cherokees into military stockades at bayonet point and then forced them to walk from their lands in the Southeast to Oklahoma, 1,000 miles west into Indian Territory. The name of the route they followed came to be called the Trail of Tears. At least 4,000 Cherokees died of disease, exposure, and hunger on their long, hard journey.

Some Indians in the South resisted removal. In 1836, after a number of violent conflicts with white settlers, troops forcibly removed the Creeks from their southern lands. In Florida, the Seminoles fought the Second Seminole War between 1835 and 1842. In the end, American troops forced most Seminoles to leave Florida.

Removal also affected Native Americans in the Midwest. In Illinois, a chief named Black Hawk led the resistance by the Sauk and Fox nations. In what became known as Black Hawk's War, they fought federal troops and local militia until crushed in 1832.

6. **Which text structure best explains how the author organized the previous passage?**

    ____ **description of important features**

    ____ **explanation of steps in a sequence**

    ____ **account of cause and effect**

    ____ **explanation of problem and solution**

    ____ **comparison/contrast of two or more things**

    Give a reason from the text for your answer. For example, if you choose description, tell what is being described. For sequence, list one or two steps explained in the text. For cause and effect, state a cause or an effect mentioned in the text. For problem/solution, tell what the problem is or describe the solution. For comparison, tell what is being compared or contrasted.

The Nullification Crisis

Protective tariffs had long been a topic of debate and discord in the United States. A tariff is a tax on imported goods for the purpose of raising revenue for the federal government and protecting American manufacturers from foreign competition. In general, the industrial North favored them, but the agricultural South disliked them.

In 1828, Congress adopted an especially high tariff. Southerners called it the Tariff of Abominations. This tariff had been designed by members of Congress not only to promote American industry but to embarrass President Adams and ensure a Jackson victory in that year's presidential election. In fact, Adams did sign the tariff, though reluctantly, and it did help bring about his defeat in 1828.

7. **What evidence in the text strongly suggests that members of Congress favored Jackson even before he was elected to the presidency?**

Calhoun Champions Nullification   Jackson's Vice President, John C. Calhoun of South Carolina, violently opposed the tariff. He was convinced that the future of slavery, which he supported, required a strong defense of states' rights. Toward that end, he began to champion the concept of nullification which meant that states could nullify, or void, any federal law deemed unconstitutional.

Calhoun and his supporters expected Jackson to reject a protective tariff. After all, Jackson was not a supporter of the tariff, and they hoped he might take action against it on his own. He did modify the tariff rates, but not enough to satisfy Calhoun.

The Crisis Deepens   In 1832, the South Carolina legislature nullified the protective tariff and prohibited the collection of federal tariff duties in South Carolina after February 1, 1833. Further, the state threatened to secede from the Union if the federal government employed force against South Carolina. Calhoun resigned the vice presidency and instead became a senator.

Jackson generally supported states' rights, and he wanted a lower tariff. He drew the line at nullification and secession, however. "Disunion by armed force is treason," Jackson thundered. He felt the Union must be perpetual and states must honor federal law. "I can have within the limits of South Carolina fifty thousand men, and in forty days more another fifty thousand. . . . The Union will be preserved. The safety of the republic, the supreme law, which will be promptly obeyed by me." Other state legislatures around the country supported him by passing resolutions rejecting nullification.

8. What was Jackson's point of view regarding states' rights and the preservation of the Union?

Webster Defends the Union   In Congress, Daniel Webster of Massachusetts became the great champion of nationalism. In an 1830 debate over nullification, he had blasted the notion in a fiery speech. "Liberty and Union, now and forever, one and inseparable," he declared. Webster defined the Union as the creation of the American people rather than of the states. In 1833, Webster led the way in pushing for passage of a Force Bill, giving Jackson authority to use troops to enforce federal law in South Carolina.

The Crisis Avoided   At the same time, with Jackson's support, Congress also reduced the tariff. This reduced South Carolina's militancy. In March, a special convention suspended that state's ordinance of nullification. Still, the convention made a political statement by nullifying the now-unnecessary Force Bill. The crisis passed. Jackson and Webster could declare victory. The difficult questions of nullification and secession, however, had been postponed rather than **resolved.**

9. What is the meaning of *resolved* in the context of the previous paragraph?

10. Analyze how Jackson used similar tactics to deal with the nullification crisis and the Native American issue. Include two similarities.

Summarize what the text says about how South Carolina caused a nullification crisis and how it was resolved.

Optional Standard 8 Assessment

Memorial of the Cherokee Nation (1830)

In his first term of office, Andrew Jackson was instrumental in removing Native Americans from the southern states to Indian Territory (present day Oklahoma). This occurred despite the legal support of the Supreme Court for the rights of the Native Americans as stated by the Cherokee nation.

We are aware that some persons suppose it will be for our advantage to remove beyond the Mississippi. We think otherwise. Our people universally think otherwise. Thinking that it would be fatal to their interests, they have almost to a man sent their memorial to Congress, deprecating the necessity of a removal. . . . It is incredible that Georgia should ever have enacted the oppressive laws to which reference is here made, unless she had supposed that something extremely terrific in its character was necessary in order to make the Cherokees willing to remove. We are not willing to remove; and if we could be brought to this extremity, it would be not by argument, nor because our judgment was satisfied, not because our condition will be improved; but only because we cannot endure to be deprived of our national and individual rights and subjected to a process of intolerable oppression.

We wish to remain on the land of our fathers. We have a perfect and original right to remain without interruption or molestation. The treaties with us, and laws of the United States made in pursuance of treaties, guaranty our residence and our privileges, and secure us against intruders. Our only request is, that these treaties may be fulfilled, and these laws executed.

But if we are compelled to leave our country, we see nothing but ruin before us. The country west of the Arkansas territory is unknown to us. From what we can learn of it, we have no prepossessions in its favor. All the inviting parts of it, as we believe, are preoccupied by various Indian nations, to which it has been assigned. They would regard us as intruders. . . . The far greater part of that region is, beyond all controversy, badly supplied with wood and water; and no Indian tribe can live as agriculturists without these articles. All our neighbors . . . would speak a language totally different from ours, and practice different customs. The original possessors of that region are now wandering savages lurking for prey in the neighborhood. . . . Were the country to which we are urged much better than it is represented to be, . . . still it is not the land of our birth, nor of our affections. It contains neither the scenes of our childhood, nor the graves of our fathers.

. . . We have been called a poor, ignorant, and degraded people. We certainly are not rich; nor have we ever boasted of our knowledge, or our moral or intellectual elevation. But there is not a man within our limits so ignorant as not to know that he has a right to live on the land of his fathers, in the possession of his immemorial privileges, and that this right has been acknowledged by the United States; nor is there a man so degraded as not to feel a keen sense of injury, on being deprived of his right and driven into exile . . .

Read the excerpt from the Memorial of the Cherokee Nation. Explain four reasons or arguments that the Cherokee present for not wising to leave their ancestral lands.

Select two reasons or arguments and, for each one, explain why you think it is or is not valid.

American History, Part III

Democracy and the Age of Jackson: More Conflicts and Crises

Andrew Jackson's presidency featured a number of conflicts and crises. Read how these helped bring about the formation of a rival political party.

The Bank War

Notwithstanding his fight over nullification, Jackson was a supporter of the agricultural South. Indeed, he longed to revive Jefferson's ideal of an agrarian republic, in which almost all white men owned farms and enjoyed a rough equality. But industrialization worked against that vision. Increasing numbers of Americans worked in cities for wages instead of on their own farms. In the cities, a gap widened between rich owners and poor workers. Wealth became more abstract and more fluid since it was measured in bank stock versus land. The changes troubled many Americans.

Jackson Opposes the Bank   Jacksonian Democrats suspected that the new economy encouraged corruption and greed. They howled when industry sought special advantages, such as protective tariffs or federal subsidies for roads and canals. Industry claimed these advantages promoted economic growth. To Jackson and his followers, they seemed mainly to enrich wealthy people at the expense of everyone else. Jacksonian Democrats promised to rescue the Republic from a new form of aristocracy they called the "Money Power."

Jacksonian Democrats especially disliked the second Bank of the United States, which had been chartered by Congress in 1816. They saw it as a dangerous, and perhaps even corrupt, special interest that favored rich investors. Many business leaders, on the other hand, valued the Bank. They believed it promoted economic growth by providing a **stable** currency, paper money, in which people could have confidence. They argued that a lack of confidence in the money supply could cause serious harm to the economy.

1. What is the meaning of *stable* in the context of the previous paragraph?

The Bank had many supporters in Congress. In 1832, they voted to renew the Bank's charter. Jackson, however, vetoed the renewal. He denounced the Bank as "unauthorized by the Constitution, subversive of the rights of the states, and dangerous to the liberties of the people." He opposed government action that led to "the advancement of the few at the expense of the many." He regretted "that the rich and powerful too often bend the acts of government to their selfish purposes." Jackson posed as the defender of "the humble members of society—the farmers, mechanics, and laborers."

2. The topic of the previous section is "Jackson Opposes the Bank." What is the central idea?

3. What evidence in the text strongly supports that Jackson and Jacksonian Democrats did not support the wealthy? Give two examples.

4. What was Jackson's point of view regarding the usefulness of the Second Bank of the United States?

5. Which text structure best explains how the author organized the previous passage?

____ description of important features

____ explanation of steps in a sequence

____ account of cause and effect

____ explanation of problem and solution

____ comparison/contrast of two or more things

Give a reason from the text for your answer. For example, if you choose description, tell what is being described. For sequence, list one or two steps explained in the text. For cause and effect, state a cause or an effect mentioned in the text. For problem/solution, tell what the problem is or describe the solution. For comparison, tell what is being compared or contrasted.

The Whig Party Forms   The Bank's supporters denounced Jackson as a power-hungry tyrant trampling on the rights of Congress. Jackson's veto shocked them because previous Presidents had so rarely used that power—only nine times in forty-two years.

In 1832, the Bank's friends formed a new political party known as the Whigs. (The name came from a British political party.) The Whigs were led by Henry Clay and Daniel Webster, two important political figures. Henry Clay served almost 40 years in the House or the Senate. Devoted to the Union, he crafted three major compromises to settle political crises that threatened to divide the nation: The Missouri Compromise, the compromise tariff in 1833 and the Compromise of 1850. In honor of these achievements, he was called "The Great Pacificator." Daniel Webster gained fame for his skill as an orator and lawyer when he argued and won several cases before the Supreme Court. Like Clay, he spent most of four decades in the U.S. House and Senate. There, he spoke forcefully in favor of preserving the union saying that he spoke, "not as a Massachusetts man, not as a Northern man, but as an American."

The Whigs were nationalists who wanted a strong federal government to manage the economy. Relying on a broad interpretation of the Constitution, they favored the American system of protective tariffs, internal improvements, and a national bank. Whigs also appealed to northern Protestants who wanted the government to promote moral reform.

The emergence of the Whigs renewed two-party politics in the United States.

For the next twenty years, Whigs challenged Jackson's Democrats in local, state, and national elections. These close contests drew growing numbers of voters to the polls.

6. The topic of the previous section is "the formation of the Whig party." What is the central idea?

7. Analyze how the policies of the Whig party and the policies of Jackson were different. Provide at least two examples.

In the presidential election of 1832, the Whigs nominated Henry Clay. Voters, however, reelected the popular Jackson in a landslide. Longtime Jackson supporter Martin Van Buren became the new Vice President. Emboldened by the public support, Jackson completed his attack on the second Bank of the United States by withdrawing federal funds and placing them in state banks. Though its charter still had several years to run, Jackson's action weakened it severely. As Secretary of the Treasury, Roger B. Taney managed Jackson's plan to undermine the Bank of the United States. When John Marshall died in 1835, Jackson rewarded Taney by appointing him Chief Justice of the United States.

Politics After Jackson

Jackson reveled in his victory, but the Bank's destruction weakened the economy. Relieved from federal regulation, state banks expanded, inflating prices with a flood of paper bank notes. The face value of bank notes exploded from $10 million in 1833 to $149 million in 1837. The inflation hurt the common people that Jackson had professed to help.

Van Buren's Presidency and the Panic of 1837   Economic trouble was still in the future when Jackson retired from politics in 1836. In that year's election, voters chose Martin Van Buren, Jackson's favorite, to become President.

Soon after Van Buren took office in 1837, the economy suffered a severe panic.

A key trigger was Jackson's decision, taken months earlier, to stop accepting paper money for the purchase of federal land. The effect was a sharp drop in land values and sales. As a result, hundreds of banks and businesses that had invested in land went bankrupt. Thousands of planters and farmers lost their land. One out of three urban workers lost his or her job. Those who kept their jobs saw their wages drop by 30 percent. The Panic of 1837 was the worst **depression** suffered by Americans to that date.

8. What is the meaning of *depression* in the context of the previous passage?

9. Analyze how two of Jackson's actions actually harmed what he described as "the humble members of society—the farmers, mechanics and laborers."

The Whigs Taste Brief Victory in the Election of 1840   The depression in 1837 revived the Whigs. In 1840, they ran William Henry Harrison for President and John Tyler for Vice President. Harrison was known as "Old Tip" for his successes at the Battle of Tippecanoe against the Indians in 1811. The Whigs ran a campaign that was light on ideas but heavy on the sort of theatrics that would become common in American politics. For example, the Whigs organized big parades and coined a catchy slogan—"Tippecanoe and Tyler too"—to garner voters' attention. With more creativity than honesty, Whig campaign managers portrayed Harrison as a simple farmer who lived in a log cabin and drank hard cider instead of the expensive champagne favored by Van Buren. Turning the political tables, the Whigs persuaded voters that Van Buren was ineffective, corrupt, and an aristocrat who threatened the Republic. This helped Harrison win the presidency, and meant that the Whigs had succeeded in capturing Congress.

10. What evidence in the text strongly supports that political campaigns are not always truthful?

The Whig victory proved brief, however. A month after assuming office, Harrison died of pneumonia. Vice President John Tyler of Virginia became the President. He surprised and horrified the Whigs by rejecting their policies. He vetoed Congress's legislation to restore the Bank of the United States. The Whigs would have to wait for a future election to exercise full control of the government.

Summarize what the text says about the conflict over the National Bank and how it was settled.

Optional Standard 8 Assessment

Henry Clay's Speech on Andrew Jackson's Veto of the Bank of the United States, 1832

In Andrew Jackson's second term of office, Congress voted to renew the charter of the Bank of the United States. While business leaders believed the Bank promoted economic growth, Jackson and his supporters regarded the Bank as a special interest of rich investors. Jackson vetoed the renewal.

A bill to re-charter the bank, has recently passed Congress, after much deliberation. In this body, we know that there are members enough who entertain no constitutional scruples, to make, with the vote by which the bill was passed, a majority of two thirds. In the House of Representatives, also, it is believed, there is a like majority in favor of the bill. Notwithstanding this state of things, the president has rejected the bill, and transmitted to the Senate an elaborate message, communicating at large his objections. The Constitution requires that we should reconsider the bill, and that the question of its passage, the president's objections notwithstanding, shall be taken by ayes and noes. Respect to him, as well as the injunctions of the Constitution, require that we should deliberately examine his reasons, and reconsider the question.

The veto is an extraordinary power, which, though tolerated by the Constitution, was not expected, by the convention, to be used in ordinary cases. It was designed for instances of precipitate legislation, in unguarded moments. Thus restricted, and it has been thus restricted by all former presidents, it might not be mischievous. During Mr. Madison's administration of eight years, there occurred but two or three cases of its exercise. During the last administration, I do not now recollect that it was once. In a period little upward of three years, the present chief magistrate has employed the veto four times. We now hear quite frequently, in the progress of measures through Congress, the statement that the president will veto them, urged as an objection to their passage. . . .

It can not be imagined that the Convention contemplated the application of the veto, to a question which has been so long, so often, and so thoroughly scrutinized, as that of the bank of the United States, by every departments of the government, in almost every stage of its existence, and by the people, and by the State legislatures. Of all the controverted questions which have sprung up under our government, not one has been so fully investigated as that of its power to establish a bank of the United States. . . .

No question has been more generally discussed, within the last two years, by the people at large, and in State Legislatures, than that of the bank. . . . And I believe it may be truly affirmed, that from the commencement of the government to this day, there has not been a Congress opposed to the bank of the United States, upon the distinct ground of a want of power to establish it. . . .

The power to establish a bank is deduced from that clause of the Constitution which confers on Congress all powers necessary and proper to carry into effect the enumerated powers. . . .

Mr. President, we are about to close one of the longest and most arduous sessions of Congress under the present Constitution; and when we return among our constituents, what account of the operations of their government shall we be bound to communicate? That the veto has been applied to the bank of the United States, our only reliance for a sound and uniform currency; that the Senate has been violently attacked for the exercise of a clear constitutional power; that the House of Representatives have been unnecessarily assailed; and that the president has promulgated a rule of action for those who have taken the oath to support the Constitution of the United States, that must, if there be practical conformity to it, introduce general nullification, and end in the absolute subversion of the government.

Read the excerpt from Henry Clay's speech on Andrew Jackson's veto of the bank of the United States. Explain four reasons or arguments that he presents why the Bank should not have been vetoed.

Select two arguments and, for each one, explain why you think it is or is not valid.

World History, Part I

The Rise of the Greek City-States

The earliest civilizations rose in fertile river valleys. However, ancient Greece was made up of valleys and islands. Read to learn about how geographic conditions influenced the rise of Greek city-states.

Geography Shapes Greece

Landscape Defines Political Boundaries   Greece is part of the Balkan peninsula, which extends southward into the eastern Mediterranean Sea. Mountains divide the peninsula into isolated valleys. Beyond the rugged coast, hundreds of rocky islands spread toward the horizon.

The Greeks who farmed the valleys or settled on the scattered islands did not create a large empire. Instead, they built many small city-states, cut off from one another by mountains or water. Each included a city and its surrounding countryside. Greeks fiercely defended the independence of their small city-states, and endless rivalry frequently led to war.

Life by the Sea   While mountains divided Greeks from one another, the seas provided a vital link to the world outside. With its hundreds of bays, the Greek coastline offered safe harbors for ships. The Greeks became skilled sailors and carried cargoes of goods throughout the eastern Mediterranean. Rapid population growth forced many Greeks to leave their own overcrowded valleys. With fertile land limited, the Greeks expanded overseas.

Governing the City-States

Types of Government Evolve   At first, the ruler of the city-state was a king. A government in which a hereditary ruler exercises central power is a monarchy. Slowly, however, power shifted to a class of noble landowners. Because only they could afford weapons and chariots, these nobles were also the military defenders of the city-states. In time, however, they won power for themselves. The result was an aristocracy, or rule by a hereditary landholding elite.

As trade expanded, a new middle class of wealthy merchants, farmers, and artisans emerged in some cities. They challenged the landowning nobles for power and came to dominate some city-states. The result was a form of government called an oligarchy. In an oligarchy, power is in the hands of a small, wealthy elite.

1. Which text structure best explains how the author organized the previous section?

    ____   description of important features

    ____   explanation of steps in a sequence

    ____   account of cause and effect

    ____   explanation of problem and solution

    ____   comparison/contrast of two or more things

    Give a reason from the text for your answer. For example, if you choose description, tell what is being described. For sequence, list one or two steps explained in the text. For cause and effect, state a cause or an effect mentioned in the text. For problem/solution, tell what the problem is or describe the solution. For comparison, tell what is being compared or contrasted.

The two most influential city-states, Athens and Sparta, developed very different ways of life. While Sparta stressed military virtues and stern discipline, Athens glorified the individual and extended political rights to more citizens.

Sparta: A Warrior Society

The Spartan government included two kings and a council of elders who advised the monarchs. An assembly made up of all citizens approved major decisions. Citizens were male, native-born Spartans over the age of 30.

Daily Life Ruled by Discipline   From childhood, a Spartan prepared to be part of a military state. Officials examined every newborn, and sickly children were abandoned to die. Spartans wanted future soldiers and the future mothers of soldiers to be healthy.

At the age of seven, boys began training for a lifetime in the military.

They moved into barracks, where they were toughened by a coarse diet, hard exercise, and rigid discipline. This strict and harsh discipline made Spartan youth excellent soldiers. To develop cunning and supplement their diet, boys were even encouraged to steal food. If caught, though, they were beaten severely.

At the age of 20, a man could marry, but he continued to live in the barracks for another 10 years and to eat there for another 40 years. At the age of 30, after further training, he took his place in the assembly.

Women of Sparta   Girls, too, had a rigorous upbringing. As part of a warrior society, they were expected to produce healthy sons for the army. They therefore were required to exercise and strengthen their bodies. Like other Greek women, Spartan women had to obey their fathers or husbands.

Sparta Stands Alone   The Spartans **isolated** themselves from other Greeks. They looked down on trade and wealth, forbade their own citizens to travel, and had little use for new ideas or the arts. While other Greeks admired the Spartans' military skills, no other city-state imitated their rigorous way of life. "Spartans are willing to die for their city," some suggested, "because they have no reason to live."

    2. What is the meaning of *isolated* in the context of the previous paragraph?

    3. Analyze how the military dominated Spartan society. Include at least two examples.

Athens Evolves Into a Democracy

As in many city-states, Athenian government **evolved** from a monarchy into an aristocracy. By 700 B.C., landowners held power. They chose the chief officials, judged major court cases, and dominated the assembly.

Demands for Change   Under the aristocracy, Athenian wealth and power grew. Yet discontent spread among ordinary people. Merchants and soldiers resented the power of the nobles. Foreign artisans, who produced many of the goods that Athens traded abroad, were resentful that foreigners were barred from becoming citizens. Farmers, too, demanded change. During hard times, many farmers were forced to sell their land to nobles. A growing number even sold themselves and their families into slavery to pay their debts. As discontent spread, Athens moved slowly toward democracy, or government by the people.

    4. What is the meaning of *evolved* in the context of the previous paragraph?

Solon Reforms Government   Solon was appointed chief official, in 594 B.C. Athenians gave him a free hand to make needed reforms. He outlawed debt slavery and freed those who had already been sold into slavery for debt. He opened high offices to more citizens, granted citizenship to some foreigners, and gave the Athenian assembly more say in important decisions.

Solon introduced economic reforms as well. He encouraged the export of wine and olive oil. This policy helped merchants and farmers by increasing demand for their products.

Despite Solon's reforms, citizenship remained limited, and many positions were open only to the wealthy. Continued and widespread unrest led to the rise of tyrants, or people who gained power by force. Tyrants often won support from the merchant class and the poor by imposing reforms to help these groups. Although Greek tyrants often governed well, the word *tyrant* has come to mean a vicious and brutal ruler.

  5. The topic of the above three paragraphs is "Solon Reforms Government." What is the central idea?

  6. What evidence in the text strongly supports that Solon's reforms did not go far enough?

Citizens Share Power and Wealth   The Athenian tyrant Pisistratus helped farmers by giving them loans and land taken from nobles. New building projects gave jobs to the poor. By giving poor citizens a greater voice, he further weakened the aristocracy.

Another reformer, Cleisthenes, broadened the role of ordinary citizens in government. He set up the Council of 500, whose members were chosen by lot from among all citizens over the age of 30. The council prepared laws considered by the assembly and supervised the day-to-day work of government. Cleisthenes made the assembly a genuine legislature, or lawmaking body, that debated laws before deciding to approve or reject them. All male citizens were members of the assembly and were expected to participate.

  7. What was Cleisthenes's point of view regarding the Athenian assembly?

  8. Analyze how Greek leaders fostered the development of Athenian democracy. Include at least two examples.

A Limited Democracy   By modern standards, Athenian democracy was quite limited. Only citizens could participate in government, and citizenship was restricted to landowning men. Women were excluded along with merchants and people whose parents were not citizens. So were the tens of thousands of Athenian slaves. Still, Athens gave more people a say in decision making than any other ancient civilization.

Women in Athens   Women in Athens had no share in political life and Greeks accepted the view that women must be guided by men. Women managed the household, lived a secluded existence and were rarely seen in public. Women played their most significant public role in religion. Their participation in sacred processions and ceremonies was considered essential for the city's well-being.

  9. The topic of the previous section is "Athenian women." What is the central idea?

Educating the Youth   Unlike girls, who received little or no formal education, boys attended school if their families could afford it. Besides learning to read and write, they studied music, memorized poetry, and studied public speaking because, as citizens in a democracy, they would have to voice their views. Although they received military training and participated in athletic contests, unlike Sparta, which put military training above all else, Athens encouraged young men to explore many areas of knowledge.

  10. What evidence in the text indicates that Athenian boys and girls were treated differently? Give two examples.

Summarize what the text says about differences between the city-states of Athens and Sparta.

Optional Standard 8 Assessment

Xenophon: "On the Policy of the Athenians"

Ancient Athens gradually evolved into a democracy helped by the actions of individuals like Solon, Pisistratus, and Cleisthenes. However, not everyone agreed with this form of government.

As for the constitution of the Athenians, their choice of this type of constitution I do not approve, for in choosing thus they choose that thieves should fare better than the elite. . . . everywhere they give the advantage to thieves, the poor, and the radical elements rather than to the elite. This is just where they will be seen to be preserving democracy. For if the poor and the common people and the worse elements are treated well, the growth of these classes will exalt the democracy; whereas if the rich and the elite are treated well the democrats strengthen their own opponents. . . . Among the elite there is very little license and injustice, very great discrimination as to what is worthy, while among the poor there is very great ignorance, disorderliness, and thievery; for poverty tends to lead them to what is disgraceful as does lack of education and the ignorance which befall some men as a result of poverty. . . .

It may be said that they ought not to have allowed everyone in turn to make speeches or sit on the Council, but only those of the highest capability and quality. As it is, anyone who wants, a thief maybe, gets up and makes a speech, and devises what is to the advantage of himself and those like him. . . . For it is the wish of the poor not that the state should be well-ordered and the poor themselves in complete subjection, but that the poor should have their freedom and be in control; disorderliness is of little consequence to it. . . .

But whenever the poor of Athens make an agreement they can lay the blame on the individual speaker or the proposer, and say to the other party that it was not present and does not approve what they know was agreed upon in full assembly; and should it be decided that this is not so, the poor have discovered a hundred excuses for not doing what they do not wish to do. If anything bad result from a decision of the Assembly, they lay the blame on a minority for opposing and working its ruin, whereas if any good comes about they take the credit to themselves. They do not allow caricature and abuse of the commons, lest they should hear themselves the butt of endless jokes, but they do allow you to caricature any person you wish to. They well know that generally the man who is caricatured is not of the poor or of the crowd, but someone rich or well-born or influential, and that few of the poor and democrats are caricatured, and they only because they are busy-bodies and try to overreach the commons; so they are not angry when such men are caricatured either.

I say, then, that the poor at Athens realize which citizens are good and which are thieves. With this knowledge, they favor those who are friendly and useful to them, even if they are thieves, whereas they hate rather the elite. This type of constitution of the Athenians I do not approve, but as they saw fit to be a democracy, in my opinion they preserve their democracy well by employing the means I have pointed out.

Read Xenophon's reasons why he does not approve of Athens democracy.

Explain four reasons or arguments that he presents in support of his opinions.

Select two reasons or arguments and, for each one, explain why it is or is not valid.

Conflict in the Greek World

Read to learn how war and conflict affected the Greek city-states.

The Persian Wars

The Persians conquered a huge empire stretching from Asia Minor to the border of India. Their subjects included the Greek city-states of Ionia in Asia Minor. Although under Persian rule, these Ionian city-states were largely self-governing. Still, they resented their situation.

In 499 B.C., Ionian Greeks rebelled against Persian rule. Athens sent ships to help them. As the historian Herodotus wrote some years later, "These ships were the beginning of mischief both to the Greeks and to the barbarians."

Athenians Win at Marathon   The Persians soon crushed the rebel cities. However, Darius I was furious at the role Athens played in the uprising. In time, Darius sent a huge force across the Aegean to punish Athens for its interference. The mighty Persian army landed near Marathon, a plain north of Athens, in 490 B.C. The Athenians asked for help from neighboring Greek city-states but received little support.

The Persians greatly outnumbered Athenian forces. Yet the invaders were amazed to see "a mere handful of men coming on at a run without either horsemen or archers." The Persians responded with a rain of arrows, but the Greeks rushed onward. They broke through the Persian line and engaged in fierce hand-to-hand combat. Overwhelmed by the fury of the assault, the Persians hastily retreated to their ships.

The Athenians celebrated their triumph. Still, the Athenian leader, Themistocles, knew the victory at Marathon had bought only a temporary lull in the fighting. He urged Athenians to build a fleet of warships and prepare other defenses.

Greek City-States Unite   Darius died before he could mass his troops for another attack. But in 480 B.C., his son Xerxes sent a much larger force to conquer Greece. By this time, Athens had persuaded Sparta and other city-states to join in the fight against Persia.

Once again, the Persians landed in northern Greece. A small Spartan force guarded the narrow mountain pass at Thermopylae. Led by the great warrior-king Leonidas, the Spartans held out heroically against the enormous Persian force, but were defeated in the end. The Persians marched south and burned Athens. The city was empty, however. The Athenians had already withdrawn to safety.

The Greeks now put their faith in the fleet of ships that Themistocles had urged them to build. The Athenians lured the Persian navy into the narrow strait of Salamis. Then, Athenian warships, powered by rowers, drove into the Persian boats with underwater battering rams. On the shore, Xerxes watched helplessly as his mighty fleet sank.

The next year, the Greeks defeated the Persians on land in Asia Minor. This victory marked the end of the Persian invasions. In a brief moment of unity, the Greek city-states had saved themselves from the Persian threat.

1. The topic of the previous section is "the Greek city-states unite." What is the central idea?

2. What evidence in the text indicates that the Spartan defeat at Thermopylae actually benefited the Athenians?

Athens Leads the Delian League   Victory in the Persian Wars increased the Greeks' sense of their own uniqueness. The gods, they felt, had protected their superior form of government—the city-state—against invaders from Asia.

Athens emerged from the war as the most powerful city-state in Greece. To continue to defend against Persia, it organized with other Greek city-states an alliance, or a formal agreement between two or more nations or powers, to cooperate and come to one another's defense. Modern scholars call this alliance the Delian League after Delos, the location where the league held meetings.

From the start, Athens **dominated** the Delian League. It slowly used its position of leadership to create an Athenian empire. It moved the league treasury from the island of Delos to Athens, using money contributed by other city-states to rebuild its own city. When its allies protested and tried to withdraw from the league, Athens used force to make them remain. Yet, while Athens was enforcing its will abroad, Athenian leaders were championing political freedom at home.

3. What is the meaning of *dominated* in the context of the previous passage?

4. What was Athens's point of view regarding their form of government?

5. Analyze how Athens violated the concept of an alliance as a member of the Delian League. Offer at least two examples.

The Age of Pericles and Direct Democracy

The years after the Persian Wars from 460 B.C. to 429 B.C. were a golden age for Athens under the able statesman Pericles. Because of his wise and skillful leadership, the economy thrived and the government became more democratic.

Athenian Democracy   Periclean Athens was a direct democracy. Under this system, citizens take part directly in the day-to-day affairs of government. By contrast, in most democratic countries today, citizens participate in government indirectly through elected representatives.

By the time of Pericles, the Athenian assembly met several times a month. A Council of 500, selected by lot, conducted daily government business. Pericles believed that all citizens, regardless of wealth or social class, should take part in government. Athens therefore began to pay a stipend, or fixed salary, to men who participated in the Assembly and its governing Council. This reform enabled poor men to serve in government.

In addition, Athenians also served on juries. A jury is a panel of citizens who have the authority to make the final judgment in a trial. Unlike a modern American trial jury, which is usually made up of 12 members, an Athenian jury might include hundreds or even thousands of jurors. Citizens over 30 years of age were chosen by lot to serve on the jury for a year.

Athenian citizens could also vote to banish, or send away, a public figure whom they saw as a threat to their democracy. This process was called ostracism. The person with the largest number of votes cast against him was ostracized, meaning that that individual would have to live outside the city, usually for a period of 10 years.

6. The topic of the previous section is "The Athenian Democracy." What is the central idea?

7. Analyze why Athenian or direct democracy may not have been an efficient form of government. Give two reasons.

8. Which text structure best explains how the author organized the previous passage?

_____   description of important features

_____   explanation of steps in a sequence

_____   account of cause and effect

_____   explanation of problem and solution

_____   comparison/contrast of two or more things

Give a reason from the text for your answer. For example, if you choose description, tell what is being described. For sequence, list one or two steps explained in the text. For cause and effect, state a cause or an effect mentioned in the text. For problem/solution, tell what the problem is or describe the solution. For comparison, tell what is being compared or contrasted.

Culture Thrives in Athens   Athens prospered during the Age of Pericles. With the empire's riches, Pericles directed the rebuilding of the Acropolis which the Persians had destroyed. With the help of an educated foreign-born woman named Aspasia, Pericles turned Athens into the **cultural** center of Greece. They encouraged the arts through public festivals, dramatic competitions, and building programs. Such building projects increased Athenians' prosperity by creating jobs for artisans and workers.

    9. What is the meaning of *cultural* in the context of the previous paragraph?

The Peloponnesian War

Many Greeks outside Athens resented Athenian domination. Before long, the Greek world was split into rival camps. To counter the Delian League, Sparta and other enemies of Athens formed the Peloponnesian League. In 431 B.C., warfare broke out between Athens and Sparta. This conflict, which became known as the Peloponnesian War, soon engulfed all of Greece. The fighting would last for 27 years.

Sparta Defeats Athens   Despite its riches and powerful navy, Athens faced a serious geographic disadvantage. Because Sparta was inland, Athens could not use its navy to attack. Sparta's powerful army, however, had only to march north to attack Athens. When the Spartan troops came near, Pericles allowed people from the countryside to move inside the city walls. The overcrowded conditions led to a terrible plague that killed many Athenians, including Pericles himself.

    As the war dragged on, each side committed savage acts against the other. Sparta even allied itself with Persia, the longtime enemy of the Greeks. Finally, in 404 B.C., with the help of the Persian navy, the Spartans captured Athens. The victors stripped the Athenians of their fleet and empire. However, Sparta rejected calls from its allies to destroy Athens.

Greek Dominion Declines   The Peloponnesian War ended Athenian domination of the Greek world. The Athenian economy eventually revived and Athens remained the cultural center of Greece. However, its spirit and vitality declined. Meanwhile, as Greeks battled among themselves, a new power rose in Macedonia, a kingdom to the north of Greece. By 359 B.C., its ambitious ruler stood poised to conquer the quarrelsome Greek city-states.

    10. What evidence in the text indicates that Sparta's attitude toward Athens was somewhat contradictory? Give an example of one negative action and one positive action.

    Summarize what the text says about why the union of city-states broke apart.

Optional Standard 8 Assessment

Thucydides: "History of the Peloponnesian War"

After the Persian Wars, many Greek city-states resented the domination of Athens. They met to consider if they should declare war on Athens. The following is taken from a speech by the Corinthians urging the other city-states to declare war.

For ourselves, all who have already had dealings with the Athenians require no warning to be on their guard against them. The states more inland and out of the highway of communication should understand that, if they omit to support the coast powers, the result will be to injure the transit of their produce for exportation and the reception in exchange of their imports from the sea; and they must not be careless judges of what is now said, as if it had nothing to do with them, but must expect that the sacrifice of the powers on the coast will one day be followed by the extension of the danger to the interior, and must recognize that their own interests are deeply involved in this discussion. For these reasons they should not hesitate to exchange peace for war.

. . . if we are now kindling war it is under the pressure of injury, with adequate grounds of complaint; and after we have chastised the Athenians we will in season desist. We have many reasons to expect success—first, superiority in numbers and in military experience, and secondly our general and unvarying obedience in the execution of orders. The naval strength which they possess shall be raised by us from our respective antecedent resources, and from the moneys at Olympia and Delphi. A loan from these enables us to seduce their foreign sailors by the offer of higher pay. For the power of Athens is more mercenary than national; while ours will not be exposed to the same risk, as its strength lies more in men than in money. . . . we need scarcely ask whether we shall be their superiors in courage. The money required . . . shall be provided by our contributions: nothing indeed could be more monstrous than the suggestion that . . . we should refuse to spend for vengeance and self-preservation the treasure which by such refusal we shall forfeit to Athenian rapacity and see employed for our own ruin.

We have also other ways of carrying on the war, such as revolt of their allies, the surest method of depriving them of their revenues, which are the source of their strength, and establishment of fortified positions in their country. . . . Let us also reflect that if it was merely a number of disputes of territory between rival neighbors, it might be borne; but here we have an enemy in Athens that is a match for our whole coalition, and more than a match for any of its members; so that unless as a body and as individual nationalities and individual cities we make an unanimous stand against her, she will easily conquer us divided and in detail. That conquest, terrible as it may sound, would, it must be known, have no other end than slavery pure and simple . . . . freedom which our fathers gave to Hellas.

. . . we must boldly advance to the war for many reasons; the god has commanded it and promised to be with us, and the rest of Hellas will all join in the struggle, part from fear, part from interest. . . .

Delay not, fellow allies, but, convinced of the necessity of the crisis and the wisdom of this counsel, vote for the war, undeterred by its immediate terrors, but looking beyond to the lasting peace by which it will be succeeded.

Read Corinth's reasons why they believe war should be declared against Athens. Explain four arguments that they present in support of their opinions.

Select two arguments and, for each one, explain why it is or is not valid.

World History, Part III

The Glory That Was Greece

Read to learn about the achievements of ancient Greek thinkers, artists, and writers.

To later admirers, Greek achievements in the arts represented the height of human development in the Western world. They looked back with deep respect on what one poet called "the glory that was Greece."

Philosophers: Lovers of Wisdom

Some Greek thinkers challenged the belief that events were caused by the whims of gods. Instead, they used observation and reason to find causes for events. The Greeks called these thinkers philosophers, meaning "lovers of wisdom."

Greek philosophers explored many subjects, from mathematics and music to logic, or rational thinking. Through reason and observation, they believed, they could discover laws that governed the universe.

Socrates Questions Tradition   Socrates was an Athenian stonemason and philosopher. Most of what we know about Socrates comes from his student Plato. Socrates himself wrote no books. Instead, he passed his days in the town square asking people about their beliefs. He said, "The unexamined life is not worth living." Using a process we now call the Socratic method, he would pose a series of questions to a student or passing citizen, and challenge them to examine the implications of their answers. To Socrates, this patient examination was a way to help others seek truth and self-knowledge. To many Athenians, however, such questioning was a threat to accepted values and traditions.

When he was about 70 years old, Socrates was put on trial. His enemies accused him of corrupting the city's youth and failing to respect the gods. Standing before a jury of 501 citizens, Socrates offered a calm and reasoned defense. But the jurors condemned him to death. Loyal to the laws of Athens, Socrates accepted the death penalty. He drank a cup of hemlock, a deadly poison.

1. The topic of the previous section is "Socrates questions traditions." What is the central idea?

2. What evidence in the text indicates that many Athenians were very certain about their beliefs?

Plato Envisions A Perfect Society   The execution of Socrates left Plato with a lifelong distrust of democracy. Like Socrates, Plato emphasized the importance of reason.

In his book *The Republic,* Plato described his vision of an ideal state. He rejected Athenian democracy because it had condemned Socrates. Instead, Plato argued that the state should regulate every aspect of its citizens' lives in order to provide for their best interests. He divided his ideal society into three classes: workers to produce the necessities of life, soldiers to defend the state, and philosophers to rule. This elite class of leaders would be specially trained to ensure order and justice. The wisest of them, a philosopher-king, would have the ultimate authority.

Aristotle Pursues the Golden Mean   Plato's most famous student, Aristotle, developed his own ideas about government. He analyzed all forms of government, from monarchy to democracy, and found good and bad examples of each. Like Plato, he was suspicious of democracy, which he thought could lead to mob rule. In the end, he favored rule by a single strong and virtuous leader.

Aristotle also addressed the question of how people ought to live. In his view, good conduct meant **pursuing** the "golden mean," a moderate course between the extremes. He promoted reason as the guiding force for learning. He left writings on politics, ethics, logic, biology, literature and many other subjects. When the first European universities evolved some 1,500 years later, their courses were based largely on the works and ideas of Aristotle.

3. What is the meaning of *pursuing* in the context of the previous paragraph?

4. What point of view regarding democracy was shared by both Plato and Aristotle?

5. Analyze how Plato's and Aristotle's views of government were alike and different.

Idealism in Architecture and Art

The work of Greek artists and architects reflected a similar concern with balance, order, and beauty.

Monumental Architecture   Greek architects sought to convey a sense of perfect balance to reflect the harmony and order of the universe. The most famous example of Greek architecture is the Parthenon, a temple dedicated to the goddess Athena.

Greek architecture has been widely admired for centuries. Today, many public buildings throughout the world have incorporated Greek architectural elements, such as columns, in their designs.

Artists Craft Lifelike Human Forms   Early Greek sculptors carved figures in rigid poses. By 450 B.C., Greek sculptors had developed a new style that emphasized more natural forms. While their work was lifelike, it was also idealistic. That is, sculptors carved gods, goddesses, athletes, and famous men in a way that showed human beings in their most perfect, graceful form. The only Greek paintings to survive are on pottery. They offer intriguing views of every day Greek life.

Greek Literature

Tragic Drama   Perhaps the most important Greek contribution to literature was in the field of drama. Plays were performed in large outdoor theaters with little or no scenery. Actors wore elaborate costumes and stylized masks. A chorus sang or chanted comments on the action taking place on stage. Greek dramas were often based on popular myths and legends. Through these familiar stories, playwrights discussed moral and social issues or explored the relationship between people and the gods.

The greatest Athenian playwrights were Aeschylus, Sophocles and Euripides. All three wrote tragedies, plays that told stories of human suffering that usually ended in disaster. The purpose of tragedy, the Greeks felt, was to stir up and then relieve the emotions of pity and fear. For example, in his play *Oresteia,* Aeschylus showed a powerful family torn apart by betrayal, murder and revenge. Audiences saw how even the powerful could be subject to horrifying misfortune and how the wrath of the gods could bring down even the greatest heroes.

In *Antigone,* Sophocles explored what happens when an individual's moral duty conflicts with the laws of the state. Antigone is a young woman whose brother has been killed leading a rebellion. King Creon forbids anyone to bury the traitor's body. When Antigone buries her brother anyway, she is sentenced to death. She defiantly tells Creon that duty to the gods is greater than human law: "For me, it was not Zeus who made that order. . . . Nor did I think your orders were so strong that you, a mortal man, could overrun the gods' unwritten and unfailing laws." Euripides's plays suggested that people, not the gods, were the cause of human misfortune and suffering. In *The Trojan Women,* he stripped war of its glamour by showing the suffering of women who were victims of war.

6. The topic of the previous section is "Tragic Drama." What is the central idea?

7. Analyze how Greek playwrights differed in their view of the gods. Give two examples.

8. Which text structure best explains how the author organized the previous passage?

 ____   description of important features

 ____   explanation of steps in a sequence

 ____   account of cause and effect

_____ explanation of problem and solution

_____ comparison/contrast of two or more things

Give a reason from the text for your answer. For example, if you choose description, tell what is being described. For sequence, list one or two steps explained in the text. For cause and effect, state a cause or an effect mentioned in the text. For problem/solution, tell what the problem is or describe the solution. For comparison, tell what is being compared or contrasted.

Greek Comedy   Almost all the surviving Greek comedies were written by Aristophanes. Unlike tragedy which focused on events of the past, comedies ridiculed individuals of the day, including political figures, philosophers, and prominent members of society. Through ridicule, comic playwrights sharply criticized society, much as political cartoonists do today.

Recording Events as History

The Greeks also applied observation, reason, and logic to the study of history. Herodotus is often called the "Father of History" in the Western World because he went beyond listing names of rulers or the retelling of ancient legends. Before writing *The Persian Wars,* Herodotus visited many lands, collecting information from people who remembered the actual events he chronicled. In fact, Herodotus used the Greek term *historie,* which means inquiry, to define his work. Our *history* comes from this word.

Herodotus cast a critical eye on his sources, noting **bias** and conflicting accounts. However, despite this special care for detail and accuracy, his writings reflected his own view that the war was a clear moral victory of Greek love of freedom over Persian tyranny. He even invented conversations and speeches for historical figures.

Another historian Thucydides, who was a few years younger than Herodotus, wrote about the Peloponnesian War. He had lived through the war and vividly described the war's savagery and corrupting influence on all those involved. Although he was an Athenian, he tried to be fair to both sides.

Both writers set standards for future historians. Herodotus stressed the importance of research. Thucydides showed the need to avoid bias.

9. What is the meaning of *bias* in the context of the previous passage?

10. What evidence in the text suggests that Thucydides may have been a better historian than Herodotus? Give two reasons.

Summarize what the text says about the role of tragic drama in the lives of the Greeks.

SOCIAL STUDIES

Optional Standard 8 Assessment

Plato's Account of Socrates' Defense

Socrates was accused of corrupting the youth of Athens and failing to respect the gods. At his trial he defended himself against the charges brought against him.

I would have you know that, if you kill such a one as I am, you will injure yourselves more than you will injure me. . . . And now, Athenians, I am not going to argue for my own sake, as you may think, but for yours, that you may not sin against the God, or lightly reject his boon by condemning me. For if you kill me you will not easily find another like me, who, if I may use such a ludicrous figure of speech, am a sort of gadfly, given to the state by the God . . . always fastening upon you, arousing and persuading and reproaching you. . . .

. . . if anyone likes to come and hear me while I am pursuing my mission, whether he be young or old, he may freely come . . . anyone, whether he be rich or poor, may ask and answer me and listen to my words. . . . And if anyone says that he has ever learned or heard anything from me in private which all the world has not heard, I should like you to know that he is speaking an untruth.

And this is a duty which the God has imposed upon me, as I am assured by oracles, visions, and in every sort of way in which the will of divine power was ever signified to anyone. . . . For if I am really corrupting the youth, and have corrupted some of them already, those of them who have grown up and have become sensible that I gave them bad advice in the days of their youth should come forward as accusers and take their revenge; and if they do not like to come themselves, some of their relatives, fathers, brothers, or other kinsmen, should say what evil their families suffered at my hands. . . . Why should they too support me with their testimony? Why, indeed, except for the sake of truth and justice, and because they know that I am speaking the truth. . . .

. . . I did not go where I could do no good to you or to myself; but where I could do the greatest good privately to everyone of you, thither I went, and sought to persuade every man among you that he must look to himself, and seek virtue and wisdom before he looks to his private interests, and look to the state before he looks to the interests of the state; and that this should be the order which he observes in all his actions. . . .

Someone will say: Yes, Socrates, but cannot you hold your tongue . . . ? Now I have great difficulty in making you understand my answer to this. For if I tell you that this would be a disobedience to a divine command, and therefore that I cannot hold my tongue, you will not believe that I am serious; and if I say again that the greatest good of man is daily to converse about virtue, and all that concerning which you hear me examining myself and others, and that the life which is unexamined is not worth living—that you are still less likely to believe. . . .

The hour of departure has arrived, and we go our ways—I to die, and you to live. Which is better God only knows.

Read the excerpt from Socrates's defense against the charges of corrupting the youth of Athens. Explain four reasons or arguments that Socrates presents in support of his innocence.

Select two arguments and, for each one, explain why it is or is not valid.

Science, Part I

Earth's Landforms: How Does Earth's Surface Change?

The Earth's surface is made up of many different features called landforms. Read to find out how the Earth's surface changes every day.

Earth's Features

Water is responsible for major changes on the Earth's surface. Over many years water continued to flow over flat land and the water dug deeper and deeper into Earth's surface to form the deep canyons we see today in several areas of our country. Even frozen waters can carve into Earth's surface. Many North American lakes, including the Great Lakes between the United States and Canada, were carved out by glaciers on the move. Glaciers are huge masses of slow moving ice. As glaciers moved, they carried along huge amounts of rock and soil that dug out the lakes' bottoms.

1. Explain how water has changed the surface of the Earth. Give two examples.

Other landforms on Earth have also been shaped by both gradual and dramatic events. Rivers shift as they carry and deposit sediments, solid particles that are moved from one place to another. Although they are flat, plateaus share with mountains their high elevation compared to the land around them. Plains are also flat but are not higher than the surrounding **areas** and they support grasslands. The Great Plains of North America is actually a huge, high plateau.

2. What is the meaning of *areas* in the context of the above paragraph?

3. Which text structure best explains how the author organized the above passage?

   ____   explanation of steps in a sequence

   ____   account of cause and effect

   ____   comparison/contrast of two or more things

   Give a reason from the text for your answer. For example, if you choose sequence, list one or two steps. If you choose cause and effect, give a cause and/or effect mentioned in the text. For comparison, tell what is being compared or contrasted.

Weathering and Erosion

Many changes on Earth's surface can only be seen over thousands of years or more. These changes are often caused by the weathering and erosion of Earth's surface. Weathering is the process of breaking down rock into smaller pieces. Some weathering takes place when forces such as water and ice break down rock. This process is called mechanical weathering. During mechanical weathering the minerals that make up the rock do not change.

Most rocks have small cracks in their surfaces. These cracks may be smaller than the width of a hair, but it is in these cracks that mechanical weathering begins. Water can seep into these cracks and freeze. The freezing water expands and pushes against the sides of the crack making it larger. When the ice melts, water moves back into the cracks again. The rock freezes and thaws over and over again, making the cracks larger each time.

Sometimes soil forms in the cracks of the rock. Plants begin to grow and their roots push the crack open even further. Some types of plants can produce chemicals that eat into rocks to cause cracks and holes.

During chemical weathering, the actual minerals that make up rock change. The change can be caused when the minerals react with other substances in the environment, such as water or oxygen, to change the mineral content of rocks.

4. Explain how freezing makes cracks in rocks get larger.

5. What evidence in the text indicates how mechanical and chemical weathering are different?

What happens to the pieces of rock when weathering breaks them apart? Erosion is the process by which soil and sediments are **transferred** from one location to another—usually by wind, water, ice, and gravity. Erosion can carry eroded materials for hundreds of kilometers. Weathering and erosion continuously change Earth's surface. Over time, these processes can flatten mountains or dig deep canyons in layers of rock.

6. The topic of the above paragraph is "erosion." What is the central idea?

7. What is the meaning of *transferred* in the context of the above paragraph?

8. What evidence in the text indicates that erosion is a very powerful process?

Soil Erosion

Erosion can have more immediate effects too. When areas of soil are not covered by plants, the soil can be eroded easily. The roots of plants help prevent soil erosion. That's one reason farmers plant cover crops. Cover crops are planted between harvests to reduce erosion. They also add nutrients to the soil.

When soil erodes, a chain of destructive events might occur. One example is what happened in the southern plains of the United States in the 1930s. Years of drought and poor farming practices left many areas of soil bare. The area became known as the Dust Bowl because of the severe dust storms that blew for eight years. The blown dust was so heavy that children wore dust masks to school. In some places the dust was so thick that people couldn't see even during the day. Dust piled up like snow drifts.

9. The topic of the above paragraph is "soil erosion." What is the central idea?

The drought affected not only the land. People had health problems. Some died. Dust damaged cars and farm equipment. Farmers lost their land. Millions of people were left without jobs. Along with the bad came the good. Farmers learned better farming methods and an era of soil conservation began. People learned to take care of the land.

10. Explain why the Dust Bowl occurred.

Summarize what the text says about weathering and how it changes Earth's surface.

Science, Part II

Earth's Landforms: How Does Water Affect Earth's Features?

Through erosion, water changes the shape and design of Earth's surface. Read to find out how this occurs.

Deposition

Did you ever get hit by a huge splash of water? If you did, you know that water can hit with quite a force. All moving water has energy, and water running downhill is the main process that shapes Earth's surface. As it flows downhill in complicated, ever-changing systems of streams and rivers, water carries and deposits many tiny pieces of rock and soil. During mechanical weathering, the high energy of running water can break down rock and soil into bits of sediments. Water can also chemically weather rock when it dissolves minerals and other materials in the rock. This process changes the mineral make-up of the rock.

The sediments that form during weathering are eroded and deposited at another location. This process of adding sediments to a new place after being carried from another is called deposition. In the process of deposition, the shape and direction of a river's flow changes.

1. Explain how water shapes Earth's surface.

Minerals in Lakes, Oceans and Caverns

As rivers flow to the ocean, they carry along sediments and dissolved minerals. Ocean plants and animals use some of these dissolved minerals to carry on life processes. Other dissolved minerals settle out of the water and form mineral deposits in lakes, along the coast, and on the ocean floor. As water flows into rock beneath the earth's surface, dissolved minerals build up in caverns and form stalagmites and stalactites.

One mineral carried by water is salt. Rivers carry an estimated four billion tons of dissolved salts to the oceans each year. As ocean water evaporates, it leaves behind dissolved salts and other minerals. As a result of this process over thousands of years, the amount of salt in the ocean has increased.

2. Which text structure best explains how the author organized the above passage?

    ____ description of important points

    ____ account of cause and effect

    ____ comparison/contrast of two or more things

    Give a reason from the text for your answer. For example, if you choose description, tell what is being described. For cause and effect, give a cause or an effect mentioned in the text. For comparison, tell what is being compared or contrasted.

3. Explain how the oceans become salty. Give two reasons.

You might picture a river as a flat, quiet body of water, but it can change quite a lot over time. Rivers and streams are **dynamic** systems; they are always changing. A stream begins on land that is higher than sea level. Its water flows because gravity pulls the water downward to a lower area. As a stream flows, other streams may join it, until a river forms. The flowing river water wears down soil and rock and carries sediment away.

4. What is the meaning of *dynamic* in the context of the above paragraph?

The sediments a river carries can be deposited in varying places. That's because as water slows down, it has less energy and can carry less sediment. Heavier sediments are deposited first. Finer, lighter ones can be carried for hundreds of kilometers. Bends in rivers can become more dramatic as sediments are deposited. Sometimes deposition can cut the bends off from the rest of the river, forming lakes. Waters often slow down at the low areas at the mouth of the river. There fine sediments are deposited in areas called river deltas. Often these deposits of sediment are fan-shaped. Fan-shaped deposits can be especially obvious where mountains drop rapidly to the water below that receives the river's sediment.

5. The topic of the above paragraph is "river sediments." What is the central idea?

6. What evidence in the text indicates how energy in moving water controls where different kinds of sediments are deposited?

7. Explain how sediments in rivers can change the land.

The Mississippi River is one of the largest river systems in the world. It begins as a stream flowing out of Lake Itasca, Minnesota. Water from 31 states drains into the Mississippi before it reaches the Gulf of Mexico. The land that is drained by a river is called its drainage basin. The river provides habitats for 241 fish **species**, 38 species of mussels, 45 amphibian species and 50 species of mammals. It also serves 40 percent of the nation's migratory birds.

8. The topic of the above paragraph is the "Mississippi River." What is the central idea?

9. What is the meaning of *species* in the context of the above paragraph?

Floodplains

When rivers and streams flood their banks, their water often slows down and sediments are deposited. Flooding can move huge amounts of sediments to places that would otherwise never receive them. A floodplain is that part of the landscape that is likely to receive the overflow water and sediment from a flooded river.

In some places farmers depend on flooding. That's because the sediments distributed in the soil are important nutrients for growing crops. Often, however, floods are very destructive. Those living in the floodplains can lose homes, villages, or even their lives.

10. What evidence in the text indicates that living on a floodplain can be a good thing?

Summarize what the text says about minerals in water.

Science, Part III

Earth's Landforms: How Do Waves Affect Coastal Landforms?

Because of waves and wind, coastal landforms are always changing.
Read to find out how this process occurs.

Wave Energy

Ocean waves carry and pass along a great deal of energy. If you've ever watched ocean waves, you probably thought that the water moves forward with the waves. But only energy moves. The water stays in the same spot, rising and falling in a circular motion. As a wave approaches, the water moves slightly forward and then downward and back in a circular loop. Each time a wave passes, the water ends up just about where it started.

As waves move near shore, the shallower ocean bottom interferes with the waves' movements. The ocean floor can cause the bottom of waves to slow down. The tops of the waves continue to move quickly, so the tops tumble forward. Eventually the waves tumble toward shore to form a breaker.

1. What evidence in the text indicates that water in waves does not move forward?

2. Which text structure best explains how the author organized the above passage?

  ____ description of important points

  ____ account of cause and effect

  ____ explanation of steps in a sequence

  Give a reason from the text for your answer. For example, if you choose description, tell what is being described. For sequence, explain two steps explained in the text. If you choose comparison, tell what is being compared or contrasted.

Causes of Waves

The familiar waves we spot at the beach are often caused by wind. These waves form in the open ocean. As winds touch ocean water, energy transfers from the wind to the water, creating waves. The size of waves depends on the speed of the wind, how long it blows, and on how much of the sea it blows over.

Waves are also formed through tectonic action. Volcanic eruptions, earthquakes, and landslides take place under water or along coasts. These events can form tsunamis, waves that travel at incredible speeds and reach great heights before they crash into the shore.

Tsunamis can cause enormous damage and loss of life. On March 11, 2011, a powerful earthquake erupted 45 miles off of the coast of the Oshika Peninsula which is on the Northeast coast of the major island of Japan. The earthquake caused a tsunami and the waves that hit the shore were estimated to be 133 feet high. The earthquake shifted the Oshika Peninsula by 17 feet towards the center of the earthquake and lowered it by 4 feet.

3. What evidence in the text indicates that wave size depends on different things?

Wave Characteristics

Scientists use certain characteristics to describe all waves including water waves. The highest part of a wave is the crest. The lowest part is the trough. If you measure the water's position before a wave passes through it to the crest or the trough, you will know a wave's amplitude or how large it is.

On a calm day, the amplitude of ocean waves is small. But when strong winds blow, the waves pick up energy, and the amplitude greatly increases.

Wavelength is the distance from one crest to the next or from one trough to the next. The wavelength of small ripples of water may only be a few millimeters. Those of huge waves may be several meters. A meter is a little over three feet.

4. **Explain how wind changes waves.**

Beaches: Dynamic Systems

With all of the **energy** carried by waves, it's not so surprising that they can dramatically **alter** an ocean beach. The great amounts of energy in large waves can cause cracks in even huge rocks. Over time, the cracks can become larger, until finally pieces of rock break off. Waves also carry sediments, such as stones and sand, that can wear down coastal landforms. When these sediments hit coastal features, they act like sandpaper to wear away rock.

5. **The topic of the above paragraph is "beaches." What is the central idea?**

6. **What is the meaning of _energy_ in the context of the above paragraph?**

7. **What is the meaning of _alter_ in the context of the above paragraph?**

Waves also build up beaches by moving sand along the shore. The way the sand moves depends on the angle at which waves strike the shore. When waves move at an angle toward the shoreline, they push water along the shoreline. The movement of water, called a longshore current, can move materials from the shoreline to an area in the water away from the shore. One landform created this way is a sandbar, which is a ridge of sand, shells, and stones. The top of a sandbar can be above or below water.

8. **The topic of the above paragraph is "waves." What is the central idea?**

Wind too can change landforms along a coast. On rocky shores, wind can shape cliffs and large rocks into amazing shapes. Along quieter, sandy coastlines, wind can blow loose sand into piles, called dunes. Beach dunes are usually small but can be very large.

Coastal landforms are constantly changing as water and wind act on them. Not all beaches are the same. The color and texture of any beach are determined by the sources of its sand and rock.

9. **Explain how waves can change the land. Give two examples.**

10. **Explain why a beach that has many storms changes more rapidly than a beach with few storms.**

Summarize what the text says about how waves and wind can change beaches.

Science, Part I

What is Inside a Cell?

Cells are the smallest living parts of any living thing. Cells have the same needs as any organism and carry out many of the same activities. Cells contain smaller parts, each with a specialized job. Read to find out more about how cells work.

What Are Cells?

A cell is the smallest part of your body that carries out the activities of life. Cells are the basic building blocks that make up all living things. The tiniest organisms are only single cells. Multicellular organisms, on the other hand, have many cells, maybe trillions. Most cells are too tiny to be seen by the eye alone. A single drop of blood would hold millions of red blood cells. You definitely need a microscope to see them.

   1. What evidence in the text indicates that a tiny organism crawling across your desk is multicellular?

Function of Cells

Cells in most living things have the same needs for survival as you do. Cells must take in food and get rid of wastes. Cells use materials in food to grow and to repair wounds. While very few cells move around, all cells have parts that move inside them. Cells sense and **respond** to changes in their surroundings. They often communicate and cooperate with other cells.

   2. What is the meaning of *respond* in the context of the above paragraph?

All cells need energy. Most cells get energy through cellular respiration. Cellular respiration is the taking in of oxygen and food, such as sugar, in order to get energy. In this process, carbon dioxide and water are made. Different cells require different amounts of energy for all the things that they do to stay alive, including growing, moving, and dividing to make new cells.

   3. Explain how cells carry out the same functions as your body does. Give two examples.

Parts of Cells

A cell is an amazing package made up of a cell membrane, a nucleus, and many other structures. Most of the things that your body does are really done inside cells. For example, you grow when your cells grow larger and divide. Your arm moves because small fibers are moving inside muscle cells.

   4. What evidence in the text indicates how the cells of a 15-year-old are different from the cells of a five-year-old?

Some Parts of Animal Cells

All cells have some of the same parts, and many parts have similar jobs. Cells have the same needs as your whole body has. For example, your body needs an outside covering of skin, a control system of nerves, a support system of bones, and places to store food and wastes in the digestive system. Some cell parts can be compared to these larger structures in your body.

The cell membrane surrounds a cell, holding the parts of the cell together. It allows needed materials, such as sugar, water, and oxygen, to enter the cell. It allows certain other materials, such as carbon dioxide and other waste products, to exit.

5. The topic of the above two paragraphs is "cell parts." What is the central idea?

6. Explain how the cell membrane and our skin are alike.

The nucleus is the part of the cell that contains chromosomes. Chromosomes are made of materials including a chemical called DNA. DNA is a chemical shaped like a twisted ladder. Chromosomes carry the instructions for the cell. By telling every cell how to do its jobs, chromosomes control how the body grows and changes. Almost every cell nucleus in your body has 46 chromosomes.

Every chromosome has small sections of DNA called genes. Genes are made of DNA. Each gene carries a single unit of information. Almost every cell in your body has the same set of thousands of genes. Heredity is the **process** of passing these genes from one generation to the next.

7. The topic of the above two paragraphs is "chromosomes." What is the central idea?

8. What is the meaning of *process* in the context of the above paragraph?

9. Explain how chromosomes work in the cell.

Cytoplasm is all the material of the cell between the cell membrane and the nucleus. Mitochrondria are the cell's power producers. They combine oxygen and food to produce energy. Vacuoles can sometimes act like a stomach, storing and breaking down material. In plants, vacuoles may store water.

The Size of Cells

Like most things, cells have a limit as to how big or small they can be. They cannot be too small, or they will not have room for all their parts. They cannot be too big, or oxygen and other materials will not be able to reach the middle of the cell fast enough to keep the cell alive. Also, wastes must be able to leave.

10. Which text structure best explains how the author organized the above passage?

_____ description of important features

_____ explanation of steps in a sequence

_____ account of cause and effect

_____ explanation of problem and solution

_____ comparison/contrast of two or more things

Give a reason from the text for your answer. For example, if you choose description, tell what is being described. For sequence, list one or two steps. For cause and effect, state a cause or effect mentioned in the text. For problem and solution, tell what the problem is or describe the solution. For comparison, tell what is being compared or contrasted.

Summarize what the text says about what each part of an animal cell does.

Science, Part II

How Do Cells Work Together?

Different types of cells are found throughout the body. Each cell's shape and structure help it perform specialized jobs. Read to find out what different cells do and how they work together.

Types of Cells and Their Work

Just as footballs and basketballs have different shapes and different purposes, so do different cells. Your body has about 200 different kinds of cells. A cell's shape is often specifically **designed** to fit its job. Also, many cells often have specialized **structures** that help them in their work.

    1. What is the meaning of *designed* in the context of the above paragraph?

    2. What is the meaning of *structures* in the context of the above paragraph?

Branching Cells

The shape of nerve cells makes them great for communicating signals between the brain and the rest of the body. Their great length helps these signals reach the brain quickly. A nerve cell's branching structure is designed to connect several parts of the body at once.

Flat Cells

Flat cells, such as skin cells, often join or overlap to cover a surface. They work something like the shingles on a building's roof. Your skin is built of many layers of flat cells, making it both strong and flexible. Flat cells are found lining many different parts of the body. For example, they line the surfaces of the mouth.

Round Cells

Red blood cells are rounded discs with two big dimples. This shape gives extra surface area for picking up and carrying oxygen. Their job is to carry oxygen to all your cells. The smooth shape of red blood cells helps these cells move easily through blood vessels.

    3. What evidence in the text indicates that a cell's shape is related to the work it does?

    4. Explain how flat and round cells are alike.

Special Cell Structure

Cells with different kinds of hair-like structures do different jobs inside the body. When a friend whispers in your ear, sound waves cause many parts of your ear to vibrate. This causes hair-like structures on cells in your inner ear to bend. The bending results in nerve signals being sent to the brain.

    Muscle cells have long fibers made of protein. The fibers are like threads that move to make the whole cell shorter. Each fiber is not very strong, but they work together in each cell. Many cells work together in bundles, making the muscles strong. In the airway of the lungs, cells have waving hair-like structures called cilia. They sweep dirt and germs out of the airways.

5. The topic of the above section is "special cell structure." What is the central idea?

6. Explain how the work of hair-like structures in the ears and the lungs are different.

7. What evidence in the text indicates that muscles can become strong even though cell fibers are weak?

Cells Form Tissues

You may have noticed that teamwork can be a great way to get work done. Cells rarely work by themselves and often work in tissues. A tissue is a group of the same kind of cells working together doing the same job. Muscle cells grouped in bundles make up muscle tissue. Bone cells grouped together make up bone tissue. Groups of nerve cells together make up nerve tissues.

Tissues Form Organs

Tissues join with other types of tissues to form organs. An organ is a grouping of different kinds of tissues combined together into one structure. These tissues work together to perform a main job in the body. Your heart, eyes, ears, and stomach are all examples of organs in your body. The largest organ that you have is your skin. Many animals have tissues and organs similar to yours. Plants have tissues and organs too. Plant organs include stems, roots, leaves, and flowers.

8. The topic of the above two paragraphs is "tissues." What is the central idea?

9. Which text structure best explains how the author organized the above paragraph?

_____ description of important features

_____ explanation of steps in a sequences

_____ account of cause and effect

_____ explanation of problem and solution

_____ comparison/contrast of two or more things

Give a reason from the text for your answer. For example, if you choose description, tell what is being described. For sequence, list one or two steps. For cause and effect, state a cause or effect mentioned in the text. For problem and solution, tell what the problem is or describe the solution. For comparison, tell what is being compared or contrasted.

Skin Cell Tissue

Skin cells form in many layers. The top section alone has about 25 layers of skin cells. When new cells form in the bottom layers, they push the other cells outward and away from any blood supply. By the time they are pushed to the outside surface, the cells are dead. It takes about one month for skin cells to get pushed to the surface. Dead cells at the outside surface simply fall off.

Other Tissues in the Skin

Your skin is more than just layers of flat skin cells. Skin has many tissues working together to do many jobs. Skin tissue protects the inside of your body, keeps out germs, and prevents too much from leaving the body. Nerve tissue helps you sense touch, pressure, and temperature. Blood vessels carry food and oxygen to cells. Oil glands keep the skin soft. When you feel cold, muscle tissue pulls the hair upright, causing goosebumps. Upright hairs help you stay warmer by trapping warm air next to the skin.

10. Explain how tissues and organs are alike and how they are different.

Summarize what the text says about what tissues are and what they do.

SCIENCE

How Do Organs Work Together?

An organ is made when tissues of different types combine together. Read to learn how organs work together.

Organ Systems

In dogs, cats, fish, ferns, and you, many cells work together in tissues. Many tissues work together in organs. Organs work together in groups too. An organ system is a group of organs and tissues that work together to carry out a life process. For instance, the mouth, stomach, intestines, and other organs work together to digest food.

Bones Form a System

Each of your bones is an organ. Together, about 200 bones make up the skeletal system. This organ system has several important jobs. It provides the body with a strong support system. Imagine what life would be like if you did not have bones to help you stand or sit up. You would move like wiggling worms! Another job of the skeletal system is to protect internal organs. The skull is made of several bones that work together to protect the brain. The rib cage protects your lungs and heart. Bones have other roles too.

Between the bone cells is a hard material that has a lot of calcium. This material makes bones hard. Other parts of the body, like muscles, also use calcium from blood to do their work. Bones store calcium until the level of calcium in the blood is low.

1. The topic of the above two paragraphs is "skeletal system." What is the central idea?

2. Which text structure best explains how the author organized the above section?

    _____ description of important features

    _____ explanation of steps in a sequence

    _____ account of cause and effect

    _____ explanation of problem and solution

    _____ comparison/contrast of two or more things

    Give a reason from the text for your answer. For example, if you choose description, tell what is being described. For sequence, list one or two steps explained in the text. For cause and effect, state a cause or effect mentioned in the text. For problem and solution, tell what the problem is or describe the solution. For comparison, tell what is being compared or contrasted.

3. Explain why the skeletal system is important to your body.

Muscles Work as a System

Muscles are organs that work together to move your body. You have about 640 muscles that you control. When you run or dance, your brain tells dozens of these muscles how to work together. In other cases, muscles work by themselves without your being aware of them. Have you ever shivered in cold weather? Shivering can help you survive the cold. When you shiver, many muscles are working together to warm the body. You do not have to think about shivering for it to happen.

Long thin muscle cells work in bundles for increased strength. Squeeze your fist tight. Several muscles work together to make your fingers form a fist. Can you feel them get tight in your lower arm? It also takes several muscles to smile.

4. What evidence in the text indicates that dancing and shivering are controlled by different kinds of muscles?

Bones and Muscles Work Together

One of the biggest jobs of your muscle and skeletal systems is to work together to move your body. Many muscles work in pairs to move bones.

Hold out your arm straight in front of you, and then bend your elbow. While you do this, the triceps muscle on the bottom of your arm **relaxes.** A muscle that is relaxed can stretch. At the same time, the biceps muscle on top of your upper arm contracts or shortens. This makes the end of the muscle pull on the bone of your forearm to bend your elbow.

The opposite happens when you straighten your elbow. In this case, the triceps muscle on the back of your upper arm contracts. The biceps muscle on the top of the arm **relaxes.** Muscles only pull on bones. They never push. That is why two or more muscles must work together to move each bone in opposite directions.

5. What is the meaning of *relaxes* in the context of the above two paragraphs?

6. Explain how muscles work together when you straighten your leg.

Nerves and Muscles

Many organ systems work together to make a **complex** organism. For example, your nervous system controls how your muscles move your bones. Nerves carry electrical signals from your brain and spinal cord to your muscles. Without nerves you would never move a muscle.

7. What is the meaning of *complex* in the context of the above paragraph?

Other Systems Work Together

Organ systems often work so closely together that some organs are in two organ systems. For example, muscles are not just connected to bones. Some of the strongest muscles in your body make up your heart. These muscles function every minute of your life to push blood through the system of blood vessels. Muscles also squeeze food through the digestive system.

Your skeletal system is very important to the circulatory system. The red and white blood cells in your body are made in bone marrow. Bone marrow is a soft material that fills cavities and spongy bone tissue inside some bones.

8. The topic of the above section is "organ systems." What is the central idea?

9. Explain how the circulatory system in our bodies depends on two other organ systems.

10. What evidence in the text indicates that organ systems work without our knowledge or awareness?

Summarize what the text says about what the skeletal system does.

Science, Part I

What Are Earth's Layers Made Of?

Earth has a variety of surface features. Beneath Earth's crust are the mantle and core. Read to find out about the structure of our Earth.

Earth's Variety

Victoria Falls is just one of Earth's many land **features.** The area around Victoria Falls is raised, flat land called a plateau. Water from the falls plunges into a gorge, or deep crack, in the plateau. In the United States, a very large plateau, the Colorado Plateau, covers areas of Utah, New Mexico, Arizona, and Colorado. At one time, this plateau was flat, but over thousands of years water has washed away some of the rock. Landforms such as the Grand Canyon are the result.

Depending on where you live, you might find other landforms, such as mountains, plains, and valleys. In the southern African desert of Namib, mountains rise high above the surrounding plains. Plains are flatlands with few trees. Valleys, such as the Napa Valley region in southern California, are found where mountains are close together.

Some of Earth's **features** are hidden by water. For example, beneath the Atlantic Ocean is a ridge, or long row, of towering mountains. Some of those mountains are volcanoes. Also below the ocean are trenches, long narrow canyons in the ocean floor.

Although these **features** differ in many ways, they all formed from processes than began deep inside Earth. To understand the process, you need to understand what Earth is like inside.

1. The topic of the above three paragraphs is "Earth's features." What is the central idea?

2. Which text structure best explains how the author organized the above passage?

   ____ description of important features

   ____ explanation of steps in a sequence

   ____ account of cause and effect

   ____ explanation of problem and solution

   ____ comparison/contrast of two or more things

   Give a reason from the text for your answer. For example, if you choose description, tell what is being described. For sequence, list one or two steps. For cause and effect, state a cause or effect mentioned in the text. For problem and solution, tell what the problem is or describe the solution. For comparison, tell what is being compared or contrasted.

3. What is the meaning of *features* in the context of the above section?

4. What evidence in the text indicates that we cannot see all of Earth's land features?

Earth's Layers

Sometimes Earth is described as a giant rock in space. In one way, that's true. Earth's surface is solid and is made of rock and soil. But Earth has different **layers,** and not all of them are solid.

Above Earth's surface is the atmosphere. Parts of the atmosphere constantly interact with Earth's land. This thin **layer** of gases is the air we breathe. Humans could not live on Earth without the atmosphere. In fact, Earth's atmosphere makes it the only planet we know of that can support life.

The outermost solid **layer** of Earth is the crust, the part of Earth we live on. It includes the soil and rock that covers Earth's surface. The thickness of the crust varies. The part of the crust covered by ocean water is about 6–11 kilometers thick. The part that is dry land is about 35–40 kilometers thick. When you think about high mountains, which are part of Earth's crust, you may think the crust is thick. Compared to the size of the Earth, the crust is just a thin shell.

The layer of Earth just below the crust is the mantle. This thick **layer** contains most of Earth's mass. The outer part of the mantle is solid, like the crust. The inner part is so hot that the rock can flow very slowly over time.

The innermost **layer** of Earth is the core which has two **layers**. The core is much denser, or compacted, than the mantle because of the weight of all the rock above it. The temperature of the core is thought to be about 7,000°C. That's as hot as the surface of the Sun. The outer core is so hot that it is a liquid. The inner core is solid.

5. What is the meaning of *layer* in the context of the above section?

6. Analyze how the mantle and the core are alike. Give two examples from the text.

7. What evidence in the text indicates that Earth is not really a giant rock in space?

8. Analyze how Earth's atmosphere and Earth's crust are different.

9. Analyze why equipment used to drill for oil cannot be used to drill into the mantle.

Earth's Plates

In some ways, the outer part of Earth is like an eggshell. If you boil an egg too long, the inner part becomes a soft solid, but the shell breaks into pieces. Earth's crust and the upper part of the mantle are called the lithosphere. Like a cracked eggshell, the lithosphere is not a continuous layer. It is broken into pieces called tectonic plates. The plates all have different shapes and sizes. Some, like the South American Plate, are the size of continents. Others, such as the Caribbean Plate, are much smaller. All the plates fit together like the pieces of a jigsaw puzzle.

The plates don't follow the edges of the continents. Many of the plates are made of both continental crust—the crust that makes up continents—and oceanic crust—the crust that makes up the floor of the ocean. Most of the United States is on the North American Plate. Much of the Atlantic Ocean is also on this plate.

10. The topic of the above two paragraphs is "Earth's plates." What is the central idea?

If you viewed Earth from space, much of the land that makes up Earth's plates is not visible. Much of Earth's lithosphere is under oceans and other bodies of water. For example, the western part of California is on the Pacific Plate, but most of this plate is covered by ocean.

Like the cracked shell of a boiled egg, Earth's plates rest on a soft solid. Recall that the lower part of the mantle can flow very slowly. The plates of the lithosphere float on top of this layer.

Summarize how the text describes the four layers of Earth.

How Do Earth's Plates Help Create Landforms?

Alfred Wegener introduced the idea that the continents drift slowly over Earth's surface. Read to find out about evidence that supported this theory.

Continental Drift

Until the early 1600s, most people thought that Earth's continents were always in the same place. Then scientists began to notice that the coastlines of some continents looked as if they could fit together like a jigsaw puzzle. Many people wondered why.

Then in 1912 Alfred Wegener, a German scientist, suggested an explanation for the fit of the coastlines. Wegener thought that about 225 million years ago the continents were joined in one large continent he called Pangaea (meaning "all Earth"). Wegener suggested that long ago Pangaea broke apart.

Wegener also introduced the idea of continental drift, the theory that continents drifted apart in the past and continue to do so. Wegener's **theory** stated that as Pangaea broke apart, its pieces moved to different parts of Earth to form today's continents.

　　1.　The topic of the above two paragraphs is "the continental drift." What is the central idea?

The shape of continents was **evidence** for Wegener's ideas, but it wasn't proof. Other evidence supported Wegener's ideas. Identical plant fossils were found in South America, Africa, India, Antarctica, and Australia. Wegener felt these similarities were impossible unless the species had once lived side by side when the continents were joined. Fossils of an ancient freshwater reptile were found in both South America and Africa. This animal could not have survived a trip across a saltwater ocean. Wegener claimed the reptile must have walked from one area to the other when the continents were connected.

Further evidence for Wegener's **theory** was found in rocks. Layers of rocks along the eastern coast of South America match layers of rocks along the western coast of Africa. Wegener said that the layers of rocks must have been joined at some time.

　　2.　What is the meaning of *theory* in the context of the above two paragraphs?

　　3.　What is the meaning of *evidence* in the context of the above two sections?

　　4.　Analyze what evidence supported Wegner's theory of Pangaea. Offer two examples.

What forces could be strong enough to move whole continents? This is the question that Wegener could not answer. As a result, most scientists did not believe the idea of continental drift. They thought that the continents did not move, even over millions of years.

The Spreading Ocean Bottom

Not much other evidence supported Wegener's theory of continental drift. Later, better methods to map the ocean floor were developed. Scientists then collected data that showed long, deep ocean trenches. They also discovered a chain of mountains along the floor of the Atlantic Ocean. These mountains are now called the Mid-Atlantic Ridge.

In 1960 scientist Harry Hess offered an explanation for the trenches and ridges. He suggested that new crust forms at ocean ridges. He explained that magma, which is molten rock, pushes up through Earth's crust. As the magma cools, it forms new crust. More magma comes up and pushes the newly formed crust and the old crust aside. This process is known as seafloor spreading.

What causes the magma to rise? As Earth's plates move away from each other, the ocean floor spreads apart, and magma rises to fill the gap. But what causes the plates to move apart?

5. The topic of the above three paragraphs is "sea floor spreading." What is the central idea?

6. Which text structure best explains how the author organized the above passage?

_____ description of important features

_____ explanation of steps in a sequence

_____ account of cause and effect

_____ explanation of problem and solution

_____ comparison/contrast of two or more things

Give a reason from the text for your answer. For example, if you choose description, tell what is being described. For sequence, list one or two steps. For cause and effect, state a cause or effect mentioned in the text. For problem and solution, tell what the problem is or describe the solution. For comparison, tell what is being compared or contrasted.

7. What evidence in the text indicates that the seafloor is constantly spreading?

In the early 1930s, Arthur Holmes had developed ideas that scientists used in the 1960s to answer the question. When a liquid is heated, particles that make up the liquid move faster and spread apart. Hot liquids therefore weigh less and float above cooler liquids. As the hot liquid rises and cools, it becomes heavier and again sinks. More hot liquid can then rise above it. This process is called convection. The mantle is not a flowing liquid, but its rocks are so hot that they flow very slowly. The result is that currents in the mantle constantly rise, circle around, and fall. When the mantle moves, the plates floating on it also move. Convection is the force that moves Earth's plates.

8. Analyze why Earth's plates move.

Proof of Continental Drift

Although the explanation for sea floor spreading helped to support Wegener's ideas, scientists needed more proof of continental drift. In the early 1960s, scientists studying the magnetism of rocks near the Mid-Ocean Ridge noticed a pattern. In some places the magnetism faced north. In other places, it faced south. Scientists found alternating rows of north/south patterns spreading out from the Mid-Ocean Ridge. What did this evidence mean?

Earth's magnetism "flips" about every half million years. When rocks form from the cooling lava of volcanoes, the particular magnetic pattern at the time is "frozen" into the rocks. The alternating magnetic patterns indicated that the rocks formed at different times. Continental drift had been occurring throughout Earth's history and is still continuing.

9. Analyze how rock magnetism supported the theory of continental drift.

10. What evidence in the text indicates that scientists demand much proof before they accept a new theory?

Summarize Wegener's theory of Pangaea and the continental drift.

Science, Part III

How Do Scientists Explain Earth's Features?

Read to learn how the theory of plate tectonics explains Earth's features such as mountains and volcanoes.

Theory of Plate Tectonics

Wegener's idea of continental drift suggested that continents moved, but it did not explain many other parts of Earth's crust. Today scientists use the theory of plate tectonics to explain why Earth's features appear as they do.

According to the theory of plate tectonics, Earth's lithosphere is broken into about 20 moving plates. The continents and the ocean floor make up the surfaces of these moving plates.

Earth's plates move in a continuous process in different directions away from, alongside, or toward each other. How do scientists know how the plates move?

Scientists can figure out how the plates move by receiving radio signals from Global Positioning System (GPS) satellites in space to determine the **precise** distance between points on different plates and how the distances change over time. For example, they know from data they have collected that the North American Plate and the Eurasian Plate are moving about two centimeters a year away from each other.

1. The topic of the above section is "plate tectonics." What is the central idea?

2. What evidence in the text indicates that the theory of plate tectonics differs from the theory of continental drift?

3. What is the meaning of *precise* in the context of the above paragraph?

The theory of plate tectonics explains many of Earth's features. Continents may break apart. Mountain chains may form where plates move together. As plates move apart, magma may rise to the surface, forming a volcano. Oceans may become larger or smaller. Throughout Earth's history, the positions of the land and the oceans have changed from the ancient Pangaea to the modern-day continents.

Scientists can **predict** where the continents will be 50 million years from now. How can they make this prediction? Evidence shows that plate movement has always taken place at about the same rate. And scientists predict that the plates will continue to move. They think it is possible that in the far distant future, the continents could come together once again to create another Pangaea-like continent.

4. What is the meaning of *predict* in the context of the above paragraph?

Plate Boundaries

Plate boundaries are areas where two plates meet. Plates move slowly in different directions. They may move apart, they may collide, or they may slide past each other. Landforms result as changes slowly happen at each kind of plate boundary.

At spreading boundaries, plates move away from each other and gaps form between the plates. Convection currents cause magma to rise from the mantle through these gaps. Huge valleys can form. This type of plate movement is responsible for seafloor spreading. The Mid-Atlantic Ridge formed at plate boundaries that were moving apart.

At fracture boundaries, plates slide past each other. This break in Earth's crust is called a fault. The movement of the plates past each other can cause strong earthquakes.

The area where two plates push against each other is called a colliding boundary. When plates collide, one plate might slide beneath the other. When plates carry continents into each other, towering mountains form. Other times, deep ocean trenches, earthquakes, and volcanoes can result.

5. Which text structure best explains how the author organized the above two paragraphs?

    ____ description of important features

    ____ explanation of steps in a sequence

    ____ account of cause and effect

    ____ explanation of problem and solution

    ____ comparison/contrast of two or more things

Give a reason from the text for your answer. For example, if you choose description, tell what is being described. For sequence, list one or two steps. For cause and effect, state a cause or effect mentioned in the text. For problem and solution, tell what the problem is or describe the solution. For comparison, tell what is being compared or contrasted.

6. Analyze how Earth's features change when plates move. Give two examples.

What Causes Earthquakes and Volcanoes?

Earthquakes are caused by the sudden shifting of rocks as tectonic plates shift positions. Volcanoes occur where magma from the mantle either flows or explodes through the crust.

Earthquakes

Plate movement takes place so slowly that you can't see or feel it. In fact, some plates don't move for many years. Jagged rock edges in the lithosphere sometimes stop the movement. Over time, pressure builds up, until suddenly the pressure is too strong. The rocks lurch forward. Earth's crust shakes. An earthquake has happened!

Earthquakes cause damage when the pressure that builds up along a fault is suddenly released. The underground point where the earthquake occurs is called the focus. The point on Earth's surface directly over the focus is called the epicenter.

The energy from an earthquake is carried by waves. The waves spread out from the focus and from the epicenter. Some waves cause the ground to move back and forth. Other waves cause the ground to move up and down or in a circular motion. As waves spread out, they lose energy. The possibility of damage is greatest close to the epicenter.

7. The topic of the above section is "earthquakes." What is the central idea?

8. Analyze why some earthquakes cause more damage than others.

9. What evidence in the text indicates that earthquakes can act very differently?

Volcanoes

A volcano is an opening in the surface of one of Earth's plates through which magma rises. Like earthquakes, most volcanoes occur near plate boundaries. The theory of plate tectonics explains why.

When one plate sinks beneath another at a plate boundary, the sinking crust melts into magma. Pressure can build up from gases trapped in the magma—somewhat like the pressure that builds when you shake a can of carbonated beverage. If the crust of the overlying plate can no longer withstand the pressure, magma explodes through it as a volcano. Magma that reaches the surface is called lava.

You never hear about most volcanoes. They take place where plate boundaries are moving *away* from each other on the ocean floor. Magma quietly flows out onto the ocean floor. New crust forms from the cooled lava.

10. Analyze why most volcanoes occur at a plate boundary.

Summarize what the text says about how plate boundaries explain Earth's features.

Life Sciences, Part I

The Digestive System

Read to find out how our digestive system works.

The digestive system has three main functions. First, it breaks down food into molecules the body can use. Then the molecules are absorbed into the blood and carried throughout the body. Finally waste is eliminated from the body.

Digestion

The process by which your body breaks down food into small nutrient molecules is called digestion. There are two kinds of digestion: mechanical and chemical. In mechanical digestion, foods are physically broken down into smaller pieces. Mechanical digestion occurs when you bite into a sandwich and chew it into small pieces. In chemical digestion, chemicals produced by the body break foods into their smaller chemical building blocks. For example, the starch in bread is broken down into individual sugar molecules.

Absorption and Elimination

After your food is digested, the molecules are ready to be transported throughout your body. Absorption is the process by which nutrient molecules pass through the wall of your digestive system into your blood. Materials that are not absorbed, such as fiber, are eliminated from the body as wastes.

1. What evidence in the text strongly supports that only two things can happen to food once it is digested?

The Mouth

Both mechanical and chemical digestion begins in the mouth. The fluid released when your mouth waters is saliva. Saliva plays an important role in both kinds of digestion.

Mechanical Digestion in the Mouth   Your teeth carry out the first stage of mechanical digestion. Your center teeth, or incisors, cut the food into bite-sized pieces. Sharp, pointy teeth called canines tear and slash the food into smaller pieces. Premolars and molars crush and grind the food. As the teeth do their work, saliva moistens the pieces of food into one slippery mass.

Chemical Digestion in the Mouth   As mechanical digestion begins, so does chemical digestion. If you take a bite of a cracker and suck on it, the cracker begins to taste sweet. It tastes sweet because a chemical in the saliva has broken down the starch molecules in the cracker into sugar molecules.

The chemical in saliva that digests starch is an enzyme. Enzymes are proteins that speed up chemical reactions in the body. Your body produces many different enzymes. Each enzyme has a **specific** chemical shape. Its shape enables it to take part in only one kind of chemical reaction.

2. The topic of the above section entitled The Mouth is "digestion in the mouth." What is the central idea?

3. Analyze why saliva is important to the digestive process.

4. What is the meaning of *specific* in the context of the above passage?

5. Which text structure best explains how the author organized the above passage?

____   description of important features

____   explanation of steps in a sequence

_____   account of cause and effect

_____   explanation of problem and solution

_____   comparison/contrast of two or more things

Give a reason from the text for your answer. For example, if you choose description, tell what is being described. For sequence, list one or two steps. For cause and effect, state a cause or effect mentioned in the text. For problem and solution, tell what the problem is or describe the solution. For comparison, tell what is being compared or contrasted.

The Esophagus

There two openings at the back of your mouth. One opening leads to your windpipe, which carries air into your lungs. As you swallow, a flap of tissue called the epiglottis seals off your windpipe, preventing the food from entering. Food goes into the esophagus, a muscular tube that connects the mouth to the stomach. The esophagus is lined with mucus, a thick, slippery substance produced by the body. Mucus makes food easier to swallow and move along.

Food remains in the esophagus for only about 10 seconds. **Contractions** of smooth muscles push the food toward the stomach. These involuntary waves of muscle contractions are called peristalsis. Peristalsis also occurs in the stomach and farther down the digestive system. These muscular waves keep food moving in one direction.

6. What is the meaning of *contractions* in the context of the above passage?

7. What evidence in the text strongly supports that you cannot breathe at the same time that you are swallowing something?

8. Analyze why the entire digestive process can occur even if you are lying flat.

The Stomach

When food leaves the esophagus, it enters the stomach, a J-shaped, muscular pouch located in the abdomen. As you eat, your stomach expands to hold all of the food that you swallow. Most mechanical digestion and some chemical digestion occur in the stomach.

Mechanical Digestion in the Stomach   The process of mechanical digestion occurs as three strong layers of smooth muscle contract to produce a churning motion which mixes the food with fluids.

Chemical Digestion in the Stomach   Chemical digestion occurs as the churning food makes contact with digestive juice, a fluid produced by cells in the lining of the stomach. Digestive juice contains the enzyme pepsin. Pepsin chemically digests the proteins in your food, breaking them down into short chains of amino acids.

Digestive juice also contains hydrochloric acid, a very strong acid. Without this strong acid, your stomach could not function properly. First, pepsin works best in an acid environment. Second, the acid kills many bacteria that you swallow with your food.

9. The topic of the above section entitled The Stomach is "digestion in the stomach." What is the central idea?

Why doesn't stomach acid burn a hole in your stomach? The reason is that cells in the stomach lining produce a thick coating of mucus, which protects the stomach lining. Also, the cells that line the stomach are quickly replaced as they are damaged or worn out.

Food remains in the stomach until all of the solid material has been broken down into liquid form. A few hours after you finish eating, the stomach completes mechanical digestion of the food. By that time, most of the proteins have been chemically digested into shorter chains of amino acids.

The food, now a thick liquid, is released into the next part of the digestive system. That is where final chemical digestion and absorption will take place.

10. Analyze why the digestive system would break down without the stomach lining. Give two reasons.

Summarize what the text says happens to a pizza from the time it enters your mouth until it is a thick liquid.

SCIENCE

The Muscular System

Read to find out how our muscular system works.

There are about 600 muscles in your body. Muscles have many functions. For example, they keep your heart beating, pull your mouth into a smile, and move the bones of your skeleton. You use your muscles to move your arms, legs, hands, feet, and head. Other muscles expand and contract your chest and allow you to breathe.

Types of Muscle

Some of your body's movements, such as smiling, are easy to control. Other movements, such as the beating of your heart, are impossible to control completely. That is because some of your muscles are not under your conscious control. Those muscles are called involuntary muscles. Involuntary muscles are responsible for such essential activities as breathing and digesting food.

The muscles that are under your conscious control are called voluntary muscles. Smiling, turning a page in a book, and getting out of your chair when the bell rings are all actions controlled by voluntary muscles.

Your body has three types of muscle tissue: skeletal muscle, smooth muscle, and cardiac muscle. Some of these muscle tissues are involuntary, and some are voluntary. Both skeletal and smooth muscles are found in many places in the body. Cardiac muscle is found only in the heart. Each muscle type performs specific **functions** in the body.

1. The topic of the above three paragraphs is "types of muscle." What is the central idea?

2. What is the meaning of *functions* in the context of the above passage?

3. Which text structure best explains how the author organized the above passage?

    ____ description of important features

    ____ explanation of steps in a sequence

    ____ account of cause and effect

    ____ explanation of problem and solution

    ____ comparison/contrast of two or more things

    Give a reason from the text for your answer. For example, if you choose description, tell what is being described. For sequence, list one or two steps. For cause and effect, state a cause or effect mentioned in the text. For problem and solution, tell what the problem is or describe the solution. For comparison, tell what is being compared or contrasted.

4. What evidence in the text strongly supports that the body contains more skeletal and smooth muscle than cardiac muscle?

Skeletal Muscle

Every time you walk across a room, you are using skeletal muscles. Skeletal muscles are attached to the bones of your skeleton and provide the force that moves your bones. At each end of a skeletal muscle is a tendon. A tendon is a strong connective tissue that attaches muscle to bone. Skeletal muscle cells appear banded, or striated. For this reason, skeletal muscle is sometimes called striated muscle.

Because you have conscious control of skeletal muscles, they are classified as voluntary muscles. One characteristic of skeletal muscles is that they react very quickly. Think about what happens during a swim meet. Immediately after the starting gun sounds, a swimmer's leg muscles push the swimmer off the block into the pool. However, another characteristic of skeletal muscles is that they tire quickly. By the end of the race, the swimmer's muscles are tired and need a rest.

5. Analyze why you could not walk if you did not have any skeletal muscle.

Smooth Muscle

The inside of many internal organs, such as the stomach and blood vessels, contain smooth muscles. Smooth muscles are involuntary muscles. They work automatically to control certain movements inside your body, such as those involved in digestion. For example, as the smooth muscles of your stomach contract, they produce a churning action. The churning mixes the food with chemicals, and helps to digest the food.

Unlike skeletal muscles, smooth muscle cells are not striated. Smooth muscles behave differently than skeletal muscles, too. Smooth muscles react more slowly and tire more slowly.

Cardiac Muscle

The tissue called cardiac muscle is found only in your heart. Cardiac muscle has some characteristics in common with both smooth muscle and skeletal muscle. Like smooth muscle, cardiac muscle is involuntary. Like skeletal muscle, cardiac muscle cells are striated. However, unlike skeletal muscle, cardiac muscle does not get tired. It can contract repeatedly. You call those repeated contractions heartbeats.

6. Analyze which type of muscle you would be aware of after running in a race and why you would be aware of it.

7. What evidence in the text strongly supports that smooth muscle is similar to cardiac muscle?

8. Analyze how smooth muscle and skeletal muscle are different. Give two separate examples.

Muscles at Work

Skeletal muscles such as the muscles in your arm do their work by contracting, becoming shorter and thicker. Muscle cells contract when they receive messages from the nervous system. Because muscle cells can contract, not extend, skeletal muscles must work in pairs. While one muscle contracts, the other muscle in a pair relaxes to its original length.

Muscles Work in Pairs   Consider the muscle action involved in bending your arm at the elbow. First, the biceps muscle on the front of your upper arm contracts to bend the elbow, lifting your forearm and hand. As the biceps contracts, the triceps on the back of your upper arm relaxes and returns to its original length. Then, to straighten your elbow, the triceps muscle contracts. As the triceps contracts to extend the arm, the biceps relaxes and returns to its original length. Another example of muscles that work in pairs are those in your thigh that bend and straighten the knee joint.

9. The topic of the above two paragraphs is "skeletal muscles." What is the central idea?

Muscular Strength and Flexibility

Regular exercise is important for maintaining both muscular strength and **flexibility**. Exercise makes individual muscle cells grow in size. As a result the whole muscle becomes thicker. The thicker a muscle is the stronger the muscle is.

10. What is the meaning of *flexibility* in the context of the above passage?

Summarize what the text says about how skeletal muscle and smooth muscle are different.

Life Sciences, Part III

The Respiratory System

Read to find out how our respiratory system works.

Your body cells need oxygen, and they get that oxygen from the air you breathe. The respiratory system moves oxygen from the outside environment into the body. It also removes carbon dioxide and water from the body.

Taking in Oxygen

Oxygen is needed for the energy-releasing chemical reactions that take place inside your cells. Like a fire, which cannot burn without oxygen, your cells cannot "burn" enough fuel to keep you alive without oxygen. The process in which oxygen and glucose undergo a complex series of chemical reactions inside cells is called respiration. Respiration is different from breathing. Breathing refers to the movement of air into and out of the lungs. Respiration, on the other hand, refers to the chemical reactions inside cells. As a result of respiration, your cells **release** the energy that fuels growth and other cell processes. In addition to the release of energy, respiration produces carbon dioxide and water. Your respiratory system eliminates the carbon dioxide and some of the water through your lungs.

1. What is the meaning of *release* in the context of the above passage?

2. Which text structure best explains how the author organized the above passage?

   ____   description of important features

   ____   explanation of steps in a sequence

   ____   account of cause and effect

   ____   explanation of problem and solution

   ____   comparison/contrast of two or more things

   Give a reason from the text for your answer. For example, if you choose description, tell what is being described. For sequence, list one or two steps. For cause and effect, state a cause or effect mentioned in the text. For problem and solution, tell what the problem is or describe the solution. For comparison, tell what is being compared or contrasted.

The Path of Air

Air contains particles such as grains of dust, plant pollen, and microorganisms. Some microorganisms can cause diseases. When you breathe in, all these materials enter your body along with the air. However, most of these materials never reach your lungs. On its way to the lungs, air passes through a **series** of structures that filter and trap particles. As air travels from the outside environment to the lungs, it passes through the following structures: nose, pharynx, trachea, and bronchi. It takes air only a few seconds to complete the route from the nose to the lungs.

3. What is the meaning of *series* in the context of the above passages?

4. What evidence in the text strongly supports that what we breathe is not always good for us?

The Nose

Air enters the body through the nose and then moves into spaces called the nasal cavities. Some of the cells lining the nasal cavities produce mucus. This sticky material moistens the air and keeps the lining from drying out. Mucus also traps particles such as dust.

The cells that line the nasal cavities have cilia, tiny hairlike extensions that can move together in a sweeping motion. The cilia sweep mucus into the throat where you swallow it. Stomach acid destroys the mucus along with everything trapped in it. Some particles and bacteria can irritate the lining of your nose or throat, causing you to sneeze which shoots the particles out of your nose and into the air.

5. The topic of the above section is "the nose." What is the central idea?

The Pharynx

Next air enters the pharynx or throat. Both the nose and the mouth connect to the pharynx.

The Trachea

From the pharynx air moves into the trachea or windpipe. The trachea, like the nose, is lined with cilia and mucus. The cilia in the trachea sweep upward, moving mucus toward the pharynx, where it is swallowed. The trachea's cilia and mucus continue the cleaning and moistening of air that began in the nose. If particles irritate the lining of the trachea, you cough. A cough, like a sneeze, sends the particles into the air. Normally, only air, not food, enters the trachea. If food does enter the trachea, the food can block the opening and prevent air from getting to the lungs. When that happens, a person chokes. Fortunately food rarely gets into the trachea. The epiglottis, a small flap of tissue that folds over the trachea, seals off the trachea while you swallow.

6. What evidence in the text strongly supports that mucus can be a good thing?

7. Analyze what might happen if the trachea is blocked.

The Bronchi and Lungs

Air moves from the trachea to the bronchi, the passages that direct air into the lungs. The lungs are the main organs of the respiratory system. The left bronchus leads into the left lung, and the right bronchus leads into the right lung. Inside the lungs, each bronchus divides into smaller and smaller tubes in a pattern that resembles the branches of a tree.

At the end of the smallest tubes are structures that look like bunches of grapes. The "grapes" are alveoli, tiny sacs of lung tissue specialized for the movement of gases between air and blood. Each alveolus is surrounded by a network of capillaries. It is here that the blood picks up its cargo of oxygen from the air.

8. The topic of the above section is "bronchi and lungs." What is the central idea?

9. Analyze how the trachea and the bronchi are alike and how they are different.

Gas Exchange

Because the walls of both the alveoli and the capillaries are very thin, certain materials can pass through them easily. After air enters an alveolus, oxygen passes through the wall of the alveolus and then through the capillary wall into the blood. Carbon dioxide and water pass from the blood into the alveoli. This whole process is known as gas exchange. Blood enters capillaries carrying a lot of carbon dioxide and little oxygen but leaves rich in oxygen and poor in carbon dioxide. This whole process is known as gas exchange.

10. Analyze how alveoli and capillaries are similar.

Summarize what the text says about how a breath of air moves from your nose to your lungs.

Earth Science, Part I

Fossils

Read to find out what fossils are and how they formed.

Millions of years ago, a fish died and sank to the bottom of a lake. Before the fish could decay completely, layers of sediment covered it. Minerals in the sediment seeped into the fish's bones. Slowly, pressure changed the sediment into solid rock. Inside the rock, the fish became a fossil.

Fossils are the preserved traces of living things. Fossils like the ancient fish provide evidence of how life has changed over time. Fossils can also help scientists **infer** how Earth's surface has changed. Fossils are clues to what past environments were like.

1. What is the meaning of *infer* in the context of the above paragraph?

How a Fossil Forms

Most fossils form when living things die and are buried by sediments. The sediments slowly harden into rock and preserve the shapes of the organisms. Fossils are usually found in sedimentary rock. Sedimentary rock is the type of rock that is made of hardened sediment, material removed by erosion. Sediment is made up of rock particles or the remains of living things. Sandstone, limestone, and coal are examples of sedimentary rocks. Most fossils form from animals or plants that once lived in or near quiet water such as swamps, lakes, or shallow seas where sediments build up.

When an organism dies, its soft parts often decay quickly or are eaten by animals. That is why only hard parts of an organism generally leave fossils. These hard parts include bones, shells, teeth, seeds, and woody stems. It is rare for the soft parts of an organism to become a fossil.

For a fossil to form, the **traces** of an organism must be protected from decay. Then several processes may cause a fossil to form. Fossils found in rock include molds and casts, petrified fossils, carbon films, and trace fossils. Other fossils form when the remains of organisms are preserved in substances such as tar, amber, or ice.

2. The topic of the above three paragraphs is "how a fossil forms." What is the central idea?

3. Which text structure best explains how the author organized the above passage?

    ____ description of important features

    ____ explanation of steps in a sequence

    ____ account of cause and effect

    ____ explanation of problem and solution

    ____ comparison/contrast of two or more things

    Give a reason from the text for your answer. For example, if you choose description, tell what is being described. For sequence, list one or two steps. For cause and effect, state a cause or effect mentioned in the text. For problem and solution, tell what the problem is or describe the solution. For comparison, tell what is being compared or contrasted.

4. What is the meaning of *traces* in the context of the above passage?

Molds and Casts

The most common fossils are molds and casts. Both copy the shape of ancient organisms. A mold is a hollow area in sediment in the shape of an organism or part of an organism. A mold forms when the hard part of the organism, such as a shell, is buried in sediment.

Later, water carrying dissolved minerals and sediment may seep into the empty space of a mold. If the water deposits the minerals and sediment there, the result is a cast. A cast is a solid copy of the shape of an organism. A cast is the opposite of its mold. Both the mold and cast preserve details of the animal's structure.

Petrified Fossils

A fossil may form when the remains of an organism become petrified. The term *petrified* means "turned into stone." Petrified fossils are fossils in which minerals replace all or part of an organism. Fossil tree trunks are examples of petrified wood. These fossils formed after sediment covered the wood. Then water rich in dissolved minerals seeped into spaces in the plant's cells. Over time, the minerals come out of solution and harden, filling in all of the spaces. Some of the original wood remains, but the minerals have hardened and preserved it.

Carbon Films

Another type of fossil is a carbon film, an extremely thin coating of carbon on rock. How does a carbon film form? All living things contain carbon. When sediment buries an organism, some of the materials that make up the organism evaporate, or become gases. These gases escape from the sediment, leaving carbon behind. Eventually, only a thin film of carbon remains. This process can preserve the delicate parts of plant leaves and insects.

Trace Fossils

Most types of fossils preserve the shapes of ancient animals and plants. In contrast, trace fossils provide evidence of the activities of ancient organisms. A fossilized footprint is one example of a trace fossil. The mud or sand that the animal stepped in was buried by layers of sediment. Slowly the sediment became solid rock, preserving the footprint for millions of years.

From fossil footprints, scientists can find answers to questions about an animal's size and behavior. Did the animal walk on two or four legs? Did it live alone or as part of a group?

Other types of trace fossils also provide clues about ancient organisms. A trail or burrow can give clues about the size and shape of an organism, where it lived, and how it obtained food.

5. Analyze why minerals are important to the formation of some kinds of fossils.

6. What evidence in the text strongly supports that scientists can learn more from trace fossils than from other kinds?

7. Analyze why sediment is important in the formation of a fossil. Give at least two examples.

Preserved Remains

Some processes preserve the remains of organisms with little or no change. For example, some remains are preserved when organisms become trapped in tar. Tar is sticky oil that seeps from Earth's surface. Many fossils preserved in tar have been found at the Rancho La Brea tar pits in Los Angeles, California. Thousands of years ago, animals came to drink the water that covered these pits. Somehow, they became stuck in the tar and then died. The tar soaked into their bones, preserving the bones from decay.

Ancient organisms also have been preserved in amber. Amber is the hardened resin, or sap, of evergreen trees. First, an insect is trapped on sticky resin. After the insect dies, more resin covers it, sealing it from air and protecting its body from decay.

Freezing can also preserve remains. The frozen remains of woolly mammoths, huge ancient relatives of elephants, have been found in very cold regions of Siberia and Alaska. Freezing has preserved even the mammoths' hair and skin.

8. What evidence in the text strongly supports that water is an important part of fossil formation?

9. The topic of the above two paragraphs is "preserved remains." What is the central idea?

10. Analyze how fossils formed by tar and resin are alike.

Summarize what the text says about how fossils form.

SCIENCE

The Relative Age of Rocks

Read to learn how and why geologists determine the age of rocks.

As sedimentary rock forms, the remains of organisms in the sediment may become fossils. Millions of years later, if you split open the rock, you might see the petrified bones of an extinct reptile or insect.

Your first question about a new fossil might be, "What is it?" Your next question would probably be, "How old is it?" Geologists have two ways to express the age of a rock and any fossil it contains. The relative age of a rock is its age compared to the ages of other rocks. You have probably used the idea of relative age when comparing your age with someone else's age. For example, if you say that you are older than your brother but younger than your sister, you are describing your relative age.

The relative age of a rock does not provide its absolute age. The absolute age of a rock is the number of years since the rock formed. It may be impossible to know a rock's absolute age exactly. But sometimes geologists can determine a rock's absolute age to within a certain number of years.

1. The topic of the above three paragraphs is "fossil age." What is the central idea?

The Position of Rock Layers

The sediment that forms sedimentary rocks is deposited in flat layers one on top of the other. Over time, the sediment hardens and changes into sedimentary rock. These rock layers provide a record of Earth's geologic history.

It can be difficult to determine the absolute age of a rock. So geologists use a method to find a rock's relative age. Geologists use the law of superposition to determine the relative ages of sedimentary rock layers. According to the law of superposition, in horizontal sedimentary rock layers the oldest layer is at the bottom. Each higher layer is younger than the layers below it.

The walls of the Grand Canyon in Arizona illustrate the law of superposition. The deeper down you go in the Grand Canyon, the older the rocks.

2. Analyze one way in which the relative age and absolute age of rocks are alike and one way in which they are different.

3. Which text structure best explains how the author organized the above passage?

_____ description of important features

_____ explanation of steps in a sequence

_____ account of cause and effect

_____ explanation of problem and solution

_____ comparison/contrast of two or more things

Give a reason from the text for your answer. For example, if you choose description, tell what is being described. For sequence, list one or two steps. For cause and effect, state a cause or effect mentioned in the text. For problem and solution, tell what the problem is or describe the solution. For comparison, tell what is being compared or contrasted.

4. What evidence in the text strongly supports that Earth formed from the bottom up?

Determining Relative Age

There are other clues besides the **position** of rock layers to the relative ages of rocks. To determine relative age, geologists also study extrusions and intrusions of igneous rock, faults, and gaps in the geologic record.

5. What is the meaning of *position* in the context of the above two passages entitled "The Position of Rock Layers" and "Determining Relative Age"?

Clues From Igneous Rock.   Igneous rock forms when magma or lava hardens. Magma is molten material beneath Earth's surface. Magma that flows onto the surface is called lava.

Lava that hardens on the surface is called an extrusion. An extrusion is always younger than the rocks below it.

Beneath the surface, magma may push into bodies of rock. There, the magma cools and hardens into a mass of igneous rock called an intrusion. An intrusion is always younger than the rock layers around and beneath it. Geologists study where intrusions and extrusions formed in relation to other rock layers. This helps geologists understand the relative ages of the different types of rock.

6. The topic of the above three paragraphs is "igneous rock." What is the central idea?

Clues From Faults   More clues come from the study of faults, a break in Earth's crust. Forces inside Earth cause movement of the rock on opposite sides of a fault.

A fault is always younger than the rock it cuts through. To determine the relative age of a fault, geologists find the relative age of the youngest layer cut by the fault.

Movements along faults can make it harder for geologists to determine the relative ages of rock layers. Rock layers no longer line up because of movement along the fault.

7. Analyze how extrusions, intrusions, and faults are similar.

Gaps in the Geologic Record   The geologic record of sedimentary rock layers is not always complete. Deposition slowly builds layer upon layer of sedimentary rock. But some of these layers may erode away, exposing an older rock surface. The deposition begins again, building new rock layers.

The surface where new rock layers meet a rock surface beneath them is called an unconformity. An unconformity is a gap in the geologic record. An unconformity shows where some rock layers have been lost because of erosion.

8. What evidence in the text strongly supports that determining the relative age of rocks is a difficult and complex process?

Using Fossils to Date Rocks

To date rock layers, geologists first give a relative age to a layer of rock at one location. Then they can give the same age to matching layers of rock at other locations.

Certain fossils, called **index** fossils, help geologists match rock layers. To be useful as an index fossil, a fossil must be widely distributed and represent a type of organism that existed only briefly. A fossil is considered widely distributed if it occurs in many different areas. Geologists look for index fossils in layers of rock. Index fossils are useful because they tell the relative ages of the rock layers in which they occur.

9. What is the meaning of *index* in the context of the above passage?

Geologists use particular types of organisms as index fossils, for example, certain types of ammonites. Ammonites were a group of hard-shelled animals that evolved in shallow seas more than 500 million years ago. They became extinct about 65 million years ago.

Ammonite fossils make good index fossils for two reasons. First, they are widely distributed. Second, many different kinds of ammonites evolved and then became extinct after a few million years.

Geologists can identify the different types of ammonites through differences in the structure of their shells. Based on these differences, geologists can identify the rock layers in which a particular type of ammonite fossil occurs.

Using Index Fossils

Scientists use index fossils to match up rock layers at locations that may be far apart. An index fossil occurs in only one time period but in several different locations.

   10. **Analyze how an index fossil helps date rocks that are in two different places.**

   Summarize what the text says about how scientists determine the relative age of rocks.

Earth Science, Part III

Radioactive Dating

Read to learn how scientists can determine the age of rocks.

In Australia, scientists have found sedimentary rocks that contain some of the world's oldest fossils. These are fossils of stromatolites, which are the remains of reefs built by organisms similar to present-day bacteria. Sediment **eventually** covered these reefs. As the sediment changed to rock, so did the reefs. Using absolute dating, scientists have determined that some stromatolites are more than 3 billion years old. To understand absolute dating, you need to learn more about the chemistry of rocks.

1. What is the meaning of *eventually* in the context of the above paragraph?

Radioactive Decay

Rocks are a form of matter. All the matter you see, including rocks, is made of tiny particles called atoms. When all the atoms in a particular type of matter are the same, the matter is an element. Carbon, oxygen, iron, lead, and potassium are just some of the more than 110 currently known elements.

Most elements are stable. They do not change under normal conditions. But some elements exist in forms that are unstable. Over time, these elements break down, or decay, by **releasing** particles and energy in a process called radioactive decay. These unstable elements are said to be radioactive. During radioactive decay, the atoms of one element break down to form atoms of another element.

Radioactive elements occur naturally in igneous rocks. Scientists use the rate at which these elements decay to calculate the rock's age. You calculate your age based on a specific day, your birthday. What's the "birthday" of a rock? For an igneous rock, that "birthday" is when it first hardens to become rock. As a radioactive element within the igneous rock decays, it changes into another element. So the composition of the rock changes slowly over time. The amount of the radioactive element goes down. But the amount of the new element goes up.

The rate of decay of each radioactive element is constant; it never changes. This rate of decay is the element's half-life. The half-life of a radioactive element is the time it takes for half of the radioactive atoms to decay.

2. The topic of the above two paragraphs is "radioactive decay." What is the central idea?

3. What is the meaning of *releasing* in the context of the above section?

4. Analyze how the composition of an igneous rock changes over time.

Determining Absolute Ages

Geologists use radioactive dating to determine the absolute ages of rocks. In radioactive dating, scientists first determine the amount of a radioactive element in a rock. Then they compare that amount with the amount of the stable element into which the radioactive element decays.

Potassium-Argon Dating

Scientists often date rocks using potassium-40. This form of potassium decays to stable argon-40 and has a half-life of 1.3 billion years. Potassium-40 is useful in dating the most ancient rocks because of its long half-life.

Carbon-14 Dating

A radioactive form of carbon is carbon-14. All plants and animals contain carbon, including some carbon-14. As plants and animals grow, carbon atoms are added to their tissues. After an organism dies, no more carbon is added. But the carbon-14 in the organism's body decays. It changes to stable nitrogen-14. To determine the age of a sample, scientists measure the amount of carbon-14 that is left in the organism's remains. From this amount, they can determine its absolute age. Carbon-14 has been used to date fossils such as frozen mammoths, as well as pieces of wood and bone. Carbon-14 even has been used to date the skeletons of prehistoric humans.

Carbon-14 is very useful in dating materials from plants and animals that lived up to about 50,000 years ago. Carbon-14 has a half-life of only 5,730 years. For this reason, it can't be used to date very ancient fossils or rocks. The amount of carbon-14 left would be too small to measure accurately.

5. The topic of the above two paragraphs is "carbon-14 dating." What is the central idea?

6. What evidence in the text strongly supports that the content of a fossil is different from its content when it was living?

7. Analyze one way in which potassium-argon dating and carbon-14 dating are alike and one way in which they are different.

Radioactive Dating of Rock Layers

Radioactive dating works well for igneous rocks, but not for sedimentary rocks. The rock particles in sedimentary rocks are from other rocks, all of different ages. Radioactive dating would provide the age of the particles. It would not provide the age of the sedimentary rock.

How, then, do scientists date sedimentary rock layers? They date the igneous intrusions and extrusions near the sedimentary rock layers.

8. Analyze why it is difficult to determine the absolute age of a sedimentary rock.

The Geologic Time Scale

Imagine squeezing Earth's 4.6-billion-year history into a 24-hour day. Earth forms at midnight. About seven hours later, the earliest one-celled organisms appear. Over the next 14 hours, simple, soft-bodied organisms such as jellyfish and worms develop. A little after 9:00 P.M., 21 hours later, larger, more complex organisms evolve in the oceans. Reptiles and insects first appear about an hour after that. Dinosaurs arrive just before 11:00 P.M., but are extinct by 11:30 P.M. Modern humans don't appear until less than a second before midnight!

Months, years, or even centuries aren't very helpful for thinking about Earth's long history. Because the time span of Earth's past is so great, geologists use the geologic time scale to show Earth's history. The geologic time scale is a record of the life forms and geologic events in Earth's history.

Scientists first developed the geologic time scale by studying rock layers and index fossils worldwide. With this information, scientists placed Earth's rocks in order by relative age. Later, radioactive dating helped determine the absolute age of the divisions in the geologic time scale.

9. What evidence in the text strongly supports that humans have not been part of most of Earth's history?

Divisions of Geologic Time

As geologists studied the fossil record, they found major changes in life forms at certain times. They used these changes to mark where one unit of geologic time ends and the next begins. Therefore the divisions of the geologic time scale depend on events in the history of life on Earth.

When speaking of the past, what names do you use for different spans of time? You probably use names such as century, decade, year, month, week, and day. Scientists use similar divisions for the geologic time scale.

Geologic time begins with a long span of time called Precambrian Time. Precambrian Time, which covers about 88 percent of Earth's history, ended 544 million years ago. After Precambrian Time, the basic units of the geologic time scale are eras and periods. Geologists divide the time between Precambrian Time and the present into three long units of time called eras. They are the Paleozoic Era, the Mesozoic Era, and the Cenozoic Era.

Eras are subdivided into units of geologic time called periods. The Mesozoic Era includes three periods: the Triassic Period, the Jurassic Period, and the Cretaceous Period.

The names of many of the geologic periods come from places around the world where geologists first described the rocks and fossils of that period. For example, the name Cambrian refers to Cambria, the old Roman name for Wales.

10. Which text structure best explains how the author organized the above passage?

_____ description of important features

_____ explanation of steps in a sequence

_____ account of cause and effect

_____ explanation of problem and solution

_____ comparison/contrast of two or more things

Give a reason from the text for your answer. For example, if you choose description, tell what is being described. For sequence, list one or two steps. For cause and effect, state a cause or effect mentioned in the text. For problem and solution, tell what the problem is or describe the solution. For comparison, tell what is being compared or contrasted.

Summarize what the text says about the process of radioactive decay in rocks.

Life Is Cellular

Read to learn about the discovery of cells and how cell theory was developed. Read to distinguish between two broad categories of cells: prokaryotes and eukaryotes.

The Discovery of the Cell

Cell Theory   "Seeing is believing," an old saying goes. It would be hard to find a better example of that than the discovery of the cell. Without the instruments to make them visible, cells remained out of sight and, therefore, out of mind for most of human history. All of this changed with a dramatic advance of technology—the invention of the microscope.

In the late 1500s, eyeglass makers in Europe discovered that using several glass lenses in combination could magnify even the smallest objects to make them easy to see. Before long they had built the first true microscopes from these lenses.

In 1865, Robert Hooke used an early compound microscope to look at a nonliving thin slice of cork, a plant material. Under the microscope, cork seemed to be made of thousands of tiny empty chambers. Hooke called these chambers "cells" because they reminded him of a monastery's tiny rooms which were called cells.

Around the same time, Anton van Leewenhoek used a single-lens microscope to observe pond water and other things. To his amazement, the microscope revealed a fantastic world of tiny living organisms that seemed to be everywhere.

Soon after van Leeuwenhock, observations by scientists made it clear that cells are the basic unit of life. In 1838, Matthias Schleiden concluded that all plants are made of cells. The next year Theodor Schwann stated that all animals are made of cells. In 1855, Rudolf Virchow concluded that new cells can be produced only from a division of existing cells. These discoveries, **confirmed** by many biologists, are summarized in the cell theory, a **fundamental** concept of biology. The cell theory states: All living things are made of cells. Cells are the basic units of structure and function in living things. New cells are produced from existing cells.

1. The topic of the above section is "cell theory." What is the central idea?

2. Analyze how evidence from various scientists supported cell theory. Include at least two different forms of evidence in your analysis.

3. What is the meaning of *confirmed* in the context of the above passage?

4. What is the meaning of *fundamental* in the context of the above passage?

5. Which text structure best explains how the author organized the above passage?

    ____ description of important features

    ____ explanation of steps in a sequence

    ____ account of cause and effect

    ____ explanation of problem and solution

    ____ comparison/contrast of two or more things

    Give a reason from the text for your answer. For example, if you choose description, tell what is being described. For sequence, list one or two steps. For cause and effect, state a cause or effect mentioned in the text. For problem and solution, tell what the problem is or describe the solution. For comparison, tell what is being compared or contrasted.

Exploring Cells   Modern biologists still use microscopes to explore the cell. But today's researchers use technology more powerful than the pioneers of biology could ever have imagined. We know

now that cells come in an amazing variety of shapes and sizes. Despite their differences, all cells, at some point in their lives, contain DNA, the molecule that carries biological information. In addition, all cells are surrounded by a thin flexible barrier called a cell membrane. There are other similarities as well.

Cells fall into two broad categories, depending on whether they contain a nucleus. The nucleus is a large membrane-enclosed structure that contains genetic material in the form of DNA and controls many of the cell's activities. Eukaryotes are cells that enclose their DNA in nuclei. Prokaryotes are cells that do not enclose DNA in nuclei.

6. The topic of the above two paragraphs is "exploring cells." What is the central idea?

Prokaryotes   Prokaryotic cells are generally smaller and simpler than eukaryotic cells, although there are many exceptions to this rule. Prokaryotic cells do not separate their genetic material within a nucleus. Despite their simplicity, prokaryotes carry out every activity associated with living things. They grow, reproduce, respond to the environment, and, in some cases, glide along surfaces or swim through liquids. The organisms we call bacteria are prokaryotes.

Eukaryotes   Eukaryotic cells are generally larger and more complex than prokaryotic cells. Most eukaryotic cells contain dozens of structures and internal membranes, and many are highly specialized. In eukaryotic cells, the nucleus separates the genetic material from the rest of the cell. Eukaryotes display great variety: some, like the ones commonly called "protists," live solitary lives as unicellular organisms; other eukaryotic cells form large, multicellular organisms—plants, animals, and fungi.

7. Analyze how prokaryotic cells and eukaryotic cells are alike and how they are different.

Cell Organization

The Role of the Cell Nucleus   The eukaryotic cell is a complex and busy place. But if you look closely at eukaryotic cells, patterns begin to emerge. For example, it's easy to divide each cell into two major parts: the nucleus and the cytoplasm. The cytoplasm is the portion of the cell outside the nucleus. The nucleus and cytoplasm work together in the business of life. Prokaryotic cells have cytoplasm too, even though they do not have a nucleus.

Many components of cells act like specialized organs. Because of this, they are known as organelles, literally "little organisms." Understanding what each organelle does helps us understand the cell as a whole.

Comparing the Cell to a Factory   In some respects, the eukaryotic cell is much like a living version of a modern factory. The different organelles of the cell can be compared to the specialized machines and assembly lines of the factory. In addition, cells, like factories, follow instructions and produce products. This comparison will help us understand how cells work.

The Nucleus   In the same way that the main office controls a large factory, the nucleus is the control center of the cell. The nucleus contains nearly all the cell's DNA and, with it, the coded instructions for making proteins and other important molecules. Prokaryotic cells lack a nucleus, but they do have DNA that contains the same kinds of instructions.

The nucleus is surrounded by a nuclear envelope composed of two membranes. The nuclear envelope is dotted with thousands of nuclear pores, which allow material to move into and out of the nucleus. Like messages, instructions, and blueprints moving in and out of a factory's main office, a steady stream of proteins, RNA, and other molecules move through the nuclear pores to and from the rest of the cell.

Chromosomes, which carry the cell's genetic information, are also found in the nucleus. Most of the time, the threadlike chromosomes are spread throughout the nucleus in the form of chromatin—a complex of DNA bound to proteins. When a cell divides, its DNA condenses into a packed chromosome and can be seen under a microscope. Most nuclei also contain a small dense region known as the nucleolus. The nucleolus is where the assembly of ribosomes begins. Ribosomes assemble protein by following instructions found on the DNA strand.

8. Analyze why the nucleus is a very important part of the cell. Offer two examples.

9. What evidence in the text strongly supports that cells can function without a nucleus?

10. What evidence in the text strongly supports that Hooke's impression of a cell as an empty chamber was inaccurate? Give two kinds of text evidence.

Summarize the role of the nucleus in eukaryotic cells.

Life Science, Part II

Cell Structure

A eukaryotic cell is like a factory and the cell nucleus can be compared to a factory's main office. Read to learn about other parts of the cell and how the jobs they perform can be compared to different parts of a factory.

What are the functions of vacuoles, lysosomes, and the cytoskeleton?   Many of the organelles or "little organs" outside the nucleus of a eukaryotic cell have specific functions, or roles. Among them are structures called vacuoles, lysosomes, and cytoskeleton. These organelles represent the cellular factory's storage space, cleanup crew, and support structures.

Vacuoles and Vesicles   Every factory needs a place to store things, and, so does every cell. Many cells contain large, saclike, membrane-enclosed structures called vacuoles. Vacuoles store materials like water, salts, proteins, and carbohydrates. In many plant cells, there is a single large central vacuole filled with liquid. The pressure of the central vacuole in these cells increases their **rigidity,** making it possible for plants to support heavy structures, such as leaves and flowers.

Vacuoles are also found in some unicellular organisms and in some animals. In addition, nearly all eukaryotic cells contain smaller membrane-enclosed structures called vesicles. Vesicles store and move materials between cell organelles, as well as to and from the cell surface.

1. What is the meaning of *rigidity* in the context of the above passage?

Lysosomes   Even the neatest, cleanest factory needs a cleanup crew, and that's where lysosomes come in. Lysosomes are small organelles filled with enzymes. Lysosomes break down lipids, carbohydrates, and proteins into small molecules that can be used by the rest of the cell. They are also involved in breaking down organelles that have outlived their usefulness. Lysosomes perform the vital function of removing "junk" that might otherwise **accumulate** and clutter up the cell. A number of serious human diseases can be traced to lysosomes that fail to function properly.

2. What is the meaning of *accumulate* in the context of the above passage?

The Cytoskeleton   As you know, a factory building is supported by steel or cement beams and by columns that hold up its walls and roof. Eukaryotic cells are given their shape and internal organization by a network of protein filaments known as the cytoskeleton. Certain parts of the cytoskeleton also help transport materials between different parts of the cell much like the conveyor belts that carry materials from one part of a factory to another. Cytoskeletal components may also be involved in moving the entire cell.

Microfilaments   Microfilaments are threadlike structures made up of a protein called actin. They form extensive networks in some cells and produce a tough flexible framework that supports the cell. Microfilaments also help cells move. Microfilament assembly and disassembly are responsible for the cytoplasmic movements that allow amoebas and other cells to crawl along surfaces.

Microtubules   Microtubules are hollow structures made up of proteins known as tubulins. In many cells, they play critical roles in maintaining cell shape. Microtubules are also important in cell division. In animal cells, organelles called centrioles are also formed from tubulins. Centrioles are located near the nucleus and help organize cell division. Centrioles are not found in plant cells.

Microtubules also help build projections from the cell surface known as cilia and flagella that enable cells to swim rapidly through liquid. Small cross-bridges between the microtubules use chemical energy to pull on, or slide along, the microtubules, producing controlled movements.

3. The topic of the above section is "microtubules." What is the central idea?

4. Analyze how microfilaments and microtubules are alike. Offer two examples.

5. Analyze why protein is a critical element in the cytoskeleton. Offer two examples.

Organelles That Build Proteins

What organelles help make and transport proteins?   Life is a dynamic process, and living things are always working, building new molecules all the time, especially proteins, which catalyze chemical reactions and make up important structures in the cell. Because proteins carry out so many of the essential functions of living things, a big part of the cell is devoted to their production and distribution.

Ribosomes   One of the most important jobs carried out in the cellular "factory" is making proteins. Proteins are assembled on ribosomes. Ribosomes are small particles of RNA and protein found throughout the cytoplasm in all cells. Ribosomes produce proteins by following coded instructions that come from DNA. Each ribosome, in its own way, is like a small machine in a factory, turning out proteins on orders that come from its DNA "boss."

Endoplasmic Reticulum   Eukaryotic cells contain an internal membrane system known as the endoplasmic reticulum or ER. The endoplasmic reticulum is where lipid or fatty components of the cell membrane are assembled, along with protein and other materials that are exported from the cell.

The portion of the ER involved in the synthesis of proteins is called rough endoplasmic reticulum, or rough ER. It is given this name because of the ribosomes found on its surface. Newly made proteins leave these ribosomes and are inserted into the rough ER, where they may be chemically modified.

Proteins made on the rough ER include those that will be released, or secreted, from the cell as well as many membrane proteins and proteins destined for other specialized locations within the cell.

The other portion of the ER is known as smooth endoplasmic reticulum (smooth ER) because ribosomes are not found on its surface. In many cells, the smooth ER contains collections of enzymes that perform specialized tasks, including the synthesis of membrane lipids and the detoxification of drugs. Liver cells, which play a key role in detoxifying drugs, often contain large amounts of smooth ER.

6. The topic of the above section is "endoplasmic reticulum." What is the central idea?

7. Which text structure best explains how the author organized the above passage?

_____   description of important features

_____   explanation of steps in a sequence

_____   account of cause and effect

_____   explanation of problem and solution

_____   comparison/contrast of two or more things

Give a reason from the text for your answer. For example, if you choose description, tell what is being described. For sequence, list one or two steps. For cause and effect, state a cause or effect mentioned in the text. For problem and solution, tell what the problem is or describe the solution. For comparison, tell what is being compared or contrasted.

8. Analyze how rough ER and smooth ER are alike and different.

9. What evidence in the text strongly supports that ribosomes may be the most important part of a cell?

Golgi Apparatus   In eukaryotic cells, proteins produced in the rough ER move next into an organelle called the Golgi apparatus, which appears as a stack of flattened membranes. As proteins leave the rough ER, molecular "address tags" get them to the right destinations. As these tags are "read" by the cell, the proteins are bundled into tiny vesicles that bud from the ER and carry them to the Golgi apparatus. The Golgi apparatus modifies, sorts, and packages proteins and other materials from the endoplasmic reticulum for storage in the cell or release outside the cell. The Golgi apparatus is somewhat like a customization shop, where the finishing touches are put on proteins before they are ready to leave the "factory." From the Golgi apparatus, proteins are "shipped" to their final destination inside or outside the cell.

10. What evidence in the text strongly supports that the Golgi apparatus functions like FedEx, UPS, or the postal service? Give two reasons.

Summarize how organelles are similar to parts of a factory.

Organelles That Capture and Release Energy

Read to learn how cell organelles or "little organs" provide energy to the cell and how cells are protected by a cell wall and cell membrane.

What are the functions of chloroplasts and mitochondria?   All living things require a source of energy. Factories are hooked up to the local power company, but how do cells get energy? Most cells are powered by food molecules that are built using energy from the sun.

Chloroplasts   Plants and some other organisms contain chloroplasts. Chloroplasts are biological equivalents of solar power plants. Chloroplasts capture the energy from sunlight and convert it into food that contains chemical energy in a process called photosynthesis. Two membranes surround chloroplasts. Inside the organelle are large stacks of other membranes, which contain the green pigment molecule, chlorophyll.

Mitochondria   Nearly all eukaryotic cells, including plants, contain mitochondria. Mitochondria are the power plants of the cell. Mitochondria **convert** the chemical energy stored in food into compounds that are more convenient for the cell to use. Like chloroplasts, two membranes—an outer membrane and an inner membrane—enclose mitochondria. The inner membrane is folded up inside the organelle.

One of the most interesting **aspects** of mitochondria is the way in which they are inherited. In humans, all or nearly all of our mitochondria come from the cytoplasm of the ovum, or egg cell. This means that when your relatives are discussing which side of the family should take credit for your best characteristics, you can tell them where you got your mitochondria!

1. What is the meaning of *convert* in the context of the above passage?

2. What is the meaning of *aspects* in the context of the above passage?

3. Analyze how chloroplasts and mitochondria are alike. Offer two examples.

4. What evidence in the text strongly supports that chloroplasts and mitochondria function like power plants? Give two kinds of evidence.

Cellular Boundaries

What is the function of the cell membrane?   A working factory needs walls and a roof to protect it from the environment outside, and also to serve as a barrier that keeps its products safe and secure until they are ready to be shipped out. Cells have similar needs, and they meet them in a similar way. As you have learned, all cells are surrounded by a barrier known as the cell membrane. Many cells, including most prokaryotes, also produce a strong supporting layer around the membrane known as a cell wall.

Cell Walls   Many organisms have cell walls in addition to cell membranes. The main function of the cell wall is to support, shape, and protect the cell. Most prokaryotes and many eukaryotes have cell walls. Animal cells do not have cell walls. Cell walls lie outside the cell membrane. Most cell walls are porous enough to allow water, oxygen, carbon dioxide, and certain other substances to pass through easily.

Cell walls provide much of the strength needed for plants to stand against the force of gravity. In trees and other large plants, nearly all of the tissue we call wood is made up of cell walls. The cellulose fiber used for paper as well as the lumber used for building comes from these walls. So if you are reading these words off a sheet of paper from a book resting on a wooden desk, you've got the products of cell walls all around you.

5. The topic of the above two paragraphs is "cell walls." What is the central idea?

6. Which text structure best explains how the author organized the above passage?

____ description of important features

____ explanation of steps in a sequence

____ account of cause and effect

____ explanation of problem and solution

____ comparison/contrast of two or more things

Give a reason from the text for your answer. For example, if you choose description, tell what is being described. For sequence, list one or two steps. For cause and effect, state a cause or effect mentioned in the text. For problem and solution, tell what the problem is or describe the solution. For comparison, tell what is being compared or contrasted.

Cell Membranes   All cells contain cell membranes, which almost always are made up of a double-layered sheet called a lipid bilayer. The lipid bilayer gives cell membranes a flexible structure that forms a strong barrier between the cell and its surroundings. The cell membrane regulates what enters and leaves the cell and also protects and supports the cell.

7. Analyze how cell walls and cell membranes are different. Offer two examples.

The Properties of Lipids   The layered structure of cell membranes reflects the chemical properties of the lipids that make them up. Many lipids have oily fatty acid chains attached to chemical groups that interact strongly with water. In the language of a chemist, the fatty acid portions of this kind of lipid are hydrophobic or "water-hating," while the opposite end of the molecule is hydrophilic or "water-loving." When these lipids, including the phospholipids that are common in animal cell membranes, are mixed with water, their hydrophobic fatty acid "tails" cluster together while their hydrophilic "heads" are attracted to water. A lipid bilayer is the result. The head groups of lipids in a bilayer are exposed to the outside of the cell, while the fatty acid tails form an oily layer inside the membrane that keeps water out.

8. Analyze how the lipid bilayer is formed from two different lipids.

The Fluid Mosaic Model   Embedded in the lipid bilayer of most cell membranes are protein molecules. Carbohydrate molecules are attached to many of these proteins. Because the proteins embedded in the lipid bilayer can move around and "float" among the lipids, and because so many different kinds of molecules make up the cell membrane, scientists describe the cell membrane as a "fluid mosaic." A mosaic is a kind of art that involves bits and pieces of different colors or materials. What are all these different molecules doing? Some of the proteins form channels and pumps that help to move material across the cell membrane. Many of the carbohydrate molecules act like chemical identification cards, allowing individual cells to identify one another. Some proteins attach directly to the cytoskeleton, enabling cells to respond to their environment by using their membranes to help move or change shape.

As you know, some things are allowed to enter and leave a factory, and some are not. The same is true for living cells. Although many substances can cross biological membranes, some are too large or too strongly charged to cross the lipid bilayer. If a substance is able to cross a membrane, the membrane is said to be permeable to it. A membrane is impermeable to substances that cannot pass across it. Most biological membranes are selectively permeable, meaning that some substances can pass across them and others cannot. Selectively permeable membranes are also called semipermeable membranes.

9. The topic of the above two paragraphs is "the cell membrane." What is the central idea?

10. What evidence in the text strongly supports that different molecules in the lipid bilayer have different functions?

Summarize how chloroplasts and mitochondria can be compared to power plants.

The Vast World Ocean

Read to learn about our oceans and how the ocean floor is studied.

How deep is the ocean? How much of Earth is covered by the global ocean? What does the ocean floor look like? Humans have long been interested in finding answers to these questions. However, it was not until relatively recently that these simple questions could be answered. Suppose, for example, that all of the water were drained from the ocean. What would we see? Plains? Mountains? Canyons? Plateaus? You may be surprised to find that the ocean conceals all of these features, and more.

The Blue Planet   The "blue planet" or the "water planet" are appropriate nicknames for Earth. Nearly 71 percent of Earth's surface is covered by the global ocean. Although the ocean makes up a much greater percentage of Earth's surface than the continents, it has only been since the late 1800s that the ocean became an important focus of study. New technologies have allowed scientists to collect large amounts of data about the oceans. As technology has advanced, the field of oceanography has grown. Oceanography is a science that draws on the methods and knowledge of geology, chemistry, physics, and biology to study all aspects of the world ocean.

Geography of the Oceans   The area of Earth is about 510 million square kilometers. Of this total, approximately 360 million square kilometers, or 71 percent, is represented by oceans and smaller seas such as the Mediterranean Sea and the Caribbean Sea. Continents and islands comprise the remaining 29 percent, or 150 million square kilometers. The world ocean can be divided into four main ocean basins—the Pacific Ocean, the Atlantic Ocean, the Indian Ocean, and the Arctic Ocean.

The Pacific Ocean is the largest ocean. In fact, it is the largest single geographic feature on Earth. It covers more than half of the ocean surface area on Earth. It is also the world's deepest ocean, with an average depth of 3940 meters.

The Atlantic Ocean is about half the size of the Pacific Ocean, and is not quite as deep. It is a relatively narrow ocean compared to the Pacific. The Atlantic and Pacific Oceans are bounded to the east and west by continents.

The Indian Ocean is slightly smaller than the Atlantic Ocean, but it has about the same average depth. Unlike the Pacific and Atlantic oceans, the Indian Ocean is located almost entirely in the southern hemisphere.

The Arctic Ocean is about 7 percent of the size of the Pacific Ocean. It is only a little more than one-quarter as deep as the rest of the oceans.

1. Which text structure best explains how the author organized the above passage?

    ____   description of important features

    ____   explanation of steps in a sequence

    ____   account of cause and effect

    ____   explanation of problem and solution

    ____   comparison/contrast of two or more things

    Give a reason from the text for your answer. For example, if you choose description, tell what is being described. For sequence, list one or two steps. For cause and effect, state a cause or effect mentioned in the text. For problem and solution, tell what the problem is or describe the solution. For comparison, tell what is being compared or contrasted.

2. Analyze how the Atlantic Ocean basin differs from the Pacific Ocean basin with regard to both size and depth.

Mapping the Ocean Floor   If all the water were drained from the ocean basins, a variety of features would be seen. These features include chains of volcanoes, tall mountain ranges, trenches, and large submarine plateaus. The topography of the ocean floor is as diverse as that of continents.

An understanding of ocean-floor features came with the development of techniques to measure the depth of the oceans. Bathymetry is the measurement of ocean depths and the charting of the shape or topography of the ocean floor.

The first understanding of the ocean floor's varied topography did not unfold until the historic three-and-a-half-year voyage of the HMS Challenger. From December 1872 to May 1876, the Challenger expedition made the first—and perhaps still the most comprehensive—study of the global ocean ever attempted by one agency. The 127,500 kilometer trip took the ship and its crew of scientists to every ocean except the Arctic. Throughout the voyage, they sampled various ocean properties. They measured water depth by lowering a long, weighted line overboard. Today's technology—particularly sonar, satellites, and submersibles—allows scientists to study the ocean floor in a more efficient and precise manner than ever before.

   3. What evidence in the text strongly supports that features of the ocean floor resemble features on land? Give two examples.

Sonar   In the 1920s, a technological breakthrough occurred with the invention of sonar, a type of electronic depth-sounding equipment. Sonar is an acronym for sound navigation and ranging. It is also referred to as echo sounding. Sonar works by transmitting sound waves toward the ocean bottom. With simple sonar, a sensitive receiver intercepts the echo reflected from the bottom. Then a clock precisely measures the time interval to fractions of a second. Depth can be calculated from the speed of sound waves in water—about 1500 meters per second—and the time required for the energy pulse to reach the ocean floor and return. The depths determined from continuous monitoring of these echoes are plotted. In this way a profile of the ocean floor is obtained. A chart of the seafloor can be produced by combining these profiles.

In the last few decades, researchers have designed even more sophisticated sonar to map the ocean floor. In contrast to simple sonar, multibeam sonar uses more than one sound source and listening device. This technique obtains a profile of a narrow strip of ocean floor rather than obtaining the depth of a single point every few seconds. These profiles are recorded every few seconds as the research vessel advances. When a ship uses multibeam sonar to make a map of a section of ocean floor, the ship travels through the area in a regularly spaced back-and-forth pattern. Not surprisingly, this method is known as "mowing the lawn."

   4. The topic of the above two paragraphs is "sonar." What is the central idea?

Satellites   Measuring the shape of the ocean surface from space is another technological breakthrough that has led to a better understanding of the ocean floor. After **compensating** for waves, tides, currents, and atmospheric effects, scientists discovered that the ocean surface is not perfectly flat. This is because gravity attracts water toward regions where massive ocean floor features occur. Therefore, mountains and ridges produce elevated areas on the ocean surface. Features such as canyons and trenches cause slight **depressions**.

The differences in ocean-surface height caused by ocean floor features are not visible to the human eye. However, satellites are able to measure these small differences by bouncing microwaves off the ocean surface. Outgoing radar pulses are reflected back to a satellite. The height of the ocean surface can be calculated by knowing the satellite's exact position. Devices on satellites can measure variations in sea-surface height as small as 3 to 6 centimeters. This type of data has added greatly to the knowledge of ocean-floor topography. Cross-checked with traditional sonar depth measurements, the data are used to produce detailed ocean-floor maps.

   5. The topic of the above two paragraphs is "satellites." What is the central idea?

   6. Analyze how sonar technologies are different from satellite technologies. Offer two examples.

7. What is the meaning of *compensating* in the context of the above passage?

8. What is the meaning of *depressions* in the context of the above passage?

Submersibles   A submersible is a small underwater craft used for deep-sea research. Submersibles are used to collect **data** about areas of the ocean that were previously unreachable by humans. Submersibles are equipped with a number of instruments ranging from thermometers to cameras to pressure gauges. The operators of submersibles can record video and photos of previously unknown creatures that live in the abyss. They can collect water samples and sediment samples for analysis.

The first submersible was used in 1934 by William Beebe. He descended to a depth of 923 meters off of Bermuda in a steel sphere that was tethered or attached to a ship. Since that time, submersibles have become more sophisticated. In 1960, Jacques Piccard descended in the untethered submersible *Trieste* to 10,912 meters below the ocean surface into the Mariana Trench. *Alvin* and *Sea Cliff II* are two other manned submersibles used for deep-sea research. *Alvin* can reach depths of 4000 meters, and *Sea Cliff II* can reach 6000 meters.

Today, many submersibles are unmanned and operated remotely by computers. These remotely operated vehicles (ROVs) can remain under water for long periods. They collect data, record video, use sonar, and collect sample organisms with remotely operated arms.

9. What evidence in the text besides depth strongly supports that Piccard's descent in a submersible was more dangerous than the descent of Beebe?

10. Analyze how the use of sonar and submersibles are alike and different.

Summarize what the text says about how scientists study the ocean floor.

Earth Sciences, Part II

Ocean Floor Features

Read about the characteristics and features of three major regions of the ocean floor.

Oceanographers studying the topography of the ocean floor have divided it into three major regions. The ocean floor regions are the continental margins, the ocean basin floor, and the mid-ocean ridge. Scientists have discovered that each of these regions has its own unique characteristics and features.

Continental Margins

The zone of transition between a continent and the adjacent ocean basin floor is known as the continental margin. In the Atlantic Ocean, thick layers of undisturbed sediment cover the continental margin. This region has very little volcanic or earthquake activity. This is because the continental margins in the Atlantic Ocean are not associated with plate boundaries, unlike the continental margins of the Pacific Ocean. In the Pacific Ocean, oceanic crust is plunging beneath continental crust. This force results in a narrow continental margin that experiences both volcanic activity and earthquakes.

1. What evidence in the text strongly supports that the Atlantic continental margin is passive, whereas the Pacific continental margin is active? Give two forms of evidence.

Continental Shelf   What if you were to begin an underwater journey eastward across the Atlantic Ocean? The first area of ocean floor you would encounter is the continental shelf. The continental shelf is the gently sloping submerged surface extending from the shoreline. The shelf is almost nonexistent along some coastlines. However, the shelf may extend seaward as far as 1500 kilometers along other coastlines. On average, the continental shelf is about 80 kilometers wide and 130 meters deep at its seaward edge. The average steepness of the shelf is equal to a drop of only about 2 meters per kilometer. The slope is so slight that to the human eye it appears to be a horizontal surface.

Continental shelves have economic and political significance. Continental shelves contain important mineral deposits, large reservoirs of oil and natural gas, and huge sand and gravel deposits. The waters of the continental shelf also contain important fishing grounds, which are significant sources of food.

Continental Slope   Marking the seaward edge of the continental shelf is the continental slope. This slope is steeper than the shelf, and it marks the boundary between continental crust and oceanic crust. Although the steepness of the continental slope varies greatly from place to place, it averages about 5 degrees. In some places the slope may exceed 25 degrees. The continental slope is a relatively narrow feature, averaging only about 20 kilometers in width.

Deep, steep-sided valleys known as submarine canyons are cut into the continental slope. These canyons may extend to the ocean basin floor. Most information suggests that submarine canyons have been eroded, at least in part, by turbidity currents. Turbidity currents are occasional movements of dense, sediment-rich water down the continental slope. They are created when sand and mud on the continental shelf and slope are disturbed—perhaps by an earthquake—and become suspended in the water. Because such muddy water is denser than normal seawater, it flows down the slope. As it flows down, it erodes and accumulates more sediment. Erosion from these muddy torrents is believed to be the major force in the formation of most submarine canyons. Narrow continental margins, such as the one located along the California coast, are marked with numerous submarine canyons.

Turbidity currents are known to be an important mechanism of sediment transport in the ocean. Turbidity currents erode submarine canyons and deposit sediments on the deep-ocean floor.

2. The topic of the above three paragraphs is "continental slope." What is the central idea?

Continental Rise   In regions where trenches do not exist, the steep continental slope merges into a more gradual incline known as the continental rise. Here the steepness of the slope drops to about 6 meters per kilometer. Whereas the width of the continental slope averages about 20 kilometers, the continental rise may be hundreds of kilometers wide.

3. Which text structure best explains how the author organized the above passages?

____ description of important features

____ explanation of steps in a sequence

____ account of cause and effect

____ explanation of problem and solution

____ comparison/contrast of two or more things

Give a reason from the text for your answer. For example, if you choose description, tell what is being described. For sequence, list one or two steps. For cause and effect, state a cause or effect mentioned in the text. For problem and solution, tell what the problem is or describe the solution. For comparison, tell what is being compared or contrasted.

4. Analyze how the continental shelf and the continental slope are different. Offer two examples.

5. Analyze how turbidity currents form submarine canyons by describing two steps in the process.

Ocean Basin Floor

Between the continental margin and mid-ocean ridge lies the ocean basin floor. The size of this region—almost 30 percent of Earth's surface—is comparable to the percentage of land above sea level. This region includes deep-ocean trenches, very flat areas known as abyssal plains, and tall volcanic peaks called seamounts and guyots.

Deep-Ocean Trenches   Deep-ocean trenches are long, narrow creases in the ocean floor that form the deepest parts of the ocean. Most trenches are located along the margins of the Pacific Ocean, and many exceed 10,000 meters in depth. A portion of one trench—the Challenger Deep in the Mariana Trench—has been measured at a record 11,022 meters below sea level. It is the deepest known place on Earth.

Trenches form at sites of plate convergence where one moving plate descends beneath another and plunges back into the mantle. Earthquakes and volcanic activity are associated with these regions. The large number of trenches and the volcanic activity along the margins of the Pacific Ocean give the region its nickname as the *Ring of Fire.*

Abyssal Plains   Abyssal plains are deep, extremely flat features. In fact, these regions are possibly the most level places on Earth. Abyssal plains have thick accumulations of fine sediment that have buried an otherwise rugged ocean floor. The sediments that make up abyssal plains are carried there by turbidity currents or deposited as a result of **suspended** sediments settling. Abyssal plains are found in all oceans of the world. However, the Atlantic Ocean has the most extensive abyssal plains because it has few trenches to catch sediment carried down the continental slope.

6. What is the meaning of *suspended* in the context of the above section?

7. What evidence in the text strongly supports that the absence of trenches plays a role in the formation of abyssal plains?

Seamounts and Guyots   The submerged volcanic peaks that dot the ocean floor are called seamounts. They are volcanoes that have not reached the ocean surface. These steep-sided cone-shaped peaks are found on the floors of all the oceans. However, the greatest number have been identified in the Pacific. Some seamounts form at volcanic hot spots. An example is the Hawaiian-Emperor Seamount chain. This chain stretches from the Hawaiian Islands to the Aleutian trench.

Once underwater volcanoes reach the surface, they form islands. Over time, running water and wave action erode these volcanic islands to near sea level. Over millions of years, the islands gradually sink and may disappear below the water surface. This process occurs as the moving plate slowly carries the islands away from the elevated oceanic ridge or hot spot where they originated. These once-active, now-submerged, flat-topped structures are called guyots.

8. The topic of the above section is "seamounts and guyots." What is the central idea?

Mid-Ocean Ridges

The mid-ocean ridge is found near the center of most ocean basins. It is an interconnected system of underwater mountains that have developed on newly formed ocean crust. This system is the longest topographic feature on Earth's surface. It **exceeds** 70,000 kilometers in length. The mid-ocean ridge winds through all major oceans similar to the way a seam winds over the surface of a baseball.

The term *ridge* may be misleading because the mid-ocean ridge is not narrow. It has widths from 1000 to 4000 kilometers and may occupy as much as one half of the total area of the ocean floor. The mid-ocean ridge is broken into segments. These are offset by large transform faults where plates slide past each other horizontally, resulting in shallow earthquakes.

9. What is the meaning of *exceed* in the context of the above section?

Seafloor Spreading   A high amount of volcanic activity takes place along the crest of the mid-ocean ridge. This activity is associated with seafloor spreading. Seafloor spreading occurs at divergent plate boundaries where two lithospheric plates are moving apart. New ocean floor is formed at mid-ocean ridges as magma rises between the diverging plates and cools.

Hydrothermal Vents   Hydrothermal vents form along mid-ocean ridges. These are zones where mineral-rich water, heated by the hot, newly-formed oceanic crust, escapes through cracks in oceanic crust into the water. As the super-heated, mineral-rich water comes in contact with the surrounding cold water, minerals containing metals such as sulfur, iron, copper, and zinc precipitate out and are deposited.

10. Analyze how volcanic activity changes the ocean floor. Offer two examples.

Summarize how the text describes trenches, abyssal plains, seamounts, and guyots.

Seafloor Sediments

Read to learn about the types of sediment that cover the seafloor
and resources that come from the seafloor.

Except for steep areas of the continental slope and the crest of the mid-ocean ridge, most of the ocean floor is covered with sediment. Some of this sediment has been deposited by turbidity currents which are sediment rich water that flows down the continental slope. The rest has slowly settled onto the seafloor from above. The thickness of ocean-floor sediments varies. In general, however, accumulations of sediment are about 500 to 1000 meters thick. Generally, coarser sediments, such as sand, cover the continental shelf and slope while finer sediments, such as clay, cover the deep-ocean floor.

Types of Seafloor Sediments

Ocean-floor sediments can be classified according to their origin into three broad categories: terrigenous sediments, biogenous sediments, and hydrogenous sediments. Ocean-floor sediments are usually mixtures of the various sediment types.

Terrigenous Sediment   Terrigenous sediment is sediment that originates on land. Terrigenous sediments consist primarily of mineral grains that were eroded from continental rocks and transported to the ocean. Larger particles such as gravel and sand usually settle rapidly near shore. Finer particles such as clay can take years to settle to the ocean floor and may be carried thousands of kilometers by ocean currents. Clay accumulates very slowly on the deep-ocean floor. To form a 1-centimeter abyssal clay layer, for example, requires as much as 50,000 years. In contrast, on the continental margins near the mouths of large rivers, terrigenous sediment accumulates rapidly and forms thick deposits.

Biogenous Sediment   Biogenous sediment is sediment that is biological in origin. Biogenous sediments consist of shells and skeletons of marine animals and algae. This debris is produced mostly by microscopic organisms living in surface waters. Once these organisms die, their hard shells sink, accumulating on the seafloor.

The most common biogenous sediment is calcareous ooze. Calcareous ooze is produced from the calcium carbonate shells of organisms. Calcareous ooze has the consistency of thick mud. When calcium carbonate shells slowly sink into deeper parts of the ocean, they begin to dissolve. In ocean water deeper than about 4500 meters, these shells completely dissolve before they reach the bottom. As a result, calcareous ooze does not accumulate in the deeper areas of ocean basins.

Other biogenous sediments include siliceous ooze that is composed primarily of the shells of single-celled algae and single-celled animals that have shells made out of silica. Phosphate-rich biogenous sediments come from the bones, teeth, and scales of fish and other marine organisms.

1. The topic of the above section is "biogenous sediment." What is the central idea?

2. Analyze how calcareous ooze and siliceous ooze are alike and different.

3. Analyze how terrigenous and biogenous sediment are alike and different.

Hydrogenous Sediment   Hydrogenous sediment **consists** of minerals that crystallize directly from ocean water through various chemical reactions. Hydrogenous sediments make up only a small portion of the overall sediment in the ocean. They do, however, have many different compositions and are distributed in many different environments.

Calcium carbonates form by precipitation directly from ocean water in warm climates. If this material is buried and hardens, a type of limestone rock forms.

Evaporites form where evaporation rates are high and there is restricted open-ocean circulation. As water evaporates from such areas, the remaining ocean water becomes saturated with dissolved minerals that then begin to precipitate. Collectively termed "salts," some evaporite minerals do taste salty, such as halite, or common table salt. Other salts do not taste salty, such as the calcium sulfate minerals anhydrite and gypsum.

4. What is the meaning of *consists* in the context of the above passage?

5. What evidence in the text strongly supports that all salts are suitable for cooking?

Resources from the Ocean Floor

The ocean floor is rich in mineral and energy resources. Recovering them, however, often involves technological challenges and high costs. As technology improves we are able to access some of these resources more efficiently.

Energy Resources

Most of the value of nonliving **resources** in the ocean comes from their use as energy products. Oil and natural gas are the main energy products currently being obtained from the ocean floor. Other **resources** have the potential to be used as a source of energy in the future.

Oil and Natural Gas   The ancient remains of microscopic organisms are the source of today's deposits of oil and natural gas. These organisms were buried within marine sediments before they could decompose. After millions of years of exposure to heat from Earth's interior and pressure from overlying rock, the remains were transformed into oil and natural gas. The percentage of world oil produced from offshore regions has increased from trace amounts in the 1930s to more than 30 percent today. Part of this increase is due to advances in the technology of offshore drilling platforms. One environmental concern about offshore petroleum exploration is the possibility of oil spills caused by accidental leaks during the drilling process.

Gas Hydrates   Gas hydrates are compact chemical structures made of water and natural gas. The most common type of natural gas is methane, which produces methane hydrate. Gas hydrates occur beneath permafrost areas on land and under the ocean floor at depths below 525 meters.

Most oceanic gas hydrates are created when bacteria break down organic matter trapped in ocean-floor sediments. The bacteria produce methane gas along with small amounts of ethane and propane. These gases combine with water in deep-ocean sediments in such a way that the gas is trapped inside a lattice-like cage of water molecules.

Vessels that have drilled into gas hydrates have brought up samples of mud mixed with chunks of gas hydrates. These chunks evaporate quickly when they are exposed to the relatively warm, low-pressure conditions at the ocean surface. Gas hydrates resemble chunks of ice but ignite when lit by a flame. The hydrates burn because methane and other flammable gases are released as gas hydrates evaporate.

An estimated 20 quadrillion cubic meters of methane are locked up in sediments containing gas hydrates. This amount is double the amount of Earth's known coal, oil, and natural gas reserves combined. One drawback to using gas hydrates as an energy source is that they rapidly break down at surface temperatures and pressures. In the future, however, these ocean-floor reserves of energy may help provide our energy needs.

6. The topic of the above section is "gas hydrates." What is the central idea?

7. Which text structure best explains how the author organized the above passage?

_____ description of important features

_____ explanation of steps in a sequence

_____ account of cause and effect

_____   explanation of problem and solution

_____   comparison/contrast of two or more things

Give a reason from the text or your answer. For example, if you choose description, tell what is being described. If you choose sequence, list one or two steps. For cause and effect, state a cause or effect mentioned in the text. For problem and solution, tell what the problem is or describe the solution. For comparison, tell what is being compared or contrasted.

8. Analyze the positive and negative aspects of mining gas hydrates.

Other Resources

Other major resources from the ocean floor include sand and gravel, evaporative salts, and manganese nodules.

Sand and Gravel   The offshore sand-and-gravel industry is second in economic value only to the petroleum industry. Sand and gravel, which include rock fragments that are washed out to sea and shells of marine organisms, are mined by offshore barges using suction devices. Sand and gravel are used for landfill, to fill in recreational beaches, and to make concrete.

   In some cases, materials of high economic value are associated with offshore sand and gravel deposits. These include gem-quality diamonds, sediments rich in tin, platinum, gold and titanium.

Manganese Nodules   Manganese nodules are hard lumps of manganese and other metals that precipitate around a smaller object. They contain high concentrations of manganese and iron, and smaller concentrations of copper, nickel, and cobalt, all of which have a variety of economic uses. With current technology, mining the deep-ocean floor for manganese nodules is possible but not economically profitable. Good locations for mining are limited; it is difficult to establish mining rights far from land and there are environmental concerns about disturbing large portions of the deep-ocean floor.

Evaporative Salts   When seawater evaporates, the salts increase in concentration until they can no longer remain dissolved. When the concentration becomes high enough, the salts precipitate out of solution and form salt deposits. These deposits can then be harvested. The most economically important salt is halite or common table salt. Halite is widely used for seasoning, curing, and preserving foods. It is also used in agriculture, in the clothing industry for dying fabric, and to de-ice roads.

9. What is the meaning of *resources* in the context of the above passage?

10. What evidence in the text strongly supports that ocean resources play an important role in our life? Offer two forms of evidence.

Summarize what the text says about the differences in three types of seafloor sediments.

Chapter
8 Teacher Answer Keys

Amelia and Eleanor Go for a Ride (Adapted)
by Pam Muñoz Ryan

1. **What does "birds of a feather" mean in the sentence, "Amelia and Eleanor were birds of a feather"?**

   Answer: *People who are alike*

   Standard 4: Determine the meaning of words and phrases as they are used in a text, including those that allude to significant characters found in mythology.

2. **Describe two ways that the author shows the similarities between Amelia and Eleanor. (2 pts.)**

   Answer: *The author describes that they both "loved the feeling of independence," and that "Eleanor was outspoken and determined and so was Amelia"* **or** *"Amelia was daring and liked to try things other women wouldn't even consider," and "Eleanor was the very same"* **or** *Both women were fun but also practical* **or** *They were both famous.*

   Standard 6: Compare and contrast the point of view from which stories are narrated.

3. **What is the central idea of the story so far?**

   Answer: *That there were two famous, independent women who were outspoken and daring and who were good friends.*

   Standard 2: Determine a central idea or theme of a text.

4. **Describe the setting of the story so far.**

   Answer: *The setting was a dinner in the White House* **or** *In the Red Room of the White House* **or** *Famous people were sitting at a dining room table.* Note: "The White House" isn't sufficient.

   Standard 3: Describe in depth a character, setting, or event in a story, drawing on specific details from the text.

5. **Using details from the story, provide one reason why there were reporters and photographers at the dinner.**

   Answer: *Because two famous people were getting together* **or** *Because Mrs. Roosevelt was the First Lady of the United States* **or** *Because Amelia was coming to give a speech.*

   Standard 1: Refer to details and examples in a text when drawing an inference.

6. **Using details from the story, provide evidence that Eleanor Roosevelt did not allow others to control her behavior.**

   Answer: *She didn't obey the Secret Service men who told her that the flight had not been approved* **or** *When the Secret Service men said, "This hasn't been approved," Eleanor said, "Nonsense! If Amelia Earhart can fly solo across the Atlantic Ocean, I can certainly take a short flight to Baltimore and back!"* **or** *The way it's typed with an exclamation point suggests she may be yelling.*

   Standard 1: Refer to details and examples in a text when drawing an inference.

7. **What does the phrase, "It's like sitting on top of the world!" mean in the paragraph above?**

   Answer: *Flying* **or** *That you can see everything* **or** *Being in complete control*

   Standard 4: Determine the meaning of words and phrases as they are used in a text, including those that allude to significant characters found in mythology.

8. **Describe the personality of Eleanor Roosevelt using two details from the text. (2 pts.)**

   Answer: *She was outspoken/determined/independent/brave/she didn't want anyone telling her what to do (any two)* **or** *She was daring because instead of going into the White House, she turned and took Amelia for a ride in her car.*

   Standard 3: Describe in depth a character, setting, or event in a story, drawing on specific details from the text.

9. **Describe how the author shows the similarity between the two women toward the end of the story.**

   Answer: *Amelia felt the same way about flying as Eleanor felt about driving* **or** *Both enjoyed these adventurous/fun activities* **or** *The author compared the feeling of flying to driving a fast car on a straightway road* **or** *After Eleanor is finished talking to the reporters "Amelia smiled. She knew just how Eleanor felt."*

Standard 6: Compare and contrast the point of view from which stories are narrated.

10. **What is the message or theme of this story?**

    Answer: *That independent women take risks and seek adventure* **or** *It shows women being independent* **or** *Be brave* **or** *Don't be scared to try something new*

    Standard 2: Determine a theme of a story, drama, or poem from details in the text

Summarize the story. The summary is evaluated by the number of elements of a story (e.g., character, initiating event, etc.) it contains. A good summary includes 70 percent of the elements listed in bold. A student must include at least one statement listed under a story element in order to receive credit for that element. Total possible = 5 points

1. **Characters** _____

    Amelia and Eleanor were alike

    Because they were outspoken/determined/daring (any one of these)

    Amelia was a pilot

    Eleanor was the first lady of the United States

2. **Initiating Event** _____

    Eleanor invited Amelia for dinner at the White House

    Eleanor asked what it was like to fly over the Capitol at night

3. **Event 1** _____

    Amelia invited Eleanor to fly to Baltimore and back

The Secret Service men said it hadn't been approved

But Eleanor went anyway _____

Eleanor enjoyed the beautiful flight

4. **Event 2** _____

    When they returned Amelia and Eleanor

    Went for a ride in Eleanor's new car

5. **Ending** _____

    They returned to the White House for dessert

Point Table   Amelia and Eleanor Go for a Ride, Grade 4

Standard		Question	Points per Question
1.	Support an inference	5 6	1 1
2.	Determine theme	3 10	1 1
3.	Explain why or how	4 8	1 2
4.	Determine word or phrase meaning	1 7	1 1
6.	Determine point of view	2 9	2 1
Total Question			12
2. Summary **Total Summary**			5 (4 acceptable)

Elementary School, Grade 4, Part II   Before you begin scoring, please review the guidelines for scoring questions on pages 40–43 and pages 56–58 for scoring summaries.

LITERATURE

Encyclopedia Brown and the Case of the Slippery Salamander

by Donald Sobol
Illustrated by Brett Helquist

1. **Whose point of view is the story told from and how do you know? (2 pts.)**

    Answer: *The point of view is third person, because the story uses words like he and his wife and not words like I* **or** *The speaker's because the speaker tells what everyone is saying* **or** *The narrator's because it doesn't say his name.*

    Standard 6: Identify the point of view from which stories are narrated.

2. **Describe the type of man Chief Brown was and use at least two details from the story. (2 pts.)**

    Answer: *Chief Brown was smart/kind/brave (any two).*

Standard 3: Describe in depth a character, setting, or event in a story, drawing on specific details in the text.

3. **Using details from the story, explain why the salamander was not on display in the aquarium like the others.**

    Answer: *They had to be sure that he was healthy (before he was put on display).*

    Standard 1: Refer to details and examples in a text when drawing an inference.

4. **What does the word** *access* **mean in the following sentence? "Employees and volunteers are the only ones who have access to the back room . . ."**

    Answer: *A way in* **or** *Entry* **or** *a key* **or** *Way to open the door* **or** *allowed into*

Standard 4: Determine the meaning of words and phrases as they are used in a text, including those that allude to significant characters found in mythology.

5. **What is the central idea of the story so far?**

    Answer: *A rare salamander has been stolen from an aquarium and Chief Brown has been brought in to investigate it and find out who stole it.*

    Standard 2: Determine a central idea or theme of a story.

6. **Describe how Encyclopedia's comment about "ancient times" shows support for Mrs. King's belief that salamanders are sacred creatures.**

    Answer: *He thinks that the belief is not unusual if you know the history* **or** *If salamanders can be used for medicine maybe that's why she believes they had magical powers* **or** *Because if the salamanders can be used as medicine they were sacred* **or** *Salamanders could have magical powers to help cure people.*

    Standard 1: Refer to details and examples in a text when drawing an inference.

7. **Describe two reasons why people thought Mrs. King stole the salamander. (2 pts.)**

    Answer: *Because she has a fascination with (or loves) salamanders* **or** *Because she has a dozen of them at her home as pets* **or** *Because she thinks that they are sacred* **or** *Because this was the first tiger salamander she'd seen she'd probably want it.*

    Standard 3: Describe in depth a character, setting, or event in a story, drawing on specific details from the text.

8. **What does the phrase "If he's a lizard expert, then I'm the queen of England!" mean?**

    Answer: *Encyclopedia is saying that Sam is lying because Encyclopedia is not the queen of England so Sam is not a lizard expert* **or** *He's saying that the statement is unbelievable.*

    Standard 4: Determine the meaning of words and phrases as they are used in a text including those that allude to significant characters found in mythology.

9. **What did Encyclopedia hope to learn when he asked how long Sam Maine had been working at the aquarium? Provide text details to support your answer.**

    Answer: *He hoped he would find a clue to the theft like the others mentioned earlier in the story* **or** *Because he thought he'd learn information important to the case like how many chances Sam had to take the salamander* **or** *To rule him out as the suspect because if Sam had been working for them a long time then they'd probably trust him.*

    Standard 1: Refer to details and examples in a text when drawing an inference.

10. **What is the message or theme of this story?**

    Answer: *That suspects give themselves away by their words or actions* **or** *Thieves are sneaky, but will usually give clues or say or do something that leads someone to believe they are guilty* **or** *Don't steal* **or** *Don't lie.*

Standard 2: Determine a theme of a story, drama, or poem from details in the text.

Summarize the story. The summary is evaluated by the number of elements of a story (e.g., character, initiating event, etc.) it contains. A good summary includes 70 percent of the elements listed in bold. A student must include at least one statement listed under a story element in order to receive credit for that element. Total possible score = 5 points

1. **Setting and Characters** _____

    Idaville looked like a normal town

    Except no one had gotten away with breaking a law

    Crimes were solved by Police Chief Brown's son, Encyclopedia

2. **Initiating Event** _____

    A salamander was stolen from an aquarium

    Chief Brown was stumped

3. **Event 1** _____

    So he talked over the case with his wife and son, Encyclopedia

    There were three suspects: Mrs. King, Dr. O'Donnell, and Sam Maine

    Each of them had an excuse for not being the thief

4. **Event 2**

    Encyclopedia thought deeply and asked a question

    Sam Maine's comment about lizards gave him away

    Salamanders are amphibians

    Encyclopedia figured out he was lying about his experience and probably was the thief

5. **Ending**

    Sam admitted it the next morning and returned the salamander

    He was fired

Point Table Encyclopedia Brown and the Case of the Slippery Salamander, Grade 4

Standard	Question	Points per Question
1. Support an inference	3	1
	6	1
	9	1
2. Determine theme	5	1
	10	1
3. Explain why or how	2	2
	7	2
4. Determine word or phrase meaning	4	1
	8	1
6. Determine point of view	1	2
Total Questions		13
2. Summary **Total Summary**		5 (4 acceptable)

LITERATURE

Grandfather's Journey (Adapted)
by Alan Say

1. Using details from the story, explain how we know that the trip from Japan to the New World was a long one.

   Answer: *He didn't see land for three weeks* **or** *And finally land appeared.*

   Standard 1: Refer to details and examples in a text when drawing an inference.

2. Describe what kind of person the narrator's grandfather is and how he reacts to new things. **(2 pts.)**

   Answer: *He was adventurous* **or** *He loved to travel to different places* **or** *He was an explorer* **or** *He was very social* **and** *shook hands with all kinds of people* **or** *He had strong emotions to what he saw (he was amazed, confused, excited, marveled). One answer should describe him in general, and one should describe how he reacts.*

   Standard 3: Describe in depth a character, setting, or event in a story, drawing on specific details from the text

3. Describe the point of view from which the story is told and how you know it. **(2 pts.)**

   Answer: First person, *because it uses the words* he *and* my **or** "The boy's point of view because he is describing his grandfather."

   Standard 6: Describe the point of view from which stories are narrated.

4. What is the central idea of the story so far?

   Answer: *the grandfather likes to see new places but ends up missing his homeland (Japan). After a while he always wants to be somewhere else.*

   Standard 2: Determine the central idea of a text.

5. What do the words "scattered our lives like leaves in a storm" mean?

   Answer: *Their lives were upset/moved/disrupted just like when the wind blows leaves around* **or** *People were scared like a bad storm coming* **or** *something bad happened and you'll never forget that moment.*

   Standard 4: Determine the meaning of words and phrases as they are used in a text, including those that allude to significant characters found in mythology

6. What does "when I cannot quiet the longing in my heart" mean?

   Answer: *When I can't stop thinking about it* **or** *When I want to go so badly that I ache* **or** *He is homesick/sad in his heart.*

   Standard 4: Determine the meaning of words and phrases as they are used in the text, including those that allude to significant characters found in mythology.

7. Using details from the story, explain why the author feels that he knows his grandfather now.

   Answer: *He understands that his grandfather loved both countries and missed one when he was in the other just like he (the author) does* **or** *Because of all the time he spent with him and all the stories his grandfather told him* **or** *He lived in the same places his grandfather did.*

   Standard 1: Refer to details and examples in a text when drawing an inference.

8. What words does the author use in the last three paragraphs to signal that the author is talking about himself?

   Answer: *In the last two paragraphs the author uses "I" because he is speaking for himself.*

   Standard 6: Compare and contrast the point of view from which stories are narrated,.

9. Describe two ways that the narrator of the story (the author) and his grandfather were alike. **(2 pts.)**

   Answer: *They were alike because both loved to travel/ explore and they both explored California* **or** *They came to love the country where they were born, Japan, and California, where they moved* **or** *When they were in one country they missed the other* **or** *They both switched countries* **or** *After they left where they were born they went back to see their friends.*

   Standard 3: Describe in depth a character, setting, or event, drawing on specific details from the text.

10. What is the theme or message of this story?

    Answer: *People are never satisfied where they are but always want something to be different* **or** *You can always go back to places you've been* **or** *Love where you are or what you have* **or** *You can love more than one place* **or** *When you love two things and can't decide, just follow your heart.*

    Standard 2: Determine a theme of a story, drama, or poem from details in the text.

Summarize the story. The summary is evaluated by the number of elements of a story (e.g., character, initiating event, etc.) it contains. A good summary includes 70 percent of the elements listed in bold. A student must include at least one statement listed under a story element in order to receive credit for that element. Total possible = 5 points

1. Characters _____

It is a story a kid tells about his grandfather

2. Initiating Event _____

The grandfather came to the "New World" (United States) as a young man

From Japan on a ship

He explored the country by walking/taking the train/boat (any one)

He liked California the best so he settled there

He married a woman from Japan and they had a daughter

3. **Event 1** _____

Later he started missing Japan

So he went back there

His daughter married and had a son

Who is the narrator of the story

The grandfather wanted to go back to California

But a war started and he couldn't go

He never was able to return to California

4. **Event 2** _____

But his grandson did and

He married and had a child

The grandson did the same things as his grandfather

5. **Ending** _____

At the end of the story he too missed his homeland of Japan

And felt that he really understood his grandfather

Point Table   Grandfather's Journey, Grade 4

Standard	Question	Points per Question
1. Support an inference	1 7	1 1
2. Determine theme	4 10	1 1
3. Explain why or how	2 9	2 2
4. Determine word or phrase meaning	5 6	1 1
6. Determine point of view	3 8	2 1
Total Questions		13
2. Summary **Total Summary**		5 (4 acceptable)

Elementary School, Grade 5, Part I
Before you begin scoring, please review the guidelines for scoring questions on pages 40–43 and pages 56–58 for scoring summaries.

LITERATURE

Leonardo da Vinci: Inventor and Artist

1. **Using details from the story, why do you think Leonardo's last name was da Vinci?**

   Answer: *because he was from the village or area called Vinci.*

   Standard #1: Quote from a text to support statements about the text.

2. **Compare and contrast how his uncle, Francesco, and his father influenced da Vinci's life.**

   Answer: *his uncle spent time with him and taught him to observe nature and his father, although he wasn't with Leonardo much, recognized his artistic talent and sent him to learn with a sculptor and painter.*

   Standard 3: Compare and contrast two or more characters, settings, or events in a story, drawing on specific details.

3. **What does the phrase "a man who awoke too early in the darkness, while the others were all still asleep" mean?**

   Answer: *he was a man born ahead of his time or A man who was unusual in the time period that he lived.*

   Standard 4: determine word meaning from context

4. **Describe how the author's point of view of da Vinci's abilities is described in the story so far.**

   Answer: *the author thinks that da Vinci is very talented because he describes all the things that da Vinci could do in addition to being a great artist or The author thought that daVinci was very interesting/fascinating because he did all those things or Admired him for his curiosity and paintings.*

   Standard 6: Describe how an author's point of view influences how events are described.

5. **What do the details in the paragraph above tell you about how Leonardo researched the object he was going to make?**

   Answer: *he was very careful to study things before he started sculpting or He learned as much as he could about what he was to sculpt.*

   Standard 1: Quote from a text to support statements about the text.

6. **Describe the theme of the story so far using text evidence to support your statement. (2 pts.)**

   Answer: *da Vinci was a man who was able to do a lot of things very well but he didn't complete a lot of them. He was more interested in learning than finishing. Evidence: he started things that he didn't finish like the Adoration of the Magi.*

   Standard 2: determine a theme of a text, drawing on how characters in a story respond to challenges.

7. **Compare and contrast daVinci's work on the horse with his painting of *The Last Supper*.**

    Answer: *he worked on the horse for 12 years and didn't complete it but he completed The Last Supper in just three years.*

    Standard 3: Compare and contrast two or more characters, settings, or events in a story, drawing on specific details.

8. **What does "rub salt into a wound" mean in the paragraph above?**

    Answer: *to make something hurt more* **or** *To hurt more.*

    Standard 4: determine word meaning from context

9. **What is a theme of this story and how does da Vinci's life show it? (2 pts.)**

    Answer: *It is best to finish what one starts; he is known for The Last Supper that he completed.* **or** *Even if someone has great talent hard work is necessary.*

    Standard 2: determine a theme of a text, drawing on how characters in a story respond to challenges.

10. **How would this story be different if Michelangelo had written it?**

    Answer: *it would be more critical of da Vinci's life.*

    Standard 6: Describe how an author's point of view influences how events are described.

Summary: The summary is evaluated by the number of elements of a story (e.g., character, initiating event, etc.) it contains. A good summary includes 70 percent of the elements listed in bold. A student must include at least one statement listed under a story element in order to receive credit for that element. Total possible = 8 points

1. **Characterization:** _____

    Leonardo da Vinci was a talented artist/inventor

2. **Setting** _____

    who was born in Vinci, Italy

    and lived in Italy his whole life, especially Milan.

3. **Initiating Event:** _____

    His father sent him to study art in Florence, Italy.

    He became a member of the artists' guild when he was 20.

    He was talented in many areas (science, sculptor, invention)

4. **Episode 1:** _____

    He started his first painting, The Adoration of the Magi,

    But moved to Milan so he didn't finish it.

He was asked by the Duke of Milan to make a bronze horse to honor the duke's father

5. **Episode 2:** _____

    Da Vinci studied horses very carefully

    When he was ready to begin to build the model

    The Duke decided he wanted the horse three times bigger than life. It took da Vinci 12 years to build a clay model

6. **Episode 3:** _____

    A war with France started

    And the bronze was needed for cannons

    So the horse was never finished

    The clay model was destroyed by rain and the French

7. **Episode 4:** _____

    Two of daVinci's works are famous

    One is the painting of the Lord's Supper

    He finished it in three years

    But he used dry plaster and it started coming off immediately

    People have been restoring it ever since.

8. **Ending:** _____

    Da Vinci and Michelangelo were in competition with each other

    Da Vinci was older and recognized as a great artist

    Michelangelo criticized da Vinci for not finishing projects

    Da Vinci was jealous of the attention that Michelangelo was getting for his sculptures, especially, David.

    Da Vinci died grieving that he didn't finish his horse.

Point Table   Leonardo da Vinci: Inventor and Artist, Grade 5

Standard	Question	Points per Question
1. Support an inference	1 5	1 1
2. Determine theme	6 9	2 2
3. Explain why or how	2 7	2 1
4. Determine word or phrase meaning	3 8	1 1
6. Determine point of view	4 10	1 1
Total Questions		13
2. Summary **Total Summary**		8 (6 acceptable)

Elementary School, Grade 5, Part II Before you begin scoring, please review the guidelines for scoring questions on pages 40–43 and pages 56–58 for scoring summaries.

Weslandia
by Paul Fleischman

1. **What does the phrase "like a nose" mean?**

   Answer: *It means that it is easy to see that Wesley is different just as it is easy to see a nose* **or** *Wesley's difference stands out just as a nose stands out.*

   Standard 4: Determine the meaning of words and phrases as they are used in a text, including figurative language such as metaphors and similes.

2. **Describe two ways that Wesley was different from other boys his age. (2 pts.)**

   Answer: *Boys his age liked pizza, soda, football, and to have half of their heads shaved (any two) and Wesley liked none of that.*

   Standard 3: Compare and contrast two or more characters, settings, or events in the story, drawing on details in the story.

3. **Describe how Wesley's attitude toward learning was different from his father's attitude.**

   Answer: *Wesley liked to learn because it says that "his thoughts shot sparks and his eyes blazed" when he realized that he could "use what he'd learned that week for a summer project." On the other hand, when his father heard Wesley say what he'd learned in school, his father mumbled, "I'm sure you'll use that knowledge often." He was being sarcastic; he didn't mean what he said literally.*

   Standard 3: Compare and contrast two or more characters, settings, or events in the story, drawing on details in the story.

4. **What is the central idea of the story so far?**

   Answer: *A young boy who was very different from his peers learns about civilizations and their staple crops so he decides to create his own civilization.*

   Standard 2: Determine a theme of a story, drama, or poem from details in the text, including how characters in a story or drama respond to challenges.

5. **Describe how the author feels about Wesley, how you know that, and how the author's feelings influence how the story is told so far (3 pts).**

   Answer: *The author likes Wesley and shows it when he presents Wesley's many talents, and as the story develops the talents become more frequent.*

   Standard 6: Describe how a narrator or speaker's point of view influences how events are described.

6. **What does the word *segments* mean in the sentence, ". . . divided the day into eight segments—the number of petals on the plant's flowers."**

   Answer: *Parts/pieces*

   Standard 4: Determine the meaning of words and phrases as they are used in a text, including figurative language such as metaphors and similes.

7. **Using details from the story, explain why "Weslandia" was a good choice as a name for Wesley's domain.**

   Answer: *Because his name was Wesley and he developed this land, so he put the two together to get Weslandia* **or** *It means the land of Wesley.*

   Standard 1: Quote accurately from a text when explaining what the text says explicitly and when drawing inferences from the text.

8. **Describe how the author feels about Wesley at this point in the story, providing evidence from the last few paragraphs.**

   Answer: *The author is impressed by what Wesley has done because he says that Wesley invented complex games that would include his schoolmates* **or** *That he became more patient with the other players' mistakes* **or** *That he created a new language.*

   Standard 6: Describe how a narrator or speaker's point of view influences how events are described.

9. **Using details from the story, explain why Wesley had no shortage of friends when he returned to school.**

   Answer: *His peers became interested in the kinds of games that he made up* **or** *His peers enjoyed playing his games* **or** *They learned to enjoy him and what he invented.*

   Standard 1: Quote accurately from a text when explaining what the text says explicitly and when drawing inferences from the text.

10. **What is the theme or message of this story?**

    Answer: *That people who are different can be fun or can do fun things* **or** *You should give kids who are different from you a chance to get to know you and you might like them.*

    Standard 2: Determine a theme of a story, drama, or poem from details in the text, including how characters in a story or drama respond to challenges.

Summarize the story. The summary is evaluated by the number of elements of a story (e.g., character, initiating event, etc.) it contains. A good summary includes 70 percent of the elements listed in bold. A student must include at least one statement listed under a story element in order to receive credit for that element. Total possible score = 5 points

   1. Characterization _____

   Wesley is very different from his peers

   He didn't like the same kinds of foods or enjoy the same games

He had no friends

2. Initiating Event _____

He learned about seeds and food crops of different civilizations in school

He realized that he could use what he'd learned to found his own civilization

3. Event 1 _____

Strange plants grew, including fruit that tasted like a mix of common fruits

He made different foods and even clothing from his crops

4. Event 2 _____

He developed a new counting system and language

He called the land Weslandia

He invented games for individuals and then for groups to include his classmates

5. Ending _____

When he returned to school in the fall he had many friends.

Point Table   Weslandia, Grade 5

Standard	Question	Points per Question
1. Support an inference	7 9	1 1
2. Determine theme	4 10	1 1
3. Explain why or how	2 3	2 1
4. Determine word or phrase meaning	1 6	1 1
6. Determine point of view	5 8	3 1
Total Questions		13
2. Summary Total Summary		5 (4 acceptable)

Elementary School, Grade 5, Part III
Before you begin scoring, please review the guidelines for scoring questions on pages 40–43 and pages 56–58 for scoring summaries.

LITERATURE

Journey to the Center of the Earth

by Jules Verne
Illustrated by Marc Sasso

Tuesday, August 20

1. **Using details from the story, explain why the men thought that there were several animals in the water.**

   Answer: *Because they think they've seen a sea lizard, crocodile, whale, turtle, and a serpent* **or** *Because they saw many body parts at great distances from each other.*

   Standard 1: Quote accurately from a text when explaining what the text says explicitly and when drawing inferences from the text.

2. **Using details from the story, explain how we know that the narrator respects Hans.**

   Answer: *Because he didn't fire his gun after Hans signals him to wait*

   Standard 1: Quote accurately from a text when explaining what the text says explicitly and when drawing inferences from the text.

3. **What is the central idea of the story so far?**

   Answer: *Two men and a boy are in a raft when they come upon huge ocean creatures. They think there are many but it turns out there are only two, but they have body parts of other creatures.*

   Standard 2: Determine a theme of a story, drama, or poem from details in the text, including how characters in a story or drama respond to challenges.

4. **What does the phrase " . . . when I see his tail rise out of the water, angrily flicked like the hugest whip you could imagine" mean?**

   Answer: *That the tail looked and acted like a giant whip* **or** *Because the tail moved like a whip.*

   Standard 4: Determine the meaning of words and phrases as they are used in a text, including figurative language such as metaphors and similes.

5. **Describe how the interaction between the narrator and his uncle show which of them knows more about the creatures.**

   Answer: *The uncle names the creatures so he is more knowledgeable.*

   Standard 3: Compare and contrast two characters, settings, or events in a story and drama, drawing on specific details in the text.

6. **Describe how the narrator's point of view toward the events in *Journey* is shown.**

Answer: *The narrator is amazed by them and so described the events in detail* **or** *The narrator expressed his fear of the sea creature* **or** *The narrator uses exclamation points to show his strong feelings.*

Standard 6: Describe how a narrator's or speaker's point of view influences how events are described.

7. **What does the phrase, "and its neck, flexible as a swan's" mean?**

    Answer: *It can move in many ways* **or** *It can curve and stretch out.*

    Standard 4: Determine the meaning of words and phrases as they are used in a text, including figurative language such as metaphors and similes.

8. **Contrast how the appearance of the sea creatures at the beginning of the story was different from the second appearance described above.**

    Answer: *The appearances were different because in the first appearance there seemed to be many reptiles but in the second appearance they realized it was only two creatures* **or** *In the first appearance they were swimming around but in the second they were fighting.*

    Standard 3: Compare and contrast two characters, settings, or events in a story and drama, drawing on specific details in the text.

9. **Compare and contrast how the events in the last three paragraphs suggest different endings to the rest of this story. (2 pts.)**

    Answer: *The monsters are hurt and one possible ending is that they could both die and the men continue to sail on safely* but *the final sentence suggests that perhaps the ichthyosaurus is hiding and tending to his wounds and will come up to the surface again to destroy the men.*

    Standard 3: Compare and contrast two characters, settings, or events in a story and drama, drawing on specific details in the text.

10. **What is the theme or message of the story?**

    Answer: *That man is powerless against nature and the characters realized it because of the size and power of the creatures compared to them* **or** *When faced with a terrifying situation, man realizes how powerless he is* **or** *There may be places on Earth yet to be discovered that have unusual creatures.*

    Standard 2: Determine a theme of a story, drama, or poem from details in the text, including how characters in a story or drama respond to challenges.

Summarize the story. The summary is evaluated by the number of elements of a story (e.g., character, initiating event, etc.) it contains. A good summary includes 70 percent of the elements listed in bold. A student must include at least one statement listed under a story element in order to receive credit for that element. Total possible = 5 points

1. **Characterization** _____

   An uncle, his nephew, and Hans were on a journey into the middle of the Earth

2. **Initiating Event** _____

   They are deep within the Earth where they come upon sea monsters

   They look like many reptiles that they've seen before, but these are much larger

   They think they are whales/turtles/crocodiles/a sea lizard (any two)

3. **Event 1**

   As they watch the reptiles fighting each other they realize that

   There are only two creatures, but they are made up of parts of familiar reptiles

   One reptile has the snout of a porpoise, the head of a lizard, and the teeth of a crocodile; it is called the ichthyosaurus

   The other is a serpent, but it has a turtle's shell; it is the plesiosaurus, or sea crocodile

4. **Event 2**

   The sea serpents fight and the plesiosaurus is killed

5. **Ending**

   The men on the raft wonder where the ichthyosaurus is and

   Whether he is waiting to destroy them

Point Table   Journey to the Center of the Earth, Grade 5

Standard	Question	Points per Question
1. Support an inference	1 2	1 1
2. Determine theme	3 10	1 1
3. Explain why or how	5 8 9	1 1 2
4. Determine word or phrase meaning	4 7	1 1
5. Determine point of view	6	1
Total Questions		11
2. Summary **Total Summary**		5 (4 acceptable)

LITERATURE

Arachne (Adapted)

by Olivia E. Coolidge

1. **Using words from the text, explain how Arachne's success depended on her father.**

   Answer: *He dyed the cloth that she used to spin into yarn and weave into cloth.*

   Standard 1: Cite textual evidence to support analysis of what the text says explicitly as well as inferences drawn from the text.

2. **Describe how what Arachne said about Athene in the last sentence sets up the plot of the story.**

   Answer: *Her response challenges Athene and sets up an interaction between Arachne and Athene.*

   Standard 3: Describe how a story's plot unfolds in a series of episodes as well as how the characters respond or change as the plot moves toward a resolution.

3. **What does the word *credit* mean in this sentence? "Nor if I had, would I give Athene credit because the girl was more skillful than I."**

   Answer: *Thanks/recognition/praise/compliment/respect/ give things to those who deserve them/fame.* Note: Be sure that students don't use the word credit in their answer.

   Standard 4: Determine the meaning of words and phrases as they are used in a text, including figurative and connotative meanings; analyze the impact of a specific word choice on meaning and tone.

4. **What is the narrator's point of view of Arachne and what words from the text support your answer? (2 pts.)**

   Answer: *The author thinks she is conceited/boastful and uses the words proud, "she lived for praise," and "she didn't believe that anyone could teach her anything" or The narrator thinks she is a skilled weaver and describes her weaving as, "So soft was her thread, so fine her cloth, that soon her products were known all over Greece. No one had even seen the like of them before."*

   Standard 6: Explain how the author develops the point of view of the narrator or speaker in a text.

5. **What does the word *challenged* mean in this sentence? "I have challenged her to a contest, but she, of course, will not come."**

   Answer: *Dare/demand/requested/asked/invited to face/ take her on/go against/ wants to battle*

   Standard 4: Determine the meaning of words and phrases as they are used in a text, including figurative and connotative meanings; analyze the impact of a specific word choice on meaning and tone.

6. **Describe how Arachne's reaction to Athene in the last paragraph moves the plot along.**

   Answer: *It sets the stage for the weaving challenge or showdown.*

   Standard 3: Describe how a particular story's or drama's plot unfolds in a series of episodes as well as how the characters respond or change as the plot moves toward a resolution.

7. **What is the narrator's point of view of Athene and how is it shown in the previous paragraph? (2 pts.)**

   Answer: *The narrator thinks Athene is a fair competitor because she is weaving in a warning to Arachne or The narrator thinks Athene is very skilled at weaving because she finished before Arachne.*

   Standard 6: Explain how the author develops the point of view of the narrator or speaker in a text.

8. **Describe how Arachne's choice of a design for her weaving added to the development of the plot.**

   Answer: *The design would make Athene mad and she would react or The design was an insult to Athene and so there would be some negative response.*

   Standard 3: Describe how a story's plot unfolds in a series of episodes as well as how the characters respond or change as the plot moves toward a resolution.

9. **Why was Arachne the cause of her own downfall? Provide supporting evidence from the text. (2 pts.)**

   Answer: *She thought she was better than anyone else, even a goddess, and she challenged a goddess to see who was the better weaver. The details are: "it displeased her greatly that people should think anyone, even a goddess, could teach her anything" or "If Athene resents my words, let her answer them herself. I have challenged her to a contest, but she, of course, will not come."*

   Standard 1: Cite textual evidence to support analysis of what the text says explicitly as well as inferences drawn from the text.

10. **What is the theme or central idea of the story? Provide two details from the text that support the theme. (3 pts.)**

    Answer: *Stubbornness and pride will harm or Never mess with the gods because you'll lose. Evidence: Arachne shows pride when she talks to those who watch her. "Nor if I had, would I give Athene credit because the girl was more skillful than I. As for Athene's weaving, how could there be finer cloth or more beautiful embroidery than mine? If Athene herself were to come down and compete with me, she could do no better than I" or She later shows her pride when she challenges Athene, a goddess, to see who is the best weaver or When Athene hits her at the end Arachne says that she can't live with that insult or In the end her pride makes Athene punish her by turning her into a spider or Athene is* *a faster weaver than Arachne and her power allowed her to turn Arachne into a spider.*

Standard 2: Determine a central idea or theme from a text and how it is conveyed through particular details.

Summarize the story. The summary is evaluated by the number of elements of a story (e.g., character, initiating event, etc.) it contains. A good summary includes 70 percent of the elements listed in bold. A student must include at least one statement listed under a story element in order to receive credit for that element. Total possible = 7 points.

1. Characterization _____

Arachne is a talented girl who weaves beautiful yarn

Dyed by her father

2. Initiating Event _____

People are watching her weaving, saying that Athene must have taught her

She reacts by saying that no one taught her

And that Athene should come down so they could see who the best weaver was

3. Event 1 _____

An old woman appears and Arachne insults her

And the old woman turns into Athene

4. Event 2 _____

Arachne won't give in because there are people watching

So she brings Athene to a loom and the contest begins

5. Event 3 _____

Athene finishes first

And when she looks at what Arachne's weaving means she sees an insult to the gods

6. Event 4 _____

So she tears Arachne's work and strikes her

Arachne tries to hang herself because she was insulted

7. Ending _____

Athene turns Arachne into a spider who will spin forever

Point Table   Arachne, Grade 6

Standard	Question	Points per Question
1. Support an inference	1	1
	9	2
2. Determine theme	10	3
3. Explain why or how	2	1
	6	1
	8	1
4. Determine word or phrase meaning	3	1
	5	1
5. Determine point of view	4	2
	7	2
Total Questions		15
2. Summary Total Summary		7 (5 acceptable)

Elementary School, Grade 6, Part II   Before you begin scoring, please review the guidelines for scoring questions on pages 40–43 and pages 56–58 for scoring summaries.

The Wounded Wolf
by Jean Craighead George

1. **What does the word *gravely* mean in this sentence? "Gravely injured, Roko pulls himself toward the shelter rock."**

   Answer: *Badly/seriously/extremely/very/seriously/greatly*

   Standard 4: Determine the meaning of words and phrases as they are used in a text, including figurative and connotative meanings; analyze the impact of a specific word choice on meaning and tone.

2. **Using words from the story, explain how the weather interfered with Roko's signal.**

   Answer: *Wind and snow blew in between Roko and his pack. Note: An answer that includes only "wind" is not correct; the snow prevented the signal from being read.*

   Standard 1: Cite textual evidence to support analysis of what the text says explicitly as well as inferences drawn from the text.

3. **What does the phrase "a ghostly presence flits around" mean?**

   Answer: *It refers to the white fox or it refers to the snow swirling around him or it means that he felt the presence of something near him but couldn't see it.*

   Standard 4: Determine the meaning of words and phrases as they are used in a text, including figurative and connotative meanings; analyze the impact of a specific word choice on meaning and tone.

4. **What is the narrator's point of view toward the ravens, fox, and owl, and which words in the text show it? (2 pts.)**

   Answer: *He doesn't like them and He uses details (e.g., they peck and stab at his eyes) to show how they try to hurt Roko.*

   Standard 6: Explain how an author develops the point of view of the narrator or speaker in a text.

5. **What is the narrator's point of view toward Roko and which words in the text show it? (2 pts.)**

Answer: *The narrator is sympathetic with Roko and shows this when the wolf is struggling to protect himself and find a place to be able to face his foes.*

Standard 6: Explain how an author develops the point of view of the narrator or speaker in a text.

6. **Using words from the story, explain why Roko has the courage to face his foes.**

    Answer: *Roko wedged himself between rocks and is protected from three sides so they can only attack him from one direction.*

    Standard 1: Cite textual evidence to support analysis of what the text says explicitly as well as inferences drawn from the text.

7. **Describe how the "roll call" moves the plot along.**

    Answer: *It introduces the idea that the pack now knows that Roko is in danger and sets up action that will follow.*

    Standard 3: Describe how a story's plot unfolds in a series of episodes as well as how characters respond or change as the plot moves toward a resolution.

8. **Describe how and why Roko's behavior toward the animals changed from earlier in the plot to now. (2 pts.)**

    Answer: *In the beginning of the story he "snarls, snaps, bites" at them because they pick at his wounds, but after he's fed by Kiglo and begins to feel better he allows them to eat his leftovers and he "wags his tail and watches." Note: One point is given if the answer explains how Roko's behavior changed and one point is given if the answer explains why Roko's behavior changed.*

    Standard 3: Describe how a story's plot unfolds in a series of episodes as well as how characters respond or change as the plot moves toward a resolution.

9. **Describe four events that are necessary to the plot of the story. (4 pts.)**

    Answer: *Roko gets injured; animals follow him and harass/bother him; he finds a place that protects him; roll call tells the pack that Roko is missing; Kiglo brings him meat; Roko gets better and returns to his pack (any four). Note: One point is given for each event, up to a maximum of four.*

    Standard 3: Describe how a story's plot unfolds in a series of episodes as well as how characters respond or change as the plot moves toward a resolution.

10. **What is the message or theme of this story? Include evidence from the story to support your answer. (2 pts.)**

    Answer: *When animals are hungry they hunt others and the example is the raven and other animals come to Roko when they think he will die* **or** *Being part of a group is helpful if one gets in trouble and the example is when the pack realizes that Roko is missing and Kiglo brings him meat so he'll get stronger* **or** *To have courage or never give up or to have hope when faced with a difficult situation and the example is when Roko defends himself against the animals that attack him and finds a good place to sit that protects him on three sides.*

Standard 2: Determine the theme or general idea of a text and how it is conveyed through particular details.

Summarize the story. The summary is evaluated by the number of elements of a story (e.g., character, initiating event, etc.) it contains. A good summary includes 70 percent of the elements listed in bold. A student must include at least one statement listed under a story element in order to receive credit for that element. Total possible = 7 points

1. **Character** _____

   Roko, a wolf, gets injured

2. **Initiating Event** _____

   While fighting with his pack

   He tries to signal to his pack that he is hurt but

   The snow gets in the way and they can't see him

3. **Event 1**_____

   A raven calls to others that death is coming

   So there will be food for them

   The raven is joined by other animals

4. **Event 2** _____

   Roko falls and they attack him

   He fights them off and sits in a more protected area

5. **Event 3** _____

   In the morning he hears the leader of his pack call, but

   He is too weak to return the call, so the pack knows he is missing

6. **Event 4**_____

   His leader finds him and brings him meat

   He eats and shares the scraps with the other animals

   This goes on for several days

7. **Ending** _____

   Finally he gets strong enough to answer the pack leader's call and

   He returns to them

Point Table   The Wounded Wolf, Grade 6

Standard	Question	Points per Question
1. Support an inference	2 6	1 1
2. Determine theme	10	2
3. Explain why or how	7 8 9	1 2 4
4. Determine word or phrase meaning	1 3	1 1
5. Determine point of view	4 5	2 2
Total Questions		17
2. Summary **Total Summary**		7 (5 acceptable)

Señor Coyote and the Tricked Trickster: A Mexican Folktale
by I.G. Edmonds

1. **Describe how the interaction between Coyote and Mouse sets up the plot.**

   Answer: *The characters are trying to trick each other, which begins the tale of them not liking each other.*

   Standard 3: Describe how a story's plot unfolds in a series of episodes as well as how the characters respond or change as the plot moves toward a resolution.

2. **Using words from the text, how does the author tell us that Coyote thought he was better than Mouse?**

   Answer: *"A big, brave, smart fellow like me"* **or** *"But everyone would laugh at a big, brave, smart fellow like me working as a slave for a mere mouse!"*

   Standard 1: Cite textual evidence to support analysis of what the text says explicitly as well as inferences drawn from the text.

3. **What is the narrator's point of view of Coyote, and which words in the story tell you about his point of view? (2 pts.)**

   Answer: *He doesn't like Coyote because he always tries to get what he wants. He whines when he doesn't get what he wants and tries to talk his way out of things. The author states: "He had done nothing for Mouse but trick him"* **or** *"'Why, how can you suggest such a thing?' Coyote cried indignantly"* **or** *"Senor Coyote groaned and cried and argued, but finally agreed when he saw that Mouse would not help him otherwise."*

   Standard 6: Explain how an author develops the point of view of the narrator or speaker in a text.

4. **Describe how Coyote's behavior has changed from the beginning of the story until now. (2 pts.)**

   Answer: *At the beginning he was whining, begging, and trying to talk his way into Mouse helping him, and he didn't want to agree to Mouse's proposal that Coyote work for him. But, now he feels he has no choice, so he agreed to do the work even though he didn't like it.*

   Standard 3: Describe how a story's plot unfolds in a series of episodes as well as how the characters respond or change as the plot moves toward a resolution.

5. **What does the phrase "a bird in the hand is worth two in the bush" mean?**

   Answer: *If you have one of what you want, like Rattlesnake had one mouse, it was assured. So why should you take the chance of losing one mouse to gain two?*

   Standard 4: Determine the meaning of words and phrases as they are used in a text, including figurative and connotative meanings; analyze the impact of a specific word choice on meaning and tone.

6. **Describe how Mouse changes to become more like the sly Coyote.**

   Answer: *Mouse begins to find ways to trick Coyote by thinking quickly* **or** *Mouse begins using his knowledge of Coyote's pride to say things that result in Coyote's helping him.*

   Standard 3: Describe how a story's plot unfolds in a series of episodes as well as how the characters respond or change as the plot moves toward a resolution.

7. **What is the narrator's point of view of Mouse, and which words in the text show you his point of view? (2 pts.)**

   Answer: *He believes Mouse is smart and this is shown when he uses his knowledge of Coyote's pride* **or** *When he tells a tale that explains how a little effort can bring great results.*

   Standard 6: Explain how an author develops the point of view of the narrator or speaker in a text.

8. **What does the word *welfare* mean in these sentences? "I am only thinking of your own welfare, Snake." . . . "but I do enough thinking about my welfare for both of us."**

   Answer: *What is good for you/well being*

   Standard 4: Determine the meaning of words and phrases as they are used in a text, including figurative and connotative meanings; analyze the impact of a specific word choice on meaning and tone.

9. **Using details from the story, explain why Mouse decided to accept that Coyote paid his debt at the end.**

   Answer: *When Snake suggests that he will show how he put Mouse in his coils, Mouse becomes afraid that if he doesn't accept Coyote's saving his life as payment of his debt Coyote would let Snake capture Mouse again.*

   Standard 1: Cite textual evidence to support analysis of what the text says explicitly as well as inferences drawn from the text.

10. **What is the theme or message of this story?**

    Answer: *If you are smaller or weaker than others, be cautious of those who play tricks on you* **or** *Use your brain to think of ways to solve problems.*

    Standard 2: Determine a central idea or theme from a text and how it is conveyed through particular details.

Summarize the story. The summary is evaluated by the number of elements of a story (e.g., character, initiating event, etc.) it contains. A good summary includes 70 percent of the elements listed in bold. A student must include at least one statement listed under a story element in order to receive credit for that element. Total possible = 7 points

1. Characterization _____

It is a story about Coyote, a trickster who has played a lot of tricks

On Mouse, which hurt him

So Mouse doesn't trust Coyote

2. Initiating Event _____

Coyote gets caught in a trap and

Wants Mouse to help him get loose

Mouse refuses for a while and Coyote tries to convince him

3. Event 1 _____

Mouse agrees if Coyote will work for him his entire life or

Save his life at some point

Coyote doesn't want to do that and

Explains why but Mouse refuses to help him

And Coyote agrees so Mouse sets him free

4. Event 2 _____

Coyote works for Mouse for a while

One day Mouse is caught by Rattlesnake so

Baby Mouse comes to Coyote for help

5. Event 3 _____

Coyote and Rattlesnake argue whether or not Mouse should be let go

Coyote tricks Rattlesnake by asking him to show how he was trapped by the rock and

How Mouse helped him

6. Event 4 _____

Coyote lays the rock back on Rattlesnake and

Rattlesnake lets go of Mouse so they can see how strong he is

7. Ending _____

Mouse is free and agrees that Coyote has paid his debt

And Coyote doesn't let Rattlesnake catch him again

Point Table   Señor Coyote and the Tricked Trickster, Grade 6

Standard	Question	Points per Question
1. Support an inference	2 9	1 1
2. Determine theme	10	1
3. Explain why or how	1 4	1 2
4. Determine word or phrase meaning	5 8	1 1
5. Determine point of view	3 7	2 2
Total Questions		13
2. Summary **Total Summary**		7 (5 acceptable)

Middle School, Grade 7, Part I   Before you begin scoring, please review the guidelines for scoring questions on pages 40–43 and pages 56–58 for scoring summaries.

LITERATURE

All Summer in a Day
by Ray Bradbury

1. **Using details from the story, provide two reasons why the setting of the story is unusual. (2 pts.)**

   Answer: *Because it is on another planet/because it is on Venus/because it rains all the time (any two).*

   Standard 1: Cite several pieces of textual evidence to support analysis of what the text says explicitly as well as inferences drawn from the text.

2. **What does, "endless shaking down of clear bead necklaces upon the roof, the walk, the gardens" describe in the previous sentence?**

   Answer: *Rain*

   Standard 4: Determine the meaning of words and phrases as they are used in a text, including figurative and connotative meanings; analyze the impact of rhymes and other repetitions of sounds on a specific verse or stanza of a poem or section of a story or drama.

3. **Analyze how the setting has shaped the children's lives.**

   Answer: *They stay inside all of the time because of the rain* or *The setting makes them dream of the brief time when they saw the sun's warmth* or *Because they don't see the sun often, their classes read and talk about the sun.*

   Standard 3: Analyze how particular elements of a story interact.

4. **Describe how the author shows Margo and William are different. (2 pts.)**

   Answer: *Margo is described as standing alone and being quiet* **or** *passive; she doesn't move when William shoves her and William is outgoing* **or** *Margot is not accepted as part of the children's group and William is popular* **or** *William isn't nice to Margot and she remains passive (doesn't respond)* *or Margot is passive (doesn't respond) when William shoves her and says to her, "speak when you're spoken to" and William is a bully.*

Standard 6: Analyze how an author develops and contrasts the points of view of different characters or narrators in a text.

5. **Explain the relationships among the children and how the relationships have begun to develop the plot. (2 pts.)**

   Answer: *The children are all against Margot and she doesn't fight back **and** these relationships set up the conflict between them that will be part of the plot.*

   Standard 3: Analyze how particular elements of a story interact.

6. **What does the phrase "a nest of octopi" mean in the following sentences? "They stopped running and stood in the jungle that covered Venus that grew and never stopped growing, tumultuously, even as you watched it. It was a nest of octopi, clustering up great arms of fleshlike weed, wavering, flowering in this brief spring."**

   Answer: *The growth of the trees was like a gray octopus with long arms.*

   Standard 4: Determine the meaning of words and phrases as they are used in a text, including figurative and connotative meanings; analyze the impact of rhymes and other repetitions of sounds on a specific verse or stanza of a poem or section of a story or drama.

7. **What does the phrase "they stood as if someone had driven them, like so many stakes, into the floor" describe?**

   Answer: *How the students stood very still after they realized that they'd forgotten that Margot was still in the closet **or** The students stood very still and were afraid to move, fearful of what they'd done to Margot.*

   Standard 4: Determine the meaning of words and phrases as they are used in a text, including figurative and connotative meanings; analyze the impact of rhymes and other repetitions of sounds on a specific verse or stanza of a poem or section of a story or drama.

8. **Contrast how the children were feeling when they first put Margo in the closet to how they are feeling now.**

   Answer: *They were happy to put Margot in the closet but now they can't look each other in the eye because they feel guilty **or** They were excited when they put her in the closet, but now feel bad about what they've done.* Note: The answer must contain both how they felt at first as well as how they feel toward the end of the story.

   Standard 6: Analyze how an author develops and contrasts the points of view of different characters or narrators in a text.

9. **Using two details from the story, explain why locking Margot in the closet on this day was an especially cruel thing to do. (2 pts.)**

   Answer: *Because she only had that one hour to see the sun and they stopped her from doing that **or** She wanted to see the sun more than the others and locking her in the closet stopped her from doing that **or** It was the only day in seven years that the sun was out and they stopped her from seeing it.*

   Standard 1: Cite several pieces of textual evidence to support analysis of what the text says explicitly as well as inferences drawn from the text.

10. **What is the theme or message of the story?**

    Answer: *Children can be cruel to someone who is different **or** Children must be tolerant and accepting of others who are different **or** Think twice before you do something mean to someone else **or** Don't judge other people because they're different; give them a chance.*

    Standard 2: Determine a theme or central idea of a text and analyze its development over the course of the text.

Summarize the story. The summary is evaluated by the number of elements of a story (e.g., character, initiating event, etc.) it contains. A good summary includes 70 percent of the elements listed in bold. A student must include at least one statement listed under a story element in order to receive credit for that element. Total possible = 7 points

1. **Setting** _____

   The story occurs on the planet Venus, where it rains all the time

   Except for one hour every seven years when the sun comes out

   The day is coming soon when the sun will come out

2. **Characterization** _____

   There is one child, Margot, who has been to Earth and seen the sun

   She is excluded by other children because she is different (she remembers the sun)

   She is also very shy and withdrawn

3. **Initiating Event** _____

   There is a boy who is bullying her

   When she describes the sun no one believes her

4. **Event 1** _____

   The children gang up on Margot and put her in the closet so that she can't see the sun

5. **Event 2** _____

   The sun comes out

   The children play (run among the trees, slip and fall, and play hide-and-seek, but mostly look at the sun)

After an hour they watch the sun fade and the rain comes again

6. Event 3 _____

They realize that Margo was right about the sun

They remember that they left Margot in the closet and feel guilty

7. Ending _____

They finally let her out of the closet

Point Table   All Summer in a Day, Grade 7

Standard	Question	Points per Question
1. Support an inference	1 9	2 2
2. Determine theme	10	1
3. Explain why or how	3 5	1 2
4. Determine word or phrase meaning	2 6 7	1 1 1
5. Determine point of view	4 8	2 1
Total Questions		14
2. Summary **Total Summary**		7 (5 acceptable)

Middle School, Grade 7, Part II   Before you begin scoring, please review the guidelines for scoring questions on pages 40–43 and pages 56–58 for scoring summaries.

LITERATURE

The Californian's Tale (Adapted)
by Mark Twain

1. Analyze how the story's location relates to the narrator.

   Answer: *The narrator used to be a prospector and is telling a story of where he once mined for gold* **or** *He used to live in California and now he is telling the story of something that happened to him there.*

   Standard 3: Analyze how particular elements of a story interact.

2. Cite two pieces of evidence from the previous paragraph to explain why the man was so grateful to see the 45-year-old man and the cottage. **(2 pts.)**

   Answer: *Because he was lonely and it lifted his spirits to see a person* **and/or** *The cottage appeared cared for* **and/or** *It had a front yard with lovely flowers* **and/or** *Because he was invited in.*

   Standard 1: Cite several pieces of textual evidence to support analysis of what the text says explicitly as well as inferences drawn from the text.

3. What does the following sentence mean? ". . . but here was a nest which had aspects to rest the tired eye and refresh that something in one's nature which, after long fasting, recognizes, when confronted by the belongings of art, howsoever cheap and modest they might be, that it has unconsciously been famishing and now has found nourishment."

   Answer: *The cabin was cared for and decorated enough to renew his spirit* **or** *The cabin contained enough modest art to fill his famishing nature/soul* **or** *The cabin was cared for and decorated enough to renew his spirit that he didn't know was lacking* **or** *The cabin's decor was a comfort to his tired eyes.* Note: the answer must make mention of the fact that the man didn't realize how much he needed to see something "pretty."

   Standard 4: Determine the meaning of words and phrases as they are used in a text, including figurative and connotative meanings; analyze the impact of rhymes and other repetitions of sounds on a specific verse or stanza of a poem or section of a story or drama.

4. Explain the phrase "drank the admiration from my face."

   Answer: *He took in/absorbed the feelings of appreciation on the man's face* **or** *The owner liked the fact that the man appreciated the picture.*

   Standard 4: Determine the meaning of words and phrases as they are used in a text, including figurative and connotative meanings; analyze the impact of rhymes and other repetitions of sounds on a specific verse or stanza of a poem or section of a story or drama.

5. Cite one piece of information that suggests why the narrator is afraid to stay until the wife comes home.

   Answer: *He feels deep longing to see her* **or** *He's afraid he might do something that would insult her husband* **or** *He's afraid that he will fall in love with her.*

   Standard 1: Cite several pieces of textual evidence to support analysis of what the text says explicitly as well as inferences drawn from the text.

6. How does the letter show the woman's point of view toward her neighbors?

   Answer: *It shows her to be very friendly and caring about them* **or** *The postscripts show she is thinking of them and has fond feelings of them.*

Standard 6: Analyze how an author develops and contrasts the points of view of different characters or narrators.

7. Analyze how the narrator and Charley differ in their reaction to Henry's asking, "You don't think anything has happened, do you?"

   Answer: *The narrator is sick of hearing it and is bothered by his guilt in feeling that way, but Charley spoke to his friend a lot, so he understands him and tries to reassure him that she will be okay.*

   Standard 6: Analyze how the author develops and contrasts the point of view of different characters or narrators in a text.

8. Analyze how the Saturday night party advances the plot.

   Answer: *It provided a reason for the men to gather at Henry's to help him wait for his wife.*

   Standard 3: Analyze how particular elements of the story interact.

9. Cite two sources of evidence that the people of the town cared about Henry. **(2 pts.)**

   Answer: *They've been coming to his house for 19 years to help him over the anniversary of her not returning from the trip* **or** *They plan a party/dance for her homecoming* **or** *They fix up the house with flowers for the party* **or** *Men come by his house and ask him to read her letter to them* **or** *They drug him so he will sleep so he won't go wild* **or** *They encourage him that she will come.*

   Standard 1: Cite several pieces of textual evidence to support analysis of what the text says explicitly as well as inferences drawn from the text.

10. What is the theme or message of the story? Provide an example of how the theme was developed over the story. **(2 pts.)**

   Answer: *One central theme is that the loss of a loved one can drive someone insane, as was seen in Henry's increasing agitation as Saturday approached and he kept asking people if they thought she'd be okay* **or** *That good friends are those that help one through the difficult times in life as the men in this story helped Henry each year.*

   Standard 2: Determine a theme or central idea of a text and analyze its development over the course of the text.

Summarize the story. The summary is evaluated by the number of elements of a story (e.g., character, initiating event, etc.) it contains. A good summary includes 70 percent of the elements listed in bold. A student must include at least one statement listed under a story element in order to receive credit for that element. Total possible = 7 points

   1. Character and Setting _____

   A man (the narrator) is walking through deserted areas of California

   In the time of the gold rush

2. Initiating Event _____

   He meets a 45-year-old man named Henry

   Whose cottage shows that it had been lived in and cared for

   He is invited in and sees the house decorated in lovely ways

3. Event 1 _____

   Henry explains that all of the decoration is his wife's doing and tells him that his wife is on a trip

   And will be coming home on Saturday night

   And that he should wait because she likes to meet new people

4. Event 2 _____

   Henry's friends come by and ask when his wife is coming home

   And Henry reads them a letter from her telling when

   Henry seems worried about his wife's return

5. Event 3 _____

   A party is held on Saturday evening to celebrate her coming home

   The men drink and play instruments and continue to toast Henry's wife

   They make sure Henry has had a lot to drink so he finally sleeps

6. Event 4 _____

   The men then tell the narrator that Henry's wife was captured by Indians on that day 19 years ago

   And ever since then Henry has been insane

   He gets bad when the anniversary of her capture comes around

7. Ending _____

   So every year his friends plan a party and decorate the house

   And talk about how soon she will come home to help him cope with it

Point Table   The Californian's Tale, Grade 7

Standard	Question	Points per Question
1. Support an inference	2 5 9	2 1 2
2. Determine theme	10	2
3. Explain why or how	1 8	1 1
4. Determine word or phrase meaning	3 4	1 1
5. Determine point of view	6 7	1 1
Total Questions		13
2. Summary **Total Summary**		7 (5 acceptable)

LITERATURE

The Third Wish

by Joan Aiken

1. **What does the word** *release* **mean in this sentence? "Nevertheless he managed to release it from the thorns . . ."**

   Answer: *Free/remove/spring/deliver*

   Standard 4: Determine the meaning of words and phrases as they are used in a text, including figurative and connotative meanings; analyze the impact of rhymes and other repetitions of sounds on a specific verse or stanza of a poem or section of a story or drama.

2. **Analyze how the king's gift will affect the story's plot.**

   Answer: *The granting of three wishes will cause conflict or obstacles* **or** *The man will make three wishes and events will happen as a result.*

   Standard 3: Analyze how particular elements of a story interact.

3. **Using two details from the story, explain who Leita was before she was Mr. Peters's wife (2 pts).**

   Answer: *She was a swan because the author describes her "with eyes as blue-green as the canal"* **or** *"Hair as dusky as the bushes,"* **or** *"Skin as white as the feathers of the swans"* **or** *She was pleased that a river was near his garden* **or** *She asks, "Do swans come up there?"*

   Standard 1: Cite several pieces of textual evidence to support analysis of what the text says explicitly as well as inferences drawn from the text.

4. **Analyze how the setting is important to a character in this story.**

   Answer: *The setting of the river is important because the man found a swan struggling near the river* **or** *The river is important because the sister swans could visit with each other* **or** *If there was no river the swan wouldn't have been near it but tangled in the bushes.*

   Standard 3: Analyze how particular elements of a story interact.

5. **What is the central conflict within one of the main characters in this story?**

   Answer: *Leita desires to return to being a swan but she loves Mr. Peters, who is a human* **or** *Leita is troubled because she is half swan and half human* **or** *Mr. Peters is troubled and doesn't know what to do.*

   Standard 2: Determine a theme or central idea of a text and analyze its development over the course of the text.

6. **How did the author develop the characters of Leita and Mr. Peters to illustrate their different points of view toward being human? (2 pts.)**

   Answer: *The author shows Leita as kind and loving and trying to make Mr. Peters happy, but she greatly misses her life as a swan* **or** *Leita loves her sister so she is torn between loving and caring for Mr. Peters and her sister and the author portrays Mr. Peters as a kind man who wants to make his wife happy as a human by doing things that humans enjoy, like traveling, but she wants to stay in their home to be near her sister.*

   Standard 6: Analyze how an author develops and contrasts the point of view of characters or narrators in a text.

7. **Using two pieces of evidence, explain why Mr. Peters used his second wish to set Leita free. (2 pts.)**

   Answer: *He wanted her to be happy* **or** *He knew how much she missed her sister* **or** *He knew she would never be happy as a human* **or** *She was growing pale and thin.*

   Standard 1: Cite several pieces of textual evidence to support analysis of what the text says explicitly as well as inferences drawn from the text.

8. **Explain the phrase, "human beings and swans are better in their own shapes."**

   Answer: *That both humans and swans should remain what they were born to be* **or** *Just as different kinds of people are meant to be who they are and shouldn't try to be something else, so a swan shouldn't try to be something else.*

   Standard 4: Determine the meaning of words and phrases as they are used in a text, including figurative and connotative meanings; analyze the impact of rhymes and other repetitions of sounds on a specific verse or stanza of a poem or section of a story or drama.

9. **Analyze the contrast between the King's and Mr. Peters's points of view of turning Leita back into a swan.**

   Answer: *The King is mean and laughs at him, thinking that Mr. Peters will use his last wish for his own needs. In contrast, Mr. Peters recognizes that he has made the right choice because humans and swans are better being themselves and he won't use his last wish to change anything.*

   Standard 6: Analyze how an author develops and contrasts the point of view of different characters or narrators.

10. **What is the theme of this story?**

    Answer: *The theme is that if you do good even when it hurts to do it you will be rewarded with kindness* **or** *be kind to others without the need for a reward* **or** *be happy with what you have* **or** *Be careful what you wish for as it may not be what is best* **or** *If you love someone and they're unhappy, set them free.*

Standard 2: Determine a theme or central idea of a text and analyze its development over the course of the text.

Summarize the story. The summary is evaluated by the number of elements of a story (e.g., character, initiating event, etc.) it contains. A good summary includes 70 percent of the elements listed in bold. A student must include at least one statement listed under a story element in order to receive credit for that element. Total possible = 7 points

1. Characters _____

A man, Mr. Peters, hears a noise as he is driving near a river

2. Initiating Event _____

He finds a swan tangled in thorns on the river bank

He helps set it free and it turns into the King of the Forest

The King gives him three wishes (leaves) and warns him to use the wishes wisely

3. Event 1 _____

Mr. Peters wishes for a wife and the next morning a beautiful woman named Leita appears and they get married

4. Event 2 _____

After a while Leita becomes sad

He finds her by the river hugging her sister, a swan whom she misses very much

Mr. Peters realizes that Leita is a swan

5. Event 3 _____

Mr. Peters offers to make her back into a swan, but she says no because she is part swan and part human

One night Leita calls her sister's name and says "take me with you"

6. Event 4 _____

Because she wouldn't be happy as a human, Mr. Peters makes her back into a swan

The King returns and laughs at how Mr. Peters used his second wish to undo his first

7. Ending _____

The swans stay nearby for his entire life

When he dies he is found with a leaf and a white feather in his hands/he doesn't use his last wish

Point Table   The Third Wish, Grade 8

Standard	Question	Points per Question
1. Support an inference	3	2
	7	2
2. Determine theme	5	1
	10	1
3. Explain why or how	2	1
	4	1
4. Determine word or phrase meaning	1	1
	8	1
5. Determine point of view	6	2
	9	1
Total Questions		13
2. Summary **Total Summary**		7 (5 acceptable)

Middle School, Grade 8, Part I
Before you begin scoring, please review the guidelines for scoring questions on pages 40–43 and pages 56–58 for scoring summaries.

LITERATURE

The Tell-Tale Heart
by Edgar Allan Poe

1. **What does "Object there was none. Passion there was none" mean in the previous paragraph, and how does it set the tone of the story? (2 pts.)**

Answer: *There was no purpose or emotion driving his plan for the killing* **and** *It makes the story seem scary or dark.* Note: A student can earn one point if the answer addresses only one part of the question.

Standard 4: Determine the meaning of words and phrases as they are used in a story, including figurative and connotative language; analyze the impact of specific word choice on meaning and tone, including analogies.

2. **Describe the evidence that most strongly suggests that the narrator is crazy.**

Answer: *He says, "I heard all things in the heaven and in the earth. I heard many things in hell" and hearing things that aren't there is an indication of mental illness* **or** *He plans to kill the old man just because he doesn't like his eye.*

Standard 1: Cite textual evidence that most strongly supports an analysis of what the text says explicitly as well as inferences drawn from the text.

3. **Analyze how the author creates a feeling of suspense through how carefully the narrator planned the murder compared to how nervous and "mad" the narrator seems in other parts of the story.**

Answer: *The author describes the narrator's madness in planning a murder based on an eye, yet he described the narrator as being kind to the old man the week before as he was planning his action carefully. Suspense occurs through the description of the "vulture eye" as does his careful sneaking around. The narrator seems both rational (careful planning) and irrational (in planning to kill the old man because of an eye).*

Standard 6: Analyze how differences in points of view of the character and audience or reader create effects such as suspense or humor.

4. **Analyze how the events of the eighth night move the plot along.**

    Answer: *The narrator is in the man's room for the eighth night in a row when the man wakes up and says, "Who's there?" Something will happen between them that will move the plot along.*

    Standard 3: Analyze how particular lines of dialogue or incidents in a story propel the action, reveal aspects of a character, or provoke a decision.

5. **What does the phrase "do you mark me well" mean in the previous sentence?**

    Answer: *Do you hear me well/do you understand what I am saying?*

    Standard 4: Determine the meaning of words and phrases as they are used in a story, including figurative and connotative language; analyze the impact of specific word choice on meaning and tone, including analogies.

6. **How does the narrator's behavior, described in the two preceding paragraphs, reveal his beliefs about himself?**

    Answer: *When he describes how he hides the body, he tells us how clever he was* **or** *His behavior shows that he is very confident that what he'd done won't be discovered.* Note: The answer must describe the man's behavior and what it says about his beliefs about himself.

    Standard 3: Analyze how particular lines of dialogue or incidents in a story propel the action, reveal aspects of a character, or provoke a decision.

7. **Analyze how your view of the narrator compares with his view of himself and explain how this increases the story's suspense. (2 pts.)**

    Answer: *The reader is waiting to see when the narrator will be found out but the narrator seems confident in himself and this difference creates tension* **or** *The reader believes that the man's bragging behavior is foolish and will lead to his discovery, but the narrator is confident he has nothing to fear, which adds suspense because the reader is anticipating that his showing off will make the murder be discovered.*

    Standard 6: Analyze how differences in the points of view of the character and the audience or reader effects such as suspense or humor.

8. **Cite the evidence that most strongly supports the inference that the source of the sound getting louder and louder was the narrator's own heart.**

    Answer: *No one else hears the sound* **or** *The police didn't hear the sound* **or** *At the beginning, we are told that he hears things that aren't there and as he gets more and more nervous the sound gets louder* **or** *Fear causes the heart to beat faster and perhaps louder, so it would seem that it was*

within him **or** *It must be the narrator's because the old man is dead and the police don't seem disturbed by any sound.*

Standard 1: Use text information that most strongly supports an inference.

9. **Analyze how the differences between the police's behavior and the narrator's behavior develop suspense in the story.**

    Answer: *At the beginning, the narrator acts normal and the officers are suspicious. Then the roles reverse and the officers act normal, but now the narrator is suspicious that the officers know the secret but are pretending not to. The reader is wondering how long it will take the officers to pick up on the narrator's abnormal behavior.*

    Standard 6: Analyze how differences in points of view of the characters creates effects such as suspense.

10. **What is a theme of this story and how does it relate to the plot of the story? (2 pts.)**

    Answer: *The plot revolves around a murder for no reason by a man who is insane. The theme that emerges is despite careful planning a murderer often either gives him/herself away by his/her own behavior and the evidence is at the end of the story* **or** *A murderer's guilt may eventually consume them, as evidenced by the end of the story* **or** *What goes around comes around, and the evidence is that the narrator killed the man and now the narrator will be punished for it. Other possible themes are: don't do something you'll live to regret (the narrator confesses to the crime in the end)* **or** *Things aren't always what they seem (the old man thought the narrator was harmless and had no idea that he was planning to kill him).*

    Standard 2: Determine a theme as related to the plot of the story.

Summarize this story. The summary is evaluated by the number of elements of a story (i.e., characters, initiating event, etc.) it contains. A good summary includes about 70 percent of the elements listed in bold. A student must include at least one statement listed under a story element in order to receive credit for that element. Total possible = 6 points

1. **Characterization _____**

    The story is about a man who lives with an old man

    Although he loves the old man

    He is afraid of his eye because it reminds him of a vulture

2. **Initiating Event _____**

    So he plans to kill him

    And for seven nights he goes to the old man's room but the eye is closed

3. **Event 1 _____**

    When he goes into the old man's room on the eighth night, the old man hears him and cries out

    The narrator feared that the neighbor would hear it

    So he killed him by putting the bed over him

Then he hid the parts of the body carefully

4. Event 2 _____

In the early morning police officers visited him

Because a neighbor reported a shriek

He took them all over the house

And even sat in the old man's room where his body was hidden

5. Event 3 _____

The narrator was fine for a while

But then became agitated that the police remained

He was hearing things and began talking constantly

The officers just sat there saying nothing

6. Ending _____

He began to think that they knew what had happened

And their silence caused him to be terrified

And he confessed ("I admitted the deed")

Point Table   The Tell-Tale Heart, Grade 8

Standard	Question	Points per Question
1. Support an inference	2	1
	8	1
2. Determine theme	10	2
3. Explain why or how	4	1
	6	1
4. Determine word or phrase meaning	1	2
	5	1
6. Determine point of view	3	1
	7	2
	9	1
Total Questions		13
2. Summary Total Summary		6 (4 acceptable)

Middle School, Grade 8, Part II   Before you begin scoring, please review the guidelines for scoring questions on pages 40–43 and pages 56–58 for scoring summaries.

LITERATURE

The Drummer Boy of Shiloh
by Ray Bradbury

1. **Cite evidence that strongly supports that the boy was afraid.**

   Answer: *The sound of the peach pit falling made him sit up quickly* **or** *His heart was beating fast* **or** *He could hear his heart beat* **or** *"Struck once, like panic, which jerked the boy upright" meaning he felt panic.*

   Standard 1: Cite evidence that most strongly supports an analysis of what the text says explicitly as well as inferences drawn from the text.

2. **What does the phrase "compounded of remote but nonetheless firm and fiery family devotion, flag-blown patriotism and cocksure immortality," mean in the previous paragraph?**

   Answer: *It describes that the soldiers were motivated by devotion to their family, patriotism,* **or** *Their belief that they would come back alive* **or** *It describes why they were willing to go into battle.*

   Standard 4: Determine the meaning of words and phrases as they are used in a text, including figurative and connotative meanings; analyze the impact of specific word choices on meaning and tone.

3. **Analyze how the boy's point of view of the other soldiers' protection differs from his view of his own protection and how these views create suspense in the story. (2 pts.)**

   Answer: *He believes that the other soldiers are better protected because they have weapons, but he has only his drum and two sticks to beat it. Because of these differences the reader wonders if he is right and what will happen to him.*

   Standard 6: Analyze how the differences in the points of view of the characters and audience **or** reader create effects as suspense or humor.

4. **Cite strong evidence that shows that the General is aware of the youth of his soldiers.**

   Answer: *He asks Joby if he shaves yet* **or** *He describes all of the soldiers as "raw"* **or** *He compares Joby's cheek to a peach* **or** *He calls him "boy."*

   Standard 1: Cite evidence that most strongly supports an analysis of what the text says explicitly as well as inferences drawn from the text.

5. **Analyze what the General believes about the war and why he feels that way, using words from the text. (2 pts.)**

   Answer: *He believes the war is wrong ("it's wrong boy, it's wrong)* **or** *He believes it is going to be a crazy time* **or** *He believes that because "not one as can spit a sparrow off a tree, or knows a horse clod from a minnieball"* **or** *"We should turn tail and train four months, they should do the same"* **or** *"More innocents will get shot out of pure enthusiasm than ever got shot before."*

Standard 3: Analyze how particular lines of dialogue or incidents in the story propel the action, reveal aspects of a character, or provoke a decision.

6. **Analyze how Joby's and the General's different points of view of Joby's role in the war create suspense. (2 pts.)**

   Answer: *Joby doesn't think his job as the drummer is valuable and suspense builds as the general explains how Joby's role is very important to the war, in fact the heart of the army* **or** *Joby doesn't believe he is prepared enough to be valuable and suspense grows as the general describes the value of Joby's role.* Note: The answer must include the different points of view of Joby and the General and how that builds suspense.

   Standard 6: Analyze how the differences in the points of view of the characters and audience or reader create effects as suspense or humor.

7. **Cite evidence from the text of how Joby's drumming could result in the loss of soldiers' lives.**

   Answer: *If he beats the drum slowly the solders would walk slowly and "drowse in the field," and "they would sleep forever" or die.*

   Standard 1: Cite evidence that most strongly supports an analysis of what the text says explicitly as well as inferences drawn from the text.

8. **What do the phrases, "Move the blood up the body and make the head proud and the spine stiff and the jaw resolute. Focus the eye and set the teeth, flare the nostrils and tighten the hands," mean in the previous paragraph?**

   Answer: *The fast and steady beat of the drum can make the men stand tall and focus on the job at hand* **or** *The beat of the drum can make the men stronger in battle* **or** *A fast drum beat motivated the men to move quicker and march faster* **or** *It shows the soldiers feeling courage and determination.*

   Standard 4: Determine the meaning of words and phrases as they are used in a text, including figurative and connotative meanings; analyze the impact of specific word choices on meaning and tone.

9. **Analyze how the General shows his leadership when he explains Joby's role.**

   Answer: *His explanation of Joby's role shows that he knows how to motivate people* **or** *His explanation of Joby's role shows that he knows a lot about war* **or** *The General knows how to make each soldier feel important and needed.*

   Standard 3: Analyze how particular lines of dialogue or incidents in a story propel the action, reveal aspects of a character, or provoke a decision.

10. **What is a theme of this story and how do the characters reveal it? (2 pts.)**

    Answer: *It is important to know that your role in a job is valued* **or** *Support of someone in charge is important for those who work with/under the leader and it is revealed through the general's explanation of what Joby's role was in the war* **or** *A theme is to never give up and the General didn't give up on Joby* **or** *With power comes responsibility and with the General's power came responsibility to see that the soldiers understood their role* **or** *It was shown when he prepares Joby to be the general in case of his death* **or** *The theme is don't let your fears stop you, revealed when Joby was able to overcome his fears because of the General's explanation of his role.*

    Standard 2: Determine a theme or central idea in a text and analyze its development over the course of the text, including its relationship to the characters, setting, and plot.

Summarize the story. The summary is evaluated by the number of elements of a story (e.g., character, initiating event, etc.) it contains. A good summary includes 70 percent of the elements listed in bold. A student must include at least one statement listed under a story element in order to receive credit for that element. (Total possible = 7 points)

1. **Setting** _____

   The story takes place on a battlefield near Shiloh during the Civil War

2. **Characterization** _____

   The boy character, Joby, is afraid when unfamiliar noises startle him

   He is afraid to fight in the war because other soldiers have shields to protect them and

   Weapons to fight with

   But he only has a drum and sticks to beat on it and feels unimportant

3. **Initiating Event** _____

   The General comes by and stops to talk with him

   About the uselessness of the war with young untrained troops

4. **Event 1** _____

   He explains that Joby's role is centrally important to the outcome of the battles

   Joby is the heart of the army

5. **Event 2** _____

   He says that how Joby beats the drum will affect how the men march into battle

   If he beats the drum slowly, the men will march slowly and will die

But if he beats it faster and stronger the men will march faster and have confidence in battle

6. Event 3 _____

He tells Joby that he is the general of the army if/when the general is left behind/dies

7. Ending

Joby realizes the importance of his job and

Settles down for the night more prepared for the day ahead

Point Table   The Drummer Boy of Shiloh, Grade 8

Standard	Question	Points per Question
1. Support an inference	1	1
	4	1
	7	1
2. Determine theme	10	2
3. Analyze	5	2
	9	1
4. Determine word or phrase meaning	2	1
	8	1
6. Determine point of view	3	2
	6	2
Total Questions		14
2. Summary **Total Summary**		7 (5 acceptable)

Middle School, Grade 8, Part III
Before you begin scoring, please review the guidelines for scoring questions on pages 40–43 and pages 56–58 for scoring summaries.

LITERATURE

The Story-Teller
by Saki (H.H. Monroe)

1. **What does "but the small girls and the small boy emphatically occupied the compartment" mean in the previous paragraph?**

   Answer: *That the children were very obviously in the compartment because of their behavior, especially noise, which sets the tone for how the children act throughout the story*

   Standard 4: Determine the meaning of words and phrases as they are used in a story, including figurative and connotative language; analyze the impact of specific word choice on meaning and tone, including analogies.

2. **Analyze how the dialogue between the aunt and Cyril reveals their personalities.**

   Answer: *Cyril is a curious and persistent child who asks probing questions. His aunt's answers to his questions are not strong answers and it shows that she is not skilled in caring for children who are curious and persistent.*

   Standard 3: Analyze how particular lines of dialogue or incidents in a story propel the action, reveal aspects of a character, or provike a decision.

3. **Cite the evidence that most strongly suggests that the man is getting disturbed.**

   Answer: *He had looked at the aunt twice* **or** *He looked at the communication cord* **or** *The man's face was deepening into a scowl.*

Standard 1: Cite the textual evidence that most strongly supports an analysis of what the text says explicitly as well as inferences drawn from the text.

4. **What does the story reveal about how the children and the narrator feel about the aunt's storytelling ability?**

   Answer: *One of the children sings a song while the aunt is telling a story and others move toward her without enthusiasm and the narrator uses several negative words when describing the aunt's storytelling ability* **or** *The narrator describes the aunt's story as "unenterprising and deplorably uninteresting"* **or** *The narrator describes the aunt's response to Cyril as "weak."*

   Standard 6: Analyze how differences in points of view of the character and the audience or reader creates effects such as suspense or humor.

5. **How does the man's comment about the aunt's ability to tell stories move the plot forward?**

   Answer: *His judgment of the aunt's storytelling sets him up for his telling a better one* **or** *it stops her boring story and progresses into his entertaining the children* **or** *The conflict between the aunt and the bachelor makes the story more exciting.*

   Standard 3: Analyze how particular lines of dialogue or incidents in a story propel the action, reveal aspects of a character, or provike a decision.

6. **What does the phrase "wave of reaction" mean in the previous paragraph and how does it affect the tone of the story? (2 pts.)**

Answer: *Response/feeling/feedback that changes the children's attitude from uninterested to interested*

Standard 4: Determine the meaning of words and phrases as they are used in a story, including figurative and connotative language; analyze the impact of specific word choice on meaning and tone, including analogies.

7. Cite the two pieces of evidence that most strongly explain why the aunt is smiling. **(2 pts.)**

    Answer: *When Cyril asked why there weren't any sheep the aunt was pleased because she had been asked the same type of questions* **or** *When Cyril asked "the inevitable question" the aunt was amused that the man received the same treatment as she had* **or** *The man is being challenged in the same way the aunt was.* Note: It isn't sufficient to simply quote Cyril; the response must include reference to the aunt receiving similar treatment.

    Standard 1: Provide the evidence that most strongly supports an inference.

8. Analyze how the man's description of the park keeps the children interested in his story.

    Answer: *His description is detailed and he has an unusual explanation for why there were no sheep in the park and this keeps the children paying attention to the story* **or** *The detailed descriptions make a picture in the children's minds and that keeps them attending to the story.* Note: The student's response needs to be more general than simply listing characteristics of the pigs; it must refer to the descriptive quality of the man's story.

    Standard 3: Analyze how lines of dialogue propel the action.

9. How do the differences between the children's and the aunt's points of view of the man's story create humor at the end?

    Answer: *The aunt's reaction to the story is negative because she thinks the moral of it is inappropriate for young children, but the children loved it* **or** *Because the children loved the story they will be asking for similar stories in the future and the aunt would not like that.*

    Standard 6: Analyze how differences in the points of view of the characters and the audience or reader creates effects such as suspense or humor.

10. **What is the central theme of** *The Story-Teller*? **Support your answer with evidence from the text. (2 pts.)**

    Answer: *That to keep children entertained you have to make things different/novel and the evidence is the detail of the story told by the bachelor* **or** *You can't judge a book*

by its cover because at first the bachelor seemed unpleasant but when he told the story he was very pleasant **or** *The most unexpected people can be what children want because although the bachelor seemed unpleasant at the beginning the children enjoyed him at the end.*

Standard 2: Determine a theme or a central idea of a text and analyze its development over the course of the text, including its relationships to the characters, setting, and plot.

Summarize the story. The summary is evaluated by the number of elements of a story (e.g., character, initiating event, etc.) it contains. A good summary includes 70 percent of the elements listed in bold. A student must include at least one statement listed under a story element in order to receive credit for that element. Total possible = 7 points

1. **Setting** _____
   The story begins on a train ride

2. **Characterization** _____
   Where three children and their aunt are sitting in a compartment
   With an unknown man who is a bachelor

3. **Initiating Event** _____
   The children are restless and bored
   The aunt is trying to keep the children entertained by telling them stories
   But they aren't very good ones
   The man is getting irritated by the interaction between the aunt and the children

4. **Event 1** _____
   And tells the aunt that she doesn't have much success as a storyteller.
   She becomes defensive and suggests that perhaps he would like to tell them one

5. **Event 2** _____
   The man's story starts out as boring as the aunt's stories
   Until he says the girl was "horribly good"
   That comment pulls the children into the story
   And he continued with a very unusual story that had lots of details
   About the girl walking in the Prince's park when a large wolf came toward her
   She hid in the bushes but her medals made a noise and the wolf ate her

6. Event 3 _____

The children agreed that this was the most beautiful story they had ever heard

The aunt, however, thought it was inappropriate to tell to small children

7. Ending _____

The story ends with the bachelor thinking to himself that at least he kept the children quiet, which was more than she could do

And that the children would be asking for improper stories in the future

Point Table   The Story-Teller, Grade 8

Standard	Question	Points per Question
1. Support an inference	3	1
	7	2
2. Determine theme	10	2
3. Explain why or how	2	1
	5	1
	8	1
4. Determine word or phrase meaning	1	1
	6	2
6. Determine point of view	4	1
	9	1
Total Questions		13
2. Summary **Total Summary**		7 (5 acceptable)

High School, Grade 9, Part I   Before you begin scoring, please review the guidelines for scoring questions on pages 40–43 and pages 56–58 for scoring summaries.

LITERATURE

Sonata for Harp and Bicycle
by Joan Aiken

1. **Analyze how the segments in italics affect the mood of the story's setting.**

   Answer: *They make the story sound ugly/creepy/scary because the description of the building is dark* **or** *Because of the reference to bats, which most people find scary.*

   Standard 4: Determine the meaning of words and phrases as they are used in text, including figurative and connotative meanings; analyze the cumulative effect of specific word choices on meaning and tone.

2. **What does the word *rustling* mean in the following sentence? "A multitudinous shuffling, a rustling as of innumerable bluebottle flies might have been heard by the attentive ear after this injunction as the employees of Moreton Wold and Company thrust their papers into cases, hurried letters and invoices into drawers . . ."**

   Answer: *Noise that all of the office workers made when they were putting their papers away at the same time* **or** *A buzz of activity.*

   Standard 4: Determine the meaning of words and phrases as they are used in text, including figurative and connotative meanings; analyze the cumulative effect of specific word choices on meaning and tone.

3. **Analyze how the interaction between Miss Golden and Mr. Ashgrove advances the plot.**

   Answer: *Their interactions occur around her knowledge of a secret about the Grimes Building, which he wants to know; the interactions suggest that the story will tell us what the secret is* **or** *Once Mr. Ashgrove realizes Miss Golden likes him, he can use it to manipulate her into telling the secret.*

   Standard 3: Analyze how complex characters (those with multiple motivations) develop over the course of the text, interact with other characters, and advance the plot or develop the theme.

4. **What does the phrase "a well of gloom sank beneath him" mean in the previous paragraph and how does it affect the tone of the story? (2 pts.)**

   Answer: *It was very dark beneath him when he got to the ninth floor* **and** *The tone is gloomy/scary* **or** *The use of the word "well" suggests that the gloom was deep* **and** *It makes the story scary.*

   Standard 4: Determine the meaning of words and phrases as they are used in text, including figurative and connotative meanings; analyze the cumulative effect of specific word choices on meaning and tone.

5. **Cite evidence to show why Jason becomes afraid when he hears the sound of the bell.**

   Answer: *No one is supposed to be in the building and Miss Golden told him about a harp and a bicycle—it could be the ring of a bicycle horn* **or** *Because no one is supposed to be in the building the ringing could be an alarm, or an indication that someone else is in the building.*

   Standard 1: Cite strong and thorough evidence to support analysis of what the text says explicitly as well as inferences drawn from the text.

6. **What do the sentences in italics suggest Jason was looking at?**

Answer: *He was looking into two eyes of a ghost because they were "carved out of expressionless air," which means they weren't attached to anything* **or** *It was a ghost because he was held by two hands, knotted together out of the width of the dark.*

Standard 1: Cite strong and thorough evidence to support an analysis of what the text says explicitly as well as inferences drawn from the text.

7. **Analyze how Jason's interactions with the bicyclist advance the plot of the story.**

   Answer: *It explains part of the mystery of what happened in the Grimes Building (the man is still looking for Daisy and finds Jason instead)* **or** *When the ghost says "you wouldn't be much loss, would you?" Jason realizes he's in love with Miss Golden, which advances the plot.*

   Standard 3: Analyze how complex characters (those with multiple motivations) develop over the course of the text, interact with other characters, and advance the plot or develop the theme.

8. **Cite evidence in the text that suggests that Jason plans a celebration for two couples.**

   Answer: *He is bringing two bottles of wine and two bunches of roses.*

   Standard 1: Cite strong and thorough textual evidence to support analysis of what the text says explicitly as well as inference drawn from the text.

9. **Provide strong evidence that Mr. Heron and Miss Bell were actually in Room 492.**

   Answer: *There was music coming from the room and there wasn't anyone else in the building* **or** *The music was sweet and triumphant, a positive sign they had gotten together* **or** *Berenice and Jason were left with a memory of a bicycle with a harp/bottle of wine/bouquet of roses.*

   Standard 1: Cite strong and thorough textual evidence to support analysis of what the text says explicitly as well as inferences drawn from the text.

Summarize the story. The summary is evaluated by the number of elements of a story (e.g., characters, initiating events, etc.) it contains. A good summary includes 70 percent of the elements listed in bold. A student must include at least one statement listed under a story element in order to receive credit for that element. Total possible = 7 points

1. **Setting** _____

   The setting of the story is a dark and mysterious office building

2. **Characterization** _____

   Jason is a new employee and Miss Golden is a young woman who has worked there for several years

3. **Initiating Event** _____

   Jason asks Miss Golden why they all have to leave the building at the same time every night

   She knows but won't tell him

   They are attracted to each other

4. **Event 1** _____

   That night he goes to the building to find out

   He meets the bicyclist in the form of a ghost

   And learns that he is looking for a woman

   Then the bicyclist tries to throw him off the fire escape

5. **Event 2** _____

   His hair turns white and Miss Golden knows where he's been

   Miss Golden tells him the entire story

   He plans to unite the ghosts and prevent the curse from happening to him

6. **Event 3** _____

   They go to the building together with wine and roses

   To unite the ghosts

   When Jason and Miss Golden go to the room

   They hear music coming from it

   They leave the wine and roses there

7. **Ending** _____

   And with a parachute on they jump off the fire escape

   With another bottle of wine and roses in their hands

10. **What is a theme of this story and how does the author communicate it to the reader? (2 pts.)**

    Answer: *Theme: love conquers all was developed through the budding romance between the two office workers. The author communicates it through several things: 1. When she knew a secret and wouldn't tell him that was teasing like flirtation. She is afraid that he'll go there and she doesn't want him hurt. 2. When he comes in with gray hair she knows where he's been and finally tells him the story. 3. He kisses her passionately and makes a plan to get rid of the curse. When they go to the building to confront the ghost 4. He brings flowers and wine for the ghosts and when 5. they jump with parachutes on they have wine and roses with them.* **or** *Theme: Courage and* *innovation wins out—communicated by the author when Jason first goes to the building at night and later when he plans to go to the building with Berenice and unite the ghosts and brings the 3 RAF parachute.* **or** *Theme: Don't assume that a person's behavior means a specific thing and this was communicated by Mr. Heron's belief that Ms. Bell had betrayed him so he jumped off the building and killed himself.*

Standard 2: Determine a theme or central idea of a text and analyze in detail its development over the course of the text, including how it emerges and is shaped and refined by specific details.

Point Table   Sonata for Harp and Bicycle, Grade 9

Standard	Question	Points per Question
1. Support an inference	5	1
	6	1
	8	1
	9	1
2. Determine theme	10	2
3. Analyze	3	1
	7	1
4. Determine word or phrase meaning	1	1
	2	1
	4	2
Total Questions		12
2. Summary **Total Summary**		7 (5 acceptable)

High School, Grade 9, Part II
Before you begin scoring, please review the guidelines for scoring questions on pages 40–43 and pages 56–58 for scoring summaries.

Blues Ain't No Mockin Bird
by Toni Cade Bambara

1. **What does Granny mean by "we ain't a bunch of trees?"**

   Answer: *That they were people to be respected, not objects to take pictures of*

   Standard 4: Determine the meaning of phrases used in the text, including figurative and connotative meaning.

2. **How do the three segments in italics affect the meaning and tone of the story? (2 pts.)**

   Answer: *The sentences are describing the beginning of a conflict between white men and a black property owner, which makes the tone tense* **or** *Granny is not happy that the men are on her property and the men are trying to win her over, and the potential conflict sets the tone as tense.*

   Standard 4: Determine the meaning of words and phrases as they are used in the text; analyze the cumulative impact of specific word choices on meaning and tone.

3. **Analyze how the author has portrayed the character of Granny by how she interacts with the photographer and provide one example of her behavior. (2 pts.)**

   Answer: *Granny is shown to be assertive by saying what she means ("Go tell that man we ain't a bunch of trees"); she also communicates her displeasure through facial expressions ("she smiled that smile"; "'Did you?' said Granny with her eyebrows").*

   Standard 3: Analyze how complex characters develop over the course of the text, interact with other characters, and advance the plot or develop the theme.

4. **Analyze how the author develops the character of the camera man by how he acts with Granny.**

   Answer: *He is persistent in doing what he was sent there to do without regard for Granny's feelings; he starts by using polite words but he doesn't ask permission to photograph Granny's property ("we'd thought we'd get a picture"); he tries flattery ("nice place you've got here"); when Granny says she doesn't want them taking pictures the camera man says, "Now Aunty" and continues to point his camera at her.*

   Standard 3: Analyze how complex characters develop over the course of a text and interact with other characters, and advance the plot or the theme.

5. **Analyze how the interaction between Granny and the men in the previous scene advances the plot of the story.**

   Answer: *The plot has developed by having male characters that come onto property without permission, express familiarity with Granny where there was none ("Now, Aunty") and most of the time Granny says very little when they ask her questions ("Granny said nothing," "Granny wasn't sayin nuthin"). The author uses Granny's nonverbal messages and the men's insistence in doing what they were sent to do to create a conflict between them that advances the plot* **or** *Granny appears strong because she is willing to stand up to the men and this adds to the tension in the plot.*

   Standard 3: Analyze how complex characters develop over the course of the text, interact with other characters, and advance the plot or develop the theme.

6. **Cite evidence to explain the connection between the story Granny is telling above and the incident between Granny and the men doing the filming.**

   Answer: *The common link is the inconsiderate behavior of folks towards others, especially black folks. Granny told the story to illustrate how inconsiderate people can be in times of trouble.*

   Standard 1: Cite strong and thorough textual evidence to support analysis of what the text says explicitly as well as inferences drawn from the text.

7. Cite evidence that explains Granny's anger in the past.

    Answer: *Granny is angry because people wouldn't pay her or would bring her boxes of old clothes or someone comes into her house and exclaims (surprised) how clean it is* **or** *She isn't shown any respect, so she is angry.*

    Standard 1: Cite strong and thorough textual evidence to support analysis of what the text says explicitly as well as inferences drawn from the text.

8. What does the sentence, "Like he'd invited them in to play cards and they'd stayed too long and all the sandwiches were gone and Reverend Webb was droppin by and it was time to go" mean?

    Answer: *His greeting was very casual, like he'd known these men and they just stopped by for a visit* **or** *It also suggests that the men have overstayed their welcome and are being asked to leave.*

    Standard 4: Determine the meaning of phrases used in the text, including figurative and connotative meaning; analyze the cumulative impact of specific word choices on meaning and tone.

9. Cite strong evidence that the author's initial portrayal of Granddaddy makes it surprising that he opened the man's camera.

    Answer: *He is portrayed as polite ("Good day, gentlemen") and a strong but silent man ("Granddaddy tall and silent and like a king") and there is no evidence that he will do anything negative.*

    Standard 1: Cite strong and thorough textual evidence to support analysis of what the text says explicitly as well as inferences drawn from the text.

Summarize the story. The summary is evaluated by the number of elements of a story (e.g., character, initiating event, etc.) it contains. A good summary includes 70 percent of the elements listed in bold. A student must include at least one statement listed under a story element in order to receive credit for that element. Total possible = 7 points

1. **Setting** _____

    The story takes place in a rural area of the south

2. **Characterization** _____

    Where Granny is working in the kitchen and

    The children are playing outside

3. **Initiating Event** _____

    Two strange men come on their property taking pictures

    Granny doesn't like it

4. **Event 1** _____

    The men ask her if they can take pictures of her property for the county

    She says no

    One of the men calls her Aunty and

She reminds him that she and his mother are not related

They continue to try to get her to do what they want and she is silent

They back away but continue to take pictures

5. **Event 2** _____

    Granny tells the children a "teaching story" about people not being considerate of others

    The narrator knows the story has something to do with how people treat Granny and

    Her getting mad and the family moving in the middle of the night

6. **Event 3** _____

    Granddaddy comes back from hunting with a hawk and

    The men take pictures of him

    Granddaddy holds out his hand for the camera

    When they hand it to him he takes it apart so the film is exposed

    Then he tells them that they're standing "in the misses' flower bed"

7. **Ending** _____

    They gather the film and back off and

    The children hear Granny humming

10. What is the theme of the story and how does Granddaddy's behavior support it? **(2 pts.)**

    Answer: *The theme is that if you want something from people you must treat them with respect. If you don't treat them that way you won't get what you want. Granddaddy's behavior shows that he isn't accepting the lack of respect for his family or his property* **or** *The theme is not to tolerate nosy people and Granddaddy doesn't.*

    Standard 2: Determine a theme or central idea of a text and analyze in detail its development over the course of the text, including how it emerges and is shaped and refined by specific details.

Point Table   Blues Ain't No Mockin Bird, Grade 9

Standard	Question	Points per Question
1. Support an inference	6	1
	7	1
	9	1
2. Determine theme	10	2
3. Analyze	3	2
	4	1
	5	1
4. Determine word or phrase meaning	1	1
	2	2
	8	1
Total Questions		13
2. Summary **Total Summary**		7 (5 acceptable)

A Problem

by Anton Chekhov

1. **Explain, using textual evidence, how the Colonel's views of Sasha's behavior differ from the views held by Ivan Markovitch.**

    Answer: *They hold very different positions. The Colonel thinks that Sasha should be punished by going to trial ("fa-mil-y ho-nor false-ly un-der-stood is a prejudice! Falsely understood! That's what I say: whatever may be the motives for screening a scoundrel, whoever he may be, and helping him to escape punishment, it is contrary to law and unworthy of a gentleman. It's not saving family honor; it's civic cowardice!") and Ivan thinks that he should be forgiven because he is a young man ("He began by saying that youth has its rights and its peculiar temptations. 'Which of us has not been young, and who has not been led astray? To say nothing of ordinary mortals, even great men have not escaped errors and mistakes in their youth.'").*

    Standard 3: Analyze how complex characters develop over the course of the text, interact with other characters, and advance the plot or develop the theme.

2. **What did Ivan Markovitch assume Sasha was feeling during the family meeting? Cite evidence from the text.**

    Answer: *That Sasha's conscience is bothering him ("he was punished as it was by his conscience and the agonies he was enduring now while waiting the sentence of his relations")*

    Standard 1: Cite strong and thorough textual evidence to support analysis of what the text says explicitly as well as inferences drawn from the text.

3. **What does the word *blot* mean in the phrase, "a blot should be cast on the escutcheon, family shield with coat of arms"?**

    Answer: *A bad mark/black mark*

    Standard 4: Determine in the text, including figurative and connotative meanings; analyze the cumulative impact of specific word choices on meaning and tone.

4. **Analyze how the Russian philosophy that criminals are not responsible for their actions because they have no free will and every crime is "the product of the pure anatomical peculiarities of the individual" is similar to and different from a crime you have heard about locally or nationally. (2 pts.)**

    Answer: *The example given should explain that in many countries it is believed that criminals are responsible for their behavior except in cases of mental illness. That view differs from the Russian philosophy because it is believed that criminals are usually responsible for their behavior, but it is similar to the Russian philosophy in cases where*

the criminal has been found to have a mental illness and therefore is not responsible for his behavior.

Standard 6: Analyze a point of view or cultural experience reflected in a work of literature from outside the United States, drawing on a wide reading of world literature.

5. **Analyze how the arguments between the uncles advance the plot.**

    Answer: *They illustrate how deeply the two uncles feel about the situation, which shows that they will continue to argue for a long time* **or** *Their deeply held views illustrate the range of consequences that could be presented and they don't agree* **or** *The tension between the uncles continues adding suspense that will lead to the climax of the story.*

    Standard 3: Analyze how complex characters develop over the course of the text, interact with other characters, and advance the plot or develop the theme.

6. **What does "they had begun to be too contemptuous of his sponging on them" mean?**

    Answer: *His friends didn't like that he was borrowing money from them, using their food and drink, etc.*

    Standard 4: Determine the meaning of words and phrases as they are used in the text, including figurative and connotative meanings; analyze the cumulative impact of specific word choices on meaning and tone.

7. **Analyze how Sasha's thinking, as explained in the previous paragraph, will advance the plot of the story.**

    Answer: *It suggests that he doesn't take responsibility for his behavior and that will likely cause problems later.*

    Standard 3: Analyze how complex characters develop over the course of the text, interact with other characters, and advance the plot or develop the theme.

Summarize the story. The summary is evaluated by the number of elements of a story (e.g., characters, initiating event, etc.) it contains. A good summary includes 70 percent of the elements listed in bold. A student must include at least one statement listed under a story element in order to receive credit for that element. Total possible = 8 points

1. **Characterization** _____

    This is a story about a young man, Sasha, and his uncles

2. **Initiating Event** _____

    Sasha has cashed a false promissory note at a bank

    And the due date for payment has passed

3. **Event 1** _____

    His two paternal uncles and one maternal uncle were arguing about what should be done.

4. Event 2 _____

One side thought that the debt should be paid to save the family's honor

The other side believed that they should do nothing and let the case go to trial

One uncle, a Colonel, believed that it was their civic duty to allow Sasha to be tried and punished

The other paternal uncle, Ivan, spoke about the scandal if the family name was in the paper

5. Event 3 _____

Ivan was kind hearted and thought that they should give Sasha a chance

Because all young people make mistakes

He argued that Sasha had lost his parents when he was young

So he grew up with little guidance

6. Event 4 _____

While this argument was going on Sasha was sitting outside the door listening

He didn't care where he ended up

He was in debt and his friends were turning against him

Because he borrowed money and ate their food

Sasha felt cashing the note wasn't his fault

Because a friend had told him he would lend him money and he didn't

He didn't like it when his uncles were calling him a scoundrel and a criminal

7. Event 5 _____

The Colonel thought that if they paid the debt that Sasha would just do something like it again.

The uncles never agreed but in the end forgave the note.

8. Ending _____

As they were leaving, Sasha asked Ivan to lend him money

His uncle looked at him unbelieving, but gave it to him

Sasha decided that in fact he was a criminal

8. What does the phrase "some uneasy weight were gradually slipping off his shoulders" mean?

Answer: *That Sasha felt some relief at the decision*

Standard 4: Determine the meaning of words and phrases as they are used in the text, including figurative and connotative meanings; analyze the cumulative impact of specific word choices on meaning and tone.

9. Determine the central ideas of the story and analyze how they are developed over the course of the entire story. Cite textual evidence to support your answer. **(2 pts.)**

Answer: *the story is based on arguments on how to punish (or not) a person who has falsified an IOU. Two uncles have strongly opposing views. One (Colonel) doesn't believe that paying the debt will mean that Sasha won't do the same thing in the future. Ivan wants to give the boy a chance because he is young and makes foolish mistakes like we all do. At the end we see that the Colonel was right, and when Sasha asks Ivan for more money Ivan realizes it too* **or** *The central idea in the story is about how different members of a Russian family define family honor. One uncle views honor as following the rules of society and the other believes that honor is not sacrificed if they give their nephew a chance.*

Std #2: Determine a theme or central idea of a text and analyze in detail its development over the course of the text, including how it emerges and is shaped and refined by specific details.

10. Cite strong and thorough text evidence to explain whether or not Sasha was a criminal.

Answer: *There are two possible arguments, but the first one is the best, I believe. Any one of the following three justifications is acceptable. Yes, he was a criminal because he forged a promissory note and he continued to take money from his Uncle Ivan with no evidence that he will pay it back; He didn't really care what the outcome of the uncles' arguments would be as he thought that without money he had no life, and he doesn't consider how to earn it; Sasha acknowledges that his actions are criminal which suggests that he does not intend to pay the money back, now or in the future* **or** *No, he isn't a criminal because he only stole from his family.*

Standard 1: Cite strong and thorough text evidence to support analysis of what the text says explicitly as well as inferences drawn from the text.

Point Table   A Problem, Grade 9/10

Standard	Question	Points per Question
1. Support an inference	2 10	1 1
2. Determine theme	9	2
3. Analyze	1 5 7	1 1 1
4. Determine word or phrase meaning	3 6 8	1 1 1
6. Determine point of view	4	2
Total Questions		12
2. Summary **Total Summary**		8 (6 acceptable)

The United States, Vast and Varied: The Northeast

1. Which text structure best explains how the author organized the above passage? **(2 pts.)**

   ____ description of important features

   ____ account of cause and effect

   ____ comparison/contrast of two or more things

   Give a reason from the text for your answer. For example, if you choose description, tell what is being described. For cause and effect, state a cause or an effect mentioned in the text. For comparison, tell what is being compared or contrasted.

   Answer: *Description; the author describes the characteristics of a region such as landforms and climates. Reasons that are not present in the text are inaccurate.*

   Standard 5: Describe the overall structure of a text.

2. What evidence in the text indicates that landforms can cross from one region to another?

   Answer: *The Appalachian Mountains begin in Canada and extend through the Northeast* **or** *extends through the Northeast into the Southeast.*

   Standard 1: Refer to details and examples in a text when explaining what the text says explicitly and when drawing inferences from the text.

3. What is the meaning of *located* in the context of the above paragraph? **(AWL level 3)**

   Answer: *Found, situated, placed, where something is*

   Standard 4: Determine the meaning of general academic and domain-specific words or phrases.

4. Explain how two changes in temperature formed Niagara Falls. **(2 pts.)**

   Answer: *The climate was cold so the glaciers formed* **and** *it got warmer so the ice melted. As a two-point question, there should be two clearly defined answers.*

   Standard 3: Explain events, procedures, ideas, or concepts based on specific information in the text.

5. How is Carl Sandburg's description of Niagara Falls ("go white, go green, go changing over the gray, the brown, the rocks") different from the description in most of the paragraph? Your answer should include both Sandberg and the author of the text.

   Answer: *Sandburg described the colors of the water; the author of the paragraph described how far the water plunges and how much water goes over the Falls* **or** *The*

author focused on science **or** *facts while Sandburg focused on the appearance or beauty* **or** *Sandburg's comments were opinion and the author's were factual.* The answer should include reference to both Sandberg and the author of the text.

   Standard 6: Compare and contrast a firsthand and secondhand account on the same event or topic.

6. The topic of the above paragraph is "The Narragansett People." What is the central idea of the paragraph?

   Answer: *At first the Narragansett and the colonists got along but then they became enemies* **or** *The author describes how the Narragansett and the colonists lived.* The answer must be clearly related to the topic. Do not accept a series of details as the central idea.

   Standard 2: Determine central idea/s.

7. What evidence in the text indicates that the Narragansett would not allow a member of their community to go without food?

   Answer: *"Whenever a family needed something done all of their neighbors as well as family helped"* **or** *They "lived in a cooperative society that worked together to get things done."*

   Standard 1: Refer to details and examples in a text when explaining what the text says explicitly and when drawing inferences from the text.

8. Explain why early Europeans and the Narragansett lived in peace.

   Answer: *Both groups benefited from or helped each other* **or** *The European traders traded goods such as axes and hoes with the Narragansett for animal furs* **or** *The settlers bought land from the Narragansett* **or** *The early settlers let the Narragansett have their own land and independence.*

   Standard 3: Explain events, procedures, ideas, or concepts based on specific information in the text.

9. What is the meaning of *resources* in the context of the above paragraph? **(AWL level 2)**

   Answer: *Products, goods, something useful or desirable*

   Standard 4: Determine the meaning of general academic and domain-specific words or phrases.

10. The topic of the above paragraph is "Resources of the Northeast." What is the central idea of the paragraph?

   Answer: *The Northeast provides many resources for the country* **or** *the author describes the resources of the Northeast.* The answer must be clearly related to the topic. Do not accept a series of details as the central idea.

   Standard 2: Determine central idea/s.

Summarize what the text says about how the relationship between Europeans and Narragansett changed over time. An acceptable text-based summary contains the following units. Students receive one point for each statement in their summary that matches the following statements in meaning.

1. An introductory statement of purpose
2. The relationship between Europeans and Narragansett was friendly at first
3. They traded with each other
4. Then the Europeans took Narragansett land
5. The Narragansett tried to keep their land
6. Fights broke out
7. Many Narragansett were killed in battle
8. Many moved away

Point Table   The Northeast, Grade 4

Standard		Question	Points per Question
1.	Support an inference	2 7	1 1
2.	Determine central idea	6 10	1 1
3.	Explain why or how/analyze	4 8	2 1
4.	Determine word meaning	3 9	1 1
5.	Determine text structure	1	2
6.	Determine point of view	5	1
Total Questions			12
2. Summary			8
Total Summary			(6 acceptable)

Elementary School, Grade 4, Part II   Before you begin scoring, please review the guidelines for scoring questions on pages 40–43 and pages 63–67 for scoring summaries.

SOCIAL STUDIES

The United States, Vast and Varied: The Southeast

1. **The topic of the above paragraph is "The Mississippi River." What is the central idea of the paragraph?**

   Answer: *The Mississippi River affects the people and land of the Southeast* **or** *The author describes the Mississippi River and its effects on the land and people.* The answer must be clearly related to the topic. Do not accept a series of details as the central idea.

   Standard 2: Determine the central idea of a text.

2. **What is the meaning of** *major* **in the context of the above paragraph? (AWL level 1)**

   Answer: *Main, most important, most popular, most common, key, chief, big*

   Standard 4: Determine the meaning of general academic and domain-specific words or phrases.

3. **Explain why the Mississippi River is still important today. Give two reasons. (2 pts.)**

   Answer: *It still affects the land and people* **and/or** *Goods are still carried to states on the river* **and/or** *The river is still a water highway for boats* **and/or** *The river still carries rich nutrients to the soil.* As a two-point question, there should be two clearly defined answers.

   Standard 3: Explain events, procedures, ideas, or concepts based on specific information in the text.

4. **What evidence in the text indicates that the delta of the Mississippi River is a good place to grow crops?**

   Answer: *The Mississippi River carries dirt, sand, and mud that have rich nutrients to the delta* **or** *The delta is flat.*

   Standard 1: Refer to details and examples in a text when explaining what the text says explicitly and when drawing inferences from the text.

5. **The topic of the above paragraph is "The Cherokee People." What is the central idea of the paragraph?**

   Answer: *There were conflicts between the Cherokee and settlers* **or** *The Cherokee changed their way of life but were forced off their land* **or** *The author describes how the Cherokee were forced off their land.* The answer must be clearly related to the topic. Do not accept a series of details as the central idea.

   Standard 2: Determine the central idea of a text.

6. **What is the meaning of** *adapting* **in the context of the above passage? (AWL level 2)**

   Answer: *Changing, fitting into, adjusting, getting used to, learning new ways*

   Standard 4: Determine the meaning of general academic and domain-specific words or phrases.

7. **Explain how the Cherokee and the European settlers felt differently about using land.**

   Answer: *The settlers wanted Cherokee land for gold; the Cherokee wanted land for hunting* **or** *The Europeans wanted to own the land and the Cherokee believed in sharing the land.* Answer should include reference to both the Cherokee and the settlers.

Standard 3: Explain events, procedures, ideas, or concepts based on specific information in the text.

8. What evidence in the text indicates that the U.S. government treated the Cherokee unfairly?

   Answer: *They ordered the Cherokee to give up their land* **or** *They forced them to walk thousands of miles without enough food or warm clothing* **or** *They let thousands of Cherokee die on the journey.*

   Standard 1: Refer to details and examples in a text when explaining what the text says explicitly and when drawing inferences from the text.

9. How is Henry Wadsworth Longfellow's description of the Southeast different from the description in most of the paragraph?

   Answer: *Longfellow wrote about scenery such as prairies, forests, and flowers; the author of the paragraph wrote about the crops grown in the Southeast and the conditions that make this possible* **or** *Longfellow focused on the beauty of the land; the author described it as it is* **or** *Longfellow's comments were opinion; the author's were factual.* The answer should include reference to both Longfellow and the author of the text.

   Standard 6: Compare and contrast a firsthand and secondhand account on the same event or topic.

10. Which text structure best explains how the author organized the above passage? **(2 pts.)**

   ___description of important points
   ___account of cause and effect
   ___explanation of a problem and solution

   Give a reason from the text for your answer. For example, if you choose description, tell what is being described. For cause and effect, state a cause or an effect mentioned in the text. For problem and solution, tell what the problem is or describe the solution.

   Answer: *Description; the author describes the crops that are grown in the Southeast* **or** *Cause/effect; the author gives*

causes why the region is excellent for farming. Reasons that are not present in the test are inaccurate.

Standard 5: Describe the overall structure in a text.

Summarize what the text says about how the Mississippi River has influenced or changed the Southeast. An acceptable text-based summary contains the following units. Students receive one point for each statement in their summary that matches the following statements in meaning.

1. An introductory statement of purpose
2. The Mississippi River carries dirt
3. It carries sand
4. It carries mud
5. These form the delta
6. They are rich with nutrients
7. The nutrients benefit the land
8. The river is a water highway
9. It is a major route for ships and barges

Point Table   The Southeast, Grade 4

Standard	Question	Points per Question
1. Support an inference	4	1
	8	1
2. Determine central idea	1	1
	5	1
3. Explain why or how/analyze	3	2
	7	1
4. Determine word meaning	2	1
	6	1
5. Determine text structure	10	2
6. Determine point of view	9	1
Total Questions		12
2. Summary		9
Total Summary		(7 acceptable)

Elementary School, Grade 4, Part III
Before you begin scoring, please review the guidelines for scoring questions on pages 40–43 and pages 63–67 for scoring summaries.

The United States, Vast and Varied: The Southwest

1. What is the meaning of *involved* in the context of the above paragraph? **(AWL level 1)**

   Answer: *Was part of, included*

   Standard 4: Determine the meaning of general academic and domain-specific words or phrases.

2. Explain how sand and rainwater eroded the Grand Canyon in different ways. **(2 pts.)**

   Answer: *Blowing sand wore away rock* **and** *Rainwater dissolved rock.* Answer should include the differences of wearing away and dissolving. As a two-point question, there should be two clearly defined answers.

   Standard 3: Explain events, procedures, ideas, or concepts based on specific information in the text.

3. What evidence in the text indicates that someone who visited the Grand Canyon several times might not notice any changes from erosion?

SOCIAL STUDIES

Answer: *Changes from erosion happen very slowly over thousands of years.*

Standard 1: Refer to details and examples in a text when explaining what the text says explicitly and when drawing inferences from the text.

4. The topic of the above paragraph is "The Grand Canyon." What is the central idea of the paragraph?

Answer: *The Grand Canyon became a national park.* The answer must be clearly related to the topic. Do not accept a series of details as the central idea.

Standard 2: Determine the central idea of a text.

5. How were Roosevelt's comments on the Grand Canyon different from the author's description of the Grand Canyon?

Answer: *Roosevelt talked about the beauty of the canyon* **or** *how it should be preserved and the author of the paragraph offered a factual description of how it was formed* **or** *Roosevelt's comments were opinion and the author's were factual.* Answer should include reference to both Roosevelt and the author.

Standard 6: Compare and contrast a firsthand and secondhand account on the same event or topic.

6. What evidence in the text indicates that the U.S. government did not understand how the Navajo lived?

Answer: *They did not understand that the Navajo did not have one primary leader, so when the government made a treaty only a few clans knew about it.*

Standard 1: Refer to details and examples in a text when explaining what the text says explicitly and when drawing inferences from the text.

7. The topic of the above paragraph is "The Navajo People." What is the central idea of the paragraph?

Answer: *The Navajo were forced off their land by the United States government* **or** *The author describes what happened to the Navajo.* The answer must be clearly related to the topic. Do not accept a series of details as the central idea.

Standard 2: Determine the central idea of a text.

8. Which text structure best explains how the author organized the above paragraph? **(2 pts.)**

___ explanation of problem and solution

___ account of cause and effect

___ comparison/contrast of two or more things

Give a reason from the text for your answer. For example, if you choose problem and solution, tell what the problem is or describe the solution. For cause/effect, state a cause or an effect mentioned in the text. For comparison/contrast, tell what is being compared or contrasted.

Answer: *Cause/effect; the author describes why the Navajo were forced to move and the effect of this move* **or** *Problem/*

solution; the author describes the problem of the U.S. government and how it was solved. Reasons that are not present in the test are inaccurate.

Standard 5: Describe the overall structure in a text.

9. What is the meaning of conflict in the context of the passage entitled "The Navajo People?" **(AWL level 5)**

Answer: *Disagreement, fight, battle, war*

Standard 4: Determine the meaning of general academic and domain-specific words or phrases.

10. Explain why the Southwest did not develop farming as a major resource.

Answer: *Oil was discovered* **or** *The oil industry became important* **or** *They also developed technology as a resource* **or** *The climate may not be good for farming.*

Standard 3: Explain events, procedures, ideas, or concepts based on specific information in the text.

Summarize what the text says about how the Grand Canyon was formed. An acceptable text-based summary contains the following units. Students receive one point for each statement in their summary that matches the following statements in meaning.

1. An introductory statement of purpose
2. Erosion formed the Grand Canyon
3. Moving glaciers caused erosion
4. Rushing river water caused erosion
5. The river carried sand
6. The river carried gravel
7. The river carried boulders
8. Rain dissolved rock
9. Wind caused erosion

Point Table   The Southwest, Grade 4

Standard	Question	Points per Question
1. Support an inference	3 6	1 1
2. Determine central idea	4 7	1 1
3. Explain why or how/analyze	2 10	2 1
4. Determine word meaning	1 9	1 1
5. Determine text structure	8	2
6. Determine point of view	5	1
Total Questions		**12**
2. Summary		9
Total Summary		(7 acceptable)

Elementary School, Grade 5, Part I
Before you begin scoring, please review the guidelines for scoring questions on pages 40–43 and pages 63–67 for scoring summaries.

Inventions and Big Business

1. The topic of the above section is "Bell's invention of the telephone." What is the central idea?

   Answer: *Bell's interest in sound and speech led to the invention of the telephone* **or** *The author described how the telephone was invented.* The answer must be clearly related to the topic. Do not accept a series of details as the central idea.

   Standard 2: Determine the central idea of a text.

2. Explain why Edison is a good model or example for any inventor. Give two reasons. **(2 pts.)**

   Answer: *He never gave up* **and/or** *He invented hundreds of inventions* **and/or** *His inventions helped people* **and/or** *He maintained a positive attitude even when things didn't work.* As a two-point question, there should be two clearly defined answers.

   Standard 3: Explain events, procedures, ideas, or concepts based on specific information in the text.

3. Which text structure best explains how the author organized the above section? **(2 pts.)**

   _____ description of important features

   _____ explanation of steps in a sequence

   _____ account of cause and effect

   _____ explanation of problem and solution

   _____ comparison/contrast of two or more things

   Give a reason from the text for your answer. For example, if you choose description, tell what is being described. For sequence, list one or two steps explained in the text. For cause and effect, state a cause or an effect mentioned in the text. For problem/solution, tell what the problem is or describe the solution. For comparison, tell what is being compared or contrasted.

   Answer: *Problem/solution; the author describes the problems faced by the inventors and the solutions they reached* **or** *Cause/effect; the author described the effects of two inventions.* Reasons that are not present in the text are inaccurate.

   Standard 5: Describe the overall structure in a text.

4. The topic of the above three paragraphs is "the rise of the steel industry." What is the central idea?

   Answer: *Bessemer and Carnegie made steel a major industry in the United States* **or** *The author describes how the steel industry developed.* The answer must be clearly related to the topic. Do not accept a series of details as the central idea.

   Standard 2: Determine the central idea of a text.

5. Explain why Carnegie chose Bessemer's way of making steel.

   Answer: *It was affordable* **or** *It made strong steel* **or** *It made it possible to produce steel in large quantities* **or** *Carnegie could produce steel at a low price.*

   Standard 3: Explain events, procedures, ideas, or concepts based on specific information in the text.

6. What evidence in the text indicates that producing steel involves other industries?

   Answer: *Mines provide iron* **or** *coal* **or** *ships* **or** *railroads deliver steel.*

   Standard 1: Quote accurately from a text when explaining what the text says explicitly and when drawing inferences from the text.

7. What is the meaning of *major* in the context of the passage entitled "The Rise of Steel"? **(AWL level 1)**

   Answer: *Very big, very important, chief, key, large*

   Standard 4: Determine the meaning of general academic and domain-specific words or phrases.

8. What is the meaning of *refinery* in the context of the above passage? **(AWL level 9)**

   Answer: *Place for changing products into something else (do not accept "places to refine something")*

   Standard 4: Determine the meaning of general academic and domain-specific words or phrases.

9. What evidence in the text indicates that the invention of the automobile helped the oil industry?

   Answer: *The automobile created a growing demand for products made from oil* **or** *Automobiles needed gasoline and motor oil.*

   Standard 1: Quote accurately from a text when explaining what the text says explicitly and when drawing inferences from the text.

10. How were Andrew Carnegie and John D. Rockefeller's points of view alike?

   Answer: *Both saw an opportunity to make a lot of money in a new process or industry (making steel and refining oil)* **or** *Both wanted to succeed* **or** *Both wanted to create something new.* The answer should focus on an individual's opinion or attitude inferred from actions and words.

   Standard 6: Analyze multiple accounts of the same event or topic, noting important similarities or differences in the point of view they represent.

Summarize what the text says about how the inventions of Bell and Edison affected people. An acceptable text-based summary contains the following units. Students receive one point for each statement in their summary that matches the following statements in meaning.

1. An introductory statement of purpose
2. Bell invented the telephone
3. People could talk to each other over wires
4. The telephone changed how people communicated with each other
5. When Bell died in 1922
6. There were over 13 million phones in use
7. Edison invented the electric light bulb
8. Electric lights became practical for everyday use
9. Edison also invented the movie camera and the phonograph

Point Table   Inventions and Big Business, Grade 5

Standard		Question	Points per Question
1.	Support an inference	6 9	1 1
2.	Determine central idea	1 4	1 1
3.	Explain why or how/analyze	2 5	2 1
4.	Determine word meaning	7 8	1 1
5.	Determine text structure	3	2
6.	Determine point of view	10	1
Total Questions			12
2. **Summary**			9
Total Summary			(7 acceptable)

Elementary School, Grade 5, Part II   Before you begin scoring, please review the guidelines for scoring questions on pages 40–43 and pages 63–67 for scoring summaries.

SOCIAL STUDIES

Immigration

1. The topic of the above two paragraphs is "immigration." What is the central idea?

   Answer: *Immigrants came from many countries to escape hardships* **or** *The author describes where immigrants came from and why they came to the United States.* The answer must be clearly related to the topic. Do not accept a series of details as the central idea.

   Standard 2: Determine the central idea of a text.

2. What evidence in the text indicates that immigrants thought life in the United States would be better than life in their homeland?

   Answer: *They were escaping many hardships such as hunger, poverty, lack of jobs, lack of freedom* **or** *religious persecution.*

   Standard 1: Quote accurately from a text when explaining what the text says explicitly and when drawing inferences from the text.

3. Explain why Ellis and Angel Islands were important steps in the immigration process.

   Answer: *At Ellis and Angel Islands, immigrants got permission to enter the United States.*

   Standard 3: Explain events, procedures, ideas, or concepts based on specific information in the text.

4. What was Walter Mrozowski's point of view regarding his new world?

   Answer: *He was on his own* **or** *There was no one to help him* **or** *He knew he had to be courageous* **or** *He realized*

he was in a new situation. The answer should focus on an individual's opinion or attitude inferred from actions and words.

Standard 6: Analyze multiple accounts of the same event or topic, noting important similarities or differences in the point of view they represent.

5. Which text structure best explains how the author organized the above paragraph? **(2 pts.)**

   ___ description of important points

   ___ explanation of steps in a sequence

   ___ account of cause and effect

   ___ explanation of problem and solution

   ___ comparison/contrast of two or more things

   Give a reason from the text for your answer. For example, if you choose description, tell what is being described. For sequence, list one or two steps explained in the text. For cause and effect, state a cause or an effect mentioned in the text. For problem/solution, tell what the problem is or describe the solution. For comparison, tell what is being compared or contrasted.

   Answer: *Problem/Solution; the author describes the problems faced by immigrants (finding housing and work) and how they solved them (going to a neighborhood where there were others from their homeland).* Reasons that are not present in the text are inaccurate.

   Standard 5: Describe the overall structure in a text.

6. What is the meaning of *adjust* in the context of the above paragraph? **(AWL level 5)**

Answer: *Fit into, get used to, adapt, become part of, make changes according to a situation*

Standard 4: Determine the meaning of general academic and domain-specific words or phrases.

7. **The topic of the above two paragraphs is "immigrant life." What is the central idea?**

   Answer: *Immigrants settled in the cities and faced many hardships* **and/or** *Immigrants in the cities faced housing problems and prejudice* or *The author described the hardships of immigrant life.* The answer must be clearly related to the topic. Do not accept a series of details as the central idea.

   Standard 2: Determine the central idea of a text.

8. **What is the meaning of *negative* in the context of the above passage? (AWL level 13)**

   Answer: *Bad, harmful, damaging, not positive, unfair*

   Standard 4: Determine the meaning of general academic and domain-specific words or phrases.

9. **What evidence in the text indicates that immigrants faced many hardships even if they found a job?**

   Answer: *They lived in tenements that were crowded* **or** *Tenements lacked heat* **or** *Tenements lacked windows* **or** *Tenements lacked fresh air* **or** *Disease spread* **or** *They faced prejudice in seeking work.*

   Standard 1: Quote accurately from a text when explaining what the text says explicitly and when drawing inferences from the text.

10. **Explain how some immigrants met the same hardships in the United States that they had faced in their homeland. Give two examples. (2 pts.)**

    Answer: *They left because of lack of jobs and it was also difficult to find jobs in the United States* **and/or** *They were poor in their homeland and they were poor in the United States* **and/or** *They faced religious persecution in their homeland and faced prejudice in the United States.* Answer should address or compare both the homeland and the

United States. As a two-point question, there should be two clearly defined answers.

Standard 3: Explain events, procedures, ideas, or concepts based on specific information in the text.

Summarize what the text says about the difficulties faced by immigrants. An acceptable text-based summary contains the following units. Students receive one point for each statement in their summary that matches the following statements in meaning.

1. An introductory statement of purpose
2. They needed to find housing
3. They needed to find jobs
4. They had to live in crowded houses
5. Houses often had no heat
6. There was no fresh air
7. Disease spread
8. Many immigrants faced prejudice

Point Table   Immigration, Grade 5

Standard	Question	Points per Question
1. Support an inference	2 9	1 1
2. Determine central idea	1 7	1 1
3. Explain why or how/analyze	3 10	1 2
4. Determine word meaning	6 8	1 1
5. Determine text structure	5	2
6. Determine point of view	4	1
Total Questions		12
2. Summary		8
Total Summary		(6 acceptable)

Elementary School, Grade 5, Part III

Before you begin scoring, please review the guidelines for scoring questions on pages 40–43 and pages 63–67 for scoring summaries.

Workers and Unions

1. **The topic of the above two paragraphs is "sweatshops." What is the central idea?**

   Answer: *Working in sweatshops was dangerous* **or** *The author describes the dangers of working in sweatshops.* The answer must be clearly related to the topic. Do not accept a series of details as the central idea.

   Standard 2: Determine the central idea of a text.

2. **What evidence in the text indicates how the owners of the Triangle Shirtwaist Company caused the death of 146 people?**

   Answer: *They refused to construct fire escapes* **and/or** *They refused to keep the workshop doors unlocked.* Answer should include the actions of the company.

   Standard 1: Quote accurately from a text when explaining what the text says explicitly and when drawing inferences from the text.

SOCIAL STUDIES

3. What evidence in the text indicates that workers had little time for recreation?

    Answer: *Workers had to work seven days a week* **and/or** *Workers worked 12 hours a day* **and/or** *Workers only got two vacation days a year.*

    Standard 1: Quote accurately from a text when explaining what the text says explicitly and when drawing inferences from the text.

4. The topic of the above two paragraphs is "unions." What is the central idea?

    Answer: *Gompers helped form unions and the AFL* **or** *The author describes how the AFL was formed.* The answer must be clearly related to the topic. Do not accept a series of details as the central idea.

    Standard 2: Determine the central idea of a text.

5. Which text structure best explains how the author organized the above two paragraphs? **(2 pts.)**

    _____ description of important features

    _____ explanation of steps in a sequence

    _____ account of cause and effect

    _____ explanation of problem and solution

    _____ comparison/contrast of two or more things

    Give a reason from the text for your answer. For example, if you choose description, tell what is being described. For sequence, list one or two steps explained in the text. For cause and effect, state a cause or an effect mentioned in the text. For problem/solution, tell what the problem is or describe the solution. For comparison, tell what is being compared or contrasted.

    Answer: *Sequence; the author describes the cigar factory strike in 1877 and how it led to the formation of the AFL in 1886* **or** *Cause/effect; unsuccessful strikes (cause) led to formation of the AFL (effect).* Reasons that are not present in the text are inaccurate.

    Standard 5: Describe the overall structure in a text.

6. What is the meaning of *tensions* in the context of the above paragraph? **(AWL level 6)**

    Answer: *Differences, disagreements, arguments, stresses, strains*

    Standard 4: Determine the meaning of general academic and domain-specific words or phrases.

7. Explain why many business owners were unwilling to raise wages.

    Answer: *Raising wages would cost them money* **or** *Profits would be lower.*

    Standard 3: Explain events, procedures, ideas, or concepts based on specific information in the text.

8. How were the points of view of Samuel Gompers and Mary Harris Jones alike?

    Answer: *They wanted to improve working conditions* **or** *They believed in the power of the unions.* The answer should focus on an individual's opinion or attitude inferred from actions and words.

    Standard 6: Analyze multiple accounts of the same event or topic, noting important similarities or differences in the point of view they represent.

9. What is the meaning of *contribution* in the context of the above passage? **(AWL level 6)**

    Answer: *Influence, role, impact, effect, achievement*

    Standard 4: Determine the meaning of general academic and domain-specific words or phrases.

10. Explain why working conditions gradually improved. Give two examples. **(2 pts.)**

    Answer: *Unions were organized* **and/or** *Religious, political* **and/or** *Business leaders helped* **and/or** *New laws were formed.* As a two-point question, there should be two clearly defined answers.

    Standard 3: Explain events, procedures, ideas, or concepts based on specific information in the text.

Summarize what the text says about the difficult conditions that workers faced. An acceptable text-based summary contains the following units. Students receive one point for each statement in their summary that matches the following statements in meaning.

1. An introductory statement of purpose
2. Workers worked for 12 hours a day
3. They worked seven days a week
4. They only got two vacation days a year
5. They were paid an average of $10 a week or less
6. Working conditions were often unsafe and dangerous
7. Workers were often injured or killed
8. Children performed dangerous jobs

Point Table   Workers and Unions, Grade 5

Standard		Question	Points per Question
1.	Support an inference	2 3	1 1
2.	Determine central idea	1 4	1 1
3.	Explain why or how/analyze	7 10	1 2
4.	Determine word meaning	6 9	1 1
5.	Determine text structure	5	2
6.	Determine point of view	8	1
Total Questions			12
2. Summary			8
Total Summary			(6 acceptable)

Elementary School, Grade 6, Part I Before you begin scoring, please review the guidelines for scoring questions on pages 40–43 and pages 63–67 for scoring summaries.

An Expanding Nation: Rails Across the Nation

1. The topic of the previous section is "traveling across the United States." What is the central idea?

   Answer: *There were two ways to get across the United States in the 1850s* **or** *The author describes how to get across the United States in the 1850s.* The answer must be clearly related to the topic. Do not accept a series of details as the central idea.

   Standard 2: Determine central idea/s of a text.

2. Which text structure best explains how the author organized the previous passage? **(2 pts.)**

   ___ description of important features

   ___ explanation of steps in a sequence

   ___ account of cause and effect

   ___ explanation of problem and solution

   ___ comparison/contrast of two or more things

   Give a reason from the text for your answer. For example, if you choose description, tell what is being described. For sequence, list one or two steps explained in the text. For cause and effect, state a cause or an effect mentioned in the text. For problem/solution, tell what the problem is or describe the solution. For comparison, tell what is being compared or contrasted.

   Answer: *Comparison/contrast; the author contrasts two different methods for traveling from the East Coast to the West Coast* **or** *sequence; the author describes the sequence of traveling from the East Coast to the West Coast* **or** *Description; the author describes how people could cross the United States.* Reasons that are not present in the text are inaccurate.

   Standard 5: Analyze the structure of the text.

3. What evidence in the text indicates that paying for each mile of track completed may have been unfair?

   Answer: *The Union Pacific began building on the broad, flat plains whereas the Central Pacific had the difficult job of building in the rugged mountains* **or** *Geography gave the Union Pacific an advantage.*

   Standard 1: Cite textual evidence to support analysis of what the text says explicitly as well as inferences drawn from the text.

4. The topic of the previous section is "the Union Pacific." What is the central idea?

   Answer: *The Union Pacific faced challenges.* The answer must be clearly related to the topic. Do not accept a series of details as the central idea.

   Standard 2: Determine central idea/s of a text.

5. What is the meaning of *challenge* in the context of the previous passage? **(AWL level 5)**

   Answer: *Trials, difficulties, something hard to do, obstacles, problems*

   Standard 4: Determine the meaning of words and phrases as they are used in a text.

6. What was the point of view of the U.S. government regarding land that the railroad crossed?

   Answer: *The government felt it did not belong to the Native Americans* **or** *The government believed the land belonged to the United States* **or** *The government felt they had a right to cross the land.* The answer should focus on an individual's opinion or attitude inferred from actions or words.

   Standard 6: Determine point of view or purpose.

7. Analyze how the workers of the Union Pacific and Central Pacific were alike and different. **(2 pts.)**

   Answer: *They both were made up of immigrants, but the Union Pacific hired Irish immigrants and the Central Pacific hired Chinese immigrants* **and/or** *The Union Pacific hired former soldiers and slaves and the Central Pacific did not.* As a two-point question, there should be two clearly defined answers. The answer should include a likeness and a difference.

   Standard 3: Analyze interactions/connections between individuals, events, and ideas.

8. What is the meaning of *immigrants* in the context of the previous passage? **(AWL level 3)**

   Answer: *People from another country who come to the United States to live, people born in another country who come to the United States to live and work, people who were not born citizens of the United States*

   Standard 4: Determine the meaning of words and phrases as they are used in a text.

9. What evidence suggests why Chinese immigrants were willing to work on the railroad?

   Answer: *They were treated unfairly in the gold mining camps.*

   Standard 1: Cite textual evidence to support analysis of what the text says explicitly as well as inferences drawn from the text.

10. Analyze why newspapers knew that describing daily progress on the railroad would sell papers.

    Answer: *The project was a source of pride for Americans, so people wanted to read about it.*

    Standard 3: Analyze interactions/connections between individuals, events, and ideas.

Summarize what the text says about the problems faced by the Union Pacific and the Central Pacific. An acceptable text-based summary contains the following units. Students receive one point for each statement in their summary that matches the following statements in meaning.

1. An introductory statement of purpose
2. The Union Pacific had difficulty in finding workers
3. The Union Pacific was building far from towns and cities
4. They hired immigrants and former slaves
5. The Central Pacific had difficulty in finding workers
6. The Central Pacific was building where people were looking for gold
7. They hired Chinese immigrants
8. The Union Pacific faced conflict with the Native Americans
9. The Native Americans did not want them on their land **and/or** Said they were scaring off the buffalo
10. The Central Pacific had to build through the mountains
11. Many workers were killed from blasting tunnels

Point Table   Rails Across the Nation, Grade 6

Standard	Question	Points per Question
1. Support an inference	3 9	1 1
2. Determine central idea	1 4	1 1
3. Explain why or how/analyze	7 10	2 1
4. Determine word meaning	5 8	1 1
5. Determine text structure	2	2
6. Determine point of view	6	1
Total Questions	10	12
2. Summary		11
Total Summary		(8 acceptable)

Elementary School, Grade 6, Part II
Before you begin scoring, please review the guidelines for scoring questions on pages 40–43 and pages 63–67 for scoring summaries.

SOCIAL STUDIES

An Expanding Nation: Conflict on the Plains

1. The topic of the previous two paragraphs is "conflict between Native Americans and the U.S. government." What is the central idea?

   Answer: *The U.S. government supported the settlers against the Native Americans or the U.S. government used force to get Lakota land.* The answer must be clearly related to the topic. Do not accept a series of details as the central idea.

   Standard 2: Determine central idea/s.

2. What was the point of view of the U.S. government regarding gold found on the Lakota reservation?

   Answer: *The government wanted the land where gold had been found or The government thought that gold was useless to the Lakota so they should give it up or The government was prepared to use force to get the gold.* The answer should focus on an individual's opinion or attitude inferred from actions or words.

   Standard 6: Determine point of view or purpose.

3. What evidence in the text indicates that money meant little to the Native Americans?

   Answer: *The government offered money and goods to the Native Americans but they did not value the white man's goods* **or** *The Lakota refused to sell their land* **or** *Move again.*

   Standard 1: Cite textual evidence to support analysis of what the text says explicitly as well as inferences drawn from the text.

4. Which text structure best explains how the author organized the previous passage? (**2 pts.**)

   ____ description of important features

   ____ explanation of steps in a sequence

   ____ account of cause and effect

   ____ explanation of problem and solution

   ____ comparison/contrast of two or more things

   Give a reason from the text for your answer. For example, if you choose description, tell what is being described. For sequence, list one or two steps explained in the text. For cause and effect, state a cause or an effect mentioned in the text. For problem/solution, tell what the problem is or describe the solution. For comparison, tell what is being compared or contrasted.

Answer: *Cause and effect; the author describes the battle and defeat at Little Big Horn (cause) and loss of freedom* **or** *Movement to a reservation for the Native Americans (effect).* Reasons that are not present in the text are inaccurate.

Standard 5: Analyze the structure of the text.

5. What is the meaning of *traditional* in the context of the previous paragraph? **(AWL level 2)**

   Answer: *A custom, practice, or belief that has been in place for a long time*

   Standard 4: Determine the meaning of words and phrases as they are used in a text.

6. The topic of the previous two paragraphs is "Chief Joseph." What is the central idea?

   Answer: *Chief Joseph was treated unfairly and he spent his life working for fair treatment of Native Americans* **or** *The author describes what happened to the Nez Perce and how Chief Joseph worked for fair treatment for Native Americans.* The answer must be clearly related to the topic. Do not accept a series of details as the central idea.

   Standard 2: Determine central idea/s.

7. What is the meaning of *convinced* in the context of the previous paragraph? **(AWL level 10)**

   Answer: *Influenced, persuaded, moved, led, talked a person into doing something, got a person to change their mind, become sure about something*

   Standard 4: Determine the meaning of words and phrases as they are used in a text.

8. Analyze what results when a person is denied liberty, according to Chief Joseph.

   Answer: *The person will be unhappy* **or** *The person may not become a law-abiding citizen.*

   Standard 3: Analyze interactions/connections between individuals, events, and ideas.

9. What evidence in the text indicates that the U.S. government lied to the Native Americans?

   Answer: *General Miles lied when he said the Nez Perce could return to Oregon if they surrendered but they were taken to a reservation* **or** *The government lied when it broke its treaty with the Lakota and forced them off their reservation.* Answer should include information from the text.

   Standard 1: Cite textual evidence to support analysis of what the text says explicitly as well as inferences drawn from the text.

10. Analyze why the Native Americans probably distrusted the U.S. government. Give two examples from the text. **(2 pts.)**

Answer: *The government signed a treaty with the Lakota and broke it* **and/or** *The government forced Native Americans onto reservations* **and/or** *The government lied to get what they wanted* **and/or** *The government used force to get what they wanted* **and/or** *The government fired upon the Lakota when they were giving up their weapons.* As a two-point question, there should be two clearly defined answers.

Standard 3: Analyze interactions/connections between individuals, events, and ideas.

Summarize what the text says about how the U.S. government treated the Lakota. An acceptable text-based summary contains the following units. Students receive one point for each statement in their summary that matches the following statements in meaning.

1. An introductory statement of purpose
2. The government made a treaty with the Lakota
3. The treaty stated that the Black Hills would belong to the Lakota forever
4. Gold was discovered in the Black Hills
5. The Lakota refused to sell their land and move
6. The government sent soldiers to force the Lakota to move
7. The Lakota defeated General Custer at Little Big Horn
8. The government forced the Lakota to move
9. Some Lakota tried to leave the reservation
10. They were surrounded by soldiers
11. When they were giving up their weapons
12. The soldiers killed 300 Lakota

Point Table   Conflict on the Plains, Grade 6

Standard	Question	Points per Question
1. Support an inference	3 9	1 1
2. Determine central idea	1 6	1 1
3. Explain why or how/analyze	8 10	1 2
4. Determine word meaning	5 7	1 1
5. Determine text structure	4	2
6. Determine point of view	2	1
Total Question		12
2. Summary		12
Total Summary		(9 acceptable)

Elementary School, Grade 6, Part III   Before you begin scoring, please review the guidelines
for scoring questions on pages 40–43 and pages 63–67 for scoring summaries.

An Expanding Nation: The Great Plains

1. The topic of the previous three paragraphs is "The Homestead Act." What is the central idea?

   Answer: *The Homestead Act gave free land to citizens and immigrants under certain conditions* **or** *The author describes the Homestead Act.* The answer must be clearly related to the topic. Do not accept a series of details as the central idea.

   Standard 2: Determine central idea/s.

2. What is the meaning of *motivate* in the context of the previous passage? **(AWL level 6)**

   Answer: *Cause, inspire, encourage, influence, prompt, cause someone to want to do something, push someone to act, convince someone to act.*

   Standard 4: Determine the meaning of words and phrases as they are used in a text.

3. Analyze how development of the Great Plains would benefit the United States.

   Answer: *Development of the Great Plains would provide land for farms* **or** *Development would result in production of more farm goods* **or** *Development would provide business for the railroads.* Answer should include a benefit to the country.

   Standard 3: Analyze interactions/connections between individuals, events, and ideas.

4. Which text structure best explains how the author organized the previous passage? **(2 pts.)**

   ____ description of important features

   ____ explanation of steps in a sequence

   ____ account of cause and effect

   ____ explanation of problem and solution

   ____ comparison/contrast of two or more things

   Give a reason from the text for your answer. For example, if you choose description, tell what is being described. For sequence, list one or two steps explained in the text. For cause and effect, state a cause or an effect mentioned in the text. For problem/solution, tell what the problem is or describe the solution. For comparison, tell what is being compared or contrasted.

   Answer: *Problem and solution; the author describes the problem of finding people who would move to the Great Plains and the solution of giving land away through the Homestead Act.* Reasons that are not present in the text are inaccurate.

   Standard 5: Analyze the structure of the text.

5. What is the meaning of *survive* in the context of the previous passage? **(AWL level 7)**

   Answer: *Live, endure, stay alive, not die*

   Standard 4: Determine the meaning of words and phrases as they are used in a text.

6. What was the point of view of pioneers about staying on the Great Plains?

   Answer: *If they stayed, they would have to rough it* **or** *They would have to work hard to survive.* The answer should focus on an individual's opinion or attitude inferred from actions or words.

   Standard 6: Determine point of view or purpose.

7. What evidence in the text indicates that many sodbusters may have given up and left the Great Plains?

   Answer: *The hard work* **or** *The harsh weather* **or** *Natural disasters* **or** *the grasshoppers.* snakes, bugs, and mice is not an acceptable answer unless one of these is also included.

   Standard 1: Cite textual evidence to support analysis of what the text says explicitly as well as inferences drawn from the text.

8. What evidence in the text indicates why trees are a valuable resource for farmers?

   Answer: *Farmers had to build sod houses because there were few trees* **or** *They had difficulty building fences to keep out the animals without trees for wood.*

   Standard 1: Cite textual evidence to support analysis of what the text says explicitly as well as inferences drawn from the text.

9. The topic of the previous two paragraphs is "immigrants on the Great Plains." What is the central idea?

   Answer: *Immigrants from Europe brought valuable skills and resources such as wheat to the Great Plains* **or** *The author described how the immigrants helped improve farming on the Great Plains.* The answer must be clearly related to the topic. Do not accept a series of details as the central idea.

   Standard 2: Determine central idea/s.

10. Analyze how the success of the Great Plains was due to the efforts of different people. Give two examples from the text. **(2 pts.)**

    Answer: *The government provided land* **and/or** *Pioneers farmed the land* **and/or** *Immigrants brought new skills and wheat to the Great Plains* **and/or** *Inventors provided new inventions to help the farmers.* The answer should include two different examples.

Standard 3: Analyze interactions/connections between individuals, events, and ideas.

Summarize how the Great Plains was settled. Include difficulties as well as factors that led to success. An acceptable text-based summary contains the following units. Students receive one point for each statement in their summary that matches the following statements in meaning.

1. An introductory statement of purpose
2. The Homestead Act gave free land to people
3. If you farmed the land for five years
4. Difficulties included harsh weather
5. Natural disasters
6. Grasshoppers
7. And hard work
8. Factors that led to success were new inventions
9. New types of windmills
10. Stronger plows
11. Barbed wire
12. And new wheat seeds
13. Skills of immigrants also led to success

Point Table   The Great Plains, Grade 6

Standard	Question	Points per Question
1. Support an inference	7 8	1 1
2. Determine central idea	1 9	1 1
3. Explain why or how/analyze	3 10	1 2
4. Determine word meaning	2 5	1 1
5. Determine text structure	4	2
6. Determine point of view	6	1
Total Question		12
2. Summary		13
Total Summary		(10 acceptable)

Middle School, American History, Part I

Before you begin scoring, please review the guidelines for scoring questions on pages 40–43 and pages 63–67 for scoring summaries.

SOCIAL STUDIES

The Constitutional Convention

1. What is the meaning of *legislative* in the context of the previous paragraph? **(AWL level 2)**

   Answer: *Having to do with making laws*

   Standard 4: Determine the meaning of words and phrases as they are used in a text.

2. What is the meaning of *foundation* in the context of the previous passage? **(AWL level 7)**

   Answer: *Basis, base, support, underpinning*

   Standard 4: Determine the meaning of words and phrases as they are used in a text.

3. What evidence in the text strongly supports that some delegates did not trust future voters?

   Answer: *A delegate said that the people should have little to do with selecting members of Congress* or *The delegates felt the people would be misled* or *Wilson warned against shutting people out.*

   Standard 1: Cite textual evidence to support analysis of what the text says explicitly as well as inferences drawn from the text.

4. The topic of the previous section is "The Great Compromise." What is the central idea?

   Answer: *The delegates compromised on representation based on population* or *The Great Compromise resulted in a two-house congress* or *The author described the terms of the Great Compromise.* The answer must be clearly related to the topic. Do not accept a series of details as the central idea.

   Standard 2: Determine central idea/s.

5. Analyze how the delegates differed with regard to forming a government. Offer two examples. **(2 pts.)**

   Answer: *They differed on the number of people who should be chief executive* **and/or** *They differed on how members should be chosen for the upper and lower houses* **and/or** *They differed on whether to include people in the election process.* As a two-point question, there should be two clearly defined answers.

   Standard 3: Analyze interactions/connections between individuals, events, and ideas.

6. What evidence in the text strongly supports that small states feared the larger states would have more power?

   Answer: *The smaller states strongly opposed representation based on population* or *To please the small states, each state would have two seats in the upper house.*

Standard 1: Cite textual evidence to support analysis of what the text says explicitly as well as inferences drawn from the text.

7. **Which text structure best explains how the author organized the previous passage? (2 pts.)**

    ___ description of important features

    ___ explanation of steps in a sequence

    ___ account of cause and effect

    ___ explanation of problem and solution

    ___ comparison/contrast of two or more things

    Give a reason from the text for your answer. For example, if you choose description, tell what is being described. For sequence, list one or two steps explained in the text. For cause and effect, state a cause or an effect mentioned in the text. For problem/solution, tell what the problem is or describe the solution. For comparison, tell what is being compared or contrasted.

    Answer: *Comparison/contrast; the author contrasts the differences between the Virginia Plan and the New Jersey Plan* **or** *Problem/solution; the author describes a problem (representation based on population) and how it was solved by a compromise* **or** *Description; the author describes the Great Compromise.* Reasons that are not present in the text are inaccurate.

    Standard 5: Analyze the structure of the text.

8. **What was the Northern delegates' point of view regarding the Three-Fifths Compromise?**

    Answer: *They did not like it* **or** *They agreed in order to keep the South in the Union.* The answer should focus on an individual's opinion or attitude inferred from actions or words.

    Standard 6: Determine the author's point of view or purpose.

9. **The topic of the previous section is "Three-Fifths Compromise." What is the central idea?**

    Answer: *The central idea is Southerners and Northerners compromised on the issue of slavery* **or** *The author explains how the North and South felt about the slave trade.* The answer must be clearly related to the topic. Do not accept a series of details as the central idea.

    Standard 2: Determine central idea/s.

10. **Analyze why slavery was the unfinished business of the Constitutional Convention.**

    Answer: *The Convention did not end slavery* **or** *The compromises allowed it to continue until 1865.* The answer should specifically refer to the decisions of the Constitutional Convention.

Standard 3: Analyze interactions/connections between individuals, events, and ideas.

Summarize what the text says about the Great Compromise. An acceptable text-based summary contains the following units. Students receive one point for each statement in their summary that matches the following statements in meaning.

1. An introductory statement of purpose
2. The Virginia Plan called for representation based on population
3. Large states with more people would have more seats
4. Small states wanted an equal number of votes
5. The Great Compromise solution was a two-house Congress
6. Representation in the lower house would be based on state population
7. Representatives would serve two-year terms
8. The Senate would have the same number of representatives from each state
9. Senators would serve six-year terms.
10. The Great Compromise was a vital step in creating the Constitution

Point Table   The Constitutional Convention, Middle School

Standard	Question	Points per Question
1. Support an inference	3	1
	6	1
2. Determine central idea	4	1
	9	1
3. Explain why or how/analyze	5	2
	10	1
4. Determine word meaning	1	1
	2	1
5. Determine text structure	7	2
6. Determine point of view	8	1
Total Question	10	12
2. Summary		10
Total Summary		(7 acceptable)
8. Explain an argument	optional	2
Total Points		
8. Evaluate an argument	optional	1
Total Points		

Optional Standard 8 Assessment
Before you begin scoring, please review the guidelines for scoring questions on pages 40–43, pages 63–67 for scoring summaries, and pages 74–77 for information on the Optional Standard 8 Assessments.

Benjamin Franklin's Speech to the Constitutional Convention on September 17, 1787

Read the excerpt from Benjamin Franklin's speech to the delegates of the Constitutional Convention. Explain two reasons or arguments that Franklin presents for signing the Constitution.

Answer: *A general government is necessary* **and/or** *All forms of government may be a blessing if well administered* **and/or** *This form is likely to be well administered for a course of years* **and/or** *The government will descend into despotism only if the people become corrupted* **and/or** *Given the prejudices, passions, errors of opinion, local interests, and selfish view of the delegates, it is doubtful if any Convention could make a better constitution* **and/or** *This system approaches perfection* **and/or** *Focus should be on having the government well administered.*

Standard 8: Trace and evaluate the argument and specific claims in a text.

Select one of the arguments you chose and explain why it is valid or not valid.

Answer: *Student explanation of validity or invalidity will vary. However, it should be relevant to the argument and should contain some supporting evidence or clarification. Examples: Franklin doubted that the delegates could make a better Constitution. This is valid because he was right and the Constitution has worked for over 200 years* **or** *Franklin stated he did not agree with all parts of the Constitution but he thought he might change his mind. This is valid because people change their minds all the time when they learn something new or when things change* **or** *Franklin said the Constitution approaches perfection. This is invalid. Nothing is perfect including the Constitution and we have amended the Constitution like for civil rights.*

Standard 8: Trace and evaluate the argument and specific claims in the text.

Middle School, American History, Part II
Before you begin scoring, please review the guidelines for scoring questions on pages 40–43 and pages 63–67 for scoring summaries.

Debating the Constitution

1. **The topic of the previous section is "the Federalist position." What is the central idea?**

   Answer: *The central idea is the Federalists wanted a strong central government with the power to enforce laws* **or** *The author describes the Federalist position on central government and enforcement of laws.* The answer must be clearly related to the topic. Do not accept a series of details as the central idea.

   Standard 2: Determine central ideas in a text.

2. **What is the meaning of *enforce* in the context of the previous passage? (AWL level 7)**

   Answer: *Make people do something, impose on, coerce, put into effect, compel obedience; be able to punish*

   Standard 4: Determine the meaning of words and phrases as they are used in a text.

3. **What evidence in the text strongly supports that law and advice are different?**

   Answer: *Hamilton wrote: "Government implies the power of making laws. It is essential to the idea of a law, that it be attended with . . . a penalty or punishment for*

disobedience" **or** "If there be no penalty . . . the resolutions or commands which pretend to be laws will, in fact, amount to nothing more than advice." The answer should include the issue of punishment.

   Standard 1: Cite textual evidence to support analysis of what the text says explicitly as well as inferences drawn from the text.

4. **The topic of the previous section is "the antifederalist position." What is the central idea?**

   Answer: *The antifederalists believed that state power and individual freedom/Bill of Rights were not protected by the constitution* **or** *The author describes the antifederalist position regarding state and individual rights.* The answer must be clearly related to the topic. Do not accept a series of details as the central idea.

   Standard 2: Determine central ideas in a text.

5. **What is the meaning of *individual* in the context of the previous passage? (AWL level 7)**

   Answer: *Personal, related to one person, related to a single person, singular, not part of a larger group*

   Standard 4: Determine the meaning of words and phrases as they are used in a text.

6. Which text structure best explains how the author organized the previous passage? **(2 pts.)**

___ description of important features

___ explanation of steps in a sequence

___ account of cause and effect

___ explanation of problem and solution

___ comparison/contrast of two or more things

Give a reason from the text for your answer. For example, if you choose description, tell what is being described. For sequence, list one or two steps explained in the text. For cause and effect, state a cause or an effect mentioned in the text. For problem/solution, tell what the problem is or describe the solution. For comparison, tell what is being compared or contrasted.

Answer: *Comparison; the passage contrasts two positions: the position of the Federalists and Antifederalists* **or** *Description; the passage describes key features of the Antifederalist and Federalist positions.* Reasons that are not present in the text are inaccurate.

Standard 5: Analyze the structure of a text.

7. What was Mason's point of view regarding a strong central government?

Answer: *Mason felt that government over a large or extensive country results in destroying people's liberties* **or** *Mason was concerned about maintaining the liberties of the people.* The answer should focus on an individual's opinion or attitude inferred from actions or words.

Standard 6: Determine the author's point of view or purpose.

8. Analyze why the Antifederalists did not support ratification of the Constitution. Give two reasons. **(2 pts.)**

Answer: *There was no provision for individual rights* **and/or** *The government could weaken the power of the states* **and/or** *The president could become a king through reelection.* As a two-point question, there should be two clearly defined answers.

Standard 3: Analyze interaction/connections between individuals, ideas, and events.

9. What evidence in the text strongly supports that state population did not matter in the ratification process?

Answer: *Without the approval of nine states, the Constitution would not go into effect* **and/or** *By then, Maryland and South Carolina had ratified, which made a total of eight state ratifications; only one more was needed.*

Standard 1: Cite textual evidence to support analysis of what the text says explicitly as well as inferences drawn from the text.

10. Analyze why it was important that all 13 states ratified the Constitution.

Answer: *The Union would not break up because of states who did not vote for ratification* **and/or** *We became a nation.*

Standard 3: Analyze the interactions between individuals, events, and ideas in a text.

Summarize what the text says were the main issues debated during the ratification process. An acceptable text-based summary contains the following units. Students receive one point for each statement in their summary that matches the following statements in meaning.

1. An introductory statement of purpose
2. The Federalists wanted a strong central government
3. A strong government could enforce laws
4. Hamilton said laws must be attended with penalty
5. Antifederalists said a strong central government would weaken states' power
6. A strong central government could also wipe out individual freedom
7. Mason said that government over an extensive country could destroy people's liberty
8. There was no provision for a Bill of Rights
9. A president could be reelected and become king
10. The government lacked checks and balances

Point Table   Debating the Constitution, Middle School

Standard	Question	Points per Question
1. Support an inference	3 9	1 1
2. Determine central idea	1 4	1 1
3. Explain why or how/analyze	8 10	2 1
4. Determine word meaning	2 5	1 1
5. Determine text structure	6	2
6. Determine point of view	7	1
Total Question		12
2. Summary		10
Total Summary		(7 acceptable)
8. Explain an argument	optional	2
Total Points		
8. Evaluate an argument	optional	1
Total Points		

Optional Standard 8 Assessment Before you begin scoring, please review the guidelines for scoring questions on pages 40–43, pages 63–67 for scoring summaries, and pages 74–77 for information on the Optional Standard 8 Assessments.

Essay in The New York Journal, December 11, 1787

Read the excerpt from the newspaper. Explain two reasons or arguments that the author presents for not ratifying the Constitution.

Answer: *The president has too much power* **and/or** *The president has the powers of a king* **and/or** *The president is not hereditary and has to be elected* **and/or** *An election will cause horror and confusion* **and/or** *The president may not wish to give up his powers* **and/or** *If a president does not want to give up his powers, it could lead the country into war.*

Standard 8: Trace and evaluate the argument and specific claims in a text.

Select one of the arguments you chose and explain why you think it is or is not valid.

Answer: Student explanation of validity or invalidity will vary. However, it should be relevant to the argument and should contain some supporting evidence or clarification. *Examples: An election will cause confusion and horror. That's not valid. Our elections cause confusion but not horror. Even if your guy loses, it's not really horror. The country still goes on* **or** *if a president does not want to give up power, it could lead to war. I don't think that's valid because it never has happened in our country. The Civil War was about slaves not about a president losing power* **or** *the president has the powers of a king. It's not valid because there are the Senate, the House, and state governments.*

Middle School, American History, Part III Before you begin scoring, please review the guidelines for scoring questions on pages 40–43 and pages 63–67 for scoring summaries.

The Bill of Rights

1. The topic of the previous section is "the Constitution." What is the central idea?

   Answer: *The Constitution needed to be changed or amended to address the rights of the people* **or** *The Constitution said nothing about the rights of the people* **or** *The Constitution allowed for change* **or** *The author described what was lacking in the Constitution.* The answer must be clearly related to the topic. Do not accept a series of details as the central idea.

   Standard 2: Determine central idea/s.

2. The topic of the previous section is "The Amendment Process." What is the central idea?

   Answer: *There are two different procedures for proposing amendments and two for ratifying amendments* **or** *The author describes how the Constitution can be amended.* The answer must be clearly related to the topic. Do not accept a series of details as the central idea.

   Standard 2: Determine central idea/s.

3. What is the meaning of *procedures* in the context of the previous passage? **(AWL level 1)**

   Answer: *Processes, actions, steps, ways*

   Standard 4: Determine the meaning of words and phrases as they are used in a text.

4. What evidence in the text strongly supports that ratification of amendments by state legislatures was the most effective procedure?

   Answer: *Twenty-six of the 27 amendments to the Constitution have been ratified in this way.*

   Standard 1: Cite textual evidence to support analysis of what the text says explicitly as well as inferences drawn from the text.

5. Analyze why it is not easy to amend the Constitution. Offer two reasons. **(2 pts.)**

   Answer: *The proposal to amend the Constitution requires two-thirds agreement from both houses of Congress* **and/or** *Two-thirds of state legislatures have to request an amendment.* **and/or** *The amendment has to be ratified by three-fourths of the states.* **and/or** *If a national or state convention is involved, it has to be organized and carried out* **and/or** *A majority of people or states have to approve the amendment.* As a two-point question, there should be two clearly defined answers.

   Standard 3: Analyze interactions and connections between individuals, events, or ideas.

6. What point of view of the Framers of the Constitution is reflected in the Ninth and Tenth Amendments?

    Answer: *The Constitution might have missed some things regarding the rights of people* **or** *The Constitution does not cover every possible issue that might come up.* The answer should focus on an individual's opinion or attitude inferred from actions or words.

    Standard 6: Determine an author's point of view or purpose.

7. What is the meaning of *assemble* in the context of the previous paragraph? (**AWL level 10**)

    Answer: *Gather, get together, convene, meet as a group*

    Standard 4: Determine the meaning of words and phrases as they are used in a text.

8. Which text structure best explains how the author organized the previous passage? (**2 pts.**)

    ____ description of important features

    ____ explanation of steps in a sequence

    ____ account of cause and effect

    ____ explanation of problem and solution

    ____ comparison/contrast of two or more things

    Give a reason from the text for your answer. For example, if you choose description, tell what is being described. For sequence, list one or two steps explained in the text. For cause and effect, state a cause or an effect mentioned in the text. For problem/solution, tell what the problem is or describe the solution. For comparison, tell what is being compared or contrasted.

    Answer: *Cause/effect; the author describes a cause for the effect of including freedom of religion in the Bill of Rights* **or** *Problem/solution; the problem of church versus state was solved by the First Amendment.* Reasons that are not present in the text are inaccurate.

    Standard 5: Describe/analyze the structure an author uses to organize a text.

9. What evidence in the text strongly supports that freedom of the press is limited?

    Answer: *Individuals may sue journalists for libel, or the publication of false and malicious information that damages a person's reputation* **and/or** *The press must present the news fairly and accurately.*

    Standard 1: Cite textual evidence to support analysis of what the text says explicitly as well as inferences drawn from the text.

10. Analyze how the colonial past influenced what was included in the Bill of Rights.

    Answer: *There was lack of freedom of religion in colonial times and they included freedom of religion in the First Amendment* **or** *The king and Parliament ignored the colonists' protests and they included the right of petition and assembly in the First Amendment.*

    Standard 3: Analyze interactions and connections between individuals, events, or ideas.

Summarize what the text says about how the Constitution can be changed. An acceptable text-based summary contains the following units. Students receive one point for each statement in their summary that matches the following statements in meaning.

1. An introductory statement of purpose
2. Changes have to be proposed and ratified
3. Congress can propose an amendment
4. Both the House and Senate have to agree by a two-thirds vote
5. State legislatures can propose an amendment
6. It needs two-thirds of the states
7. State legislatures can ratify an amendment
8. It needs a yes vote of three-quarters of the states
9. State conventions can ratify an amendment
10. It needs three-quarters of the states

Point Table   The Bill of Rights, Middle School

Standard	Question	Points per Question
1. Support an inference	4 9	1 1
2. Determine central idea	1 2	1 1
3. Explain why or how/analyze	5 10	2 1
4. Determine word meaning	3 7	1 1
5. Determine text structure	8	2
6. Determine point of view	6	1
Total Questions	10	12
2. Summary		10
Total Summary		(7 acceptable)
8. Explain an argument	optional	2
Total Points		
8. Evaluate an argument	optional	1
Total Points		

Optional Standard 8 Assessment
Before you begin scoring, please review the guidelines for scoring questions on pages 40–43, pages 63–67 for scoring summaries, and pages 74–77 for information on the Optional Standard 8 Assessments.

James Madison's Letter to Thomas Jefferson, October 17, 1788

Read the excerpt from James Madison's letter to Thomas Jefferson. Explain two reasons or arguments that Madison presents for having or for not having a Bill of Rights.

Answer: *For Having a Bill of Rights: It might be of use, and if properly executed could not be of disservice* **and/or** *Political truths declared in a solemn manner become fundamental rules of free government* **and/or** *A Bill of Rights will be grounds for appeal if the government oppresses the people* **and/or** *The government may subvert liberty and a Bill of Rights would be a precaution.*

Not Having a Bill of Rights: Repeated violations of a Bill of Rights have occurred in every state **and/or** *A Bill of Rights has been inefficient in the past* **and/or** *The rights in question are reserved by the manner in which the federal powers are granted* **and/or** *Experience proves the inefficiency of a Bill of Rights on those occasions when its control is most needed* **and/or** *The limited powers of the federal Government and the jealousy of the subordinate state governments afford security.*

Standard 8: Trace and evaluate the argument and specific claims in a text.

Select one of the arguments you chose and explain why it is or is not valid.

Answer: Student explanation of validity or invalidity will vary. However, it should be relevant to the argument and should contain some supporting evidence or clarification. Examples: *Madison said there were repeated violations of a Bill of Rights in Virginia. It's not valid because people break laws all the time but that doesn't mean you shouldn't have them* **or** *Madison said a Bill of Rights would be grounds for appeal if the government becomes too powerful. That's valid because a lot of governments take away people's rights and even though ours is pretty good, you read about other countries in the newspaper every day* **or** *Madison called a Bill of Rights a precaution. It's valid because it is a good idea to cover all your bases kind of like knowing where the emergency exit is when you go into a theater.*

Middle School, World History, Part I
Before you begin scoring, please review the guidelines for scoring questions on pages 40–43 and pages 63–67 for scoring summaries.

The Roman Republic

1. **What point of view did the early Roman patricians have about plebeians holding office?**

   Answer: *They did not think plebeians were capable of holding office in the government of the republic.* The answer should focus on an individual's opinion or attitude inferred from words or actions.

   Standard 6: Determine point of view or purpose.

2. **What evidence in the text strongly supports that the senate primarily controlled the consuls?**

   Answer: *The consuls almost always did what the senate advised.*

   Standard 1: Cite textual evidence to support analysis of what the text says explicitly as well as inferences drawn from the text.

3. **What evidence in the text strongly supports that the Romans did not completely trust the office of consul?**

   Answer: *Consuls could only rule for a year* **or** *Both consuls had to agree before they could act* **or** *A dictator could take over if they did not agree* **or** *They knew the government would not work if the counsels disagreed.*

   Standard 1: Cite textual evidence to support analysis of what the text says explicitly as well as inferences drawn from the text.

4. **The topic of the previous section is the "the office of consul." What is the central idea?**

   Answer: *Consuls were the chief officials/executives in the Roman government* **or** *The author is describing the role of consuls in the Roman government* **or** *The author is describing what the consuls did.* The answer must be clearly related to the topic. Do not accept a series of details as the central idea.

   Standard 2: Determine central idea/s.

5. **The topic of the previous section is the "Patricians versus Plebeians." What is the central idea?**

   Answer: *Patricians and Plebeians had different attitudes and interests* **or** *The author describes the differences between the Patricians and Plebeians.* The answer must be clearly related to the topic. Do not accept a series of details as the central idea.

Standard 2: Determine central idea/s.

6. **Analyze why patricians and plebeians were against each other. Give two reasons. (2 pts.)**

   Answer: *Patricians had wealth, land, and power; plebeians did not* **or** *Patricians thought of themselves as leaders* **or** *wanted control of the government; plebeians wanted a voice in government* **or** *respect and fair treatment* **or** *did not trust the government* **or** *Patricians used slaves and did not hire plebeians;* **or** *Plebeians needed jobs.* As a two-point question, there should be two clearly defined answers.

   Standard 3: Analyze interactions/connections between individuals, events, and ideas.

7. **Which text structure best explains how the author organized the previous passage? (2 pts.)**

   ___ description of important features

   ___ explanation of steps in a sequence

   ___ account of cause and effect

   ___ explanation of problem and solution

   ___ comparison/contrast of two or more things

   Give a reason from the text for your answer. For example, if you choose description, tell what is being described. For sequence, list one or two steps explained in the text. For cause and effect, state a cause or an effect mentioned in the text. For problem/solution, tell what the problem is or describe the solution. For comparison, tell what is being compared or contrasted.

   Answer: *Comparison/contrast; the author contrasts patricians and plebeians and tells how they are different* **or** *Cause/effect; the author lists causes for the troubles between patricians and plebeians and the effect, which was refusal to fight in the army* **or** *Problem/solution; the plebeians had the problem of inequality and their solution was not to fight, which led to the Laws of the Twelve Tables.* Reasons that are not stated in the text are inaccurate.

   Standard 5: Analyze the structure of the text.

8. **Analyze why the army was important to the patricians.**

   Answer: *The patricians got their money and slaves from conquests by armies* **or** *Patricians would lose their wealth if there were no armies.*

   Standard 3: Analyze interactions/connections between individuals, events, and ideas.

9. **What is the meaning of *civil* in the context of the previous passage? (AWL level 4)**

   Answer: *Internal, occurring within the state, related to citizens, political*

Standard 4: Determine the meaning of words and phrases as they are used in a text.

10. **What is the meaning of *elements* in the context of the previous passage? (AWL level 4)**

    Answer: *Parts, features, components, basics*

    Standard 4: Determine the meaning of words and phrases as they are used in a text.

Summarize what the text says about how the government of the Roman Republic was organized. An acceptable text-based summary contains the following units. Students receive one point for each statement in their summary that matches the following statements in meaning.

1. An introductory statement of purpose
2. The Senate was the legislative body
3. The Senate was composed of patricians
4. Two consuls led the government
5. The Senate advised the consuls
6. Consuls ruled for one year
7. Consuls had to agree before acting
8. If consuls did not agree
9. A dictator would be appointed
10. The appointment was for six months
11. Praetors served as judges

Point Table   The Roman Republic, Middle School

Standard	Question	Points per Question
1. Support an inference	2 3	1 1
2. Determine central idea	4 5	1 1
3. Explain why or how/analyze	6 8	2 1
4. Determine word meaning	9 10	1 1
5. Determine text structure	7	2
6. Determine point of view	1	1
Total Questions		12
2. Summary		11
Total Summary		(8 acceptable)
8. Explain an argument	optional	2
Total Points		
8. Evaluate an argument	optional	1
Total Points		

Optional Standard 8 Assessment
Before you begin scoring, please review the guidelines for scoring questions on pages 40–43, pages 63–67 for scoring summaries, and pages 74–77 for information on the Optional Standard 8 Assessments.

Suetonius: The Lives of the Caesars

Explain two of Suetonius's reasons or arguments that indicate he thought Caesar was a great man.

Answer: *His death was foretold by signs (weeping horses, soothsayer, bird)* **and/or** *He and his wife dreamt that he would die* **and/or** *Many brought gifts to the funeral* **and/or** *Two "beings" suddenly appeared and set fire to the body* **and/or** *People threw their robes and jewels into the fire* **and/or** *He was formally declared a god* **and/or** *The common people believed he was a god* **and/or** *A comet shone for seven days in his honor* **and/or** *None of his assassins survived for more than three years* **and/or** *None died a natural death.*

Standard 8: Trace and evaluate the argument and specific claims in a text.

Select one reason or argument and explain why you think it is or is not valid.

Answer: *Student explanation of validity or invalidity will vary. However, it should be relevant to the argument and should contain some supporting evidence or clarification. Examples: Suetonius said Caesar's death was foretold by horses that wouldn't eat and they cried. This is not valid because horses will always eat if they are hungry and they don't cry* **or** *The common people believed he was a god. I agree it's valid because that would be a lot of people and if a lot of people believe something, it can be important even if it's not true* **or** *A comet shone for seven days. It's not valid because comets are not related to what people do; they are part of nature.*

Middle School, World History, Part II
Before you begin scoring, please review the guidelines for scoring questions on pages 40–43 and pages 63–67 for scoring summaries.

The Roman Empire

1. The topic of the previous two paragraphs is "governing conquered peoples." What is the central idea?

   Answer: *Romans did not force their way of life on conquered people* **or** *The author describes how the Romans treated conquered people.* The answer must be clearly related to the topic. Do not accept a series of details as the central idea.

   Standard 2: Determine central idea/s.

2. Analyze why conquered peoples did not rise up against Rome and attempt to gain their freedom. Give two reasons. **(2 pts.)**

   Answer: *They could live their life as they did prior to being conquered* **and/or** *They could keep their religion* **and/or** *They could run their local governments* **and/or** *They were prosperous* **and/or** *They were at peace* **and/or** *Rome did not force them to change their way of life.* As a two-point question, there should be two clearly defined answers.

   Standard 3: Analyze interactions/connections between individuals, events, and ideas.

3. Which text structure best explains how the author organized the previous passage? **(2 pts.)**

_____ description of important features

_____ explanation of steps in a sequence

_____ account of cause and effect

_____ explanation of problem and solution

_____ comparison/contrast of two or more things

Give a reason from the text for your answer. For example, if you choose description, tell what is being described. For sequence, list one or two steps explained in the text. For cause and effect, state a cause or an effect mentioned in the text. For problem/solution, tell what the problem is or describe the solution. For comparison, tell what is being compared or contrasted.

Answer: *Cause/effect; the author lists causes why the conquered people lived in peace with the Romans (no interference in daily lives, religion, local government) and the effect (peace)* **or** *description; the author describes how the Romans ruled conquered people.* Reasons that are not stated in the text are inaccurate.

Standard 5: Analyze the structure of the text.

4. What was Rome's point of view regarding the treatment of conquered people?

Answer: *Rome wanted peaceful provinces so they would not interfere or force their way of life on conquered people as long as there was peace* **or** *Rome wanted raw materials from the provinces* **or** *They wanted people to buy their goods* **or** *They wanted people to pay taxes.* The answer should focus on an individual's opinion or attitude inferred from words or actions.

Standard 6: Determine point of view or purpose.

5. **What evidence in the text strongly supports that the ancient Romans enjoyed watching fights?**

   Answer: *The Colosseum held 50,000 spectators* **and/or** *The Colosseum was the site of combats between people and animals* **and/or** *The floor could be flooded for mock naval battles* **and/or** *The Colosseum was the greatest Roman building.*

   Standard 1: Cite textual evidence to support analysis of what the text says explicitly as well as inferences drawn from the text.

6. **The topic of the previous section is "roads and aqueducts." What is the central idea?**

   Answer: *Romans built roads and aqueducts that improved their way of life* **or** *The author describes the importance of roads and aqueducts to Roman life.* The answer must be clearly related to the topic. Do not accept a series of details as the central idea.

   Standard 2: Determine central idea/s.

7. **What is the meaning of *structure* in the context of the previous passage? (AWL level 1)**

   Answer: *Buildings, something that was built, pieces of architecture, something built by man*

   Standard 4: Determine the meaning of words and phrases as they are used in a text.

8. **What evidence in the text strongly supports that Romans were skilled in matters of science?**

   Answer: *The Romans made advances in using the arch* **or** *They developed cement* **or** *They built roads to every part of the empire* **or** *They constructed great aqueducts.*

   Standard 1: Cite textual evidence to support analysis of what the text says explicitly as well as inferences drawn from the text.

9. **Analyze why Roman technology helped the empire last for a long time.**

   Answer: *The Coliseum and aqueducts provided benefits to the people* **or** *Roads made traveling fast and comfortable and helped trade* **or** *Roads helped maintain military control.* The answer should include the concept that technology benefited the Romans.

Standard 3: Analyze interactions/connections between individuals, events, and ideas.

10. **What is the meaning of *code* in the context of the previous paragraph? (AWL level 4)**

    Answer: A system, organized collection

    Standard 4: Determine the meaning of words and phrases as they are used in a text.

Summarize what the text says were the accomplishments of the Roman Empire. An acceptable text-based summary contains the following units. Students receive one point for each statement in their summary that matches the following statements in meaning.

1. An introductory statement of purpose
2. The Empire ruled conquered peoples in peace
3. Rome made improvements in architecture
4. And made improvements in technology
5. They built roads
6. They built aqueducts
7. They built large buildings such as the Coliseum
8. They invented concrete
9. And made advances in the use of the arch
10. They set up a code of laws
11. Roman law was passed to other cultures

Point Table   The Roman Empire, Middle School

Standard		Question	Points per Question
1.	Support an inference	5 8	1 1
2.	Determine central idea	1 6	1 1
3.	Explain why or how/analyze	2 9	2 1
4.	Determine word meaning	7 10	1 1
5.	Determine text structure	3	2
6.	Determine point of view	4	1
Total Question		10	12
2. Summary			11
Total Summary			(8 acceptable)
8.	Explain an argument	optional	2
Total Points			
8.	Evaluate an argument	optional	1
Total Points			

Optional Standard 8 Assessment
Before you begin scoring, please review the guidelines for scoring questions on pages 40–43, pages 63–67 for scoring summaries, and pages 74–77 for information on the Optional Standard 8 Assessments.

Tacitus: The Reign of Augustus

Explain two of Tacitus's reasons or arguments that indicate he did not admire Augustus.

Answer: *Augustus won over the people with money (gifts to the soldiers and cheap corn for the populace)* **and/or** *He was unopposed because the bold had died in battle or been condemned* **and/or** *He gave the nobles wealth and promotions* **and/or** *He gave relatives important posts although they were young boys* **and/or** *The two who would succeed him were savage and cruel and lacked experience* **and/or** *His successors would tear the State apart.*

Standard 8: Trace and evaluate the argument and specific claims in a text.

Select one reason or argument and explain why you think it is or is not valid.

Answer: Student explanation of validity or invalidity will vary. However, it should be relevant to the argument and should contain some supporting evidence or clarification. *Examples: Augustus won over the people with gifts and cheap corn. That's a valid reason for not liking him because that's bribery and bribery is a crime. Good rulers like Lincoln did not bribe people to get into office* **or** *He gave relatives important posts even though they were boys. That's valid for not liking Augustus. You should get a job because you are qualified. Senators and representatives have to have certain qualifications or they don't get voted for* **or** *His successors would tear the State apart. That's not valid for not admiring Augustus because it doesn't work that way. You can't blame a president for what the one who comes after him does. Same goes for the head of a business.*

Middle School, World History, Part III
Before you begin scoring, please review the guidelines for scoring questions on pages 40–43 and pages 63–67 for scoring summaries.

The Fall of Rome

1. **Analyze why so many of the Roman emperors after Commodus were assassinated.**

   Answer: *The emperors were dishonest; they stole money for themselves* **or** *They were generals; they probably did not know much about politics* **or** *They paid for loyalty; they didn't earn it* **or** *The government and senate had no power to support an emperor* **or** *The economy was weak so people would be unhappy.* Answer should offer a possible cause for assassination mentioned in the text.

   Standard 3: Analyze interactions/connections between individuals, events, and ideas.

2. **What evidence in the text strongly supports why a mercenary army was less effective than one loyal to the empire?**

   Answer: *Mercenaries were motivated by money, not loyalty to the empire* **or** *They often switched sides* **or** *They were not loyal to Rome.*

   Standard 1: Cite textual evidence to support analysis of what the text says explicitly as well as inferences drawn from the text.

3. **What is the meaning of *economic* in the context of the previous passage? (AWL level 1)**

   Answer: *Related to money or finance*

   Standard 4: Determine the meaning of words and phrases as they are used in a text.

4. **The topic of the previous two paragraphs is "economic problems." What is the central idea?**

   Answer: *Serious economic problems weakened Rome.* The answer must be clearly related to the topic. Do not accept a series of details as the main idea.

   Standard 2: Determine central idea/s.

5. **Analyze why Rome experienced economic problems. Give two reasons. (2 pts.)**

   Answer: *Rome did not have new sources of wealth from conquered lands* **and/or** *They had to raise taxes to get money* **and/or** *The government did not have enough silver to put in coins and money had little value* **and/or** *There was severe unemployment in the empire* **and/or** *There was uncontrolled inflation.* As a two-point question, there should be two clearly defined answers.

Standard 3: Analyze interactions/connections between individuals, events, and ideas.

6. Which text structure best explains how the author organized the previous passage? **(2 pts.)**

   ____ description of important features

   ____ explanation of steps in a sequence

   ____ account of cause and effect

   ____ explanation of problem and solution

   ____ comparison/contrast of two or more things

   Give a reason from the text for your answer. For example, if you choose description, tell what is being described. For sequence, list one or two steps explained in the text. For cause and effect, state a cause or an effect mentioned in the text. For problem/solution, tell what the problem is or describe the solution. For comparison, tell what is being compared or contrasted.

   Answer: *Cause/effect; the author describes the causes of economic problems (lack of sources of new wealth, raises in taxes, scarce food, lack of silver) and the effects (unemployment, less value for money and inflation).* Reasons that are not stated in the text are inaccurate.

   Standard 5: Analyze the structure of the text.

7. The topic of the previous two paragraphs is "efforts to stop the decline." What is the central idea?

   Answer: *Diocletian and Constantine both tried to stop Rome's decline* **or** *The author describes efforts to stop Rome's decline.* The answer must be clearly related to the topic. Do not accept a series of details as the main idea.

   Standard 2: Determine central idea/s.

8. What is the meaning of *decline* in the context of the previous passage? **(AWL level 1)**

   Answer: *Weakening, getting worse, losing power, failing*

   Standard 4: Determine the meaning of words and phrases as they are used in a text.

9. What evidence in the text strongly supports that Constantine was a strong and powerful ruler?

   Answer: *He reigned for 25 years* **or** *He moved the capitol of the Empire* **or** *He moved the power of the Empire to the east.*

   Standard 1: Cite textual evidence to support analysis of what the text says explicitly as well as inferences drawn from the text.

10. What was Constantine's point of view with regard to saving the empire?

    Answer: *He thought moving the capital of the empire from Rome to the east would strengthen the empire.* The answer should focus on an individual's opinion or attitude inferred from words or actions.

    Standard 6: Determine point of view or purpose.

Summarize what the text says were the problems that led to the fall of Rome. An acceptable text-based summary contains the following units. Students receive one point for each statement in their summary that matches the following statements in meaning.

1. An introductory statement of purpose
2. Roman emperors were corrupt
3. The senate lost power
4. The army was made up of mercenaries
5. Who had no loyalty to Rome
6. The Empire grew too big
7. Enemies attacked Rome
8. Conquered territories regained independence
9. There were serious economic problems
10. Such as unemployment
11. And inflation

Point Table   The Fall of Rome, Middle School

Standard	Question	Points per Question
1. Support an inference	2 9	1 1
2. Determine central idea	4 7	1 1
3. Explain why or how/analyze	1 5	1 2
4. Determine word meaning	3 8	1 1
5. Determine text structure	6	2
6. Determine point of view	10	1
Total Questions	10	12
2. Summary		11
Total Summary		(8 acceptable)
8. Explain an argument	optional	2
Total Points		
8. Evaluate an argument	optional	1
Total Points		

Optional Standard 8 Assessment   Before you begin scoring, please review the guidelines for scoring questions on pages 40–43, pages 63–67 for scoring summaries, and pages 74–77 for information on the Optional Standard 8 Assessments.

Ammianus Marcellinus: The Luxury of the Rich in Rome

Explain two of Marcellinus's reasons or arguments for the fall of Rome.

Answer: *There was a whirlpool of banquets* **and/or** *Romans drove recklessly* **and/or** *They had huge bodies of slaves* **and/or** *People were lazy* **and/or** *Instead of philosophers and orators they play music and engage in silly arts* **and/or** *When there was famine they expelled those who were accomplished but kept actresses and dancing girls* **and/or** *Lower classes spend all night drinking* **and/or** *They spend all their time watching chariot races.*

Standard 8: Trace and evaluate the argument and specific claims in a text.

Select one reason or argument and explain why you think it is or is not valid.

Answer: Student explanation of validity or invalidity will vary. However, it should be relevant to the argument and should contain some supporting evidence or clarification. Examples: *Romans drove recklessly. It's not valid because a lot of people drive that way today and it doesn't mean our government is falling* **or** *People were lazy. It's valid because if people don't work they don't really contribute anything and this could hurt the country but it really depends on how many are lazy. We have lazy people in our country but most people aren't* **or** *They spend all their time watching chariot races. This is not valid because people spend a lot of time watching sports like the Super Bowl and basketball and it isn't hurting our government.*

High School, American History, Part I   Before you begin scoring, please review the guidelines for scoring questions on pages 40–43 and pages 63–67 for scoring summaries.

Democracy and the Age of Jackson: The Election of 1824

1. **What evidence in the text strongly supports that Jackson had little respect for John Quincy Adams or Henry Clay?**

   Answer: *Jackson accused them of making a corrupt bargain in which Clay supported Adams in order to become Secretary of State* **or** *Jackson denounced Adams's policies as "aristocratic" and favoring the wealthy over the common people.*

   Standard 1: Cite textual evidence to support analysis of what the text says explicitly as well as inferences drawn from the text.

2. **The topic of the previous three paragraphs is "new state constitutions." What is the central idea?**

   Answer: *New state constitutions expanded the electorate but denied the votes to blacks and woman* **or** *The author describes how new state constitutions changed and defined the electorate.* The answer must be clearly related to the topic. Do not accept a series of details as the central idea.

   Standard 2: Determine central idea/s.

3. **Analyze how the new state constitutions both expanded and limited the democratic process (2 pts.)**

   Answer: *They expanded the vote by removing the property requirement* **and/or** *Any man who paid a tax could vote* **and/or** *They limited the vote to white men* **and/or** *Blacks, women, and Native Americans could not vote.* Answer should include both expansion and limitation. As a two-point question, there should be two clearly defined answers.

   Standard 3: Analyze interactions/connections between individuals, events, and ideas.

4. **What is the meaning of *projected* in the context of the previous passage? (AWL level 4)**

   Answer: *Portrayed, described, represented, made himself look like, displayed himself, showed himself as*

   Standard 4: Determine the meaning of words and phrases as they are used in a text.

5. **The topic of the previous section is "Jackson Emerges." What is the central idea?**

   Answer: *Jackson became a popular figure to the common people* **or** *Jackson became a symbol of American democracy*

or *The author explains why Jackson appealed to the common people. Answer should include the reason for his popularity, not just that he became popular.* The answer must be clearly related to the topic. Do not accept a series of details as the central idea.

Standard 2: Determine central idea/s.

6. **Analyze why Jackson was an appealing candidate. Give two reasons. (2 pts.)**

   Answer: *He supported/celebrated majority rule* **and/or** *He celebrated the dignity of the common people* **and/or** *He projected himself as a common man, not an aristocrat* **and/or** *He was a military hero* **and/or** *He was not from Virginia or Massachusetts.* As a two-point question, there should be two clearly defined answers.

   Standard 3: Analyze interactions/connections between individuals, events, and ideas.

7. **Which text structure best explains how the author organized the previous passage? (2 pts.)**

   ____ description of important features

   ____ explanation of steps in a sequence

   ____ account of cause and effect

   ____ explanation of problem and solution

   ____ comparison/contrast of two or more things

   Give a reason from the text for your answer. For example, if you choose description, tell what is being described. For sequence, list one or two steps explained in the text. For cause and effect, state a cause or an effect mentioned in the text. For problem/solution, tell what the problem is or describe the solution. For comparison, tell what is being compared or contrasted.

   Answer: *Comparison/contrast; the author is contrasting two views on offering jobs as rewards for political loyalty* **or** *Description; the author is describing a new party structure.* Reasons that are not present in the text are inaccurate.

   Standard 5: Analyze the structure of a text.

8. **What is the meaning of** *innovated* **in the context of the previous passage? (AWL level 7)**

   Answer: *Changed, remodeled, transformed, revolutionized, did something in a new way, created something new*

   Standard 4: Determine the meaning of words and phrases as they are used in a text.

9. **What was the point of view of William Marcy regarding the Democrats' use of jobs as rewards for political loyalty?**

   Answer: *He favored the practice because he defended it to Congress.* The answer should focus on an individual's opinion or attitude inferred from actions or words.

   Standard 6: Determine the author's point of view or purpose.

10. **What evidence in the text strongly supports that Jackson and his party initiated new practices for political campaigning? Include at least two kinds of evidence. (2 pts.)**

   Answer: *The Democrats developed a disciplined system of committees and conventions* **and/or** *They rewarded the faithful with government jobs* **and/or** *They carried out carefully planned appeals to voters* **and/or** *They held public rallies* **and/or** *They cast out anyone who broke with party discipline* **and/or** *They used professional managers.* As a two-point question, there should be two clearly defined answers.

   Standard 1: Cite textual evidence to support analysis of what the text says explicitly as well as inferences drawn from the text.

Summarize what the text says about how Andrew Jackson won the presidency in 1828. An acceptable text-based summary contains the following units. Students receive one point for each statement in their summary that matches the following statements in meaning.

1. An introductory statement of purpose
2. Jackson traveled across the country
3. He supported the importance of the common man
4. He projected himself as a common man
5. He formed a partnership of southern planters and northern common people
6. He promised a return to Jeffersonian principles
7. They would not interfere in slavery and state rights
8. The party developed a strong system of committees, conventions, and rallies

Point Table   The Election of 1824, High School

Standard	Question	Points per Question
1. Support an inference	1 10	1 2
2. Determine central idea	2 5	1 1
3. Explain why or how/analyze	3 6	2 2
4. Determine word meaning	4 8	1 1
5. Determine text structure	7	2
6. Determine point of view	9	1
Total Question	10	14
2. Summary		8
Total Summary		(6 acceptable)
8. Explain an argument	optional	4
Total Points		
8. Evaluate an argument	optional	2
Total Points		

Optional Standard 8 Assessment Before you begin scoring, please review the guidelines for scoring questions on pages 40–43, pages 63–67 for scoring summaries, and pages 74–77 for information on the Optional Standard 8 Assessments.

Andrew Jackson's State of the Nation Address, 1829

Read the excerpt from Andrew Jackson's State of the Nation Address. Explain four reasons or arguments that Jackson presents for amending the Constitution.

Answer: *The people's choice of president should not be defeated by the electoral college or the House of Representatives* **and/or** *Members of the electoral college or the House may be unfaithful or err* **and/or** *The vote of one state may be controlled by an individual representative* **and/or** *An individual representative may be motivated by a possible reward* **and/or** *Even without corruption, the will of the people can be misrepresented through ignorance or conviction* **and/or** *If a minority candidate is elected he can not enjoy the confidence necessary to successful discharge of his duties.*

Standard 8: Trace and evaluate the argument and specific claims in a text.

Select two reasons or arguments and, for each one, explain why you think it is or is not valid.

Answer: Student explanation of validity or invalidity will vary. However, it should be relevant to the argument and should contain some supporting evidence or clarification. Examples: *If a minority candidate is elected he will not have the people's confidence. This is valid because, whatever he does, the majority who did not vote for him will disagree. You see this in the papers all the time. The Dems don't agree with the GOP and vice versa* **or** *The vote of one state may be controlled by an individual representative. This is not valid; it may happen for one state but probably not for all the states* **or** *Members of the electoral college or the House may be unfaithful and err. This is valid because people can always make a mistake or not do what they should do and they can be bribed* **or** *An individual representative might be motivated by a possible reward. This is not valid. While one individual might be motivated by a reward, you can't assume that the entire electoral college or House will be.*

High School, American History, Part II Before you begin scoring, please review the guidelines for scoring questions on pages 40–43 and pages 63–67 for scoring summaries.

Democracy and the Age of Jackson: Conflicts and Crises

Native American Removal

1. The topic of the previous four paragraphs is "Native Americans in the South." What is the central idea?

   Answer: *Jackson agreed with southern voters that Native Americans should be removed despite their adoption of white culture* or *The author describes Jackson's view regarding Native Americans in the South.* The answer must be clearly related to the topic. Do not accept a series of details as the central idea.

   Standard 2: Determine central idea/s.

2. What evidence in the text strongly supports that Jackson's view of Native Americans as "savages" was not true? Include at least two reasons. **(2 pts.)**

   Answer: *Native Americans had adopted white culture* **and/or** *Many practiced Christianity* **and/or** *Many owned private property* **and/or** *Many formed constitutional governments* **and/or** *The Cherokees had a writing system* **and/or** *They printed newspapers and books* **and/or** *They*

established schools. As a two-point question, there should be two clearly defined answers.

   Standard 1: Cite textual evidence to support analysis of what the text says explicitly as well as inferences drawn from the text.

3. The topic of the previous two paragraphs is "Indian land." What is the central idea?

   Answer: *The Supreme Court and Jackson took different positions on Native American land* **or** *The author compares the position of the Supreme Court and Jackson with regard to Native American land* **or** *The author describes Jackson's position with regard to Native Americans in the South. Answer should include mention of Jackson.* The answer must be clearly related to the topic. Do not accept a series of details as the central idea.

   Standard 2: Determine central idea/s.

4. Analyze why many white men, including Jackson, wanted Native Americans removed from the southeast. Include at least two reasons. **(2 pts.)**

   Answer: *They did not believe that Native Americans were civilized* **and/or** *Gold had been discovered on Native*

American land **and/or** *The land was valuable for farming* **and/or** *Jackson believed Native Americans were unwilling to submit to state laws* **and/or** *They wanted the land* **and/or** *Jackson said it was to preserve the Native Americans from annihilation.* As a two-point question, there should be two clearly defined answers.

Standard 3: Analyze interactions/connections between individuals, events, and ideas.

5. What is the meaning of *liberal* in the context of the previous paragraph? **(AWL level 5)**

   Answer: *Appropriate, fitting, unselfish, more than should be expected, favorable, more than fair*

   Standard 4: Determine the meaning of words and phrases as they are used in a text.

6. Which text structure best explains how the author organized the previous passage? **(2 pts.)**

   ___ description of important features

   ___ explanation of steps in a sequence

   ___ account of cause and effect

   ___ explanation of problem and solution

   ___ comparison/contrast of two or more things

   Give a reason from the text for your answer. For example, if you choose description, tell what is being described. For sequence, list one or two steps explained in the text. For cause and effect, state a cause or an effect mentioned in the text. For problem/solution, tell what the problem is or describe the solution. For comparison, tell what is being compared or contrasted.

   Answer: *Sequence; the author sequentially describes events in the forcible removal of several tribes* **or** *Problem/solution; the author explains how a problem of Jackson's administration (the desire to remove Native Americans from the south) was solved* **or** *Cause/effect; desire for land was the cause of forcing Native Americans off their land and the effect was death and war.* Reasons that are not present in the text are inaccurate.

   Standard 5: Analyze the structure of the text.

7. What evidence in the text strongly suggests that members of Congress favored Jackson even before he was elected to the presidency?

Answer: *Congress passed The Tariff of Abominations partly in order to embarrass President Adams and ensure Jackson's victory.*

Standard 1: Cite textual evidence to support analysis of what the text says explicitly as well as inferences drawn from the text.

8. What was Jackson's point of view regarding states' rights and the preservation of the Union?

   Answer: *He supported states' rights and he believed that the Union must be preserved* **or** *States must honor federal law* **or** *He believed that states did not have the power to nullify a federal law* **or** *He believed nullification was treason* **or** *He believed federal law must be preserved.* The answer should include Jackson's view on states' rights and the preservation of Union. The answer should focus on an individual's opinion or attitude inferred from actions or words.

   Standard 6: Determine the author's point of view or purpose.

9. What is the meaning of *resolved* in the context of the previous paragraph? **(AWL level 4)**

   Answer: *Solved, decided, agreed upon, fixed, no longer an issue, ended a problem*

   Standard 4: Determine the meaning of words and phrases as they are used in a text.

10. Analyze how Jackson used similar tactics to deal with the nullification crisis and the Native American issue. Include two similarities. **(2 pts.)**

    Answer: *He was ready to use force* **and** *He worked with Congress to pass laws that favored his position.* As a two-point question, there should be two clearly defined answers.

    Standard 3: Analyze interactions/connections between individuals, events, and ideas.

Summarize what the text says about how South Carolina caused a nullification crisis and how it was resolved. An acceptable text-based summary contains the following units. Students receive one point for each statement in their summary that matches the following statements in meaning.

1. An introductory statement of purpose

2. Congress passed a high tariff

3. It was very unpopular in the South

4. South Carolina nullified this law or prohibited collection of the tariff

5. The state threatened to secede from the Union

6. If the federal government used force against the state

7. Jackson felt a state had no right to nullify a federal law

8. Congress gave Jackson the power to use force

9. Jackson convinced Congress to reduce the tariff

10. South Carolina suspended the nullification ordinance

Point Table   Conflicts and Crises, High School

Standard	Question	Points per Question
1. Support an inference	2 7	2 1
2. Determine central idea	1 3	1 1
3. Explain why or how/analyze	4 10	2 2
4. Determine word meaning	5 9	1 1
5. Determine text structure	6	2
6. Determine point of view	8	1
Total Questions		14
2. Summary		10
Total Summary		(7 acceptable)
8. Explain an argument	optional	4
Total Points		
8. Evaluate an argument	optional	2
Total Points		

Optional Standard 8 Assessment   Before you begin scoring, please review the guidelines for scoring questions on pages 40–43, pages 63–67 for scoring summaries, and pages 74–77 for information on the Optional Standard 8 Assessments.

SOCIAL STUDIES

Memorial of the Cherokee Nation (1830)

Read the excerpt from the Memorial of the Cherokee Nation. Explain four reasons or arguments that the Cherokee present for not wising to leave their ancestral lands.

Answer: *Leaving would be fatal to their interests* **and/or** *They cannot endure being deprived of national and individual rights* **and/or** *They cannot endure being subjected to oppression* **and/or** *They wish to remain in the land of their fathers* **and/or** *They have a perfect and original right to remain by virtue of U.S. treaties and laws* **and/or** *Where they will have to go is unknown territory* **and/or** *They would be regarded as intruders by other Indians* **and/or** *The land is not fit for agriculture* **and/or** *The present inhabitants have different languages and customs* **and/or** *The land is not the land of their birth or affections* **and/or** *Man has a right to live on the land of his fathers.*

Standard 8: Trace and evaluate an argument and specific claims in a text.

Select two reasons or arguments and, for each one, explain why you think it is or is not valid.

Answer: Student explanation of validity or invalidity will vary. However, it should be relevant to the argument and should contain some supporting evidence or clarification. Examples: *They have a right to remain by virtue of U.S. treaties and laws. This is valid because a nation should not break a treaty or laws just to get someone's land. They shouldn't break a treaty at all once they signed it* **or** *The present inhabitants have different language and customs. This is not valid because the Cherokee could learn their language and customs and learn to get along. It would be hard but it's possible* **or** *Man has a right to live in the land of his fathers. This is valid because no one should be forced to move where he doesn't want to go, not if America is the land of the free. And it was their land. They were there first.*

High School, American History, Part III Before you begin scoring, please review the guidelines for scoring questions on pages 40–43 and pages 63–67 for scoring summaries.

Democracy and the Age of Jackson: More Conflicts and Crises

1. What is the meaning of *stable* in the context of the previous paragraph? **(AWL level 6)**

   Answer: *Secure, steady, unchanging, constant, retains value*

   Standard 4: Determine the meaning of words and phrases as they are used in a text.

2. The topic of the previous section is "Jackson Opposes the Bank." What is the central idea?

   Answer: *Jackson opposed the bank because he felt it favored the rich* **or** *The author describes why Jackson did not support the bank.* The answer must be clearly related to the topic. Do not accept a series of details as the central idea.

   Standard 2: Determine central idea/s.

3. What evidence in the text strongly supports that Jackson and Jacksonian Democrats did not support the wealthy? Give two examples. **(2 pts.)**

   Answer: *They opposed tariffs and subsidies because they thought they enriched the wealthy* **and/or** *They thought the Bank of the United States favored rich investors* **and/or** *Jackson opposed government action that advanced a few at the expense of many* **and/or** *Jackson said the rich and powerful were selfish* and/or *bent government to their purposes.* As a two-point question, there should be two clearly defined answers.

   Standard 1: Cite textual evidence to support analysis of what the text says explicitly as well as inferences drawn from the text.

4. What was Jackson's point of view regarding the usefulness of the Second Bank of the United States? **(2 pts.)**

   Answer: *He was opposed to the bank because he believed it was not authorized by the Constitution* **and/or** *It undermined the rights of the states* **and/or** *It was dangerous to people's liberty* **and/or** *It favored the rich.* The answer should focus on an individual's opinion or attitude inferred from actions or words.

   Standard 6: Determine the author's point of view or purpose.

5. Which text structure best explains how the author organized the previous passage?

   ____ description of important features

   ____ explanation of steps in a sequence

   ____ account of cause and effect

   ____ explanation of problem and solution

   ____ comparison/contrast of two or more things

Give a reason from the text for your answer. For example, if you choose description, tell what is being described. For sequence, list one or two steps explained in the text. For cause and effect, state a cause or an effect mentioned in the text. For problem/solution, tell what the problem is or describe the solution. For comparison, tell what is being compared or contrasted.

   Answer: *Comparison/contrast; the author is contrasting two different views of the Second Bank of the United States: Jackson's view and the view of the Bank's supporters.*

   Standard 5: Analyze the structure of the text.

6. The topic of the previous section is "the formation of the Whig party." What is the central idea?

   Answer: *The central idea is the Whig party was formed in opposition to Jackson's policies* **or** *The author explains who led the Whigs and what their policies were.* The answer must be clearly related to the topic. Do not accept a series of details as the central idea.

   Standard 2: Determine central idea/s.

7. Analyze how the policies of the Whig party and the policies of Jackson were different. Provide at least two examples. **(2 pts.)**

   Answer: *The Whigs wanted the federal government to support/manage the economy and Jackson promoted states' rights and individual liberty* **and/or** *The Whigs favored a system of protective tariffs and internal improvements and Jackson saw these as favoring the wealthy* **and/or** *The Whigs wanted the renewal of the Bank of the United States and Jackson opposed the Bank.* As a two-point question, there should be two clearly defined answers.

   Standard 3: Analyze interactions/connections between individuals, events, and ideas.

8. What is the meaning of *depression* in the context of the previous passage? **(AWL level 10)**

   Answer: *Slump in the economy, decline in business and trade, a bad time when people lose money and jobs*

   Standard 4: Determine the meaning of words and phrases as they are used in a text.

9. Analyze how two of Jackson's actions actually harmed what he described as "the humble members of society—the farmers, mechanics and laborers." **(2 pts.)**

   Answer: *The destruction of the bank caused inflation, which hurt the common people* **and** *Jackson's decision to not accept paper money caused a drop in land values and sales* **and/or** *Both resulted in a severe depression where people lost land and jobs.* As a two-point question, there should be two clearly defined answers.

Standard 3: Analyze interactions/connections between individuals, events, and ideas.

10. **What evidence in the text strongly supports that political campaigns are not always truthful?**

    Answer: *The author describes the Whigs' portrayal of Harrison and Van Buren as more creative than honest* **and/or** *The campaign is described as "light on ideas"* **and/ or** *The campaign was described as "heavy on theatrics."*

Standard 1: Cite textual evidence to support analysis of what the text says explicitly as well as inferences drawn from the text.

Summarize what the text says about the conflict over the National Bank and how it was settled. An acceptable text-based summary contains the following units. Students receive one point for each statement in their summary that matches the following statements in meaning.

1. An introductory statement of purpose
2. Jacksonian Democrats did not like the Bank
3. They thought it favored rich investors
4. Business leaders valued the bank and felt it promoted economic growth
5. Congress voted to renew the Bank's charter
6. Jackson vetoed it
7. Bank supporters called Jackson power hungry
8. After Jackson's reelection, he weakened the bank

9. By withdrawing federal funds
10. And placing them in state banks

Point Table   More Conflicts and Crises, High School

Standard	Question	Points per Question
1. Support an inference	3 10	2 1
2. Determine main idea	2 6	1 1
3. Explain why or how/analyze	7 9	2 2
4. Determine word meaning	1 8	1 1
5. Determine text structure	5	2
6. Determine point of view	4	1
Total Questions		14
2. Summary		10
Total Summary		(7 acceptable)
8. Explain an argument	optional	4
Total Points		
8. Evaluate an argument	optional	2
Total Points		

Optional Standard 8 Assessment

Before you begin scoring, please review the guidelines for scoring questions on pages 40–43, pages 63–67 for scoring summaries, and pages 74–77 for information on the Optional Standard 8 Assessments.

Henry Clay's Speech on Andrew Jackson's Veto of the Bank of the United States, 1832

Read the excerpt from Henry Clay's speech on Andrew Jackson's veto of the bank of the United States. Explain four reasons or arguments that he presents why the Bank should not have been vetoed.

Answer: *The veto should not be used in ordinary cases, only in instances of precipitate legislation* **and/or** *The president has used the veto four times, more than any other president* **and/or** *The existence of the Bank has been long and thoroughly scrutinized* **and/or** *The question of the Bank has been discussed by the people and state legislatures* **and/or** *No Congress has been opposed to the Bank* **and/ or** *The power to establish a Bank is deduced from the Constitution* **and/or** *The Bank is the only reliance for a sound and uniform currency* **and/or** *The Senate and House have been violently attacked* **and/or** *The veto as used by the president can end in subversion of the government.*

Standard 8: Trace and evaluate an argument and specific claims in a text.

Select two arguments and, for each one, explain why you think it is or is not valid.

Answer: Student explanation of validity or invalidity will vary. However, it should be relevant to the argument and should contain some supporting evidence or clarification. Examples: *The president has used the veto four times, more than any other president. This is not valid because it's not how many times you do something, but why you do it that matters* **or** *The existence of the Bank has been long and thoroughly scrutinized. This is not valid because Clay does not offer any details of how long and how thoroughly it was scrutinized or who did it* **or** *No Congress has been opposed to the Bank. This is valid because Congress involves a lot of different people* **or** *The power to establish a Bank is deduced from the Constitution. This is valid because if this is so, then the president is going against the Constitution. But Clay may just be saying it is so and it really isn't in the Constitution and then it would be invalid.*

SOCIAL STUDIES

SOCIAL STUDIES

The Rise of the Greek City-States

1. **Which text structure best explains how the author organized the previous section? (2 pts.)**

   ___ description of important features

   ___ explanation of steps in a sequence

   ___ account of cause and effect

   ___ explanation of problem and solution

   ___ comparison/contrast of two or more things

   Give a reason from the text for your answer. For example, if you choose description, tell what is being described. For sequence, list one or two steps explained in the text. For cause and effect, state a cause or an effect mentioned in the text. For problem/solution, tell what the problem is or describe the solution. For comparison, tell what is being compared or contrasted.

   Answer: *Comparison/contrast; the author contrasts three forms of government: monarchy, aristocracy, and oligarchy* **or** *Description; the author describes the distinguishing features of three forms of government* **or** *Cause/effect; the author describes causes that led to each type of government (effect) such as affording weapons and trade expansion* **or** *Sequence; the author describes the sequence of changes in government.* Reasons that are not present in the text are inaccurate.

   Standard 5: Analyze the structure of a text.

2. **What is the meaning of** *isolated* **in the context of the previous paragraph? (AWL level 7)**

   Answer: *Separated, stayed or kept apart, kept away from, left alone, disconnected*

   Standard 4: Determine the meaning of words and phrases as they are used in a text.

3. **Analyze how the military dominated Spartan society. Include at least two examples. (2 pts.)**

   Answer: *Spartans abandoned sickly children because they wanted future soldiers to be healthy* **and/or** *Boys began training for the military at age seven* **and/or** *Men spent their lives in the military* **and/or** *Men were subjected to strict and harsh discipline* **and/or** *Spartans encouraged boys to steal to develop cunning* **and/or** *Men lived in barracks until age 30* **and/or** *Men ate in barracks for most of their life* **and/or** *Women were expected to produce healthy sons for the army.* As a two-point question, there should be two clearly defined answers.

   Standard 3: Analyze interactions/connections between individuals, events, and ideas.

4. **What is the meaning of** *evolved* **in the context of the previous paragraph? (AWL level 5)**

   Answer: *Changed, grew into, developed, became different*

   Standard 4: Determine the meaning of words and phrases as they are used in a text.

5. **The topic of the above three paragraphs is "Solon Reforms Government." What is the central idea?**

   Answer: *Solon opened government to more citizens; however, citizenship remained limited and unrest continued* **or** *The author describes Solon's reform and their effect.* The answer must be clearly related to the topic. Do not accept a series of details as the central idea.

   Standard 2: Determine central idea/s; provide an objective summary.

6. **What evidence in the text strongly supports that Solon's reforms did not go far enough?**

   Answer: *Citizenship remained limited* **and/or** *Many positions were open only to the wealthy* **and/or** *Unrest led to the rise of tyrants.*

   Standard 1: Cite textual evidence to support analysis of what the text says explicitly as well as inferences drawn from the text.

7. **What was Cleisthenes's point of view regarding the Athenian assembly?**

   Answer: *He believed that it should actually debate, approve,* and/or *reject laws* **or** *He believed that debating, approving,* **or** *Rejecting laws should be open to ordinary citizens.* The answer should include actual participation in government. The answer should focus on an individual's opinion or attitude inferred from actions or words.

   Standard 6: Determine the author's point of view or purpose.

8. **Analyze how Greek leaders fostered the development of Athenian democracy. Include at least two examples. (2 pts.)**

   Answer: *Solon opened high offices to more citizens and gave the assembly more say in important decisions* **and/or** *Pisistratus gave the poor a greater voice in government* **and/or** *Cleisthenes increased the role of ordinary citizens in government* **and/or** *Cleisthenes set up a genuine lawmaking body.* As a two-point question, there should be two clearly defined answers.

   Standard 3: Analyze interactions/connections between individuals, events, and ideas.

9. **The topic of the previous section is "Athenian women." What is the central idea?**

   Answer: *Women had limited roles in Athenian society* **or** *The author describes the role of women in society.* The answer must be clearly related to the topic. Do not accept a series of details as the central idea.

Standard 2: Determine central idea/s; provide an objective summary.

10. **What evidence in the text indicates that Athenian boys and girls were treated differently? Give two examples. (2 pts.)**

    Answer: *Girls received little formal education and boys attended school* **and/or** *Boys could become citizens and vote; girls lived a secluded life* **and/or** *Girls played an important role in religion; boys played an important role in government.* As a two-point question, there should be two clearly defined answers.

    Standard 1: Cite textual evidence to support analysis of what the text says explicitly as well as inferences drawn from the text.

Summarize what the text says about differences between the city-states of Athens and Sparta. An acceptable text-based summary contains the following units. Students receive one point for each statement in their summary that matches the following statements in meaning.

1. An introductory statement of purpose
2. Athens evolved into a democracy
3. Sparta remained a monarchy
4. Athens valued trade with other city-states
5. Sparta remained isolated by choice
6. Athens valued the arts
7. Sparta valued physical fitness and the military
8. Athenian women played an important role in religion
9. Spartan women were expected to produce healthy sons for the military

Point Table   The Rise of the Greek City-States, High School

Standard	Question	Points per Question
1. Support an inference	6 10	1 2
2. Determine central idea	5 9	1 1
3. Explain why or how/analyze	3 8	2 2
4. Determine word meaning	2 4	1 1
5. Determine text structure	1	2
6. Determine point of view	7	1
Total Questions		14
2. Summary		9
Total Summary		(7 acceptable)
8. Explain an argument	optional	4
Total Points		
8. Evaluate an argument	optional	2
Total Points		

Optional Standard 8 Assessment   Before you begin scoring, please review the guidelines for scoring questions on pages 40–43, pages 63–67 for scoring summaries, and pages 74–77 for information on the Optional Standard 8 Assessments.

Xenophon: "On the Policy of the Athenians"

Read Xenophon's reasons why he does not approve of Athens democracy. Explain four reasons or arguments that he presents in support of his opinions.

Answer: *The Athenians give the advantage to thieves, the poor, and the radical elements rather than to the elite* **and/ or** *Among the elite there is little license and injustice, and great discrimination as to what is worthy* **and/or** *Among the poor there is very great ignorance, disorderliness, and thievery* **and/or** *Anyone who wants, even a thief, can make a speech to the advantage of himself and those like him* **and/or** *If anything bad results from a decision of the assembly, they lay the blame on a minority for opposing and working its ruin, whereas if any good comes about they take the credit themselves* **and/or** *They make fun of the rich, well-born, or influential, and not the poor* **and/or** *The poor favor those who are friendly and useful to them even if they are thieves.*

Select two reasons or arguments and, for each one, explain why it is or is not valid.

Answer: Student explanation of validity or invalidity will vary. However, it should be relevant to the argument and should contain some supporting evidence or clarification. Examples: *Among the poor there is very great ignorance, disorderliness, and thievery. This is not valid because there are many poor people who are smart and honest and follow the laws in every country* **or** *They make fun of the rich, well-born, or influential, and not the poor. This is not valid because this happens all the time in our country like on Saturday Night Live* **or** *Anyone who wants, even a thief, can make a speech to the advantage of himself and others. This is not valid because just because a person is a thief, that doesn't mean he can't have good ideas and if you have free speech, a thief can say what he wants* **or** *If anything good comes about the assembly takes the credit. This is not valid because people do this all the time and not just in*

SOCIAL STUDIES

Athens; they take credit for what is good but not for what is bad, like when no one says it's their fault that a team lost **or** *Among the elite there is little license and injustice, and great discrimination as to what is worthy. This is valid*

because I think the elite are the important people and if they are bad, a lot of people will follow them and it can't be good for the government.

SOCIAL STUDIES

Conflict in the Greek World

The Persian Wars

1. **The topic of the previous section is "the Greek city-states unite." What is the central idea?**

    Answer: *The Greek city-states united and defeated the Persians* **or** *The author explained why the city-states united and the results of the union.* The answer should include the concepts of union and defeat of the Persians. The answer must be clearly related to the topic. Do not accept a series of details as the central idea.

    Standard 2: Determine central idea/s; provide an objective summary.

2. **What evidence in the text indicates that the Spartan defeat at Thermopylae actually benefited the Athenians?**

    Answer: *The Spartans held off the Persians long enough for the Athenians to flee Athens to safety.*

    Standard 1: Cite textual evidence to support analysis of what the text says explicitly as well as inferences drawn from the text.

3. **What is the meaning of** *dominated* **in the context of the previous passage? (AWL level 3)**

    Answer: *Controlled, had the most power, overpowered, told others what to do, ruled over, took over*

    Standard 4: Determine the meaning of words and phrases as they are used in a text.

4. **What was Athens's point of view regarding their form of government?**

    Answer: *They believed the gods had protected them because of their form of government* **or** *They believed that they should control the other city-states* **or** *They felt they were unique.* The answer should focus on an individual's opinion or attitude inferred from actions or words.

    Standard 6: Determine the author's point of view or purpose.

5. **Analyze how Athens violated the concept of an alliance as a member of the Delian League. Offer two examples. (2 pts.)**

    Answer: *Athens used the League to enrich itself* **and/or** *Athens dominated the league* **and/or** *Athens used money contributed by others to rebuild its cities* **and/or** *Athens*

used force to prevent members from leaving the league **and/or** *Athens used the League to create an Empire.* As a two-point question, there should be two clearly defined answers.

    Standard 3: Analyze interactions/connections between individuals, events, and ideas.

6. **The topic of the previous section is "The Athenian Democracy." What is the central idea?**

    Answer: *Athenian democracy was a direct democracy where citizens take part in day-to-day affairs of the government* **or** *The author describes how Athenian direct democracy worked.* The answer must be clearly related to the topic. Do not accept a series of details as the central idea.

    Standard 2: Determine central idea/s; provide an objective summary.

7. **Analyze why Athenian or direct democracy may not have been an efficient form of government. Give two reasons. (2 pts.)**

    Answer: *All citizens directly took part in Athenian democracy; this could be difficult to manage* **or** *The Athenian assembly was chosen by lot, not by vote, so some individuals might be unfit to serve or not want to serve* **or** *Athenian juries included hundreds or even thousands of jurors; this could be difficult to manage.* As a two-point question, there should be two clearly defined answers. Answer should offer a characteristic of Athenian democracy and then explain why it was inefficient.

    Standard 3: Analyze interactions/connections between individuals, events, and ideas.

8. **Which text structure best explains how the author organized the previous passage? (2 pts.)**

    ____ **description of important features**

    ____ **explanation of steps in a sequence**

    ____ **account of cause and effect**

    ____ **explanation of problem and solution**

    ____ **comparison/contrast of two or more things**

    Give a reason from the text for your answer. For example, if you choose description, tell what is being described. For sequence, list one or two steps explained in the text. For cause and effect, state a cause or an effect mentioned in the text. For problem/solution, tell what the problem is or describe the solution.

For comparison, tell what is being compared or contrasted.

Answer: *Description; the author describes key features of Athenian or direct democracy* **or** *Comparison; the author compares direct democracy with modern democracies. Reasons that are not present in the text are inaccurate.*

Standard 5: Analyze the structure of a text.

9. What is the meaning of *cultural* in the context of the previous paragraph? **(AWL level 2)**

    Answer: *Related to the arts, such as music, drama, dance*

    Standard 4: Determine the meaning of words and phrases as they are used in a text.

10. What evidence in the text indicates that Sparta's attitude toward Athens was somewhat contradictory? Give an example of one negative action and one positive action. **(2 pts.)**

    Answer: *Negative: They formed the Peloponnesian league* **or** *They allied themselves with their former enemy, Persia* **or** *They fought a war against Athens* **or** *They committed savage acts against Athens. Positive: Although victorious against Athens, they refused to destroy the city.*

    Standard 1: Cite textual evidence to support analysis of what the text says explicitly as well as inferences drawn from the text.

Summarize what the text says about why the union of city-states broke apart. An acceptable text-based summary contains the following units. Students receive one point for each statement in their summary that matches the following statements in meaning.

1. An introductory statement of purpose
2. Athens dominated the Delian League
3. Athens used a position of leadership to create an empire
4. Athens used League money to rebuild their city
5. Athens used force to keep city-states in the League
6. The other city-states resented Athens
7. They formed their own league
8. War broke out between Athens and Sparta

Point Table   Conflict in the Greek World, High School

Standard	Question	Points per Question
1. Support an inference	2 10	1 2
2. Determine central idea	1 6	1 1
3. Explain why or how/analyze	5 7	2 2
4. Determine word meaning	3 9	1 1
5. Determine text structure	8	2
6. Determine point of view	4	1
Total Questions	10	14
2. Summary		8
Total Summary		(6 acceptable)
8. Explain an argument	optional	4
Total Points		
8. Evaluate an argument	optional	2
Total Point		

Optional Standard 8 Assessment Before you begin scoring, please review the guidelines for scoring questions on pages 40–43, pages 63–67 for scoring summaries, and pages 74–77 for information on the Optional Standard 8 Assessments.

Thucydides: "History of the Peloponnesian War"

Read Corinth's reasons why they believe war should be declared against Athens. Explain four arguments that they present in support of their opinions.

Answer: *Their reception and export of goods will be injured* **and/or** *The danger will extend to the interior* **and/or** *They have been injured and have adequate grounds of complaint* **and/or** *They have many reasons to expect success (superiority in numbers and in military experience and unvarying obedience in the execution of orders)* **and/or** *They can get loans to increase their naval power and seduce the foreign sailors by the offer of higher pay*

and/or *Our strength lies in men and we shall be their superiors in courage* **and/or** *The money shall be provided by our contributions; we should not refuse to spend for vengeance and self-preservation* **and/or** *Unless we make an unanimous stand against her, Athens will easily conquer us* **and/or** *If we are conquered it will be slavery pure and simple* **and/or** *The god has commanded war and promised to be with us* **and/or** *The rest of Hellas will all join in the struggle* **and/or** *The result of victory will be lasting peace.*

Select two arguments and, for each one, explain why it is or is not valid.

Answer: Student explanation of validity or invalidity will vary. However, it should be relevant to the argument and should contain some supporting evidence or clarification.

SOCIAL STUDIES

Examples: *They have many reasons to expect success. That's valid because only a fool starts a war that he knows he can't win* **or** *The god has commanded war and promised to be with us. That's not valid because they can say this but where is the proof that the god did it? People should back up their claims* **or** *They have been injured and have adequate grounds for complaint. That's valid if they really do have adequate grounds because no one should go to war without a good reason, but sometimes, like in World War I, both sides thought they were right* **or** *We shall be their superiors in courage. This is not valid because how do they really know this? It's like sportscasters saying which team will win and then they are wrong* **or** *They have many reasons to expect success (superiority in numbers and in military experience and unvarying obedience in the execution of orders). This is valid because this is what wins wars: more men who are experienced soldiers and who obey leaders who know what they are doing.*

High School, World History, Part III   Before you begin scoring, please review the guidelines for scoring questions on pages 40–43 and pages 63–67 for scoring summaries.

SOCIAL STUDIES

The Glory That Was Greece

1. **The topic of the previous section is "Socrates questions traditions." What is the central idea?**

   Answer: *Socrates's questions threatened Athenian values and led to his death* **or** *Socrates believed that questions led to truth and self-knowledge, but this led to his death.* The answer must be clearly related to the topic. The answer should include the concept of death as a result of questioning. Do not accept a series of details as the central idea.

   Standard 2: Determine central idea/s; provide an objective summary.

2. **What evidence in the text indicates that many Athenians were very certain about their beliefs?**

   Answer: *The Athenians regarded Socrates's questions as a threat to their values and traditions* **or** *The Athenians condemned Socrates to death for corrupting their youth and failing to respect the gods.*

   Standard 1: Cite textual evidence to support analysis of what the text says explicitly as well as inferences drawn from the text.

3. **What is the meaning of *pursuing* in the context of the previous paragraph? (AWL level 5)**

   Answer: *Striving for, fulfilling, believing in, practicing, promoting, trying to accomplish, working toward.* Do not accept a definition of looking for someone or chasing after someone.

   Standard 4: Determine the meaning of words and phrases as they are used in a text.

4. **What point of view regarding democracy was shared by both Plato and Aristotle?**

   Answer: *They both distrusted democracy* **or** *They both preferred government by a single ruler.* The answer should focus on an individual's opinion or attitude inferred from actions or words.

   Standard 6: Determine the author's point of view or purpose.

5. **Analyze how Plato's and Aristotle's views of government were alike and different. (2 pts.)**

   Answer: *Alike: Both Plato and Aristotle favored rule by a single leader. Both were suspicious of democracy. Different: Plato described an ideal state divided into three classes* **or** *Plato believed the state should regulate every aspect of citizens' lives. Aristotle did not describe an ideal state but found good and bad examples of all forms of government* **or** *Aristotle believed in a moderate course.* Answer should include both a similarity and a difference. As a two-point question, there should be two clearly defined answers.

   Standard 3: Analyze interactions/connections between individuals, events, and ideas.

6. **The topic of the previous section is "Tragic Drama." What is the central idea?**

   Answer: *Greece made an important contribution to the field of drama* **or** *The author describes the contributions of Greece to the field of drama.* The answer must be clearly related to the topic. Do not accept a series of details as the central idea.

   Standard 2: Determine central idea/s; provide an objective summary.

7. **Analyze how Greek playwrights differed in their view of the gods. Give two examples. (2 pts.)**

   Answer: *Different playwrights believed events were caused by the gods and the wrath of the gods could bring down anyone* **and/or** *Duty to the gods is greater than human law* **and/or** *People, not gods, were causes of misfortune and suffering.* As a two-point question, there should be two clearly defined answers.

   Standard 3: Analyze interactions/connections between individuals, events, and ideas.

8. **Which text structure best explains how the author organized the previous passage? (2 pts.)**

   _____ description of important features

___ explanation of steps in a sequence

___ account of cause and effect

___ explanation of problem and solution

___ comparison/contrast of two or more things

Give a reason from the text for your answer. For example, if you choose description, tell what is being described. For sequence, list one or two steps explained in the text. For cause and effect, state a cause or an effect mentioned in the text. For problem/solution, tell what the problem is or describe the solution. For comparison, tell what is being compared or contrasted.

Answer: *Comparison/contrast; the author is comparing three Greek playwrights and their views on human suffering and moral duty* **or** *Description; the author is describing the key features of three Greek playwrights.* Reasons that are not present in the text are inaccurate.

Standard 5: Analyze the structure of a text.

9. What is the meaning of *bias* in the context of the previous passage? **(AWL level 8)**

   Answer: *Prejudice, preference, favoritism, unfairness*

   Standard 4: Determine the meaning of words and phrases as they are used in a text.

10. What evidence in the text suggests that Thucydides may have been a better historian than Herodotus? Give two reasons. **(2 pts.)**

    Answer: *Herodotus' writings reflected his own views or biases* **and/or** *Herodotus invented speeches* **and/or** *Thucydides tried to be fair to both Athens and Sparta* **and/or** *Thucydides avoided bias.* As a two-point question, there should be two clearly defined answers.

    Standard 1: Cite textual evidence to support analysis of what the text says explicitly as well as inferences drawn from the text.

Summarize what the text says about the role of tragic drama in the lives of the Greeks. An acceptable text-based summary contains the following units. Students receive one point for each statement in their summary that matches the following statements in meaning.

1. An introductory statement of purpose

2. Greek dramas were often based on myths and legends

3. Playwrights used these to discuss moral or social issues

4. They also explored the relationship between people and the gods

5. Aeschylus: The gods could bring down the greatest heroes

6. Sophocles: What could happen when individual moral duty conflicts with the law

7. Euripides: People were the cause of misfortune and suffering

8. The purpose of tragedy was to stir up and relieve emotions of pity and fear

Point Table   The Glory That Was Greece, High School

Standard	Question	Points per Question
1. Support an inference	2 10	1 2
2. Determine central idea	1 6	1 1
3. Explain why or how/analyze	5 7	2 2
4. Determine word meaning	3 9	1 1
5. Determine text structure	8	2
6. Determine point of view	4	1
Total Questions	10	14
2. Summary		8
Total Summary		(6 acceptable)
8. Explain an argument	optional	4
Total Points		
8. Evaluate an argument	optional	2
Total Points		

Optional Standard 8 Assessment

Before you begin scoring, please review the guidelines for scoring questions on pages 40–43, pages 63–67 for scoring summaries, and pages 74–77 for information on the Optional Standard 8 Assessments.

Plato's Account of Socrates's Defense

Read the excerpt from Socrates's defense against the charges of corrupting the youth of Athens. Explain four arguments that Socrates presents in support of his innocence.

Answer: *Killing me will injure Athens more because you will sin against the God* **and/or** *You will not find another like me to arouse and reproach you* **and/or** *I have no regular disciples but converse with everyone in public and not for pay* **and/or** *God has imposed this duty upon me through oracles and visions* **and/or** *If I corrupted the youth, they or their relatives should complain but they support me* **and/or** *I went where I could do the greatest good by persuading every man that he must look to himself and seek virtue and wisdom* **and/or** *Holding my tongue* *would be disobedience to a divine command* **and/or** *A life which is unexamined is not worth living.*

Select two arguments and, for each one, why it is or is not valid.

Answer: Student explanation of validity or invalidity will vary. However, it should be relevant to the argument and should contain some supporting evidence or clarification. Examples: *I went where I could do the greatest good by persuading every man that he seek virtue and wisdom. It's valid because how can you argue with virtue and wisdom? Ministers are always saying this* or *You will not find another like me to arouse and reproach you. It's valid because Socrates was an individual and when an individual dies, no one will ever be like him* or *God has imposed this duty on me through oracles and visions. It's not valid because how can he prove this? He can't show the vision to people* or *I converse with everyone in public and not for pay. It's not valid because where you do something and whether you get paid doesn't really matter. If he is corrupting youth, he could just as well do it in and for pay.*

Elementary School, Grade 4, Part I
Before you begin scoring, please review the guidelines for scoring questions on pages 40–43 and pages 63–67 for scoring summaries.

SCIENCE

Earth's Landforms: How Does Earth's Surface Change?

1. Explain how water has changed the surface of the Earth. Give two examples **(2 pts)**.

   Answer: *Water dug deep into the Earth's surface and formed canyons* **and/or** *Frozen water (glaciers) carved into Earth's surface* **and/or** *Glaciers carried rock and soil* **and/or** *Glaciers carved out lakes.* As a two-point question, there should be two clearly defined answers.

   Standard 3: Explain events, procedures, ideas, or concepts based on specific information in the text.

2. What is the meaning of *areas* in the context of the above paragraph? **(AWL level 1)**

   Answer: *Parts, regions, sections, places, amounts of land*

   Standard 4: Determine the meaning of general academic and domain-specific words or phrases.

3. Which text structure best explains how the author organized the above passage? **(2 pts.)**

   ____ explanation of steps in a sequence

   ____ account of cause and effect

   ____ comparison/contrast of two or more things

   Give a reason from the text for your answer. For example, if you choose sequence, list one or two steps. For cause and effect, give a cause or effect mentioned in the text. For comparison, tell what is being compared or contrasted.

   Answer: *Comparison/contrast; the author contrasts different landforms/land features such as rivers, plateaus, and plains* **or** *Cause/effect; the author explains how different landforms/features were formed.* Reasons that are not present in the text are inaccurate.

   Standard 5: Describe the overall structure in a text.

4. Explain how freezing makes cracks in rocks get larger.

   Answer: *When water gets in a crack and freezes, the crack gets larger. Because the crack is larger, more water can get in. When water freezes again, the additional water makes the crack larger.*

Standard 3: Explain events, procedures, ideas, or concepts based on specific information in the text.

5. What evidence in the text indicates how mechanical weathering and chemical weathering are different?

   Answer: *During mechanical weathering, the minerals in the rock do not change. During chemical weathering, the minerals change* **or** *Mechanical weathering breaks rocks into small pieces and chemical weathering changes minerals in rock.*

   Standard 1: Refer to details and examples in a text when explaining what the text says explicitly and when drawing inferences from the text.

6. The topic of the above paragraph is "erosion." What is the central idea?

   Answer: *Erosion transfers soil and sediments from one location to another* **or** *The author describes what erosion does.* The answer must be clearly related to the topic. Do not accept a series of details as the central idea.

   Standard 2: Determine the central idea of a text.

7. What is the meaning of *transferred* in the context of the above paragraph? **(AWL level 2)**

   Answer: *Moved, put somewhere else*

   Standard 4: Determine the meaning of general academic and domain-specific words or phrases.

8. What evidence in the text indicates that erosion is a very powerful process?

   Answer: *Erosion can flatten mountains* **or** *It can dig deep canyons* **or** *It can carry materials for hundreds of kilometers.*

   Standard 1: Refer to details and examples in a text when explaining what the text says explicitly and when drawing inferences from the text.

9. The topic of the above paragraph is "soil erosion." What is the central idea?

   Answer: *Soil erosion caused the Dust Bowl* **or** *Erosion can cause destruction.* The answer must be clearly related to the topic. Do not accept a series of details as the central idea.

Standard 2: Determine the central idea of a text.

10. **Explain why the Dust Bowl occurred.**

    Answer: *Drought and poor farming practices left bare soil.*

    Standard 3: Explain events, procedures, ideas, or concepts based on specific information in the text.

Summarize what the text says about weathering and how it changes Earth's surface. An acceptable text-based summary contains the following units. Students receive one point for each statement in their summary that matches the following statements in meaning.

1. An introductory statement of purpose
2. Weathering breaks rocks into smaller pieces
3. Mechanical weathering is caused mostly by water and ice
4. Water seeps into cracks in rocks
5. Freezing makes the cracks larger
6. Soil and roots can also make cracks larger
7. Mechanical weathering does not change minerals in rocks

8. Chemical weathering changes minerals
9. Minerals react with substances in the environment and change

Point Table   How Does Earth's Surface Change?
Grade 4

Standard		Question	Points per Question
1.	Support an inference	5 8	1 1
2.	Determine central idea	6 9	1 1
3.	Explain why or how/analyze	1 4 10	2 1 1
4.	Determine word meaning	2 7	1 1
5.	Determine text structure	3	2
Total Questions			12 points
2. Summary **Total Summary**			9 points (7 points acceptable)

Elementary School, Grade 4, Part II   Before you begin scoring, please review the guidelines for scoring questions on pages 40–43 and pages 63–67 for scoring summaries.

SCIENCE

Earth's Landforms: How Does Water Affect Earth's Features?

1. **Explain how water shapes Earth's surface.**

   Answer: *Water carries and deposits rock and soil* **or** *Water breaks down rock and soil.*

   Standard 3: Explain events, procedures, ideas, or concepts based on specific information in the text.

2. **Which text structure best explains how the author organized the above passage? (2 pts.)**

   ___ description of important points

   ___ account of cause and effect

   ___ comparison/contrast of two or more things

   Give a reason from the text for your answer. For example, if you choose description, tell what is being described. For cause and effect, give a cause or an effect mentioned in the text. For comparison, tell what is being compared or contrasted.

   Answer: *Description; the author describes how waters carry minerals to various places* **or** *Cause/effect; the author describes the effects of minerals in water.* Reasons that are not present in the text are inaccurate.

   Standard 5: Describe the overall structure in a text.

3. **Explain how the oceans become salty. Give two reasons (2 pts).**

   Answer: *Salt comes from rivers that go into the oceans* **and** *When ocean water evaporates it leaves the salt behind.* As

a two-point question, there should be two clearly defined answers.

Standard 3: Explain events, procedures, ideas, or concepts based on specific information in the text

4. **What is the meaning of *dynamic* in the context of the above paragraph? (AWL level 7)**

   Answer: *Changing, active, powerful, forceful*

   Standard 4: Determine the meaning of general academic and domain-specific words or phrases.

5. **The topic of the above paragraph is "river sediments." What is the central idea?**

   Answer: *Rivers deposit sediments in different places* **or** *The author describes how rivers deposit sediment.* The answer must be clearly related to the topic. Do not accept a series of details as the central idea.

   Standard 2: Determine the central idea of a text.

6. **What evidence in the text indicates how energy in moving water controls where different kinds of sediments are deposited?**

   Answer: *When water slows down it has less energy and can carry less sediment, so it deposits the heavier sediment first.*

   Standard 1: Refer to details and examples in a text when explaining what the text says explicitly and when drawing inferences from the text.

7. **Explain how sediments in rivers can change the land.**

Answer: *Deposits of sediments can change the bend in rivers* **or** *Sediments can cut off bends in rivers and form lakes* **or** *Sediments can be deposited at the mouth of a river.*

Standard 3: Explain events, procedures, ideas, or concepts based on specific information in the text.

8. The topic of the above paragraph is the "Mississippi River." What is the central idea?

   Answer: *The Mississippi River is one of the largest river systems.* **or** *The author describes why the Mississippi River is a large river system.* The answer must be clearly related to the topic. Do not accept a series of details as the central idea.

   Standard 2: Determine the central idea of a text.

9. What is the meaning of *species* in the context of the above paragraph? (**AWL level 7**)

   Answer: *Kind, class, type, group*

   Standard 4: Determine the meaning of general academic and domain-specific words or phrases.

10. What evidence in the text indicates that living on a floodplain can be a good thing?

    Answer: *Floods deposit sediments that contain nutrients for growing crops.*

    Standard 1: Refer to details and examples in a text when explaining what the text says explicitly and when drawing inferences from the text.

Summarize what the text says about minerals in water. An acceptable text-based summary contains the following units. Students receive one point for each statement in their summary that matches the following statements in meaning.

1. An introductory statement of purpose
2. Rivers carry dissolved minerals to the ocean
3. Ocean plants and animals use the minerals
4. They use them for life processes
5. Some minerals settle out of water
6. And form deposits
7. Water flows beneath earth's surface
8. Minerals in this water forms stalagmites and stalactites
9. Rivers carry tons of salt to the ocean each year
10. And transfer sediments from one place to another

Point Table   How Does Water Affect Earth's Features? Grade 4

Standard	Question	Points per Question
1. Support an inference	6 10	1 1
2. Determine central idea	5 8	1 1
3. Explain why or how/analyze	1 3 7	1 2 1
4. Determine word meaning	4 9	1 1
5. Determine text structure	2	2
Total Questions		12 points
2. Summary **Total Summary**		10 points (7 points acceptable)

Elementary School, Grade 4, Part III   Before you begin scoring, please review the guidelines for scoring questions on pages 40–43 and pages 63–67 for scoring summaries.

SCIENCE

Earth's Landforms: How Do Waves Affect Coastal Landforms?

1. What evidence in the text indicates that water in waves does not move forward?

   Answer: *Water stays in the same spot and rises and falls* **or** *Water moves up and down in a circular motion* **or** *When a wave passes, the water ends up where it started.*

   Standard 1: Refer to details and examples in a text when explaining what the text says explicitly and when drawing inferences from the text.

2. Which text structure best explains how the author organized the above passage? (**2 pts.**)

   ____ description of important points

   ____ comparison of two or more things

   ____ explanation of steps in a sequence

   Give a reason from the text for your answer. For example, if you choose description, tell what is being described. For sequence, explain one or two steps explained in the text. If you choose comparison, tell what is being compared or contrasted.

Answer: *Description; the author describes how waves move* or *Sequence; the author describes the sequence of wave movement.* Reasons that are not present in the text are inaccurate.

Standard 5: Describe the overall structure in a text.

3. What evidence in the text indicates that wave size depends on different things?

    Answer: *The size of waves depends on the speed of the wind* or *How long it blows* or *How much of the sea it blows over* or *Through tectonic action.* Answer should address the issue of different factors contributing to wave size.

    Standard 1: Refer to details and examples in a text when explaining what the text says explicitly and when drawing inferences from the text.

4. Explain how wind changes waves.

    Answer: *When winds blow, the waves pick up energy and the amplitude or size of the wave increases* or *The higher the wind the greater the amplitude of the waves.*

    Standard 3: Explain events, procedures, ideas, or concepts based on specific information in the text.

5. The topic of the above paragraph is "beaches." What is the central idea?

    Answer: *Ocean waves can change a beach* or *The author describes how waves can change a beach.* The answer must be clearly related to the topic. Do not accept a series of details as the central idea.

    Standard 2: Determine the central idea of a text.

6. What is the meaning of *energy* in the context of the above paragraph? **(AWL level 5)**

    Answer: *Power, force*

    Standard 4: Determine the meaning of general academic and domain-specific words or phrases.

7. What is the meaning of *alter* in the context of the above paragraph? **(AWL level 5)**

    Answer: *Change*

    Standard 4: Determine the meaning of general academic and domain-specific words or phrases.

8. The topic of the above paragraph is "waves." What is the central idea?

    Answer: *Waves build up beaches* or *The author describes how waves build up beaches.* The answer must be clearly related to the topic. Do not accept a series of details as the central idea.

    Standard 2: Determine the central idea of a text.

9. Explain how waves can change the land. Give two examples. **(2 pts.)**

Answer: *Waves can cause cracks/wear down rocks* **and/or** *Waves can build up beaches* **and/or** *Waves can wear down landforms* **and/or** *Waves can create a sandbar.* As a two-point answer, there should be two clearly defined answers.

Standard 3: Explain events, procedures, ideas, or concepts based on specific information in the text.

10. Explain why a beach that has many storms changes more rapidly than a beach with few storms.

    Answer: *Wind and waves change landforms and storms have strong winds and waves* **and/or** *Waves carry sediment that wears down landforms* **and/or** *Waves build up beaches by moving sand.*

    Standard 3: Explain events, procedures, ideas, or concepts based on specific information in the text.

Summarize what the text says about how waves and wind can change beaches. An acceptable text-based summary contains the following units. Students receive one point for each statement in their summary that matches the following statements in meaning.

1. An introductory statement of purpose
2. Waves carry energy
3. Energy in waves can break up rocks
4. Waves carry stones and sand
5. That can wear away landforms
6. Waves build up beaches by moving sand
7. And creating sandbars
8. Coastal winds can shape rocks and cliffs
9. And create sand dunes

Point Table   How Do Waves Affect Coastal Landforms? Grade 4

Standard	Question	Points per Question
1. Support an inference	1 3	1 1
2. Determine central idea	5 8	1 1
3. Explain why or how/analyze	4 9 10	1 2 1
4. Determine word meaning	6 7	1 1
5. Determine text structure	2	2
Total Questions		12 points
2. Summary **Total Summary**		9 points (7 points acceptable)

Elementary School, Grade 5, Part I Before you begin scoring, please review the guidelines for scoring questions on pages 40–43 and pages 63–67 for scoring summaries.

What Is Inside a Cell?

1. **What evidence in the text indicates that a tiny organism crawling across your desk is multicellular?**

   Answer: *Most cells are too tiny to be seen by the eye* **or** *A single drop of blood would hold millions of red blood cells.*

   Standard 1: Refer to details and examples in a text when explaining what the text says explicitly and when drawing inferences from the text.

2. **What is the meaning of *respond* in the context of the above paragraph? (AWL level 1)**

   Answer: *React, do something, change, adapt. Do not accept "answer back" or "reply."*

   Standard 4: Determine the meaning of general academic and domain-specific words or phrases.

3. **Explain how cells carry out the same functions as your body does. Give two examples. (2 pts.)**

   Answer: *Cells take in food* **and/or** *Cells get rid of waste* **and/or** *Cells grow* **and/or** *Cells repair wounds* **and/or** *Cells use energy from food* **and/or** *Cells take in oxygen* **and/or** *Cells engage in respiration* **and/or** *Cells move.* As a two-point question, there should be two clearly defined answers.

   Standard 3: Explain events, procedures, ideas, or concepts based on specific information in the text.

4. **What evidence in the text indicates how the cells of a 15-year-old are different from the cells of a five-year-old?**

   Answer: *You grow when your cells grow larger and divide, so a 15-year-old would have more* **or** *Larger cells than a five-year-old.*

   Standard 1: Refer to details and examples in a text when explaining what the text says explicitly and when drawing inferences from the text.

5. **The topic of the above two paragraphs is "cell parts." What is the central idea?**

   Answer: *Cell parts can be compared to body parts* **or** *The author describes what cell parts do.* The answer must be clearly related to the topic. Do not accept a series of details as the central idea.

   Standard 2: Determine the central idea of a text.

6. **Explain how the cell membrane and our skin are alike.**

   Answer: *The membrane surrounds a cell and skin surrounds the body.*

   Standard 3: Explain events, procedures, ideas, or concepts based on specific information in the text.

7. **The topic of the above section is "chromosomes." What is the central idea?**

   Answer: *Chromosomes control growth and change* **or** *Chromosomes carry instructions for the cell* **or** *The author describes what chromosomes do.* The answer must be clearly related to the topic. Do not accept a series of details as the central idea.

   Standard 2: Determine the central idea of a text.

8. **What is the meaning of *process* in the context of the above paragraph? (AWL level 1)**

   Answer: *Method, manner, way, procedure, orderly stage, cycle, systematic steps, step by step.*

   Standard 4: Determine the meaning of general academic and domain-specific words or phrases.

9. **Explain how chromosomes work in the cell.**

   Answer: *Chromosomes control how the body grows and changes* **or** *Chromosomes tell the cell how to do its job* **or** *Chromosomes carry genes.*

   Standard 3: Explain events, procedures, ideas, or concepts based on specific information in the text.

10. **Which text structure best explains how the author organized the above passage? (2 pts.)**

    ____ **description of important features**

    ____ **explanation of steps in a sequence**

    ____ **account of cause and effect**

    ____ **explanation of problem and solution**

    ____ **comparison/contrast of two or more things**

    Give a reason from the text for your answer. For example, if you choose description, tell what is being described. For sequence, list one or two steps. For cause and effect, state a cause or effect mentioned in the text. For problem and solution, tell what the problem is or describe the solution. For comparison, tell what is being compared or contrasted.

    Answer: *Cause and effect; the author offers different causes for the effect of cell size.* Reasons that are not present in the text are inaccurate.

    Standard 5: Describe the overall structure in a text.

Summarize what the text says about what each part of an animal cell does. An acceptable text-based summary contains the following units. Students receive one point for each statement in their summary that matches the following statements in meaning.

1. An introductory statement of purpose

2. The cell membrane holds the parts of the cell together

3. The nucleus contains the chromosomes
4. Chromosomes tell the cell how to do its job
5. Chromosomes carry genes
6. Cytoplasm is the material of the cell
7. Vacuoles store materials
8. Vacuoles break down materials
9. Mitochrondria produce energy

Point Table   What Is Inside a Cell? Grade 5

Standard	Question	Points per Question
1. Support an inference	1 4	1 1
2. Determine central idea	5 7	1 1
3. Explain why or how/analyze	3 6 9	2 1 1
4. Determine word meaning	2 8	1 1
5. Determine text structure	10	2
Total Question		12
2. Summary **Total Summary**		9 (7 acceptable)

Elementary School, Grade 5, Part II
Before you begin scoring, please review the guidelines for scoring questions on pages 40–43 and pages 63–67 for scoring summaries.

SCIENCE

How Do Cells Work Together?

1. **What is the meaning of *designed* in the context of the above paragraph? (AWL level 2)**

   Answer: *Made, built, constructed, made for a reason, made for a purpose, made for a job*

   Standard 4: Determine the meaning of general academic and domain-specific words or phrases.

2. **What is the meaning of *structures* in the context of the above paragraph? (AWL level 1)**

   Answer: *Parts, forms, frameworks, systems, arrangements*

   Standard 4: Determine the meaning of general academic and domain-specific words or phrases

3. **What evidence in the text indicates that a cell's shape is related to the work it does?**

   Answer: *The length of nerve cells allows them to reach the brain and connect parts of the body quickly* **or** *Flat cells overlap to cover a surface and make it strong and flexible* **or** *Round cells have extra surface area for picking up and carrying oxygen.*

   Standard 1: Refer to details and examples in a text when explaining what the text says explicitly and when drawing inferences from the text.

4. **Explain how flat and round cells are alike.**

   Answer: *They are both cells* **or** *They both have special purposes* **or** *Their shape is related to their purpose* **or** *They are both in the human body.*

   Standard 3: Explain events, procedures, ideas, or concepts based on specific information in the text.

5. **The topic of the above section is "special cell structure." What is the central idea?**

   Answer: *Structures in cells perform different jobs* **or** *Cells in the ear and muscles perform different jobs* **or** *The author explains what special cell structures do.* The answer must be clearly related to the topic. Do not accept a series of details as the central idea.

   Standard 2: Determine the central idea of a text.

6. **Explain how the work of hair-like structures in the ears and lungs are different.**

   Answer: *Hair-like structures in the ears sends nerve impulses to the brain. In the lungs, hair-like structures keep dirt and germs out of the airways.*

   Standard 3: Explain events, procedures, ideas, or concepts based on specific information in the text.

7. **What evidence in the text indicates that muscles can become strong even though cell fibers are weak?**

   Answer: *Fibers work together in each cell* **or** *Muscle cells work together in bundles.*

   Standard 1: Refer to details and examples in a text when explaining what the text says explicitly and when drawing inferences from the text.

8. **The topic of the above two paragraphs is "tissues." What is the central idea?**

   Answer: *Cells form tissues and tissues form organs* **or** *The author describes how tissues and organs are formed.* The answer must be clearly related to the topic. Do not accept a series of details as the central idea.

   Standard 2: Determine the central idea of a text.

9. **Which text structure best explains how the author organized the above paragraph? (2 pts.)**

   ____ description of important features

   ____ explanation of steps in a sequence

____ account of cause and effect

____ explanation of problem and solution

____ comparison/contrast of two or more things

Give a reason from the text for your answer. For example, if you choose description, tell what is being described. For sequence, list one or two steps. For cause and effect, state a cause or effect mentioned in the text. For problem and solution, tell what the problem is or describe the solution. For comparison, tell what is being compared or contrasted.

Answer: *Description; the author describes an organ and what it does in your body and in plants.* Reasons that are not present in the text are inaccurate.

Standard 5: Describe the overall structure in a text.

10. **Explain how tissues and organs are alike and how they are different. (2 pts.)**

    Answer: *Alike: Both animals and plants have tissues and organs* **and/or** *Tissues and organs all work for the body* **and/or** *Both are made up of cells. Different: Organs are made of different kinds of tissues* **or** *Tissues are groups of cells that do the same job and organs are formed of different kinds of tissues that perform a main job.* As a two-point question, there should be two clearly defined answers.

    Standard 3: Explain events, procedures, ideas, or concepts based on specific information in the text.

Summarize what the text says about what tissues are and what they do. An acceptable text-based summary contains the following units. Students receive one point for each statement in their summary that matches the following statements in meaning.

1. An introductory statement of purpose
2. Tissues are groups of the same kind of cells
3. Tissues all do the same job or work as a team
4. Bone cells make bone tissue
5. Nerve cells make nerve tissue
6. Muscle cells make muscle tissue
7. Tissues join with other tissues to form organs
8. These tissues or organs work together to perform a main job
9. The heart, eyes, ears, stomach, and skin are examples of organs

Point Table   How Do Cells Work Together? Grade 5

Standard	Question	Points per Question
1. Support an inference	3 7	1 1
2. Determine main idea	5 8	1 1
3. Explain why or how/analyze	4 6 10	1 1 2
4. Determine word meaning	1 2	1 1
5. Determine text structure	9	2
Total Question		12
2. Summary **Total Summary**		9 (7 acceptable)

Elementary School, Grade 5, Part III

Before you begin scoring, please review the guidelines for scoring questions on pages 40–43 and pages 63–67 for scoring summaries.

SCIENCE

How Do Organs Work Together?

1. **The topic of the above two paragraphs is "skeletal system." What is the central idea?**

   Answer: *The skeletal system supports the body, protects organs and stores calcium* **or** *The author describes what the skeletal systems does.* The answer must be clearly related to the topic. Do not accept a series of details as the central idea.

   Standard 2: Determine the central idea of a text.

2. **Which text structure best explains how the author organized the above section? (2 pts.)**

   _____ description of important features

   _____ explanation of steps in a sequence

   _____ account of cause and effect

   _____ explanation of problem and solution

   _____ comparison/contrast of two or more things

Give a reason from the text for your answer. For example, if you choose description, tell what is being described. For sequence, list one or two steps explained in the text. For cause and effect, state a cause or effect mentioned in the text. For problem and solution, tell what the problem is or describe the solution. For comparison, tell what is being compared or contrasted.

Answer: *Description; the author describes the skeletal system and what it does in the body.* Reasons that are not present in the text are inaccurate.

Standard 5: Describe the overall structure in a text.

3. **Explain why the skeletal system is important to your body.**

   Answer: *It provides the body with a support system* **or** *It protects internal organs* **or** *It stores calcium until it is needed.*

Standard 3: Explain events, procedures, ideas, or concepts based on specific information in the text.

4. **What evidence in the text indicates that dancing and shivering are controlled by different kinds of muscles?**

   Answer: *Your brain tells muscles how to work in dancing, but you do not have to think about shivering for it to happen. Answer should include both dancing and shivering.*

   Standard 1: Refer to details and examples in a text when explaining what the text says explicitly and when drawing inferences from the text.

5. **What is the meaning of** *relaxes* **in the context of the above two paragraphs? (AWL level 9)**

   Answer: *rests, loosens, eases, becomes less tight, calms down*

   Standard 4: Determine the meaning of general academic and domain-specific words or phrases.

6. **Explain how muscles work together when you straighten your leg.**

   Answer: *One contracts or shortens and the other relaxes or stretches.*

   Standard 3: Explain events, procedures, ideas, or concepts based on specific information in the text.

7. **What is the meaning of** *complex* **in the context of the above paragraph? (AWL level 2)**

   Answer: *Having many parts, complicated*

   Standard 4: Determine the meaning of general academic and domain-specific words or phrases.

8. **The topic of the above two paragraphs is "organ systems." What is the central idea?**

   Answer: *Organ systems work very closely together* **or** *The author describes how organ systems work together.* The answer must be clearly related to the topic. Do not accept a series of details as the central idea.

   Standard 2: Determine the central idea of a text.

9. **Explain how the circulatory system depends on two other organ systems. (2 pts.)**

   Answer: *The muscle system works to push blood through blood vessels* **and** *Blood cells are made in bone marrow, which is part of the skeletal system.* As a two-point question, there should be two clearly defined answers.

   Standard 3: Explain events, procedures, ideas, or concepts based on specific information in the text.

10. **What evidence in the text indicates that some organ systems work without our knowledge or awareness?**

   Answer: *We are not aware when our blood stores calcium* **and/or** *We are not aware of nerves sending signals from our brain* **and/or** *We are not aware of the muscles that make us shiver* **and/or** *We are not aware when muscles push blood through blood vessels* **and/or** *We are not aware when muscles squeeze blood through the digestive system.*

   Standard 1: Refer to details and examples in a text when explaining what the text says explicitly and when drawing inferences from the text.

Summarize what the text says about what the skeletal system does. An acceptable text-based summary contains the following units. Students receive one point for each statement in their summary that matches the following statements in meaning.

1. An introductory statement of purpose
2. About 200 bones make up the skeletal system
3. The skeletal system provides the body with a strong support system
4. So you can sit or stand
5. The skeletal system also protects internal organs
6. Bones in the skull protect the brain
7. Bones in the rib cage protect the lungs
8. Bones protect the heart
9. Bones store calcium

Point Table   How Do Organs Work Together? Grade 5

Standard	Question	Points per Question
1. Support an inference	4 10	1 1
2. Determine central idea	1 8	1 1
3. Explain why or how/analyze	3 6 9	1 1 2
4. Determine word meaning	5 7	1 1
5. Determine text structure	2	2
Total Question		12
2. Summary **Total Summary**		9 (7 acceptable)

SCIENCE

What Are Earth's Layers Made Of?

1. The topic of the above three paragraphs is "Earth's features." What is the central idea?

    Answer: *Earth has many different land features* **or** *The author describes Earth's land features.* The answer must be clearly related to the topic. Do not accept a series of details as the central idea.

    Standard 2: Determine the main idea of a text.

2. Which text structure best explains how the author organized the above? **(2 pts.)**

    ___ description of important features

    ___ explanation of steps in a sequence

    ___ account of cause and effect

    ___ explanation of problem and solution

    ___ comparison/contrast of two or more things

    Give a reason from the text for your answer. For example, if you choose description, tell what is being described. For sequence, list one or two steps. For cause and effect, state a cause or effect mentioned in the text. For problem and solution, tell what the problem is or describe the solution. For comparison, tell what is being compared or contrasted.

    Answer: *Description; the author describes Earth's land features.* Reasons that are not present in the text are inaccurate.

    Standard 5: Describe the overall structure of the text.

3. What is the meaning of *features* in the context of the above section? **(AWL level 2)**

    Answer: *Structures, parts, landforms, things like a mountain or a river, a land area, kinds of land*

    Standard 4: Determine the meaning of general academic and domain-specific words or phrases.

4. What evidence in the text indicates that we cannot see all of Earth's land features?

    Answer: *Some features are hidden by water* **or** *There are mountains and trenches beneath the ocean* **or** *It depends on where you live.*

    Standard 1: Refer to details and examples in a text when explaining what the text says explicitly and when drawing inferences from the text.

5. What is the meaning of *layer* in the context of the above section? **(AWL level 3)**

    Answer: *Cover, coating, level, slice, section, something stacked on top, a single thickness.* Answer must contain the concept of a level or a coating.

    Standard 4: Determine the meaning of general academic and domain-specific words or phrases.

6. Analyze how the mantle and the core are alike. Give two examples from the text. **(2 pts.)**

    Answer: *Both are beneath the Earth's crust* **and/or** *Both have two parts/layers* **and/or** *Both have an inner part and an outer part* **and/or** *Both have a solid part and a liquid part.* As a two-point question, there should be two clearly defined answers.

    Standard 3: Explain events, procedures, ideas, or concepts based on specific information in the text.

7. What evidence in the text indicates that Earth is not really a giant rock in space?

    Answer: *Earth has different layers and some are not solid* **or** *Earth's atmosphere is a gas* **or** *The inner part of the mantle is not solid* **or** *The outer core of the earth is liquid.*

    Standard 1: Refer to details and examples in a text when explaining what the text says explicitly and when drawing inferences from the text.

8. Analyze how Earth's atmosphere and Earth's crust are different.

    Answer: *Earth's atmosphere is a layer of gases and Earth's crust is solid rock* **and/or** *We breathe the atmosphere and we live on the crust.* Answer should include a description of both the atmosphere and the crust.

    Standard 3: Explain events, procedures, ideas, or concepts based on specific information in the text.

9. Analyze why equipment used to drill for oil cannot be used to drill into the mantle.

    Answer: *The distance to the mantle may be too great* **or** *The mantle may be too deep to reach* **or** *The mantle may be so hot that it will melt the drill.*

    Standard 3: Explain events, procedures, ideas or concepts based on specific information in the text.

10. The topic of the above two paragraphs is "Earth's plates." What is the central idea?

    Answer: *Earth's plates are different sizes and shapes and all fit together* **or** *The author is describing Earth's plates.* The answer must be clearly related to the topic. Do not accept a series of details as the central idea.

    Standard 2: Determine the main idea of a text.

Summarize how the text describes the four layers of Earth. An acceptable text-based summary contains the following units. Students receive one point for each statement in their summary that matches the following statements in meaning.

1. An introductory statement of purpose

2. The outermost layer is the crust

3. The crust is solid

4. The layer just below the crust is the mantle

5. The mantle contains most of Earth's mass

6. The outer part of the mantle is solid

7. The inner part of the mantle is hot rock

8. The innermost layer of Earth is the core

9. The core is very dense

10. It is the temperature of the sun

11. The outer layer is liquid

12. The inner core is solid

Point Table   What Are Earth's Layers Made Of?
Grade 6

Standard	Question	Points per Question
1. Support an inference	4	1
	7	1
2. Determine central idea	1	1
	10	1
3. Explain why or how/analyze	6	2
	8	1
	9	1
4. Determine word meaning	3	1
	5	1
5. Determine text structure	2	2
Total Question		12
2. Summary Total Summary		12 (9 acceptable)

Elementary School, Grade 6, Part II   Before you begin scoring, please review the guidelines
for scoring questions on pages 40–43 and pages 63–67 for scoring summaries.

SCIENCE

How Do Earth's Plates Help Create Landforms?

1. **The topic of the above section is "the continental drift." What is the central idea?**

   Answer: *Wegener introduced the theory that a single continent (Pangaea) broke apart to form the continents* **or** *The author explains Wegner's idea of one continent drifting apart.* The answer must be clearly related to the topic. Do not accept a series of details as the main idea.

   Standard 2: Determine the central idea of a text.

2. **What is the meaning of** *theory* **in the context of the above paragraph? (AWL level 1)**

   Answer: *Concept, idea, explanation, something that makes sense but is not yet proven*

   Standard 4: Determine the meaning of general academic and domain-specific words or phrases.

3. **What is the meaning of** *evidence* **in the context of the above two paragraphs? (AWL level 5)**

   Answer: Sign, suggestion, indication, data. Do not accept "proof" as an answer.

   Standard 4: Determine the meaning of general academic and domain-specific words or phrases.

4. **Analyze what evidence supported Wegner's theory of Pangaea. Offer two examples. (2 pts.)**

   Answer: *The shape of the continents' coastlines* **and/or** *Plant fossils found in different parts of the world* **and/or** *Fossils of an ancient reptile that could not have crossed the ocean* **and/or** *Matching rock layers from South America*

   and Africa. As a two-point question, there should be two clearly defined answers.

   Standard 3: Explain events, procedures, ideas, or concepts based on specific information in the text.

5. **The topic of the above three paragraphs is "sea floor spreading." What is the central idea?**

   Answer: *The ocean bottom spreads to form trenches and ridges* **or** *Trenches and ridges are formed by plate movement and magma* **or** *The author describes how the ocean floor spreads.* The answer must be clearly related to the topic. Do not accept a series of details as the main idea.

   Standard 2: Determine the central idea of a text.

6. **Which text structure best explains how the author organized the above passage? (2 pts.)**

   ____ description of important features

   ____ explanation of steps in a sequence

   ____ account of cause and effect

   ____ explanation of problem and solution

   ____ comparison/contrast of two or more things

   Give a reason from the text for your answer. For example, if you choose description, tell what is being described. For sequence, list one or two steps. For cause and effect, state a cause or effect mentioned in the text. For problem and solution, tell what the problem is or describe the solution. For comparison, tell what is being compared or contrasted.

   Answer: *Cause/effect; the author explains what causes trenches* **or** *ridges in the ocean bottom* **or** *What causes* *magma to form trenches and ridges* **or** *Sequence; the author describes the sequence or steps in the formation of ridges and trenches.* Reasons that are not stated in the text are inaccurate.

Standard 5: Describe the overall structure of a text.

7. **What evidence in the text indicates that the seafloor is constantly spreading?**

   Answer: *Magma (molten rock) comes up and pushes new and old crust aside.*

   Standard 1: Refer to details and examples in a text when explaining what the text says explicitly and when drawing inferences from the text.

8. **Analyze why Earth's plates move.**

   Answer: *Hot currents in Earth's mantle constantly move or rise, circle around, and fall. When the mantle moves, the plates floating on it also move.*

   Standard 3: Explain events, procedures, ideas, or concepts based on specific information in the text.

9. **Analyze how rock magnetism supported the theory of continental drift.**

   Answer: *Magnetic patterns in rocks indicate that rocks were formed at different times.*

   Standard 3: Explain events, procedures, ideas, or concepts based on specific information in the text.

10. **What evidence in the text indicates that scientists demand much proof before they accept a new theory?**

    Answer: *Despite evidence of continent shapes, fossils, and rocks, scientists refused to accept the theory of continental drift until they found more proof (convection and magnetic patterns).*

    Standard 1: Refer to details and examples in a text when explaining what the text says explicitly and when drawing inferences from the text.

Summarize Wegener's theory of Pangaea and the continental drift. An acceptable text-based summary contains the following units. Students receive one point for each statement in their summary that matches the following statements in meaning.

1. An introductory statement of purpose
2. All the continents were once a single continent (Pangaea)
3. Pangaea drifted apart to form today's continents
4. Wegener based his theory on the shape of continents
5. Some coastlines looked like they could fit together
6. He also based his theory on rocks
7. He also based it on fossils
8. Identical rocks and fossils were found on different continents
9. He believed this was impossible
10. Unless the species had lived side by side

Point Table   How Do Earth's Plates Help Create Landforms? Grade 6

Standard	Question	Points per Question
1. Support an inference	7 10	1 1
2. Determine central idea	1 5	1 1
3. Explain why or how/analyze	4 8 9	2 1 1
4. Determine word meaning	2 3	1 1
5. Determine text structure	6	2
Total Question		12
2. Summary **Total Summary**		10 (7 acceptable)

Elementary School, Grade 6, Part III   Before you begin scoring, please review the guidelines for scoring questions on pages 40–43 and pages 63–67 for scoring summaries.

SCIENCE

How Do Scientists Explain Earth's Features?

1. **The topic of the above section is "plate tectonics." What is the central idea?**

   Answer: *Scientists figure out how plates move through radio signals* **or** *The author describes the way scientists learn about plate movement* **or** *Earth's plates move in a continuous process.* The answer must be clearly related to the topic. Do not accept a series of details as the main idea.

   Standard 2: Determine the central idea of a text.

2. **What evidence in the text indicates that the theory of plate tectonics is different from the theory of continental drift?**

   Answer: *The theory of continental drift suggested that the continents moved but did not explain parts of the Earth's crust* **or** *The theory of plate tectonics explains many of earth's features.*

   Standard 1: Refer to details and examples in a text when explaining what the text says explicitly and when drawing inferences from the text.

3. **What is the meaning of** *precise* **in the context of the above paragraph? (AWL level 5)**

   Answer: *Exact, accurate*

   Standard 4: Determine the meaning of general academic and domain-specific words or phrases.

4. What is the meaning of *predict* in the context of the above paragraph? (AWL level 4)

   Answer: *Forecast, tell in advance, explain the future, say what is going to happen next, calculate.* Do not accept "guess" as an answer.

   Standard 4: Determine the meaning of general academic and domain-specific words or phrases.

5. Which text structure best explains how the author organized the above two paragraphs? (2 pts.)

   ___ description of important features

   ___ explanation of steps in a sequence

   ___ account of cause and effect

   ___ explanation of problem and solution

   ___ comparison/contrast of two or more things

   Give a reason from the text for your answer. For example, if you choose description, tell what is being described. For sequence, list one or two steps. For cause and effect, state a cause or effect mentioned in the text. For problem and solution, tell what the problem is or describe the solution. For comparison, tell what is being compared or contrasted.

   Answer: *Comparison; the author compares three types of plate boundaries* **or** *Description; the author describes three types of plate boundaries.* Reasons that are not stated in the text are inaccurate.

   Standard 5: Describe the overall structure of a text.

6. Analyze how Earth's features change when plates move. Give two examples. (2 pts.)

   Answer: *Valleys can form* **and/or** *Earthquakes can happen* **and/or** *Mountains can form* **and/or** *Volcanoes can form* **and/or** *Ocean trenches can form* **and/or** *Seafloor spreading can occur.* As a two-point question, there should be two clearly defined answers.

   Standard 3: Explain events, procedures, ideas, or concepts based on specific information in the text.

7. The topic of the above section is "earthquakes." What is the central idea?

   Answer: *Earthquakes release energy that is carried by waves* **or** *Earthquakes occur when pressure is released* **or** *The author describes how earthquakes occur and cause damage.* The answer must be clearly related to the topic. Do not accept a series of details as the main idea.

   Standard 2: Determine the central idea of a text.

8. Analyze why some earthquakes cause more damage than others.

   Answer: *The energy/pressure that is released may be a factor* **or** *The movement of the waves may be a factor* **or** *How long the wave movements occur can be a factor* **or** *An area close to the epicenter will probably have more damage*

   Standard 3: Explain events, procedures, ideas, or concepts based on specific information in the text.

9. What evidence in the text indicates that earthquakes can act very differently?

   Answer: *Some waves can cause the ground to move back and forth and others can cause the ground to move up and down or in a circular motion.*

   Standard 1: Refer to details and examples in a text when explaining what the text says explicitly and when drawing inferences from the text.

10. Analyze why most volcanoes occur at a plate boundary.

    Answer: *When one plate sinks beneath the other, the sinking plate melts into magma. Pressure builds up. If the crust of the overlying plate can no longer stand the pressure, the magma explodes as a volcano.*

    Standard 3: Explain events, procedures, ideas, or concepts based on specific information in the text.

Summarize what the text says about how plate boundaries explain Earth's features. An acceptable text-based summary contains the following units. Students receive one point for each statement in their summary that matches the following statements in meaning.

1. An introductory statement of purpose
2. Two plates meet at plate boundaries
3. Plates move away from each other at spreading boundaries
4. Valleys can form
5. Plates slide past each other at fracture boundaries
6. This can cause earthquakes
7. When plates collide
8. They can form mountains
9. They can form trenches
10. They can form earthquakes
11. They can form volcanoes

Point Table   How Do Scientists Explain Earth's Features? Grade 6

Standard	Question	Points per Question
1. Support an inference	2 9	1 1
2. Determine central idea	1 7	1 1
3. Explain why or how/analyze	6 8 10	2 1 1
4. Determine word meaning	3 4	1 1
5. Determine text structure	5	2
Total Questions	10	12 points
2. Summary **Total Summary**		11 points (8 points acceptable)

Middle School, Life Science, Part I
Before you begin scoring, please review the guidelines for scoring questions on pages 40–43 and pages 63–67 for scoring summaries.

The Digestive System

1. **What evidence in the text strongly supports that only two things can happen to food once it is digested?**

   Answer: *The text says that digested food either passes into the blood stream or is eliminated as waste* **and/or** *Digested food can either be absorbed or eliminated.* Answer should include mention of both options.

   Standard 1: Cite textual evidence to support analysis of what the text says explicitly as well as inferences drawn from the text.

2. **The topic of the above section entitled The Mouth is "digestion in the mouth." What is the central idea?**

   Answer: *Mechanical and chemical digestion occurs in the mouth* **or** *The author describes how mechanical and chemical digestion occurs in the mouth.* The answer must be clearly related to the topic. Do not accept a series of details as the central idea.

   Standard 2: Determine central idea/s.

3. **Analyze why saliva is important to the digestive process.**

   Answer: *Saliva contains an enzyme (or chemical) that digests starch* **or** *Saliva contains an enzyme that speeds up chemical reactions* **or** *Saliva moistens food pieces into a slippery mass.*

   Standard 3: Analyze interactions/connections between individuals, events, and ideas.

4. **What is the meaning of *specific* in the context of the above passage? (AWL level 1)**

   Answer: *Special, distinctive, particular, individual, exact*

   Standard 4: Determine the meaning of words and phrases as they are used in the text.

5. **Which text structure best explains how the author organized the above passage? (2 pts.)**

   ____ **description of important features**

   ____ **explanation of steps in a sequence**

   ____ **account of cause and effect**

   ____ **explanation of problem and solution**

   ____ **comparison/contrast of two or more things**

   Give a reason from the text for your answer. For example, if you choose description, tell what is being described. For sequence, list one or two steps. For cause and effect, state a cause or effect mentioned in the text. For problem and solution, tell what the problem is or describe the solution. For comparison, tell what is being compared or contrasted.

   Answer: *Comparison and contrast; the author compares mechanical and chemical digestion in the mouth* **or** *Description; the author describes the beginning of the digestion process that occurs in the mouth* **or** *Sequence; the author explains the sequence of the first steps of the digestive process.* Reasons that are not present in the text are inaccurate.

   Standard 5: Analyze the structure of the text.

6. **What is the meaning of *contractions* in the context of the above passage? (AWL level 1)**

   Answer: *Movements, pushes, muscular waves, involuntary waves*

   Standard 4: Determine the meaning of words and phrases as they are used in the text.

7. **What evidence in the text strongly supports that you cannot breathe at the same time that you are swallowing something?**

   Answer: *When you swallow, the epiglottis/flap of tissue seals off your windpipe.*

   Standard 1: Cite textual evidence to support analysis of what the text says explicitly as well as inferences drawn from the text.

8. **Analyze why the entire digestive process can occur even if you are lying flat.**

   Answer: *Muscle contractions or peristalsis move the food, not gravity or position.*

   Standard 3: Analyze interactions and connections between individuals, events, and ideas.

9. **The topic of the above section entitled "The Stomach" is "digestion in the stomach." What is the central idea?**

   Answer: *The central idea is mechanical and chemical digestion breaks down food in the stomach* **or** *Most mechanical and chemical digestion occurs in the stomach.* The answer must be clearly related to the topic. Do not accept a series of details as the central idea.

   Standard 2: Determine central idea/s.

10. **Analyze why the digestive system would break down without the stomach lining. Give two reasons (2 pts).**

    Answer: *There would be no digestive juices because they are produced in the lining of the stomach* **and** *Stomach acid would burn a hole in your stomach because stomach lining produces mucus that protects from acid.* As a two-point question, there should be two clearly defined answers.

    Standard 3: Analyze interactions/connections between individuals, events, and ideas.

Summarize what the text says happens to a pizza from the time it enters your mouth until it is a thick liquid. An acceptable text-based summary contains the following units. Students receive one point for each statement in their summary that matches the following statements in meaning.

1. An introductory statement of purpose
2. Mechanical digestion starts in the mouth
3. When you chew the food into small pieces
4. Chemical digestion breaks the food into molecules
5. Swallowing pushes the food into the esophagus
6. Muscle contractions move food to the stomach
7. Mechanical digestion mixes the food with fluids
8. Chemical digestion occurs when food mixes with digestive juices
9. Digestive juices turn food into liquid
10. Food remains in the stomach until all solids are liquid

Point Table   The Digestive System, Middle School

Standard	Question	Points per Question
1. Support an inference	1	1
	7	1
2. Determine central idea	2	1
	9	1
3. Explain why or how/analyze	3	1
	8	1
	10	2
4. Determine word meaning	4	1
	6	1
5. Determine text structure	5	2
Total Question		12
2. Summary **Total Summary**		10 (7 acceptable)

Middle School, Life Science, Part II
Before you begin scoring, please review the guidelines for scoring questions on pages 40–43 and pages 63–67 for scoring summaries.

SCIENCE

The Muscular System

1. **The topic of the above three paragraphs is "types of muscle." What is the central idea?**

   Answer: *Muscles can be voluntary or involuntary and skeletal, smooth or cardiac* **or** *The author describes different types of muscles.* The answer must be clearly related to the topic. Do not accept a series of details as the central idea.

   Standard 2: Determine central idea/s.

2. **What is the meaning of *functions* in the context of the above passage? (AWL level 1)**

   Answer: *Purposes, roles, jobs, tasks, activities. Do not accept "things," "parts," "movements," "abilities."*

   Standard 4: Determine the meaning of words and phrases as they are used in the text.

3. **Which text structure best explains how the author organized the above passage? (2 pts.)**

   ___ description of important features

   ___ explanation of steps in a sequence

   ___ account of cause and effect

   ___ explanation of problem and solution

   ___ comparison/contrast of two or more things

   Give a reason from the text for your answer. For example, if you choose description, tell what is being described. For sequence, list one or two steps. For cause and effect, state a cause or effect mentioned in the text. For problem and solution, tell what the problem is or describe the solution. For comparison, tell what is being compared or contrasted.

   Answer: *Description; the author describes types of muscles and muscle tissue found in the body* **or** *Comparison/ contrast; the author compares voluntary and involuntary muscles and three types of muscle tissue.* Reasons that are not present in the text are inaccurate.

   Standard 5: Analyze the structure of the text.

4. **What evidence in the text strongly supports that the body contains more skeletal and smooth muscle than cardiac muscle?**

   Answer: *Both skeletal and smooth muscles are found in many places in the body. Cardiac muscle is found only in the heart.* Answer should include reference to all three muscle types.

   Standard 1: Cite textual evidence to support analysis of what the text says explicitly as well as inferences drawn from the text.

5. **Analyze why you could not walk if you did not have any skeletal muscle.**

   Answer: *Skeletal muscle is attached to bones and provides the force that moves your bones.* Answer should include provision of force.

   Standard 3: Analyze interactions/connections between individuals, events, and ideas.

6. **Analyze which type of muscle you would be aware of after running in a race and why you would be aware of it.**

   Answer: *You would be aware of skeletal muscle because your muscles would be tired and possibly ache* **or** *You would be aware of cardiac muscle when you feel your heart beating faster.*

Standard 3: Analyze interactions/connections between individuals, events, and ideas.

7. **What evidence in the text strongly supports that smooth muscle is similar to cardiac muscle?**

   Answer: *Like smooth muscle, cardiac muscle is involuntary* **or** *Smooth muscles tire more slowly and cardiac muscle does not get tired.*

   Standard 1: Cite textual evidence to support analysis of what the text says explicitly as well as inferences drawn from the text.

8. **Analyze how smooth muscle and skeletal muscle are different. Give two separate examples. (2 pts.)**

   Answer: *Skeletal muscles are voluntary and smooth muscles are involuntary* **and/or** *Skeletal muscles are striated and smooth muscles are not* **and/or** *Skeletal muscles react quickly and smooth muscles react more slowly* **and/or** *Skeletal muscles tire easily and smooth muscles tire more slowly* **and/or** *Smooth muscle is found in internal organs and skeletal muscle is found on bones.* As a two-point question, there should be two clearly defined answers.

   Standard 3: Analyze interactions/connections between individuals, events, and ideas.

9. **The topic of the above two paragraphs is "skeletal muscles." What is the central idea?**

   Answer: *The central idea is that skeletal muscles work in pairs* **or** *They work by contracting and relaxing.* The answer must be clearly related to the topic. Do not accept a series of details as the central idea.

   Standard 2: Determine central idea/s.

10. **What is the meaning of *flexibility* in the context of the above passage? (AWL level 6)**

    Answer: *Easy to move, can bend easily, not stiff or rigid, elastic*

    Standard 4: Determine the meaning of words and phrases as they are used in the text.

Summarize what the text says about how skeletal muscle and smooth muscle are different. An acceptable text-based summary contains the following units. Students receive one point for each statement in their summary that matches the following statements in meaning.

1. An introductory statement of purpose
2. Skeletal muscles are attached to bones
3. Smooth muscles are inside internal organs
4. Skeletal muscle is voluntary
5. Smooth muscle is involuntary
6. Skeletal muscle is striated
7. Smooth muscle is not striated
8. Skeletal muscle tires easily
9. Smooth muscle does not tire easily
10. Skeletal muscle reacts quickly
11. Smooth muscle reacts more slowly

Point Table   The Muscular System, Middle School

Standard	Question	Points per Question
1. Support an inference	4 7	1 1
2. Determine central idea	1 9	1 1
3. Explain why or how/analyze	5 6 8	1 1 2
4. Determine word meaning	2 10	1 1
5. Determine text structure	3	2
Total Question		12
2. Summary **Total Summary**		11 (8 acceptable)

Middle School, Life Science, Part III
Before you begin scoring, please review the guidelines for scoring questions on pages 40–43 and pages 63–67 for scoring summaries.

The Respiratory System

1. **What is the meaning of *release* in the context of the above passage? (AWL level 7)**

   Answer: *Letting something go, letting something out, freeing*

   Standard 4: Determine the meaning of words and phrases as they are used in the text.

2. **Which text structure best explains how the author organized the above passage? (2 pts.)**

   ____ description of important features

   ____ explanation of steps in a sequence

   ____ account of cause and effect

   ____ explanation of problem and solution

   ____ comparison/contrast of two or more things

   Give a reason from the text for your answer. For example, if you choose description, tell what is being described. For sequence, list one or two steps. For cause and effect, state a cause or effect mentioned in the text.

For problem and solution, tell what the problem is or describe the solution. For comparison, tell what is being compared or contrasted.

Answer: *Description; the author describes the key features of oxygen, respiration, and breathing* **or** *Comparison/contrast; the author compares respiration and breathing.* Reasons that are not present in the text are inaccurate.

Standard 5: Analyze the structure of the text.

3. What is the meaning of *series* in the context of the above passages? **(AWL level 4)**

    Answer: *Things one after another, a sequence of steps*

    Standard 4: Determine the meaning of words and phrases as they are used in the text.

4. What evidence in the text strongly supports that what we breathe is not always good for us?

    Answer: *Air contains dust, pollen, and microorganisms that can cause disease.*

    Standard 1: Cite textual evidence to support analysis of what the text says explicitly as well as inferences drawn from the text.

5. The topic of the above section is "the nose." What is the central idea?

    Answer: *Mucus and cilia in nasal cavities work to move air into the throat* **or** *The author describes what mucus and cilia do.* The answer must be clearly related to the topic. Do not accept a series of details as the central idea.

    Standard 2: Determine central idea/s.

6. What evidence in the text strongly supports that mucus can be a good thing?

    Answer: *Mucus in the nasal cavities moistens the air and traps particles such as dust* **or** *Mucus in the trachea continues the cleaning and moistening of air.*

    Standard 1: Cite textual evidence to support analysis of what the text says explicitly as well as inferences drawn from the text.

7. Analyze what might happen if the trachea is blocked.

    Answer: *If the trachea is blocked no air could get into the lungs and a person could suffocate* **or** *Die.*

    Standard 3: Analyze interactions/connections between individuals, events, and ideas.

8. The topic of the above section is "bronchi and lungs." What is the central idea?

    Answer: *Air moves from the trachea to the bronchi to the alveoli.* The answer must be clearly related to the topic. Do not accept a series of details as the central idea.

    Standard 2: Determine central idea/s.

9. Analyze how the trachea and the bronchi are alike and how they are different **(2 pts)**.

Answer: *Alike: They are part of the respiratory process* **or** *They both move air into the lungs. Different: The trachea moves air into the bronchi and the bronchi move air directly into the lungs or the alveoli* **or** *The trachea has one part but the bronchi has two parts.* As a two-point question, there should be two clearly defined answers.

Standard 3: Analyze interactions/connections between individuals, events, and ideas.

10. Analyze how alveoli and capillaries are similar.

    Answer: *Alveoli and capillaries both have thin walls that allow materials such as oxygen, carbon dioxide and water to pass through* **or** *Both are located in bronchi* **or** *Both play an important role in gas exchange.*

    Standard 3: Analyze interactions/connections between individuals, events, and ideas.

Summarize what the text says about how a breath of air moves from your nose to your lungs. An acceptable text-based summary contains the following units. Students receive one point for each statement in their summary that matches the following statements in meaning.

1. An introductory statement of purpose
2. Air enters the nasal cavities
3. Mucus moistens the air
4. And traps some particles
5. Air enters the pharynx or throat
6. And moves into the trachea
7. Cilia and mucus continue to clean
8. And moisten the air
9. Air then goes into the bronchi
10. That lead to the lungs
11. The air reaches the alveoli
12. Where the blood picks up oxygen

Point Table   The Respiratory System, Middle School

Standard	Question	Points per Question
1. Support an inference	4	1
	6	1
2. Determine central idea	5	1
	8	1
3. Explain why or how/analyze	7	1
	9	2
	10	1
4. Determine word meaning	1	1
	3	1
5. Determine text structure	2	2
Total Question		12
2. Summary **Total Summary**		12 (9 acceptable)

SCIENCE

Middle School, Earth Science, Part I Before you begin scoring, please review the guidelines for scoring questions on pages 40–43 and pages 63–67 for scoring summaries.

Fossils

1. **What is the meaning of *infer* in the context of the above paragraph? (AWL level 7)**

   Answer: *Figure out, conclude, reason, determine, make an educated guess. Do not accept "guess" or "predict."*

   Standard 4: Determine the meaning of general academic and domain-specific words or phrases.

2. **The topic of the above three paragraphs is "how a fossil forms." What is the central idea?**

   Answer: *Fossils form from hard parts of organisms that are protected from decay* **or** *Fossils form when dead organisms are buried by sediment or preserved in substances* **or** *The author describes the process of fossil formation.* The answer must be clearly related to the topic. Do not accept a series of details as the central idea.

   Standard 2: Determine the central idea of a text.

3. **Which text structure best explains how the author organized the above passage?**

   ___ description of important features

   ___ explanation of steps in a sequence

   ___ account of cause and effect

   ___ explanation of problem and solution

   ___ comparison/contrast of two or more things

   Give a reason from the text for your answer. For example, if you choose description, tell what is being described. For sequence, list one or two steps. For cause and effect, state a cause or effect mentioned in the text. For problem and solution, tell what the problem is or describe the solution. For comparison, tell what is being compared or contrasted.

   Answer: *Description; the author lists different kinds of fossils and describes how they are formed through decay, protection, and preservation* **or** *Cause/effect; the author lists causes for fossil formation such as decay, protection, and preservation.* Reasons that are not stated in the text are inaccurate.

   Standard 5: Analyze the structure of the text.

4. **What is the meaning of *traces* in the context of the above passage? (AWL level 7)**

   Answer: *Sign, remains, small amounts, something left behind, evidence*

   Standard 4: Determine the meaning of general academic and domain-specific words or phrases.

5. **Analyze why minerals are important to the formation of some kinds of fossils.**

   Answer: *Cast fossils form when water deposits minerals into a mold* **or** *When minerals get into plant cells, they harden and preserve petrified fossils.*

Standard 3: Explain events, procedures, ideas, or concepts based on specific information in the text.

6. **What evidence in the text strongly supports that scientists can learn more from trace fossils than from other kinds?**

   Answer: *Trace fossils provide evidence of the activities of ancient organisms, not just their shape* **or** *Scientists can use trace fossils to find answers about size, shape, and behavior.*

   Standard 1: Refer to details and examples in a text when explaining what the text says explicitly and when drawing inferences from the text.

7. **Analyze why sediment is important in the formation of a fossil. Give at least two examples. (2 pts.)**

   Answer: *Fossils form when living things die and are covered by sediment* **and/or** *Sediment hardens and preserves the shape of the organism* **and/or** *Sediment forms a cast fossil* **and/or** *Petrified wood is formed after sediment covers the wood* **and/or** *Sediment turns into rock and preserves trace fossils.* As a two-point question, there should be two clearly defined answers.

   Standard 3: Explain events, procedures, ideas, or concepts based on specific information in the text.

8. **What evidence in the text strongly supports that water is an important part of fossil formation?**

   Answer: *Most fossils form from animals or plants that once lived in or near quiet water where sediments build up* **or** *Water carrying minerals and sediment seeps into a mold, and if water deposits the minerals and sediment, the result is a cast* **or** *Water rich in dissolved minerals seeped into spaces in the plant's cells* **or** *Freezing can preserve remains, even hair and skin.*

   Standard 1: Refer to details and examples in a text when explaining what the text says explicitly and when drawing inferences from the text.

9. **The topic of the above two paragraphs is "preserved remains." What is the central idea?**

   Answer: *Some organisms are preserved with little or no change* **or** *Some organisms are preserved in tar and amber and by freezing* **or** *The author explains how remains are preserved.* The answer must be clearly related to the topic. Do not accept a series of details as the central idea.

   Standard 2: Determine the central idea of a text.

10. **Analyze how fossils formed by tar and resin are alike.**

    Answer: *Both were preserved with little or no change* **or** *Both were protected from decay* **or** *Both were trapped in sticky materials.*

    Standard 3: Explain events, procedures, ideas, or concepts based on specific information in the text.

Summarize what the text says about how fossils form. An acceptable text-based summary contains the following units. Students receive one point for each statement in their summary that matches the following statements in meaning.

1. An introductory statement of purpose
2. Living things die
3. Their soft parts decay or are eaten
4. The hard parts are covered by sediment
5. The sediment becomes rock
6. The shape of the fossil is preserved
7. Fossils found in rock include molds and casts
8. Petrified fossils
9. Carbon films
10. And trace fossils
11. Other fossils are preserved by tar
12. Amber
13. And freezing

Point Table Fossils, Middle School

Standard	Question	Points per Question
1. Support an inference	6	1
	8	1
2. Determine central idea	2	1
	9	1
3. Explain why or how/analyze	5	1
	7	2
	10	1
4. Determine word meaning	1	1
	4	1
5. Determine text structure	3	2
Total Question		12
2. Summary **Total Summary**		13 (10 acceptable)

Middle School, Earth Science, Part II
Before you begin scoring, please review the guidelines for scoring questions on pages 40–43 and pages 63–67 for scoring summaries.

The Relative Age of Rocks

1. The topic of the above three paragraphs is "fossil age." What is the central idea?

   Answer: *The age of fossils is determined by its relative age and absolute age* **or** *The author describes the relative age and absolute age of fossils.* The answer must be clearly related to the topic. Do not accept a series of details as the central idea.

   Standard 2: Determine central idea/s.

2. Analyze one way in which the relative age and absolute age of rocks are alike and one way in which they are different **(2 pts.)**

   Answer: *Alike: Both are rock ages* **and/or** *Both absolute age and relative age can be estimated. Different: Absolute age is the exact number of years since the rock formed; relative age is age in relation to other rocks* **or** *Determining absolute age may be impossible or estimated but it is possible to determine relative age by superposition.* As a two-point question, there should be two clearly defined answers.

   Standard 3: Analyze interactions/connections between individuals, events, and ideas.

3. Which text structure best explains how the author organized the above passage? **(2 pts.)**

   ___ description of important features
   ___ explanation of steps in a sequence
   ___ account of cause and effect
   ___ explanation of problem and solution
   ___ comparison/contrast of two or more things

   Give a reason from the text for your answer. For example, if you choose description, tell what is being described. For sequence, list one or two steps. For cause and effect, state a cause or effect mentioned in the text. For problem and solution, tell what the problem is or describe the solution. For comparison, tell what is being compared or contrasted.

   Answer: *Problem/solution; the author describes the problem of determining the relative age of rocks and how it was solved through the law of superposition* **or** *Description; the author describes the process of superposition to determine the relative age of rocks* **or** *Comparison; the author compares absolute age and relative age.* Reasons that are not stated in the text are inaccurate.

   Standard 5: Analyze the structure of the text.

4. What evidence in the text strongly supports that Earth formed from the bottom up?

   Answer: *Sediment is deposited in layers one on top of the other* **or** *According to the law of superposition, the oldest layer is at the bottom* **or** *Each higher layer is younger than the layers below it* **or** *The deeper you go in the Grand Canyon, the older the rocks.*

Standard 1: Cite textual evidence to support analysis of what the text says explicitly as well as inferences drawn from the text.

5. **What is the meaning of** *position* **in the context of the above two passages entitled "The Position of Rock Layers" and "Determining Relative Age"? (AWL level 10)**

    Answer: *Location, site, placement, where something is*

    Standard 4: Determine the meaning of words and phrases as they are used in the text.

6. **The topic of the above three paragraphs is "igneous rock." What is the central idea?**

    Answer: *The relative age of rocks can be determined from igneous rock/intrusions.* The answer must be clearly related to the topic. Do not accept a series of details as the central idea.

    Standard 2: Determine central idea/s.

7. **Analyze how extrusions, intrusions, and faults are similar.**

    Answer: *They are all younger than the rocks that surround them.*

    Standard 3: Analyze interactions/connections between individuals, events, and ideas.

8. **What evidence in the text strongly supports that determining the relative age of rocks is a difficult and complex process?**

    Answer: *The geologic record is not always complete* **or** *Layers may erode exposing an older layer* **or** *Rock layers may be lost because of erosion.*

    Standard 1: Cite textual evidence to support analysis of what the text says explicitly as well as inferences drawn from the text.

9. **What is the meaning of** *index* **in the context of the above passage? (AWL level 6)**

    Answer: *Key, indicator, used as a catalog, used to organize, used to identify, a fossil used to match layers.* The answer should contain the meaning of "index" as a matching or organizing tool. Do not accept an answer that ties "index" to a book.

    Standard 4: Determine the meaning of words and phrases as they are used in the text.

10. **Analyze how an index fossil helps date rocks that are in two different places.**

    Answer: *If both places contain the same index fossil, then the rocks are about the same age.*

    Standard 3: Analyze interactions/connections between individuals, events, and ideas.

Summarize what the text says about how scientists determine the relative age of rocks. An acceptable text-based summary contains the following units. Students receive one point for each statement in their summary that matches the following statements in meaning.

1. An introductory statement of purpose
2. Scientists use the law of superposition
3. The oldest layer of rock is at the bottom
4. They also use extrusions **and/or** Intrusions
5. That are formed by magma or igneous rock
6. These are always younger than the rock
7. That is around and beneath them
8. They also study faults
9. Which are always younger than the rock they cut
10. They also use index fossils to match up rock layers

Point Table   The Relative Age of Rocks, Middle School

Standard	Question	Points per Question
1. Support an inference	4 8	1 1
2. Determine central idea	1 6	1 1
3. Explain why or how/analyze	2 7 10	2 1 1
4. Determine word meaning	5 9	1 1
5. Determine text structure	3	2
Total Question		12
2. Summary **Total Summary**		10 (7 acceptable)

Middle School, Earth Science, Part III   Before you begin scoring, please review the guidelines for scoring questions on pages 40–43 and pages 63–67 for scoring summaries.

SCIENCE

Radioactive Dating

1. **What is the meaning of** *eventually* **in the context of the above paragraph? (AWL level 8)**

    Answer: *Finally, in time, in the end, later, after time passes, in due time.* Do not accept an answer that includes "soon."

    Standard 4: Determine the meaning of general academic and domain-specific words or phrases.

2. **The topic of the above section is "radioactive decay." What is the central idea?**

    Answer: *The rate of radioactive decay is used to determine the age of rocks* **or** *The author describes the* process of radioactive decay **or** *How radioactive decay changes rocks.* The answer must be clearly related to the topic. Do not accept a series of details as the main idea.

Standard 2: Determine central idea/s.

3. **What is the meaning of** *releasing* **in the context of the above section? (AWL level 7)**

   Answer: *Letting out, letting loose, letting go, discharging*

   Standard 4: Determine the meaning of general academic and domain-specific words or phrases.

4. **Analyze how the composition of an igneous rock changes over time.**

   Answer: *Radioactive elements in igneous rocks decay and change into other elements* **or** *The amount of the radioactive element in a rock goes down over time and the amount of the new element goes up.*

   Standard 3: Explain events, procedures, ideas, or concepts based on specific information in the text.

5. **The topic of the above two paragraphs is "carbon-14 dating." What is the central idea?**

   Answer: *The rate of radioactive decay is used to determine the age of rocks* **or** *The author describes the process of radioactive decay* **or** *How radioactive decay changes rocks.* The answer must be clearly related to the topic. Do not accept a series of details as the main idea.

   Standard 2: Determine central idea/s.

6. **What evidence in the text strongly supports that the content of a fossil is different from its content when it was living?**

   Answer: *As plants and animals grow, carbon atoms are added to their tissues. After an organism dies, no more carbon is added* **or** *Carbon-14 decays and changes to stable nitrogen.*

   Standard 1: Refer to details and examples in a text when explaining what the text says explicitly and when drawing inferences from the text.

7. **Analyze one way in which potassium-argon dating and carbon-14 dating are alike and one way in which they are different. (2 pts.)**

   Answer: *Alike: Both are used to determine the ages of rocks and fossils* **and/or** *Both are forms of radioactive dating. Different: Potassium-argon has a long half-life and carbon-14 has a short half-life* **and/or** *Carbon-14 is useful in dating plants and animals that lived up to 5,730 years ago, not ancient rocks or fossils, and potassium-argon is useful in dating the most ancient rocks.* As a two-point question, there should be two clearly defined answers.

Standard 3: Explain events, procedures, ideas, or concepts based on specific information in the text.

8. **Analyze why it is difficult to determine the absolute age of a sedimentary rock.**

   Answer: *Sedimentary rock contains particles from other rocks and different time periods* **or** *Radioactive dating can provide the age of the different particles but not the age of the rock.*

   Standard 3: Explain events, procedures, ideas, or concepts based on specific information in the text.

9. **What evidence in the text strongly supports that humans have not been part of most of Earth's history?**

   Answer: *If Earth's 4.6-billion-year history is squeezed into a 24-hour day, humans do not appear until less than a second before midnight.*

   Standard 1: Refer to details and examples in a text when explaining what the text says explicitly and when drawing inferences from the text.

10. **Which text structure best explains how the author organized the above passage? (2 pts.)**

    ____ description of important features

    ____ explanation of steps in a sequence

    ____ account of cause and effect

    ____ explanation of problem and solution

    ____ comparison/contrast of two or more things

    Give a reason from the text for your answer. For example, if you choose description, tell what is being described. For sequence, list one or two steps. For cause and effect, state a cause or effect mentioned in the text. For problem and solution, tell what the problem is or describe the solution. For comparison, tell what is being compared or contrasted.

    Answer: *Sequence; the author explains the sequence of different geologic time periods. Reasons that are not stated in the text are inaccurate.*

    Standard 5: Analyze the structure of the text.

    Summarize what the text says about the process of radioactive decay in rocks. An acceptable text-based summary contains the following units. Students receive one point for each statement in their summary that matches the following statements in meaning.

    1. An introductory statement of purpose
    2. Some elements in rocks are stable/do not change
    3. Some are unstable/break down

4. And they release particles and energy

5. This is called radioactive decay

6. When the atoms break down/decay

7. They form atoms of another element

8. The rate of decay is an element's half-life

9. When a rock is fully decayed

10. It becomes a different element

Point Table   Radioactive Dating, Middle School

Standard		Question	Points per Question
1.	Support an inference	6 9	1 1
2.	Determine central idea	2 5	1 1
3.	Explain why or how/analyze	4 7 8	1 2 1
4.	Determine word meaning	1 3	1 1
5.	Determine text structure	10	2
Total Question			12
2. Summary **Total Summary**			10 (7 acceptable)

High School, Life Science, Part I   Before you begin scoring, please review the guidelines for scoring questions on pages 40–43 and pages 63–67 for scoring summaries.

SCIENCE

Life Is Cellular

1. The topic of the above section is "cell theory." What is the central idea?

   Answer: *Different individuals contributed to the formation of cell theory* **or** *The author describes different contributions to cell theory.* The answer must be clearly related to the topic. Do not accept a series of ideas as the central idea.

   Standard 2: Determine central idea/s.

2. Analyze how evidence from various scientists supported cell theory. Include at least two different forms of evidence in your analysis. **(2 pts).**

   Answer: *Hooke discovered cells when looking at cork under the microscope* **and/or** *Van Leeuwenhoek discovered living organisms in pond water* **and/or** *Schleiden concluded that all plants are made of cells* **and/or** *Schwann stated that all animals are made of cells* **and/or** *Virchow concluded that new cells are produced by cell division.* Answer should include two scientists and what they learned about cells. As a two-point question, there should be two clearly defined answers.

   Standard 3: Analyze interactions/connections between individuals, events, and ideas.

3. What is the meaning of *confirmed* in the context of the above passage? **(AWL level 7)**

   Answer: *Settled, established as true, proven, agreed upon, accepted, observed more than once, supported with evidence from different scientists, concluded*

   Standard 4: Determine the meaning of words and phrases as they are used in the text.

4. What is the meaning of *fundamental* in the context of the above passage? **(AWL level 5)**

   Answer: *Basic, central, major, important, elementary*

   Standard 4: Determine the meaning of words and phrases as they are used in the text.

5. Which text structure best explains how the author organized the above passage? **(2 pts.)**

   ____ description of important features

   ____ explanation of steps in a sequence

   ____ account of cause and effect

   ____ explanation of problem and solution

   ____ comparison/contrast of two or more things

   Give a reason from the text for your answer. For example, if you choose description, tell what is being described. For sequence, list one or two steps. For cause and effect, state a cause or effect mentioned in the text. For problem and solution, tell what the problem is or describe the solution. For comparison, tell what is being compared or contrasted.

   Answer: *Sequence; the author relates the sequence of discoveries that led to the cell theory* **or** *Description; the author describes the discoveries about the cell that led to the cell theory* **or** *Cause/effect; the invention of the microscope (cause) led to the discovery of cell theory (effect).* Reasons that are not present in the text are inaccurate.

   Standard 5: Analyze the structure of the text.

6. The topic of the above two paragraphs is "exploring cells." What is the central idea?

Answer: *Cells are different but also alike* **or** *The author describes how cells are different and alike.* The answer must be clearly related to the topic. Do not accept a series of ideas as the central idea.

Standard 2: Determine central idea/s.

7. Analyze how prokaryotic cells and eukaryotic cells are alike and how they are different. **(2 pts.)**

    Answer: *Alike: Both contain DNA* **and/or** *Both are surrounded by a cell membrane. Different: Prokaryotic cells do not enclose DNA in a nucleus and eukaryotic cells do* **and/or** *Eukaryotic cells are larger and more complex than prokaryotic cells.* Answer should include a likeness and a difference. As a two-point question, there should be two clearly defined answers.

    Standard 3: Analyze interactions/connections between individuals, events, and ideas.

8. Analyze why the nucleus is a very important part of the cell. Offer two examples. **(2 pts.)**

    Answer: *The nucleus is the control center* **and/or** *The nucleus contains genetic information in DNA* **and/or** *It contains instruction for making proteins and other important molecules* **and/or** *The nucleus contains genetic information in packed chromosomes.* As a two-point question, there should be two clearly defined answers.

    Standard 3: Analyze interactions/connections between individuals, events, and ideas.

9. What evidence in the text strongly supports that cells can function without a nucleus?

    Answer: *Cells fall into two categories depending on whether they have a nucleus* **or** *Prokaryotic cells do not separate genetic material within a nucleus* **or** *Prokaryotic cells do not have/lack a nucleus.*

    Standard 1: Cite textual evidence to support analysis of what the text says explicitly as well as inferences drawn from the text.

10. What evidence in the text strongly supports that Hooke's impression of a cell as an empty chamber was inaccurate? Give two kinds of text evidence. **(2 pts.)**

    Answer: *The cell is a complex and busy place* **and/or** *The cell is much like a living version of a modern factory* **and/or** *Many components of cells act like specialized organs*

and/or *The different organelles of the cell can be compared to machines and assembly lines of the factory* **and/or** *Cells follow instructions and produce products.*

Standard 1: Cite textual evidence to support analysis of what the text says explicitly as well as inferences drawn from the text.

Summarize the role of the nucleus in eukaryotic cells. An acceptable text-based summary contains the following units. Students receive one point for each statement in their summary that matches the following statements in meaning.

1. An introductory statement of purpose
2. The nucleus is the control center
3. It contains the cell's DNA
4. And instructions for making proteins
5. The nucleus is surrounded by an envelope
6. That has thousands of pores
7. These pores allow materials to move out of the nucleus
8. The nucleus also contains the cell's genetic information
9. Which is carried by chromosomes
10. The nucleus contains a nucleolus
11. Which produces ribosomes

Point Table   Life Is Cellular, High School

Standard	Question	Points per Question
1. Support an inference	9 10	1 2
2. Determine central idea	1 6	1 1
3. Explain why or how/analyze	2 7 8	2 2 2
4. Determine word meaning	3 4	1 1
5. Determine text structure	5	2
Total Question		15
2. Summary **Total Summary**		11 (8 acceptable)

High School, Life Science, Part II   Before you begin scoring, please review the guidelines for scoring questions on pages 40–43 and pages 63–67 for scoring summaries.

Cell Structure

1. What is the meaning of *rigidity* in the context of the above passage? **(AWL level 9)**

    Answer: *Stiffness, firmness, does not bend easily*

    Standard 4: Determine the meaning of words and phrases as they are used in the text.

2. What is the meaning of *accumulate* in the context of the above passage? **(AWL level 8)**

    Answer: *Build up, pile up, increase. Do not accept "gather."*

    Standard 4: Determine the meaning of words and phrases as they are used in the text.

SCIENCE

3. The topic of the above section is "microtubules." What is the central idea?

   Answer: *Microtubules play roles in maintaining cell shape, cell division, and cell movement* **or** *The author described the roles that microtubules play in cells.* The answer must be clearly related to the topic. Do not accept a series of details as the central idea.

   Standard 2: Determine central idea/s.

4. Analyze how microfilaments and microtubules are alike. Offer two examples. **(2 pts.)**

   Answer: *Both are part of the cytoskeleton* **and/or** *Both are made of protein* **and/or** *Both are involved in cell shape/ structure/framework/stability* **and/or** *Both are involved in cell movement.* As a two-point question, there should be two clearly defined answers.

   Standard 3: Analyze interactions/connections between individuals, events, and ideas.

5. Analyze why protein is a critical element in the cytoskeleton. Offer two examples. **(2 pts.)**

   Answer: *The cytoskeleton contains microfilaments that are made of protein and they produce a framework/ support/shape of a cell* **and/or** *The cytoskeleton also contains microtubules that are made of protein and they are important in cell division/maintaining cell shape/cell movement.* Answer should include reference to specific components of importance. As a two-point question, there should be two clearly defined answers.

   Standard 3: Analyze interactions/connections between individuals, events, and ideas.

6. The topic of the above section is "endoplasmic reticulum." What is the central idea?

   Answer: *Rough ER is involved in the synthesis of proteins and smooth ER performs specialized tasks* **or** *The author describes what the rough and smooth ERs do.* The answer must be clearly related to the topic. Do not accept a series of details as the central idea.

   Standard 2: Determine central idea/s.

7. Which text structure best explains how the author organized the above passage? **(2 pts.)**

   ____ description of important features

   ____ explanation of steps in a sequence

   ____ account of cause and effect

   ____ explanation of problem and solution

   ____ comparison/contrast of two or more things

   Give a reason from the text for your answer. For example, if you choose description, tell what is being described. For sequence, list one or two steps. For cause and effect, state a cause or effect mentioned in the text.

For problem and solution, tell what the problem is or describe the solution. For comparison, tell what is being compared or contrasted.

Answer: *Comparison; the author compares the function of the rough ER and the smooth ER* **or** *Description; the author describes the parts and functions of the rough ER and the smooth ER.* Reasons that are not present in the text are inaccurate.

Standard 5: Analyze the structure of the text.

8. Analyze how rough ER and smooth ER are alike and different. **(2 pts.)**

   Answer: *Alike: Both are part of eukaryotic cells* **and/or** *Both are part of an internal membrane system involved in assembling cell components* **and/or** *Each has a distinct function in the cell. Different: Rough ER has ribosomes on its surface and smooth ER does not* **and/or** *Rough ER makes proteins that are released and smooth ER contains enzymes that perform specialized tasks.* Answer should include reference to a likeness and a difference. As a two-point question, there should be two clearly defined answers.

   Standard 3: Analyze interactions/connections between individuals, events, and ideas.

9. What evidence in the text strongly supports that ribosomes may be the most important part of a cell?

   Answer: One of the most important jobs in the cell is making proteins, which are assembled on ribosomes **or** Proteins carry out many of the essential functions of living things.

   Standard 1: Cite textual evidence to support analysis of what the text says explicitly as well as inferences drawn from the text.

10. What evidence in the text strongly supports that the Golgi apparatus functions like FedEx, UPS, or the postal service? Give two reasons. **(2 pts.)**

    Answer: *The Golgi apparatus sorts cell materials for storage or release* **and/or** *It packages materials* **and/or** *It ships proteins to their final destination.* Answer should not include modification or customization, as these are not activities of FedEx, UPS, or the post office. As a two-point question, there should be two clearly defined answers.

    Standard 3: Analyze interactions/connections between individuals, events, and ideas.

Summarize how organelles are similar to parts of a factory. An acceptable text-based summary contains the following units. Students receive one point for each statement in their summary that matches the following statements in meaning.

1. An introductory statement of purpose

2. Factories have storage space

3. Cell vacuoles and vesicles provide storage

4. Factories have cleanup crews

5. Lysosomes are the cell's cleanup crew

6. A factory has supports

7. The cytoskeleton is the cell's support structure

8. Factories move things/have conveyor belts

9. Parts of the cytoskeleton transport materials from part of the cell to another

10. Factories produce goods

11. Organelles produce protein

Point Table   Cell Structure, High School

Standard	Question	Points per Question
1. Support an inference	9 10	1 2
2. Determine central idea	3 6	1 1
3. Explain why or how/analyze	4 5 8	2 2 2
4. Determine word meaning	1 2	1 1
5. Determine text structure	7	2
Total Question		15
2. Summary **Total Summary**		11 (8 acceptable)

High School, Life Science, Part III   Before you begin scoring, please review the guidelines for scoring questions on pages 40–43 and pages 63–67 for scoring summaries.

SCIENCE

Organelles That Capture and Release Energy

1. **What is the meaning of *convert* in the context of the above passage? (AWL level 7)**

   Answer: *Change, transform. Do not accept "join a new cause."*

   Standard 4: Determine the meaning of words and phrases as they are used in the text.

2. **What is the meaning of *aspects* in the context of the above passage? (AWL level 2)**

   Answer: *Features, characteristics, traits, parts*

   Standard 4: Determine the meaning of words and phrases as they are used in the text.

3. **Analyze how chloroplasts and mitochondria are alike. Offer two examples. (2 pts.)**

   Answer: *Both are part of plant cells* **and/or** *Both convert energy* **and/or** *Both are surrounded by two membranes* **and/or** *Both function like power plants.* As a two-point question, there should be two clearly defined answers.

   Standard 3: Analyze interactions/connections between individuals, events, and ideas.

4. **What evidence in the text strongly supports that chloroplasts and mitochondria function like power plants? Give two kinds of evidence. (2 pts.)**

   Answer: *Chloroplasts capture energy from the sun and convert it into food* **and/or** *Chloroplasts are the biological equivalents of solar power plants* **and/or** *Mitochrondria are the power plants of the cell* **and/or** *Mitochrondria convert chemical energy in food into compounds* **and/or** *Most cells are powered by molecules that use energy from the sun.* As a two-point answer, there should be two clearly defined answers.

   Standard 1: Cite textual evidence to support analysis of what the text says explicitly as well as inferences drawn from the text.

5. **The topic of the above two paragraphs is "cell walls." What is the central idea?**

   Answer: *The cell walls support shape and protect the cell* **or** *The author describes what cell walls do.* The answer must be clearly related to the topic. Do not accept a series of details as the central idea.

   Standard 2: Determine central idea/s.

6. **Which text structure best explains how the author organized the above passage? (2 pts.)**

   ____ description of important features

   ____ explanation of steps in a sequence

   ____ account of cause and effect

___ explanation of problem and solution

___ comparison/contrast of two or more things

Give a reason from the text for your answer. For example, if you choose description, tell what is being described. For sequence, list one or two steps. For cause and effect, state a cause or effect mentioned in the text. For problem and solution, tell what the problem is or describe the solution. For comparison, tell what is being compared or contrasted.

Answer: *Description; the author describes cell walls and their functions* **or** *Comparison; the author compares plant and animal cell walls.* Reasons that are not present in the text are inaccurate.

Standard 5: Analyze the structure of the text.

7. Analyze how cell walls and cell membranes are different. Offer two examples. **(2 pts.)**

   Answer: *All organisms contain cell membranes but not all contain cell walls* **and/or** *Cell walls provide strength for plants against the force of gravity; cell membranes provide a barrier between the cell and its surroundings and protect the cell.* The answer should clearly differentiate walls from membranes. As a two-point question, there should be two clearly defined answers.

   Standard 3: Analyze interactions/connections between individuals, events, and ideas.

8. Analyze how the lipid bilayer is formed from two different lipids. **(2 pts.)**

   Answer: *Some fatty acids 'love' or are drawn to water. Some "hate" water. The water-loving lipids form an outside layer exposed to water, The water-hating lipids form an oily inside layer that keeps water out.* As a two-point question, there should be two clearly defined answers. Answer should explain both forms of lipids.

   Standard 3: Analyze interactions/connections between individuals, events, and ideas.

9. The topic of the above two paragraphs is "the cell membrane." What is the central idea?

   Answer: *The cell membrane contains many different kinds of molecules that float in the lipid bilayer* **or** *The cell membrane can be compared to a fluid mosaic* **or** *The author describes molecules and the lipid bilayer in the cell membrane.* The answer must be clearly related to the topic. Do not accept a series of details as the central idea.

   Standard 2: Determine central idea/s.

10. What evidence in the text strongly supports that different molecules in the lipid bilayer have different functions?

    Answer: *Some form channels and pumps* **or** *Some act like identification cards* **or** *Some attach directly to the cytoskeleton.*

    Standard 3: Cite textual evidence to support analysis of what the text says explicitly as well as inferences drawn from the text.

Summarize how chloroplasts and mitochondria can be compared to power plants. An acceptable text-based summary contains the following units. Students receive one point for each statement in their summary that matches the following statements in meaning.

1. An introductory statement of purpose
2. Chloroplasts are like solar power plants
3. They capture energy from the sun
4. And convert it into food for the cell
5. This process is called photosynthesis
6. Nearly all eukaryotic cells contain mitochondria
7. Mitochondria are the cell's power plant
8. They convert the chemical energy in food into compounds that the cell can use
9. A power plant is protected by walls
10. Both chloroplasts and mitochondria are protected by two membranes

Point Table   Organelles That Capture and Release Energy, High School

Standard	Question	Points per Question
1. Support an inference	4 10	2 1
2. Determine central idea	5 9	1 1
3. Explain why or how/analyze	3 7 8	2 2 2
4. Determine word meaning	1 2	1 1
5. Determine text structure	6	2
Total Question		15
2. Summary **Total Summary**		10 (7 acceptable)

High School, Earth Science, Part I Before you begin scoring, please review the guidelines for scoring questions on pages 40–43 and pages 63–67 for scoring summaries.

The Vast World Ocean

1. Which text structure best explains how the author organized the above passage? **(2 pts.)**

    ___ description of important features

    ___ explanation of steps in a sequence

    ___ account of cause and effect

    ___ explanation of problem and solution

    ___ comparison/contrast of two or more things

    Give a reason from the text for your answer. For example, if you choose description, tell what is being described. For sequence, list one or two steps. For cause and effect, state a cause or effect mentioned in the text. For problem and solution, tell what the problem is or describe the solution. For comparison, tell what is being compared or contrasted.

    Answer: *Comparison; the author compares the four ocean basins* **or** *Description; the author describes the four ocean basins.* Reasons that are not present in the text are inaccurate.

    Standard 5: Analyze the structure of the text.

2. Analyze how the Atlantic Ocean basin differs from the Pacific Ocean basin with regard to both size and depth. **(2 pts.)**

    Answer: *The Pacific Ocean is deeper than the Atlantic* **and** *The Pacific Ocean is the largest ocean* **or** *The Atlantic is half the size of the Pacific* **or** *The Atlantic Ocean is relatively narrow compared to the Pacific.* As a two-point question, there should be two clearly defined answers.

    Standard 3: Analyze interactions/connections between individuals, events, and ideas.

3. What evidence in the text strongly supports that features of the ocean floor resemble features on land? Give two examples. **(2 pts.)**

    Answer: *Similar features include volcanoes* **and/or** *Mountain ranges* **and/or** *Trenches* **and/or** *Plateaus* **and/or** *The topography of the ocean floor is as diverse as that of continents.* As a two-point question, there should be two clearly defined answers.

    Standard 1: Cite textual evidence to support analysis of what the text says explicitly as well as inferences drawn from the text.

4. The topic of the above two paragraphs is "sonar." What is the central idea?

    Answer: *Sonar uses sound waves to map the ocean floor* **or** *How sonar works.* The answer must be clearly related to the topic. Do not accept a series of details as the main idea.

5. The topic of the above two paragraphs is "satellites." What is the central idea?

    Answer: *Satellites can measure ocean-surface height by bouncing microwave off the ocean surface* **or** *The author describes how satellites measure ocean surface height.* The answer must be clearly related to the topic. Do not accept a series of details as the main idea.

    Standard 2: Determine central idea/s.

6. Analyze how sonar technologies are different from satellite technologies. Offer two examples. **(2 pts.)**

    Answer: *Sonar uses sound waves and satellite technology uses microwaves* **and** *Sonar receives information on the ocean depth and satellite technology receives information on ocean surface height.* Answer should include two separate comparisons of sonar and satellite technologies.

    Standard 3: Analyze interactions/connections between individuals, events, and ideas.

7. What is the meaning of *compensating* in the context of the above passage? **(AWL level 3)**

    Answer: *Paying attention to, adjusting for, making up for, counteracting, taking account of*

    Standard 4: Determine the meaning of words and phrases as they are used in the text.

8. What is the meaning of *depressions* in the context of the above passage? **(AWL level 10)**

    Answer: *Hollows, dips, sunken places, an area lower than the surrounding surface*

    Standard 4: Determine the meaning of words and phrases as they are used in the text.

9. What evidence in the text besides depth strongly supports that Piccard's descent in a submersible was more dangerous than the descent of Beebe?

    Answer: *Beebe's submersible was tethered to the ship and could not get loose.*

    Standard 1: Cite textual evidence to support analysis of what the text says explicitly as well as inferences drawn from the text.

10. Analyze how the use of sonar and submersibles is alike and different. **(2 pts.)**

    Answer: *Alike: The purpose of both is to learn about the sea floor* **or** *Both collect data about the sea floor.* Different: *Sonar sends waves down into the ocean from a ship on the surface and submersibles actually go into the ocean* **or** *People on a ship control sonar and do not actually enter the ocean; submersibles may be controlled by an individual inside the submersible who goes into the ocean* **or** *Humans* *in submersibles actually see the ocean bottom; people working with sonar do not.* As a two-point question, there should be two clearly defined answers.

Standard 3: Analyze interactions/connections between individuals, events, and ideas.

Summarize what the text says about how scientists study the ocean floor. An acceptable text-based summary contains the following units. Students receive one point for each statement in their summary that matches the following statements in meaning.

1. An introductory statement of purpose
2. HMS Challenger measured ocean depth
3. By lowering long weighted lines overboard
4. Sonar transmits sound waves to the ocean floor
5. And uses the echo from the bottom to measure depth
6. Multibeam sonar uses more than one sound source
7. And obtains a profile of a narrow strip of ocean
8. Satellite technology bounces microwaves off the ocean surface

9. And cross checks this data with sonar measurements
10. Submersibles collect data by actually going into the ocean

Point Table   The Vast World Ocean, High School

Standard	Question	Points per Question
1. Support an inference	3 9	2 1
2. Determine central idea	4 5	1 1
3. Explain why or how/analyze	2 6 10	2 2 2
4. Determine word meaning	7 8	1 1
5. Determine text structure	1	2
Total Question	10	15
2. Summary **Total Summary**		10 (7 acceptable)

High School, Earth Science, Part II   Before you begin scoring, please review the guidelines for scoring questions on pages 40–43 and pages 63–67 for scoring summaries.

SCIENCE

Ocean Floor Features

1. **What evidence in the text strongly supports that the Atlantic continental margin is passive, whereas the Pacific continental margin is active? Give two forms of evidence. (2 pts.)**

   Answer: *In the Atlantic margin, there is very little volcanic or earthquake activity. The Pacific margin experiences both volcanic and earthquake activity* **and/or** *The Atlantic margin has thick layers of undisturbed sediment and in the Pacific margin, oceanic crust plunges beneath continental crust* **and/or** *The Atlantic margin is not associated with plate boundaries; the Pacific margin is.* Answer should include reference to both margins. As a two-point question, there should be two clearly defined answers.

   Standard 1: Cite textual evidence to support analysis of what the text says explicitly as well as inferences drawn from the text.

2. **The topic of the above three paragraphs is "continental slope." What is the central idea?**

   Answer: *The continental slope is steep and contains canyons formed by turbidity currents* **or** *The author describes the continental slope and how it is formed.* The answer must be clearly related to the topic. Do not accept a series of ideas as the central idea.

Standard 2: Determine central idea/s.

3. **Which text structure best explains how the author organized the above passages? (2 pts.)**

   ____ description of important features

   ____ explanation of steps in a sequence

   ____ account of cause and effect

   ____ explanation of problem and solution

   ____ comparison/contrast of two or more things

   Give a reason from the text for your answer. For example, if you choose description, tell what is being described. For sequence, list one or two steps. For cause and effect, state a cause or effect mentioned in the text. For problem and solution, tell what the problem is or describe the solution. For comparison, tell what is being compared or contrasted.

   Answer: *Description; the author describes the continental shelf, the continental slope, and the continental rise* **or** *Comparison; the author compares the continental shelf, the continental slope, and the continental rise.* Reasons that are not present in the text are inaccurate.

   Standard 5: Analyze the structure of the text.

4. Analyze how the continental shelf and the continental slope are different. Offer two examples **(2 pts)**.

    Answer: *The continental shelf begins at the shoreline; the continental slope begins in the ocean at the end of the continental shelf* **and/or** *The continental shelf is a gentle slope; the continental slope is steeper* **and/or** *The continental shelf is about 80 kilometers wide; the continental slope is narrow and only about 20 kilometers in width.* Answer should include reference to both the shelf and the slope. As a two-point question, there should be two clearly defined answers.

    Standard 3: Analyze interactions/connections between individuals, events, and ideas.

5. Analyze how turbidity currents form submarine canyons by describing two steps in the process. **(2 pts.)**

    Answer: *Turbidity currents are formed of dense sediment-rich water* **and/or** *They flow down the continental slope* **and/or** *They erode the slope* **and/or** *They accumulate more sediment.* As a two-point question, there should be two clearly defined answers.

    Standard 3: Analyze interactions/connections between individuals, events, and ideas.

6. What is the meaning of *suspended* in the context of the section? **(AWL level 2)**

    Answer: *Distributed, floating, hung, scattered or loose in something*

    Standard 4: Determine the meaning of words and phrases as they are used in the text.

7. What evidence in the text strongly supports that the absence of trenches plays a role in the formation of abyssal plains?

    Answer: *The Atlantic Ocean has the most extensive abyssal plains because there are few trenches to catch the sediment.*

    Standard 1: Cite textual evidence to support analysis of what the text says explicitly as well as inferences drawn from the text.

8. The topic of the above section is "seamounts and guyots." What is the central idea?

    Answer: *Seamounts and guyots are forms of underwater volcanoes* **or** *The author describes two forms of underwater volcanoes* **or** *What seamounts and guyots are.* The answer must be clearly related to the topic. Do not accept a series of ideas as the central idea.

    Standard 2: Determine central idea/s.

9. What is the meaning of *exceed* in the context of the above section? **(AWL level 6)**

    Answer: *Be more or greater than, go above, go beyond, get bigger*

    Standard 4: Determine the meaning of words and phrases as they are used in the text.

10. Analyze how volcanic activity changes the ocean floor. Offer two examples. **(2 pts.)**

    Answer: *Volcanic activity is associated with the formation of deep ocean trenches* **and/or** *Volcanic activity is associated with seafloor spreading* **and/or** *Volcanoes form peaks or seamounts* **and/or** *Volcanoes play a part in the deposition of minerals.* As a two-point question, there should be two clearly defined answers.

    Standard 3: Analyze interactions/connections between individuals, events, and ideas.

Summarize how the text describes trenches, abyssal plains, seamounts, and guyots. An acceptable text-based summary contains the following units. Students receive one point for each statement in their summary that matches the following statements in meaning.

1. An introductory statement of purpose
2. Most trenches are located in the Pacific Ocean
3. They are long narrow creases
4. And are the result of plate activity
5. Trenches represent the deepest places on Earth
6. They form at sites of plate convergence
7. Abyssal plains are deep level features
8. They are formed by thick accumulations of sediment
9. They are carried by turbidity currents
10. Seamounts are submerged volcanic peaks
11. Guyots are islands that have sunk below the surface

Point Table   Ocean Floor Features, High School

Standard	Question	Points per Question
1. Support an inference	1 7	2 1
2. Determine central idea	2 8	1 1
3. Explain why or how/analyze	4 5 10	2 2 2
4. Determine word meaning	6 9	1 1
5. Determine text structure	3	2
Total Question	10	15
2. Summary **Total Summary**		11 (8 acceptable)

SCIENCE

High School, Earth Science, Part III Before you begin scoring, please review the guidelines for scoring questions on pages 40–43 and pages 63–67 for scoring summaries.

Seafloor Sediments

1. The topic of the above section is "biogenous sediment." What is the central idea?

   Answer: *There are different kinds of biogenous sediment* **or** *Biogenous sediment is composed of different things* **or** *The author describes the composition of biogenous sediment.* The answer must be clearly related to the topic. Do not accept a series of details as the main idea.

   Standard 2: Determine central idea/s.

2. Analyze how calcareous ooze and siliceous ooze are alike and different. (**2 pts.**)

   Answer: *Alike: They both have the consistency of thick mud* **and/or** *They are both examples of biogenous sediment* **and/or** *They both come from organisms or shells. Different: Calcareous ooze is formed from calcium carbonate shells; siliceous ooze is formed from shells made of silica* **and/or** *Calcareous ooze is not found below depths of 4500 meters; siliceous ooze is.* Answer should include both likeness and difference. As a two-point question, there should be two clearly defined answers.

   Standard 3: Analyze interactions/connections between individuals, events, and ideas.

3. Analyze how terrigenous and biogenous sediment are alike and different. (**2 pts.**)

   Answer: *Alike: Both are found on the ocean floor. Different: Terrigenous sediment originates on land and biogenous sediment originates in the ocean* **or** *Terrigenous sediment consists of mineral grains eroded from rocks; biogenous sediment consists of shells, skeletons of marine animals, and algae.* Answer should include both likeness and difference. As a two-point question, there should be two clearly defined answers.

   Standard 3: Analyze interactions/connections between individuals, events, and ideas.

4. What is the meaning of *consists* in the context of the above passage? (**AWL level 1**)

   Answer: *Contains, are made of, are composed of*

   Standard 4: Determine the meaning of words and phrases as they are used in the text.

5. What evidence in the text strongly supports that all salts are suitable for cooking?

   Answer: *Other salts do not taste salty, such as the calcium sulfate minerals anhydrite and gypsum.*

   Standard 1: Cite textual evidence to support analysis of what the text says explicitly as well as inferences drawn from the text.

6. The topic of the above section is "gas hydrates." What is the central idea?

   Answer: *Gas hydrates produce methane and other flammable gases* **or** *The author describes the presence of methane in gas hydrates.* The answer must be clearly related to the topic. Do not accept a series of details as the main idea.

   Standard 2: Determine central idea/s.

7. Which text structure best explains how the author organized the above passage? (**2 pts.**)

   ____ description of important features

   ____ explanation of steps in a sequence

   ____ account of cause and effect

   ____ explanation of problem and solution

   ____ comparison/contrast of two or more things

   Give a reason from the text for your answer. For example, if you choose description, tell what is being described. If you choose sequence, list one or two steps. For cause and effect, state a cause or effect mentioned in the text. For problem and solution, tell what the problem is or describe the solution. For comparison, tell what is being compared or contrasted.

   Answer: *Description. The author describes gas hydrates, how they are formed, where they are found and their possible use as energy.* Reasons that are not present in the text are inaccurate.

   Standard 5: Analyze the structure of a text.

8. Analyze the positive and negative aspects of mining gas hydrates. (**2 pts.**)

   Answer: *Positive: A lot of methane is contained in gas hydrates* **and/or** *The amount of methane in gas hydrates is double the amount of present energy resources* **and/or** *Gas hydrates could help provide for our energy needs. Negative: Gas hydrates evaporate quickly when they are removed from the ocean* **and/or** *Gas hydrates rapidly break down when brought to the surface.* As a two point question, there should be two clearly defined answers. One should focus on positive aspects and the other on negative aspects.

   Standard 3: Analyze interactions/connections between individuals, events, and ideas.

9. What is the meaning of *resources* in the context of the above passages? (**AWL level 2**)

   Answer: *Assets, things that can be put to use, things that can be used in a helpful way, things used for a purpose.* Do not accept "energy" or "minerals."

   Standard 4: Determine the meaning of words and phrases as they are used in the text.

10. What evidence in the text strongly supports that ocean resources play an important role in our life? Offer two forms of evidence. **(2 pts.)**

    Answer: *Most of the value of nonliving resources comes from their use as energy products* **and/or** *Sand and gravel harvested from the ocean are used for landfill, filling in recreational beaches, and making concrete* **and/or** *Salt harvested from the ocean is widely used for preserving food, in agriculture, for dying clothes, and for de-icing roads.* As a two-point question, there should be two clearly defined answers.

    Standard 1: Cite textual evidence to support analysis of what the text says explicitly as well as inferences drawn from the text.

Summarize what the text says about the differences in three types of seafloor sediments. An acceptable text-based summary contains the following units. Students receive one point for each statement in their summary that matches the following statements in meaning.

1. An introductory statement of purpose
2. Types of seafloor sediments are based on their origin
3. Terrigenous sediments originate on land
4. And consist of mineral grains eroded from rocks
5. And transported to the ocean
6. They can form gravel, sand, and clay
7. Biogenous sediments consist of shells and skeletons of marine animals and algae
8. Biogenous sediments include calcareous ooze and siliceous ooze
9. Hydrogenous sediments come from minerals crystallized from ocean water
10. They are only a small part of overall sediment
11. But have many different forms

Point Table Seafloor Sediments, High School

Standard	Question	Points per Question
1. Support an inference	5 10	1 2
2. Determine central idea	1 6	1 1
3. Explain why or how/analyze	2 3 8	2 2 2
4. Determine word meaning	4 9	1 1
5. Determine text structure	7	2
Total Question	10	15
2. Summary **Total Summary**		11 (8 acceptable)

References

Abrami, P. C., Bernard, R. M., Borokhovski, E., Wade, A., Surkes, M. A., Tamim, R., et al. (2008). Instructional interventions affecting critical thinking skills and dispositions: A stage 1 meta-analysis. *Review of Educational Research, 78,* 1102–1134.

ACT, Inc. (2012). The condition of college and career readiness. Retrieved September 3, 2013, from www.act.org/readiness/2012

Afflerbach, P. (1990). The influence of prior knowledge on expert readers' main idea construction strategies. *Reading Research Quarterly, 25,* 31–46.

Afflerbach, P. (2007). Best practices in literacy assessment. In L. B. Gambrell, L. M. Morrow, & M. Pressley (Eds.), *Best practices in literacy instruction* (3rd ed.), pp. 264–282. New York, NY: The Guilford Press.

Afflerbach, P. & Cho, B. (2011), The classroom assessment of reading. In M. L, Kamil, P. D. Pearson, E. B. Moje & P, P. Afflerbach (Eds.), Handbook of reading research (Vol IV, pp. 487–515). New York: Routledge.

Afflerbach, P. & Cho, B. (2009). Identifying and describing constructively responsive comprehension strategies in new and traditional forms of reading. In S. E. Israel & G. G. Duffy (Eds.), *Handbook of research on reading comprehension* (pp. 69–91). New York, NY: Routledge.

Akhondi, M., Malayeri, F. A., & Samad, A. A. (2011). How to teach expository text structure to facilitate reading comprehension. *The Reading Teacher, 64,* 368–372.

Alexander, P. A., & Jetton, T. L. (2000). Learning from text: A multidimensional and developmental perspective. In M. L. Kamil, P. B. Moesenthal, P. D. Pearson, & R. Barr (Eds.), *Handbook of reading research* (Vol. 3, pp. 285–310). Mahwah, NJ: Erlbaum.

Almasi, J. F., & Garas-York, K. (2009). Comprehension and discussion of text. In S. E. Israel & G. G. Duffy (Eds.), *Handbook of research on reading comprehension* (pp. 470–493). New York, NY: Routledge.

Anderson, L. W., & Krathwohl, D. (2001). *A taxonomy for learning, teaching and assessing: A revision of Bloom's taxonomy of educational objectives.* New York, NY: Addison Wesley Longman.

Applegate, M. D., Quinn, K. B., & Applegate, A. (2002). Levels of thinking required by comprehension questions in informal reading inventories. *The Reading Teacher, 56,* 174–180.

Baumann, J. F. (2009). Vocabulary and comprehension: The nexus of meaning. In S. E. Israel & G. G. Duffy (Eds.), *Handbook of research on reading comprehension* (pp. 323–346). New York, NY: Routledge.

Baumann, J. F., & Graves, M. F. (2010). What is academic vocabulary? *Journal of Adolescent & Adult Literacy, 54,* 4–12.

Baumann, J. F., Ware, D., & Edwards, E. C. (2007). "Bumping into spicy, tasty words that catch your tongue": A formative experiment on vocabulary instruction. *The Reading Teacher, 62,* 108–122.

Baumann, J. F., Edwards, E. B., Font, G., Tereshinski, C. A., Kame'enui, E. J., & Olejnik, S. (2002). Teaching morphemic and contextual analysis to fifth-grade students. *Reading Research Quarterly, 37,* 150–176.

Beck, I. L., McKeown, M. G., Hamilton, R. L., & Kucan, L. (1997). *Questioning the author: An approach for enhancing student engagement with text.* Newark, DE: International Reading Association.

Beck, I. L., McKeown, M. G., & Kucan, L. L. (2002). *Bringing words to life: Robust vocabulary instruction.* New York, NY: The Guilford Press.

Betts, E. (1946). Foundations of reading instruction. New York, NY: American Books.

Betts, E. (1957). *Foundations of reading instruction, with emphasis on differentiated guidance* (4th ed.). New York, NY: American Books.

Blachowicz, C. L., & Fisher, P. (2000). Vocabulary instruction. In M. L. Kamil, P. B. Moesenthal, P. D. Pearson, & R. Barr (Eds.), *Handbook of reading research* (Vol. 3, pp. 503–524). Mahwah, NJ: Erlbaum.

Black, P., & Wiliam, W. (1998). Assessment and classroom learning. *Assessment in Education: Principles, Policy, and Practice, 5,* 7–74.

Block, C. C., & Pressley, M. (2007). Best practices in teaching comprehension. In L. B. Gambrell, L. M. Morrow, & M. Pressley (Eds.), *Best practices in literacy instruction* (3rd ed., pp. 220–243). New York, NY: The Guilford Press.

Bloom, B., & Krathwohl, D. (1956). *Taxonomy of educational objectives: The classification of educational goals.* New York, NY: Longmans Green.

Booth, W. C. (1983). *The rhetoric of fiction.* Chicago, IL: University of Chicago Press.

Bransford, J. D., Brown, A. L., & Cocking, R. R. (2000). *How people learn: Brain, mind, experience, and school.* Washington, DC: National Academy Press.

Brozo, W. G., Moorman, G., Meyer, C., & Stewart, T. (2013). Content area reading and disciplinary literacy: A case for the radical center. *Journal of Adolescent & Adult Literacy, 56,* 353–357.

Buehl, D. (2011). *Developing readers in the academic disciplines.* Newark, DE: International Reading Association.

Caldwell, J. S., & Leslie, L. (2013). *Intervention strategies to follow informal reading inventory assessment: So what do I do now?* (3rd ed.). Boston, MA: Pearson.

Calkins, L., Ehrenworth, M. D., & Lehman, C. (2012). *Pathways to the common core: Accelerating achievement.* Portsmouth, NJ: Heinemann.

Campbell, K. H. (2007). Less is more: Teaching literature with short texts, Grades 6–12. Portland, ME: Stenhouse Publishers.

Carlisle, J. F. (2010). Effects of instruction in morphological awareness on literacy achievement: An integrative review. *Reading Research Quarterly, 45,* 464–487.

Carnegie Council on Advancing Adolescent Literacy (2010). *A time to act: An agenda for advancing adolescent literacy for college and career success.* New York, NY: Carnegie Corporation of New York. Retrieved September 16, 2009, from carnegie.org

Carpenter, R. D., & Paris, S. G. (2005). Issues of validity and reliability in early reading assessments. In S. G. Paris & S. A. Stahl (Eds.), *Children's reading comprehension and assessment* (pp. 279–305). Mahwah, NJ: Erlbaum.

Chall, J. S., & Dale, E. (1995). *Manual for the new Dale-Chall readability formula.* Cambridge, MA: Brookline.

Chanock, K. (2000). Comments on essays: Do students understand what tutors write? *Teaching in Higher Education, 5,* 95–105.

Ciardiello, A. V. (1998). Did you ask a good question today? Alternative cognitive and metacognitive strategies. *Journal of Adolescent & Adult Literacy, 42,* 210–219.

Clancy, J., & Ballard, B. (1981). *Essay writing for students: A practical guide.* Melbourne: Longman.

Coleman, D., & Pimental, S. (2011). *Publishers' criteria for the common core state standards in English language arts and literacy: Grades 3–12.* Retrieved March 13, 2012, from www.corestandards.org

Conley, M. W. (2008). Literacy assessment for adolescents: What's fair about it? In K. A. Hinchman & H. K. Sheridan-Thomas (Eds.), *Best practices in adolescent literacy instruction* (pp. 297–312). New York: Guilford Press.

Conley, M. W. (2009). Improving adolescent comprehension: Developing comprehension strategies in the content areas. In S. E. Israel & G. G. Duffy (Eds.), *Handbook of research on reading comprehension* (pp. 531–551). New York: Routledge.

Council of Chief State School Officers (CCSSO) & National Governor's Association (NGA) (2010). *Common core state standards for English language arts & literacy in history/social studies, science and technical subjects.* Retrieved September 28, 2010, from www.corestandards.org

Council of Chief State School Officers (CCSSO) & National Governor's Association (NGA) (2010). Appendix A. Retrieved September 28, 2010 from www.corestandards.org

Coxhead, A. (2000). A new academic word list. *TESOL Quarterly, 34,* 213–238.

Cresswell, J. W. (2008). *Educational research.* Upper Saddle River, NJ: Pearson Merrill Prentice Hall.

Davis, F. B. (1968). Research in comprehension in reading. *Reading Research Quarterly, 3,* 499–545.

Davis, F. B. (1972). Psychometric research on comprehension in reading. *Reading Research Quarterly, 7,* 628–678.

Dobler, E. (2013). Authentic reasons for close reading: How to monitor students to take another look. *Reading Today, 30*(6), 13–15.

Dole, J. A., Nokes, J. D., & Drits, D. (2009). Cognitive strategy instruction. In S. E. Israel & G. G. Duffy (Eds.), *Handbook of research on reading comprehension* (pp. 347–373). New York, NY: Routledge.

Duke, N. K., Roberts, K. L., & Norman, R. R. (2011). Young children's understanding of specific graphical devices in informational text. Poster presented at the annual meeting of the International Reading Association, Orlando, FL.

Dymock, S. (2007). Comprehension strategy instruction: Teaching narrative text structure awareness. *The Reading Teacher, 61,* 161–167.

Dymock, S., & Nicholson, T. (2010). "High 5!" Strategies to enhance comprehension of expository text. *The Reading Teacher, 64,* 166–178.

Fang, Z. (2008). Going beyond the Fab Five: Helping students cope with the unique linguistic challenges of expository reading in intermediate grades. *Journal of Adolescent & Adult Literacy, 51,* 478–287.

Fang, Z. (2012). Approaches to developing content area literacies: A synthesis and a critique. *Journal of Adolescent & Adult Literacy, 56,* 103–108.

Farr, J. N., Jenkins, J. J., & Paterson, D. G. (1951). Simplification of Flesch reading ease formula. *Journal of Applied Psychology, 35,* 333–337.

Ferretti, R. P., & De La Paz, S. (2011). On the comprehension and production of written texts: Instructional activities that support content-area literacy. In R. E. O'Connor & P. F. Vadasy (Eds.), *Handbook of reading interventions* (pp. 326–412). New York, NY: The Guilford Press.

Fisher, D., & Frey, N. (2012). Close reading in elementary schools. *The Reading Teacher, 66,* 179–187.

Fisher, D., Frey, N., & Lapp, D. (2012). *Text complexity: Raising rigor in reading.* Newark, DE: International Reading Association.

Flanagan, K., Templeton, S., & Hayes, L. (2012). What's in a word? Using content vocabulary to generate growth in general academic vocabulary. *Journal of Adolescent & Adult Literacy, 56,* 132–140.

Flesch, R. (1948). A new readability yardstick. *Journal of Applied Psychology, 32,* 221–233.

Freebody, P., & Freiberg, J. M. (2011). The teaching and learning of critical literacy: Beyond "a show of wisdom." In M. L. Kamil, P. D. Pearson, E. B. Moje, & P. P. Afflerbach (Eds.), *Handbook of reading research* (Vol. 4, pp. 432–453). New York, NY: Routledge.

Fry, E. (2002). Readability versus leveling. *The Reading Teacher, 56,* 286–291.

Funk & Wagnalls New International Dictionary of the English Language. (1997). Chicago, IL: Ferguson Publishing Company.

Glasswell, K., & Ford, M. P. (2010). Teaching flexibly with leveled texts: More power for your reading block. *The Reading Teacher, 64,* 57–60.

Graesser, A. C., McNamara, D. S., & Louwerse, M. M. (2011). Methods of animated text analysis. In M. L. Kamil, P. D. Pearson, E. B. Moje, & P. P. Afflerbach (Eds.), *Handbook of reading research* (Vol. 4, pp. 34–53). New York, NY: Routledge.

Graesser, A., Ozuru, Y., & Sullins, J. (2010). What is a good question? In M. G. McKeown & L. Kucan (Eds.), *Bringing reading research to life* (pp. 112–141). New York, NY: The Guilford Press.

Graesser, A. C., & Person, N. K. (1994). Question asking during tutoring. *American Educational Research Journal, 31,* 104–137.

Graham, S. (2006). Strategy instruction and the teaching of writing: A meta-analysis. In C. A. MacArthur, S. Graham, & J. Fitzgerald (Eds.), *Best practices in writing instruction* (pp. 187–207). New York, NY: The Guilford Press.

Graham, S., & Harris, K. (2007). Best practices in teaching planning. In S. Graham, C. A. MacArthur, & J. Fitzgerald (Eds.), *Best practices in writing instruction* (pp. 119–140). New York, NY: The Guilford Press.

Gunn, T. M., & Pomahac, G. A. (2008). Critical thinking in the middle school science classroom. *The International Journal of Learning, 15,* 239–247.

Gunn, T., Grigg, L., & Pomahac, G. (2006). Critical thinking and bioethical decision making in the middle school classroom. *The International Journal of Learning, 13,* 129–136.

Guthrie, J. (2013). Attaining the CCSS is impossible. *Reading Today Online: From the Literacy Research Panel.* Retrieved September 4, 2013, from www.reading.org/general/Publications/blog.aspx

Halladay, J. L. (2012). Revisiting key assumptions of the reading level framework. *The Reading Teacher, 66,* 53–61.

Hannus, M., & Hyona, J. (1999). Utilization of illustrations during learning of science textbook passages among low- and high-ability children. *Contemporary Educational Psychologist, 24*(2), 95–123.

Helsel, L., & Greenberg, D. (2007). Helping struggling writers succeed: A self-regulated strategy instruction program. *The Reading Teacher, 60,* 752–760.

Hiebert, E. (2013). Supporting students' movement up the staircase of text complexity. *The Reading Teacher, 66,* 459–469.

Hiebert, E. H., & Mesmer, H. A. (2013). Upping the ante of text complexity in the Common Core Standards: Examining its potential impact on young readers. *Educational Researcher, 42,* 44–51.

International Reading Association Common Core State Standards Committee (2012). *Literacy implementation guidance for the ELA Common Core State Standards.* Newark, DE: International Reading Association.

Jennings, J. H., Caldwell, J. S., & Lerner, J. W. (2014). *Reading problems: Assessment and teaching strategies* (7th ed.). Boston, MA: Pearson.

Jetton, T. L., & Lee, R. (2012). Learning from text: Adolescent literacy from the past decade. In T. L. Jetton & C. Shanahan (Eds.), *Adolescent literacy in the academic disciplines: General principles and practical strategies* (pp. 1–33). New York, NY: The Guilford Press.

Jitendra, A. K., & Gajria, M. (2011). Main idea and summarizing instruction to improve reading comprehension. In R. E. O'Connor & P. F. Vadasy (Eds.), *Handbook of reading interventions* (pp. 198–219). New York, NY: The Guilford Press.

Johnston, P. J., Ivey, G., & Faulkner, A. (2011). Talking in class: Remembering what is important about classroom talk. *The Reading Teacher, 65,* 232–237.

Kintsch, W. (1998). Comprehension: A paradigm for cognition. London, UK: Cambridge University Press.

Kintsch, W. (2004). The construction-integration model of text comprehension and its implications for instruction. In R. B. Ruddell & N. J. Unrau (Eds.), *Theoretical models and processes of reading* (5th ed., pp. 1270–1328). Newark, DE: International Reading Association.

Kintsch, W. (2012). Psychological models of reading comprehension and their implications for assessment. In J. P. Sabatini, E. Albro, & T. O'Reilly (Eds.), *Measuring up: Advances in how to assess reading ability* (pp. 21–39). Lanham, MA: Rowman & Littlefield Publishers.

Kintsch, W., & van Dijk, T. A. (1978). Toward a model of text comprehension and production. *Psychological Review, 85,* 366–394.

Klingner, J. K., Morrison, A., & Eppolito, A. (2011). Metacognition to improve reading comprehension. In R. E. O'Connor & P. F. Vadasy (Eds.), *Handbook of reading interventions* (pp. 220–254). New York, NY: The Guilford Press.

Kuhn, D. (1999). A developmental model of critical thinking. *Educational Researcher, 28,* 16–26.

Leslie, L., & Caldwell, J. (2009). Formal and informal measures of reading comprehension. In S. E. Israel & G. G. Duffy (Eds.), *Handbook of research on reading comprehension* (pp. 403–427). New York, NY: Routledge.

Leslie, L., & Caldwell, J. S. (2011). *Qualitative reading inventory 5.* Boston, MA: Pearson.

Mariage, T. V., & Englert, C. S. (2010). Constructing access and understanding in inclusive middle-grade content classrooms: A sociocognitive apprenticeship in literacy with bilingual students and those with language/learning disabilities. In G. Li & P. A. Edwards (Eds.), *Best practices in ELL instruction* (pp. 151–188). New York, NY: The Guilford Press.

Mayer, R. E., & Wittrock, M. C. (2006). Problem solving. In P. A. Alexander & P. H. Winne (Eds.), *Handbook of educational psychology* (pp. 287–303). Mahwah, NJ: Erlbaum.

McCormack, R. L., Paratore, J. R., & Dahlene, K. F. (2004). Establishing instructional congruence across learning settings: One path to success for struggling third-grade readers. In R. L. McCormack, J. R. Paratore (Ed.), *After early intervention, then what?* (pp. 117–136). Newark, DE: International Reading Association.

McCutchen, D., & Logan, B. (2011). Inside incidental word learning: Children's strategic use of morphological information to infer word meanings. *Reading Research Quarterly, 46,* 334–349.

McKeown, M. G., Beck, I. L., & Blake, R. G. (2009). Rethinking reading comprehension: A comparison of instruction for strategies and content approaches instruction. *Reading Research Quarterly, 44,* 218–253.

McKeown, M. G., Beck, I. L., Sinatra, G. M., & Loxterman. J. A. (1992). The contribution of prior knowledge and coherent text to comprehension. *Reading Research Quarterly, 27,* 78–93.

McNamara, D. S., Graesser, A., & Louwerse, M. (2012). Sources of text difficulty: Across genres and grades. In J. P. Sabatinim, E. Albro, & T. O'Reilly (Eds.), *Measuring up: Advances in how to assess reading ability* (pp. 89–118). Lanham, MD: Rowman & Littlefield Publishers.

McNamara, D. S., Kintsch, E., Songer, N. B., & Kintsch, W. (1996). Are good texts always better? Text coherence, background knowledge, and levels of understanding in learning of text. *Cognition and Instruction, 14,* 1–43.

McTigue, E., & Flowers, A. (2011). Science visual literacy: Learners' perceptions and knowledge of diagrams. *The Reading Teacher, 64*(8), 578–589.

MetaMetrics (2013). Retrieved August 24, 2013, from www.metametricsinc.com

Moje, E. B. (2008). Foregrounding the disciplines in secondary literacy teaching and learning: A call for change. *Journal of Adolescent & Adult Literacy, 52,* 96–107.

Monte-Sano, C., & De La Paz, S. (2012). Using writing tasks to elicit adolescents' historical reasoning. *Journal of Literacy Research, 44,* 273–299.

Morgan, D. N., & Rasinski, T. V. (2012). The power and potential of primary sources. *The Reading Teacher, 65,* 584–594.

Morsy, L., Kieffer, M., & Snow, C. E. (2010). *Measure for measure: A critical consumers' guide to reading comprehension assessments for adolescents.* New York, NY: Carnegie Corporation of New York. Retrieved December 8, 2010, from carnegie.org

Mosenthal, P. (1996). Understanding the strategies of document literacy and their condition of use. *Journal of Educational Psychology, 88,* 314–332.

Moss, B. (2006). Teaching English language learners about expository text structure. In T. A. Young & N. L. Hadaway (Eds.), *Supporting the literacy development of English learners: Increasing success in all classrooms* (pp. 132–147). Newark, DE: International Reading Association.

Nagy, W. E. (2010). The word game. In M. G. McKeown & L. Kucan (Eds.), *Bringing reading research to life* (pp. 72–91). New York, NY: The Guilford Press.

Nagy, W., & Townsend, D. (2012). Words as tools: Learning academic vocabulary as language acquisition. *Reading Research Quarterly, 47,* 91–108.

National Center for Education Statistics (2013). *The nation's report card: Trends in academic progress 2012.* National Assessment of Educational Progress. Retrieved July 15, 2013, http://nces.ed.gov/nationsreportcard/pubs/main2012/2013456.aspx

Neufeld, P. (2005). Comprehension instruction in content area classes. *The Reading Teacher, 59,* 302–312.

Ogle, D. M. (1986). K-W-L: A teaching model that develops active rereading of expository text. *The Reading Teacher, 39,* 564–570.

Paris, S. G., & Hamilton, E. E. (2009). The development of children's reading comprehension. In S. E. Israel & G. G. Duffy (Eds.), *Handbook of research on reading comprehension* (pp. 32–54). New York, NY: Routledge.

Pearson, P. D., & Hamm, D. N. (2005). The assessment of reading comprehension: A review of practices—past, present, and future. In S. G. Paris & S. A. Stahl (Eds.), *Children's reading comprehension and assessment* (pp. 13–70). Mahwah, NJ: Erlbaum.

Perfetti, C., & Adlof, S. M. (2012). Reading comprehension: A conceptual framework from word meaning to text meaning. In J. P. Sabatini, E. Abro, & T. O'Reilly (Eds.), *Measuring up: Advances in how to assess reading ability* (pp. 3–20). Lanham, MD: Rowman & Littlefield Publishers.

Perin, D. (2007). Best practices in teaching writing to adolescents. In S. Graham, C. A. MacArthur, & J. Fitsgerald (Eds.), *Best practices in writing instruction* (pp. 242–264). New York, NY: The Guilford Press.

Pressley, M., & Afflerbach, P. (1995). *Verbal protocols of reading: The nature of constructively responsive reading.* Hillsdale, NJ: Erlbaum.

Questar Association, Inc. (2013). Retrieved August 24, 2013, from http://www.questarai.com

RAND Reading Study Group. (2002). *Reading for understanding: Toward an R&D program in reading comprehension.* Washington, DC: RAND Education.

Raphael, T. E. (1982). Question-answering questions for children. *The Reading Teacher, 36,* 186–190.

Raphael, T. E. (1986). Teaching question-answer relationships, revisited. *The Reading Teacher, 39,* 516–522

Raphael, T. E., Highfield, K., & Au, K. (2006). *QAR now: Question answer relationships.* New York, NY: Scholastic.

Rasinski, T. V., Padak, N., Newton, J., & Newton, E. (2011). The Latin-Greek connection: Building vocabulary through morphological study. *The Reading Teacher, 65,* 133–141.

Roberts, K. L., Norman, R. R., Duke, N. K., Morsink, P., Martin, N. M., & Knight, J. A. (2013). Diagrams, timelines and tables—Oh, my! *The Reading Teacher, 67*(1), 12–23.

Robertson, D. A., Dougherty, S., Ford-Connors, E., & Paratore, J. R. (2014). Re-envisioning Instruction: Mediating Complex Text for Older Readers, *The Reading Teacher, 67*(7), 547–559. DOI: 10.1002/trtr.1247.

Rosenshine, B., Meister, C., & Chapman, S. (1996). Teaching students to generate questions: A review of intervention studies. *Review of Educational Research, 66,* 181–221.

Saddler, B. (2007). Improving sentence construction skills through sentence-combining practice. In S. Graham, C. A. MacArthur, & J. Fitzgerald (Eds.), *Best practices in writing instruction* (pp. 163–178). New York, NY: The Guilford Press.

Salkind, N. J. (2011). Statistics for people who (think they) hate statistics. Thousand Oaks, CA: Sage Publications.

Scholastic Aptitude Test. (2012). The SAT report on college and career readiness. Retrieved September 3, 2013, from media.collegeboard.com/homeOrg/content/pdf/sat-report-college-career-readiness-2012.pdf

Scott, C. M. (2009). A case for the sentence in reading comprehension. *Language, speech and hearing services in schools, 40,* 184–191.

Shanahan, C. (2009). Disciplinary comprehension. In S. E. Israel & G. G. Duffy (Eds.), *Handbook of research on reading comprehension* (pp. 240–261). New York, NY: Routledge.

Shanahan, C., Shanahan, T., & Misischia, C. (2011). Analysis of three readers in three disciplines: History, mathematics and chemistry. *Journal of Literacy Research, 43,* 293–430.

Shanahan, T. (2011). Common core standards: Are we going to lower the fence or teach kids to climb? *Reading Today, 28*(7), 20–21.

Sheridan-Thomas, H. K. (2008). Assisting struggling readers with textbook comprehension. In K. A. Hinchman & H. K. Sheridan-Thomas (Eds.), *Best practices in adolescent literacy instruction* (pp. 164–184). New York, NY: The Guilford Press.

Sinatra, G. M., Brown, K., & Reynolds, R. E. (2002). Implications of cognitive resource allocation for comprehension strategies instruction. In C. C. Block & M. Pressley (Eds.), *Comprehension instruction: Research-based practices* (pp. 62–76). New York, NY: The Guilford Press.

Smith, M. W., & Wilhelm, J. D. (2010). *Fresh takes on teaching literary elements: How to teach what really matters about character, setting, point of view and theme.* Urbana, IL: NCTE.

Snow, C. E. (2010). Academic language and the challenge of reading for learning about science. *Science, 328,* 450–452.

Snow, C. E. (2013). Cold versus warm close reading: Building students' stamina for struggling with text. *Reading Today, 30*(6), 18–19.

Stevens, R. J., Van Meter, P., & Warcholak, N. D. (2010). The effects of explicitly teaching story structure to primary grade children. *Journal of Literacy Research, 42,* 159–198.

Stead, T. (2014). Nurturing the Inquiring Mind Through the Nonfiction Read-aloud. *The Reading Teacher, 67* (7), 488–495. DOI: 10.1002/trtr.1254.

Sweet, A. P. (2005). Assessment of reading comprehension: The RAND Reading Study Group Vision. In S. G. Paris & S. A. Stahl (Eds.), *Children's reading comprehension and assessment* (pp. 3–12). Mahwah, NJ: Erlbaum.

Thomas, M. (1995). *The effect of genre-specific story grammar instruction on recall, comprehension and writing of tenth grade students.* Unpublished doctoral dissertation. Milwaukee, WI: Marquette University.

Trabasso, T., & Magliano, J. P. (1996). Conscious understanding during reading. *Discourse Processes, 21,* 255–287.

van den Broek, P., Lorch, R. F., Linderholm, T., & Gustafson, M. (2001). The effects of readers' goals on inference generation and memory for text. *Memory and Cognition, 29,* 1081–1087.

Vidal-Abarca, E., Martinez, E., & Gilabert, R. (2000), Effects on memory and learning. *Journal of Educational Psychology, 92,* 107–116.

Wharton-McDonald, R., & Swiger, S. (2009). Developing higher order comprehension in the middle grades. In S. E. Israel & G. G. Duffy (Eds.), *Handbook of research on reading comprehension* (pp. 510–531). New York: Routledge.

Wilkinson, I. A., & Son, E. H. (2011). A dialogic turn in research on learning and teaching to comprehend. In M. L. Kamil, P. D. Pearson, E. B. Moje, and P. P. Afflerbach (Eds.), *Handbook of reading research* (Vol. 4, pp. 359–388). New York, NY: Routledge.

Williams, J. P., & Pao, L. S. (2011). Teaching narrative and expository text structure to improve comprehension. In R. E. O'Connor & P. F. Vadasy (Eds.), *Handbook of reading interventions* (pp. 254–279). New York, NY: The Guilford Press.

Wood, K. D., Taylor, B., Drye, B., & Brigman, M. J. (2007). Assessing students' understanding of informational text in intermediate- and middle-level classrooms. In J. R. Paratore & R. L. McCormack (Eds.), *Classroom literacy assessment: Making sense of what students know and do* (pp. 195–210). New York, NY: The Guilford Press.

Yeh, S. S. (2001). Tests worth teaching to: Constructing state-mandated tests that emphasize critical thinking. *Educational Researcher, 30,* 12–17.

Zeno, S. M., Ivens, S. H., Millard, R. T., & Duvvuri, R. (1995). *The educator's word frequency guide.* Brewster, NY: Touchstone Applied Science Associates, Inc.

Zywica, J., & Gomez, K. (2008). Annotation to support learning in the content areas: Teaching and learning science. *Journal of Adolescent & Adult Literacy, 52,* 155–165.

Children's Literature

Cisneros, S. (1991). *The house on mango street.* New York, NY: Vintage Books.

Finney, J. (1956). *The contents of the dead Man's pocket.* Originally published in Good Housekeeping Magazine of New York.

Gish, J. (1984). *The white umbrella.* In A. Mazer (Ed.), *America Street: A multicultural anthology of stories.* Logan, IA: Perfection Learning.

Hurst, J. (1998). *The scarlet ibis: The collection of wonder/creative short stories.* New York, NY: Creative Education. Originally published in 1960 in the Atlantic Monthly.

Mazer, A. (1993). *America Street: A multicultural anthology of stories.* Logan, IA. Perfection Learning.

Poe, E. A. (1846). *The cask of amontillado.* New York, NY: Godey's Lady's Book.

Scieszka, J. (1996). *The true story of the three little pigs.* New York, NY: Penguin Books.

Shihab Nye, N. (1999). *Hamadi.* In A. Mazer (Ed.), *America Street: A multicultural anthology of stories.* Logan, IA: Perfection Learning.

Thurber, J. (1945). The secret life of Walter Mitty. In *The Thurber Carnival* (pp. 55–60). New York, NY: Harper and Brothers.

Twain, M. (1865). *The celebrated jumping frog of Calaveras County.* Originally published by the Saturday Press. Published in 1997 by Oxford Press of New York.

Index